Advances in Audio and Speech Signal Processing:

Technologies and Applications

Hector Perez-Meana
National Polytechnic Institute, Mexico

IDEA GROUP PUBLISHING

Hershey • London • Melbourne • Singapore

Acquisition Editor:	Kristin Klinger
Senior Managing Editor:	Jennifer Neidig
Managing Editor:	Sara Reed
Assistant Managing Editor:	Sharon Berger
Development Editor:	Kristin Roth
Copy Editor:	Kim Barger
Typesetter:	Jamie Snavely
Cover Design:	Lisa Tosheff
Printed at:	Yurchak Printing Inc.

Published in the United States of America by
Idea Group Publishing (an imprint of Idea Group Inc.)
701 E. Chocolate Avenue
Hershey PA 17033
Tel: 717-533-8845
Fax: 717-533-8661
E-mail: cust@idea-group.com
Web site: http://www.idea-group.com

and in the United Kingdom by
Idea Group Publishing (an imprint of Idea Group Inc.)
3 Henrietta Street
Covent Garden
London WC2E 8LU
Tel: 44 20 7240 0856
Fax: 44 20 7379 0609
Web site: http://www.eurospanonline.com

Library of Congress Cataloging-in-Publication Data

Advances in audio and speech signal processing : technologies and applications / Hector Perez Meana, editor.
p. cm.
Summary: "This book provides a comprehensive approach of signal processing tools regarding the enhancement, recognition, and protection of speech and audio signals. It offers researchers and practitioners the information they need to develop and implement efficient signal processing algorithms in the enhancement field"--Provided by publisher.
Includes bibliographical references and index.
ISBN 978-1-59904-132-2 (hardcover) -- ISBN 978-1-59904-134-6 (ebook)
1. Sound--Recording and reproducing. 2. Signal processing--Digital techniques. 3. Speech processing systems. I. Meana, Hector Perez, 1954-
TK7881.4.A33 2007
621.389'32--dc22
2006033759

British Cataloguing in Publication Data
A Cataloguing in Publication record for this book is available from the British Library.

Advances in Audio and Speech Signal Processing:

Technologies and Applications

Table of Contents

Section IV
Feature Extraction Algorithms and Speech Speaker Recognition

Foreword

Speech is no doubt the most essential medium of human interaction.

By means of modern digital signal processing, we can interact, not only with others, but also with machines. The importance of speech/audio signal processing lies in preserving and improving the quality of speech/audio signals. These signals are treated in a digital representation where various advanced digital-signal-processing schemes can be carried out adaptively to enhance the quality.

Here, special care should be paid to defining the goal of "quality." In its simplest form, signal quality can be measured in terms of signal distortion (distance between signals). However, more sophisticated measures such as perceptual quality (the distance between human perceptual representations), or even service quality (the distance between human user experiences), should be carefully chosen and utilized according to applications, the environment, and user preferences. Only with proper measures can we extract the best performance from signal processing.

Thanks to recent advances in signal processing theory, together with advances in signal processing devices, the applications of audio/speech signal processing have become ubiquitous over the last decade. This book covers various aspects of recent advances in speech/audio signal processing technologies, such as audio signal enhancement, speech and speaker recognition, adaptive filters, active noise canceling, echo canceling, audio quality evaluation, audio and speech watermarking, digital filters for audio effects, and speech technologies for language therapy.

I am very pleased to have had the opportunity to write this foreword. I hope the appearance of this book stimulates the interest of future researchers in the area and brings about further progress in the field of audio/speech signal processing.

Tomohiko Taniguchi, PhD
Fujitsu Laboratories Limited

Tomohiko Taniguchi (PhD) was born in Wakayama Japan on March 7, 1960. In 1982 he joined the Fujitsu Laboratories Ltd. were he has been engaged in the research and development of speech coding technologies. In 1988 he was a visiting scholar at the Information System Laboratory, Stanford University, CA, where he did research on speech signal processing. He is director of The Mobile Access Laboratory of Fujitsu Laboratories Ltd., Yokosuka, Japan. Dr. Taniguchi has made important contributions to the speech and audio processing field which are published in a large number of papers, international conference and patents. In 2006, Dr. Taniguchi became a fellow member of the IEEE in recognition for his contributions to speech coding technologies and development of digital signal processing- (DSP) based communication systems. Dr. Taniguchi is also a member of the IEICE of Japan.

Preface

With the development of the VLSI technology, the performance of signal processing devices (DSPs) has greatly improved making possible the implementation of very efficient signal processing algorithms that have had a great impact and contributed in a very important way in the development of large number of industrial fields. One of the fields that has experience an impressive development in the last years, with the use of many signal processing tools, is the telecommunication field. Several important developments have contributed to this fact, such as efficient speech coding algorithm (Bosi & Goldberg, 2002), equalizers (Haykin, 1991), echo cancellers (Amano, Perez-Meana, De Luca, & Duchen, 1995), and so forth. During the last several years very efficient speech coding algorithms have been developed that have allowed reduction of the bit/s required in a digital telephone system from 32Kbits/s, provided by the standard adaptive differential pulse code modulation (ADPCM), to 4.8Kbits/s or even 2.4Kbits/s, provided by some of the most efficient speech coders. This reduction was achieved while keeping a reasonably good speech quality (Kondoz, 1994). Another important development with a great impact on the development of modern communication systems is the echo cancellation (Messershmitt, 1984) which reduces the distortion introduced by the conversion from bidirectional to one-directional channel required in long distance communication systems. The echo cancellation technology has also been used to improve the development of efficient full duplex data communication devices. Another important device is the equalizers that are used to reduce the intersymbol interference, allowing the development of efficient data communications and telephone systems (Proakis, 1985).

In the music field, the advantages of the digital technology have allowed the development of efficient algorithms for generating audio effects such as the introduction of reverberation in music generated in a studio to do it more naturally. Also the signal processing technology allows the development of new musical instruments or the synthesis of musical sounds produced by already available musical instruments, as well as the generation of audio effects required in the movie industry.

The digital audio technology is also found in many consumer electronics equipments to modify the audio signal characteristics such as modifications of the spectral characteristics of audio signal, recoding and reproduction of digital audio and video, edition of digital material, and so forth. Another important application of the digital technology in the audio field is the restoration of old analog recordings, achieving an adequate balance between the storage space, transmission requirements, and sound quality. To this end, several signal processing algorithms have been developed during the last years using analysis and synthesis techniques of audio signals (Childers, 2000). These techniques are very useful for generation of new and already known musical sounds, as well as for restoration of already recorded audio signals, especially for restoration of old recordings, concert recordings, or recordings obtained in any other situation when it is not possible to record the audio signal again (Madisetti & Williams, 1998).

One of the most successful applications of the digital signal processing technology in the audio field is the development of efficient audio compression algorithms that allow very important reductions in the storage requirements while keeping a good audio signal quality (Bosi & Goldberg, 2002; Kondoz, 1994). Thus the researches carried out in this field have allowed the reducing of the 10Mbits required by the WAV format to the 1.41Mbits/s required by the compact disc standard and recently to 64Kbits/s required by the standard MP3PRO. These advances in the digital technology have allowed the transmission of digital audio by Internet, the development of audio devices that are able to store several hundreds of songs with reasonable low memory requirements while keeping a good audio signal quality (Perez-Meana & Nakano-Miyatake, 2005). The digital TV and the radio broadcasting by Internet are other systems that have taken advantage of the audio signal compression technology.

During the last years, acoustic noise problem has become more important as the use of large industrial equipment such as engines, blowers, fans, transformers, air conditioners and motors, and so forth increases. Because of its importance, several methods have been proposed to solve this problem, such as enclosures, barriers, silencers, and other passive techniques that attenuate the undesirable noise (Tapia-Sánchez, Bustamante, Pérez-Meana, & Nakano-Miyatake, 2005; Kuo & Morgan, 1996). There are mainly two types of passive techniques: the first type uses the concept of impedance change caused by a combination of baffles and tubes to silence the undesirable sound. This type, called reactive silencer, is commonly used as mufflers in internal combustion engines. The second type, called resistive silencers, uses energy loss caused by sound propagation in a duct lined with sound-absorbing material. These silencers are usually used in ducts for fan noise. Both types of passive silencers have been successfully used during many years in several applications; however, the attenuation of passive silencers is low when the acoustic wavelength is large compared with the silencer's dimension (Kuo & Morgan, 1996). Recently, with the developing of signal processing technology, during the last several years have been developed efficient active noise cancellation algorithms using single- and multi-channel structures, which use a secondary noise source that destructively interferes with the unwanted noise. In addition, because these systems are adaptive, they are able to track the amplitude, phase, and sound velocity of the undesirable noise, which are in most cases non-stationary. Using the active noise canceling technology, headphones with noise canceling capability, systems to reduce the noise aircraft and cabins, air condition ducts, and so forth have been developed. This technology, which must be still improved, is expected to become an important tool to reduce the acoustic noise problem (Tapia et al., 2005).

Another important field in which the digital signal processing technology has been successfully applied is the development of hearing aids systems, speech enhancement of persons with oral communication problems such as the alaryngeal speakers. In the first case, the signal processing device performs selective signal amplification on some specific frequency bands, in a similar form as an audio equalizer, to improve the patient hearing capacity. While improving the alaryngeal speech several algorithms have been proposed. Some of them intend to reduce the noise produced by the electronic larynx, which is a widely used for alaryngeal persons, while the second group intends to restore the alaryngeal speech providing a more natural voice, at least when a telecommunication system, such as a telephone, is used (Aguilar, Nakano-Miyatake, & Perez-Meana, 2005). Most of these methods are based on patterns recognition techniques.

Several speech and audio signal processing applications described previously, such as the echo and noise canceling; the reduction of intersymbol interference, and the active noise canceling, strongly depend on adaptive digital filters using either time domain or frequency domain realization forms that have been a subject of active research during the last 25 years (Haykin, 1991). However, although several efficient algorithms have been proposed during this time, some problems still remain to be solved, such as the development of efficient IIR adaptive filters, as well as non-linear adaptive filters, which have been less studied in comparison with their linear counter parts.

The development of digital signal processing technology, the widespread use of data communication networks, such as the Internet, and the fact that the digital material can be copied without any distortion, has created the necessity to develop mechanisms that permit the control of the illegal copy and distribution of digital audio, images, and video, as well as the authentication of a given digital material. A suitable way to do that is by using the digital watermarking technology (Bender, Gruhl, Marimoto, & Lu, 1996; Cox, Miller, & Bloom, 2001).

Digital watermarking is a technique used to embed a collection of bits into a given signal, in such way that it will be kept imperceptible to users and the resulting watermarked signal remains with nearly the same quality as the original one. Watermarks can be embedded into audio, image, video, and other formats of digital data in either the temporal or spectral domains. Here the temporal watermarking algorithms embed watermarks into audio signals in their temporal domain, while the spectral watermarking algorithms embed watermarks in certain transform domain. Depending on their particular application, the watermarking algorithms can be classified as robust and fragile watermarks, where the robust watermarking algorithms are used for copyright protection, distribution monitoring, copy control, and so forth, while the fragile watermark, which will be changed if the host audio is modified, is used to verify the authenticity of a given audio signal, speech signal, and so forth. The watermarking technology is expected to become a very important tool for the protection and authenticity verification of digital audio, speech, images, and video (Bender et al., 1996; Cox et al., 2001).

Another important application of the audio and speech signal processing technology is the speech recognition, which has been a very active research field during the last 30 years; as a result, several efficient algorithms have been proposed in the literature (Lee, Soong, & Paliwal, 1996; Rabiner & Biing-Hwang, 1993). As happens in most pattern recognition algorithms, the pattern under analysis, in this case the speech signal, must be characterized to extract the most significant as well as invariant features, which are then fed into the recognition stage. To this end several methods have been proposed, such as the linear predictions coefficients (LPC) of the speech signal and LPC-based cepstral coefficients, and recently the used phonemes to characterize the speech signal, instead of features extracted from its waveform, has attracted the attention of some researchers. A related application that also has been widely studied consists of identifying not the spoken voice, but who spoke it. This application, called speaker recognition, has been a subject of active research because of its potential applications for access control to restricted places or information. Using a similar approach it is possible also to identify natural or artificial sounds (Hattori, Ishihara, Komatani, Ogata, & Okuno, 2004). The sound recognition has a wide range of applications such as failure diagnosis, security, and so forth.

This book provides a review of several signal processing methods that have been successfully used in speech and audio fields. It is intended for scientists and engineers working in enhancing, restoration, and protection of audio and speech signals. The book is also expected to be a valuable reference for graduate students in the fields of electrical engineering and computer science.

The book is organized into XIV chapters, divided in four sections. Next a brief description of each section and the chapters included is provided.

Chapter I provides an overview of some the most successful applications of signal processing algorithms in the speech and audio field. This introductory chapter provides an introduction to speech and audio signal analysis and synthesis, audio and speech coding, noise and echo canceling, and recently proposed signal processing methods to solve several problems in the medical field. A brief introduction of watermarking technology as well as speech and speaker recognition is also provided. Most topics described in this chapter are analyzed with more depth in the remaining chapters of this book.

Section I analyzes some successful applications of the audio and speech signal processing technology, specifically in applications regarding the audio effects, audio synthesis, and restoration. This section consists of three chapters, which are described in the following paragraphs.

Chapter II presents the application of digital filters for introducing several effects in the audio signals, taking into account the fact that the audio editing functions that change the sonic character of a recording, from loudness to tonal quality, enter the realm of *digital signal processing* (DSP), removing parts of the sound, such as noise, and adding to the sound elements that were not present in the original recording, such as reverb, improving the music in a studio, which sometimes does not sound as natural as for example music performed in a concert hall. These and several other signal processing techniques that contribute to improve the quality of audio signals are analyzed in this chapter.

Chapter III provides a review of audio signal processing techniques related to sound generation via additive synthesis, in particular using the sinusoidal modeling. Here, firstly the processing stage required to obtaining a sinusoidal representation of audio signals is described. Next, suitable synthesis techniques that allow reconstructing an audio signal, based on a given parametric representation, are presented. Finally, some audio applications where sinusoidal modeling is successfully employed are briefly discussed.

Chapter IV provides a review of digital audio restoration techniques whose main goal is to use digital signal processing techniques to improve the sound quality, mainly, of old recordings, or the recordings that are difficult to do again, such as a concert. Here a conservative goal consists on eliminating only the audible spurious artifacts that either are introduced by analog recording and playback mechanisms or result from aging and wear of recorded media, while retaining as faithfully as possible the original recorded sound. Less restricted approaches are also analyzed, which would allow more intrusive sound modifications, such as elimination of the audience noises and correction of performance mistakes in order to obtain a restored sound with better quality than the original recording.

Section II provides an analysis of recently developed speech and audio watermarking methods. The advance in the digital technology allows an error free copy of any digital material, allowing the unauthorized copying, distribution, and commercialization of copyrighted digital audio, images, and videos. This section, consisting of two chapters, provides an analysis of the watermarking techniques that appear to be an attractive alternative to solving this problem.

Chapters V and **VI** provide a comprehensive overview of classic watermark embedding, recovery, and detection algorithms for audio and speech signals, providing also a review of the main factors that must be considered to design efficient audio watermarking systems together with some typical approaches employed by existing watermarking algorithms. The watermarking techniques, which can be divided into robust and fragile, presented in these chapters, are presently deployed in a wide range of applications including copyright protection, copy control, broadcast monitoring, authentication, and air traffic control. Furthermore, these chapters describe the signal processing, geometric, and protocol attacks together with some of the existing benchmarking tools for evaluating the robustness performance of watermarking techniques as well as the distortion introduced in the watermarked signals.

Section III. The adaptive filtering has been successfully used in the solution of an important amount of practical problems such as echo and noise canceling, active noise canceling, speech enhancement, adaptive pulse modulation coding, spectrum estimation, channel equalization, and so forth. Section III provides a review of some successful adaptive filter algorithms, together with two of the must successful applications of this technology such as the echo and active noise cancellers. Section III consists of four chapters, which are described in the following paragraphs.

Chapter VII provides an overview of adaptive digital filtering techniques, which are a fundamental part of echo and active noise canceling systems provided in Chapters VIII and IX, as well as of other important telecommunications systems, such as equalizers, widely used in data communications, coders, speech and audio signal enhancement, and so forth. This chapter presents the general framework of adaptive filtering together with two of the most widely used adaptive filter algorithms—the LMS (least-mean-square) and the RLS (recursive least-square) algorithms—together with some modification of them. It also provides a review of some widely used filter structures, such as the transversal FIR filter, the transform-domain implementations, multirate structures and IIR filters realization forms, and so forth. Some important audio applications are also described.

Chapter VIII presents a review of the echo cancellation problem in telecommunication and teleconference systems, which are two of the most successful applications of the adaptive filter technology. In the first case, an echo signal is produced when mismatch impedance is present in the telecommunications system, due to the two-wires-to-four-wires transformation required because the amplifiers are one-directional devices, and as a consequence a portion of the transmitted signal is reflected to the transmitter as an echo that degrades the system quality. A similar problem affects the teleconference systems because of the acoustical coupling between the speakers and microphones, in each room, used in such systems. To avoid the echo problem in both cases, an adaptive filter is used to generate an echo replica, which is then subtracted from the signal to be transmitted. This chapter analyzes the factors to consider in the development of efficient echo canceller systems, such as the duration of the echo canceller impulse response, the convergence rate of adaptive algorithm, and computational complexity, because these systems must operate in real time, and how to handle the simultaneous presence of both the echo signal and the near end speaker voice.

Chapter IX provides a review of the active noise cancellation problem together with some of its most promising solutions. In this problem, which is closely related with the echo canceling, adaptive filters are used to reduce the noise produced in automotive equipment, home appliances, industrial equipment, airplanes cabin, and so forth. Here active noise canceling is achieved by introducing an antinoise wave through an appropriate array of secondary sources, which are interconnected through electronic adaptive systems with a particular cancellation configuration. To properly cancel the acoustic noise signal, the adaptive filter generates an antinoise, which is acoustically subtracted from the incoming noise wave. The resulting wave is then captured by an error microphone and used to update the adaptive filter coefficients such that the total error power is minimized. This chapter analyzes the filter structures and adaptive algorithms, together with other several factors to be considered in the development of active noise canceling systems; this chapter also presents some recently proposed ANC structures that intend to solve some of the already existent problems, as well as a review of some still remaining problems that must be solved in this field.

Chapter X presents a recurrent neural network structure for audio and speech processing. Although the performance of this artificial neural network, called differentially fed artificial neural network, was evaluated using a prediction configuration, it can be easily used to solve other non-linear signal processing problems.

Section IV. The speech recognition has been a topic of active research during the last 30 years. During this time a large number of efficient algorithms have been proposed, using hidden Markov models, neural networks, and Gaussian mixtures models, among other several paradigms to perform the recognition tasks. To perform an accurate recognition task, besides the paradigm used in the recognition stage, the feature extraction has also great importance. A related problem that has also received great attention is the speaker recognition, where the task is to determine the speaker identity, or verify if the speaker is who she/he claims to be. This section provides a review of some of the most widely used feature extraction algorithms. This section consists of four chapters that re described in the following paragraphs.

Chapters XI and **XII** present the state-of-the-art automatic voice recognition (ASR), which is related to multiple disciplines, such as processing and analysis of speech signals and mathematical statistics, as well as applied artificial intelligence and linguistics among some of the most important. The most widely used paradigm for speech characterization in the developing of ASR has been the phoneme as the essential information unit. However, recently the necessity to create more robust and versatile systems for speech recognition has suggested the necessity of looking for different approaches that may improve the performance of phoneme based ASR. A suitable approach appears to be the use of more complex units such as syllables, where the inherent problems related with the use of phonemes are overcome to a greater cost of the number of units, but with the advantage of being able to approach using the form in which really the people carry out the learning and language production process. These two chapters also analyze the voice signal characteristics in both the time frequency and domain, the measurement and extraction of the parametric information that characterizes the speech signal, together with an analysis of the use of artificial neuronal networks, vector quantification, hidden Markov models, and hybrid models to perform the recognition process.

Chapter XIII presents the development of an efficient speaker recognition system (SRS), which has been a topic of active research during the last decade. SRSs have found a large number of potential applications in many fields that require accurate user identification or user identity verification, such as shopping by telephone, bank transactions, access control to restricted places and information, voice mail and law enforcement, and so forth. According to the task that the SRS is required to perform, it can be divided into speaker identification system (SIS) or speaker verification systems (SVS), where the SIS has the task to determine the most likely speaker among a given speakers set, while the SVS has the task of deciding if the speaker is who she/he claims to be. Usually a SIS has M inputs and N outputs, where M depends on the feature vector size and N on the size of the speaker set, while the SVS usually has M inputs, as the SRS, and two possible outputs (accept or reject) or in some situations three possible outputs (accept, reject, or indefinite). Together with an overview of SRS, this chapter analyzes the speaker features extraction methods, closely related to those used in speech recognition presented in Chapters XI and XII, as well as the paradigms used to perform the recognition process, such as vector quantizers (VQ), artificial neural networks (ANN), Gaussian mixture models (GMM), fuzzy logic, and so forth.

Chapter XIV presents the use of speech recognition technologies in the development of a language therapy for children with hearing disabilities; it describes the challenges that must be addressed to construct an adequate speech recognizer for this application and provides the design features and other elements required to support effective interactions. This chapter provides to developers and educators the tools required to work in the developing of learning methods for individuals with cognitive, physical, and sensory disabilities.

Advances in Audio and Speech Signal Processing: Technologies and Applications, which includes contributions of scientists and researchers of several countries around the world and analyzes several important topics in the audio and speech signal processing, is expected to be a valuable reference for graduate students and scientists working in this exciting field, especially those involved in the fields of audio restoration and synthesis, watermarking, interference cancellation, and audio enhancement, as well as in speech and speaker recognition.

References

Aguilar, G., Nakano-Miyatake, M., & Perez-Meana, H. (2005). Alaryngeal speech enhancement using pattern recognition techniques. *IEICE Trans. Inf. & Syst., E88-D*(7), 1618-1622.

Amano, F., Perez-Meana, H., De Luca, A., & Duchen, G. (1995). A multirate acoustic echo canceler structure. *IEEE Trans. on Communications, 43*(7), 2173-2176.

Bender, W., Gruhl, D., Marimoto, N., & Lu. (1996). Techniques for data hiding. *IBM Systems Journal, 35*, 313-336.

Bosi, M., & Goldberg, R. (2002). *Introduction to digital audio coding and standards.* Boston: Kluwer Academic Publishers.

Childers, D. (2000). *Speech processing and synthesis toolboxes.* New York: John Wiley & Sons.

Cox, I., Miller, M., & Bloom, J. (2001). *Digital watermark: Principle and practice.* New York: Morgan Kaufmann.

Hattori, Y., Ishihara, K., Komatani, K., Ogata, T., & Okuno, H. (2004). Repeat recognition for environmental sounds. In *Proceedings of IEEE International Workshop on Robot and Human Interaction* (pp. 83-88).

Haykin, S. (1991). *Adaptive filter theory.* Englewood Cliffs, NJ: Prentice Hall.

Kondoz, A. M. (1994). *Digital speech.* Chinchester, England: Wiley & Sons.

Kuo, S., & Morgan, D. (1996). *Active noise control system: Algorithms and DSP implementations.* New York: John Wiley & Sons.

Lee, C., Soong, F., & Paliwal, K. (1996). *Automatic speech and speaker recognition.* Boston: Kluwer Academic Publishers.

Madisetti, V., & Williams, D. (1998). *The digital signal processing handbook.* Boca Raton, FL: CRC Press.

Messershmitt, D. (1984). Echo cancellation in speech and data transmission. *IEEE Journal of Selected Areas in Communications, 2*(3), 283-297.

Perez-Meana, H., & Nakano-Miyatake, M. (2005). Speech and audio signal applications. In *Encyclopedia of information science and technology* (pp. 2592-2596). Idea Group.

Proakis, J. (1985). *Digital communications.* New York: McGraw Hill.

Rabiner, L., & Biing-Hwang, J. (1993). *Fundamentals of speech recognition.* Englewood Cliff, NJ: Prentice Hall.

Tapia-Sánchez, D., Bustamante, R., Pérez-Meana, H., & Nakano-Miyatake, M. (2005). Single channel active noise canceller algorithm using discrete cosine transform. *Journal of Signal Processing, 9*(2), 141-151.

Acknowledgments

The editor would like to acknowledge the help of all involved in the collation and review process of the book, without whose support the project could not have been satisfactorily completed.

Deep appreciation and gratitude is due to the National Polytechnic Institute of Mexico, for ongoing sponsorship in terms of generous allocation of online and off-line Internet, WWW, hardware and software resources, and other editorial support services for coordination of this yearlong project.

Most of the authors of chapters included in this also served as referees for articles written by other authors. Thanks go to all those who provided constructive and comprehensive reviews that contributed to improve the chapter contents. I also would like to thanks to Dr. Tomohiko Taniguchi of Fujitsu Laboratories Ltd. of Japan, for taking some time of his very busy schedule to write the foreword of this book.

Special thanks also go to all the staff at Idea Group Inc., whose contributions throughout the whole process from inception of the initial idea to final publication have been invaluable. In particular, to Kristin Roth who continuously prodded via e-mail for keeping the project on schedule and to Mehdi Khosrow-Pour, whose enthusiasm motivated me to initially accept his invitation for taking on this project.

Special thanks go to my wife, Dr. Mariko Nakano-Miyatake, of the National Polytechnic Institute of Mexico, who assisted me during the reviewing process, read a semi-final draft of the manuscript, and provided helpful suggestions for enhancing its content; also I would like to thank her for her unfailing support and encouragement during the months it took to give birth to this book.

In closing, I wish to thank all of the authors for their insights and excellent contributions to this book. I also want to thank all of the people who assisted me in the reviewing process. Finally, I want to thank my daughter Anri for her love and support throughout this project.

Hector Perez-Meana, PhD
National Polytechnic Institute
Mexico City, Mexico
December 2006

Chapter I

Introduction to Audio and Speech Signal Processing

Hector Perez-Meana, National Polytechnic Institute, Mexico

Mariko Nakano-Miyatake, National Polytechnic Institute, Mexico

Abstract

The development of very efficient digital signal processors has allowed the implementation of high performance signal processing algorithms to solve an important amount of practical problems in several engineering fields, such as telecommunications, in which very efficient algorithms have been developed to storage, transmission, and interference reductions; in the audio field, where signal processing algorithms have been developed to enhancement, restoration, copy right protection of audio materials; in the medical field, where signal processing algorithms have been efficiently used to develop hearing aids systems and speech restoration systems for alaryngeal speech signals. This chapter presents an overview of some successful audio and speech signal processing algorithms, providing to the reader an overview of this important technology, some of which will be analyzed with more detail in the accompanying chapters of this book.

Introduction

The advances of the VLSI technology have allowed the development of high performance digital signal processing (DSP) devices, enabling the implementation of very efficient and sophisticated algorithms, which have been successfully used in the solution of a large amount of practical problems in several fields of science and engineering. Thus, signal processing techniques have been used with great success in telecommunications to solve the echo problem in telecommunications and teleconference systems (Amano, Perez-Meana, De Luca, & Duchen, 1995), to solve the inter-symbol interference in high speed data communications systems (Proakis, 1985), as well as to develop efficient coders that allow the storage and transmission of speech and audio signals with a low bit rate keeping at the same time a high sound quality (Bosi & Golberg, 2002; Kondoz, 1994). Signal processing algorithms have also been used for speech and audio signal enhancement and restoration (Childers, 2000; Davis, 2002) to reduce the noise produced by air conditioning equipment and motors (Kuo & Morgan, 1996), and so forth, and to develop electronic mufflers (Kuo & Morgan, 1996) and headsets with active noise control (Davis, 2002). In the educational field, signal processing algorithms that allow the time scale modification of speech signals have been used to assist the foreign language students during their learning process (Childers, 2000). These systems have also been used to improve the hearing capability of elder people (Davis, 2002).

The digital technology allows an easy and error free reproduction of any digital material, allowing the illegal reproduction of audio and video material. Because this fact represents a huge economical loss for the entertainment industry, many efforts have been carried out to solve this problem. Among the several possible solutions, the watermarking technology appears to be a desirable alternative for copyright protection (Bassia, Pitas, & Nikoladis, 2001; Bender, Gruhl, Marimoto, & Lu, 1996). As a result, several audio and speech watermarking algorithms have been proposed during the last decade, and this has been a subject of active research during the last several years. Some of these applications are analyzed in the remaining chapters of this book.

This chapter presents an overview of signal processing systems to storage, transmission, enhancement, protection, and reproduction of speech and audio signals that have been successfully used in telecommunications, audio, access control, and so forth.

Adaptive Echo Cancellation

A very successful speech signal processing application is the adaptive echo cancellation used to reduce a common but undesirable phenomenon in most telecommunications systems, called echo. Here, when mismatch impedance is present in any telecommunications system, a portion of the transmitted signal is reflected to the transmitter as an echo, which represents an impairment that degrades the system quality (Messershmitt, 1984). In most telecommunications systems, such as a telephone circuit, the echo is generated when the long distant portion consisting of two one-directional channels (four wires) is connected with a bidirectional channel (two wires) by means of a hybrid transformer, as shown in Figure 1. If the hybrid impedance is perfectly balanced, the two one-directional channels are

Figure 1. Hybrid circuit model

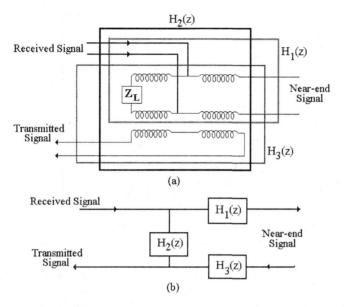

Figure 2. Echo cancellation configuration

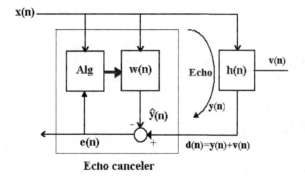

Echo canceler

uncoupled, and no signal is returned to the transmitter side (Messershmitt, 1984). However, in general, the bridge is not perfectly balanced because the required impedance to properly balance the hybrid depends on the overall impedance network. In this situation part of the signal is reflected, producing an echo.

To avoid this problem, an adaptive filter is used to generate an echo replica, which is then subtracted from the signal to be transmitted as shown in Figure 2. Subsequently the adaptive filter coefficients are updated to minimize, usually, the mean square value of the residual

Figure 3. Acoustic echo cancellation configuration

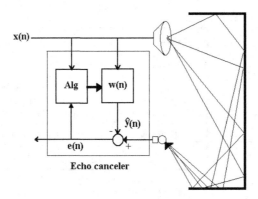

echo (Madisetti & Williams, 1998). To obtain an appropriate operation, the echo canceller impulse response must be larger than the longer echo path to be estimated. Thus, assuming a sampling frequency of 8kHz and an echo delay of about 60ms, an echo canceller with 256 or more taps is required (Haykin, 1991). Besides the echo path estimation, another important problem is how to handle the double talk, that is, the simultaneous presence of the echo and the near speech signal (Messershmitt, 1984). The problem is that it is necessary to avoid if the adaptive algorithm modifies the echo canceller coefficients in a domed-to-fail attempt to cancel it.

A critical problem affecting speech communication in teleconferencing systems is the acoustic echo shown in Figure 3. When a bidirectional line links two rooms, the acoustic coupling between loudspeaker and microphones in each room causes an acoustic echo perceivable to the users in the other room. The best way to handle it appears to be the adaptive echo cancellation. An acoustic echo canceller generates an echo replica and subtracts it from the signal picked up by the microphones. The residual echo is then used to update the filter coefficients such that the mean square value of approximation error is kept to a minimum (Amano et al., 1995; Perez-Meana, Nakano-Miyatake, & Nino-de-Rivera, 2002). Although the acoustic echo cancellation is similar to that found in other telecommunication systems, such as the telephone ones, the acoustic echo cancellation presents some characteristics that present a more difficult problem. For instance the duration of the acoustic echo path impulse response is of several hundred milliseconds as shown in Figure 4, and then, echo canceller structures with several thousands FIR taps are required to properly reduce the echo level. Besides that, the acoustic echo path is non-stationary, because it changes with the speaker's movement, and the speech signal is non-stationary. These factors challenge the acoustic echo canceling, presenting a quite difficult problem because it requires a low complexity adaptation algorithms with a fact enough convergence rate to track the echo path variations. Because conventional FIR adaptive filters, used in telephone systems, do not meet these requirements, more efficient algorithms using frequency domain and subband approaches have been proposed (Amano et al., 1995; Perez-Meana et al., 2002).

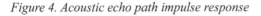

Figure 4. Acoustic echo path impulse response

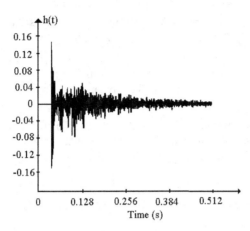

Figure 5. Adaptive filter operating with a noise cancellation configuration

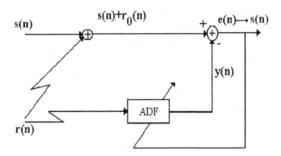

Adaptive Noise Cancellation

The adaptive noise canceller, whose basic configuration is shown in Figure 5, is a generalization of the echo canceller in which a signal corrupted with additive noise must be enhanced. When a reference signal correlated with the noise signal but uncorrelated with the desired one is available, the noise cancellation can be achieved by using an adaptive filter to minimize the total power of the output of the difference between the corrupted signal and the estimated noise, such that the resulting signal becomes the best estimate, in the mean square sense, of the desired signal as given by equation (1) (Widrow & Stearns, 1985).

$$E\left[\left[r_0(n) - y(n)\right]^2\right]_{\min} = E\left[\left[e(n) - s(n)\right]^2\right]_{\min}. \tag{1}$$

This system works fairly well when the reference and the desired signal are uncorrelated among them (Widrow & Stearns, 1985). However, in other cases (Figure 6), the system performance presents a considerable degradation, which increases as the signal-to-noise ratio between $r(n)$ and $s_0(n)$ decreases, as shown in Figure 7.

To reduce the degradation produced by the crosstalk, several noise-canceling algorithms have been proposed, which present some robustness in the presence of crosstalk situations. One of these algorithms is shown in Figure 8 (Mirchandani, Zinser, & Evans, 1992), whose performance is shown in Figure 9 when the SNR between $r(n)$ and $s_0(n)$ is equal to 0dB.

Figure 9 shows that the crosstalk resistant ANC (CTR-ANC) provides a fairly good performance, even in the presence of a large amount of crosstalk. However, because the transfer function of the CTR-ANC is given by (Mirchandani et al., 1992):

$$E_1(z) = \frac{D_1(z) - A(z)D_2(z)}{1 - A(z)B(z)},$$

it is necessary to ensure that the zeros of 1-A(z)B(z) remain inside the unit circle to avoid stabilty problems.

A different approach, developed by Dolby Laboratories, is used in the Dolby noise reduction systems in which the dynamic range of the sound is reduced during recording and expanded during the playback (Davis, 2002). Several types of Dolby noise reduction systems have been developed including the A, B, C, and HXpro. Most widely used is the Dolby B, which allows acceptable playback, even on devices without noise reduction. The Dolby B noise reduction system uses a pre-emphasis that allows masking the background hiss of a tape with a stronger audio signal, especially at higher frequencies. This effect is called psycho-acoustic masking (Davis, 2002).

Figure 6. Noise canceling in presence of crosstalk

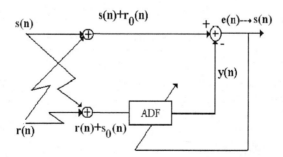

Figure 7. ANC Performance with different amount of crosstalk. (a) Corrupted signal with a signal to noise ratio (SNR) between s(n) and r0(n) equal to 0 dB. (b) Output error when s0(n)=0. (c) Output error e(n) when the SNR between r(n) and s0(n) is equal to 10 dB. (c) Output error e(n) when the SNR between r(n) and s0(n) is equal to 0 dB.

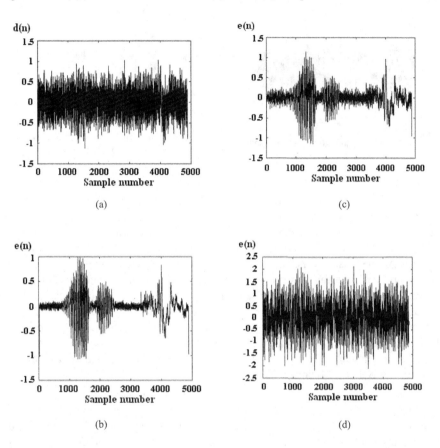

Figure 8. Crosstalk resistant adaptive noise canceller scheme

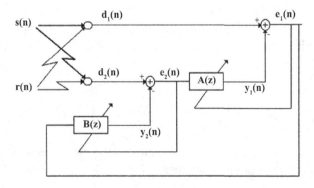

Figure 9. Noise canceling performance of crosstalk resistant ANC system. (a) Original signal where the SNR of $d_1(n)$ and $d_2(n)$ is equal to 0 dB. (b) ANC output error.

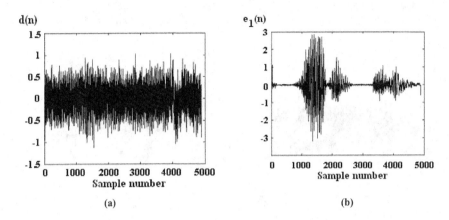

(a)   (b)

A related problem to noise cancellation is the active noise cancellation, which intends to reduce the noise produced in closed places by several electrical and mechanical equipments, such as home appliances, industrial equipment, air condition, airplanes turbines, motors, and so forth. Active noise is canceling achieved by introducing a canceling antinoise wave through an appropriate array of secondary sources, which are interconnected through an electronic system using adaptive noise canceling systems, with a particular cancellation configuration. Here, the adaptive noise canceling generates an antinoise that is acoustically subtracted from the incoming noise wave. The resulting wave is captured by an error microphone and used to update the noise canceller parameters, such that the total error power is minimized, as shown in Figure 10 (Kuo & Morgan, 1996; Tapia-Sánchez, Bustamante, Pérez-Meana, & Nakano-Miyatake, 2005).

Although the active noise-canceling problem is similar to the noise canceling describe previously, there are several situations that must be taken in account to get an appropriate operation of the active noise-canceling system. Among them we have the fact that the error signals presents a delay time with respect to the input signals, due to the filtering, analog-to-digital and digital-to-analog conversion, and amplification tasks, as shown in Figure 11. If no action is taken to avoid this problem, the noise-canceling system will be only able to cancel periodic noises. A widely used approach to solve this problem is shown in Figure 12. The active noise-canceling problem is described with detail in Chapter IX.

The ANC technology has been successfully applied in earphones, electronic mufflers, noise reduction systems in airplane cabin, and so forth (Davis, 2002; Kuo & Morgan, 1996).

Speech and Audio Coding

Besides interference cancellation, speech and audio signal coding are other very important signal processing applications (Gold & Morgan, 2000; Schroeder & Atal, 1985). This is

Figure 10. Principle of active noise canceling

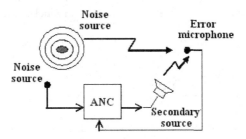

Figure 11. Bloc diagram of a typical noise canceling system

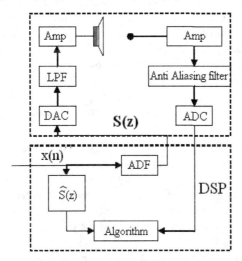

Figure 12. Block diagram of a filtered-X noise-canceling algorithm

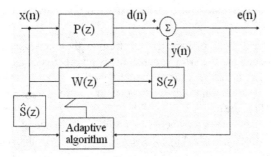

because low bit rate coding is required to minimize the transmission costs or to provide a cost efficient storage. Here we can distinguish two different groups: the narrowband speech coders used in telephone and some video telephone systems, in which the quality of telephone-bandwidth speech is acceptable, and the wideband coders used in audio applications, which require a bandwidth of at least 20 kHz for high fidelity (Madisetti & Williams, 1998).

Narrowband Speech Coding

The most efficient speech coding systems for narrowband applications use the analysis-synthesis-based method, shown in Figure 13, in which the speech signal is analyzed during the coding process to estimate the main parameters of speech that allow its synthesis during the decoding process (Kondoz, 1994; Schroeder & Atal, 1985; Madisetti & Williams, 1998). Two sets of speech parameters are usually estimated: (1) the linear filter system parameters, which model the vocal track, estimated using the linear prediction method, and (2) the excitation sequence. Most speech coders estimate the linear filter in a similar way, although several methods have been proposed to estimate the excitation sequence that determines the synthesized speech quality and compression rates. Among these speech coding systems we have the multipulse excited (MPE) and regular pulse excited (RPE) linear predictive coding, the codebook exited linear predictive coding (CELP), and so forth, that achieve bit rates among 9.6 Kb/s and 2.4 kb/s, with reasonably good speech quality (Madisetti & Williams, 1998). Table 1 shows the main characteristics of some of the most successful speech coders.

The analysis by synthesis codecs split the input speech $s(n)$ into frames, usually about 20 ms long. For each frame, parameters are determined for a synthesis filter, and then the excitation to this filter is determined by finding the excitation signal, which, passed into the given synthesis filter, minimizes the error between the input speech and the reproduced speech. Finally, for each frame the encoder transmits information representing the synthesis filter parameters and the excitation to the decoder, and at the decoder, the given excitation, is passed through the synthesis filter to give the reconstructed speech. Here the synthesis filter is an all pole filter, which is estimated by using linear prediction methods, assuming that the speech signal can be properly represented by modeling it as an autoregressive process. The synthesis filter may also include a pitch filter to model the long-term periodicities presented in voiced speech. Generally MPE and RPE coders will work without a pitch filter, although their performance will be improved if one is included. For CELP coders, however, a pitch filter is extremely important, for reasons discussed next (Schroeder & Atal, 1985; Kondoz, 1994).

The error-weighting filter is used to shape the spectrum of the error signal in order to reduce the subjective loudness of the error signal. This is possible because the error signal in frequency regions where the speech has high energy will be at least partially masked by the speech. The weighting filter emphasizes the noise in the frequency regions where the speech content is low. Thus, the minimization of the weighted error concentrates the energy of the error signal in frequency regions where the speech has high energy, allowing that the error signal be at least partially masked by the speech, reducing its subjective importance. Such weighting is found to produce a significant improvement in the subjective quality of the reconstructed speech for analysis by synthesis coders (Kondoz, 1994).

Figure 13. Analysis by synthesis speech coding. (a) encoder and (b) decoder

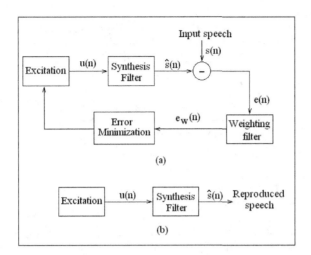

The main feature distinguishing the MPE, RPE, and CELP coders is how the excitation waveform $u(n)$ for the synthesis filter is chosen. Conceptually every possible waveform is passed through the filter to see what reconstructed speech signal this excitation would produce. The excitation that gives the minimum weighted error between the original and the reconstructed speech is then chosen by the encoder and used to drive the synthesis filter at the decoder. This determination of the excitation sequence allows the analysis by synthesis coders to produce good quality speech at low bit rates. However, the numerical complexity required determining the excitation signal in this way is huge; as a result, some means of reducing this complexity, without compromising the performance of the codec too badly, must be found (Kondoz, 1994).

The differences between MPE, RPE, and CELP coders arise from the representation of the excitation signal $u(n)$ to be used. In MPE the excitation is represented using pulses not uniformly distributed, typically eight pulses each 10ms (Bosi & Goldberg, 2002; Kondoz, 1994). The method to determine the position and amplitude of each pulse is through the minimization of a given criterion, usually the mean square error, as shown in Figure 13. The regular pulse is similar to MPE, in which the excitation is represented using a set of 10 pulses uniformly in an interval of 5ms. In this approach the position of the first pulse is determined, minimizing the mean square error. Once the position of the first pulse is determined, the positions of the remaining nine pulses are automatically determined. Finally the optimal amplitude of all pulses is estimated by solving a set of simultaneous equations. The pan-European GSM mobile telephone system uses a simplified RPE codec, with long-term prediction, operating at 13kbits/s. Figure 14 shows the difference between both excitation sequences.

Although MPE and RPE coders can provide good speech quality at rates of around 10kbits/s and higher, they are not suitable for lower bit rates. This is due to the large amount of information that must be transmitted about the excitation pulses positions and amplitudes. If

Figure 14. Multi-pulse and regular pulse excitation sequences

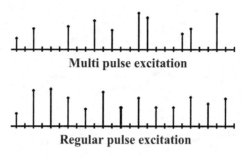

Multi pulse excitation

Regular pulse excitation

we attempt to reduce the bit rate by using fewer pulses, or coarsely quantizing their amplitudes, the reconstructed speech quality deteriorates rapidly. It is necessary to look for other approaches to produce good quality speech at rates below 10kbits/s. A suitable approach to this end is the CELP proposed by Schroeder and Atal in 1985, which differs from MPE and RPE in that the excitation signal is effectively vector quantized. Here the excitation is given by an entry from a large vector quantizer codebook and a gain term to control its power. Typically the codebook index is represented with about 10 bits (to give a codebook size of 1,024 entries), and the gain is coded with about 5 bits. Thus the bit rate necessary to transmit the excitation information is greatly reduced. Typically it requires around 15 bits compared to the 47 bits used for example in the GSM RPE codec.

Early versions of the CELP coders use codebooks containing white Gaussian sequences. This is because it was assumed that long- and short-term predictors would be able to remove nearly all the redundancy from the speech signal to produce a random noise-like residual signal. Also, it was shown that the short-term probability density function (pdf) of this residual error was nearly Gaussian (Schroeder & Atal, 1985), and then using such a codebook to produce the excitation for long and short-term synthesis filters could produce high quality speech. However, to choose which codebook entry to use in an analysis-by-synthesis procedure meant that every excitation sequence had to be passed through the synthesis filters to see how close the reconstructed speech it produced would be to the original. Because this procedure requires a large computational complexity, much work has been carried out for reducing the complexity of CELP codecs, mainly through altering the structure of the codebook. Also, large advances have been made with the speed possible from DSP chips, so that now it is relatively easy to implement a real-time CELP codec on a single, low cost DSP chip. Several important speech-coding standards have been defined based on the CELP, such as the American Defense Department (DoD) of 4.8kbits/s and the CCITT low delay CELP of 16kbits/s (Bosi & Goldberg, 2002; Kondoz, 1994).

The CELP codec structure can be improved and used at rates below 4.8kbits/s by classifying speech segments into voiced, unvoiced, and transition frames, which are then coded differently with a specially designed encoder for each type. For example, for unvoiced frames the encoder will not use any long-term prediction, whereas for voiced frames such prediction is vital but the fixed codebook may be less important. Such class-dependent codecs are ca-

Table 1. Digital speech coding standards

Rate Kb/s	Application	Type of Coder	Year
64	Public Switched Telephone Network	Pulse Code Modulation (PCM)	1972
2.4	U.S. Government Federal Standard	Linear Predictive Coding	1977
32	Public Switched Telephone Network	Adaptive Differential PCM	1984
9.6	Skyphone	Multii-Pulse Linear Predictive Coding (MPLPC)	1990
13	Pan-European Digital Mobile Radio (DMR) Cellular System (GSM)	Regular Pulse Excitation Linear Prediction Coding (RPE-LPC)	1991
4.8	U.S. Government Federal Standard	Codebook Excited Linear Prediction Coding (CELP).	1991
16	Public Switched Telephone Network	Low Delay CELP (LD-CELP)	1992
6.7	Japanese Digital Mobile Radio (DMR)	Vector Sum Excited Linear Prediction Coding (VSELP)	1977

pable of producing reasonable quality speech at bit rates of 2.4kbits/s. Multi-band excitation (MBE) codecs work by declaring some regions the frequency domain as voiced and others as unvoiced. They transmit for each frames a pitch period, spectral magnitude and phase information, and voiced/unvoiced decisions for the harmonics of the fundamental frequency. This structure produces a good quality speech at 8kbits/s. Table 1 provides a summary of some of the most significant CELP coders (Kondoz, 1994).

Higher bandwidths than that of the telephone bandwidth result in major subjective improvements. Thus a bandwidth of 50 to 20 kHz not only improves the intelligibility and naturalness of audio and speech, but also adds a feeling of transparent communication, making speaker recognition easier. However, this will result in the necessity of storing and transmitting a much larger amount of data, unless efficient wideband coding schemes are used. Wideband speech and audio coding intend to minimize the storage and transmission costs while providing an audio and speech signal with no audible differences between the compressed and the actual signals with 20kHz or higher bandwidth and a dynamic range equal of above 90 dB. Four key technology aspects play a very important role to achieve this goal: the perceptual coding, frequency domain coding, window switching, and dynamic bit allocation. Using these features the speech signal is divided into a set of non-uniform subbands to encode with more precision the perceptually more significant components and with fewer bits the perceptually less significant frequency components. The subband approach also allows the use of the masking effect in which the frequency components close to those with larger amplitude are masked, and then they can be discharged without audible degradation. These features, together with a dynamic bit allocation, allow significant reduction of the total bits required for encoding the audio signal without perceptible degradation of the audio signal quality. Some of the most representative coders of this type are listed in Table 2 (Madisetti & Williams, 1998).

Table 2. Some of the most used wideband speech and audio coders

Coder	Bit Rate	Application
CCITT G.722	64 kbits/s 56 kbits/s 48 kbits/s	Speech
Low Delay CELP	32 kbits/s	Speech
Compact Disc	1.41Mbits/s	Audio
Perceptual Audio Coder	128 kbits/s	Audio
MP3(MPEG-1 layer III)	96 kbits/s	Audio
Windows Media Audio	64 kbits/s	Audio
VQF	80 kbits/s	Audio
MP3PRO	64 kbits/s	Audio
OGG Vorbis	96 kbits/s	Audio
WAV	10 Mbits/m	Audio

Medical Applications of Signal Processing Technology

Signal processing has been successfully used to improve the life quality of persons with hearing and speaking problems (Davis, 2002). Among them we have the development of hearing aids devices, which attempt to selectively amplify the frequencies in the sound that is not properly perceived. The enhancement of alaryngeal speech is another successful application in which signal processing and pattern recognition methods are used to improve the intelligibility and speech quality of persons whose larynx and vocal cords have been extracted by a surgical operation (Aguilar, Nakano-Miyatake, & Perez-Meana, 2005). Signal processing algorithms have also been developed to modify the time scale of speech signal to improve the hearing capabilities of elderly people (Childers, 2000; Nakano-Miyatake, Perez-Meana, Rodriguez-Peralta, & Duchen-Sanchez, 2000).

Enhancement and Restoration of Alaryngeal Speech Signals

Persons who suffer from diseases such as throat cancer require that their larynx and vocal cords be extracted by a surgical operation and then require rehabilitation in order to be able to reintegrate to their individual, social, familiar, and work activities. To accomplish this, different methods have been used, such as the esophageal speech, the use of tracheoesophagical prosthetics, and the artificial larynx transducer (ALT), also known as "electronic larynx." Among them the esophageal speech and ALT, which has been used by alaryngeal patients for over the last 40 years without essential changes, are the most widely used rehabilitation method.

Figure 15. Alaryngeal speech enhancement system

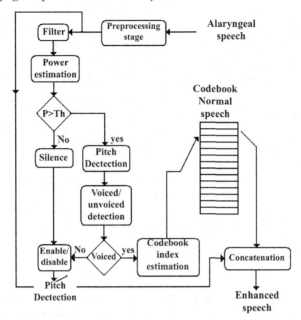

The esophageal speech is produced by injecting air to the mouth, from the stomach through the esophagus, which is then modulated by the mouth movement. When the patient is able to learn how to produce the esophageal speech, this method is very convenient because it does not require any additional device. However, although the esophageal speech is an attractive alternative, its quality is low.

The ALT, which has the form of a handheld device, introduces an excitation in the vocal track by applying a vibration against the external walls of the neck. This excitation is then modulated by the movement of the oral cavity to produce the speech sound. This transducer is attached to the speaker's neck, and in some cases in the speaker's cheeks. The ALT is widely recommended by voice rehabilitation physicians because it is very easy to use, even for new patients, although the voice produced by these transducers is unnatural and with low quality, and besides that it is distorted by the ALT produced background noise. This results in a considerable degradation of the quality and intelligibility of speech, a problem for which an optimal solution has not yet been found.

To improve the speech quality of alaryngeal speech signal, Aguilar et al. (2005) proposed an enhancement alaryngeal speech algorithm whose block diagram is shown in Figure 15, in which the voiced segments of alaryngeal speech are replaced by their equivalent voiced segments of normal speech, while the unvoiced and silence segments are kept without change. The main reason about it is the fact that the voiced segments have more impact on the speech quality. To achieve this goal, the following steps are carried out:

- **Step 1:** First the alaryngeal speech signal is processed to reduce the background noise.

- **Step 2:** The preprocessed signal is filtered with a low pass filter with cutoff frequency of 900Hz and then the silence segments are estimated using the time average of the power signal as proposed. Here, if a silence segment is detected, the switch is enabled, and the segment is concatenated with the previous one to produce the output signal.

- **Step 3:** If voice activity is detected, the speech segment is analyzed to determine if it is a voiced or unvoiced one. To do this the signal is segmented in blocks of 30ms, with 50% of overlap, to estimate the pitch period using the autocorrelation method [10] and [11]. If no pitch is detected the segment is unvoiced and concatenated at the output with the previous segments.

- **Step 4:** If pitch periods are detected, the segment is considered as voiced, and the codebook index estimation is performed.

- **Step 5:** The first 12 linear prediction coefficients (LPCs) of the voiced segment are estimated using the Levinson Durbin method.

- **Step 6:** The LPCs estimated in Step 5 are fed into a multilayer ANN, to estimate the optimum codebook index. Here, first a multilayer ANN was used to identify the vowel present in the voiced segment; the ANN structure has a 12-9-5 structure, that is, 12 neurons in the input layer, 9 in the hidden, and 5 in the output layer. Once the vowel is identified, the same LPCs are fed into a second ANN with a 12-23-8 structure. This structure performs more accurate voiced segment identification by identifying the vowel-consonant combination. All neural networks are trained using the backpropagation algorithm, as described in Aguilar et al. (2005), with 650 different alaryngeal voiced segments with a convergence factor equal to 0.009, achieving a mean square error of 0.1 after 400,000 iterations.

- **Step 7:** Once the voiced segment is identified, it is replaced by its equivalent voiced segment of normal speech stored in a codebook and concatenated with the previous segments.

Evaluation results show that a fairly good enhancement performance can be obtained.

Watermarking

Digital watermarking is a technique used to embed a collection of bits into a signal, in such way that it will be kept imperceptible to users and the resulting watermarked signal remains with almost the same quality as the original one. Watermarks can be embedded into audio, image, video, and other formats of digital data in either the temporal or spectral domains (Bender et al., 1996; Cox, Millar, & Bloom, 2001). Here the temporal watermarking algorithms embed watermarks into audio signals in their temporal domain, while the spectral watermarking algorithms embed watermarks in certain transform domains, such as Fourier transform domain, wavelet domain, or cepstrum domain (Bassia et al., 2001; Kim & Choi, 2003; Kwang, Lee, & Sung-Ho, 2000). Depending on their particular application, the watermarking algorithms can be classified as robust or fragile watermarks. Here the robust watermarking algorithms, which cannot be removed by common signal processing operations, are used for copyright protection, distribution monitoring, copy control, and so forth, while the fragile watermark, which will be changed if the host audio is modified, is used to verify the authenticity of audio signal, speech signal, and so forth. Because of its importance and potential use in digital material protection and authentication, this topic is analyzed with detail in Chapters V and VI.

Other Successful Applications

Besides the applications described previously, signal processing technology has found wide acceptance in the audio and speech in applications such as natural sound and recognition, cross language conversion, speaker recognition, musical instruments synthesis and audio effects, and so forth.

Natural sound recognition has found a wide acceptance in applications such as machine preventive maintenance and failure diagnostic (Hattori, Ishihara, Komatani, Ogata, & Okuno, 2004). Here, analyzing the noise produced by a given machine, it is possible to determine a possible failure preventing in this way that it would broken down. In the military field the analysis of the sound produced by a given aircraft, ship, or submarine is widely used to determine if it is an enemy or not.

The speech recognition, which can be divided into isolate word recognition and continuous speech recognition, is one of the most developed signal processing applications in the speech field (Kravchenko, Basarab, Pustoviot, & Perez-Meana, 2001). The main difference among them is the fact that, while in isolate speech recognition the target is to recognize a single spoken word, in continuous speech recognition the target is to recognize a spoken sentence. Thus, although both approaches present many similarities, both of them also have strong differences that gave as a result a separate development of both fields (Rabiner & Biing-Hwang, 1993; Rabiner & Gold, 1975). Accompanying chapters in this book provide a complete description of speech recognition algorithms. Voice conversion is a related problem, whose purpose is to modify the speaker voice to sound as if a given target speaker had spoken it. Voice conversion technology offers a large number of useful applications such as personification of text-to-speech synthesis, preservation of the speaker characteristics in interpreting systems and movie doubling, and so forth (Abe, Nakamura, Shikano, & Kawaba, 1988; Childers, 2000; Narayanan & Alwan, 2005).

Speech signal processing can also contribute to solving security problems such as the access control to restricted information or places. To this end, several efficient speaker recognition algorithms, which can be divided in speaker classification, whose target is to identify the person who emitted the voice signal, and speaker verification, and whose goal is to verify if this person is who he/she claims to be, have been proposed (Lee, Soong, & Paliwal, 1996; Simancas, Kurematsu, Nakano-Miyatake, & Perez-Meana, 2001). This topic is analyzed in an accompanying chapter of this book.

Finally, the music field has also take advantage of the signal processing technology through the development of efficient algorithms for generation of synthetic music and audio effects (Childers, 2000; Gold & Morgan, 2000).

Open Issues

The audio and speech processing have achieved an important development during the last three decades; however, several problems that must be solved still remain, such as to develop more efficient echo canceller structures with improved double talk control systems. In adaptive noise canceling, a very important issue that remains unsolved is the crosstalk problem. To get efficient active noise cancellation systems, it is necessary to cancel the antinoise wave that is inside the reference microphone, which distorts the reference signal to reduce the computational complexity of ANC systems, as well as to develop a more accurate secondary path estimation. Another important issue is to develop low distortion speech coders for bit rates below of 4.8kbits/s. Another important issue is to increase the convergence speed of adaptive equalizers, to allow the tracking of fast time varying communication channels. The speech and audio processing systems will also contribute to improve the performance of medical equipments such as hearing aids and alaryngeal speech enhancement systems, as well as in security through the development of efficient and accurate speaker recognition and verification systems. Finally, in recent years, the digital watermarking algorithms has grown rapidly; however, several issues remain open, such as development of an efficient algorithm taking in account the human auditory system (HAS), solving synchronization problems using multi-bits watermarks, as well as developing efficient watermarking algorithms for copy control.

Conclusion

Audio and speech signal processing have been fields of intensive research during the last three decades, becoming an essential component for interference cancellation and speech compression and enhancement in telephone and data communication systems, high fidelity broadband coding in audio and digital TV systems, speech enhancement for speech and speaker recognition systems, and so forth. However, despite the development that speech and audio systems have achieved, the research in those fields is increasing in order to provide new and more efficient solutions in the previously mentioned fields, and several others such as the acoustic noise reduction to improve the environmental conditions of people working in the airports, in factories, and so forth, to improve the security of restricted places through speaker verification systems and improve the speech quality of alaryngeal people through more efficient speech enhancement methods. Thus it can be predicted that the speech and audio processing will contribute to more comfortable living conditions during the following years.

References

Abe, M., Nakamura, S., Shikano, K., & Kawaba, H. (1988). Voice conversion through vector quantization. In *Proceedings of ICASSP* (pp. 655-658).

Aguilar, G., Nakano-Miyatake, M., & Perez-Meana, H. (2005). Alaryngeal speech enhancement using pattern recognition techniques. *IEICE Trans. Inf. & Syst. E88-D,*(7), 1618-1622.

Amano, F., Perez-Meana, H., De Luca, A., & Duchen, G. (1995). A multirate acoustic echo canceler structure. *IEEE Trans. on Communications, 43*(7), 2173-2176.

Bender, W., Gruhl, D., Marimoto, N., & Lu. (1996). Techniques for data hiding. *IBM Systems Journal, 35*, 313-336.

Bosi, M., & Goldberg, R. (2002). *Introduction to digital audio coding and standards.* Boston: Kluwer Academic Publishers.

Bassia, P., Pitas, I., & Nikoladis, N. (2001). Robust audio watermarking in time domain. *IEEE Transactions on Multimedia, 3*, 232-241.

Childers, D. (2000). *Speech processing and synthesis toolboxes.* New York: John Wiley & Sons.

Cox, I., Miller, M., & Bloom, J. (2001). *Digital watermark: Principle and practice.* New York: Morgan Kaufmann.

Davis, G. (2002). *Noise reduction in speech applications.* New York: CRC Press.

Gold, B., & Morgan, N. (2000). *Speech and audio signal processing.* New York: John Wiley & Sons.

Hattori, Y., Ishihara, K., Komatani, K., Ogata, T., & Okuno, H. (2004). Repeat recognition for environmental sounds. In *Proceedings of IEEE International Workshop on Robot and Human Interaction* (pp. 83-88).

Haykin, S. (1991). *Adaptive filter theory.* Englewood Cliffs, NJ: Prentice Hall.

Kim, H. J., & Choi, Y. H. (2003). A novel echo-hiding scheme with backward and forward kernels. *IEEE Transactions on Circuits and Systems for Video and Technology, 13*(August), 885-889.

Kondoz, A. M. (1994). *Digital speech.* Chinchester, England: Wiley & Sons.

Kwang, S., Lee, & Sung-Ho, Y. (2000). Digital audio watermarking in the cepstrum domain. *IEEE Transactions on Consumer Electronics, 46*(3), 744-750.

Kravchenko, V., Basarab, M., Pustoviot, V., & Perez-Meana, H. (2001). New construction of weighting windows based on atomic functions in problems of speech processing. *Journal of Doklady Physics, 377*(2), 183-189.

Kuo, S., & Morgan, D. (1996). *Active noise control system: Algorithms and DSP implementations.* New York: John Wiley & Sons.

Lee, C., Soong, F., & Paliwal, K. (1996). *Automatic speech and speaker recognition.* Boston: Kluwer Academic Publishers.

Madisetti, V., & Williams, D. (1998). *The digital signal processing handbook.* Boca Raton, FL: CRC Press.

Messershmitt, D. (1984). Echo cancellation in speech and data transmission. *IEEE Journal of Selected Areas in Communications, 2*(3), 283-297.

Mirchandani, G., Zinser, R., & Evans, J. (1992). A new adaptive noise cancellation scheme in presence of crosstalk. *IEEE Trans. on Circuit and Systems, 39*(10), 681-694.

Nakano-Miyatake, M., Perez-Meana, H., Rodriguez-Peralta, P., & Duchen-Sanchez, G. (2000). Time scaling modification in speech signal applications. In *The International Symposium of Information Theory and its Applications* (pp. 927-930). Hawaii.

Narayanan, A., & Alwan, A. (2005). *Text to speech synthesis.* Upper Saddle River, NJ: Prentice Hall.

Perez-Meana, H., Nakano-Miyatake, M., & Nino-de-Rivera, L. (2002). Speech and audio signal application. In G. Jovanovic-Dolecek (Ed.), *Multirate systems design and applications* (pp. 200-224). Hershey, PA: Idea Group Publishing.

Proakis, J. (1985). *Digital communications.* New York: McGraw Hill.

Rahim, M. (1994). *Artificial neural networks for speech analysis/synthesis.* London: Chapman & Hall.

Rabiner, L., & Gold, B. (1975). *Digital processing of speech signals.* Englewood Cliffs, NJ: Prentice Hall.

Rabiner, L., & Biing-Hwang, J. (1993). *Fundamentals of speech recognition.* Englewood Cliff, NJ: Prentice Hall.

Schroeder, M., & Atal, B. (1985). Code excited linear prediction (CELP): High quality speech at very low bit rates. In *Proceedings of ICASSP* (pp. 937-940).

Simancas, E., Kurematsu, A., Nakano-Miyatake, M., & Perez-Meana, H. (2001). Speaker recognition using Gaussian Mixture Models. In *Lecture notes in computer science, bio-inspired applications of connectionism* (pp. 287-294). Berlin: Springer Verlag.

Tapia-Sánchez, D., Bustamante, R., Pérez–Meana, H., & Nakano–Miyatake, M.(2005). Single channel active noise canceller algorithm using discrete cosine transform. *Journal of Signal Processing, 9*(2), 141-151.

Yeo, I., & Kim, H. (2003). Modified patchwork algorithm: A novel audio watermarking scheme. *IEEE Transactions on Speech and Audio Processing, 11*(4), 381-386.

Widrow, B., & Stearns, S. (1985). *Adaptive signal processing.* Englewood Cliffs, NJ: Prentice Hall.

Section I

Audio and Speech Signal Processing Technology

This section analyzes some successful applications of the audio and speech signal processing technology, specifically in applications regarding the audio effects, audio synthesis, and restoration.

Chapter II

Digital Filters for Digital Audio Effects

Gordana Jovanovic Dolecek, National Institute of Astrophysics, Mexico

Alfonso Fernandez-Vazquez, National Institute of Astrophysics, Mexico

Abstract

This chapter introduces several digital filters useful for sound generation and transformation as well as for production of audio effects. It also argues that the applications of digital filters give rise to new possibilities in creating sound effects, which would be difficult and almost impossible by analog means. The problem of how to eliminate desired frequencies and noise from speech signal is considered first. Then, the effect of delay and echo is investigated, whereby single and multiple echo filters are considered. Comb filter and its modification useful for obtaining a more natural reverberation effect are also considered. Two filters proposed by Schroeder for a realization of the artificial reverberation are also given. Finally, the filters using variable delays to produce flanging and chorus effect and equalizers are described. The authors hope that this introductory text about digital filters will be useful in further investigation and applications of digital filters in generating digital audio effects.

Introduction

The goal of this chapter is to explore different digital filters useful in generating and transforming sound and producing audio effects. "Audio editing functions that change the sonic character of a recording, from loudness to tonal quality, enter the realm of *digital signal processing* (DSP)" (Fries & Fries, 2005, p. 15). Applications of digital filters enable new possibilities in creating sound effects, which would be difficult and impossible to do by analog means (Pellman, 1994.)

Music generated in a studio does not sound as natural as for example music performed in a concert hall. In a concert hall there exists an effect called natural reverberation, which is produced by the reflections of sounds off surfaces (Duncan, 2003; Gold & Morgan, 2000.) In fact, some of the sounds travel directly to the listener, while some of the sounds from the instrument reflect off the walls, the ceiling, the floor, and so forth before reaching the listener, as indicated in Figure 1(a). Because these reflections have traveled greater distances, they

Figure 1. Natural reverberation

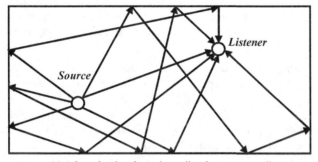

(a) A few of paths of sound traveling from source to listener

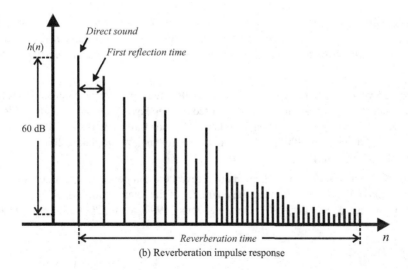

(b) Reverberation impulse response

will reach the listener later than the direct sound. The amount and quality of reverberation in a natural environment are influenced by certain factors: the volume and dimensions of the space and the type, shape, and number of surfaces that the sound encounters (Dodge & Jerse, 1997).

The natural reverberation is presented by the impulse response of the room, obtained as room's response over time to a very short burst (an impulse). A typical impulse response of a reverberated sound is shown in Figure 1(b), where the parameters called the reverberation time and the first reflection time are depicted.

The reverberation time is the amount of time it takes for the sound to die away to 60 dB of its original amplitude. The first reflection time is the amount of time separating the direct sound from the first reflection.

Natural reverberation typically follows a quasi-exponential curve that reaches a peak and decays more or less slowly. In general, an irregular time interval between peaks is desirable in a concert hall. Regularly spaced peaks indicate "ringing" resonant frequencies in the hall, which can be annoying (Curtis, 2002). Lower frequencies of sound are reflected more efficiently than higher frequencies. As a consequence, high frequency sounds have a lower reverberation time (McClellan, Schafer, & Yoder, 1998; Orfanidis, 1996; Pellman, 1994).

Audio effects, also known as artificial reverberation, are artificially generated, manipulated, and combined in order to get a stereo high quality sound recording that looks natural. This effect spatializes sounds, thus leading to the illusion of sounds emerging from imaginary environments.

From a signal processing point of view, an artificial reverberator is a filter with an impulse response that resembles the impulse response of a room (Curtis, 2002). Effective simulation of natural reverberation requires high echo density (Dodge & Jerse, 1997.) Fries and Fries (2005) make an analogy of the sound processing with the word processing (font manipulation): "*You can adjust the size and style of your fonts, bold them for emphasis, and apply dramatic effects to grab a reader's attention*" (p. 38).

Further, Pellman (1994) says that:

The effect of signal processors on a sound should perhaps be thought of in the same way as that of spices in cooking." Pellman also makes remark that "*too much artificial reverberation can have just as unsatisfactory a result as an excess of oregano in a pasta salad.* (p. 68)

For the past 25 years an extensive research has been devoted to the electronic techniques for simulating natural reverberation, and different techniques have been proposed to achieve real-auralization in virtual acoustic environments (Fouad, Ballas, & Brock, 2000; Green, 2003; Mitra, 2006; Tsingos, 2001, 2005; Tsingos, Emmanuel, & Drettakis, 2004; Wenzel, Miller, & Abel, 2000; etc.).

The use of digital techniques to simulate natural reverberation permits a great deal of control over the parameters that determine the character of the reverberation (Belanger, 2000; Darlington, Daudet, & Sandler, 2002; Dodge & Jerse, 1997; Mitra, 2006; Steiglitz, 1996; Tempelaars, 1996).

Here we present methods for generating different sound effects using appropriate digital filters. In order to better understand the process of generating sound effects, the filters are described in both the time and the transform domain using Fourier and z-transform. Filters are designed using MATLAB, and the corresponding effects are illustrated on the speech signal. The rest of the chapter is organized as follows. The next section introduces the speech signal used to illustrate different sound effects. Some basic filtering operations are also discussed. The following section deals with the single echo filter, followed by sections discussing multiple echo filters, allpass filters, and lowpass reverberation filters. Finally, natural sounding reverberation filters, filters using variable delays, and equalizers are presented.

Loading the Speech Signal and the
Basic Filtering Operations

In this text we use the speech signal file from MATLAB (The MathWorks Inc., 2000). To load the signal and to analyze its frequency content we use the following MATLAB command:

load mtlb

This signal is "Matlab" and has 4,001 samples. The sampling frequency *Fs* is 7418 Hz. The signal is shown in Figure 2(a), and its power spectral density is shown in Figure 2(b).

We now apply basic filtering operations on this speech signal. The lowpass filtering applied to the speech removes all high-frequency components. We use two lowpass filters. The first one keeps all frequencies below 1000 Hz and eliminates all frequencies higher than 2000 Hz.

The second filter preserves the frequencies less than 500 Hz, and attenuates the frequencies higher than 1000 Hz. The corresponding cut-off digital frequencies in radians for the first filter are as follows.

Passband frequency:

$$\omega_p = \frac{f_p}{F_s/2} = \frac{1000}{7418/2} = 0.2696 \tag{1}$$

Stopband frequency:

$$\omega_s = \frac{f_s}{F_s/2} = \frac{2000}{7418/2} = 0.5392 \tag{2}$$

Similarly, for the second filter we have:

$$\omega_p = 0.1348, \quad \omega_s = 0.2696 \tag{3}$$

Figure 2. Speech signal

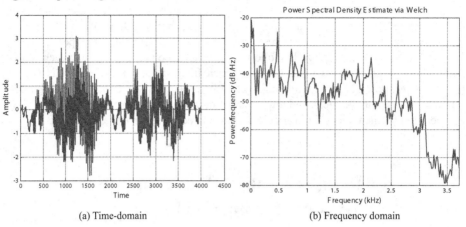

(a) Time-domain   (b) Frequency domain

Figure 3. Lowpass filters

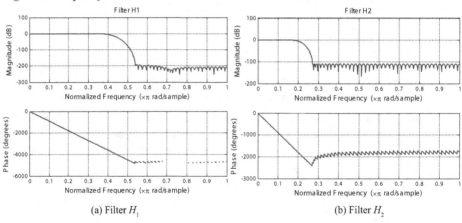

(a) Filter H_1 (b) Filter H_2

Magnitude and phase responses for both filters are shown in Figure 3.

The speech signal from Figure 2 is filtered using lowpass filters shown in Figure 3. The corresponding outputs are given in Figure 4(a) and 4(b). Note that as a result of lowpass filtering the output signal is "smoother" than the input. The zooms of the output signals (samples from 3000-3200), shown in Figures 4(c) and 4(d) demonstrate that the filtering by a narrower lowpass filter results in a smoother response. The corresponding power spectral densities of the outputs from the filters H_1 and H_2 are shown in Figures 4(e) and 4(f), respectively.

We now add noise at 2500Fz and 3200 Hz:

$$noise = \sin(2\pi \times 2500t) + 0.9\sin(2\pi \times 3200t) \qquad (4)$$

Figure 4. Filtered speech signals

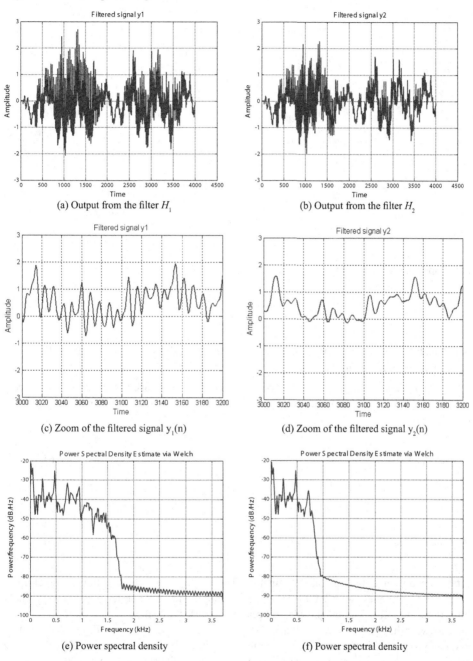

(a) Output from the filter H_1

(b) Output from the filter H_2

(c) Zoom of the filtered signal $y_1(n)$

(d) Zoom of the filtered signal $y_2(n)$

(e) Power spectral density

(f) Power spectral density

Figure 5. Speech signal with added noise

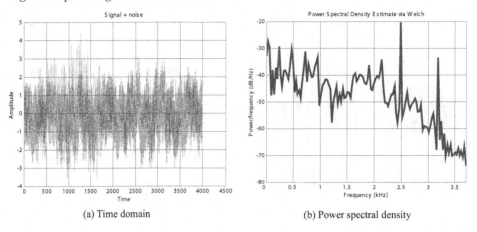

(a) Time domain   (b) Power spectral density

to the speech signal *x* from Fig.2 to get the signal:

$$xx = x + noise,$$ (5)

which is shown in Figure 5(a). Its power spectral density is shown in Figure 5(b). Notice that the power spectral density has two peaks corresponding to the frequencies of the noise.

We now consider how to design filters for the elimination of noise (Fernandez-Vazquez & Jovanovic-Dolecek, 2006b). We calculate the corresponding normalized digital frequencies in radians:

$$\omega_1 = 2\pi f_1 / Fs,$$ (6)

and,

$$\omega_2 = 2\pi f_2 / Fs.$$ (7)

First, consider the 2500 Hz noise elimination. The corresponding notch filter, which eliminates noise at frequency f_1=2500 Hz, has a zero on the unit circle at the frequency ω_1. The filter order N_1 is 14. The magnitude and phase responses are shown in Figure 6(a), while the corresponding power spectral density of the filtered signal is shown in Figure 6(b). Note that the noise at frequency 2500 Hz is eliminated. Similarly, the second notch filter, which eliminates noise at frequency 3200 Hz, has a zero on the unit circle at the frequency ω_2, and the filter order N_2=6. The corresponding magnitude and phase characteristics of the filters are shown in Figure 6(c). The power spectral density of the filtered signal shows that the noise

Figure 6. Eliminating the noise in the speech signal

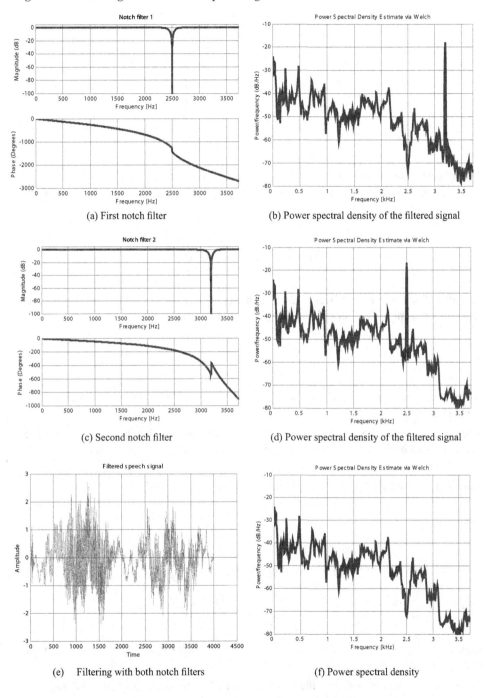

(a) First notch filter

(b) Power spectral density of the filtered signal

(c) Second notch filter

(d) Power spectral density of the filtered signal

(e)   Filtering with both notch filters

(f) Power spectral density

Figure 7. Single echo filter

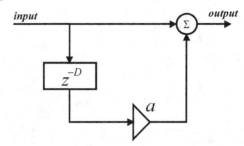

at frequency 3200 Hz is eliminated. The noise is completely eliminated if the output of the first notch filter is filtered by the second notch filter, as illustrated at Figures 6(e) and 6(f).

Single Echo Filter

A single reflection or echo of signal can be implemented by the following filter, which adds to the direct signal an attenuated and delayed copy of itself:

$$y(n) = x(n) + ax(n - D), \tag{8}$$

where D is time delay and a is a measure of the reflection and propagation losses so that $|a| \leq 1$ (Figure 7).

The delay is one of the simplest effects, but it is very valuable when used properly. The delay is also a building block for a number of more complex effects such as reverb, flanging, and chorusing.

From (8) we compute the system function of the filter:

$$H(z) = 1 + az^{-D}, \tag{9}$$

where z is the complex value, and the transfer function, as:

$$H(e^{j\omega}) = 1 + ae^{-j\omega D}. \tag{10}$$

Figure 8 shows magnitude and phase responses of the filter (9) for different values of the constant a and the delay D.

We analyze the effect changing the parameter a for the constant value of D set to 2000. The corresponding echo signals are shown in Figure 9 for a set to 0.1, 0.5, 0.8, and 0.9, respectively.

Figure 8. Magnitude and phase responses for single echo filter

(a) *D*=5, *a*=0.2

(b) *D*=5, *a*=0.9

(c) *D*=50, *a*=0.9

(d) *D*=500, *a*=0.9

Figure 9. Echo signals for different values of constant a

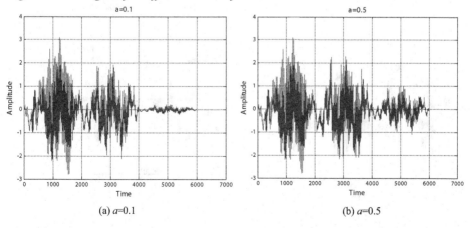

(a) *a*=0.1

(b) *a*=0.5

Figure 9. continued

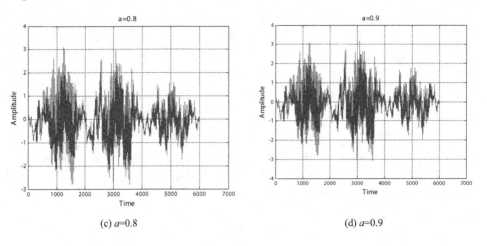

(c) *a*=0.8   (d) *a*=0.9

Figure 10. Echo signals for different values of delays

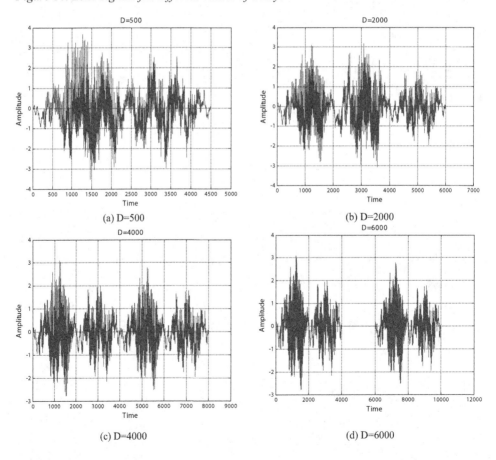

(a) D=500   (b) D=2000

(c) D=4000   (d) D=6000

Figure 11. Magnitude and phase responses for single echo filter (10)

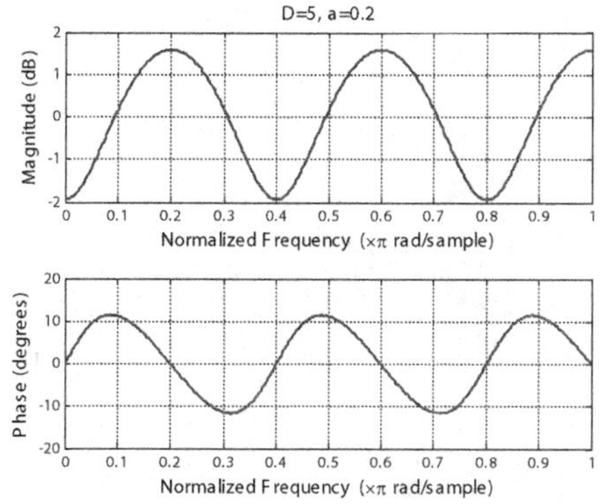

(a) $D=5$, $a=0.2$

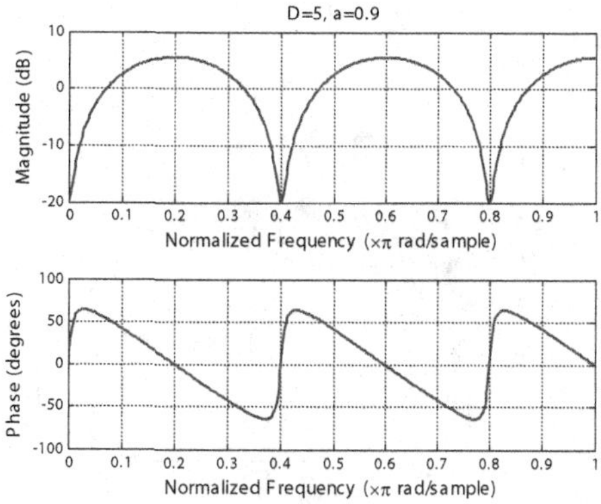

(b) $D=5$, $a=0.9$

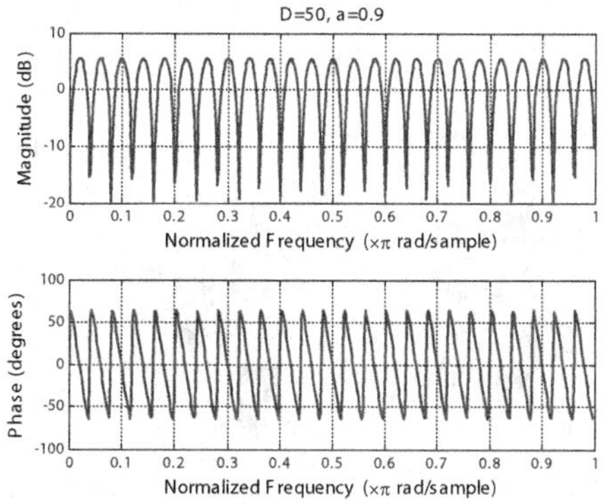

(c) $D=50$, $a=0.9$

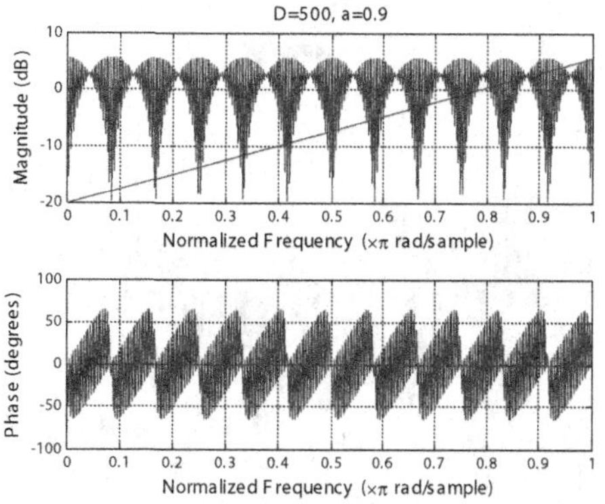

(d) $D=500$, $a=0.9$

Likewise, for the constant value of a equal to 0.9, we investigate the effect of varying delay on the echo signal, by considering D equal to 500, 2000, 4000, and 6000. The resulting echo signals are shown in Figure 10.

Instead of adding the echo, we can subtract it to obtain:

$$y(n) = x(n) - ax(n - D).$$ (11)

From Equation (11) the corresponding system function of the filter is:

$$H(z) = 1 - az^{-D},$$ (12)

Figure 12. Echo signals for different values of delays

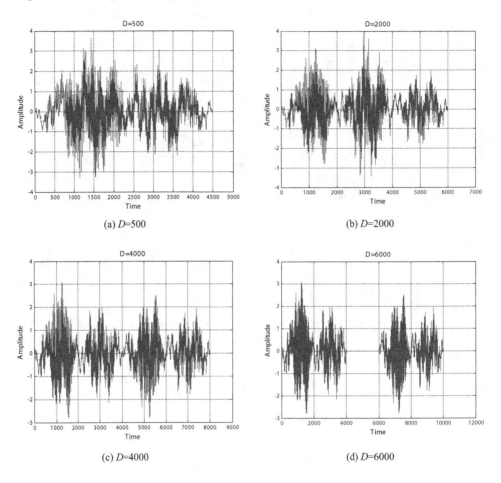

(a) $D=500$

(b) $D=2000$

(c) $D=4000$

(d) $D=6000$

where z is the complex value and the transfer function is:

$$H(e^{j\omega}) = 1 - ae^{-j\omega D}.$$ (13)

Figure 11 shows magnitude and phase responses of the filter (11) for the same values of the constant a and delays D as in Figure 8. The corresponding echo signals are shown in Figure 12.

Figure 13. Multiple echo filter

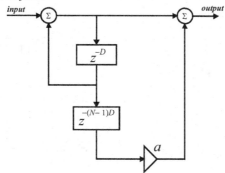

Multiple Echo Filters

If we add multiple echoes spaced D sampling periods apart and scaled with exponentially decaying amplitudes, we get the following signal:

$$y(n) = x(n) + ax(n-D) + a^2 x(n-2D) + ... + a^{N-1} x(n-(N-1)D) \tag{14}$$

The multiple echo filter has the system function:

$$H(z) = 1 + az^{-D} + a^2 z^{-2D} + ... + a^{N-1} z^{-(N-1)D}, \tag{15}$$

which can be expressed in the recursive form,

$$H(z) = \frac{1 - a^N z^{-ND}}{1 - az^{-D}}. \tag{16}$$

The corresponding block diagram is given in Figure13.

Its transfer function is given as:

$$H(e^{j\omega}) = \frac{1 - a^N e^{-j\omega ND}}{1 - ae^{-j\omega D}} = \frac{1 - a^N \cos(\omega ND) + ja^N \sin(\omega ND)}{1 - a\cos(\omega D) + ja\sin(\omega D)}. \tag{17}$$

Figure 14 illustrates the magnitude responses for a=0.9, D=50, and for N=4 and N=10 of this filter.

In the following, we demonstrate the multiple echo filtering of the speech signal using the same parameters as in Figure 14. The echo speech signals are shown in Figure 15.

Figure 14. Multiple echo filters

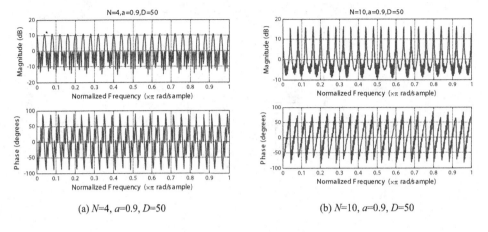

(a) N=4, a=0.9, D=50   (b) N=10, a=0.9, D=50

Figure 15. Multiple echo signals

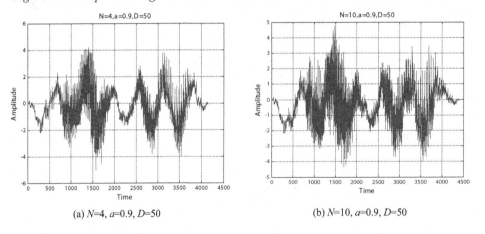

(a) N=4, a=0.9, D=50   (b) N=10, a=0.9, D=50

For N approaching infinity, the result is an IIR filter with an impulse response:

$$y(n) = x(n) + ax(n-D) + a^2 x(n-2D) + ... + a^3 x(n-3D) + ...$$ (18)

The corresponding multiple echo filter has the system function:

$$H(z) = 1 + az^{-D} + a^2 z^{-2D} + a^3 z^{-3D} + ...,$$ (19)

Figure 16. IIR comb filter

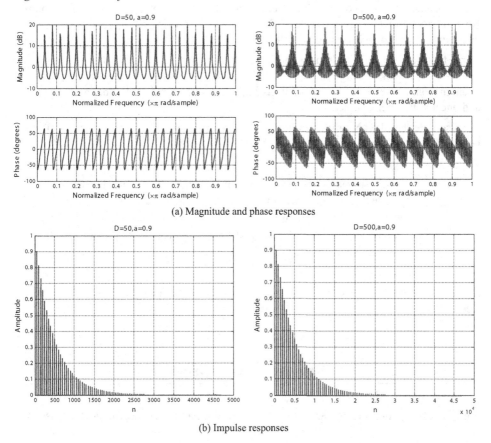

(a) Magnitude and phase responses

(b) Impulse responses

which can be expressed as,

$$H(z) = \frac{1}{1 - az^{-D}}.$$ (20)

The transfer function of this infinite impulse response (IIR) filter is:

$$H(e^{j\omega}) = \frac{1}{1 - ae^{-j\omega D}}.$$ (21)

Figure 16(a) illustrates the resulting magnitude responses for a=0.9, D=50, and D=500, while Figure 16(b) indicates the impulse responses.

The filter (20) is also known as a comb filter (Steiglitz, 1996) since the magnitude response resembles the teeth on a comb. The higher the sample delay, the more "teeth" on the comb. Note that the finite impulse response (FIR) filter (9) is just reciprocal of the filter (11). It is consequently called an inverse comb filter.

Comb filters are versatile building blocks for making sounds of all sorts. "*A comb filter gets you a lot for a little*" (Steiglitz, 1996, p. 125) in the sense that it models a basic physical phenomenon, the return of an echo, but its implementation needs only one multiplication and one addition per sample.

We also note that the comb filter is not good enough for providing natural sound effects because of the following reasons (Green, 2003):

1.   Its magnitude response is not constant for all frequencies. The filter boosts some frequencies, while attenuating others, thus resulting in a "coloration" of many musical sounds that are often undesired for listening purpose.

2.   The impulse response of the filter has equally spaced peaks, while natural echo signals have increasingly dense spikes as time progresses.

In the next section we consider filters with constant magnitude response over all frequencies.

The Allpass Filter

For natural-sounding echoes an allpass filter, which has a flat magnitude response, is used,

$$y(n) = ay(n - D) - ax(n) + x(n - D). \tag{22}$$

The block diagram is shown in Figure 17.

Figure 17. Block diagram of the first order allpass filter

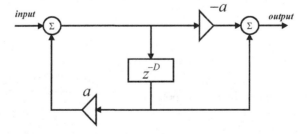

Figure 18. The magnitude and phase responses of allpass filters

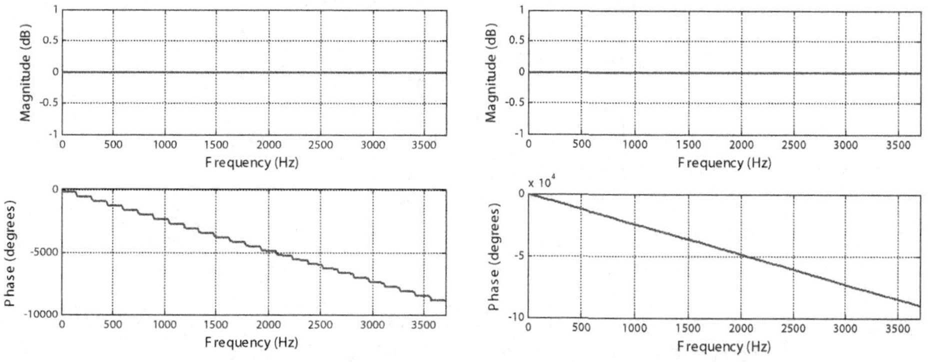

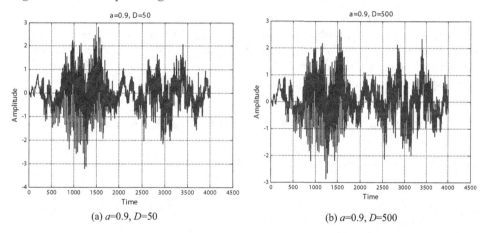

(a) a=0.9, D=50   (b) a=0.9, D=500

Figure 19. Filtered speech signals

(a) a=0.9, D=50   (b) a=0.9, D=500

The system function and the transfer function are, respectively:

$$H(z) = \frac{-a + z^{-D}}{1 - az^{-D}},$$ (23)

$$H(e^{j\omega}) = \frac{-a + e^{-j\omega D}}{1 - ae^{-j\omega D}}.$$ (24)

The magnitude response of the filter for a=0.9, and D=50, and D=500, are shown in Figure, 18. Note that the magnitude response is flat over all frequencies. Therefore, the allpass filter

Figure 20. Lowpass reverberation filter

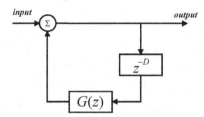

passes all frequencies with equal magnitude and has a significant impact on the phase of the incoming signal. The corresponding filtered signals are shown in Figure 19.

Lowpass Reverberation Filter

Karplus and Strong (1983) proposed a very interesting modification of the comb filter for obtaining a more natural reverberation effect. Their idea is to insert a lowpass filter in the feedback loop. The presence of the lowpass filter in the feedback causes each echo to spread out more and more, resulting in a more diffuse reverberation response. Lowpass reverberation filter is obtained by introducing a lowpass filter $g(n)$ in (18), resulting in:

$$y(n) = x(n) + ag(n)x(n-D) + a^2(g*g)x(n-2D) + a^3(g*g*g)x(n-3D) + ..., \quad (25)$$

where * means the convolution. From (25) we have the following system function,

$$H(z) = \frac{1}{1 - aG(z)z^{-D}}. \quad (26)$$

The corresponding structure is shown in Figure 20.

Consider the following simple lowpass filter:

$$G(z) = 0.5(1 + z^{-1}). \quad (27)$$

The magnitude response of this filter has a cosine form and is shown in Figure 21.

$$G(e^{j\omega}) = e^{-j\omega/2} \cos(\omega/2). \quad (28)$$

Figure 21. Reverberation lowpass filter

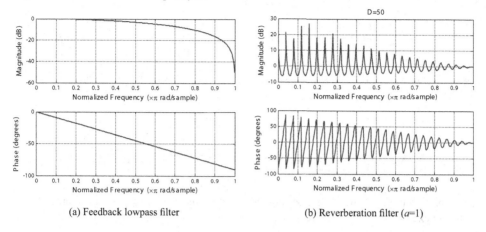

(a) Feedback lowpass filter (b) Reverberation filter ($a=1$)

Figure 22. Filtered speech signals

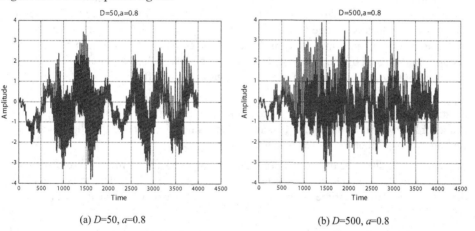

(a) D=50, a=0.8 (b) D=500, a=0.8

Note that the filter (28) is a modest filter that sloped down to zero at the *Fs*/2 (Nyquist frequency). However, it does a nice job because otherwise the high frequency components of the input signal would get wiped out too fast. (Steiglitz, 1996).

Replacing (27) into (26) we arrive at:

$$H(z) = \frac{1}{1 - 0.5az^{-D} - 0.5az^{-(D+1)}}. \tag{29}$$

The corresponding transfer function is:

$$H(e^{j\omega}) = \frac{1}{1 - e^{-j\omega(0.5+D)}a\cos(\omega/2)}. \tag{30}$$

Figure 22 shows the filtered speech signals using filter (30) with a=0.8 and D=50 and D=500.

A Natural Sounding Reverberation Filter

Reverberation filters create the echoes and add them to the original signal. The comb filter (14) is an example of the simple reverberation filter, but it does not provide natural-sounding reverberations.

The comb reverberator (14) and the allpass reverberator (5) can be combined to generate more natural reverberation effects. The comb filters should be connected in parallel to minimize the spectral disturbances, while allpass filters should be connected in cascade, since they are colorless (Dodge & Jerse, 1997; Tempelaars, 1996). For example, a frequency that passes through one comb filter might be attenuated by another. Because of the phase distortion introduced by the allpass filter, connecting allpass filters in parallel can result in a non-uniform amplitude response due to phase cancellation effect.

Figure 23 presents two filters proposed by Schroeder for a realization of the artificial reverberation. An impulse applied to the reverberator of Figure 23(a) initiates a decaying train of echoes from each of the comb filters, that are then summed and fed to the allpass cascade. Cascaded allpass filters increase the echo density.

Similarly, in the structure of Figure 23(b), the five cascaded allpass filters serve to increase pulse density (Dodge & Jerse, 1997). For a natural sound it is important to choose delay times that are relatively prime to one another (i.e., that have no common divisor) (Moorer, 1977, 1979).

The following example considers the Schroeder reverberators using the following delays of the comb filters: D_1=221, D_2=277, D_3 =311, and D_4=327, and the values of a equal to 0.8,

Figure 23. Schroeder Reverberators

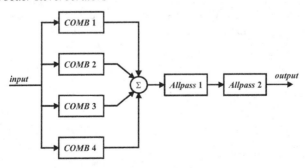

Figure 24. Impulse response

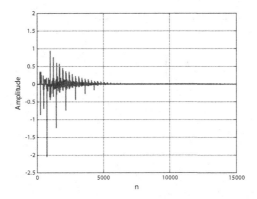

Figure 25. Output signals

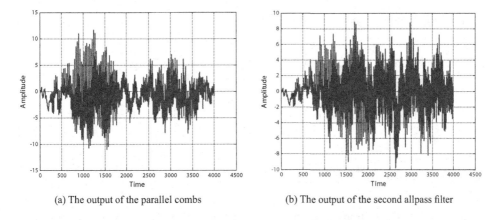

(a) The output of the parallel combs   (b) The output of the second allpass filter

0.7, 0.5, and 0.3, respectively. The corresponding parameters for the allpass filters are 0.6 and 718 for the first allpass filter, and 0.8 and 243 for the second allpass filter. The resulting impulse response and the output signals are shown in Figures 24 and 25.

Filters using Variable Delays

Certain effects can be realized on sounds by using delay lines whose delay time varies on a sample-to-sample basis (Dodge & Jerse, 1997). A delay technique called *flanging* can have a particularly dramatic effect on a sound (Pellman, 1994). In this case the fixed delay is substituted with a time varying delay. In the early days, the flanging effect was created by playing the music piece simultaneously through two tape players and alternately slowing

Figure 26. Flanging effect

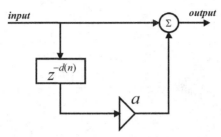

down each tape manually (Orfanidis, 1996). By changing the constant delay D by $d(n)$ in (8) we get:

$$y(n) = x(n) + ax(n - d(n)), \tag{31}$$

as shown in Figure 26. Because the variable delay d can take non-integer values, the desired effect can be accomplished by truncation, rounding, or linear interpolation. (Orfanidis, 1996).

For example, a delay varying sinusoidally between 0 and D will be (Mitra, 2006; Orfanidis, 1996):

$$d(n) = \frac{D}{2}(1 - \cos(\omega_0 n)), \tag{32}$$

where ω_0 is a low pass frequency. The parameter a controls the depth of the notches that occur at odd multiples of π/d.

The chorus effect is the effect of generating same sounds at the same time but with small changes in the amplitudes and small timing differences. The small variations in the time delays and amplitude can be simulated by varying them slowly and randomly replacing the delay as follows:

$$z^{-D} \to z^{-\beta(n)}, \tag{33}$$

where $\beta(n)$ is a low frequency random signal. The technique entails the use of several variable delay lines connected in parallel as shown in Figure 27.

Figure 27. Generation of the chorus effect with variable delays

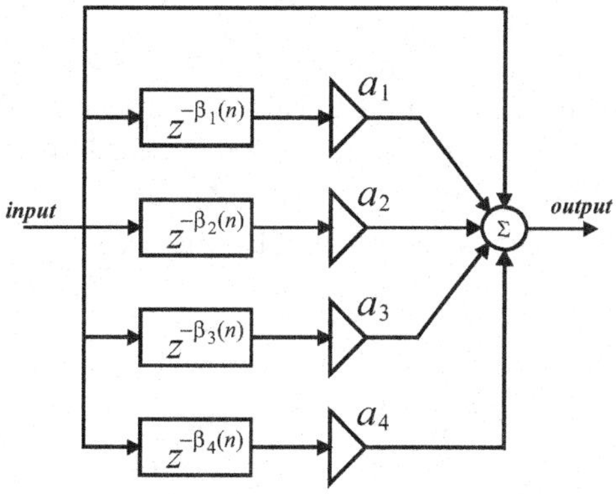

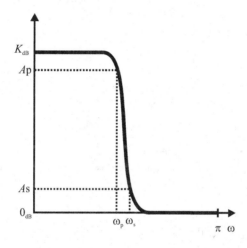

Figure 28. Design parameters for lowpass shelving filter

Equalizers

Two of the most commonly used IIR filters in audio equalization are shelving filters and peaking filters (Keiler & Zölzer, 2004; Mitra, 2006). Shelving filters provide boost or cut equalization, where the cut case is the inverse of the boost case, that is, they amplify or attenuate a certain frequency band while not affecting the remaining frequency range. Peaking filters can have bandpass or stopband frequency responses to provide boot or cut equalization, respectively.

Shelving Filters

In this section, we present the design of shelving filters, which have flat magnitude response in both passband and stopband. The design parameters are the gain K_{dB}, the passband droop A_p, stopband attenuation A_s, passband frequency ω_p, and stopband frequency ω_s, which are shown in Figure 28 for the lowpass case.

The lowpass and highpass shelving filters are given by Mitra (2006):

$$G_{LP}^{(s)} = K \cdot H_{LP}(z) + H_{HP}(z), \tag{34}$$

$$G_{HP}^{(s)} = H_{LP}(z) + K \cdot H_{HP}(z), \tag{35}$$

where $H_{LP}(z)$ and $H_{HP}(z)$ are stable lowpass and highpass filters, respectively.

If the filters $H_{LP}(z)$ and $H_{HP}(z)$ satisfy the power complementary property (Vaidyanathan, 1993), equations (34) and (35) can be rewritten as:

$$G_{LP}^{(s)} = \frac{K}{2}[A_0(z) + A_1(z)] + \frac{1}{2}[A_0(z) - A_1(z)], \tag{36}$$

$$G_{HP}^{(s)} = \frac{1}{2}[A_0(z) + A_1(z)] + \frac{K}{2}[A_0(z) - A_1(z)], \tag{37}$$

where $A_0(z)$ and $A_1(z)$ are stable and real allpass filters.

Figure 29 shows the resulting structures for the filters $G_{LP}^{(s)}(z)$ and $G_{HP}^{(s)}(z)$. The magnitude responses of $G_{LP}^{(s)}(z)$ and $G_{HP}^{(s)}(z)$ can be written as:

$$\left|G_{LP}^{(s)}\right| = \left|\frac{K}{2}[1 + A(z)] + \frac{1}{2}[1 - A(z)]\right|, \tag{38}$$

$$\left|G_{HP}^{(s)}\right| = \left|\frac{1}{2}[1 + A(z)] + \frac{K}{2}[1 - A(z)]\right|, \tag{39}$$

where $A(z) = A_1(z)/A_0(z)$ is an allpass filter of order N (N odd), which is defined by Mitra (2006):

$$A(z) = \frac{a_N + a_{N-1}z^{-1} + a_{N-2}z^{-2} + \cdots + z^{-N}}{1 + a_1 z^{-1} + a_2 z^{-2} + \cdots + a_N z^{-N}}, \tag{40}$$

and a_n, $n = 1,\ldots,N$, are real coefficients.

In Fernandez-Vazquez and Jovanovic-Dolecek (2006a), a new method for designing allpass filters $A(z)$ is proposed, and it provides flat magnitude response for both lowpass and highpass filters (38) and (39). The allpass filter coefficients are expressed by:

Figure 29. Shelving filter structures

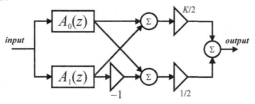

(a) Lowpass shelving filter structure

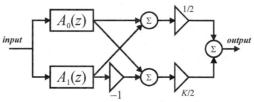

(b) Highpass shelving filter structure

$$a_n = \begin{cases} \dbinom{N}{n} & n \text{ even} \\ \dbinom{N}{n} C & n \text{ odd} \end{cases}, \tag{41}$$

where the binomial coefficient is given by:

$$\binom{N}{n} = \frac{N!}{n!(N-n)!}, \tag{42}$$

and the constant C is selected such that the design parameters (see Figure 28) are satisfied. Based on results (Fernandez-Vazquez & Jovanovic-Dolecek, 2006a), the value of C is computed as:

$$C = -\frac{\tan(\cos^{-1}(x_p)/2) + (-1)^{(N-1)/2} \tan^N(\omega_p/2)}{\tan(\cos^{-1}(x_p)/2) - (-1)^{(N-1)/2} \tan^N(\omega_p/2)}, \tag{42}$$

where

$$x_p = \frac{2}{10^{K_{dB}/10} - 1} 10^{-Ap/10} - \frac{10^{K_{dB}/10} + 1}{10^{K_{dB}/10} - 1}, \tag{43}$$

and K_{dB} is the value of K in dB, that is, $20\log_{10}(K)$.

From (42) it follows that the order of the filter N is given by:

$$N = \left\lceil \frac{\log\left(\dfrac{\tan(\cos^{-1}(x_s)/2)}{\tan(\cos^{-1}(x_p)/2)}\right)}{\log\left(\dfrac{\omega_s'}{\omega_p'}\right)} \right\rceil, \tag{44}$$

where $\lceil \cdot \rceil$ is the ceiling function and,

$$x_s = \frac{2}{10^{K_{dB}/10}-1}10^{-As/10} - \frac{10^{K_{dB}/10}+1}{10^{K_{dB}/10}-1}, \tag{45}$$

$$\omega_p' = \tan\left(\frac{\omega_p}{2}\right), \tag{46}$$

$$\omega_s' = \tan\left(\frac{\omega_s}{2}\right). \tag{47}$$

Example 1: We design a lowpass (boost) shelving filter using the following specifications: $K_{dB} = 20$ dB, Ap $= 16.5$ dB, As $= 10$ dB, $\omega_p = 0.35\pi$, and $\omega_s = 0.5\ \pi$. Additionally, we design a lowpass (cut) shelving filter using $K_{dB} = -20$ dB, Ap $= -16.5$ dB, and As $= -10$ dB, and with the same passband and stopband frequencies as given for the boost filter.

Figure 30. Magnitude responses of the boost and cut filters $G_{LP}^{(s)}(z)$

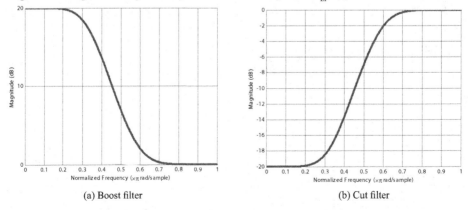

(a) Boost filter   (b) Cut filter

Figure 31. Filtered speech signals using shelving lowpass filters

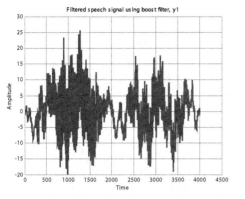

(a) Output from the boost lowpass filter

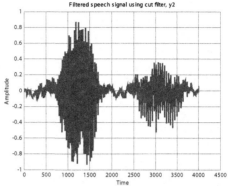

(b) Output from the cut lowpass filter

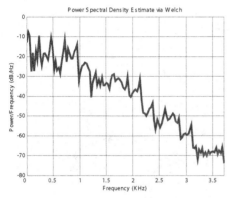

(c) Power spectral density for the boost case

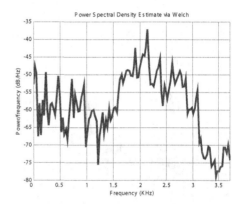

(d) Power spectral density for the cut case

Using equation (44), the order of the allpass filter $A(z)$ is 3. Figure 30(a) shows the magnitude response of $G_{LP}^{(o)}(z)$ for the boost case, while the magnitude response of $G_{LP}^{(s)}(z)$ for the cut case is illustrated in Figure 30(b).

The speech signal given in Figure 2 is filtered by the filters shown in Figure 30. Figures 31(a) and 31(b) show the outputs of the boost and cut filters, respectively. The corresponding power spectral densities are shown in Figures 31(c) and 31(d).

By replacing the parameters x_s and x_p with $-x_s$ and $-x_p$ into (42), (44), and (45), we can design highpass shelving filters. The following example illustrates the procedure.

Example 2: The design parameters of the shelving filters for the boost case are $K_{dB} = 20$, Ap = 17.5 dB, As = 10 dB, $\omega_p = 0.7\pi$, and $\omega_s = 0.65\pi$, while for the cut case are $K_{dB} = -20$, Ap = −17.5 dB, As = −10 dB, $\omega_p = 0.7\pi$, and $\omega_s = 0.65\pi$.

Figure 32. Magnitude response of the highpass shelving filter for the boost and cut cases

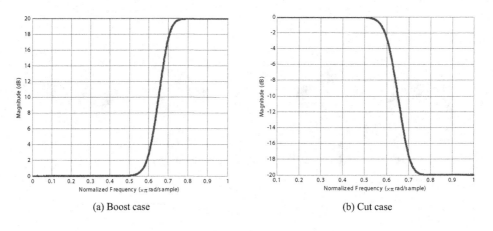

(a) Boost case   (b) Cut case

Figure 33. Filtered speech signals using shelving highpass filters

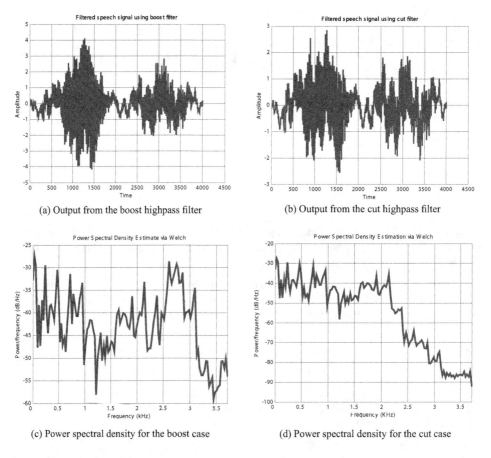

(a) Output from the boost highpass filter   (b) Output from the cut highpass filter

(c) Power spectral density for the boost case   (d) Power spectral density for the cut case

It follows from equation (44) that the order of the allpass filter $A(z)$ is 7. Figure 32(a) shows the magnitude response of $G_{HP}^{(s)}(z)$ for the boost case, while the magnitude response of $G_{HP}^{(s)}(z)$ for the cut case is given in Figure 32(b).

The speech signal example of Figure 2 is filtered using the filters shown in Figure 32, and the filtering outputs are given in Figures 33(a) and 33(b). Additionally, the power spectral density for the outputs of the boost and cut filters are provided in Figures 33(c) and 33(d), respectively.

Peaking Filters

In the following we review the design of peaking filters. The design parameters are the gain K_{dB}, the central frequency ω_c, the bandwidth BW, and the attenuation A_B, at which BW is defined (see Figure 34).

For the boost and the cut cases, a second order peaking filter based on allpass filter $A_2(z)$ is given by Zölzer and Boltze (1995):

$$G_{BP}^{(p)} = \frac{K}{2}[1 - A_2(z)] + \frac{1}{2}[1 + A_2(z)].$$

(48)

Figure 35 shows the structure of the peaking filter based on (48).

The allpass filter $A_2(z)$ can be expressed as:

$$A_2(z) = -\frac{\alpha - \beta(1+\alpha)z^{-1} + z^{-2}}{1 - \beta(1+\alpha)z^{-1} + \alpha},$$

(49)

where $\beta = \cos(\omega_0)$, ω_0 is the central frequency and,

Figure 34. Design parameters for the bandpass peaking filter

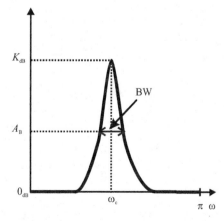

Figure 35. Structure for peaking filters

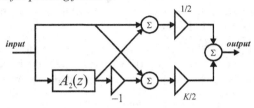

$$\alpha = \begin{cases} \dfrac{1-\tan(BW/2)}{1+\tan(BW/2)} & \text{boost case} \\[2em] \dfrac{K-\tan(BW/2)}{K+\tan(BW/2)} & \text{cut case} \end{cases} \qquad (50)$$

the parameter BW is the bandwidth. It is most common to use $A_B = K_{dB} - 3$ (Keiler & Zölzer, 2004; Mitra, 2006).

Example 3: The peaking filters have the following parameters: for the boost case $K_{dB} = 10$ dB, $\omega_0 = 0.4\pi$, and BW $= 0.1\pi$, and for the cut case $K_{dB} = -10$ dB, $\omega_0 = 0.4\pi$, and $BW = 0.2\pi$. Figure 36 illustrates the magnitude responses of the designed filters.

Figure 37 illustrates the outputs and the corresponding power spectra densities for each output obtained by filtering the speech signal using boost and cut peaking filters.

Figure 36. Magnitude responses of the peaking filter for the boost and cut cases

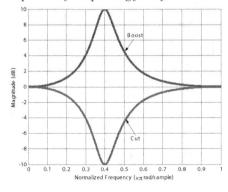

Figure 37. Filtered speech signals using peaking filters

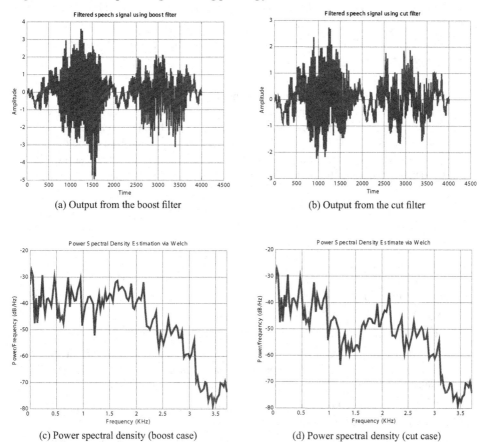

(a) Output from the boost filter

(b) Output from the cut filter

(c) Power spectral density (boost case)

(d) Power spectral density (cut case)

Conclusion

Music generated in a studio does not sound natural compared, for example, to the music performed in a concert hall. In a concert hall there is an effect called *natural reverberation*, which is produced by the reflections of sounds off surfaces. Some sounds travel directly to the listener, while some sounds from the instrument reflect off the walls, the ceiling, the floor, and so forth, before reaching the listener.

The amount and quality of reverberation in a natural environment are influenced by certain factors: the volume and dimensions of the space and the type, shape, and number of surfaces that the sound encounters. The overall natural reverberation is described by the impulse response of the room.

Natural reverberation typically follows a quasi-exponential curve that reaches a peak and decays more or less slowly. In general, an irregular time interval between peaks is desirable in a concert hall.

Music signal processing includes a wide variety of effects and filtering techniques. We have examined some important building blocks used for developing more natural reverberation.

Specifically, reverberation filters create the echoes and add them to the original signal. The comb filter is an example of a simple reverberation filter, but it does not provide natural-sounding reverberations.

The comb reverberators and the allpass reverberators can be combined to generate more natural reverberation effects. The comb filters should be connected in parallel to minimize the spectral disturbances, while allpass filters should be connected in a cascade, since they are colorless. Certain effects, such as flanging and chorus effects, can be realized on sounds by using delay lines whose delay time varies on a sample-to-sample basis. The design of high order shelving filters and second orders peaking filters for audio equalization, which allow independent control of the gain is presented. The filter designs are based on the design of allpass filters.

References

Belanger, M. (2000). *Digital processing of signals, theory and practice* (3rd ed.). Chichester, England: John Wiley & Sons Ltd.

Curtis, R. (2002). *The computer music tutorial*. Cambridge, MA: MIT Press.

Darlington, D., Daudet, L., & Sandler, M. (2002). Digital audio effects in the wavelet domain. In *Proceedings of Conference on Digital Audio Effects, DAFX2002* (pp. 7-12). Hamburg, Germany.

Dodge, C., & Jerse, T. A. (1997). *Computer music, synthesis, composition, and performance* (2nd ed.). New York: Schrimer Books.

Duncan Luce, R., (1993). *Sound & hearing a conceptual introduction*. Hillsdale, NJ: Lawrence Erlbaum Associates, Publishers.

Fernandez-Vazquez, A., & Jovanovic-Dolecek, G. (2006 a). A new method for the design of IIR filters with flat magnitude response. *IEEE Transactions on Circuits and Systems I: Regular Papers*.

Fernandez-Vazquez, A., & Jovanovic-Dolecek, G. (2006 b). Design of IIR notch filter with maximally flat or equiripple Magnitude Characteristics. *European Signal Processing Conference, EUSIPCO 2006*.

Filter Design Toolbox For Use with MATLAB: User's Guide. (2000). Natick, MA: The MathWorks, Inc.

Fouad, H., Ballas, J. A., & Brock, D. (2000). An extensible toolkit for creating virtual sonic environments. In *Proceedings of the ICAD 2000* (pp. 32-37). Atlanta, Georgia.

Fries, B., & Fries, M. (2005). Digital audio essentials. Sebastopol, CA: O'Reilly Media.

Gold, B., & Morgan, N. (2000). *Speech and audio signal processing*. New York: John Wiley & Sons.

Green, D. W. (2003). *Reverberation filters*. pp. 1-15. Retrieved March 13, 2003, from http://padre.ca/green/reverb.pdf

Karplus, K., & Strong, A. (1983). Digital synthesis of plucked string and drum timbres. *Computer Music Journal, 7*(2), 43-55.

Keiler, F., & Zölzer, U. (2004). Parametric second- and fourth-order shelving filters for audio applications. In *IEEE 6th workshop on Multimedia signal Processing, Siena Italy* (pp. 231-234). New York: IEEE

McClellan, J. H., Schafer, R. W., & Yoder, M. A. (1998). *DSP first: A multimedia approach*. Upper Saddle River, NJ: Prentice Hall.

Mitra, S. K. (2006). *Digital signal processing: A computer-based approach* (3rd ed.). New York: McGraw Hill.

Moorer, J. A. (1977). Signal processing aspects of computer music. In *Proceedings of IEEE, 65*(8), 1108-1132.

Moorer, J. A. (1979). About this reverberation business. *Computer Music Journal, 3*(2), 13-28.

Orfanidis, S. J. (1996). *Signal processing*. Upper Saddle River, NJ: Prentice Hall.

Pellman, S. (1994). *An introduction to the creation of electroacoustic music*. Belmont, CA: Wadswort Publishing Company.

Steiglitz, K. (1996). *A digital signal processing primer with applications to digital audio and computer music*. Menlo Park, CA: Addison Wesley Publishing Company.

Tempelaars, S. (1996). *Signal processing, speech and music*. Lisse, Netherlands: Swets & Zeitlinger B.V.

Tsingos, N. (2001). A versatile software architecture for virtual audio simulation. In *Proceedings of the 2001 International Conference on Auditory Display* (pp. ICAD01-1-ICAD01-6). Espoo, Finland.

Tsingos, N. (2005). Scalable perceptual mixing and filtering of audio signals using augmented spectral representation. In *Proceedings of the Eighth Conference on Digital Audio Effects, (DAFx'05)* (pp. DAFX-1-DAFX-6). Madrid.

Tsingos, N., Emmanuel, G., & Drettakis, G. (2004). Perceptual audio rendering of complex virtual environments. *ACM Transactions on Graphics, 23*(3), 545-552.

Vaidyanathan, P. P. (1993). *Multirate systems and filter banks*. Englewood Cliffs, NJ: Prentice Hall.

Wenzel, E. M., Miller, J. D., & Abel, J. S. (2000). A software-based system for interactive spatial sound synthesis. In *Proceedings of International Conference on Auditory Display, ICAD 2000* (pp. 151-156).

Zölzer, U., & Boltze, T. (1995). *Parametric digital filters structures*. Paper presented at the 99th Audio Engineering Society Convention New York, AES preprint 4099.

Chapter III

Spectral-Based Analysis and Synthesis of Audio Signals

Paulo A.A. Esquef, Nokia Institute of Technology, Brazil

Luiz W.P. Biscainho, Federal University of Rio de Janeiro, Brazil

Abstract

This chapter reviews audio signal processing techniques related to sound generation via additive synthesis. Particular focus will be put on sinusoidal modeling. Each processing stage involved in obtaining a sinusoidal representation for audio signals is described. Then, synthesis techniques that allow reconstructing an audio signal based on a given parametric representation are presented. Finally, some audio applications where sinusoidal modeling is employed are briefly discussed.

Introduction

There is a family of real-world sounds to which the idea of "pitch" can be associated. According to psychoacoustics (Meddis & Hewitt, 1991; Hartmann, 1996), pitch can be loosely seen as the perceived frequency, so that one can speak of low- or high-pitched signals. The voiced part of speech, singing voice, and most of musical instruments have discernible pitches, to which musical notes are directly linked. The "tonal" aspect of these audio signals reflects into peaky spectra; that means slowly decaying periodic components, which can be modeled as non-decaying oscillations during short periods of time.

Additive synthesis is a method specially suited to accurately generate pitched sounds. Its strength comes from the inherent generality of the idea behind the method, that is, that sounds can be generated by a sum of sinusoids with varying frequency, amplitude, and phase. A diagram of such scheme is depicted in Figure 1 (Cook, 2002). It can be noted that, in addition to the controllable oscillators, there is a noise source that can be shaped in frequency as well. The latter accounts for representing the stochastic components present in the signal to be synthesized (Serra & Smith, 1990).

Naturally, depending on the complexity of the sound to be synthesized, determining manually the amplitude and frequency control functions for each oscillator over time can be an

Figure 1. Additive synthesis method. Functions $A_i(t)$ and $F_i(t)$ control the amplitude and frequency of the sinusoidal oscillators, respectively. Adapted from Figure 6.13 of Cook (2002).

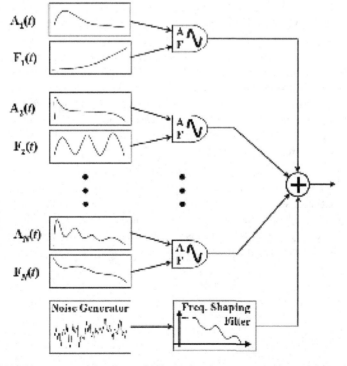

unfeasible task. Although the general structure of additive synthesis gives freedom to generating experimental or synthetic types of sound, when it comes to imitating the sound of real-world musical instruments, automated ways of determining the control functions based on the waveform of recorded sounds are one of the main goals. To attain such objectives, spectral analysis of the signal is required.

There are many tools available for spectral analysis. One of the most useful is the discrete Fourier transform (DFT), which gained popularity due to a family of fast algorithms to compute it, generically named as fast Fourier transform (FFT). Spectral analysis can be realized by other means, such as model-based methods (Kay, 1988; Hayes, 1996), where a model is fitted to the time waveform of the signal and then, the spectral information is derived from the estimated model. The most commonly used spectral analysis techniques for additive synthesis are covered by Cook (2002).

The phase vocoder (Flanagan & Golden, 1966) was one of the earliest attempts to automatically provide control functions to the additive synthesis method. The main drawbacks of the phase vocoder in the original formulation are the high computational cost and latency, due to the use of a non-decimated filterbank, as well as the assumption of dealing with harmonic signals. Further on, a formulation of the phase vocoder using FFT (Portnoff, 1976) helped to improve the computational efficiency but the limitation to analysis and synthesis of harmonic signals remained (Puckette, 1995).

Since the advent of the phase vocoder, many other ways of either implementing or obtaining control functions to additive synthesis have been proposed. More focused on obtaining the control functions, the works of McAulay and Quatieri (1986) as well as of Smith and Serra (1987) have become the fundamental basis of what today is called sinusoidal modeling. It is also worth mentioning a technique called FFT^{-1} proposed by Rodet and Depalle (1992), in which the burden of controlling a possibly large set of resonators was alleviated by devising a specially shaped spectrum and synthesizing the signal by means of inverse FFT within an overlap-and-add scheme.

Practical applications of sinusoidal modeling include artistic-oriented issues such as controlled time- and/or frequency-modification of signals (Bonada, 2000; Laroche, 1998), for example, pitch correction of a mistuned singer; study of expressiveness in musical interpretation (S2S^2, 2006), for example, obtaining sound inflections generated by different musicians; and automatic transcription of music (Klapuri & Davy, 2006), for example, transcription of a jazz improvisation. For all that the topic is specially rewarding and stimulating from both R&D and commercial perspectives.

The remaining sections of this chapter are organized as follows. The processing stages used in sinusoidal modeling to obtain a parametric representation of an analyzed signal are described in the next four sections. The corresponding synthesis stage, that is, recovering the signal waveform from the parametric representation, is described in the following section. After that, brief descriptions of applications in which sinusoidal modeling is a useful tool are given. Finally, conclusions are drawn.

Signal Segmentation

On the Parameter Choices

The first step in time-frequency analysis of an audio signal concerns signal segmentation. Segmentation is needed because of the non-stationary behavior of audio signals. Roughly speaking, this means that frequency information is changing over time in audio signals. Therefore, the choice of frame lengths in the segmentation stage should reflect an average duration over which the frequency information can be considered unaltered. Typically, for audio and speech signals, this duration ranges around 10 to 30 ms.

If spectral analysis is performed via the DFT, the length of the frames also determines the minimum resolution attained in the frequency domain. For a signal sampled at f_s Hz, a frame of length N (in samples) implies a frequency resolution of f_s/N in the DFT domain. This relation establishes the fundamental tradeoff between time and frequency resolutions.

Zero-Padding

Segmentation can be interpreted as the result of multiplying the signal to be analyzed by a rectangular window. Therefore, the resulting spectrum is a convolution of the signal spectrum with that of the window. Due to the time-frequency duality, the less localized a signal is in time, the more localized it is in frequency. Thus, zero-padding, which consists of appending a certain number of zero-valued samples to the segment to be analyzed, implies increasing the apparent length of the analysis windows and that of the DFT buffer. As a consequence, frequency resolution is increased, since a finer frequency-sampling grid is attained, which helps to better define the spectral shape.

However, one must not overestimate the zero-padding benefits. Except for normalization, the DFT representation of a windowed signal converges to that of the discrete-time Fourier transform (DTFT) (Diniz, da Silva, & Netto, 2002) when an infinite zero-padding extension is applied. Once the signal is windowed in time, frequency resolution is bounded by the shape of window spectrum. For instance, the DTFT of the windowed sum of two sinusoids extremely close in frequency is composed by the sum of two copies of the window spectrum, centered at the frequencies of each signal component. One can easily deduce that the resulting spectrum will probably exhibit a unique peak, thus preventing discrimination of the individual components. In such cases, zero-padding is of no avail.

Besides being a tool for frequency interpolation, zero-padding can be used for example to extend the frame size up to a power of 2. Thus, one can take advantage of faster computation of the DFT. One side effect of zero-padding is that it tends to spread signal energy among adjacent bins. However, despite the effects of zero-padding, segmentation itself always tends to bias the spectrum to some extent.

Window Types

In general, the most used windows in spectral analysis, such as the Hanning, Hamming, and Kaiser windows (Harris, 1978), have a low-pass characteristic in the frequency domain and a Gaussian-like shape in time. The main purpose of using a fading window is to avoid abrupt boundary discontinuities during signal segmentation.

The two most important features related to a window of a given length are the width of its passband (main lobe) and the attenuation of its rejection band (side lobes). As pointed out in the previous section, the width of the main lobe imposes a limit to the minimum distance between two peaks that could be resolved in frequency, since, if they are closer than the width of the main lobe, they will be integrated into a single peak. Of course, increasing the window length yields narrower main lobes and helps with resolving closely spaced spectral peaks.

Zero-Phase Windowing

When segmenting a signal for spectral analysis, it has to be decided to which time instant the extracted spectral information belongs. The most obvious choice is to associate this instant with the middle of the window. However, applying a causal window would imply a time-shift of half of the window length. This delay also affects the phase information measured in the frequency domain. To overcome problems related to the phase information a zero-phase window can be adopted. The zero-phase windowing scheme is described by Smith and Serra (1987). Basically, it suffices to properly fill in an FFT buffer of length N (preferably a power of 2) with samples of an M-length segment ($M \leq N$), as illustrated in Figure 2. For convenience M is set an odd value. The steps to perform the zero-phase windowing follow:

Figure 2. Zero-phase windowing scheme

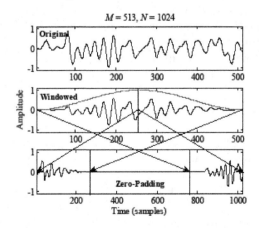

1. Initialize the FFT buffer with N null samples;

2. Multiply the M-length input segment with the chosen window, also of length M;

3. Take the first $(M–1)/2$ samples of the windowed segment and store them on the end of the FFT buffer, that is, from $N–(M–1)/2$ to $N–1$;

4. Store the remaining $(M–1)/2$ samples on the beginning of the FFT buffer, that is, from 0 to $(M–1)/2$.

Note that in this scheme, if M<N, the zero-padding is done automatically in the middle of the FFT buffer.

Window Hopping and Overlap-and-Add

Apart from the window-related parameters, another parameter that needs to be properly chosen is the length of the window hop R. This parameter dictates the time advance of the analysis window, that is, the difference in samples between the beginnings of each analyzed segment. If $R=0$, the advance will be null and the same frame keeps being analyzed forever. Of course, that is not the idea. Setting $R=1$ implies advancing sample-by-sample. This, however, may not be a wise choice, since it would lead to data explosion, that is, with each signal sample there would be associated a non-unitary set of parameters. On the other hand, short values of R are sometimes used for spectral smoothing purposes, such as in periodogram computation (Hayes, 1996).

On average, the spectra of audio and speech signals vary slowly. Therefore, a sample-by-sample hopping is not always necessary. Instead, a longer value of hopping can be afforded. As a rule of thumb, values of R corresponding to time periods between 5 ms and 10 ms yield good results. In some situations it is convenient to tie together the values of R and M, for example, $R=M/2$.

There are applications where overlap-and-add windowing schemes play an important role. Examples of such applications are the analysis-by-synthesis sinusoidal modeling (George & Smith, 1992, 1997) and signal reconstruction from spectral information (Rodet & Depalle, 1992). In these cases, in order to prevent amplitude modulations due to windowing, it is required that overlapping windows sum up to a constant value, that is,

$$Q_w(n) = \sum_{m=-\infty}^{\infty} w(n-mR) = K, \tag{1}$$

where $Q_w(n)$ is the amplitude gain as a function of time index n and $w(n)$ is a given window type. Ideally, the window type and the overlap factor should be chosen so that $Q_w(n)$ be equal to 1 for all n. This way the amplitude of the original signal is guaranteed to be preserved. A more relaxed criterion is to ensure $Q_w(n)$ equal to a constant for all n. Thus, one rules out any amplitude modulations due to windowing. For example, Hanning windows sum up to $Q_w(n)=1$ when overlapped at 50% and up to $Q_w(n)=2$ when overlapped at 75%.

Segmentation Strategies

Fixed Segmentation

The simplest way of segmenting a signal is to set fixed values for the window length and the hop size. These values can be chosen based on the characteristics of the signal to be analyzed. Rapidly changing signals usually require shorter windows and a smaller hop size. On the other hand, larger values can be adopted for more stationary or steady signals.

Adaptive Segmentation

Real-life audio signals contain both steady or slow varying portions and rapid transients. A typical problem appears when an abrupt transient pops up inside and far from the beginning of an analysis frame. In those cases, a phenomenon called pre-echo occurs. It is due to the violation of the hypothesis by which the spectral behavior of the signal would not change within the time spanned by the analysis window.

An illustration of the pre-echo phenomenon is shown in Figure 3. The top subplot shows an onset signal (solid line) and the overlapping windows (dashed lines). The middle subplot shows the reconstructed signal, which was obtained by interpolating the spectral information along the three time instants associated with the centers of the windows, that is, at time indices equal to 500, 1000, and 1500 samples. Note that the amplitudes of the sinusoids start from zero at time index 500 and are linearly interpolated up to their values at time index 1500. Therefore, the sharp transient that occurs at time 1000 is smeared, as it

Figure 3. Pre-echo phenomenon. The subplot on the top depicts an example of signal analysis through overlapping Hanning windows (dashed lines) in a case where the signal in question contains an abrupt transient (solid line). The reconstructed signal is seen on the subplot in the middle. The error between the original signal and the reconstructed version is displayed on subplot on the bottom.

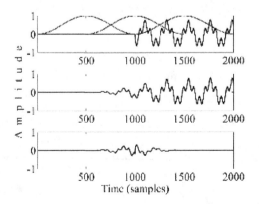

can be verified from the bottom subplot, which displays the error between the original and reconstructed signals.

A curious issue related to pre-echo is non-causal signal masking. A high-amplitude stimulus can inhibit the perception of a previous low-amplitude one, if they occur sufficiently near each other. In practical applications, such as perceptual audio coders (Bosi & Goldberg, 2002), some residual pre-echo can be admitted, provided that it is masked by the next stimuli.

The pre-echo phenomenon calls for adaptive ways of performing signal segmentation. Adaptive segmentation is mainly applicable to methods that do not require the perfect amplitude reconstruction constraint of equation (1), which is the case of sinusoidal modeling. An example of adaptive segmentation is the optimized procedure proposed by Goodwin (1996), where the cost function to be minimized is the reconstruction error. An alternative strategy for signal segmentation was proposed by Masri (1996). It lies in synchronizing the beginning or end of the windows according to the onset time of detected transients. Thus, the lengths of the windows are either squeezed or enlarged so that whenever a sharp transient occurs, the current window ends just before it and the following window starts together with its onset time.

An illustration of the principle behind the adaptive signal segmentation is seen in Figure 4. Here, the same test signal used in Figure 3 is segmented in a different way: when the transient is detected, the large Hanning window is shortened to be overlapped with a much shorter analysis window, as seen on the top subplot. When the transient is over, larger analysis windows are employed again. As a result, the pre-echo phenomenon is substantially reduced, as observed from the middle subplot, which shows the reconstructed signal, and from the bottom subplot, which displays the error between the original and the reconstructed signal.

Finally, if the signal to be analyzed is strongly tonal, such as in voiced speech or in monophonic quasi-harmonic signals, a pitch-synchronous segmentation minimizes the effects

Figure 4. Reduction of the pre-echo phenomenon via adaptive segmentation. The subplot on the top illustrates an adaptive segmentation analysis of test signal (solid line) that contains an abrupt transient. The subplot in the middle shows the reconstructed signal, whereas the subplot on the bottom displays the error between the original and reconstructed signals.

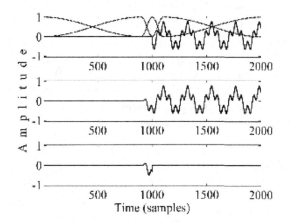

of boundary discontinuities associated with windowing. In this case, the output of a pitch detector guides the selection of the window length over time. In general, it is recommended to choose the length of the window equal to at least three times the fundamental period of the signal (McAulay & Quatieri, 1986). This makes sense, since in low-pitched signals, spectral peaks occur well clustered in frequency. Therefore, longer analysis windows are required to achieve enough resolution for resolving the peaks in frequency.

Peak Detection Strategies

The next step after signal segmentation consists of identifying prominent resonances present in the signal of interest. In this context, the natural choice is to transform the signal to the frequency domain and look for prominent peaks in its magnitude spectrum. A selection of possible strategies for peak detection is described in the following sections.

Take All Peaks

The easiest way of performing peak detection is to take all possible peaks in the magnitude spectrum of a signal given frame. In such strategy, the importance of a peak is not taken into account. It is up to the peak continuation stage (see the section on Peak Continuation or Tracking) to decide on whether a spectral peak corresponds to a real resonance or a noise component in the signal (Serra, 1997).

Usually, most practical applications deal with real-valued signals. Therefore, due to spectral symmetry, peak search needs to be performed only in the positive frequency range. A peak occurs in the magnitude spectrum whenever the criterion $|S(k-1)| < |S(k)|$ and $|S(k+1)| < |S(k)|$, for $k = 1, 2, ..., N/2-1$, is satisfied, where $S(i)$ is the N-length DFT of a given frame, being $i = 0, 1, ..., N-1$ the indices of the DFT bins.

A practical way of performing peak detection is looking for signal changes in the slope of $|S(k)|$. From a computational point of view, it suffices initially to obtain the sequences $D_1(k) \equiv \text{sign}\{|S(k+1)| - |S(k)|\}$ and $D_2(k) \equiv D_1(k+1) - D_1(k)$. Then, if $D_2(\tilde{k}) = -2$ for a given index $\tilde{k}$, it can be guaranteed that $|S(\tilde{k}+1)|$ is a spectral peak.

The main drawback of the take-all-peaks approach is that many irrelevant low-amplitude peaks are unnecessarily taken. This will overload the peak continuation stage. Another and more serious problem is related to spurious peaks, which appear due to the inevitable windowing of the signal for spectral analysis. For instance, if the analysis window has side lobes, peak detection of a single sinusoidal component will not lead to a single peak, since the side lobes of the window will be considered peaks as well.

Include Only the Most Prominent Peaks

One way to reduce the number of spectral peaks to deal with is to select only the most prominent spectral peaks. This can be achieved through comparing the magnitude spectrum against the value of a certain user-defined threshold.

Constant Threshold

Choosing a suitable threshold value to be used in all signal frames would be a difficult task. The main reason for this is related to the huge variations in dynamic that can occur in audio signals. To overcome this problem a relative anchor should be set for each frame. Usually, the anchor is chosen as the global maximum of the magnitude spectrum. As rule of thumb, and due to psychoacoustic reasons, the value of the threshold is set somewhere around 60 to 80 dB below the maximum (Serra, 1997).

Opting for an anchored constant-valued threshold is likely to leave high-frequency peaks un-detected, since the average energy distribution of audio signals along frequency is usually of a low-pass characteristic. Furthermore, the anchored constant threshold may be useless when there are no prominent peaks in the spectrum, as it may occur in noise-like passages of the signal.

Variable Threshold

Variable threshold techniques aim at overcoming the aforementioned drawbacks. The idea is to use an estimate of either the background noise spectrum or the spectrum envelope as a variable threshold. Once one of the thresholds is obtained, one can compare the magnitude spectrum with an offset version of it. Alternatively, the variable threshold can be used to first compensate for the original spectral tilt, after which a constant anchored threshold can be applied.

On the one hand, spectral envelope can be obtained by means of low-order autoregressive modeling of the audio signal (Hayes, 1996). For instance, spectral envelope computation via linear predictive coding (LPC) is widely used in speech coding. On the other hand, esti-mation of the background noise spectrum can be carried out by non-linear techniques such as the two-pass split window (TPSW) filtering (Struzinski & Lowe, 1984) and recursive smoothing filters (Macleod, 1992). Another interesting possibility would be to compute the masking threshold (Beerends & Stemerdink, 1992) for the spectrum at hand and select only those peaks whose magnitudes are above the value of the masking curve.

An example that compares different threshold techniques is shown in Figure 5. The take-all-peaks approach, shown in the upper left plot, is unsuitable, since a large number of spurious peaks are taken. The situation gets better with the selection of peaks above a fixed threshold (upper right plot). Note, however, that some high-frequency peaks are not selected. When it comes to selecting only prominent spectral peaks, the variable-threshold approaches yield better results, as shown in the bottom plots.

Note that thresholding is used here as a way of selecting the most prominent spectral peaks in a given signal frame. Estimation of the peak parameters, that is, frequency, amplitude, and phase, is covered in the following section.

Figure 5. Peak Detection—comparison among four different schemes: Take all peaks (top left), constant anchored threshold (top right), variable threshold using TPSW-based background spectrum (bottom left), and variable threshold using LPC-based spectral envelope (with an offset of -10 dB) (bottom right)

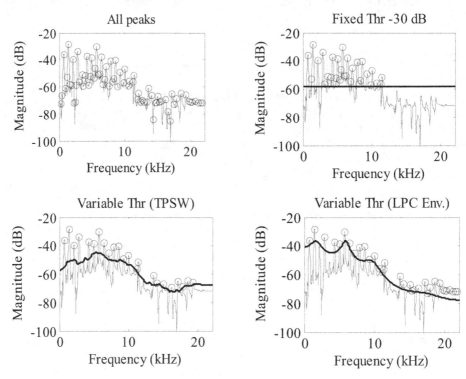

Estimation of Frequency, Amplitude, and Phase of Peaks

At this stage, it is assumed that the most prominent spectral peaks in a given frame have been already detected. Hence, the goal now is to estimate precisely the peak parameters, namely, frequency, amplitude, and phase. A selection of techniques for attaining that purpose is described in the following sections.

It should be noticed for completeness that specific strategies can be employed to find the correct amplitudes of individual resonances even if they are clustered into a single peak, as long as the frequencies of the underlying components are known beforehand (Quatieri & McAulay, 1998).

Plain DFT

Let $x(n)=s(n)w(n)$ be an M-length windowed signal frame, with $s(n)$ and $w(n)$ being, respectively, the original signal and the window function. Moreover, assume that the N-length DFT of $x(n)$ is denoted by $X(k)$. If k_p is an integer index associated with a selected peak, the corresponding frequency and amplitude of this peak are given by:

$$f_{k_p} = k_p \frac{f_s}{N} \text{ and} \tag{2}$$

$$a_{k_p} = \frac{|X(k_p)|}{W(0))} \tag{3}$$

respectively, where f_s is the sampling rate and $W(0) = \sum_{n=0}^{M} w(n)$ is the DFT of the window at DC.

Note that in this scheme, f_{k_p} can only assume the values given in equation (2). Therefore, if the resonance frequency in the original signal does not coincide with f_{k_p}, errors will occur. The frequency readability can be increased by increasing N, for instance, via zero-padding. To achieve frequency errors below 0.1%, a zero-padding factor of around 1000 is required (Serra, 1997), that is, the length of the FFT buffer should be set $N > 1000M$. Although it is possible to compute long-size FFTs in nowadays computers, using this resource would raise unnecessarily the computational cost of the procedure. Furthermore, custom digital signal processors usually have limitations on the size of the FFT buffer. Fortunately, a similar performance level for peak frequency estimation can be achieved by more intelligent ways, for instance, by interpolating along FFT bins, as described in the following section.

Parabolic Interpolation

The shape of the main lobe of the magnitude spectrum of a typical window resembles a parabola. For the Gaussian window the main lobe is an exact parabola (Harris, 1978). Furthermore, it is known that if the input signal has a single resonance, its magnitude spectrum (continuous version) corresponds to the magnitude spectrum of the window modulated to the resonance frequency. Thus, one way to improve the frequency estimation of detected peaks consists of:

1.   Fitting a parabola to three points: the peak itself and its left and right neighbors;

2.   Taking the coordinates of the maximum associated with the fitted parabola as the frequency and amplitude of the peak.

Performing parabolic interpolation on the dB scale was shown experimentally to yield better results by Smith and Serra (1987). Thus, let the magnitude spectrum of $x(n)$ on the dB scale be denoted by $X_{dB}(k) = 20\log_{10}|X(k)|$. Moreover, define the magnitude of a given peak and its neighbors as:

$$A_1 = X_{dB}(k_p-1),\ A_2 = X_{dB}(k_p),\ \text{and}\ A_3 = X_{dB}(k_p+1), \tag{4}$$

where, as before, k_p is the integer DFT index of a selected resonance peak.

It can be shown (Smith & Serra, 1987) that the frequency associated with the maximum of the fitted parabola is given by:

$$f_{\hat{k}_p} = (k_p + d)\frac{f_s}{N} \tag{5}$$

where,

$$d = \frac{1}{2}\frac{A_1 - A_3}{A_1 - 2A_2 + A_3}. \tag{6}$$

As for the peak amplitude, the estimated value in dB can be computed via:

$$a_{\hat{k}_{p,dB}} = A_2 - \frac{d}{4}(A_1 - A_3). \tag{7}$$

If the phase of a resonance is of any interest, the parabolic fitting has to be done separately for the real and imaginary parts of the complex spectrum. More specifically, d can be computed as before and the phase is given by:

Figure 6. Parabolic interpolation (Adapted from Smith and Serra, 1987)

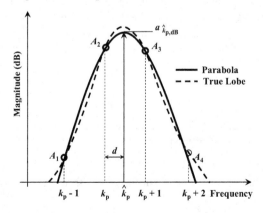

$$\theta_{k_p} = -\arctan\left\{\frac{a_{k_{p,imag}}}{a_{k_{p,real}}}\right\} \tag{8}$$

where $a_{k_{p,imag}}$ and $a_{k_{p,real}}$ are computed similarly to equation (7). However, when computing $a_{k_{p,imag}}$ and $a_{k_{p,real}}$, variables A_i represent the imaginary and real parts of the complex spectrum, respectively. A schematic illustration of the parabolic interpolation is shown in Figure 6.

Triangular Window Technique

A similar approach to the parabolic interpolation is the triangular window technique (Keiler & Zölzer, 2001). The key idea is to design a window whose main lobe in the magnitude spectrum approximates the shape of a triangle. Thus, the intersection point of two lines fitted to the slopes of the triangle defines the frequency and amplitude of the peak.

The desired spectral magnitude of the triangular window is given by:

$$W_{tri}(k) = \begin{cases} 1 - \dfrac{k}{S}, & 0 \le k < S \\ 0, & S \le k \le N - S \\ 1 - \dfrac{N-k}{S} & N - S < k < N, \end{cases} \tag{9}$$

where S is the number of frequency bins in the slope region of the window and N is the length of the FFT buffer.

The time domain window is designed by computing the IDFT of $W_{tri}(k)$ and applying a proper shifting of $N/2$. Figure 7 illustrates an example for $N=32$ and $S=4$.

Once a suitable analysis window is designed, it is used in signal segmentation within a regular DFT-based spectral analysis. The starting point is to select from the sampled magnitude spectrum a peak occurring at frequency index k_p. The remaining steps required in the triangular method follow:

Figure 7. Triangular window: frequency and time responses

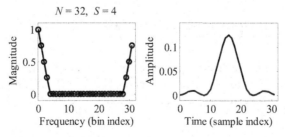

1.   For convenience the selected peak is modulated down to the origin. This implies subtracting k_p from all DFT bin indices;

2.   Decide whether k_p is on the positive (left-hand side) or negative (right-hand side) slope of the triangle. If $|X(k_p - 1)| > |X(k_p + 1)|$, then k_p belongs to the right-hand side of the triangle;

3.   Compute the angular and linear coefficients of the slopes, that is, a and b such that:

$$h_l(k) = ak + b, \text{ with } a > 0, \tag{10}$$

$$h_r(k) = -a(k-2S) - b, \tag{11}$$

where $h_l(k)$ and $h_r(k)$ are, respectively, the left and right lines to be fitted to the peak. The values of a and b are computed using a least-squares error criterion as described by Keiler and Zölzer (2001);

4.   Obtain a refined estimate for the frequency of the peak as:

$$f_{\hat{k}_{p,tri}} = \underbrace{\left(k_p + S - \frac{b}{a} \right)}_{\hat{k}_{p,tri}} \frac{f_s}{N}; \tag{12}$$

5.   Obtain an initial estimate for the amplitude of the peak as:

$$a_{\hat{k}_{p,tri}} = 2Sa, \tag{13}$$

and then, refine it by a polynomial approximation of the error function (obtained from reference signals). Further details can be found from Keiler and Zölzer (2001).

The value of S defines the width of the main lobe of the window spectrum. Increasing S leads to better peak parameter estimation under noisy conditions for isolated peaks. As a side effect, as the width of the main lobe increases, resolving closely spaced peaks in frequency becomes more difficult. To reduce the effect of measurement noise on the peak parameter estimates, only the first $S-1$ points from top to down are used when computing the slope parameters a and b.

Frequency Reassignment and Related Methods

An interesting idea born from time-frequency representation for continuous signals is the so-called time- and frequency-reassignment (Auger & Flandrin, 1995; Hainsworth & Macleod, 2003). Consider in particular frequency reassignment in the short-time Fourier transform

(STFT) domain, where $X_t(\omega)$ is the STFT of a continuous signal $s(t)$ segmented by a fixed window $w(t)$ centered at t. A given spectral peak at ω can be more accurately relocated to $\hat{\omega}$, at the center of gravity of the corresponding energy distribution in the time-frequency space. It can be shown that $\hat{\omega}$ is simply the instantaneous frequency at ω, which can be obtained if one knows two STFTs of $x(t)$ at w, computed respectively for windows $w(t)$ and $w'(t)$, the latter being the first derivative of $w(t)$.

A discrete-time version of the method (Fitz & Haken, 2002) can be formulated in terms of a window $w(n)$ centered at n. A peak at frequency f_k in Hz corresponding to bin k in the spectrum of a signal $x(n)$ can be relocated to $\hat{f}_k$ by knowing two discrete STFTs of $x(n)$ at k, $X_n(k)$ and $X'_n(k)$, computed respectively for windows $w(n)$ and $w'(n)$, the latter being a frequency-weighted version of $w(n)$:

$$\hat{f}_k = f_k \left\{ 1 + \Im \left[\frac{X'_n(k) X^*_n(k)}{|X_n(k)|^2} \right] \right\}, \tag{14}$$

where $*$ and $\Im$ stand for complex conjugate and imaginary part, respectively. The efficiency of the method is related to the complexity of the discrete STFTs. Choosing the Hanning window (Hainsworth & Macleod, 2003) yields to an implementation based on two DFTs.

An alternative approach approximates the instantaneous frequency by the phase difference between two STFTs whose windows start at contiguous samples. Once more the Hanning window is a suitable choice (Brown & Puckette, 1993). The idea is successfully recalled and generalized by David and Szczupak (1996) on an iterative basis.

It is curious to find that the Hanning window is an excellent choice for the methods described, not only for its efficient implementation as a combination of three rectangular windows (Brown & Puckette, 1993), but also for the exceptionally stable behavior it lends to the phase derivative around resonances.

From a quite different reasoning comes a similar method, the so-called DFT[1], introduced by (Desainte-Catherine & Marchand, 2000). It refines the frequency estimation through the knowledge of the signal derivative: the relocated frequency is proportional to the ratio between the Fourier transforms of the derivative and of the signal itself. In discrete-time domain, the derivative is once more approximated by a first-order difference. The basic steps of the DFT[1] algorithm follow.

For an M-length signal segment $s(n)$:

1. Compute the first derivative of $s(n)$, that is, $s'(n) = [s(n) - s(n-1)]f_s$;

2. Multiply $s(n)$ and $s'(n)$ by a M-length window $w(n)$. This leads to $x(n) = s(n)w(n)$ and $x'(n) = s'(n)w(n)$;

3. Compute N-length DFTs (zero-phase windowing can be used) for $x(n)$ and $x'(n)$, here denoted by $X(k)$ and $X'(k)$;

4. Compute $|X(k)|$ and $|X'(k)|$ and multiply the latter by $F(k) = 2f_s \sin\left(2\pi k \frac{f_s}{N}\right)$ to

compensate for the spectral tilt due to the differentiation;

5.   Obtain a more accurate frequency estimate of the peak selected at index k_p via:

$$f_{\hat{k}_{p,\mathrm{diff}}} = \frac{1}{2\pi} \frac{|X'(k_p)|}{|X(k_p)|}. \tag{15}$$

6.   Consider the estimate valid only if $\left(k_p - \dfrac{1}{2}\right) < \hat{k}_p < \left(k_p + \dfrac{1}{2}\right)$;

7.   Compute the estimate for the peak amplitude as:

$$a_{\hat{k}_{p,\mathrm{diff}}} = 2 \frac{|X(k_p)|}{|W(e^{j2\pi \Delta f/f_\mathrm{s}})|}, \tag{16}$$

where $\Delta f = \left| f_{\hat{k}_{p,\mathrm{diff}}} - k_p\, f_\mathrm{s}/N \right|$ and $W(e^{j2\pi f/f_\mathrm{s}})$ is the continuous spectrum of the window $w(n)$.

The performance of the algorithm, which requires two DFTs, is dependent on the window type, the best results being attained with the Hanning window. According to Desainte-Catherine and Marchand (2000), the DFT[1] algorithm outperforms the parabolic interpolation method in estimation of the peak frequency for the Hanning and Blackman windows. The parabolic interpolation performs better for the rectangular and Hamming windows, though. For the Gaussian window, which favors the parabolic interpolation, the performance of both methods is equivalent. As for the peak amplitude estimates the derivative method achieves better results for the Hanning, Hamming, and Blackman windows.

A comprehensive survey of spectral peak parameter estimation was elaborated by Keiler and Marchand (2002) and Hainsworth and Macleod (2003).

Least-Squares Spectral Optimization Using Windows without Side-Lobes

Another approach to estimate spectral peak parameters is based on writing a parametric model $\hat{S}(f)$ for each frame spectrum and optimizing the parameters as to match best the observed spectrum $S(f)$. A general spectral model for a windowed signal would be (Depalle & Hélie, 1997):

$$\hat{S}(f) = \sum_{k=1}^{K} \frac{a_k}{2} \left(e^{j\theta_k} W(f - f_{k_p}) + e^{-j\theta_k} W(f + f_{k_p}) \right), \tag{17}$$

where k is an index associated with the number K of selected peaks, not to be confused with the FFT bin index, a_k and θ_k are, respectively, the amplitude and phase associated with the peaks, and $W(f)$ is the Fourier transform of the analysis window.

Both $\hat{S}(f)$ and $S(f)$ can be sampled on an N-length equally-spaced frequency grid, leading to the vectors $\hat{S}$ and S, respectively. The best estimate of S would be attained by minimizing the cost $\|S - \hat{S}\|$. This is not a trivial task because $\hat{S}$ is non-linear in the f_k parameter, although it is linear in terms of a_k and $e^{j\theta_k}$.

To solve the minimization problem, an iterative algorithm is required. First, rough estimates of f_k are given to the algorithm. A simple peak-picking method would do in this case. Then, assuming the values of f_k are known, estimates of a_k and θ_k are computed. Then the estimates f_k are further refined. See Depalle and Hélie (1997) for implementation details. Indeed, f_k are forced to converge to the local maxima of the magnitude response of the modulated windows.

The method is sensitive to the presence of two or more peaks very close to each other in frequency. This type of occurrence drives the optimization procedure ill posed. To overcome this problem only one of the peaks is retained, and the residual signal (original minus modeled) is submitted again to the optimization.

Another concern when using the method is related to the choice of the window. The initial guesses for the frequencies of the peaks can be sometimes far from the true values. Thus, instead of converging toward the local maximum of the main lobe of the modulated window—where the true value is located—the estimates may be stuck at the maximum of a sidelobe. A solution that prevents this type of occurrence consists of employing a window whose magnitude response does not have side lobes. Such window can be attained, for instance, by truncating a Gaussian window with a power of a triangular window (Harris, 1978).

Nonlinearly Spaced Spectrum Descriptions

At this point, after examining several methods based on the DFT, it is fair to mention two alternative descriptions that are distinguished by non-linear spacing of spectral bins. The motivation behind them can be summarized as follows. Spectral resolution of human hearing (Zwicker & Fastl, 1999) can be associated to critical bands, which can be loosely modeled as a bank of contiguous bandpass filters geometrically spaced along frequency.

This representation matches well the usual western music equal-tempered scale, which is organized in contiguous semitones whose frequency ratio is $\sqrt[12]{2}$. For this reason, describing the auditory spectrum (ranging from 20 to 20000 Hz) along a linearly spaced frequency scale may lead to undesirable coarseness in low frequencies as well as unnecessary refinement at high frequencies.

In Brown (1991), the so-called Constant-Q transform (CQT) is introduced. It can be seen as a discrete transform where each bin is computed through a different-sized DFT, in order to obtain progressively spaced channels, for example, according to a factor $\sqrt[24]{2}$, for a quarter-tone spacing. Of course, such strategy prevents the efficient use of FFTs. However, a fast algorithm that approximates the CQT was later proposed by Brown and Puckette (1992).

Another approach cited by Klapuri (1997) is the Bounded-Q transform, which divides the spectrum in successive octaves, that is, half spectra, from high to low frequencies. Each octave is further divided, but this time in equal-spaced channels. The algorithm approximates a geometric spacing in frequency, but it allows an FFT-based implementation.

Some care should be taken when dealing with the previous methods, regarding the time scales related to different frequency bins, since they correspond to different-sized analysis windows.

Other Parametric Methods

Similarly to the Least-Squares Spectral Optimization method described before, there are several other parametric methods aiming at the estimation of spectral peak parameters. Among them it is worth mentioning the Analysis-by-Synthesis/Overlap-Add (George & Smith, 1992). In this method, peak by peak, the associated resonance parameters are estimated. Then, a signal component is synthesized and subtracted from the signal under analysis. The resulting residue is submitted again to the analysis-by-synthesis procedure until the energy of the residue becomes lower than a certain value.

Other approaches assign a model for the analyzed signal and, from the model parameters, such as pole or zero locations, the parameters of the spectral peaks can be drawn. Usually, autoregressive (AR) or moving-average autoregressive (ARMA) models are used (Hayes, 1996; Kay, 1988). AR models are easier to handle; however, high-order models are required for proper modeling of audio signals. Furthermore, model order selection, which is directly related to the number of resonance peaks present in the signal, may be a crucial issue in this matter. Examples and applications of parametric spectrum estimation can be found from Laroche (1989, 1993) and Sandler (1990). The main drawback of model-based parametric methods lies on their high computational costs, which may prevent use in real-time applications.

In regard to deciding between a non-parametric and a parametric method, the choice can be dictated by the problem and computational resources at hand. In general, one should consider, among other aspects, robustness to corrupting noise, computational cost, and processing latency. As expected, in all methods the tradeoff between time and frequency resolutions exists to some extent. Parametric methods, however, tend to be preferred, for they provide higher frequency resolution than non-parametric spectrum analysis (Hayes, 1996).

Peak Continuation or Tracking

As seen in the previous sections, peak detection and resonance mode estimation are carried out frame-by-frame, and for each frame in isolation. This means that no inter-frame information is generated up to those stages.

The role of the peak continuation procedure is to track down the history of each peak throughout the frames, by setting paths along the peaks. In other words, the point here is to determine when a given spectral peak appeared, how it evolved along time, and when it vanished. This is definitely a complicated task to perform. There are heuristic or rule-based methods as well as statistical solutions to the peak continuation problem. These methodologies are reviewed in the following sections.

Rule-Based Methods

A well-known rule-based algorithm for peak matching was introduced by McAulay and Quatieri (1986) for tracking partials of speech signals. Modifications and extensions of this approach to audio signals were described by Quatieri and McAulay (1998), Serra (1997), and Smith and Serra (1987).

Basically, in most of the rule-based methods, frequency proximity is the key criterion to determine whether two peaks in adjacent frames belong to a same frequency track. However, as the number of peaks varies from frame to frame, there may be several conflicts to be solved. The criteria reproduced next follow the ideas used in the PARSHL program (Smith & Serra, 1987).

The starting point consists of defining an entity called track. A track is a given path followed by a set of spectral peaks along consecutive frames. Thus, during the procedure, each peak will be invariably associated with a given track. Moreover, there are three possible statuses for a track: (1) emerging track, (2) evolving track, and (3) vanishing track. Tracks in the first two statuses are considered as active, whereas those in the third status are taken as inactive.

With exception of the first frame, where all peaks are directly associated with emergent tracks, the process of track formation always uses peak information within two consecutive frames. Now, consider that the spectral peaks present in frame m are to be matched to active tracks in frame $m-1$. In addition, suppose that there are p tracks in frame $m-1$ and their frequencies are labeled $f_1, f_2, ..., f_p$. On the other hand, there are r peaks in frame m and their frequencies are labeled $g_1, g_2, ..., g_r$.

For all active tracks i in frame $m-1$ a search in frame m is performed in order to find a peak whose frequency lies inside an interval around f_i. In other words, track i claims a peak g_j in frame m such as $|f_i - g_j| < \Delta f_i$. The interval Δf_i can be frequency dependent, for instance, a semitone around f_i. Now, there are two possible situations:

I.   If track i does not find a continuation, its status changes from active to inactive, in this case, a vanishing track. In reality, a vanishing track in frame $m-1$ vanishes in frame m, since the track is extended to frame m through a peak with the same frequency but null amplitude.

II.   If track i finds a continuation, its status remains active, that is, evolving. Moreover, peak g_j, which is the closest in frequency to f_i, inherits the track index. Note that more than one peak in frame m can satisfy the frequency matching criterion. The problem is not yet solved. Within this scenario there are other two possibilities:

   1. g_j is a "free" peak, that is, it has not been claimed by another active track in $m-1$. In this case there is no conflict, and g_j is assigned to track i immediately.

   2. g_j has been already claimed by another track in frame $m-1$ other than f_i. Suppose then that tracks f_u and f_v are claiming the same peak g_j, and f_v is the track that is

currently claiming g_j. In this case, the conflict can be solved by means of verifying two frequency distance measures, $d_u = |f_u - g_j|$ and $d_v = |f_v - g_j|$. Now, there are two alternatives:

a. If $d_v > d_u$, the current track f_v loses the conflict and simply picks the best available peak. If this peak exists, the track remains active; if not, the track status is changed to inactive.

b. If $d_v > d_u$, the current track f_v wins the conflict and calls the matching search procedure on behalf of the track f_u. Logically, f_u is now the track that is currently claiming a peak. It will claim again g_j and will lose the conflict. Thus, according to the previous item (exchanging indices u and v), it will take either the best available peak, if existent, and keep its status or be set inactive otherwise.

The previously described process is repeated for all active tracks in $m-1$ until they all have an updated status. As mentioned before, those tracks whose status was turned inactive are then extended up to frame m, where they will vanish with the same frequency as in $m-1$ but with null amplitude. For those peaks in m that remained unmatched new tracks are created. The initial status of the new tracks is set to emerging. Indeed, similar to what was done to the vanishing tracks, the new tracks that appear in frame m are extended backwards to frame $m-1$, where they start with null amplitude and the same frequency as the associated peaks in m.

A refinement to the aforementioned procedure consists of including some hysteresis associated with the decision to start a new track or discontinue an existing one. For instance, hysteresis is useful when a certain partial suffers from amplitude modulation. In such case, the amplitude of the partial may stay below the peak detection threshold for certain frames. As a result, the peak continuation algorithm will shut down the track whenever the partial peak disappears in a given frame. However, the algorithm will start a new track a few frames later, when the peak reappears. This will lead to segmented tracks instead of a continuous one, as it should be.

Adding hysteresis to status changing from evolving to vanishing would consist of giving a certain number of chances to a "track to be discontinued," before effectively changing its status to inactive. Note that implementing a hysteresis scheme would demand the existence of an intermediate status, sleeping, between active and inactive. A practical way to avoid the burden of working with that intermediate status is given next:

1. Impute a counter to the track whenever it is to be assigned an inactive status.

2. Delay the status changing until the counter reaches a certain value. This implies extending the track to a succeeding frame by adding peaks with the same amplitude and frequency.

3. Increment the counter at each new frame processed.

4. Repeat the procedure until the counter reaches its maximum value. If meanwhile the track finds a matching peak, reset the counter and proceed normally. Otherwise, confirm the status change. In this case, the artificially created peaks used to extend the

track should be deleted from the track, which is then to be discontinued at the frame in which it was initially set to be so.

A similar strategy can be used to devise a hysteresis for the emergent tracks. In this case, the idea is to avoid that spurious peaks initialize new tracks that are going to be very short, since they do not correspond to resonances in the signal. Thus, an emerging track would only be confirmed if it remains active for a certain number of frames. An illustration of the peak continuation scheme is shown in Figure 8.

The performance of a peak tracking procedure is affected by several parameters. A basic requirement is that the peak parameters, especially the peak frequency, be well estimated. Apart from that, two other parameters must be carefully chosen: the hope size R between frames and the frequency matching interval Δf_i. The choice of R depends on the characteristics of the signal at hand. The faster the frequency and amplitude of the sinusoidal components of the signal evolve, the smaller should be the value of R. In summary, if the value of R is improperly chosen, there is not much hope to expect a good performance of the peak continuation stage.

Now, supposing that the value of R is suitably selected, the choice of the value of Δf_i will depend on the depth (in frequency) of the partial fluctuations. Therefore, if an estimate of the partial fluctuations (in a vibrato, for instance) is known, the value of Δf_i should be set so that $\Delta f_i / 2R$ be greater than the maximum slope associated with the variation in frequency of a certain partial.

A challenging problem in peak continuation occurs when the trajectories of two or more tracks cross each other. The first problem is that, at the intersection point, the resonances collapse into a single peak. Even if they do not merge into a single peak, the frequency distance criterion used to guide the track continuation becomes fragile. Using long-term

Figure 8. Peak tracking scheme (Adapted from Figure 6 of Serra, 1997)

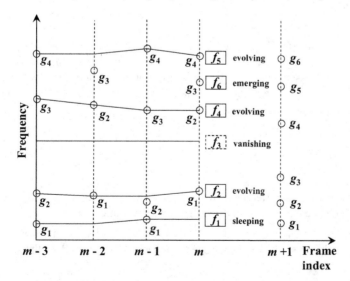

information on the peak trajectories would help solve the conflict. For instance, when partial tracks exhibit oscillations due to vibrato, an enhanced track continuation scheme can be attained via an autoregressive-based linear prediction applied over the known part of a given track trajectory (Lagrange, Marchand, Raspaud, & Rault, 2003). Another alternative to improve track continuation would be to add a second dimension in the proximity criterion, such as the peak amplitudes. Of course, the complexity of the matching procedure would also increase.

Statistical Methods

A more sophisticated way of performing peak continuation is through statistical methods. In Depalle, Garcia, and Rodet (1993), a scheme based on hidden Markov models (HMM) (Rabiner, 1989) is employed to perform the task. In this scheme the HMM states define all possible peak continuations between all peaks on two successive frames. The observation is defined as the number of peaks of those two frames. It is not necessary to say that this method is much more expensive computationally than the ruled-based ones. In its more general implementation the number of states will be huge, and also, one has to consider that the number of peaks may change from frame to frame as well as the number of tracks.

Synthesis Methods

Once the spectral information has been extracted from the signal frames and partial tracks have been traced, it is possible to re-synthesize a signal from the obtained sinusoidal modeling parameters.

Basic Principles

The synthesizer consists of a set of second-order resonators, one for each track present on a given frame. Now, for the sake of simplicity, consider sound re-synthesis based on the sinusoidal parameters associated with Ψ_m tracks present in a single frame with index m. Each track with index r will have three associated parameters $(a_{r,m}, f_{r,m}, \theta_{r,m})$. Signal re-synthesis is then accomplished by:

$$s_m(n) = \sum_{r=1}^{\Psi_m} a_{r,m} \cos(2\pi n f_{r,m}/f_s + \theta_{r,m}), \tag{18}$$

where $s_m(n)$ is the synthesis buffer and $n=0, 1, ..., R-1$, with R being the length of the synthesis buffer, which is equal to the length of the synthesis frame hop.

In order to avoid clicks and spurious distortions in the synthesized signal from frame to frame, the final goal is to smoothly interpolate the values of $(a_{r,m}, f_{r,m}, \theta_{r,m})$ throughout the frames.

The amplitude parameters will be interpolated linearly. As for the frequency and phase a joint interpolation scheme is used, since frequency is the first derivative of phase. In this context, the sets $(a_{r,m-1}, f_{r,m-1}, \theta_{r,m-1})$ and $(a_{r,m}, f_{r,m}, \theta_{r,m})$ are the track parameters pertinent to frames $m-1$ and m, respectively. These values represent the signal characteristic at the beginning of the frame.

The interpolated amplitude of a given track r at an instant n within the synthesis buffer is then given by:

$$A_{r,m}(n) = a_{r,m-1} + \frac{a_{r,m} - a_{r,m-1}}{R} n. \tag{19}$$

For simplicity, it is convenient to label $\omega_{r,m} = 2\pi\, f_{r,m}/f_s$ as the angular frequency of a given track r at frame m. The joint estimation of the instantaneous frequency and phase involves a cubic interpolation scheme. Without going into details, which can be found in McAulay and Quatieri (1986), the instantaneous phase of a given track r can be obtained by:

$$\theta_{r,m}(n) = \theta_{r,m-1} + \omega_{r,m-1} n + \alpha\, n^2 + \beta\, n^3, \tag{20}$$

where,

$$\alpha = \frac{3}{R^2}(\theta_{r,m} - \theta_{r,m-1} - \omega_{r,m-1} R + 2\pi G) - \frac{1}{R}(\omega_{r,m} - \omega_{r,m-1}), \tag{21}$$

$$\beta = \frac{-2}{R^3}(\theta_{r,m} - \theta_{r,m-1} - \omega_{r,m-1} R + 2\pi G) - \frac{1}{R^2}(\omega_{r,m} - \omega_{r,m-1}), \tag{22}$$

and G is the integer closest to μ, with:

$$\mu = \frac{1}{2\pi}\left[(\theta_{r,m-1} + \omega_{r,m-1} R - \theta_{r,m}) + (\omega_{r,m} - \omega_{r,m+1})\frac{R}{2} \right]. \tag{23}$$

Finally, the synthesis formula becomes:

$$s_m(n) = \sum_{r=1}^{\Psi_m} A_{r,m}(n)\cos\left[\theta_{r,m}(n)\right]. \tag{24}$$

The main drawback of time-domain synthesis methods is related to the possibly high computational cost of realizing, for a large number of tracks, the interpolation of sinusoidal parameters, from frame to frame. An attempt to overcome this problem is to employ frequency-domain synthesis schemes.

One example of frequency-domain synthesis is a scheme based on the inverse DFT called FFT^{-1} synthesis (Rodet & Depalle, 1992). In the FFT^{-1} method, the most prominent spectral peaks are selected, and an artificial spectrum consisting of overlapping modulated window spectra is built. Then, signal synthesis is carried out by applying an inverse FFT to the so-devised spectrum. An overlap-and-add scheme is used to guarantee a smooth continuation of the signal frames in time. The main advantages of the FFT^{-1} synthesis are its computational efficiency, precise control and modeling of noisy components in the signal, and the easiness of control from the user point of view (Rodet & Depalle, 1992).

Sinusoids + Noise

In its basic form presented in the previous section, sinusoidal modeling synthesis assumes that sinusoidal variations present in the analyzed signal are slow. As a consequence, there will be a limit to how fast the re-synthesized signal can vary, both in amplitude and frequency. In other words, fast transients and noise-like components are bound to be absent from the re-synthesized version of the signal. For example, the sounds generated by bow friction noise in violin playing or blowing noise in flute playing are typical cases. However, these sounds are inherent characteristics of those musical instruments and, therefore, should be present in high-quality sound synthesis.

In Serra and Smith (1990), a scheme for signal decomposition into a deterministic and a stochastic part is introduced. The deterministic component of the signal is obtained through conventional sinusoidal modeling analysis and synthesis. The stochastic component is obtained by subtracting the deterministic part from the original signal. If phase information is taken into account during sound synthesis, time-domain subtraction can be straightforwardly performed. Otherwise, subtraction of the deterministic part should be done on the magnitude spectrum domain.

Modeling of the stochastic component can be carried out in a simple way by estimating the envelope of its magnitude spectrum. This estimate can be obtained by various ways. For instance, standard low-order AR models can be used for spectral envelope estimation. Alternatively, a piece-wise linear approximation of the magnitude spectrum was found to be sufficient for representing the stochastic component (Serra & Smith, 1990). In this case, the spectral envelope is obtained by drawing straight lines that pass through local maxima of the magnitude spectrum. Finally, the stochastic component is synthesized by computing the inverse DFT of a complex spectrum formed by the so-estimated magnitude envelope and a random phase.

An example of the sinusoids+noise modeling scheme is illustrated in Figure 9. The plot on the left shows the original spectrum of a short excerpt of one-voice singing *a capella*. The plot in the middle shows the magnitude spectrum of the stochastic part, obtained after removing the prominent sinusoids from the original signal. The plot on the left shows again the latter spectrum in dashed line and an estimate of its envelope in solid line.

Sinusoids + Noise + Transients

The sinusoids+noise synthesis scheme is suitable for modeling originally noisy signals with

Figure 9. Sinusoids+noise synthesis scheme

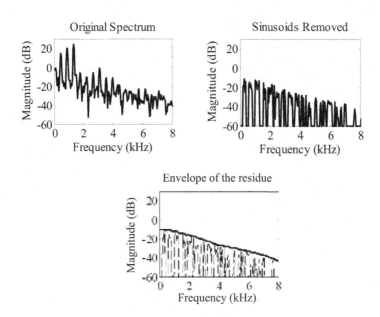

slowly varying noise components. Fast transients such as drum kicks will not be properly re-synthesized. This calls for a decomposition of the stochastic part into slowly varying filtered noise and fast transients.

A practical way to handle transients is to detect and isolate them from the stochastic part and reinsert them back to the synthesized signal. Although this resource works, it is not flexible enough to deal with sound modifications. Besides, the transients should be stored in wavetables, introducing a non-parametric element to the sinusoidal modeling approach.

A more flexible way of coping with transients within the sinusoidal modeling is the model-based approach proposed by Verma, Levine, and Meng (1997). As before, the transients are first located in the stochastic signal. Then, each transient is modeled separately and subtracted from the stochastic part, which after that should meet the assumption of being a slowly varying noise. After obtaining models for both the noise and the transients, those components can be re-synthesized and added together to the deterministic component. A block diagram of the sinusoids+noise+transient scheme is depicted in Figure 10.

Modeling of transients plays with the duality between time and frequency representations: short signals in time are represented by long signals in frequency and vice-versa. Therefore, instead of trying to model transients in the time domain, each detected transient is transformed to the frequency domain via a block discrete cosine transform (DCT). Then, a sinusoidal representation is obtained for the transformed signal. Finally, an inverse DCT is employed to transform back to the time-domain a re-synthesized version of the transient signal. Further developments related to transient modeling can be found in Boyer and Abed-Meraim (2002) and Verma and Meng (1998, 2000).

The main advantage of modeling transients instead of just sampling them is that signal

Figure 10. Sinusoids+noise+transients synthesis scheme (Adapted from Figure 1 of Verma, Levine, & Meng, 1997)

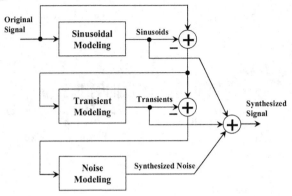

eterized.

Applications

Representing audio signals through sinusoidal parameters, noise, and transient components finds applications in various areas of audio signal processing. Naturally, one of the main applications of sinusoidal modeling is music synthesis. In this area, there are three main goals: (1) to re-synthesize sounds as close as possible perceptually to the original source; (2) to reduce the dimension of the parameter space; and (3) to allow easy control over sound transformations through the models.

The purpose of this section is to provide brief descriptions on selected audio applications that use sinusoidal modeling other than sound synthesis. The coverage starts with sound processing such as time- and frequency-scale modifications, and morphing. Then, it passes through audio interpolation, sound source separation, and audio de-noising, before concluding with low-bit audio coding. The interested reader is referred to the works of Amatriain, Bonada, Loscos, and Serra (2001), Cook (2002), Laroche (1998), Laroche and Dolson (1999), Macon (1993), Maher (1991), Quatieri and McAulay (1986), and Wright, Beauchamp, Fitz, Rodet, Röbel, Serra, and Wakefield (2000) for thorough descriptions of those applications.

Signal Modifications

Time-Scale Modifications

Time scaling means performing temporal modifications to an audio signal, such as shortening its duration while keeping the pitch unchanged (Laroche, 1998). There are several ways to realize time scaling (Cook, 2002). In the context of sinusoidal modeling, once a parametric representation is obtained for an audio segment, time scaling can be carried out by changing the value of the hop size parameter R during synthesis, in comparison with that used during analysis. In other words, if a certain value of R was used during analysis and a higher value is adopted during synthesis, the generated signal becomes stretched and, therefore, longer in duration. On the contrary, the signal is rendered shorter if a smaller value of R is chosen.

Apart from the previous situation, it is also possible to adapt the ratio between the analysis and synthesis hop sizes over time. Variable time-scale modifications find use in several applications. One example is adding variations to rhythmic patterns in audio recordings in order to render the playing performance more expressive (Gouyon, Fabig, & Bonada, 2003). Another use is in synchronization matters, such as rhythmic matching between two or more audio excerpts or between audio and video sources.

An important aspect of time scaling concerns handling transient occurrences. For example, it is desirable that, even after time stretching an audio signal, its transients are perceived as short as in the original time basis. Hence, ideally, those transients should not have their time basis modified, but just be dislodged to coincide with the corresponding locations in the stretched signal. In this regard, sinusoidal parameterization with transient modeling (Verma, Levine, & Meng, 1997) offers a suitable solution to the problem. Last but not least, a typical side effect of time-scale modifications is a change in the perceived sound ambience due to phase distortions (Puckette, 1995). Propositions to overcome this problem can be found in the relevant literature (Macon, 1993; Puckette, 1995).

Frequency-Scale Modifications

Frequency scaling refers to signal modifications that alter the perceived pitch of a given signal without changing its duration. As with time scaling, there are several means of realizing frequency-scale modifications. A comprehensive coverage of the topic can be found in Cook (2002).

Within sinusoidal modeling analysis and synthesis, frequency modifications can be carried out by tweaking the track frequencies during synthesis. For instance, pitch shifting can be implemented by simply multiplying the frequency of all tracks by a proper constant. If this constant is equal to two, the resulting signal is likely to be perceived one octave higher than the original source. Recalling that signal resampling can be seen as time- and frequency-scale simultaneous modifications, it is simple to devise an alternative scheme for frequency scaling in which a time-scaled signal is resampled in such a way that the first operation is undone by the second, leaving only the frequency-scaling effect (Laroche, 1998).

Apart from pitch shifting, more sophisticated frequency modifications can be performed by modulating over time the value of the track frequencies. For instance, artificial vibrato can be added to a steady clarinet tone if the track frequencies are properly modulated by a sinusoidal function. Moreover, frequency distortions present in the original source, such as wow and flutter, can be corrected if a pitch variation curve is made available.

In the examples mentioned so far, frequency scaling was partial dependent, in the sense that all tracks are affected in the same way. This may not be necessarily desirable in some applications related to audio effects. For example, if the goals are to render inharmonic an originally harmonic signal or to change the timbre characteristic of a given sound, only a subset of tracks can be subject to frequency change.

A particular class of frequency-scale modifications is the so-called shape-invariant. It concerns altering the pitch of the sound without changing its original spectral envelope (Macon, 1993; Quatieri & McAulay, 1992). This type of modification finds applications in speech and musical instrument sound synthesis, where timbre of the original sound should be preserved despite any pitch alteration.

A point worth mentioning is that frequency scaling may lead to undesirable artifacts in the re-synthesized signal. One pertinent concern is frequency aliasing (Diniz, da Silva, & Netto, 2002), which happens if certain track frequencies become higher than the Nyquist frequency. Another issue is the perception of some signal components as a function of frequency. For instance, low-frequency components that, in the original signal, would lie in a perceptually less salient frequency range can become overemphasized if moved to a more sensitive region of the auditory system (Zwicker & Fastl, 1999).

Audio Morphing

One of the most interesting applications of sinusoidal modeling is audio morphing. The terminology comes from image processing, where the form, or *morph* in Greek, of objects can be changed by means of image transformations. In audio, the goal is either to smoothly concatenate sounds with different timbre characteristics or devise sounds with hybrid timbres (Serra, 1994; Tellman, Haken, & Holloway, 1995).

Audio morphing is more complex than pure crossfading two different sound excerpts. In crossfading, the frequency components of the sounds are just added together in such a way that the amplitude of one sound will gradually vanish, while those of the other sound will gradually rise. On the contrary, in audio morphing, not only the frequency components, but also their amplitudes, are smoothly interpolated from one sound to the other.

An illustration that compares sound morphing against crossfading is shown in Figure 11. In this artificial example, a low-pitched harmonic sound is both crossfaded (left image) and morphed (right image) with a higher-pitched harmonic signal. The sound fusion is performed between frames 100 and 200.

Audio morphing finds applications in the entertainment industry, such as in movie soundtracks and advertisement for television. One of the most famous examples of audio morphing was the re-creation of Farinelli's voice for a moving picture about the life of the famous castrato of the eighteenth century (Depalle & Rodet, 1994). In that case, the voices of a coloratura-soprano and a counter-tenor have been morphed to give birth to the castrato register. Still in the singing voice synthesis arena, propositions for timbre mutations, such as from solo to choir (Bonada, 2005) or voice impersonation in karaoke systems appeared in the literature (Cano, Loscos, Bonada, de Boer, & Serra, 2000).

Signal Interpolation

A sinusoidal representation of sounds can be also useful for signal interpolation and extrapolation purposes. For instance, if a portion of the analyzed signal is missing for some

Figure 11. Crossfading (top image) versus morphing (bottom image)

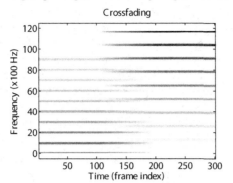

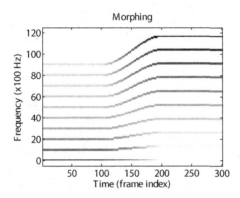

reason, the signal gap can be filled in by assuming that the missing signal is likely to behave similarly as the signal that surrounds the gap. Thus, the goal consists of matching the tracks present at the boundaries of the gap and reconstructing their trajectories over the gap by means of linear interpolation (Maher, 1991).

In situations where the track frequencies are modulated over time, such as in vibrato sounds, linear interpolation may become inadequate. Instead, it is preferable to fit low-order autoregressive models to the tracks and extrapolate their parameters across the gap based on the model (Lagrange, Marchand, & Rault, 2005). In contrast to conventional autoregressive-based interpolation methods, which are suitable for short gaps only, audio interpolation using sinusoidal modeling was reported to handle better signal reconstruction over long gaps (Godsill & Rayner, 1998; Lagrange, Marchand, & Rault, 2005; Maher, 1991).

Sound Source Separation

Sinusoidal modeling is also a core component of source separation schemes. The goal of source separation is to identify and re-synthesize separately all individual sound sources present in a given audio mixture.

The first step of the separation procedure is to analyze the sound mixture and obtain a sinusoidal representation of it. After that, one proceeds to the analysis of the obtained parameters, that is, frequency, amplitude, phase, onset time, and offset time of the tracks. The goal is to meaningfully *group* tracks that are related to a same sound source. For this purpose, pattern similarities associated with the observed tracks are pursued. For instance, tracks whose frequencies are related harmonically are likely to belong to the same sound source. Also, coherent frequency variations over time of some tracks, such as those observed in instrument sounds having vibrato, are indicative of a sound coming from the same source. The same goes for tracks that start at the same instant.

To date, separation of sound sources from complex mixtures is not feasible. Typical difficulties are to isolate different sources when the frequency trajectories of their tracks cross each other or when partials of distinct sources share same frequency tracks (Depalle, Garcia, & Rault, 1993). Therefore, in general, the performance of source separation systems tends to decrease with the number of sources to be separated. Successful separation of sound sources from a mixture of five different monophonic instruments was reported by Virtanen and Klapuri (2000, 2001).

Audio De-Noising

As seen in the last two subsections on synthesis methods, sinusoidal modeling allows separating the deterministic and stochastic components of the signal. If the stochastic components are an inherent part of the sound to be synthesized, they should be included in the synthesis scheme. On the other hand, if stochastic components are undesirable, such as in a signal corrupted with hiss noise, they can be ignored during the synthesis stage. Thus, the resulting synthesized signal will be free of the disturbing noise (Maher, 1991).

Sinusoidal modeling can be also useful for removing periodical interferences affecting audio signals, for example hum and buzz caused by grounding problems in power supply nets. In such cases, a source separation approach can be adopted in order to segregate the sinusoidal components associated with the interference source from the observed mixture. Then, denoising is accomplished by leaving those components out of the synthesis stage.

Low Bit-Rate Audio Coding

Sinusoidal modeling is also used in low bit-rate audio/speech coding. Again, the key idea is count on the slowness associated with the signal variations in time and frequency and represent the signal sparsely and parametrically through sinusoids, noise, and transient components. This way, instead of transmitting the signal through a channel, the sinusoidal parameters are transmitted and the signal is synthesized at the receiver end.

Further developments have been made in order to reduce the number of parameters to be transmitted. For instance, sinusoidal components can be grouped into harmonic-related ones and individual ones. Hence, if a harmonic tone is to be transmitted, instead of sending all track parameters, it suffices to send a package containing the parameters of the fundamental frequency and the spectral envelope of the tone. Noise components are compactly represented by their amplitude and spectral envelopes, as seen in the second subsection on synthesis methods. Furthermore, individual sinusoidal components can be allocated to account for inharmonic components. This strategy is adopted in the MPEG-4 standard for low bit-rate audio coding and is called harmonic and individual lines plus noise (HILN) parametric audio coding (Ahmadi & Spanias, 1996; Brandenburg & Bosi, 1997; Edler, Purnhagen, & Ferekidis, 1996; ISO/IEC, 2001; Purnhagen, 1999).

Conclusion

This chapter reviewed spectral-based sound synthesis, in particular, additive synthesis through sinusoidal modeling. The basic processing stages for obtaining a parametric representation of an audio signal were described. They include signal segmentation, spectral analysis, peak detection, estimation of peak parameters, and track formation. In the sequel, signal re-synthesis based on the extracted sinusoidal parameters was addressed, as well as extensions to the model to account for parameterization and re-synthesis of noise and transient components.

Finally, a selection of audio applications that use sinusoidal modeling was discussed. Typical application examples include time- and frequency-scaling, signal interpolation, audio de-noising, sound source separation, and low bit-rate audio coding.

Acknowledgments

The authors would like to thank the reviewer for the pertinent comments that helped to improve the quality of the manuscript. Acknowledgement is also due to Mr. Leonardo de Oliveira Nunes for his contribution in the Frequency Reassignment section.

References

Ahmadi, S., & Spanias, A. (1996). New techniques for sinusoidal coding of speech at 2400 BPS. In *Proceedings of the 30th Asilomar Conference on Signals, Systems, & Computers*. (pp. 770-774). Pacific Grove, CA: IEEE.

Amatriain, X., Bonada, J., Loscos, A., & Serra, X. (2001). Spectral modeling for higher-level sound transformation. In *Proceedings of MOSART Workshop on Current Research Directions in Computer Music*. Barcelona, Spain.

Auger, F., & Flandrin, P. (1995). Improving the readability of time-frequency and time-scale representations by the reassignment method. *IEEE Transactions on Signal Processing, 43*(5), 1068-1089.

Beerends, J. G., & Stemerdink, J. A. (1992). A perceptual audio quality measure based on a psychoacoustic sound representation. *Journal of the Audio Engineering Society, 40*(12), 963-978.

Bonada, J. (2000). Automatic technique in frequency domain for near loss-less time-scale modification of audio. In *Proceedings of the International Computer Music Conference,* (pp. 396-399). Berlin, Germany.

Bonada, J. (2005, May). *F-2 voice solo to unison choir transformation.* Paper presented at the 118th Convention of the Audio Engineering Society Convention, Barcelona, Spain. Preprint 6362.

Bosi, M., & Goldberg, R. E. (2002). *Introduction to digital audio coding and standards.* Norwell, MA: Kluwer.

Boyer, R., & Abed-Meraim, K. (2002). Audio transients modeling by damped & delayed sinusoids (DDS). In *Proceedings of the IEEE International Conference of Acoustics, Speech, Signal Processing (ICASSP'02),* (vol. 2) (pp. 1729-1732). Orlando, FL.

Brandenburg, K., & Bosi, M. (1997). Overview of MPEG audio: Current and future standards for low bit rate audio coding. *Journal of the Audio Engineering Society, 45*(1/2), 4-21.

Brown, J. C. (1991). Calculation of a constant Q spectral transform. *Journal of the Acoustical Society of America, 89*(1), 425-434.

Brown, J. C., & Puckette, M. S. (1992). An efficient algorithm for the calculation of a constant Q transform. *Journal of the Acoustical Society of America, 92*(5), 2698-2701.

Brown, J. C., & Puckette, M. S. (1993). A high resolution fundamental frequency determination based on phase changes of the fourier transform. *Journal of the Acoustical Society of America, 94*(2), 662-667.

Cano, P., Loscos, A., Bonada, J., de Boer, M., & Serra, X. (2000). *Voice morphing system for impersonating in karaoke applications. In Proceedings of the International Computer Music Conference* (pp. 109-112). *Berlin, Germany.*

Cook, P. R. (2002). *Real sound synthesis for interactive applications.* Wellesley, MA: A K Peters.

David, P.A. M.-S., & Szczupak, J. (1996). Refining the digital spectrum. In *Proceedings of the IEEE 39th Midwest Symposium on Circuits and Systems* (vol. 2) (pp. 767-770). Ames, IA.

Depalle, P., Garcia, G., & Rodet, X. (1993). Tracking of partials for additive sound synthesis using Hidden Markov Models. In *Proceedings of the IEEE International Conference of Acoustics, Speech, and Signal Processing,* (vol. 1, pp. 225-228). Minneapolis, MN.

Depalle, P., & Hélie, T. (1997). Extraction of spectral peak parameters using a short-time fourier transform modeling and no sidelobe windows. In *Proceedings of the IEEE ASSP Workshop on Applications of Signal Processing to Audio and Acoustics.* New Paltz, NY.

Depalle, P., & Rodet, X. (1994). A virtual castrato (?!). In *Proceedings of the International Computer Music Conference,* Copenhagen, Denmark.

Desainte-Catherine, M., & Marchand, S. (2000). High-precision analysis of sounds using signal derivatives. *Journal of the Audio Engineering Society, 48*(7/8), 654-667.

Diniz, P. S. R., da Silva, E. A. B., & Netto, S. L. (2002). *Digital signal processing—System analysis and design.* Cambridge, UK: Cambridge University Press.

Edler, B., Purnhagen, H., & Ferekidis, C. (1996). ASAC-analysis/synthesis audio codec for very low-bit rates. *Presented at the 100ᵗʰ Convention of the Audio Engineering Society.* AES Preprint 4179.

Fitz, K., & Haken, L. (2002). On the use of time-frequency reassignment in additive sound modeling. *Journal of the Audio Engineering Society, 50*(11), 879-893.

Flanagan, J. L., & Golden, R. M. (1966). Phase vocoder. *Bell System Technical Journal, 45*, 1493-1509.

George, E. B., & Smith, M. J. T. (1992). Analysis-by-synthesis/overlap-add sinusoidal modeling applied to the analysis and synthesis of musical tones. *Journal of the Audio Engineering Society, 40*(6), 497-516.

George, E. B., & Smith, M. J. T. (1997). Speech analysis/synthesis and modification using an analysis-by-synthesis/overlap-add sinusoidal model. *IEEE Transaction on Speech and Audio Processing, 5*(5), 389-406.

Godsill, S. J., & Rayner, P. J. W. (1998). *Digital audio restoration—A statistical model based approach.* London, UK: Springer-Verlag.

Goodwin, M. (1996). Residual modeling in music analysis-synthesis. In *Proceedings of the IEEE International Conference of Acoustics, Speech, and Signal Processing* (vol. 2 pp. 1005-1008). Atlanta, GA.

Gouyon, F., Fabig, L., & Bonada, J. (2003). Rhythmic expressiveness transformations of audio recordings: Swing modifications. In *Proceedings of the Sixth International Conference of Digital Audio Effects (DAFx-03).* London.

Hainsworth, S., & Macleod, M. D. (2003). *Time frequency reassignment: A review and analysis* (Tech. Rep. CUED/F-INFENG/TR.459). Cambridge, UK: Cambridge University, Engineering Dept.

Harris, F. J. (1978). On the use of windows for harmonic analysis with the discrete fourier transform. *Proceedings of the IEEE, 66*(1), 51-83.

Hartmann, W. M. (1996). Pitch, periodicity, and auditory organization. *Journal of the Acoustical Society of America, 100*(6), 3491-3502.

Hayes, M. H. (1996). *Statistical signal processing and modeling.* West Sussex, UK: John Wiley.

ISO/IEC. (2001). *Coding of audio-visual objects—Part 3: Audio* (MPEG-4 Audio Edition 2001). ISO/IEC Int. Std. 144963:2001.

Kay, S. M. (1988). *Modern spectral estimation.* Englewood Cliffs, NJ: Prentice-Hall.

Keiler, F., & Marchand, S. (2002). Survey of extraction of sinusoids in stationary sounds. In *Proceedings of the Fifth International Conference of Digital Audio Effects (DAFx-02)* (pp. 51-58). Hamburg, Germany.

Keiler, F., & Zölzer, U. (2001). Extracting sinusoids from harmonic signals. *Journal of New Music Research, 30*(3), 243-258.

Klapuri, A. (1997). *Automatic transcription of music.* Unpublished master's thesis, Tampere University of Technology, Department of Information of Technology, Tampere, Finland.

Klapuri, A., & Davy, M. (Eds.) (2006). *Signal processing methods for music transcription.* Berlin, Germany: Springer-Verlag.

Lagrange, M., Marchand, S., Raspaud, M., & Rault, J.-B. (2003). Enhanced partial tracking using linear prediction. In *Proceedings of the Sixth International Conference of Digital Audio Effects (DAFx-03)* (pp. 141-146). London, UK.

Lagrange, M., Marchand, S., & Rault, J.-B. (2005). Long interpolation of audio signals using linear prediction in sinusoidal modeling. *Journal of the Audio Engineering. Society, 53*(10), 891-905.

Laroche, J. (1989). A new analysis/synthesis system of musical signals using Prony's Method—Application to heavily damped percussive sounds. In *Proceedings of the IEEE International Conference of Acoustics, Speech, and Signal Processing* (vol. 3 pp. 2053-2056). Glasgow, UK.

Laroche, J. (1993). The use of the matrix pencil method for the spectrum analysis of musical signals. *Journal of the Acoustical Society of America, 94*(4), 1958-1965.

Laroche, J. (1998). Time and pitch scale modifications of audio signals. In M. Karhs & K. Brandenburg (Eds.), *Applications of digital signal processing to audio and acoustics* (pp. 279-309). Boston, MA: Kluwer.

Laroche, J., & Dolson, M. (1999). New phase-vocoder techniques for realtime pitch shifting, chorusing, harmonizing, and other exotic audio modifications. *Journal of the Audio Engineering Society, 47*(11), 928-936.

Macleod, M. D. (1992). Nonlinear recursive smoothing filters and their use for noise floor estimation. *IEEE Electronic Letters, 28*(21), 1952-1953.

Macon, M. W. (1993). *Applications of sinusoidal modeling to speech and audio signal processing.* Unpublished doctoral dissertation, Atlanta, GA, Georgia Institute of Technology, School of Electrical Engineering.

Maher, R. C. (1991). Sinewave additive synthesis revisited. Presented at the 91st AES Convention. New York, NY. AES Preprint no. 3138.

Masri, P. (1996). *Computer modeling of sound for transformation and synthesis of musical signals.* Unpublished doctoral dissertation, University of Bristol, UK.

McAulay, R. J., & Quatieri, T. F. (1986). Speech analysis/synthesis based on sinusoidal representation. *IEEE Transactions on Acoustics, Speech, and Signal Processing, 34*(4), 744-754.

Meddis, R., & Hewitt, M. J. (1991). Virtual pitch and phase sensitivity of a computer model of the auditory periphery I: Pitch identification. *Journal of the Acoustical Society of America, 89*(6), 2866-2882.

Portnoff, M. R. (1976). Implementation of the digital phase vocoder using the fast fourier transform. *IEEE Transactions on Acoustics, Speech, and Signal Processing, 24*(3), 243-248.

Puckette, M. (1995). Phase-locked vocoder. In *Proceedings of the IEEE ASSP Workshop on Applications of Signal Processing to Audio and Acoustics* (pp. 222-225). New

Paltz, NY.

Purnhagen, H. (1999). Advances in parametric audio coding. In *Proceedings of the IEEE Workshop Applications of Signal Processing to Audio and Acoustics* (pp. 31-34). New Paltz, NY.

Quatieri, T. F., & McAulay, R. J. (1986). Speech transformations based on a sinusoidal representation. *IEEE Transactions on Acoustics, Speech, and Signal Processing, 34*(6), 1449-1464.

Quatieri, T. F., & McAulay, R. J. (1992). Shape invariant time-scale and pitch modification of speech. *IEEE Transactions on Signal Processing, 40*(3), 497-510.

Quatieri, T. F., & McAulay, R. J. (1998). Audio signal processing based on sinusoidal analysis and synthesis. In M. Kahrs & K. Brandenburg (Eds.), *Applications of digital signal processing to audio and acoustics* (pp. 314-416). Boston: Kluwer Academic Publishers.

Rabiner, L. R. (1989). A tutorial on Hidden Markov Models and selected applications in speech recognition. *Proceedings of the IEEE, 77*(2), 257-286.

Rodet, X., & Depalle, P. (1992). Spectral envelopes and inverse FFT synthesis. Presented at the 93rd AES Convention. San Francisco. AES Preprint 3393.

S2S². (2006). Music performance modeling—Trend analysis. *Sound to Sense, Sense to Sound.* Retrieved June 10, 2006, from http://www.s2s2.org/content/view/102/124

Sandler, M. B. (1990). Analysis and synthesis of atonal percussion using high order linear predictive coding. *Applied Acoustics (Special Issue on Musical Acoustics), 30*(2/3), 247-264.

Serra, X. (1994). Sound hybridization techniques based on a deterministic plus stochastic decomposition model. In *Proceedings of the International Computer Music Conference.* (pp. 348-351). San Francisco.

Serra, X. (1997). Musical sound modeling with sinusoids plus noise. In C. Roads, S. Pope, A. Picialli, & G. De Poli (Eds.), *Musical signal processing.* Lisse, The Netherlands: Swets & Zeitlinger.

Serra, X., & Smith, J. O. (1990). Spectral modeling synthesis: A sound analysis/synthesis system based on a deterministic plus stochastic decomposition. *Computer Music Journal, 14*(4), 12-24.

Smith III, J. O., & Serra, X. (1987). PARSHL: An analysis/synthesis program for non-harmonic sounds based on a sinusoidal representation. In *Proceedings of the International Computer Music Conference.* Champaign-Urbana, IL.

Struzinski, W. A., & Lowe, E. D. (1984). A performance comparison of four noise background normalization schemes proposed for signal detection systems. *Journal of the Acoustical Society of America, 76*(6), 1738-1742.

Tellman, E., Haken, L., & Holloway, B. (1995). Timbre morphing of sounds with unequal number of reatures. *Journal of the Audio Engineering Society, 43*(9), 678-689.

Verma, T., Levine, S. N., & Meng, T. H. Y. (1997). Transient modeling synthesis: A flexible analysis/synthesis tool for transient signals. In *Proceedings of the International Computer Music Conference* (pp. 164-167). Thessaloniki, Greece.

Verma, T. S., & Meng, T. H. Y. (1998). An analysis/synthesis tool for transient signals that allows a flexible sines+transients+noise model for audio. In *Proceedings of the IEEE International Conference of Acoustics, Speech, Signal Processing (ICASSP'98)* (vol. 6) (pp. 3573-3576). Seattle, WA.

Verma, T. S., & Meng, T. H. Y. (2000). Extending spectral modeling synthesis with transient modeling synthesis. *Computer Music Journal, 24*(2), 47-59.

Virtanen, T., & Klapuri, A. (2000). Separation of harmonic sound sources using sinusoidal modeling. In *Proceedings of the IEEE International Conference of Acoustics, Speech, Signal Processing (ICASSP'00)* (vol. 2, pp. 765-768). Istanbul, Turkey.

Virtanen, T., & Klapuri, A. (2001). Separation of harmonic sounds using multipitch analysis and iterative parameter estimation. In *Proceedings of the IEEE Workshop Applications of Signal Processing to Audio and Acoustics (WASPAA'01)* (pp. 83-86). New Paltz, NY.

Wright, M., Beauchamp, J., Fitz, K., Rodet, X., Röbel, A., Serra, X., & Wakefield, G. (2000). Analysis/synthesis comparison. *Organized Sound, 4*(3), 173-189.

Zwicker, E., & Fastl, H. (1999). *Psychoacoustics: Facts and models* (2nd ed.). Berlin, Germany: Springer-Verlag.

Chapter IV

DSP Techniques for Sound Enhancement of Old Recordings

Paulo A.A. Esquef, Nokia Institute of Technology, Brazil

Luiz W.P. Biscainho, Federal University of Rio de Janeiro, Brazil

Abstract

This chapter addresses digital signal processing techniques for sound restoration and enhancement. The most common sound degradations found in audio recordings, such as thumps, pops, clicks, and hiss are characterized. Moreover, the most popular solutions for sound restoration are described, with emphasis on their practical applicability. Finally, critical views on the performance of currently available restoration algorithms are provided, along with discussions on new tendencies observed in the field.

Introduction

A Brief History of Recording Technology

The history of recorded sound starts around 1877 when Thomas A. Edison demonstrated a tinfoil cylinder phonograph that was capable of recording and reproducing human voice for the first time. The following decades were marked by continuous attempts to find more accurate ways to record and reproduce sounds. It is possible to divide the sound recording history roughly into three eras. The acoustic era lasted until the mid-20s when means to record and reproduce sound via electro-mechanical transducers were launched. The electric era witnessed the emergence and development of magnetic tape as well as stereophonic recordings. It reigned until about the beginning of the eighties, when digital recordings came about boosted by the finalization of the compact disc standard in 1980, being a direct consequence of the developments of electronic computers, in conjunction with the ability to record data onto magnetic or optical media.

Nowadays, digital audio technology is found in most consumer audio appliances. Its objectives range from improving the quality of modern and old recording/reproduction techniques to achieving an adequate balance between storage space or transmission capacity requirements and sound quality. A comprehensive timeline with descriptions of the most prominent events that marked the recording technology history is provided by Coleman (2004), Morton (2000), and Schoenherr (2005).

Aims and Processing Chain

The primary purpose of digital audio restoration is to employ digital signal processing to improve the sound quality of old recordings. A conservative goal consists of eliminating only the audible spurious artifacts that either are introduced by recording and playback mechanisms or result from aging and wear of recorded media, while retaining as faithfully as possible the original recorded sound (Godsill & Rayner, 1998a). Less restricted approaches would allow more intrusive sound modifications, such as elimination of the audience noises and correction of performance mistakes. An even more audacious concept could target at overcoming the intrinsic limitations of the recording media in order to obtain a restored sound with better quality than the originally recorded one.

In any case, a typical audio restoration chain starts with capturing the sound from old matrices and transferring it to a digital form. This stage is crucial for a successful restoration job, since it is likely to substantially affect the final sonic quality of the results. Sound transfer can be a tricky task due to the usual lack of standardization associated with obsolete recording and playback systems. The process may involve searching for the original matrices or best sounding copies and choosing the best way to play back a given matrix. Such job includes finding the right reproducing apparatus in good condition, as well as dealing with diverse recording equalization curves, among other issues.

Prior to the digital era it was already common to transfer sound from old medium types to more modern ones, for instance from 78 RPM (revolutions per minute) to LP (long-playing) disks. Also frequently seen during the electric era were attempts to enhance the sound quality of the recordings by analog means, either within the sound transfer process or at the playback stage (Burwen, 1978; Craven & Gerzon, 1975; Kinzie, Jr. & Gravereaux, 1973). The advent of the digital era and the progressive increases in computation power of digital processors made it possible to employ more and more involved signal processing techniques to digitized audio data. As a consequence, nowadays, audio restoration is mostly carried out through customized DSP algorithms meant to suppress and reduce audible undesirable noises or distortions that are still present in the signal after the sound transfer. Still within the digital domain, the de-noised signal can be further processed if necessary, for example, equalized, prior to the final remastering, which concludes the audio restoration chain.

Typical Degradations

Most of the undesirable noises found in old recordings can be roughly classified, for didactic reasons, between global and localized disturbances (Godsill & Rayner, 1998a). As these names suggest, global disturbances affect the signal as a whole, whereas localized noises corrupt only limited portions of the signal. Typical examples of global degradations are continuous background disturbances or interferences, such as broadband noise (hiss), buzz, and hum. As for localized degradations, the most obvious examples are short-time impulsive noises, such as clicks, crackles, and pops, as well as low-frequency pulses, also known as thumps. Other common types of degradations, which may not fall clearly into the previous two classes, are slow and fast frequency modulations, which are known as wow and flutter, respectively, and nonlinear distortions, such as amplitude clipping and compression.

From Older to Newer Ideas

In the analog era, restoration was restricted to some simplistic (although not always trivial) procedures. For example, a general way to reduce surface noise was low-pass filtering the recording according to the rule "the noisier the signal, the more radically filtered." Local-ized disturbances could be literally cut from a magnetic-tape copy, in spite of the resulting timing squeeze. In case of long portions of lost signal, the recording could be patched by copies of similar passages. Besides being time-consuming, this kind of job demanded too many manual skills for sometimes poor final results.

The digital era opened new avenues for audio processing. However, some general principles were retained, such as search-and-cleaning of localized defects in time-based methods, and overall, possibly non-linear, filtering of global distortions in frequency-based methods. Only recently new paradigms have been launched, for instance, sound restoration by resynthesis (see the section on "Future Directions").

In spite of all commercial interest in audio restoration (or perhaps for this very reason), the related literature is scarce. To the authors' knowledge, in 2006 the only book in print dealing exclusively with digital audio restoration is by Godsill and Rayner (1998a). Other books, like the ones by Ó Ruanaidh and Fitzgerald (1996), Vaseghi (2006), and Veldhuis (1990), grew around particular topics on this subject, but developed into more extended contents.

Chapter Organization

The purpose of this chapter is to review digital signal processing techniques used in audio restoration for treating disturbances such as thumps, clicks, and hiss. The presentation follows the order of precedence in which the problems are usually tackled. Methods and algorithms devised for dealing with other types of degradations can be found elsewhere (Godsill & Rayner, 1998a). In addition to this brief introduction, the section on "Long Pulse Removal" describes techniques for removal of long pulses of low-frequency content from audio signals. The section on "Audio De-Clicking" reviews a common model-based method for impulsive noise detection in audio signals, covering algorithms for signal reconstruction as well. The section on "Audio De-Hissing" addresses reduction of corrupting broadband noise in audio signals. The chapter concludes with a discussion on future directions concerning the digital audio restoration field.

Long-Pulse Removal

Large discontinuities on the groove walls of a disk, such as those provoked by deep scratches or breakages on the disk surface, are bound to excite the mechanical parts of the playback mechanism in an abnormal way. As a consequence, the resulting reproduced signal becomes contaminated by additive long pulses of low-frequency content that are heard as thumps.

The next sections are devoted to first qualify the degradation and then review three methods of long-pulse removal. The first employs a template matching scheme; the second is based on separation of autoregressive (AR) models; and the third is built upon non-linear filtering techniques.

Degradation Characterization

A typical long pulse is usually preceded by a short-time impulsive disturbance of high amplitude. The pulse shape after this impulsive transient is related to the impulse response of the stylus-arm set. Therefore, it is acceptable to assume that, ideally and for a given playback equipment, the pulse shape is invariable, only changing in amplitude.

The pulse tail is composed of varying low-frequency components within the range from 5 to 100 Hz, modulated in amplitude by a decaying envelope (Vaseghi, 1988). Moreover, it can be observed that the oscillations become slower as the pulse decays.

In practice, the impulsive-like excitations that drive the stylus-arm mechanism can be far from an ideal impulse, thus implying changes to the shape of the long pulses associated with certain equipment. Moreover, it may happen that the pulses occur in a clustered way, for instance, when there are two or more scratches very close to each other on a disk surface. As a result, new pulses can be generated while the response of the previous one has not yet vanished, yielding the so-called superimposed pulses. The resulting shape of superimposed and isolated pulses can differ substantially from each other. Figure 1 depicts both situations.

Figure 1. Examples of long pulses: (a) Isolated pulse, (b) superimposed pulses

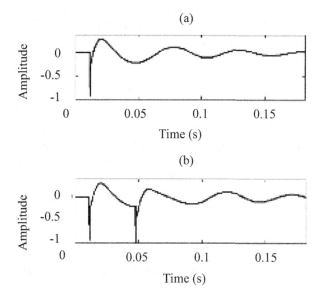

Template Matching

The template matching method for detecting and suppressing long pulses was introduced by Vaseghi (1988) and Vaseghi and Frayling-Cork (1992) and figures among the first propositions to appear in the literature. A block diagram of the processing stages of the template matching scheme for pulse removal is shown in Figure 2.

The key-point behind the method is the assumption of shape similarity among the pulse occurrences. Thus, if the assumption is valid, each pulse occurrence is considered a version of the template, possibly scaled in amplitude. Provided the availability of a pulse template, the corrupting pulses are detected in the signal by means of cross-correlating the template with the observed noisy signal and looking for values of the cross-correlation coefficient that are close to unity in magnitude. Once detected, a corrupting pulse can be suppressed by subtracting a scaled version of the template from the signal, after proper synchronization.

Figure 2. Block diagram of the template matching method for long-pulse removal, (adapted from Vaseghi and Frayling-Cork (1992)

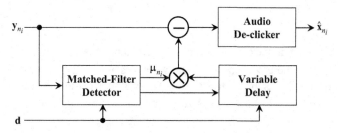

Degradation Model

In mathematical terms, a segment of the observed signal corrupted with a long pulse can be modeled as:

$$\mathbf{y}_n = \mathbf{x}_n + \mu\mathbf{d}, \tag{1}$$

where $\mathbf{y}_n = [y_n, y_{n+1}, \ldots, y_{n+N-1}]^{\mathrm{T}}$ is a segment containing the corrupted signal, $\mathbf{x}_n = [x_n, x_{n+1}, \ldots, x_{n+N-1}]^{\mathrm{T}}$ is the corresponding clean version, $\mathbf{d} = [d_0, d_1, \ldots, d_{N-1}]^{\mathrm{T}}$ is the pulse template containing N samples, and μ is a scaling factor.

Template Estimation

A pulse template can be obtained from a noise-only excerpt of the signal, if such an occurrence is available. If not, an estimate for the pulse shape has to be obtained from a "noisy" version of the pulse, that is, a pulse that also contains information on the clean signal $\mathbf{x}_n$.

Since the signal of interest is the pulse tail, which contains only low frequencies, the noisy pulse can be passed through a low-pass filter, with cutoff frequency of about 100 Hz, in order to reduce the information associated with the clean signal in the template.

Another possibility consists of using an adaptive template estimation scheme integrated to the pulse detection procedure (Vaseghi, 1988). In this approach the pulse detection algorithm begins with a noisy template. As long as other pulses are being detected, a scheme that averages the detected pulses can be applied to filter out the information associated with the clean audio components. This way, the pulse estimate is progressively refined.

Pulse Detection

As mentioned before, the samples of the detection signal used in the template matching scheme are the cross-correlation coefficients computed between the template and signal segments contained in a window that slides over the observed signal. This procedure can be realized by filtering the noisy signal through a matched filter whose impulse response is simply formed by a time-reversed version of the template, so that the output of the filter at a given time instant n is computed as:

$$\mathbf{z}_{\mathrm{DET},n} = \mathbf{d}^{\mathrm{T}}\mathbf{y}_n. \tag{2}$$

However, in order to obtain the cross-correlation coefficients it is necessary to divide $\mathbf{z}_{\mathrm{DET},n}$ by $c = (N-1)\sqrt{\sigma_x^2 \sigma_h^2}$, where σ_x^2 and σ_h^2 are the variances associated with the input signal segment and the matched filter, respectively. Thus, the cross-correlation coefficient sequence is given by:

$$r_{\mathbf{xh},n} = \frac{\mathbf{z}_{\mathrm{DET},n}}{c}. \tag{3}$$

By property, the values of the cross-correlation coefficients are within the range $-1 \le r_{\mathbf{xh},n} \le 1$. Moreover, values of $\left|r_{\mathbf{xh},n}\right|$ close to the unity indicate a strong correlation between the input signal and the template. Thus, pulse detection can be carried out by searching for time instants n_i associated with the local maxima of $\left|r_{\mathbf{xh},n}\right|$ whose values are above a user-defined threshold.

Pulse Suppression

Suppose that a certain pulse is detected and its starting point occurs at instant n_i. The pulse suppression is simply realized by subtracting a scaled version of the template from the corrupted signal. Thus, an estimate of the clean signal is computed as:

$$\hat{\mathbf{x}}_{n_i} = \mathbf{y}_{n_i} - \mu_{n_i}\mathbf{d}, \tag{4}$$

where the amplitude scaling factor can be shown to be determined by (Vaseghi, 1988),

$$\mu_{n_i} = \frac{\mathbf{z}_{\mathrm{DET},n}}{\mathbf{d}^{\mathrm{T}}\mathbf{d}}. \tag{5}$$

It should be noticed that the pulse suppression described in equation (5) is only meant to remove the low-frequency part of the pulse. The initial high-amplitude click that drives the pulse remains still to be treated. For this purpose any standard de-clicking method can be applied (see the section on "Audio De-Clicking").

Performance

Besides its simplicity, another advantage of the template matching method is that it serves to both detect and suppress long pulses. The main drawback of the method is the lack of robustness to deal with pulses whose shape varies over time as well as with superimposed pulses. As regards the former issue, Vaseghi (1988) proposed the use of a database of pulse templates with different shapes, so that the system would search for the best template match the observed pulses. The solution, of course, increases the computational cost of the method. Nonetheless, it leaves unsolved the problem with superimposed pulses, especially when the inter-pulse delay varies over time, as it happens in the case of crossed scratches. The previous shortcomings have motivated the design of more sophisticated algorithms to treat long pulses, as the AR-separation method described in the following section.

AR Separation

The AR separation method for long-pulse removal was introduced by Godsill (1993). The proposed formulation assumes that both the underlying clean signal and the corrupting pulse are independent stochastic processes governed by AR models (see equation (15) for their definition). As before, each pulse is considered to be an additive disturbance to the audio signal, leading thus to a corrupted signal that can be thought of as a mixture of two AR processes. Provided that the model parameters for both processes can be estimated, signal restoration can be accomplished by separating one of the processes from the mixture.

Signal and Pulse Models

The mixture of the two AR processes that compose the corrupted signal is given by:

$$\mathbf{y} = \sum_{i=1}^{2} \mathbf{x}_i ,$$ (6)

where, by convention, index $i=1$ will be related to the underlying signal process. Moreover, each of the independent AR processes $\mathbf{x}_i$ is assumed to follow a Gaussian distribution (Godsill & Rayner, 1998a),

$$p_{\mathbf{x}_i}(\mathbf{x}_i) = \frac{1}{(2\pi\sigma_{e_i}^2)^{\frac{N-p_i}{2}}} \exp\left(-\frac{1}{2\sigma_{e_i}^2} \mathbf{x}_i^{\mathrm{T}} \mathbf{A}_i^{\mathrm{T}} \mathbf{A}_i \mathbf{x}_i \right),$$ (7)

where $\sigma_{e_i}^2$ is the variance of the process excitation (which, in this context, consists of white noise), N is the number of samples of the observed process, p_i is the AR-model order, and $\mathbf{A}_i$ is an $(N-p_i) \times N$ matrix of the form:

$$\mathbf{A}_i = \begin{bmatrix} -a_{i_{p_i}} & \cdots & -a_{i_1} & 1 & 0 & \cdots & 0 \\ 0 & -a_{i_{p_i}} & \cdots & -a_{i_1} & 1 & 0 & \cdots \\ \vdots & \ddots & -a_{i_{p_i}} & \cdots & -a_{i_1} & 1 & \vdots \\ 0 & \cdots & 0 & -a_{i_{p_i}} & \cdots & -a_{i_1} & 1 \end{bmatrix},$$ (8)

whose nonzero elements are the AR-model coefficients.

In the AR separation method both the initial click and the low-frequency tail are modeled by the same AR model. However, the variance of the excitation associated with the click part is much higher than that related to the tail. Godsill (1993) then formulates the separation problem in terms of a switched AR model in which the diagonal correlation matrix $\mathbf{\Lambda}$ of the excitation noise process has elements defined by:

$$\lambda_k = \sigma_{e_{2,t}}^2 + j_k(\sigma_{e_{2,c}}^2 - \sigma_{e_{2,t}}^2), \tag{9}$$

where $\sigma_{e_{2,t}}^2$ and $\sigma_{e_{2,c}}^2$ are variances of the tail and click parts of the noise process, respectively, whereas j_k is a binary indicator made equal to 1 for those indices k associated with pulse samples that are considered driving clicks.

Separation Formula

It can be shown that the maximum *a posteriori* (MAP) estimate of the underlying signal process can be computed by (Godsill & Rayner, 1998a):

$$\mathbf{x}_1^{MAP} = \left(\frac{\mathbf{A}_1^T \mathbf{A}_1}{\sigma_{e_1}^2} + \mathbf{A}_2^T \mathbf{\Lambda}^{-1} \mathbf{A}_2 \right)^{-1} \mathbf{A}_2^T \mathbf{\Lambda}^{-1} \mathbf{A}_2 \mathbf{y}. \tag{10}$$

The practical problem is then reduced to the estimation of the model parameters and the indicator j_k.

An issue that cannot be overlooked is that, even in the ideal case of known model parameters, the separation performance is dependent on excitation variances. Intuitively, high-power processes are more easily separable than low-power ones.

Parameter Estimation

The estimation of the model parameters associated with the underlying signal can be realized by standard AR model estimators, such as the Yule-Walker and Burg's methods (Hayes, 1996; Kay, 1988; Makhoul, 1977). Models of orders around 50 suffice for the aimed purpose (Godsill & Rayner, 1998a; Janssen, Veldhuis, & Vries, 1986). Since a typical long pulse can last longer than a period within which audio signals can be considered stationary, it is necessary to employ a block-based AR separation scheme. For instance, segments of about 1000 samples can be used, considering signals sampled at 44.1 kHz.

Counting on the assumption of local signal stationarity, Godsill and Tan suggest taking the signal portion that immediately precedes the beginning of the pulse as the source of model estimation for the subsequent block. One can adopt a similar strategy to treat the succeeding blocks, that is, as long as a signal frame is treated it is used as the observation data upon which to estimate the model of the subsequent frame. It should be noticed, however, that such a scheme is prone to propagation errors. Another possibility, devised to reduce the computational costs of the procedure, consists of treating only the signal portion composed of the initial click and the beginning of the pulse tail, leaving the rest of the pulse to be removed by standard high-pass filtering (Godsill, 1993).

When it comes to the estimation of the model parameters associated with the pulse, if a clean pulse is available, the AR model parameters can be estimated from that observation. Of course, this approach counts on the similarity among pulse occurrences. In the lack of a clean pulse, it is possible to use a fixed second order model with coefficients a_2=2 and a_1=

−1 as a reasonable approximation. The variances $\sigma^2_{e_{2,t}}$ and $\sigma^2_{e_{2,c}}$ must be set experimentally. Moreover, it is recommended to decrease $\sigma^2_{e_{2,t}}$ exponentially toward the end of the pulse tail (Godsill & Tan, 1997).

The indicators j_k can be obtained by inverse filtering the corrupted segment through an estimate of its AR model. A similar procedure is used in click detection (see the section on "Click Detection").

Performance

The AR-separation method has been reported to offer an effective solution for long-pulse removal. Moreover, since no specific shape is assumed for the pulses, it is capable of treating pulses whose form varies over time as well as superimposed pulse occurrences. Another advantage is the joint suppression of the initial click and low-frequency parts of the pulse. The main disadvantage of the AR-separation method lies in its heavy computational load. This issue can be alleviated by employing a separation scheme based on Kalman filtering (Godsill & Tan, 1997).

Nonlinear Filtering

A more recent proposition for audio de-thumping, which was presented by Esquef, Biscainho, and Välimäki (2003), makes use of non-linear filtering techniques for estimating the waveform of long pulses. As with the previous methods, the degradation model is additive, but no hypothesis is made on the pulse shape. It is only assumed that the tail part of the pulse is composed of low-frequency components.

The pulse estimation procedure is divided into two stages: the first is meant to obtain an initial estimate of the pulse shape and is based on a procedure called two-pass split window (TPSW); the second stage employs a polynomial filtering scheme to refine the estimate.

TPSW Filtering

The two-pass split window was proposed by Struzinski (1984) and Struzinski and Lowe (1984) as a tool to estimate the background noise magnitude in peaky spectra. The key idea consisted of submitting the sampled magnitude spectrum to a couple of linear filters with a non-linear signal modification in between the two filtering steps.

In the first pass a rectangular moving average filter with a center gap, as shown in Figure 3, is employed. Provided that the length of the gap is large enough to encompass the width of observed spectral peaks, the first pass of the procedure produces an average magnitude spectrum in which the influence of the peak values on the average is mitigated at the peak locations. This happens because, at those locations, the peaks and the filter gap coincide. The peaks, however, may still induce on the filtered spectrum an average bias around their locations.

Figure 3. Example of split window

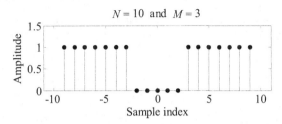

$$N = 10 \text{ and } M = 3$$

The second pass is meant to correct the aforementioned bias. Prior to it, a sample substitution criterion is applied to the intermediate signal so that, around the peak locations, the original magnitude spectrum is recovered. The output of the second filter, which now can be an ordinary moving average, yields a smooth background magnitude spectrum with little influence of the spectral peaks.

The TPSW filtering procedure can be easily adapted to deal with the problem of long pulse estimation. In this case, the waveform of the pulse tail plays the role of the background spectrum. In mathematical terms, the first pass of the TPSW procedure is realized by a conventional discrete convolution between the noisy signal $\mathbf{y}_n$ and a split window defined by:

$$\mathbf{h}_{\mathrm{SW},n} = \begin{cases} 0, & |n| < M \\ 1, & M \le |n| < N \end{cases}, \qquad (11)$$

where N and M are odd-valued parameters related to the lengths of the window and its middle gap, respectively. For instance, the split window shown in Figure 3 was generated with parameters $N=10$ and $M=3$. The modification of the intermediate signal prior to the second pass is governed by the following criterion:

$$\mathbf{y}_{\mathrm{M},n} = \begin{cases} \mathbf{y}_{\mathrm{I},n}, & \text{if } \left| \mathbf{y}_n - \mathbf{y}_{\mathrm{I},n} \right| > \alpha \left| \mathbf{y}_{\mathrm{I},n} \right| \\ \mathbf{y}_n, & \text{otherwise} \end{cases}, \qquad (12)$$

where, by convention, $\mathbf{y}_{\mathrm{I},n}$ refers to the intermediate signal that results from the first pass and $\alpha \ge 1$ is a parameter that controls the click rejection capability. It should be noticed that no prior information on the location of the pulse clicks is taken into account.

The second pass can be carried out by convolving an ordinary square window with the modified intermediate signal $\mathbf{y}_{\mathrm{M},n}$. This leads to the TPSW-based estimate of the long pulse:

$$\hat{\mathbf{d}}_{\mathrm{TPSW},n} = \frac{1}{2N-1} \sum_{k=-N}^{N} y_{\mathrm{M},n-k}. \qquad (13)$$

The effects of the passes are illustrated on subplots (a) and (b) of Figure 4. In the shown examples, the length of the split window was 111 samples with a middle gap of 31 samples,

Figure 4. TPSW results: (a) Input signal (thin solid line) showing an example of the beginning of a superimposed pulse and output of the first pass (bold solid line); (b) intermediate signal (thin solid line) after signal substitution and output of the second pass (bold solid line); (c) input signal (thin solid line) and output of a moving-average filter (bold solid line)

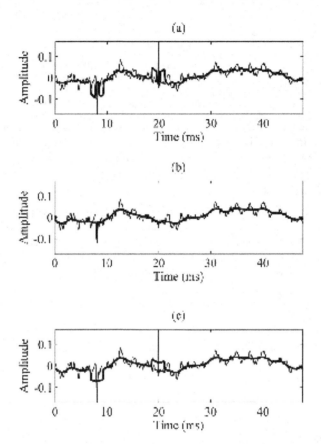

that is, $N=55$ and $M=15$, respectively. The value of α was set experimentally to 8. From subplot (a) it is possible to notice that the pulse clicks are pointing downward and upward at time instants 8 and 20 ms, respectively. Moreover, one can observe how those clicks move the output of the first pass downward and upward, respectively, in their surroundings.

After the second pass, however, the bias is substantially reduced and a signal that approximates the pulse waveform is obtained. Just for comparison purposes, the signal that would result by submitting the noisy signal to a conventional moving-average filter is shown on subplot (c), where the harmful peak influence can be more clearly seen.

Esquef, Biscainho, and Välimäki (2003) show the necessity of adjusting the length of the split windows over time, in order to cope with the frequency variations present in the pulse tail. The adjustment can be done by either changing the effective length of the window over time or using a splicing scheme to merge together three TPSW-based pulse estimates obtained from different split-window sizes.

Polynomial Fitting

The pulse estimates obtained by the procedures described in the previous section may still contain valuable information on the signal to be restored. This accounts for the need of additional processing to further refine the pulse estimates. To achieve a suitably smooth pulse estimate, an overlap-and-add polynomial fitting scheme is proposed by Esquef, Biscainho, and Välimäki (2003).

In the presented method, the TPSW-based estimate $\hat{\mathbf{d}}_{TPSW,n}$ is first sub-divided into overlapping short frames. Then a low-order polynomial is fitted to each frame. Finally, the pulse estimate is obtained by adding together the fitted curves. A schematic view of the piece-wise polynomial fitting is depicted in Figure 5.

The level of smoothing attained by the procedure can be controlled by three parameters: the frame overlap percentage, the polynomial order, and the length of the frames. For practical reasons, it is convenient to freeze the overlap factor at 50% or 75% and set the polynomial order to 2. Thus, the user only needs to adjust the length of the frame to control the global smoothness of the pulse estimate. In this case, the longer the frame, the smoother the pulse estimates. Practical values for the frame length range from 50 to 200 samples, considering a sample rate of 44.1 kHz.

In the end, the waveform that results from the polynomial fitting procedure, and which represents final pulse estimate $\hat{\mathbf{d}}_{POLY,n}$, is subtracted from the corrupted signal to yield the de-thumped signal.

Figure 5. Illustration of the piece-wise polynomial fitting over segments of a TPSW-based pulse estimate

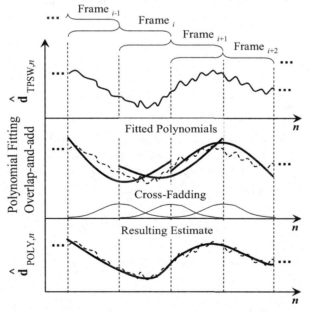

Performance

As with the template matching, the TPSW-based de-thumping method only takes care of suppressing the low-frequency transient of long pulses. The initial pulse click has to be removed later by a de-clicking algorithm (see the section on "Audio De-Clicking"). This should not be considered an extra burden, since de-clicking is usually required as a de-thumping follow up in a typical sound restoration processing chain.

According to Esquef, Biscainho, and Välimäki (2003), the TPSW-based de-thumping method can perform as effectively as the AR-separation method, also when treating superimposed pulses. However, from a computational point of view and for typical values of the processing parameters, the TPSW-based solution can be up to two orders of magnitude less expensive. Comparisons were conducted be means of a set of objective measures and confirmed by informal listening tests.

Discussion

Among the three de-thumping methods presented, the template matching is the only one that offers a solution for long pulse detection. The AR-separation and the TPSW-based schemes assume the location of the pulses as well as those of the driving initial clicks as *a priori* known information. The template matching is perhaps the most adequate solution when the shape similarity among the corrupting pulses can be accepted as a valid hypothesis.

For more general situations of pulse suppression, including superimposed pulses, the user can opt for either the AR-separation method or the TPSW-based scheme. If keeping the computational costs low is an issue of concern, the most suitable choice would be the TPSW-based solution. Finally, it is important to emphasize that all methods described in this section require a certain degree of interaction with the user, which is needed to choose the values of some processing parameters. Therefore, full automatism cannot be claimed for any of them.

Audio De-Clicking

Discontinuities of very short duration present in audio signal are usually heard as clicks. More often, those discontinuities are produced during playback by superficial scratches, accumulated dust or particles, and intrinsic irregularities on a disk surface (Wilson, 1965).

A general model for impulsive noise corruption assumes an additive type of degradation of the form:

$$y_n = x_n + j_n d_n,$$

(14)

where y_n is the corrupted signal, x_n is the wanted clean signal, and $j_n d_n$ is the noise component, with j_n being a binary indicator of corrupted samples, that is, $j_{n_i} = 1$ if the sample y_{n_i} is found to be corrupted.

Digital audio de-clickers operate in general between two processing stages: click detection and signal reconstruction. The following sections are meant to describe those stages in more detail.

Click Detection

One of the most obvious ways to perform click detection is to explore the contrast in frequency content between typical audio signals and clicks. Short-time discontinuities such as clicks contain strong energy on high frequencies as opposed to audio signals, whose energy is more concentrated on low frequencies. Therefore, a straightforward means to produce a detection signal for click location consists of high-pass filtering the signal.

Figure 6 exemplifies the effect of high-pass filtering an audio signal contaminated by clicks. In this case, the audio signal, sampled at 44.1 kHz, was submitted to a 15th-order FIR half-band high-pass filter. It can be noticed that, on the original waveform, it is harder to detect all clicks by amplitude discrimination, especially those with small amplitudes. On the contrary, click occurrences are enhanced in the high-pass filtered version of the signal, $y_{\text{HP}, n}$, due to the energy attenuation on the frequency range more associated with the wanted audio content. This reduction on the signal-to-noise ratio (SNR) allows the use of threshold-based amplitude discrimination criteria to locate clicks in the corrupted signal.

Figure 6. Click detection via high-pass filtering: (a) Corrupted signal and (b) magnitude of its high-pass filtered version

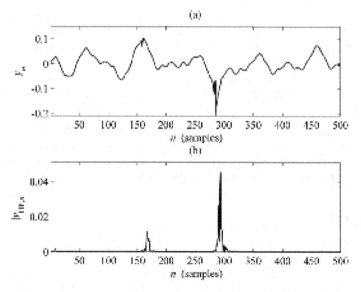

Model-Based Approach

Another option to ease click detection through amplitude criteria is to employ a model-based scheme. A common approach in this direction is to assume that the underlying signal follows an autoregressive (AR) model. High values of the modeling error in relation to the observed data indicate the presence of clicks.

In mathematical terms, the desired clean signal is modeled as:

$$x_n = \sum_{k=1}^{p} a_k x_{n-k} + e_n, \tag{15}$$

where a_k, with $a_0=1$, are the coefficients of the pth order AR model and e_n is the modeling error at time instant n. An alternative interpretation takes e_n as the excitation signal at the input of an all-pole filter that generates x_n at its output.

In practice, the observed signal must be segmented into short-time frames of N samples in order to render more plausible the hypothesis of local stationarity of audio signals. As a rule of thumb, it suffices to choose a value of N that corresponds to a duration ranging from 20 to 50 ms. Moreover, the available noisy data are used as the observation upon which the estimation of the AR coefficients are carried out. For this purpose any well-known AR model estimator can be employed, such as the autocorrelation or the covariance methods (Hayes, 1996).

Now, assuming that the model is known, a detection signal can be obtained via inverse filtering the observed corrupted data y_n through the model. In other words, y_n is passed through an FIR filter whose coefficients are $(1, a_1, -a_2, ..., -a_p)$, yielding the signal e_n. The initial p samples of e_n are affected by the filter's transient; hence, they should be discarded for click detection purposes.

As with the high-pass filtering approach, the inverse filtering scheme aims at reducing the SNR of the observed data as a means to increase the amplitude contrast between corrupted and clean signal samples. However, the filtering procedure inevitably smears the clicks in time (Vaseghi, 1988), thus hindering their precise location. The higher the filter order, the more prominent the spread of clicks in the detection signal. Therefore, it is recommended to adopt low-order filters, for example, within the range between 10 and 40. It should be noticed that even if those low orders are insufficient to fully model the underlying signal, this is not to worry about, since the primary goal here is click detection, not strict signal modeling.

A suitable click detection criterion is to consider as clicks samples of the corrupted signal that correspond to samples of a detection signal whose magnitude exceed the value of a given threshold. Consider, for instance, a segment of N samples of the detection signal $y_{DS,n}$ associated with of the signal y_n. The click indicator can be obtained as:

$$j_n = \begin{cases} 1, & |y_{DS,n}| \geq T \\ 0, & \text{otherwise} \end{cases}, \text{ for } n_i \leq n \leq n_i+N-1, \tag{16}$$

where T is an adaptive threshold that can be computed as:

$$T = K \, \mathrm{median}\left(\left|y_{DS,n_i}\right|, \left|y_{DS,n_i+1}\right|, \ldots, \left|y_{DS,n_i+N-1}\right|\right),\tag{17}$$

with K being a scalar parameter to be adjusted by the user.

The detection signal $y_{DS,n}$ can be either the high-pass filtered version $y_{HP,n}$ of the noisy signal or the modeling error sequence e_n. The value of the threshold T varies over time according to the variance of the background component of $y_{DS,n}$. That variance can be estimated in a robust way, for example, via the median operator (Donoho, 1992). The value of K, which should be chosen experimentally, controls the balance between missed and false click detections in the signal.

Figure 7 illustrates the effect of inverse filtering on an audio sequence corrupted by impulsive noise. In this case, a 20th order AR model was estimated from the noisy data using Burg's method (Hayes, 1996). It is possible to verify that the magnitude of the detection signal obtained via inverse filtering, $\left|e_n\right|$, is composed by a small-magnitude background signal, associated with the stochastic component of x_n, and by bursts of high-valued magnitude associated with the corrupting clicks. As with the high-pass filtering case, it seems easier to detect click occurrences by a threshold-based amplitude criterion. A block diagram showing the typical processing stages of an AR-based audio de-clicker is depicted in Figure 8.

Performance Improvements

Several means to improve the performance of model-based click detectors have been proposed in the literature. For example, the use of a two-sided linear prediction was suggested

Figure 7. AR-based inverse filtering for click detection: (a) Corrupted signal and (b) its model error (in solid line) compared with a threshold T, with K=5 (in dashed line)

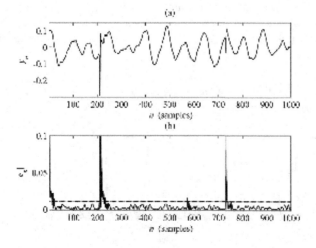

Figure 8. Processing stages of an AR-based audio de-clicker, (Adapted from Vaseghi & Frayling-Cork, 1992)

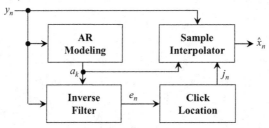

by Vaseghi and Rayner (1990). Frequency-warped linear prediction applied to click detection was investigated by Esquef, Karjalainen, and Välimäki (2002). A further improvement on the click detection capability, especially of low-amplitude clicks, is to submit the detection signal to a matched filter, in which the template signal consists of a time-reversed version of the inverse filter coefficients (Vaseghi, 1988). The main drawback of such resource is that it contributes an additional spread to the click occurrences, which may be critical when dealing with clicks well clustered in time.

An example of the effect of passing the detection signal of Figure 7 through a matched filter can be seen in Figure 9. It can be noticed that, for example, the detection of the small-amplitude one-sample click that occurs around sample 570 is greatly facilitated by the matched filter. The costs for that detection gain are the longer filter's transient and the substantial spread that afflicts the clicks in the detection signal.

The threshold-based criterion of equation (15) may fail to provide the precise location and extension of a click. Apart from the signal spread, which, by delaying the end of a click, tends to cause the overestimation of its duration, there is the possibility of intermediate samples of the detection signal associated with a click occurrence having a magnitude that lies below the threshold value (see, for instance, the click occurrence around sample 250 in Figure 9). As a result, a given click can be undesirably split into several parts.

Solutions for the previous problems were proposed by Esquef, Biscainho, Diniz, and Freeland (2000). In the described double-threshold scheme, a higher threshold is used for click detection, whereas a lower threshold is set as a reference for defining the duration of a given detected click. Moreover, a heuristic criterion is adopted to merge into a single

Figure 9. Detection signal given by the magnitude of the matched-filter's output (in solid line) compared against a fixed threshold T=0.5 (in dashed line)

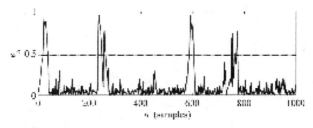

occurrence clicks that appear close to each other. An alternative for a more precise click location consists of locating the beginning of the clicks using the original detection signal, obtained via inverse filtering, and estimating the end of the clicks in a similar fashion, but this time inverse filtering the time-reversed version of the corrupted signal (Esquef et al., 2002; Godsill & Rayner, 1998a).

Performance

Model-based detectors offer a suitable and simple solution for click detection in audio signals. There are, however, limitations in a few situations. For example, there is the risk that genuine impulsive-like events present in the recorded signal be mistaken by clicks. Thus, it is likely that percussive events, such as whip sounds and drum kicks, be detected as clicks. Attempts to restore those sounds may smooth out their original sharp transients.

Another difficult situation for model-based click detection happens when dealing with audio signals that possess a strong harmonic or quasi-harmonic frequency structure (Vaseghi, 1988). In such cases, the low-order models employed within the inverse filtering stage are insufficient to destroy the long-term correlations of samples in the detection signal. As a result, those correlations show up as periodical bursts of high-magnitude values, thus, being susceptible to be taken as click occurrences.

Advanced Methods

Besides model-based methods there exist other means to detect and locate clicks in audio signals. One of those methods is based on wavelet decomposition of the corrupted signal (Montresor, Valiere, Allard, & Baudry, 1991). As a multiscale transform, the discrete wavelet transform (Mallat, 1999) offers a natural signal decomposition for click detection, since impulsive-like events are bound to appear clearly on the finest scales, thus facilitating their detection.

More advanced techniques employ statistical modeling of both the underlying signal and the noise components. In that direction, powerful tools that employ statistical data detection, inference, and classification based on Bayesian methods have been proposed in the literature (Godsill & Rayner, 1998a).

Signal Recovery

In de-clicking techniques, once the corrupting clicks are located in time, there arises the problem of reconstruction of the audio material in the damaged portions. A variety of DSP solutions for signal recovery exists in the literature. Among the available techniques it is relevant to mention band-limited recovery (Ferreira, 2001; Papoulis, 1975), interpolators based on sinusoidal modeling (George & Smith, 1992; Godsill & Rayner, 1998a; Maher, 1994; Quatieri & McAulay, 1998), waveform substitution schemes (Goodman, Lockhart, Waen, & Wong, 1986; Niedzwiecki & Cisowski, 2001), sub-band methods (Chen & Chen,

1995; Cocchi & Uncini, 2001; Montresor, Valiere, Allard, & Baudry, 1991), and interpolators based on autoregressive models (Godsill & Rayner, 1992, 1998b; Janssen, Veldhuis, & Vries, 1986; Vaseghi, 1988). A comprehensive coverage on interpolators for audio signals can be found in the works of Godsill and Rayner (1998a) and Veldhuis (1990).

Autoregressive processes have been demonstrated to be well suited to model short-time portions of general audio signals. It is no surprise that AR-based interpolators figure among the most adequate techniques for signal reconstruction over short-time portions of audio signals. Therefore, in the next sections, the attention will be focused on AR-based interpolators. First, an interpolator devised to perform a joint signal reconstruction across several distinct gaps of missing samples within a frame of audio signal is described. Its inclusion here is justified by its effective performance and simplicity of formulation. Then, a solution for signal reconstruction over long gaps of missing samples is outlined. It involves the use of AR-based signal extrapolators and signal decomposition into sub-bands.

Least Squares AR Interpolator

The least squares AR (LSAR) interpolator was introduced by Janssen, Veldhuis and Vries, (1986) and Vaseghi (1988) and attempts to recover the audio information in damaged or missing portions of a signal frame by minimizing the modeling error with respect to signal samples to be restored. In matrix notation, the pth order AR model stated in equation (15) can be reformulated as:

$$\mathbf{e} = \mathbf{A}\mathbf{x}, \tag{18}$$

where $\mathbf{x} = [x_0, x_1, \ldots, x_{N-1}]^T$ and $\mathbf{A}$ is the $(N-p) \times N$ matrix previously defined in equation (8). Moreover, it is convenient to split the observation vector $\mathbf{x}$ into two parts: one vector containing the known or clean samples $\mathbf{x}_k$ and another with those to be recovered $\mathbf{x}_u$. Thus, it is possible to re-write equation (18) as:

$$\mathbf{e} = \mathbf{A}_u \mathbf{x}_u + \mathbf{A}_k \mathbf{x}_k, \tag{19}$$

where $\mathbf{A}_u$ and $\mathbf{A}_k$ are, respectively, column-wise partitions of matrix $\mathbf{A}$ with direct correspondence to the partition performed on $\mathbf{x}$. By minimizing the cost function $C = \mathbf{e}^T \mathbf{e}$ with respect to the vector of unknown samples $\mathbf{x}_u$ one obtains the LS interpolator solution, which can be shown (Godsill & Rayner, 1998a) to be given by:

$$\hat{\mathbf{x}}_u = -\left(\mathbf{A}_u^T \mathbf{A}_u\right)^{-1} \mathbf{A}_u^T \mathbf{A}_k \mathbf{x}_k. \tag{20}$$

Performance

The LSAR interpolator is known to perform suitably when filling in short portions of missing samples, say, up to 2 ms. From a practical point of view, it is expected that a given signal block to be treated contains many more known than unknown samples. That helps to assure a less biased and statistically more significant modeling of the underlying signal. Besides, the lower the number of samples to be recovered, the less taxing computationally the interpolation becomes.

When it comes to the choice of the AR model order, it should be taken into account that the objective is to fill in very short gaps in the signal, and not to fit the best model to the signal. Thus, adopting model orders within the range from 40 to 80 usually suffice. Figure 10 demonstrates the performance of the LSAR interpolator over an excerpt of audio signal that contains three artificial gaps of lengths 50, 100, and 200. In this simulation $p=40$ was adopted.

There are some drawbacks associated with running the LSAR interpolator with low-order models. The first occurs when dealing with signals that possess strong harmonic content. In those cases, interpolation of long excerpts may be too smooth or decay in energy toward the middle of the gap. Means to improve the interpolation performance in the previous situations include the use of a pitch-based extended AR model (Vaseghi & Rayner, 1990) and an AR-based interpolator appended with a sinusoidal basis representation (Godsill & Rayner, 1998a).

Another issue associated with AR-based interpolation, especially when treating long gaps, is its inability to reconstruct stochastic components present in the underlying signal. This limitation is directly linked to the minimization of the modeling error, as part of the estimation of the unknown samples. As the stochastic components of the signal appear in the modeling error, the resulting recovered signal tends to be smoother than the surrounding portions. Among possible ways to overcome this problem, one finds solutions such as the use of random sampling techniques (Ó Ruanaidh & Fitzgerald, 1994) and sample estimation procedures that impose a lower bound to the minimization of the modeling error (Rayner & Godsill, 1991; Niedzwiecki, 1993).

Figure 10. Performance of the LSAR interpolator. The original signal is depicted in dashed line, whereas the interpolated is shown in solid line. Gap locations are delimited by vertical dotted lines.

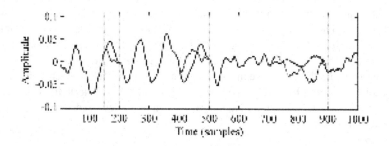

Interpolation Across Long Gaps

As mentioned in the previous section, reconstructing long portions of missing audio data can be a difficult job for the LSAR interpolator. When referring to long gaps, one should keep in mind that the non-stationary nature of audio signals in general imposes an upper limit to the extent of signal excerpts that can be meaningfully recovered. Considering that local stationarity can only be assumed within short blocks up to approximately 50 ms, recovering fragments of such duration is already an extreme situation for the AR-based method described.

Perhaps, the most trivial way of improving the performance of AR-based interpolators when dealing with long gaps consists of increasing the model order. However, the number of observation samples needs to be at least equal to, but preferably greater than, the chosen model order. Therefore, depending on the length of the gap to fill in, there may not be many samples left within a stationary frame centered on a given gap, available for model estimation.

Moreover, the time-frequency characteristics of the passage that immediately antecedes a long gap may differ from those of the succeeding excerpt. This fact has motivated the proposition of interpolators that use two different AR models: one for the segment that precedes the gap and another for the ensuing portion. In a work by Etter (1996) an LS solution for a dual AR model interpolation is introduced. In the same direction, an interpolator that merges forward- and backward-extrapolated signals based upon two distinct AR models is presented by Kauppinen, Kauppinen, and Saarinen (2001) and Kauppinen and Roth (2002b). These interpolators are able to fill in long gaps of missing samples better than the LSAR solution, but at the cost of employing high model orders. Of course, the higher the adopted model order, the higher the computational complexity required by the interpolator.

Multirate AR-Based Interpolator

As an attempt to find a better balance between qualitative performance and computational load, Esquef and Biscainho (2006) proposed an AR-based multirate interpolation scheme. The proposed method is composed of two stages: a fullband interpolation, in which a slightly modified version of the interpolator presented by Kauppinen, Kauppinen, & Saarinen. (2001), Kauppinen and Kauppinen (2002), and Kauppinen and Roth (2002b) is used; then follows the multirate stage, where the interpolator of Kauppinen and Kauppinen (2002) is applied to the signals of the lowest sub-bands.

The original proposition of Kauppinen and Kauppinen (2002) carries out pure signal extrapolation to accomplish audio reconstruction. Taking the forward extrapolation as an example, that means that a high-order AR model is estimated for a fragment of the signal that precedes a gap. Then, appropriate initial states for the AR synthesis filter are obtained and the truncated unforced response of this filter is taken as the forward-extrapolated signal. The same formulation is applied to produce a backward-extrapolated fragment, which is seamlessly merged with the forward-extrapolated one via a cross-fading scheme. The modified scheme of Esquef and Biscainho (2006) uses the same AR synthesis filter and initial states, but excites the filter with the modeling error sequence reversed in time. All other processing steps are identical.

That simple change allows adopting low-order models and yet obtaining non-decaying extrapolated signals, which account for a better signal reconstruction in terms of energy preservation across the gap, at a substantially lower cost. Nonetheless, low-frequency arti-facts can be perceived in the restored signals. Here it comes into place the multirate stage, which is meant to reduce the audibility of those disturbances.

The multirate stage decomposes the output of the first stage into six octave sub-bands via a maximally decimated filterbank. Then, the interpolator of Kauppinen and Kauppinen (2002) is applied to the signals of the two lowest sub-bands prior to resynthesis. In those sub-bands, the already filled gap regions and surrounding segments are squeezed in length by the decimation factor of 32. Therefore, re-interpolation of those signals can be performed using low-order AR models, thus easing the interpolation task. Further details on imple-mentation issues and choice of processing parameters can be found in the work by Esquef and Biscainho (2006).

Performance

The multirate AR-based interpolator described by Esquef and Biscainho (2006) has been confronted against the formulation presented by Kauppinen and Kauppinen (2002), for a case study in which a gap of 1800 samples, at 44.1 sample rate, was to be concealed. Results from formal listening tests revealed that, on average, the multirate scheme can perform comparably to the original method. However, while the latter required AR models with orders of about 1000 to satisfactorily accomplish the task, the former demanded interpola-tors with orders as low as 50, thus accounting for a reduction of one order of magnitude in computational cost.

Figure 11. Performance comparisons among the interpolator of Kauppinen and Kauppinen (2002), with model orders 100 and 1000, and that of Esquef and Biscainho (2006) with order 50

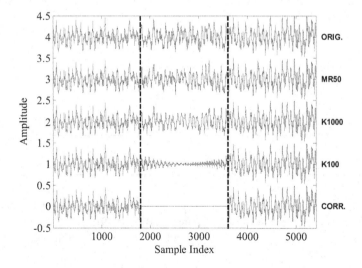

Figure 11 offers comparative results between the two interpolators, for the task of filling in a gap of 1800 samples within an excerpt of rich orchestral music. The corrupted signal, which is labeled as **CORR.**, appears on the bottom of the image. Kauppinen's interpolator with order 100 produced the segment denoted by **K100**. Increasing the order to 1000 yields the recovered signal **K1000**. The interpolation task, as realized by the multirate scheme with interpolators of order 50, generated the signal **MR50**. The original signal, marked as **ORIG.**, is depicted on the top of the figure as a reference. The plots have been shifted in amplitude for clarity.

The computational cost to obtain the signals **K100** and **MR50** is approximately the same. However, it can be observed that, for the length of the gap in question and with order 100, the interpolator of Kauppinen and Kauppinen (2002) suffers from the problem of energy decay toward the middle of the gap. To remedy this problem one can increase the model order to 1000, at the cost of a ten-fold increase in the computational load. Alternatively, the multirate scheme offers similar results at a much lower cost. Additional comparisons among the multirate scheme and competing AR-based interpolators can be found in a work by Esquef and Biscainho (2006).

Audio De-Hissing

Audio contamination by additive broadband noise, which is perceived as hiss, is a rather common type of signal degradation associated usually with measurement noise. Among the many sources of hiss it is possible to mention thermal noise associated with the transducers and electric amplification circuitry, electro-magnetic interferences, quantization errors in analog to digital conversion, and intrinsic characteristics of the recording media. In the latter matter, magnetic tape and 78 RPM recordings are notable for suffering from hiss contamination.

Compared to the removal of localized disturbances, hiss reduction is a much more taxing problem to solve effectively. Apart from the fact that almost all samples of the signal are affected by the degradation, there is the commonly unavoidable overlap between the audio and noise spectra. And separation of the noise and audio spectra is a key point in well-known de-hissing methods.

The following sections will tackle the fundamentals of two methods for audio de-hissing, namely, the short-time spectral attenuation (STSA) and the wavelet shrinkage.

Short-Time Spectral Attenuation

Formulation

Short-time spectral attenuation is the most popular class of methods for audio de-hissing and originates in noise removal from speech signals (Boll, 1979a, 1979b; Lim, 1978, 1986; Lim & Oppenheim, 1978). The main assumption behind STSA is that the corrupted signal can be modeled as:

$$y_n = x_n + d_n, \tag{21}$$

where x_n is an ergodic stationary process corresponding to the clean signal and d_n is an additive zero-mean process uncorrelated with x_n. It is trivial to demonstrate that the power spectral density (PSD) of the corrupted signal is given by:

$$S_{y,\omega} = S_{x,\omega} + S_{d,\omega}, \tag{22}$$

where $S_{x,\omega}$ and $S_{d,\omega}$ are the PSD associated with the underlying clean signal and the noise process, respectively, with ω denoting frequency. Thus, a direct estimate of the PSD of the clean signal can be attained as:

$$\hat{S}_{x,\omega} = S_{y,\omega} - S_{d,\omega}. \tag{23}$$

If d_n can be considered white noise, then $S_{d,\omega}$ is constant over frequency and proportional to the variance σ_d^2 of the noise process.

In practice, audio signals can only be considered stationary within frames of short duration. Therefore, a block-based overlap-and-add signal analysis procedure must be employed (Cappé & Laroche, 1995; Godsill, Rayner, & Cappé, 1998). For convenience, it is recommended to adopt window types and overlap factors that guarantee that the windows sum up to a constant value. For instance, Hanning windows, overlapped at 50% and 75% sum up to one and two, respectively. Otherwise, amplitude compensation must be applied to the synthesized signal (Godsill & Rayner 1998a).

Moreover, considering a block of N samples of the noisy signal y_n, its PSD can be approximated by the sampled power spectrum of the observed data, computed via the discrete Fourier transform (DFT) (Hayes, 1996):

$$\hat{S}_{y,\omega_k} \approx \frac{\left| \mathrm{DFT}_k \left\{ y_n \right\} \right|^2}{N} \equiv \left| Y_k \right|^2, \tag{24}$$

with k standing for frequency bin index. As the same approximation holds true for the noise component, the estimated PSD of the clean signal can be approximated by:

$$\left| \hat{X}_k \right|^2 = \begin{cases} \left| Y_k \right|^2 - \alpha \left| D_k \right|^2, & \left| Y_k \right|^2 > \alpha \left| D_k \right|^2, \\ 0, & \text{otherwise} \end{cases} \tag{25}$$

where α is a gain factor. The component $\left| D_k \right|^2$ can be estimated *a priori* from noise-only portions of the signal. In case of white noise, one can count on the expected spectral flatness of $\left| D_k \right|^2$ and replace it with an average level for all k. Alternatively, an estimate of this level can be obtained, for instance, by averaging the upper-quarter part of the observed power spectrum $|Y_k|^2$, where it is plausible to assume that the energy of noise component is dominant over that of the signal.

Once an estimate for the magnitude spectrum of the clean signal is obtained, the corresponding estimate of the clean signal itself is produced by taking the inverse DFT of the complex signal, which is formed by $|\hat{X}_k|e^{j\angle Y_k}$, where $j = \sqrt{-1}$ is the imaginary unity and the symbol $\angle$ stands for phase. Figure 12 summarizes in a functional diagram the processing stages of a standard STSA scheme.

The suppression rule given in equation (25) is the so-called power spectrum subtraction. In general, it is possible to formulate the most common suppression rules as:

$$|\hat{X}_k| = H_k |Y_k|, \tag{26}$$

where H_k can be considered a time-varying filter that appropriately attenuates the magnitude spectrum of the noisy signal based upon an estimate of the local SNR measured at each frequency bin k. Moreover, the attenuation factor can assume the general form (Lorber & Hoeldrich, 1997):

$$H_k = H_{b,k} = \begin{cases} \left(1 - \left(\alpha \dfrac{|D_k|}{|Y_k|} \right)^b \right)^{\frac{1}{b}}, & |Y_k|^2 > \alpha |D_k|^2, \\ 0, & \text{otherwise} \end{cases} \tag{27}$$

where b is a selection factor that defines the type of selection rule. For example, adopting $b=1$ yields the so-called spectral subtraction rule, whereas setting $b=2$ leads to the previously seen power spectrum subtraction rule. The well-known Wiener estimator, which minimizes the mean square error between the noisy and clean signals, is just given by $H_k = H_{2,k}^2$.

In order to gain more insight on the effect of suppression rules, it is convenient to set $\alpha=1$ and re-write $H_{b,k}$ as a function of the signal-to-noise ratio, defined as $R_k \equiv |X_k|^2 / |D_k|^2$. This leads to:

$$H_{b,k} = \begin{cases} \left(1 - \left(\dfrac{1}{R_k + 1} \right)^{\frac{b}{2}} \right)^{\frac{1}{b}}, & R_k > 0 \\ 0, & \text{otherwise} \end{cases} \tag{28}$$

from where one can infer that, as intuitively expected, $H_{b,k}$ decreases with R_k. Figure 13 compares the attenuation levels associated with the suppression rules $H_{2,k}$ (power spectrum subtraction), $H_{1,k}$ (spectral subtraction), and $H_{2,k}^2$ (Wiener) as a function of R_k.

From Figure 13 it is possible to verify that the power spectrum subtraction rule offers the least intense magnitude spectrum attenuation, whereas the spectral subtraction rule provides the most severe. The Wiener rule rests in between the previous two curves.

Figure 12. Block diagram of a typical STSA procedure, (Adapted from Wolfe and Godsill (2003)

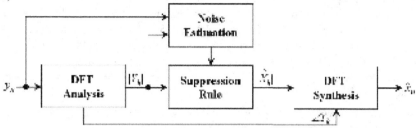

Performance

The conventional implementation of an STSA-based de-hisser can produce notable reduction of the audible background noise. However, the attained results can be marred by two main distortions: the inevitable suppression of valuable high-frequency content from the underlying signal and the annoying audibility of a random tonal noise associated with the remaining components of the noise process left in the signal after restoration. The latter phenomenon, which is also known as musical noise, has its roots on the fragile assumption on the flatness of $|D_k|^2$ over frequency. In reality, in a given frame, the value of $|D_k|^2$ varies around a certain constant average level. Therefore, R_k will be underestimated for an arbitrary set of frequency bins, which varies from frame to frame. As a consequence, at those frequencies, which are randomly distributed along the spectrum, the noise component is less attenuated than it ideally should be and becomes audible for a brief period of time,

Figure 13. Comparison among the level of spectral attenuation produced by the power spectrum subtraction, spectral subtraction, and Wiener suppression rules as a function of the signal-to-noise ratio.

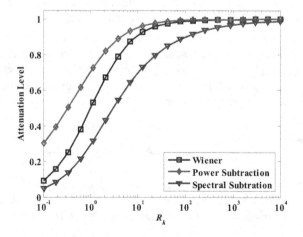

especially on the high-frequency range.

There have been proposed several means to reduce the musical noise in de-hissed audio signals. Perhaps the simplest solution consists of overestimating the level of the noise power (Berouti, Schwartz, & Makhoul, 1979; Boll, 1979a, 1979b; Lorber & Hoeldrich, 1997; Vaseghi, 1988; Vaseghi & Rayner, 1988). This can be easily carried out by setting $\alpha>1$ in equation (27). The side effect of this option is an even greater loss of valuable components of the recorded signal, especially on the high-frequency range, rendering the restored sound too muffled.

Other straightforward ways of reducing the audibility of musical noise repose on the use of spectral averaging within the computation of the suppression rules (Boll, 1979b), on the adoption of a minimum attenuation level for $H_{b,k}$ (Berouti, Schwartz, & Makhoul, 1979; Lorber & Hoeldrich, 1997), and on the application of heuristic rules over the values of $H_{b,k}$, measured during a set of consecutive processed frames (Vaseghi & Frayling-Cork, 1992). All those options attempt to set a suitable balance among the audibility of a residual noise floor, that of the musical noise, and a faithful preservation of the recorded content on the restored signal.

A more sophisticated solution for decreasing the audibility of musical noise was proposed by Ephraim and Malah (1983, 1984, 1985), and it is known as the Ephraim and Malah suppression rule (EMSR). The EMSR figures as the optimal, in the minimum mean square error sense, amplitude estimator of a short-time sinusoid marred in additive white noise. Its formulation requires the knowledge of both the *a priori* and the *a posteriori* SNRs associated with a given frequency bin. In a practical implementation, the *a posteriori* SNR refers to R_k measured from the signal frame being processed as before. In its turn, the *a priori* SNR is guessed from a non-linear decision-directed scheme involving previously processed frames.

The EMSR has been demonstrated to be an effective de-hissing method in terms of attaining significant levels of noise reduction without being much afflicted by the presence of musical noise (Cappé, 1994). As regards variants of the EMSR, simpler alternatives to the EMSR were proposed by Wolfe and Godsill (2001b, 2003). Moreover, the incorporation of psychoacoustic criteria within suppression rules used in STSA-based de-hissing methods has been also registered in the literature (Kauppinen & Roth, 2002a; Lorber & Hoeldrich, 1997; Tsoukalas, Mourjopoulos, & Kokkinakis, 1997; Tsoukalas, Paraskevas, & Mourjopoulos, 1993; Wolfe & Godsill, 2000, 2001a) as providing suitable results.

As with de-clicking algorithms, STSA-based de-hissing schemes are unable to discern between spurious noises and genuine noise-like occurrences in audio signals, such as unvoiced speech, drum brushing, and blowing noise in wind instrument sounds. Those events are likely to be mistaken by corrupting noise, thus being subject to either unwanted suppression or severe distortions by the restoration procedure.

Wavelet Shrinkage

Besides the use of the short-time DFT for signal de-noising, another non-parametric signal analysis tool that has gained substantial attention in the field is the Discrete Wavelet Transform (DWT) (Burrus, Gopinath, & Guo, 1997; Daubechies, 1992; Mallat, 1999). As opposed to the DFT, the DWT projects a given input signal into an orthogonal basis composed of functions that are localized in both time and frequency—all of them scaled and delayed versions of the same "mother-wavelet." This property allows a parsimonious multi-resolution representation for a variety of signals, in that the most relevant signal information is captured by few large-valued DWT coefficients, whereas less important information is mapped into a large number of small-valued coefficients. It must be noted that this capability depends strongly on the choice of the DWT-basis: the more the wavelet resembles the signal to be decomposed, the more compact a faithful representation can be. The DWT has been successfully employed in tasks such as signal compression and de-noising, where its ability to reduce the data space dimension while preserving important details and edges of the signal is much praised.

Theoretical fundamentals and implementation of the DWT can be readily found from the vast available literature and DSP simulation softwares. Thus, without going through its strict formulations and properties, simply consider that $W_{j,k}$ is the set of DWT coefficients associated with a signal frame of $N = 2^J$ samples, contaminated with zero-mean Gaussian white noise with variance σ^2, uncorrelated with the underlying signal. In this context J refers to the maximum number of scales of the DWT, being $j = 0, \ldots, J-1$ the scale index and $k = 0, \ldots, 2^j - 1$ the coefficient index within a given scale. Index $j=0$ refers to the coarsest scale level, whereas $j = J-1$ relates to the finest one.

Due to the orthogonality of the transformation, the DWT of a white noise process yields also a set of white noise coefficients with the same variance. Thus, the DWT of a signal corrupted with white noise results in a set of DWT coefficients where the energy of the noise component spreads equally across the scales. On the other hand, the energy associated with a wide range of real-world smooth signals decays approximately exponentially toward the finest scale (Cheng, 1997). By exploring this contrast, Donoho and Johnstone (1994) proposed two threshold-based coefficient shrinkage schemes for signal denoising (Berger, Coifman, & Goldberg, 1994; Donoho, 1995; Donoho & Johnstone, 1994; Teolis & Benedetto, 1994; Whitmal, Rutledge, & Cohen, 1995).

In one of those schemes, called hard-thresholding, the DWT coefficients are either kept or discarded according to the following criterion:

$$\hat{W}_{j,k}^{\text{hard}} = \begin{cases} W_{j,k}, & |W_{j,k}| > \lambda \\ 0, & \text{otherwise} \end{cases}, \tag{29}$$

where λ is an adequately chosen threshold value. The other possibility consists of employing a soft-thresholding scheme in which the DWT coefficients values are either modified or discarded based on the rule:

$$\hat{W}_{j,k}^{\text{soft}} = \begin{cases} \text{sign}(W_{j,k}) \, (|W_{j,k}| - \lambda), & |W_{j,k}| > \lambda \\ 0, & \text{otherwise}. \end{cases} \tag{30}$$

After the application of the thresholding criterion over the DWT coefficients, the last step of the wavelet shrinkage is to re-synthesize the signal from $W_{j,k}^{\text{hard}}$ or $W_{j,k}^{\text{soft}}$ via the inverse DWT

(IDWT) correspondent to the DWT used in the analysis stage.

The threshold choice has been extensively discussed, leading to different criteria. A simple solution (Donoho & Johnstone, 1994) that attains a bounded deviation from the minimax mean square error is $\lambda = \hat{\sigma}\sqrt{2\log(N)}$, with $\hat{\sigma}$ being an estimate of the noise standard deviation. In practice, $\hat{\sigma}$ can be determined from noise-only excerpts of the input signal or from the coefficients of the finest scale, where the noise components tend to be stronger than the desired signal information.

De-noising by soft-thresholding shrinkage has been demonstrated to almost achieve the minimax mean square error and provide a restored signal at least as smooth as the original clean signal (Donoho, 1995). Apart from the simple aforementioned thresholding rules, DWT coefficient shrinkage can be approached from several other more involved means, for example, Bayesian statistics methods (Abramovich, Sapatinas, & Silverman, 1998; Vidakovic, 1998). For a comprehensive coverage on the most common DWT coefficient shrinkage techniques see the work by Nason (1995).

Performance

From a computational point of view, wavelet shrinkage is a rather appealing de-noising method, since fast algorithms exist for computing both the DWT and its inverse. These algorithms, which are based on maximally decimated octave-band filterbanks, demand only $O(N)$ floating-point multiplications (Mallat, 1999) to realize either a DWT or an IDWT.

As opposed to STSA methods, which are known for strongly attenuating high-frequency components of the signals and distorting its sharp transients, wavelet shrinkage is capable of preserving fast transients in the restored signal, provided that they overpower the noise level. However, as with STSA methods, wavelet-based de-noising also suffers from the audibility of artifacts derived from the residual noise left in the signal and from non-canceled aliasing components that arise as the result of processing the DWT coefficients prior to signal resynthesis. Moreover, the method cannot discern between originally recorded noise-like broadband sounds and spurious noises.

Other Methods

Besides non-parametric solutions to audio de-hissing, such as the STSA and Wavelet shrinkage methods, a number of alternatives to tackle the problem have been proposed. For example, autoregressive-based noise reduction of speech sounds was presented by Lim and Oppenheim (1978), and joint treatment of impulsive and broadband noises using AR and ARMA models was demonstrated by Godsill (1993), Godsill and Rayner (1996), Niedzwiecki (1994), and Niedzwiecki and Cisowski (1996).

An adaptive filtering scheme for broadband noise elimination when two copies of the recorded sound source are available was described by Vaseghi (1988) and Vaseghi and Frayling-Cork (1992). Adaptive strategies for audio de-noising that employ Kalman filter techniques were reported by Bari, Canazza, De Poli, and Mian (1999) and Niedzwiecki and Cisowski (1996).

Last but not least, hybrid approaches figure in the literature among available solutions for audio de-hissing. For example, a technique that combines sub-band processing with STSA was presented by Jebara, Benazza-Benyahia, and Khelifa (2000), Moorer and Berger (1986), and Ramarapu and Maher (1998), and the use of AR modeling within STSA was covered by Kauppinen and Roth (2002b).

Future Directions

The audio de-noising techniques described in this chapter can attain a certain level of automatism in carrying out the tasks at hand, provided a judicious choice of the processing parameters. As far as the judgment of restored signals go, it is up to a skilled audio restorer to determine whether the sonic quality of the final results have reached an acceptable quality standard. As this process involves subjective assessment of the restored signals, it is dependent among other issues on how well informed the restorer is regarding the contents of the audio program being processed.

It seems reasonable to speculate that in the future audio restoration algorithms can benefit from the incorporation of high-level information about the content of the signal under processing. On a lower layer, knowledge of important facets related to the signal content, such as music genre, sound sources present in the mixture, and recording ambience can be used for guidance of the type of algorithm to employ as well as of a suitable choice of a set of processing parameters. On a more advanced layer, audio content could be embedded as *a priori* information within model-based techniques for signal restoration.

A more audacious and challenging goal would consist of realizing sound restoration by resynthesis. Putting aside issues associated with the artistic fidelity of the results, from a technical point of view such strategy would be multidisciplinary, involving among others audio content analysis; computational auditory scene analysis within a structured-audio framework (Bregman, 1990; Dixon, 2004; Ellis, 1996; Rosenthal & Okuno, 1998; Scheirer, 1999; Vercoe, Gardner, & Scheirer, 1998); sound source modeling and synthesis of musical instrument, speech, and singing voice sounds (Cook, 2002; Miranda, 2002; Serra, 1997; Smith, 1991; Tolonen, 2000; Välimäki, Pakarinen, Erkut, & Karjalainen, 2006); psychoacoustics (Järveläinen, 2003; Zwicker & Fastl, 1999); and auditory modeling (Beerends, 1998). Although in an embrionary stage, restoration by resynthesis has already given signs of practical usability in restricted scenarios (Berger & Nichols, 1994; Esquef, 2004), thus cementing its way as a promising and stimulating long-term research area.

References

Abramovich, F., Sapatinas, T., & Silverman, B. W. (1998). Wavelet thresholding via a Bayesian approach. *Journal of the Royal Statistic Society, Series B, 60*, 725-749.

Bari, A., Canazza, S., De Poli, G., & Mian, G. A. (1999). Some key points on restoration of audio documents by the extended Kalman filter. In *Proceedings of the Diderot Forum on Mathematics and Music* (pp. 37-47). Vienna, Austria.

Beerends, J. G. (1998). Audio quality determination based on perceptual measurement techniques. In M. Kahrs & K. Brandenburg (Eds.), *Applications of digital signal processing to audio and acoustics* (pp. 1-38). Norwell, MA: Kluwer.

Berger, J., Coifman, R. R., & Goldberg, M. J. (1994). Removing noise from music using local trigonometric bases and wavelet packets. *Journal of the Audio Engineering Society, 42*(10), 808-818.

Berger, J., & Nichols, C. (1994). Brahms at the piano: An analysis of data from the Brahms cylinder. *Leonardo Music Journal, 4*, 23-30.

Berouti, M., Schwartz, R., & Makhoul, J. (1979). Enhancement of speech corrupted by acoustic noise. In *Proceedings of the IEEE International Conference of Acoustics, Speech, and Signal Processing* (vol. 4, pp. 208-211), Washington DC: IEEE.

Boll, S. F. (1979a). A spectral subtraction algorithm for suppression of acoustic noise in speech. In *Proceedings of the IEEE International Conference of Acoustics, Speech, and Signal Processing* (vol. 4, pp. 200-203). Washingtond DC: IEEE.

Boll, S. F. (1979b). Suppression of acoustic noise in speech using spectral subtraction. *IEEE Transactions on Acoustics, Speech, and Signal Processing, ASSP-27*(2), 113-120.

Bregman, A. S. (1990). *Auditory scene analysis*. Cambridge, MA: MIT.

Burrus, C. S., Gopinath, R. A., & Guo, H. (1997). *Wavelets and wavelet transform—A primer*. Upper Saddle River, NJ: Prentice-Hall.

Burwen, R. S. (1978). *Suppression of low level impulsive noise*. Presented at the 61st Convention of the AES, New York. AES Preprint 1388.

Cappé, O. (1994). Elimination of the musical noise phenomenon with the Ephraim and Malah noise suppressor. *IEEE Transactions on Speech and Audio Processing, 2*(2), 345-349.

Cappé, O., & Laroche, J. (1995). Evaluation of short-time spectral attenuation techniques for the restoration of musical recordings. *IEEE Transactions on Speech and Audio Processing, 3*(1), 84-93.

Chen, B.-S., & Chen, Y.-L. (1995). Multirate modeling of AR/ARMA stocastic signals and its application to the combined estimation-interpolation problem. *IEEE Transactions on Signal Processing, 43*(10), 2302-2312.

Cheng, C. (1997). High frequency compensation of low sample-rate audio files: A wavelet-based excitation algorithm. In *Proceedings of the International Computer Music Conference* (pp. 458-461). Thessaloniki, Greece.

Cocchi, G., & Uncini, A. (2001). Subbands audio signal recovering using neural nonlinear prediction. In *Proceedings of the IEEE International Conference of Acoustics, Speech, and Signal Processing*, (vol. 2, pp. 1289-1292). Salt Lake City, UT.

Coleman, M. (2004). *Playback: From Victrola to MP3, 100 years of music, machines, and money*. Cambridge, MA: Da Capo.

Cook, P. R. (2002). *Real sound synthesis for interactive applications*. Wellesley, MA: A K Peters.

Craven, P. G., & Gerzon, M. A. (1975). *The elimination of scratch noise from 78 RPM records.* Presented at the 50th Convention of the AES. AES Preprint L-37.

Czyzewski, A. (1997). Learning algorithms for audio signal enhancement, Part I: Neural network implementation for the removal of impulsive distortions. *Journal of the Audio Engineering Society, 45*(10), 815-831.

Daubechies, I. (1992). *Ten lectures on wavelets.* Philadelphia: SIAM.

Dixon, S. (2004). Analysis of musical content in digital audio. In J. DiMarco (Ed.), *Computer graphics and multimedia: Applications, problems, and solutions* (pp. 214-235). Hershey, PA: Idea Group.

Donoho, D. (1992). Wavelet shrinkage and W.V.D: A 10 minute tour. In Y. Meyer & S. Roques (Eds.), *Progress in wavelet analysis and applications* (pp. 109-128). Gig-sur-Yvette, France: Frontières.

Donoho, D., & Johnstone, I. (1994). Ideal spatial adaptation by wavelet shrinkage. *Biometrika, 81*(3), 425-455.

Donoho, D. L. (1995). De-noising by soft-thresholding. *IEEE Transactions on Information Theory, 41*(3), 613-627.

Ellis, D. (1996). *Prediction-driven computational auditory scene analysis.* Unpublished doctoral dissertation, MIT, Department of Electrical Engineering and Computer Science, Cambridge, MA.

Ephraim, Y., & Malah, D. (1983). Speech enhancement using optimal non-linear spectral amplitude estimation. In *Proceedings of the IEEE International Conference of Acoustics, Speech, and Signal Processing,* (vol. 8, pp. 1118-1121) Boston MA.

Ephraim, Y., & Malah, D. (1984). Speech enhancement using a minimum mean-square error short-time spectral amplitude estimator. *IEEE Transactions on Acoustics, Speech, and Signal Processing, 32*(6), 1109-1121.

Ephraim, Y., & Malah, D. (1985). Speech enhancement using a minimum mean-square error log-spectral amplitude estimator. *IEEE Transactions on Acoustics, Speech, and Signal Processing, 33*(2), 443-445.

Esquef, P. A. A. (2004). *Model-based analysis of noisy musical recordings with application to audio restoration.* Unpublished doctoral dissertation, Lab of Acoustics and Audio Signal Processing, Helsinki University of Technology, Espoo, Finland. Retrieved June 30, 2006 from http://lib.hut.fi/Diss/2004/isbn9512269503/.

Esquef, P. A. A., & Biscainho, L. W. P. (2006). An efficient method for reconstruction of audio signals across long gaps. *IEEE Transactions on Speech and Audio Processing, 14*(4), 1391-1400.

Esquef, P. A. A., Biscainho, L. W. P., Diniz, P. S. R., & Freeland, F. P. (2000). A double-threshold-based approach to impulsive noise detection in audio signals. In *Proceedings of the X European Signal Processing Conf.* (vol. 4, pp. 2041-2044). Tampere, Finland.

Esquef, P. A. A., Biscainho, L. W. P., & Välimäki, V. (2003). An efficient algorithm for the restoration of audio signals corrupted with low-frequency pulses. *Journal of the Audio Engineering Society, 51*(6), 502-517.

Esquef, P. A. A., Karjalainen, M., & Välimäki, V. (2002), Detection of clicks in audio signals using warped linear prediction. In *Proceedings of the 14th IEEE International Conference of on Digital Signal Processing (DSP2002)* (vol. 2, pp. 1085-1088). Santorini, Greece.

Etter, W. (1996). Restoration of a discrete-time signal segment by interpolation based on the left-sided and right-sided autoregressive parameters. *IEEE Transactions on Signal Processing, 44*(5), 1124-1135.

Ferreira, P. J. S. G. (2001). Iterative and noniterative recovery of missing samples for 1-D band-limited signals. In F. Marvasti (Ed.), *Nonuniform sampling—Theory and practice* (pp. 235-281). New York: Kluwer/Plenum.

George, E. B., & Smith, M. J. T. (1992). Analysis-by-synthesis/overlap-add sinusoidal modeling applied to the analysis and synthesis of musical tones. *Journal of the Audio Engineering Society, 40*(6), 497-516.

Godsill, S. J. (1993). *The restoration of degraded audio signals.* Unpublished doctoral dissertation, Engineering Department, Cambridge University, Cambridge, England. Retrieved June 30, 2006 from http://www-sigproc.eng.cam.ac.uk/»sjg/thesis/

Godsill, S. J., & Rayner, P. J. W. (1992). A Bayesian approach to the detection and correction of error bursts in audio signals. In *Proceedings of the IEEE International Conference of Acoustics, Speech, and Signal Processing* (vol. 2, pp. 261-264). San Fransisco, CA.

Godsill, S. J., & Rayner, P. J. W. (1996). Robust noise reduction for speech and audio signals. In *Proceedings of the IEEE International Conference of Acoustics, Speech, and Signal Processing* (vol. 2, pp. 625-628). Atlanta, GA.

Godsill, S. J., & Rayner, P. J. W. (1998a). *Digital audio restoration—A statistical model based approach.* Berlin, Germany: Springer-Verlag.

Godsill, S. J., & Rayner, P. J. W. (1998b). Statistical reconstruction and analysis of autoregressive signals in impulsive noise using the Gibbs sampler. *IEEE Transactions on Speech and Audio Processing, 6*(4), 352-372.

Godsill, S. J., Rayner, P. J. W., & Cappé, O. (1998). Digital audio restoration. In M. Kahrs & K. Brandenburg (Eds.), *Applications of digital signal processing to audio and acoustics* (pp. 133-194). Boston: Kluwer.

Godsill, S. J., & Tan, C. H. (1997). Removal of low frequency transient noise from old recordings using model-based signal separation techniques. In *Proceedings of the IEEE ASSP Workshop on Applications of Signal Processing to Audio and Acoustics.* New Paltz, NY.

Goodman, D. J., Lockhart, G. B., Waen, O. J., & Wong, W. C. (1986). Waveform substitution techniques for recovering missing speech segments in packet voice communications. *IEEE Transactions on Acoustics, Speech, and Signal Processing, ASSP-34*(6), 1440-1448.

Hayes, M. H. (1996). *Statistical signal processing and modeling.* West Sussex, England: John Wiley.

Jaffe, D., & Smith, J. O. (1983). Extension of the Karplus-Strong plucked string algorithm. *Computer Music Journal, 7*(2), 56-69.

Janssen, A. J. E. M., Veldhuis, R. N. J., & Vries, L. B. (1986). Adaptive interpolation of discrete-time signals that can be modeled as autoregressive processes. *IEEE Transactions on Acoustics, Speech, Signal Processing, ASSP-34*(2), 317-330.

Järveläinen, H. (2003). *Perception of attributes in real and synthetic string instrument sounds*. Unpublished doctoral dissertation, Helsinki University of Technology—Lab of Acoustics and Audio Signal Processing, Espoo, Finland. Retrieved June 30, 2006 from http://lib.hut.fi/Diss/2003/isbn9512263149/

Jebara, S. B., Benazza-Benyahia, A., & Khelifa, A. B. (2000). Reduction of musical noise generated by spectral subtraction by combining wavelet packet transform and Wiener filtering. In *Proceedings of the X European Signal Processing Conference* (vol. 2, pp. 749-752). Tampere, Finland.

Kauppinen, I., & Kauppinen, J. (2002). Reconstruction method for missing or damaged long portions in audio signal. *Journal of the Audio Engineering Society, 50*(7/8), 594-602.

Kauppinen, I., Kauppinen, J., & Saarinen, P. (2001). A method for long extrapolation of audio signals. *Journal of the Audio Engineering Society, 49*(12), 1167-1180.

Kauppinen, I., & Roth, K. (2002a). Adaptive psychoacoustic filter for broadband noise reduction in audio signals. In *Proceedings of the 14th International Conference of Digital Signal Processing* (vol. 2, pp. 962-966). Santorini, Greece.

Kauppinen, I., & Roth, K. (2002b). Audio signal extrapolation—Theory and applications. In *Proceedings of the Fifth IInternational Conference on Digital Audio Effects* (pp. 105-110). Hamburg, Germany. Retrieved June 30, 2006 from http://www.unibw-hamburg.de/EWEB/ANT/dafx2002/papers.html

Kay, S. M. (1988). *Modern spectral estimation*. Upper Saddle River, NJ: Prentice-Hall.

Kinzie, Jr., G. R., & Gravereaux, D. W. (1973). Automatic detection of impulsive noise. *Journal of the Audio Engineering Society, 21*(3), 331-336.

Lim, J. (1978). Evaluation of a correlation subtraction method for enhancing speech degraded by additive white noise. *IEEE Transactions on Acoustics, Speech, and Signal Processing, 26*(5), 471-472.

Lim, J. (1986). Speech enhancement. In *Proceedings of the IEEE International Conference of Acoustics, Speech, and Signal Processing* (vol. 11, pp. 3135-3142). Tokyo, Japan.

Lim, J., & Oppenheim, A. V. (1978). All-pole modeling of degraded speech. *IEEE Transactions on Acoustics, Speech, and Signal Processing, 26*(3), 197-210.

Lorber, M., & Hoeldrich, R. (1997). A combined approach for broadband noise reduction. In *Proceedings of the IEEE ASSP Workshop on Applications of Signal Processing to Audio and Acoustics*. New Paltz, NY.

Maher, R. C. (1994). A method for extrapolation of missing digital audio data. *Journal of the Audio Engineering Society, 42*(5), 350-357.

Makhoul, J. (1977). Stable and efficient lattice methods for linear prediction. *IEEE Transactions on Acoustics, Speech, and Signal Processing, ASSP-25*(5), 423-428.

Mallat, S. (1999). *A wavelet tour of signal processing*. San Diego, CA: Academic Press.

Miranda, E. R. (2002). *Computer sound design: Synthesis techniques and programming.* Oxford, UK: Focal Press.

Montresor, S., Valiere, J. C., Allard, J. F., & Baudry, M. (1991). *Evaluation of two interpolation methods applied to old recordings restoration.* Presented at the 90th Convention of the AES, Paris, France. AES Preprint 3022.

Moorer, J. A., & Berger, M. (1986). Linear-phase bandsplitting: Theory and applications. *Journal of the Audio Engineering Society, 34*(3), 143-152.

Morton, D. (2000). *The technology and culture of sound recording in America.* Piscataway, NJ: Rutgers University Press.

Nason, G. P. (1995). Choice of threshold parameter in wavelet function estimation. In A. Antoniadis & G. Oppenheim (Eds.), *Lecture Notes in statistics* (Vol 103, pp. 261-280). New York: Springer-Verlag.

Niedzwiecki, M. (1993). Statistical reconstruction of multivariate time series. *IEEE Transactions on Signal Processing, 41*(1), 451-457.

Niedzwiecki, M. (1994). Recursive algorithms for elimination of measurement noise and impulsive disturbances from ARMA signals. In *Signal Processing VII: Theories and Applications* (pp. 1289-1292). Edinburgh, UK.

Niedzwiecki, M., & Cisowski, K. (1996). Adaptive scheme for elimination of broadband noise and impulsive disturbances from AR and ARMA signals. *IEEE Transactions on Signal Processing, 44*(3), 528-537.

Niedzwiecki, M., & Cisowski, K. (2001). Smart copying—A new approach to reconstruction of audio signals. *IEEE Transactions on Signal Processing, 49*(10), 2272-2282.

Ó Ruanaidh, J. J., & Fitzgerald, W. J. (1994). Interpolation of missing samples for audio restoration. *Electronics Letters, 30*(8), 622-623.

Ó Ruanaidh, J. J., & Fitzgerald, W. J. (1996). *Numerical Bayesian methods applied to signal processing.* Berlin, Germany: Springer-Verlag.

Papoulis, A. (1975). A new algorithm in spectral analysis and band-limited extrapolation. *IEEE Transactions on Circuits Syst., 22*(9), 735-742.

Quatieri, T. F., & McAulay, R. J. (1998). Audio signal processing based on sinusoidal analysis and synthesis. In M. Kahrs & K. Brandenburg (Eds.), *Applications of digital signal processing to audio and acoustics* (pp. 314-416). Boston: Kluwer.

Ramarapu, P. K., & Maher, R. C. (1998). Methods for reducing audible artifacts in a wavelet-based broadband de-noising system. *Journal of the Audio Engineering Society, 46*(3), 178-190.

Rayner, P. J. W., & Godsill, S. J. (1991). The detection and correction of artifacts in degraded gramophone recordings. In *Proceedings of the IEEE ASSP Workshop on Applications of Signal Processing to Audio and Acoustics* (pp. 151-152). New Paltz, NY.

Rosenthal, D., & Okuno, H. G. (Eds.). (1998). *Computational auditory scene analysis.* Mahwah, NJ: Lawrence Erlbaum.

Scheirer, E. D. (1999). Structured audio and effects processing in the MPEG-4 multimedia standard. *Multimedia Systems, 7*(1), 11-22.

Schoenherr, S. (2005). *Recording technology history*. Retrieved July 6, 2005, from http://history.acusd.edu/gen/recording/notes.html

Serra, X. (1997). Musical sound modeling with sinusoids plus noise. In C. Roads, S. Pope, A. Picialli, & G. De Poli (Eds.), *Musical signal processing* (pp. 91-122). Lisse, Netherlands: Swets & Zeitlinger.

Smith, J. O. (1991). Viewpoints on the history of digital synthesis. In *Proceedings of the International Computer Music Conference* (pp. 1-10). Montreal, Canada.

Struzinski, W. A. (1984). A new normalization algorithm for detection systems. *Journal of the Acoustical Society of America, Supplement, 75*(S1), S43.

Struzinski, W. A., & Lowe, E. D. (1984). A performance comparison of four noise background normalization schemes proposed for signal detection systems. *Journal of the Acoustical Society of America, 76*(6), 1738-1742.

Teolis, A., & Benedetto, J. J. (1994). Noise suppression using a wavelet model. In *Proceedings of the IEEE International Conference of Acoustics, Speech, and Signal Processing* (vol. 1, pp. 17-20).

Tolonen, T. (2000). *Object-based sound source modeling*. Unpublished doctoral dissertation, Helsinki University of Technology, Espoo, Finland. Retrieved June 30, 2006 from http://lib.hut.fi/Diss/2000/isbn9512251965/

Tsoukalas, D., Mourjopoulos, J., & Kokkinakis, G. (1997). Perceptual filters for audio signal enhancement. *Journal of the Audio Engineering Society, 45*(1/2), 22-36.

Tsoukalas, D., Paraskevas, M., & Mourjopoulos, J. (1993). Speech enhancement using psychoacoustic criteria. In *Proceedings of the IEEE International Conference of Acoustics, Speech, and Signal Processing* (vol. 2, pp. 359-362).

Välimäki, V., Pakarinen, J., Erkut, C., & Karjalainen, M. (2006). Discrete-time modeling of musical instruments. *Reports on Progress in Physics, 69*(1), 1-78.

Vaseghi, S. V. (1988). *Algorithms for restoration of archived gramophone recordings*. Unpublished doctoral dissertation, Engineering Department, Cambridge University, Cambridge, England.

Vaseghi, S. V. (2006). *Advanced digital signal processing and noise reduction* (3rd ed.). West Sussex, England: John Wiley.

Vaseghi, S. V., & Frayling-Cork, R. (1992). Restoration of old gramophone recordings. *Journal of the Audio Engineering Society, 40*(10), 791-801.

Vaseghi, S. V., & Rayner, P. J.W. (1988). A new application of adaptive filters for restoration of archived gramophone recordings. In *Proceedings of the IEEE International Conference of Acoustics, Speech, and Signal Processing* (vol. 5, pp. 2548-2551). New York: IEEE.

Vaseghi, S. V., & Rayner, P. J. W. (1990). Detection and suppression of impulsive noise in speech communication systems. *IEEE Proceedings, 137*(1), 38-46.

Veldhuis, R. (1990). *Restoration of lost samples in digital signals*. Upper Saddle River, NJ: Prentice-Hall.

Vercoe, B. L., Gardner, W. G., & Scheirer, E. D. (1998). Structured audio: Creation, transmission, and rendering of parametric sound representations. *Proc. IEEE, 86*(5), 922-940.

Vidakovic, B. (1998). Non-linear wavelet shrinkage with Bayes rules and Bayes factors. *Journal of the American Statistical Association, 93*(441), 173-179.

Whitmal, N. A., Rutledge, J. C., & Cohen, J. (1995). Wavelet-based noise reduction. In *Proceedings of the IEEE International Conference of Acoustics, Speech, and Signal Processing* (vol. 5, pp. 3003-3006). Detroit, MI.

Wilson, P. (1965). Record contamination: Causes and cure. *Journal of the Audio Engineering Society, 13*(2), 166-176.

Wolfe, P. J., & Godsill, S. J. (2000). Towards a perceptually optimal spectral amplitude estimator for audio signal enhancement. In *Proceedings of the IEEE International Conference of Acoustics, Speech, and Signal Processing* (vol. 2, pp. 821-824). Istanbul.

Wolfe, P. J., & Godsill, S. J. (2001a). Perceptually motivated approaches to music restoration. *Journal of New Music Research—Special Issue: Music and Mathematics, 30*(1), 83-92.

Wolfe, P. J., & Godsill, S. J. (2001b). Simple alternatives to the Ephraim and Malah suppression rule for speech enhancement. In *Proceedings of the 11th IEEE Signal Processing Workshop on Statistical Signal Processing* (pp. 496-499). Singapore.

Wolfe, P. J., & Godsill, S. J. (2003). Efficient alternatives to the Ephraim and Malah suppression rule for audio signal enhancement. *EURASIP Journal on Applied Signal Processing—Special Issue on Digital Audio for Multimedia Communications, 2003*(10), 1043-1051.

Zwicker, E., & Fastl, H. (1999). *Psychoacoustics: Facts and models* (2nd ed.). Berlin, Germany: Springer-Verlag.

Section II

Speech and Audio Watermarking Methods

This section provides an analysis of recently developed speech and audio watermarking methods to avoid unauthorized copying, distribution, and commercialization of copyrighted digital audio and speech digital signals.

Chapter V

Digital Watermarking Techniques for Audio and Speech Signals

Aparna Gurijala, Michigan State University, USA

John R. Deller, Jr., Michigan State University, USA

Abstract

The main objective of this chapter is to provide an overview of existing speech and audio watermarking technology and to demonstrate the importance of signal processing for the design and evaluation of watermarking algorithms. This chapter describes the factors to be considered while designing speech and audio watermarking algorithms, including the choice of the domain and signal features for watermarking, watermarked signal fidelity, watermark robustness, data payload, security, and watermarking applications. The chapter presents several state-of-the-art speech and audio watermarking algorithms and discusses their advantages and disadvantages. The various applications of watermarking and developments in performance evaluation of watermarking algorithms are also described.

Introduction

Representation of information in digital form has many significant benefits relative to more conventional forms—among them the possibility of creating an unlimited number of essentially perfect copies of the digital record. This benefit, however, is an obvious cause for concern among intellectual property owners and content providers. Widespread use of the Internet and modern advances in data compression and streaming techniques facilitate efficient distribution of digital content. The ease and accuracy with which digital media can be inexpensively replicated and distributed, however, poses a severe challenge to those with copyright and intellectual property interests in the materials. Copyright laws protecting analog information are generally not applicable to digital information. As a result, there is a need to develop techniques for protecting the ownership of digital content, for tracking intellectual piracy, and for authenticating multimedia data. While traditional methods of providing information security, such as encryption, protect the data during transmission, the data are again vulnerable after decryption. A response to the unprecedented need to protect intellectual property has been the emergence of an active research effort into digital watermarking strategies. Computer-based signal processing has emerged as a premier tool for design and evaluation of these technologies.

The watermarking concept has its origins in the ancient Greek technique of steganography or "covered writing"—interpreted as hiding information in other information (Cox, Miller, & Bloom, 2002). Digital watermarking is the process of embedding data (comprising the *watermark*), ideally imperceptibly, into a host signal (the *coversignal*) to create a *stegosignal*. Although the term "coversignal" is commonly used in watermarking literature (Cox et al., 2002) to denote the host signal (data to be protected), the name used for the watermarked result, the "stegosignal," is borrowed from steganography (Johnson, Duric, & Jajodia, 2000). The watermark is typically a pseudo-noise sequence, or a sequence of symbols mapped from a message. Unlike cryptography, watermarking does not restrict access to the host signal. A watermark offers copyright protection by providing identifying information accessible only to the owner of the material. Watermarked versions of the copyrighted material are released to the public. When copyright questions arise, the watermark is recovered from the stegosignal as evidence of title. Watermarking has been argued to be an advantageous solution to this modern copyright problem, and there is strong evidence that the practice will be accepted by the courts as proof of title (Seadle, Deller Jr., & Gurijala, 2002).

In its modern usage, the term "steganography" refers to another branch of data hiding. Audio steganography is the covert communication of messages embedded within host audio data. Unlike watermarking, in steganography the hidden message is of primary importance and the host signal is merely a medium for secret communication.

Watermarks embedded in image or video material may be visible or invisible, depending on their intended purpose. Visible watermarks are easily perceptible to a human observer and are typically composed of the logo of an organization. As an example, news channel broadcasts include their logo at one end of the screen. While visible watermarks readily provide identification information, they are less secure because they can be more easily removed. Most watermarking applications require the embedded information to be imperceptible. In broad terms, the design of a watermarking strategy involves the balancing of two principal criteria. First, embedded watermarks must be imperceptible, that is, the stegosignal must

Figure 1. A general watermarking system

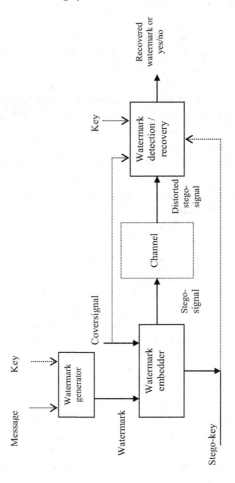

be of high *fidelity*. Second, watermarks must be *robust*, that is, they must be able to survive *attacks* (Voloshynovskiy, Pereira, Pun, Su, & Eggers, 2001)—those deliberately designed to destroy or remove them, as well as distortions inadvertently imposed by technical processes (e.g., compression) or by systemic processes (e.g., channel noise). These fidelity and robustness criteria are generally competing, as greater robustness requires more watermark energy and more manipulation of the coversignal, which, in turn, lead to noticeable distortion of the original content. Related measures of a watermark's efficacy include *data payload*—the number of watermark bits per unit of time (Cox et al., 2002)—and watermark *security*—the inherent protection against unauthorized removal, embedding, or detection (Cox et al., 2002). A watermarking scheme implements security from secret codes or patterns (*keys*) that are used to embed the watermark in the coversignal. Only a breach of keying strategies should compromise the security of a watermarking technique; public knowledge of the technical method should not lesson its effectiveness (Cox et al., 2002).

A general watermarking system consists of a watermark generator, an embedder, and a watermark detector as depicted in Figure 1. The transmission channel represents possible attacks or distortion on the stegosignal from the time the watermark is embedded until there is a need for watermark detection or recovery. Certain inputs are indicated by dotted lines in Figure 1, meaning that they may not be present in all techniques. There are two kinds of keys that may be used in a watermarking system. The watermark key (key in Figure 1) is used to encrypt the watermark so that the message contained in the watermark is not obvious. In Figure 1, the stego-key determines the locations in the coversignal where the watermark is to be embedded and thus introduces additional protection by making the watermark's location unknown. A watermark may take different forms—an encrypted or modulated speech sequence or an image, least significant bit manipulations, a pseudo-random sequence, and so forth. Consequently, the inputs to watermark generators are highly diverse.

In addition to copyright protection, watermarking has been deployed in applications such as fingerprinting, authentication, copy control, owner identification, broadcast monitoring, security control, and tamper proofing (Cox et al., 2002). Watermarking requirements vary depending on the application(s) in which they are employed. For example, in many authentication applications, watermark robustness to compression is desired, while robustness to high-level information tampering is not required.

Watermark embedding techniques vary widely in method and purpose. Watermarks may be additive, multiplicative, or quantization-based, and may be embedded in the time domain, or in a transform domain. Each technical variation tends to be more robust to some forms of attack than to others, and for this and other application-specific reasons, particular strategies may be better suited to certain tasks. Watermark detection (or recovery) is classified as being *blind* or *informed*. In informed detection, a copy of the unmarked host signal is required. Some informed watermark detectors require only partial information about the host signal. Detectors that do not require a representation of the host signal for watermark detection are called blind detectors. The additional information available during watermark detection and recovery in informed detection can be used to better satisfy watermarking requirements. For example, the coversignal information available at the detector can serve as a registration pattern to undo any temporal or geometric distortions of the host signal as it appears in the stegosignal (Cox et al., 2002). In case of a "cropping attack," wherein speech samples are randomly deleted, a dynamic programming algorithm can be used for watermark recovery from the desynchronized stegosignal (Gurijala & Deller Jr., 2001). On the other hand, blind watermarking can be deployed for a wider range of applications. For applications in which watermark detection must be performed by the public, not just by the content owner or distributors, informed watermarking is inapplicable.

A common approach to watermark detection employs classic binary decision theory (Poor, 1994). The hypotheses are $H_0 : Z_R = X$ and $H_1 : Z_R = X + W$, where Z_R is the received signal, X is the original signal, and W is the watermark signal (Barni, Bartolini, Rosa, & Piva, 2003; Hernandez, Amado, & Perez-Gonzalez, 2000). A Bayesian or Neyman-Pearson paradigm is followed in deriving the detection thresholds. Many of these approaches do not consider the effect of noise while designing the detector. Several watermark detectors are based on correlation detection in the time or in transform domain (Linnartz, Kalker, & Depovere, 1998; Miller & Bloom, 1999). That is, the correlation between the original and recovered watermarks, or the correlation between the original watermark and the possibly distorted stegosignal (the *recovered signal*) is compared against a threshold. Correlation detectors are optimal when the watermark and noise are jointly Gaussian, or, in case of blind detectors, when the watermarked signal and noise are jointly Gaussian. This is true for watermark patterns that are spectrally white.

The main objective of the present chapter is to provide a comprehensive overview of classic watermark embedding, recovery, and detection algorithms for audio and speech signals. Another important objective is to provide a comprehensive overview of the factors to be considered while designing an audio watermarking system and the typical approaches employed by existing watermarking algorithms. The watermarking techniques presented in this chapter are presently deployed in a wide range of applications including copyright protection, copy control, broadcast monitoring, authentication, and air traffic control. Audio and speech watermarking techniques can be broadly categorized into spread-spectrum-based, quantization-based, and parametric-modeling-based approaches. Although the main focus of the chapter will be watermarking algorithms specifically designed for speech/audio signals, techniques developed for other multimedia content that are applicable for speech/audio signals will also be discussed. Furthermore, the chapter will describe the (commonly employed) signal processing, geometric, and protocol attacks on speech/audio watermarking techniques. Finally, existing benchmarking tools (Petitcolas, 2000; Petitcolas & Anderson, 1999; Steinebach, Lang, & Dittmann, 2002; Steinebach, Petitcolas, Raynal, Dittmann, Fontaine, Seibel, & Fates, 2001) for evaluating the robustness performance of these techniques will be discussed. The various speech/audio watermarking applications and the algorithmic requirements will also be described in detail.

Background

Digital Watermarking Challenges

The design of a watermarking system involves balancing several conflicting requirements. Watermark robustness, stegosignal fidelity, watermark data payload, and security are important requirements of any watermarking system. In the case of fragile watermarking algorithms, robustness to selective manipulations or attacks is desired. The fidelity and robustness criteria are generally competing, as greater robustness requires more watermark energy and more manipulation of the coversignal, which, in turn, lead to distortion of the original content. In fact, when stegosignal fidelity parameter is fixed, robustness and data payload cannot be increased simultaneously (Cvejic & Seppänen, 2003). A trade-off also exists between watermark security and stegosignal fidelity as evidenced by the fact that visible watermarking algorithms tend to be less secure. The computational complexity of watermarking algorithms is also a factor for consideration, especially for real-time applications.

Digital Watermarking Applications

Digital watermarking is currently deployed for a wide range of applications (Cox et al., 2002) as discussed next.

Content Authentication: Watermarking is used for establishing the authenticity of multimedia content. Traditional cryptographic authentication schemes involve hash functions and are used to ensure that every bit in the data stream is unmodified. In case of multimedia data, minor changes can often be made to their content without affecting the perceptual quality. Moreover, multimedia content is typically subjected to non-malicious, yet distorting, signal-processing operations and channel noise, which result in minor perceptual changes to the content. For multimedia authentication, fragile watermarking provides a flexible alternative to techniques based on cryptographic hash functions or digital signatures. Authentication is performed by determining whether certain defining characteristics and rules present in the original signal exist in the test signal (Wu & Liu, 2004). Two important issues to be addressed while designing an authentication system include: (a) choice of features to embed, and (b) security considerations to prevent forgery or manipulation of embedded data (Wu & Liu, 2004).

Broadcast Monitoring: Digital watermarking is used for tracking the broadcast and distribution of information over television, radio, and the Internet. In broadcast monitoring applications, the content is embedded with a unique identification tag and optional information about the content owner or distributor. Such a scheme can be used for automatically monitoring the broadcast of advertisements by a particular television station, for example. A watermark decoder determines the number of times an advertisement was broadcast and whether the advertisement was broadcast at the contracted time slot. This information is conveyed to the content owner or distributor. Digital watermarking for broadcast monitoring helps ensure broadcast compliance and detects unauthorized use of content.

Content Management: Digital watermarks can be used as tags containing identifying or supporting information for content management. In this case, the embedded digital watermarks may link to a central server or remote system containing metadata, keywords, rights and permissions, and other pertinent information. This application of watermarking will greatly facilitate content management in environments such as digital libraries where large databases are to be handled.

Copy Control: Watermarks can be used for preventing unauthorized copying and subsequent distribution of digital content. Attempts to integrate digital watermarking technology into DVD and CD writers have been variously successful. To prevent unauthorized DVD copying, watermarks containing copy-control instructions are embedded into the content. As an example, the watermark may include instructions indicating whether or not a single copy of the content may be made, or if not further copying is permitted. This application of watermarking is of great interest to the movie and music industries for the prevention of piracy.

Copyright Protection: Traditional copyright protection mechanisms for analog content are generally inapplicable to digital content. Hence, watermarking of digital content for the communication of copyright and ownership information has been proposed as a solution. Watermarking facilitates detection of unauthorized use of the content, and as witnessed by the recent Napster case, there is evidence that the courts will consider watermarks as a legitimate form of copyright protection (Seadle et al., 2002). Additionally, watermarking is also deployed for owner identification (Cox et al., 2002). Application of digital watermarking for copyright protection has always been a controversial issue. This is mainly because such an application entails robustness to a wide range of attacks that no existing (perhaps future) watermarking algorithm exhibits.

Transaction Tracking: Digital watermarks are also used for transaction and traitor tracking. Every copy of the digital content is securely embedded with unique identification information before distribution. If an unauthorized copy of the content is found, the extracted watermarks will track the last authorized recipient.

A related data hiding technology is digital *fingerprinting*, a term that is used to denote two slightly different techniques. The term fingerprinting may be used to denote the process of securely embedding unique identification codes in each copy of a particular multimedia signal for the purpose of traitor tracing. More significantly, digital fingerprinting is used to extract unique features from multimedia content and store them in association with metadata (identification data) (Cano, Batlle, Kalker, & Haitsma, 2002). At a later time, the stored features may be compared with newly extracted features from a given multimedia file for identification purposes. Applications of fingerprinting include preventing the distribution of copyrighted material, monitoring audio broadcasts, and providing consumers with supplementary information about the digital content.

Audio and Speech Watermarking

In the last decade many algorithms have been proposed for multimedia watermarking. Early work emphasized watermarking algorithms that could be universally applied to a wide spectrum of multimedia content, including images, video, and audio. This versatility was deemed conducive to the implementation of multimedia watermarking on common hardware (Cox, Kilian, Leighton, & Shamoon, 1997). However, many watermarking applications (such as copyright protection for digital speech libraries [Ruiz & Deller Jr., 2000], embedding patient information in medical records [Anand & Niranjan, 1998; Miaou, Hsu, Tsai, & Chao, 2000], or television broadcast monitoring (Kalker, Depovere, Haitsma, & Maes, 1999), involve the embedding of information into a single medium. Attacks and inherent processing distortions vary depending on the nature of the multimedia content. For example, an attack on watermarked images may involve rotation and translation operations to disable watermark detection. However, such an attack is not applicable to audio data. Hiding information in audio signals is also complicated by the wider dynamic range of the human auditory system (HAS) (Bender, Gruhl, Marimoto, & Lu, 1996). That is, the HAS is sensitive to power in the range of one billion to one and perceives frequency in the range of one thousand to one. Watermarking algorithms that are specifically designed for particular multimedia content can exploit well-understood properties of that content to better satisfy robustness, fidelity, and data payload criteria.

Designing an Audio Watermarking System

This section discusses in detail the existing trends and the factors to be considered while developing audio watermarking algorithms.

Choice of Domain and Audio Features for Watermarking

Audio watermarks may be embedded in either the time or transform domain of the signal. Many audio watermarking algorithms exploit the smaller differential range of the HAS because of which louder sounds tend to mask weaker sounds in both the frequency and the time domain. Some of the early developments in audio watermarking involved hiding data in the time domain (Bassia & Pitas, 1998). However, the constraints imposed on watermarking due to the highly competing requirements of robustness, fidelity, and data payload necessitated embedding data in various transform domains.

Time-domain audio watermarking techniques are based on the premise that the HAS cannot detect slight changes in certain temporal regions of an audio signal (Bassia & Pitas, 1998). Time-domain audio watermarking techniques exploit temporal masking properties of the HAS, the details of which are discussed in detail in a later section. Bassia and Pitas (1998) proposed one of the earliest time-domain robust audio watermarking algorithms. Audio watermarks are embedded in the time domain by modifying each audio sample according to its amplitude. Stocker and Kummer (2005) proposed the time-domain R2O watermarking algorithm. The authors argue that since the HAS-based psychoacoustic auditory model cannot be naturally exploited in the time domain, audio watermarking techniques based in the time domain tend to survive HAS-based audio encoding operations such as MPEG compression.

Frequency-domain watermarking techniques tend to provide greater versatility in balancing the competing requirements of robustness and fidelity. Many spread-spectrum watermarking techniques operate in the discrete cosine transform (DCT) domain. In spread-spectrum watermarking, a narrow-band watermark signal is hidden in the wide-band host signal (Cox et al., 1997). Watermark information is typically embedded in the low frequency or the mid frequency components. Many frequency-domain audio watermarking techniques tend to exploit the HAS-based MPEG-1 Layer 3 psychoacoustic auditory model in order to preserve stegosignal fidelity (Cox et al., 1997). Some existing audio watermarking techniques take into consideration both temporal and frequency information during the embedding process. Boney, Tewfik, and Hamdy (1996) generate a watermark by filtering a pseudo-noise (PN) sequence with a filter that approximates the frequency-masking characteristics of the HAS. The filtered PN sequence is also weighted in the time domain to account for temporal masking. Audio watermarking in the discrete-wavelet domain exploits the multi-resolution property of wavelets to embed information at different scales. Watermarking in the wavelet domain provides simultaneous spatial localization and frequency spread, resulting in increased robustness to highly disparate attacks such as filtering and cropping (Petitcolas, Anderson, & Kuhn, 1998; Voloshynovskiy et al., 2001).

Audio watermarking can also be performed in other time-frequency domains using transforms such as spectrogram and Wigner distribution. For example, watermarks may be embedded by modifying the singular value decomposition coefficients of the spectrogram of an audio signal (Ozer, Sankur, & Memon, 2005). Additionally, watermarking can be done in a parameter domain such as the cepstral domain or the linear prediction (LP) domain in case of speech signals. Embedding information in a parameter domain implies alteration of signal properties that are not linearly related to the signal samples. This renders the embedded information more difficult to separate from the signal samples. Some existing speech watermarking techniques operate in the LP domain by embedding watermark information in LP coefficients of speech signals. In the cepstral domain, audio watermarks may be weighted according to the distribution of cepstral coefficients and the cepstral masking of the HAS for imperceptible modification of cepstral coefficients (Deller Jr., Hansen, & Proakis, 2000). Watermarking algorithms have also been developed to operate in the bit-stream domain of compressed audio signals (Neubauer & Herre, 2000; Siebenhaar, Neubauer, & Herre, 2001).

Depending on whether audio watermarking is performed in the time or transform domain, several parameters or features of audio signals may be altered for hiding the watermarks. A simple way to embed audio watermarks is by modifying the amplitude of audio samples in the time domain. Alternately, audio watermarks can be created by modifying the magnitude or phase coefficients in the DCT or FFT domain, wavelet coefficients, cepstral coefficients, or the LP coefficients. One of the earliest watermarking techniques involves least-significant-bit (LSB) (Van Schyndel, Tirkel, & Osborne, 1994) modification through the use of PN sequences. The techniques are highly sensitive to noise and are not robust. Watermarking techniques based on echo hiding encode watermark information in the audio signal through the use of echoes of different delays representing either a binary zero or a binary one. Echo hiding techniques provide good robustness against MPEG audio compression and D/A conversion, but are not effective for speech signals with frequent silence intervals. Many existing audio watermarking algorithms (Foote, Adcock, & Girgensohn, 2003) involve modification of the time scale of an audio signal. Watermarks are embedded imperceptibly in an audio signal by changing the time duration of the signal without modifying the pitch and other spectral characteristics (Foote et al., 2003). Foote et al. (2003) embed watermarks by either compressing or expanding short time sections of an audio signal in accordance with a watermark function. The sequence and amount of compression or expansion encode the watermark information.

Stegosignal Fidelity

Fidelity is a measure of perceptual similarity between the coversignal and the stegosignal. It is important to differentiate fidelity from *signal quality* (Cox et al., 2002). Audio signal quality might be low even prior to watermarking. However, the resulting watermarked signal can be of high fidelity. It is almost impossible to achieve perfect imperceptibility of the embedded watermarks with acceptable robustness properties. The goal is always to achieve the best perceptibility for a targeted application. The watermarking process must not affect the fidelity of the audio signal beyond an application-dependent standard. Hence two important issues to be confronted for ensuring stegosignal fidelity are the following: how to adjust and ensure the imperceptibility of the embedded watermarks, and how to measure or assess stegosignal fidelity.

In order to ensure the inaudibility of embedded watermarks, audio watermarking techniques exploit temporal and/or frequency masking properties of the HAS. Typically the watermarking process involves either a time- or transform-domain scaling parameter or shaping the information to be hidden using the HAS-based psychoacoustic auditory model. If $X = \{x_i\}_{i=1}^{N}$ represents the values of the original audio signal in the time or frequency domain, $W = \{w_i\}_{i=1}^{N}$ is the watermark to be embedded, and α is a scaling parameter, then the resulting watermarked signal $Y = \{y_i\}_{i=1}^{N}$ is obtained as,

$$y_i = x_i(1+\alpha w_i), \quad i=1, 2, ..., N. \tag{1}$$

Equation (1) represents a simple and effective way to control the stegosignal fidelity using a scaling parameter α (Cox et al., 1997; Cox et al., 2002). When the signal values x_i are small, $\alpha \prec 1$ ensures that the corresponding watermark values are also low in magnitude and the stegosignal is not distorted noticeably.

Another common strategy for embedding imperceptible watermarks involves the use of HAS-based perceptual models, which are employed extensively in audio compression technology. Psychoacoustic models are based on a model of audio processing in the human brain. Psychoacoustic audio models are used for sound waveform compression due to their ability to highlight the most important features for audition and perception. Psychoacoustic perceptual models take into consideration the temporal and frequency masking properties and loudness sensitivity of the human ear. In audio watermarking, the masking properties of HAS-based psychoacoustic models are used to embed less-perceptible watermarks while simultaneously ensuring that the watermark information is not discarded by compression techniques that rely on similar psychoacoustic models.

The adult human can typically hear sounds in the 20 Hz to 16 kHz range. The effective frequency range is 300 Hz to 3.4 kHz for telephone quality speech, and wideband speech has an audible frequency range of 50 Hz to 7 kHz. The effect of frequency on the human ear is not linear, but logarithmic. The loudness of a sound is perceived differently depending on the frequency. Sensitivity of the HAS is determined by measuring the minimum sound intensity level required for perception at a given frequency (Cox et al., 2002). Also, loud sounds tend to mask faint, but barely audible, sounds. Temporal masking can be classified into pre-masking and post-masking effects. In pre-masking, a faint signal is rendered inaudible before the occurrence of the louder masker. While in post-masking, a faint signal immediately following a loud masker is rendered inaudible. If two signals occur close together in frequency, then the stronger signal masks the weaker signal resulting in frequency masking. The masking threshold depends on frequency, the intensity level, and noise-like or tone-like nature of the masker and masked signal. A sinusoidal masker will require greater intensity or loudness to mask a noise-like signal, than conversely.

In audio watermarking, HAS-based psychoacoustic perceptual models have been used to generate imperceptible watermarks (Boney et al., 1996) and to identify embedding regions of the coversignal that are robust against compression. Psychoacoustic perceptual models such as MPEG-1 Layer 3 have been effectively used to generate highly imperceptible watermarks by PN sequences spectrally shaped by filters approximating the frequency masking characteristics of HAS (Boney et al., 1996). Psychoacoustic models are also used to identify tonal masking components of an audio signal for robust data hiding (Lee & Lee, 2005).

Measuring the fidelity of a watermarked signal is a complex problem. Objective evaluation functions or subjective evaluations may be employed. Proper subjective evaluation of fidelity involving a large number of human observers is rare. Many claims of fidelity are made via experiments involving a single listener and on a small subset of trials (Cox et al., 2002). Since auditory sensitivity varies slightly across individuals, credible evaluation requires a large number of listeners and a large number of experiments.

Objective evaluation of fidelity is less expensive and more definitive for a given model, without the logistical difficulties and subjective nature of human evaluation. However, it is difficult to find an objective evaluation model that closely approximates human evaluation. Objective evaluation models attempt to quantify the differences between the coversignal and the stegosignal. A commonly used objective evaluation model in audio watermarking algorithms is the mean squared error (MSE) function:

$$MSE = \frac{1}{N}\sum_{n=1}^{N}(y_n - x_n)^2 \tag{2}$$

The MSE between the stegosignal and the coversignal is used as an indicator of fidelity. MSE does not accurately capture perceptual impact of the changes to the host signal as it weighs all changes equally (Cox et al., 2002).

Another simple and mathematically tractable measure of fidelity is the signal-to-noise ratio (SNR), or, in the watermarking context, *coversignal-to-watermark (power) ratio* (CWR), defined as:

$$CWR = 10\log_{10}\frac{E_X}{E_W} = 10\log_{10}\frac{\sum_{n=1}^{N}x_n^2}{\sum_{n=1}^{N}w_n^2}, \tag{3}$$

where $w_n = y_n - x_n$ is the sample-wise difference between the stegosignal and the coversignal at time n. The CWR averages the distortion of the coversignal over time and frequency. However, CWR is a poor measure of audio and speech fidelity for a wide range of distortions. The CWR is not related to any subjective attribute of fidelity, and it weights the time-domain errors equally (Deller Jr. et al., 2000).

A better measure of fidelity, for speech signals, can be obtained if the CWR is measured and averaged over short speech frames. The resulting fidelity measure is known as *segmental* CWR (Deller Jr. et al., 2000), defined as:

$$CWR_{seg} = \frac{1}{K}\sum_{j=1}^{K}10\log_{10}\left[\sum_{l=k_j-L+1}^{k_j}\frac{x_l^2}{(y_l - x_l)^2}\right], \tag{4}$$

where $k_1, k_2,..., k_K$ are the end-times for the K frames, each of length L. The segmentation of the CWR assigns equal weight to the loud and soft portions of speech. For computing CWR_{seg}, the duration of speech frames is typically 15-25 mS with frames of 15 mS used for the experimental results presented in this chapter. Some of the other objective measures of quality (fidelity, in the present case) of speech signals include the Itakura distance (Deller Jr. et al., 2000), the weighted-slope spectral distance, and the cepstral distance. According to Wang, Sekey, and Gersho (1992), CWR_{seg} is a much better correlate to the auditory experience than the other objective measures mentioned previously.

Watermark Data Payload, Robustness, and Security

Embedded watermark messages vary across applications. These messages are typically coded or mapped into symbols or vectors before being embedded into the host signal. The watermark data payload, or *information embedding rate*, is measured in terms of number of bits embedded per unit time of the host signal. If an N bit (binary) watermark is embedded, then the watermark detector must identify which one of the 2^N possible watermarks is present in the audio signal. For many audio watermarking algorithms, the watermark payload increases at least linearly with an increase in the sampling rate. Different audio watermarking applications require different data payloads. Copy control applications may require four to eight bits of watermark information to be embedded in every 10 seconds of music (Cox et al., 2002). Broadcast monitoring may require 24 bits of information per second of the broadcast segment such as a commercial (Cox et al., 2002).

When watermarking is deployed for applications such as content protection, authentication, or copy control, the watermarked signal may be subjected to various deliberate and inadvertent attacks (Petitcolas et al., 1998; Voloshynovskiy et al., 2001). It is common for multimedia data to be subjected to processing such as compression, format conversion, and so on. Additionally, an attacker might try to deliberately remove the watermark or prevent its detection. Robustness refers to the ability of the watermark to tolerate distortion from any source to the extent that the quality of the coversignal is not affected beyond a set fidelity standard, or that the watermark detection or recovery processes are not hindered. Even watermarks for fragile watermarking applications are required to be selectively robust against certain attacks. Some of the factors affecting the robustness include the length of the audio or speech signal frame to be watermarked, the choice of watermark sequence, the relative energy of the watermark, the spectral content of the watermark, and the temporal locations and duration of the watermarks in the stegosignal. In broader terms, watermark robustness also depends on the watermark embedding, recovery, and detection algorithms. Cox et al. (1997) argue that watermarks must be embedded in perceptually significant components of the host signal to achieve robustness to common signal distortion and malicious attacks (Petitcolas et al., 1998; Voloshynovskiy et al., 2001). The perceptually irrelevant components of an audio signal can be easily removed by lossy compression other signal manipulations without much loss in signal fidelity. A trade-off also occurs between the quantity of embedded data and the robustness to host signal manipulation. While robustness is an indispensable characteristic of watermarking algorithms, there is no existing watermarking algorithm that is robust to all possible attacks. Some of the important attacks on audio watermarking systems are discussed next.

Noise and signal processing operations: Multimedia content may be subjected to signal processing operations such as lossy compression, digital-to-analog (D/A) conversion, analog-to-digital (A/D) conversion, filtering, quantization, amplification, and noise reduction. High frequency regions are not appropriate for robust data hiding, since lossy compression algorithms remove substantial information from this part of the spectrum. Speech signals may also be subjected to pitch modification. Finally, watermarks must be robust to additive noise for content transmitted across channels.

Geometric attacks: A *geometric attack* distorts the watermark through temporal modifications of the stegosignal. Audio watermarks may be attacked by geometric distortions such as jitter and cropping. Speech and audio signals may also be subjected to delay and temporal scaling attacks. In a jitter attack or a cropping attack, arbitrary samples of the stegosignal either are duplicated or removed (Petitcolas et al., 1998). If the audio watermarking technique involves an additive operation during the watermark embedding and recovery processes, cropping and jitter attacks result in desynchronization of the coversignal and the stegosignal and watermark detection is hindered.

Protocol attacks: *Protocol attacks* exploit loopholes in the security of watermarking algorithms. Collusion, averaging, brute force key search, oracle, watermark inversion, ambiguity (Craver, Memon, Yeo, & Yeung, 1998), and copy attacks are categorized as protocol attacks (Voloshynovskiy et al., 2001). In a *collusion attack*, an attacker or a group of attackers having access to a number of differently watermarked versions of a work, conspire to obtain a watermark-free copy of the work. In an *inversion* or a *dead-lock attack*, the attacker inserts his or her own watermark into the watermarked signal, in such a way that it is also present in the inaccessible and non-public host signal. In a *copy attack*, a watermark is copied from one audio signal to another, without any prior knowledge of the watermarking algorithm (Kutter, Voloshynovskiy, & Herrigel, 2000). This can be particularly devastating for authentication applications. Many protocol attacks compromise watermark security.

A watermark's security refers to its ability to withstand attacks designed for unauthorized removal, detection, or embedding. For example, if the purpose of watermarking is copyright protection, an adversary may be interested in removing the watermark or replacing the existing watermark in the content with his or her own copyright information, or in confirming if a watermark is indeed present. A watermarking technique must not rely on the secrecy of the algorithm for its security. A watermarking scheme generally derives its security from secret codes or patterns (*keys*) that are used to embed the watermark. Additionally, cryptographic algorithms may be employed to encrypt the watermark before it is embedded in the content. Only a breach of keying strategies should compromise the security of a watermarking technique; public knowledge of the technical method should not lesson its effectiveness (Cox et al., 2002).

Watermarking technology is also vulnerable to the problem of the *analog hole*. When watermarked digital content is played back in analog form, the watermark information is lost. The analog content can then be reconverted to digital content without any watermark information. Generally there is a loss in audio signal quality due to D/A and A/D conversions. The significance of the analog hole problem is related to the amount of perceptual distortion that can be tolerated on the attacked watermarked signal.

Audio Watermarking Techniques

This section will provide a description of some of the state-of-art audio watermarking algorithms. Spread spectrum, echo hiding, and quantization index modulation (QIM) watermarking are some of the commonly used audio watermarking approaches. This section also discusses robust bit-stream watermarking of compressed audio content and transform encryption coding based audio watermarking. Due to the existence of a large number of diverse audio watermarking algorithms, it is impossible to provide a description of all important algorithms.

Spread Spectrum Watermarking

The *spread spectrum* (SS) technique originally proposed by Cox et al. (1997) is one of the earliest and best-known watermarking algorithms for multimedia data. Several audio watermarking algorithms proposed in the literature are based on SS watermarking. The amount of manipulation to each audio signal component is limited by fidelity constraints. To overcome this limitation, a narrowband watermark is spread and embedded into a wideband channel that is the coversignal. The watermark is embedded in perceptually significant components of a signal, thereby providing sufficient robustness to attack. Tampering with perceptually significant components will destroy audio fidelity before destroying the watermark.

For instance, the watermark may be embedded in the N (typically 1000) highest magnitude discrete cosine transform (DCT) coefficients, predominantly from the low frequency regions, not including the zero frequency component (Cox et al., 1997). For increased security, the perceptually significant frequency components can be selected randomly. Also, the precise magnitude of embedded watermark information is only known to the designer. Since the watermark is spread across a number of host-signal frequencies, the watermark energy present in any single frequency is not perceptible. Moreover, HAS-based perceptual models may be used to increase the watermark signal energy embedded into individual host-signal components. Each value of the watermark $W = \{w_i\}_{i=1}^{N}$ is drawn independently from a unit normal, or a uniform distribution, that is $w_i \in N(0,1)$. The watermark values are selected to be continuous, and not binary, for better robustness against collusion attacks. If $\{x_i\}_{i=1}^{N}$ represents the N perceptually significant DCT components, then the watermark can be embedded in any one of the following ways:

$$y_i = x_i + \alpha_i w_i, \tag{5a}$$

$$y_i = x_i(1 + \alpha_i w_i), \tag{5b}$$

$$y_i = x_i(e^{\alpha_i w_i}), \tag{5c}$$

where $\{y_i\}_{i=1}^{N}$ represents the resulting watermarked components and $\{\alpha_i\}_{i=1}^{N}$ are multiple scaling parameters to account for different levels of perturbation tolerance exhibited by each host-signal spectral component. The modified coefficients are used to reconstruct the water-marked signal Y. One main advantage of SS watermarking is that watermark detection may be blind. The watermark detector must be aware of the temporal location of the watermark information, which is then concentrated into a shorter, higher-SNR, signal for detection. At the detector, a watermark is extracted from the possibly distorted watermarked signal Z and is correlated with the original watermark. If the resulting correlation value is above an application-defined threshold, the watermark is deemed to be present in the received signal.

SS watermarking is robust to a wide range of attacks including linear filtering, additive noise, A/D and D/A conversions, resampling, requantization, lossy compression, cropping, and scaling. Audio-specific extensions of the original SS watermarking algorithm (Boney et al., 1996) employ frequency and temporal masking to render enhanced security and robustness. Other variations of SS watermarking include modifications to the encoding and detection algorithms proposed by Kirovski and Malvar (2003) in order to improve watermark robustness and perceptual transparency, to prevent desynchronization and removal attacks, and to establish covert communications over public audio channels.

Echo Hiding

Bender et al. (1996) used homomorphic signal processing techniques to place information imperceptibly into audio signals through the introduction of closely-spaced echoes. The distortion due to data hiding is similar to the effect of resonances present in a room because of walls and furniture. Typically echoes of delay 20 mS or less are imperceptible. Four major parameters of an echo are considered: initial amplitude, decay rate, "one" offset (delay), and "zero" offset (one offset + delta). The echo blends with the original signal as the offset parameter is reduced. This generally happens even before the offset parameter becomes zero and is a function of the original speech, the echo, and the HAS. According to Bender et al. (1996), this fusion usually occurs around one thousandth of a second for most sounds and speakers. The offset parameter is selected to be below this threshold of perceptible watermarking. Binary "one" and "zero" information is encoded in the offset or delay parameters of an echo (Bender et al., 1996). Since the echoes are scaled by much smaller valued watermark coefficients, the louder coversignal masks some components of the echoes. The decay rate of the echoes is also adjusted to be below the audibility threshold of the HAS.

Binary watermarks are embedded using two different system functions (*kernels*). In the simplest case, the system functions are two impulses representing the "one" echo and the "zero" echo. Convolving the coversignal with any one of the kernels creates an encoded signal. The two kernels are characterized by different delay parameters (δ_1 and δ_0 seconds). Multiple watermark bits are embedded by dividing the coversignal into smaller frames and encoding either a zero or a one echo into each frame. The stegosignal is reconstructed by combining all the individual frames. Perceptible distortion is introduced when different bits (not all zeros or ones) are embedded into adjacent frames. In order to alleviate this distortion, the entire coversignal is first encoded by both the echoes. The echoed versions of the coversignal are then combined by using one and zero mixer signals. The zero (one) mixer signal is composed of ones (zeros) in the frames where a zero is to be encoded, and is composed of zeroes (ones) in the frames where a one is to be encoded. In the transition regions between frames, the mixer signals are composed of numbers between zero and one such that the sum of the two signals is always unity. While reconstructing the stegosignal, the one coversignal is multiplied by the one mixer signal, and the zero coversignal is multiplied by the zero mixer signal, and the resulting sequences are then added. This results in a smooth transition between adjacent frames encoding different bits, thus preventing perceptible changes in the stegosignal.

In echo hiding, the individual watermark bits are decoded by detecting the spacing between echoes. This is accomplished by examining the magnitude of the autocorrelation of the received signal's cepstrum. In the cepstral domain, the echoes are separated from the coversignal. The echoes are periodic in nature as determined by the offset parameters. Detection of the echoes is hindered by the fact that the magnitude of echo coefficients is much smaller than that of the coversignal coefficients. This is overcome by taking the autocorrelation of the cepstrum of the stegosignal, which gives the power of the signal at each delay. By determining whether the signal power is greater at δ_1 or δ_0 seconds, the watermark is decoded.

Quantization Index Modulation

Quantization index modulation (Chen & Wornell, 2001) is a class of quantization-based watermarking techniques that can be used to achieve good trade-offs between information embedding rate, watermark robustness, and stegosignal fidelity. QIM techniques are different from quantize-and-replace strategies such as watermarking through LSB modification (Van Schyndel et al., 1994). In LSB modification schemes, the host signal is first quantized and the LSBs in the quantization are replaced by the binary representation of the watermark. Because perceptually significant bits are not used for data hiding, LSB-based watermarking schemes are not robust.

In QIM, the embedding function $Y(X;W)$ is composed of an ensemble of functions of the host signal (X) indexed by the watermark message (W) such that:

$$Y(X;W) \approx X \tag{6}$$

for all W. Thus the distortion due to watermark embedding is small. The coversignal X may be composed of audio samples, frequency coefficients, or LP coefficients. For better robustness, the points in the range of one function should be as far away as possible from the points in the range of any other function. Every point from one function $Y(X;W_1)$ should be different from all the points of a different function $Y(X;W_0)$ for the watermark to be unambiguously recovered. This is known as the *non-intersection property*, and this leads to the rejection of host signal interference.

Quantizers are good generators of functions with the non-intersection property and the approximate identity property of equation (6). In QIM schemes, information is embedded by modulating an index, or sequence of indices, containing the watermark information, then quantizing the coversignal with the associated quantizer or sequence of quantizers. For example, two different quantizers are required to embed one bit of information $W=\{0,1\}$ in a frame of the host signal. If $W=1$ is to be embedded, then all the coefficients of the coversignal are quantized by the quantizer $Y(X;W_1)$ corresponding to $W=1$. The properties of the ensemble of quantizers are related to robustness, information embedding rate, and distortion. The number of quantizers in the ensemble determines the information embedding rate R_W. The sizes and shapes of the quantization cells determine the fidelity. Watermark robustness is determined by the minimum distance parameter d_{min} given by:

$$d_{min} \triangleq \min_{(i,j):i \neq j} \min_{(X_i, X_j)} \left\| Y(X_i; i) - Y(X_j; j) \right\|. \tag{7}$$

This equation evaluates the minimum distance between sets of reconstruction points from different quantizers in the ensemble.

A minimum-distance decoder is used for watermark detection. A copy of the coversignal is not required at the decoder. For blind watermark detection, the minimum distance decoder must consider all the reconstruction points from all the quantizers and not just the reconstruction points of the host signal. If the quantizers $Y(X; W)$ map X to the nearest reconstruction point, then the watermark decoding rule is given by:

$$\hat{W}(Y) = \arg\min_{W} \left\| Z - Y(Z; W) \right\|, \tag{8}$$

where Z is the possibly distorted stegosignal. Chen and Wornell (2001) proposed an implementation of QIM known as *dither modulation* (DM). In DM, dithered quantizers are used as the ensemble of quantizers. In dithered quantizers, the quantization cells and reconstruction points of one quantizer are a shifted version of the quantization cells and reconstruction points of another quantizer in the ensemble (Chen & Wornell, 2001). The shifts correspond to pseudo-random vectors known as *dither vectors*. The dither vector is modulated with the watermark vector or signal, constituting a unique dithered quantizer. The host signal is then quantized using the dithered quantizer resulting in the watermarked signal.

QIM has been used to embed data in the frequencies of sinusoidal tones of audio signals (Liu & Smith, 2003, 2004). The quantization step size or the spacing between adjacent reconstruction points of different quantizers was linear below 500 Hz and log-scaled above 500 Hz. Quantized sinusoidal parameters are then used to reconstruct the stegosignal. The embedded watermarks were robust to MP3 compression and an information hiding rate of 50 bps was achieved.

Bit-Stream Watermarking

Robust audio watermarking algorithms have also been developed for MPEG bit streams (Neubauer & Herre, 2000; Siebenhaar et al., 2001). Audio content is mainly stored and distributed in a compressed format. *Bit-stream watermarking* is used to protect the copyright and to prevent the distribution of illicit copies of compressed audio. Neubauer and Herre (2000) proposed a watermarking technique for the state-of-the-art MPEG-2 advanced audio coding (AAC) audio compression standard. In MPEG-2 AAC bit-stream watermarking, the audio bit stream is partly decoded, and an imperceptible watermark is embedded in the frequency domain. The resulting signal is then quantized and coded. Watermarking the bit stream generally leads to a small increase (typically 3% or less) in the bit rate of the output bit stream.

The MPEG-2 AAC audio coder consists of four main components: analysis filterbank, perceptual modeling, quantization and coding, and bit-stream multiplexing components. In the analysis filterbank, a critically subsampled modified discrete cosine transform (MDCT) is applied to the input audio samples, with a 50% overlap between adjacent analysis windows. The HAS-based psychoacoustic masking model is used for perceptual modeling. Both time and frequency-domain masking effects are considered, and the masking threshold is computed. The quantizer step size is then determined by ensuring that the quantization error is at or below the masking threshold. There exists a tradeoff between maintaining a low bit-rate for high compression rates and ensuring that the bit-rate is sufficiently high for the quantization noise to not exceed the masking threshold. Groups of frequencies quantized by the same quantization step size are called scalefactor bands. Generally, the actual quantization noise is slightly higher or lower than the masking threshold. The bit-stream multiplexing component assembles the output bit stream, consisting mainly of the quantized frequency coefficients and scalefactors. The MPEG-2 AAC decoder consists of a bit-stream demultiplexing component, decoding and inverse quantization component, and a synthesis filterbank. By sending the MPEG-2 AAC bit stream through the decoder, the audio signal is reconstructed.

The quantization, coding, and multiplexing components of the MPEG-2 AAC decoder and encoder are used for watermarking the audio bit stream. Thus, the bit stream is only partially decoded. For watermarking, the input bit stream is parsed in the demultiplexing component. The scale factors are also obtained as a result of parsing. This is followed by Huffman decoding. The inverse quantization component is used to obtain the MDCT representation of the signal.

The binary watermark message is cyclically repeated for better robustness. The low-bandwidth watermark data is spread to match the channel bandwidth of the host audio signal (e.g., 16 kHz). The resulting high-bandwidth watermark signal is shaped in the frequency domain through the application of a time-varying filter. The filter ensures that the watermark signal is below the masking threshold and hence is imperceptible. The masking threshold information is conveyed to the watermarking system as a separate data file. This does not lead to an increase in the ultimate bit rate, as the masking information is not transmitted with the watermarked bit stream. The masked watermark signal is added to the MDCT representation of the audio signal. Finally, the composite spectrum is quantized again using the scale factors and quantization step sizes from the original bit stream. The original audio bit stream is not required for watermark detection. A matched filter is used to detect the spread spectrum watermark in the bit stream (Neubauer & Herre, 2000).

Audio Watermarking through Transform Encryption Coding

Another interesting audio watermarking technique is the method based on *transform encryption coding* (TEC) (Ruiz & Deller Jr., 2000). TEC involves the application of all-pass pre/post filters to conventional transform coding to improve noise resilience, to increase the coding efficiency, and to facilitate secure transmission of coded images (Kuo, Deller, & Jain, 1996). The all-pass pre-filter scrambles the phase component of the signal prior to transform coding. If the all-pass filter is selected to have pseudo-random coefficients, the resulting pre-filtered image is encrypted and is unintelligible. Further, use of such a pre-filter results in uncorrelated transform coefficients that are Gaussian distributed and hence independent. The forward TEC operation on a signal frame $X = [x_1, x_2, \ldots, x_N]$ is defined by:

$$X' = \mathrm{T}(X) = FT^{-1}\{|FT(X)|\ e^{j\Theta(X)}e^{j\Phi}\}, \tag{9}$$

where Φ is the phase spectrum of a particular all-pass filter and FT represents the Fourier transform. Quasi m-arrays are generally used to obtain the phase coefficients of the all-pass filter (Kuo & Rigas, 1991; Kuo et al., 1996). The two-dimensional quasi m-arrays are arranged into a row vector before the application of TEC. The signal X is uniquely recoverable from the TEC-encrypted signal X' using the following inverse operation:

$$X = T^{-1}(X') = FT^{-1}\{|FT(X')|\ e^{j\Theta(X')}e^{-j\Phi}\}. \tag{10}$$

In TEC-based audio watermarking, the watermark (image, speech, or audio signal) is encrypted in accordance with equation (9) by using a set of quasi m-arrays Φ_W. The host audio signal is similarly encrypted using a different set of quasi m-arrays Φ_X. In order to ensure watermark imperceptibility, the encrypted watermark signal is scaled by a gain factor k, which is determined by a pre-specified *coversignal-to-watermark* (CWR_{dB}) ratio. The CWR_{dB} is a number that denotes the following relation:

$$CWR_{dB} = 10 \log_{10} \frac{\displaystyle\sum_{i=m-\frac{L_w}{2}}^{m+\frac{L_w}{2}} x_i^2}{k[m] \times \displaystyle\sum_{i=m-\frac{L_w}{2}}^{m+\frac{L_w}{2}} w_i'^2} = 10 \log_{10} \frac{X[m]}{k[m] \times W'[m]} \tag{11}$$

In this equation, $X[m]$ and $W'[m]$ represent the short-term energy measures for the host signal and the encrypted watermark, respectively, at time m. The short-term energy measures are calculated over a rectangular window of size L_w and centered at m. The gain factor is determined for every audio frame of size L_w by:

$$k[m] = \frac{X[m]}{W'[m]} 10^{-\frac{CWR_{dB}}{10}}. \tag{12}$$

The encrypted watermark is then embedded into an encrypted host audio signal resulting in the encrypted stegosignal, Y',

$$Y' = T_X(X) + k \times T_W(W) = X' + k \times W'. \tag{13}$$

The stegosignal is reconstructed by decrypting [equation (10)] the encrypted audio and this process encrypts the already-encrypted embedded watermark. Thus, the embedded watermark is twice encrypted,

$$Y = X + T_X^{-1}\{k \times T_W(W)\} = X + k \times W''. \tag{14}$$

If there is a need to recover the watermark from the stegosignal then the coversignal is subtracted from the received stegosignal to obtain an estimate of the twice-encrypted watermark,

$$\hat{W}'' = Z - X. \tag{15}$$

An estimate of the embedded watermark is obtained by applying the inverse TEC operations,

$$\hat{W} = \hat{k}^{-1} \times T_W^{-1}\{T_X\{\hat{W}''\}\}. \tag{16}$$

Knowledge of the two sets of quasi m-arrays is necessary for watermark recovery, and this contributes to increased watermark security. There are several other watermarking algorithms based on modifying the phase of audio signals (Ansari, Malik, & Khokhar, 2004; Dong, Bocko, & Ignjatovic, 2004). Phase-based watermarking techniques are vulnerable to MPEG coding and IIR filtering.

Speech Watermarking Techniques

Unlike general audio, speech is characterized by intermittent periods of voiced (periodic) and unvoiced (noise-like) sounds. Speech signals are characterized by a relatively narrow bandwidth, with most information present below 4 kHz. Broadband audio watermarking algorithms involving HAS-based perceptual models (Boney et al., 1996) may not be effective for speech. Several watermarking algorithms have been proposed specifically for speech signals. Many of these algorithms are based on developments in key speech technology areas such as coding, enhancement, and recognition. Existing robust speech watermarking algorithms are mostly based on one of three approaches: spread-spectrum signaling, synthesis-based, and parameter-based. A particular example of a fragile speech watermarking algorithm is presented along with these three basic types.

Spread-Spectrum Signaling

In *spread spectrum signaling* (Cheng & Sorensen, 2001) a narrow-band SS watermark signal is embedded in perceptually significant coefficients of the host signal, much like SS watermarking described previously. The watermark message and a PN sequence are first modulated using binary phase-shift keying (BPSK). The center frequency of the carrier is 2025 Hz, and the chip rate of the PN sequence is 1775 Hz. The SS watermark signal is lowpass filtered before modulation using a seventh order IIR Butterworth filter with a cut-off frequency of 3400 Hz. Linear predictive coding is used to embed high-energy watermark signals while ensuring imperceptibility. Linear predictive analysis involves the estimation of the all-pole component of speech of the form $A(z) = 1/(a_0 + a_1 z^{-1} + \ldots + a_p z^{-P})$. The LP coefficients of a p^h order all-pole LP model are typically computer using the Levinson-Durbin recursion (Deller Jr. et al., 2000). In general, the coversignal is assumed to generated by the LP model,

$$x_n = \sum_{p=1}^{P} a_p x_{n-p} + \xi_n. \tag{17}$$

The sequence $\{\xi_n\}_{n=1}^{N}$ is the prediction residual associated with the estimated model. In SS signaling, a bandwidth expansion operation is performed on the host signal. The poles are moved closer to the center of the unit circle, thereby increasing the bandwidth of their resonances. This is because the all-pole filter tends to have narrow spectral peaks. Frequencies near the peaks are subjected to masking effects and are unlikely to be perceived by an observer. By expanding the bandwidth of these resonances, more watermark frequencies can be effectively masked, and this facilitates the embedding of more robust watermarks. A bandwidth parameter $\gamma = (0,1), \gamma \in \mathbb{R}$, is used to scale the LP parameters. For $i = [1,2,\ldots,P]$, $\dot{a}_i = \gamma a_i$.

The modulated watermark signal is shaped by the LP spectrum of the coversignal. The filtered watermark signal is scaled by an instantaneous gain factor. The latter measure reduces perceptual distortion. In regions of silence in the coversignal, the watermark signal is scaled by a constant gain factor and then added to the coversignal. Watermarking contributes to a small amount of noise, which is not uncommon to any recording. Let E_{ξ_n} be the normalized per sample energy of the prediction residual associated with the all-pole model for one frame and E_{x_n} be the normalized per sample energy of the speech signal for one frame. In regions of speech activity, the watermark gain (g_n) is calculated as a linear combination of the gains for silence (λ_0), normalized per sample energy of the prediction residual associated with the all-pole model (λ_1), and normalized per sample energy of the speech signal (λ),

$$g_n = \lambda_0 + \lambda_1 E_{\xi_n} + \lambda E_{x_n}. \tag{18}$$

The possibly distorted stegosignal can be expressed as $z_n = w_n + x_n + I_n = y_n + I_n$, where w_n is the watermark signal and I_n represents the distortion. The LP coefficients of the received signal $\{z_n\}$ are estimated. This is followed by inverse LP filtering of the received signal resulting in the signal $\{\hat{\bar{w}}_n\}$. The inverse-filtering operation converts voiced speech into periodic pulses and unvoiced speech into white noise. The inverse filtering also decorrelates the speech samples. For watermark detection, a correlation detector is constructed. The estimate $\{\hat{\bar{w}}_n\}$ is compared with the synchronized and BPSK-modulated spreading function for the current speech frame, $\{\bar{w}_n\}$. That is,

$$\sum_{n=1}^{N} \bar{w}_n \hat{\bar{w}}_n \underset{H_0}{\overset{H_1}{\gtrless}} 0. \tag{19}$$

The watermark receiver requires perfect synchronization between the whitened stegosignal and the PN spreading sequence. These techniques have been tested in low-noise environments such as in the presence of additive white Gaussian noise with a 20 dB SNR (Cheng & Sorensen, 2001).

Parametric Watermarking

Parametric watermarking (Gurijala & Deller Jr., 2003; Gurijala, Deller Jr., Seadle, & Hansen, 2002) has both spectrum-spreading and integration-by-synthesis aspects, but is fundamentally different from these approaches. The well-known robustness of the LP model to practical anomalies occurring in coding, recognition, and other applications, suggests that some representation of these parameters might provide an effective basis for embedding durable watermarking data. There is a difference in the way LP modeling is applied in this watermarking application relative to its conventional deployment in speech coding and analysis. In coding applications, the goal is to find a set of LP coefficients that optimally model quasi-stationary regions of speech. In parametric watermarking, the LP parameters are derived according to the usual optimization criterion—to minimize the total energy in the residual (Deller Jr. et al., 2000)—with the understanding that the aggregate time-varying dynamics will be distributed between the *long-term* parametric code and the residual sequence.

The coversignal or a particular frame of the coversignal $\{x_n\}$ is assumed to be generated by a pth order LP model,

$$x_n = \sum_{p=1}^{P} a_p x_{n-p} + \xi_n. \tag{20}$$

The sequence $\{\xi_n\}$ is the prediction residual associated with the estimated model. The autocorrelation method may be used for deriving the LP coefficients $\{a_p\}_{p=1}^{P}$ (Deller Jr. et al., 2000). The prediction residual is obtained by using the LP parameters in an inverse-filter configuration,

$$\xi_n = x_n - \sum_{p=1}^{P} a_p x_{n-p}. \tag{21}$$

Once computed for a frame of speech to be watermarked, the LP parameters are modified in a predetermined way to produce a new set, $\{\tilde{a}_p\}$. The perturbations to the parameters constitute the watermark $\{w_p = \tilde{a}_p - a_p\}$. The stegosignal is constructed by using the modified LP parameters as a suboptimal predictor of the coversignal and by adding the prediction residual $\{\xi_n\}$.

$$y_n = \sum_{p=1}^{P} \tilde{a}_p x_{n-p} + \xi_n. \tag{22}$$

The watermark information is concentrated in the few LP coefficients during the watermark-embedding and recovery processes, while it is dispersed in time and spectrally otherwise. The coversignal is required for watermark recovery. The watermark recovery process involves least-square-error (LSE) estimation of modified LP coefficients, and this further contributes to watermark robustness. First, the prediction residual associated with the coversignal is subtracted from the possibly distorted stegosignal z_n,

$$d_n = z_n - \xi_n. \tag{23}$$

The modified LP coefficients are estimated by computing the LSE solution, say, $\{\hat{\tilde{a}}_p\}_{p=1}^{P}$, to the over-determined system of equations: $d_n \approx \sum_{p=1}^{P} \alpha_p y_{n-p}$. The watermark is recovered by subtracting the original LP coefficients from the estimated LP coefficients,

$$\hat{w}_p = \hat{\tilde{a}}_p - a_p. \tag{24}$$

The watermark detection is treated as a binary decision problem in the presence of additive noise in the LP domain (Gurijala & Deller Jr., 2005). A correlation detector is implemented based on the hypotheses,

$$H_0 : \hat{w}_p = v_p$$
$$H_1 : \hat{w}_p = w_p + v_p.$$

The null hypothesis is that no watermark is present, and only noise is transmitted $\{v_p\}_{p=1}^{P}$, while under H_1, both watermark $\{\hat{w}_p\}_{p=1}^{P}$ and noise samples $\{v_p\}_{p=1}^{P}$ are present in additive combination. The noise in the LP domain v_p is approximated by the distribution $N(\mu, \sigma^2)$, when noise $\{I_n\}_{n=1}^{N}$ is added to the stegosignal in the time domain such that the SNR is:

$$S = 10 \log_{10} \frac{\sum_{n=1}^{N} \tilde{y}_n^2}{\sum_{n=1}^{N} I_n^2}.$$

To account for possible deviations from the true LP noise distribution, the detection threshold is selected to be a value several (l) standard deviations away from the mean.

$$\sum_{p=1}^{P} \hat{w}_p w_p \underset{H_0}{\overset{H_1}{\gtrless}} \mu + l\sigma. \tag{25}$$

Fragile Speech Watermarking

A *fragile speech watermarking algorithm* for authentication applications is based on pitch and duration modification of quasi-periodic speech segments (Celik, Sharma, & Tekalp, 2005). The significance of these features makes them suitable for watermarking, and the natural variability of these features facilitates imperceptible data embedding. The coversignal is segmented into phonemes. A phoneme is a fundamental unit of speech that conveys linguistic meaning (Deller Jr. et al., 2000). Certain classes of phonemes such as vowels, semivowels, diphthongs, and nasals are quasi-periodic in nature. The periodicity is characterized by the fundamental frequency or the pitch period. The *pitch synchronous overlap and add* (PSOLA) *algorithm* is used to parse the coversignal and to modify the pitch and duration of the quasi-periodic phonemes (Molines & Charpentier, 1990). The pitch periods $\{\rho_m\}$ are determined for each segment of the parsed coversignal. The average pitch period is then computed for each segment,

$$\rho_{avg} = \sum_{m=1}^{M} \rho_m / M. \tag{26}$$

The average pitch period is modified to embed the pth watermark bit w_p by using dithered QIM (Chen & Wornell, 2001),

$$\rho_{avg}^{w} = Q_w \left(\rho_{avg} + \eta \right) - \eta, \tag{27}$$

where Q_w is the selected quantizer and η is the pseudo-random dither value. The individual pitch periods are then modified such that:

$$\rho_m^{w} = \rho_m + \left(\rho_{avg}^{w} - \rho_{avg} \right). \tag{28}$$

The PSOLA algorithm is used to concatenate the segments and synthesize the stegosignal. The duration of the segments is modified for better reproduction of the stegosignal. As required by authentication applications, watermark detection does not use the original speech. At the detector, the procedure is repeated, and the modified average pitch values are determined for each segment. Using the modified average pitch values, the watermark bits are recovered.

The algorithm is robust to low-bit-rate speech coding. This is because it uses features that are preserved by low-bit-rate speech coders such as QCELP, AMR, and GSM-06.10 (Spanias, 1994). Robustness to coding and compression is necessary for authentication applications. On the other hand, the fragile watermarking algorithm is designed to detect malicious operations such as re-embedding and changes to acoustic information (e.g., phonemes).

Performance Evaluation and Benchmarking

Since the mid 1990s, numerous watermarking algorithms have been developed for multimedia, text, software, and integrated circuits. An important unsolved challenge is to objectively evaluate the performance of these algorithms in terms of watermark robustness to deliberate inadvertent attacks, stegosignal fidelity, data payload, watermark security, and complexity. Generally, authors of published papers experimentally evaluate the performance of their watermarking algorithms. Because of the wide range of possible attacks against watermarking systems it is impossible to evaluate performance in the presence of every attack scenario. This leads to great variations in the way watermarking algorithms are evaluated, subsequently masking the merits and demerits of various algorithms. Hence, there have been efforts to benchmark the performance of watermarking algorithms and facilitate trusted third-party evaluation.

Audio Stirmark is the most commonly used benchmark available for evaluating audio watermarking algorithms (Steinebach et al., 2001; Steinebach et al., 2002). Audio Stirmark creates a common test environment and uses the same host audio signals for performance testing. Stirmark is written in C language and is freely available for both Windows and Linux. Stirmark enables researchers and software developers to provide a table of results summarizing the performance of their algorithms to the Stirmark tests. Stirmark evaluates the robustness of watermarking algorithms to attacks such as amplitude normalization, pitch shifting, time scaling, modulation, resampling, equalization, linear filtering, lossy compression, smoothing, additive noise, addition of echoes, and so on. In addition to robustness evaluation, Stirmark also tests the performance in terms of watermark perceptibility, data payload, and complexity. Because of application-specific variations in watermarking requirements, Stirmark provides the user with an option to customize the evaluation by selecting the tests to be executed (Steinebach et al., 2001; Steinebach et al., 2002). Public benchmarking tools specifically targeted at speech watermarking are not yet publicly available.

Conclusion

The chapter described the principles of audio and speech watermarking. The main considerations for audio watermarking such as the intended application, choice of domain and audio features, and stegosignal fidelity, watermark robustness, data payload, and security requirements are discussed in detail. Audio watermarking requirements vary depending on the application. The chapter also described some important audio and speech watermarking algorithms. Advances in the development of tools for the performance evaluation of existing audio watermarking algorithms were discussed.

References

Anand, D., & Niranjan, U. C. (1998, October). *Watermarking medical images with patient information.* Paper presented at IEEE EMBS Conference, Hong Kong.

Ansari, R., Malik, H., & Khokhar, A. (2004, May). *Data-hiding in audio using frequency-selective phase alteration.* Paper presented at IEEE International Conference on Acoustics Speech and Signal Processing, Montreal, Canada.

Barni, M., Bartolini, F., Rosa, A. D., & Piva, A. (2003). Optimal decoding and detection of multiplicative watermarks. *IEEE Transactions on Signal Processing, 51*(4).

Bassia, P., & Pitas, I. (1998, September). *Robust audio watermarking in the time domain.* Paper presented at IX European Signal Processing Conference, Rhodes, Greece.

Bender, W., Gruhl, D., Marimoto, N., & Lu, A. (1996). Techniques for data hiding. *IBM Systems Journal, 35*, 313-336.

Boney, L., Tewfik, A. H., & Hamdy, K. N. (1996, June). *Digital watermarks for audio signals.* Paper presented at IEEE International Conference on Multimedia Computing and Systems, Hiroshima, Japan.

Cano, P., Batlle, E., Kalker, T., & Haitsma, J. (2002, December). *A review of algorithms for audio fingerprinting.* Paper presented at International Workshop on Multimedia Signal Processing, U.S. Virgin Islands.

Celik, M., Sharma, G., & Tekalp, A. M. (2005, March). *Pitch and duration modification for speech watermarking.* Paper presented at IEEE International Conference on Acoustics Speech and Signal Processing, Philadelphia.

Chen, B., & Wornell, G. W. (2001). Quantization index modulation: A class of provably good methods for digital watermarking and information embedding. *IEEE Transactions on Information Theory, 47*(4).

Cheng, Q., & Sorensen, J. (2001, May). *Spread spectrum signaling for speech watermarking.* Paper presented at IEEE International Conference on Acoustics Speech and Signal Processing, Salt Lake City, UT.

Cox, I. J., Kilian, J., Leighton, T., & Shamoon, T. (1997). Secure spread spectrum watermarking for multimedia. *IEEE Transactions on Image Processing, 6*(3), 1673-1687.

Cox, I. J., Miller, M. L., & Bloom, J. A. (2002). *Digital watermarking.* San Diego, CA: Academic Press.

Craver, S. A., Memon, N., Yeo, B. L., & Yeung, M. (1998). Resolving rightful ownerships with invisible watermarking techniques: Limitations, attacks, and implications. *IEEE Journal of Selected Areas in Communications—Special issue on Copyright and Privacy Protection, 16*(4), 573-586.

Cvejic, N., & Seppänen, T. (2003, September). *Robust audio watermarking in wavelet domain using frequency hopping and patchwork method.* Paper presented at 3rd International Symposium on Image and Signal Processing and Analysis, Rome, Italy.

Deller Jr., J. R., Hansen, J. H. L., & Proakis, J. G. (2000). *Discrete time processing of speech signals* (2nd ed.). New York: IEEE Press.

Dong, X., Bocko, M., & Ignjatovic, Z. (2004, May). *Data hiding via phase modification of audio signals.* Paper presented at IEEE International Conference on Acoustics Speech and Signal Processing, Montreal, Canada.

Foote, J., Adcock, J., & Girgensohn, A. (2003, July). *Time base modulation: A new approach to watermarking audio.* Paper presented at IEEE International Conference on Multimedia and Expo, Baltimore.

Gurijala, A., & Deller Jr., J. R. (2001, May). *Robust algorithm for watermark recovery from cropped speech.* Paper presented at IEEE International Conference on Acoustics Speech and Signal Processing, Salt Lake City, UT.

Gurijala, A., & Deller Jr., J. R. (2003, September). *Speech watermarking by parametric embedding with an l_∞ fidelity criterion.* Paper presented at Interspeech Eurospeech, Geneva, Switzerland.

Gurijala, A., & Deller Jr., J. R. (2005, July). *Detector design for parametric speech watermarking.* Paper presented at IEEE International Conference on Multimedia and Expo, Amsterdam, The Netherlands.

Gurijala, A., Deller Jr., J. R., Seadle, M. S., & Hansen, J. H. L. (2002, September). *Speech watermarking through parametric modeling.* Paper presented at International Conference on Spoken Language Processing, Denver, CO.

Hagmüller, M., Horst, H., Kröpfl, A., & Kubin, G. (2004, September). *Speech watermarking for air traffic control.* Paper presented at 12th European Signal Processing Conference, Vienna, Austria.

Hatada, M., Sakai, T., Komatsu, N., & Yamazaki, Y. (2002). Digital watermarking based on process of speech production. In *Proceedings of SPIE: Multimedia systems and applications V.* Boston.

Haykin, S. (1996). *Adaptive filter theory* (3rd ed.). NJ: Prentice-Hall.

Hernandez, J. J., Amado, M., & Perez-Gonzalez, F. (2000). DCT-domain watermarking techniques for still images: Detector performance analysis and a new structure. *IEEE Transactions on Image Processing, 9*(1).

Johnson, K. F., Duric, Z., & Jajodia, S. (2000). *Information hiding: Steganography and watermarking—Attacks and countermeasures.* MA: Kluwer Academic Publishers.

Kalker, T., Depovere, G., Haitsma, J., & Maes, M. (1999, January). *A video watermarking system for broadcast monitoring.* Paper presented at IS\&T/SPIE's 11th Annual Symposium on Electronic Imaging '99: Security and Watermarking of Multimedia Contents, San Jose, CA.

Kirovski, D., & Malvar, H. S. (2003). Spread spectrum watermarking of audio signals. *IEEE Transactions on Signal Processing, 51*(4), 1020-1033.

Kundur, D., & Hatzinakos, D. (1998, May). *Digital watermarking using multiresolution wavelet decomposition.* Paper presented at IEEE International Conference on Acoustics, Speech and Signal Processing, Seattle, WA.

Kuo, C. J., Deller, J. R., & Jain, A. K. (1996). Pre/post-filter for performance improvement of transform coding. *Signal Processing: Image Communication Journal, 8*(3), 229-239.

Kuo, C. J., & Rigas, H. B. (1991). Quasi M-arrays and gold code arrays. *IEEE Transactions on Information Theory, 37*(2), 385-388.

Kutter, M., Voloshynovskiy, S., & Herrigel, A. (2000, January). *The watermark copy attack.* Paper presented at SPIE Security and Watermarking of Multimedia Contents II, San Jose, CA.

Lee, H. S., & Lee, W. S. (2005). Audio watermarking through modification of tonal maskers. *ETRI Journal, 27*(5), 608-616.

Linnartz, J. P. M. G., Kalker, A. C. C., & Depovere, G. F. (1998). Modeling the false-alarm and missed detection rate for electronic watermarks. In L. D. Aucsmith (Ed.), *Notes in computer science* (vol. 1525*)* (pp. 329-343). Springer-Verlag.

Liu, Y. W., & Smith, J. O. (2003, April). *Watermarking parametric representations for synthetic audio.* Paper presented at IEEE International Conference on Acoustics Speech and Signal Processing, Hong Kong, China.

Liu, Y. W., & Smith, J. O. (2004, May). *Watermarking sinusoidal audio representations by quantization index modulation in multiple frequencies.* Paper presented at IEEE International Conference on Acoustics Speech and Signal Processing, Montreal, Canada.

Lu, C. S., Liao, H. Y. M., & Chen, L. H. (2000, September). *Multipurpose audio watermarking.* Paper presented at 15th International Conference on Pattern Recognition, Barcelona, Spain.

Miaou, S. G., Hsu, C. H., Tsai, Y. S., & Chao, H. M. (2000, July). *A secure data hiding technique with heterogeneous data-combining capability for electronic patient records.* Paper presented at World Congress on Medical Physics and Biomedical Engineering: Electronic Healthcare Records, Chicago, IL.

Miller, M. L., & Bloom, M. A. (1999, September). *Computing the probability of false watermark detection.* Paper presented at the Third Workshop on Information Hiding, Dresden, Germany.

Molines, E., & Charpentier, F., (1990). Pitch-synchronous waveform processing techniques for text-to-speech synthesis using diphones. *Speech Communication*, pp. 453-467.

Neubauer, C., & Herre, J. (2000, February). *Audio watermarking of MPEG-2 AAC bits streams.* Paper presented at 108th Audio Engineering Society Convention, Paris, France.

Ozer, H., Sankur, B., & Memon, N. (2005, August). *An SVD-based audio watermarking technique.* Paper presented at seventh ACM Workshop on Multimedia and Security, New York.

Petitcolas, F. A. P. (2000). Watermarking schemes evaluation. *IEEE Signal Processing Magazine, 17.*

Petitcolas, F. A. P., & Anderson, R. J. (1999, June). *Evaluation of copyright marking systems.* Paper presented at IEEE Multimedia Systems, Florence, Italy.

Petitcolas, F. A. P., Anderson, R. J., & Kuhn, M. G. (1998, April). *Attacks on copyright marking systems.* Paper presented at Second Workshop on Information Hiding, Portland, OR.

Poor, H. V. (1994). *An introduction to signal detection and estimation* (2nd ed.). Springer-Verlag.

Ruiz, F. J., & Deller Jr., J. R. (2000, June). *Digital watermarking of speech signals for the National Gallery of the Spoken Word.* Paper presented at International Conference on Acoustics, Speech and Signal Processing, Istanbul, Turkey.

Seadle, M. S., Deller Jr., J. R., & Gurijala, A. (2002, July). *Why watermark? The copyright need for an engineering solution.* Paper presented at ACM/IEEE Joint Conference on Digital Libraries, Portland, OR.

Siebenhaar, F., Neubauer, C., & Herre, J. (2001, March). *Combined compression/watermarking for audio signals.* Paper presented at 110th Audio Engineering Society Convention, Amsterdam, The Netherlands.

Spanias, A. (1994). Speech coding: A tutorial review. In *Proceedings of the IEEE, 82*(10), 1541-1582.

Steinebach, M., Lang, A., & Dittmann, J. (2002, January). *StirMark benchmark: Audio watermarking attacks based on lossy compression.* Paper presented at Security and Watermarking of Multimedia Contents IV, Electronic Imaging 2002, Photonics West, San Jose, CA.

Steinebach, M., Petitcolas, F. A. P., Raynal, F., Dittmann, J., Fontaine, C., Seibel, C., & Fates, N. (2001, April). *Stirmark benchmark: Audio watermarking attacks.* Paper presented at International Conference on Information Technology: Coding and Computing, ITCC 2001, Special Session in Multimedia Security and Watermarking Applications, Las Vegas, NV.

Stocker, D., & Kummer, J. C. (2005, May). *R2O audio watermarking technology.* Paper presented at 118th Audio Engineering Society Convention, Barcelona, Spain.

Van Schyndel, R. G., Tirkel, A. G., & Osborne, C. F. (1994, November). *A digital watermark.* Paper presented at IEEE International Conference on Image Processing, Austin, TX.

Voloshynovskiy, S., Pereira, S., Pun, T., Su, J. K., & Eggers, J. J. (2001). Attacks and benchmarking. *IEEE Communication Magazine, 39*(8).

Wang, S., Sekey, A., & Gersho, A. (1992). An objective measure for predicting subjective quality of speech coders. *IEEE Journal on Selected Areas in Communications, 10*(5), 819-829.

Wu, M., & Liu, B. (2004). Data hiding in binary image for authentication and annotation. *IEEE Transactions on Multimedia, 6*(4), 528-538.

Chapter VI

Audio and Speech Watermarking and Quality Evaluation

Ronghui Tu, University of Ottawa, Canada

Jiying Zhao, University of Ottawa, Canada

Abstract

In this chapter, we will introduce digital watermarking systems and quality evaluation algorithms for audio and speech signals. Originally designed for copyright protection, digital watermarking is a technique that embeds some data to the host signal to show the copyright information. The embedded data, or the watermark, cannot be eliminated from the host signal with normal use or even after some attacks. In the first part of this chapter, we introduce a generic framework of digital watermarking systems. Several properties and application of the watermarking systems are then described. Focused on audio and speech signals, we divide the watermarking algorithms into robust and fragile ones. Different concerns and techniques are described for each category. In the second part of this chapter, a novel watermarking algorithm for audio and speech quality evaluation is introduced together with some conventional quality evaluation standards.

Introduction

Digital watermarking is a technique to embed a collection of bits into a signal. We refer to this collection of bits as a watermark. A well-designed watermarking algorithm will keep the watermark imperceptible to users. In other words, the resulting signal remains almost the same quality as the original signal. Watermarks can be embedded into audio, image, video, and other formats of digital data. There are different concerns to different formats of data in watermarking system design. In this chapter, we narrow our scope to audio and speech watermarking systems, or simply audio watermarking systems.

There are several ways to categorize audio watermarking systems. They can be classified as temporal and spectral watermarking. Temporal watermarking algorithms embed watermarks into audio signals in their temporal domain. Spectral watermarking algorithms embed watermarks in certain transform domain, such as Fourier transform domain, wavelet domain, or cepstrum domain.

Watermarking algorithms can also be categorized as robust and fragile ones. Watermarks in robust algorithms cannot be removed by common signal processing operations. On the contrary, a fragile watermark will be changed if the host audio is modified. In this chapter, we will follow this classification.

In recent years, digital watermarking algorithms boomed rapidly, especially in the image watermarking field. Compared to image, the research on audio watermarking is not as mature. The most important reason is the difference between the human visual system (HVS) and human auditory system (HAS). In general, HAS is more sensitive to distortions than the visual system. Therefore, it is challenging to implement imperceptible audio watermarks.

The rest of this chapter is organized as follows. In the first section, a generic digital watermarking framework is presented. A variety of properties and applications of watermarking algorithms are described. In the second section we provide a classification of attacks and a benchmark for audio watermarking systems. Several techniques for robust audio watermarking algorithms are described in the third section. Example algorithms for each technique are introduced. The fourth section is designated for fragile audio watermarking. Since there are not many algorithms for fragile audio watermarking, we combine semi-fragile watermarking in this section. In the last section, we introduce traditional audio and speech quality evaluation methods and a watermark-based evaluation algorithm.

Introduction to Digital Watermarking Technology

With the rapid growth of Internet, personal computers, and a variety of new digital devices, the digital format of media becomes more and more popular. The variety of software makes it convenient for consumers to create, manipulate, and store the digital multimedia data. Internet and wireless network provide a channel to transmit and to exchange the multimedia information. In the recent decades, these new formats of data have brought many changes to our life. However, they also pose the danger of illegal copy, redistribution, and various malicious attacks. Therefore, the protection of ownership and the prevention of the unauthorized tampering of digital multimedia data become important concerns.

The most common method for security issue is to use cryptographic techniques. In cryptography, the data is encrypted before its transmission, and it can be viewed after decryption. Once the data are decrypted, the digital signature is removed and there is no more proof of ownership. In other words, cryptography can protect digital data only in transit, but once decrypted, the data has no further protection.

Watermarking is a new technique that has the potential to protect digital data even after they are decrypted. A watermark is a data stream embedded into the original signal imperceptibly. Once a watermark is embedded, it is never removed during normal usage. When the host signal is modified, the watermark undergoes the same transformations as the host signal does. The watermark can be used to identify the copyright holder, to prevent illegal copy, and to verify whether the content is modified.

The idea of using digital watermarks for copyright protection arose in 1994 by Brassil, Low, Maxemchuk, and O'Gorman (1994). From the following year, digital watermarking has gained a lot of attention and has evolved quickly. A lot of practical working methods and systems have been developed.

Generic Digital Watermarking Framework

In general, a digital watermarking system consists of an embedder, a detector, and a watermark, as shown in Figure 1. The embedder E takes two inputs. One is the watermark that is only known by the author, and the other one is the original signal in which we want to embed the watermark. In most cases, the watermark is a collection of bits, which may come from an encoded character string, from a pattern, from some executable agents, or others (Wu, 2001). The watermark embedder incorporates the watermark W into the signal A and generates a watermarked signal A'. The embedding algorithm is defined as (Xu, Wu, & Sun, 1999):

$$A' = E(A,W). \tag{1}$$

The watermarked signal A' is then delivered to the communication network where the signal may be distorted by some attacks such as compression, filtering, and additive noise. When watermark detection is required, the watermarked signal is presented as an input to the detector.

The watermark detector D extracts the watermark from the watermarked signal, which may or may not have undergone attacks. The input of the detector A'' may differ from the original signal A and the watermarked signal A'. The difference is referred to as noise. The detector can be defined as (Xu et al., 1999):

$$W' = D(A'', A). \tag{2}$$

Figure 1. A generic watermarking system

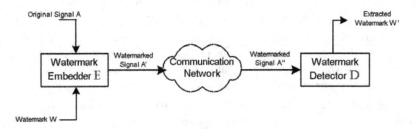

The extracted watermark W' will be compared with the original watermark W to check whether the signal is encoded with the watermark or not. Note that in equation (2) the original signal A may not be required by detector D in some algorithms.

Properties

Watermarking systems are required to have a number of properties. In a later section, several applications of digital watermarking will be introduced. We will find that different applications may have different properties. Therefore, there is no unique set of properties that all watermarking techniques must satisfy. The importance of each property varies in different applications. In this part, we highlight six properties.

- **Robustness:** Robustness refers to the ability to detect the watermark after common signal processing operations such as filtering, lossy compression, distortions, and additive noise. Different host signals may face certain types of transformations. For example, image watermarks may need to be robust against rotation, which is never a concern in audio watermarking algorithms. Even for one certain type of host signal, a watermarking algorithm need not be robust to all possible signal processing operations. It is application dependent.

- **Imperceptibility:** The embedded watermark should not be noticed by the user, and it cannot destroy the quality of the original signal. In other words, the data embedding process should not introduce any perceptible artifacts into the host data. Unlike robustness, this property should be achieved in all watermarking algorithms.

- **Data payload:** Data payload is the number of bits a watermark encoded within a host signal. Different applications may require different data payload. The online applications such as broadcast monitoring require embedding a segment of watermark in every short-time interval. The total amount of watermark bits required for such applications is then huge. On the contrary, an application for copyright protection may need only a small amount of information to be incorporated in the signal.

- **Detection blindness:** In the previous section, we learned that a watermark detector may take the original audio A and the audio A'' as its input. But this is not a general case. In some applications, the watermark detector does not require any information related to the original signal. We refer it as blind detection. Different from equation (2), a blind detector is formulized as $W' = D(A'')$. In the watermarking literature, systems that use blind detection are called public watermarking systems, whereas those that require access to the original signal are called private watermarking systems.

- **Security:** The security of a watermarking system means that an unauthorized user can neither embed a watermark, nor detect if a given signal contains a watermark. If security is required in a watermarking system, at least one secret key has to be used for the embedding and extraction process. For example, in many schemes, the embedded watermarks are pseudorandom signals. In this case, the seed of the pseudorandom number generator may be used as a secret key.

- **Computational cost:** Different applications require the watermark detection to be done at different speeds and complexity. In broadcast monitoring, the detector is required to work in real time. The computational cost should be low enough to make the decoder keep up with the real time broadcasts. However, speed is not an issue when using watermarks to track illegal copies.

The importance of each property listed above is dependent on the requirements of applications. In fact, it is not possible to achieve all of these properties in one watermarking system at the same time, since there are some tradeoffs among them. In order to make a watermark difficult to remove, the watermark must be placed in the perceptually "important" parts of the host signal. For example, the audio watermark should be placed in the portions of the audio that most affect human hearing. However, placing the watermark in the "important" parts is against the goal of reducing the perceptual effect of the watermark. Thus, the robustness and the imperceptibility of a watermark cannot be maximized at the same time. The similar conflict occurs between the data payload and the imperceptibility of the watermark. The more bits we embed into the signal, the more likely people will notice the presence of the watermark. Therefore, we should optimize these properties according to the specific application.

Applications

There are quite a number of watermarking systems developed based on different applications (Cox, Miller, & Bloom, 1999). In recent years, some new applications of digital watermarking have been discovered. For example, in a later section, we will introduce an audio watermarking algorithm designed for audio and speech quality evaluation. This is the first time that people use digital watermarking for quality evaluation. In this section, we list out five main applications of digital watermarking: copyright protection, content authentication, broadcast monitoring, copy control, and fingerprinting.

- **Copyright protection:** One of the motivations of introducing digital watermarking is copyright protection. The idea is to embed information of the copyright or the owner(s) into the data to prevent other parties from claiming to be the rightful owner(s) of the data. A watermark used for this purpose is known only by the author of the digital source and is supposed to be very robust against various attacks intended to remove it. It also has to be unambiguous and still resolve rightful ownership after other parties embed additional watermarks. The data payload for this application does not need to be high.

- **Content authentication:** In content authentication, the signature information is embedded to the source, and later is used to verify whether the content has been tampered with or not. In this application, the robustness of the watermark is not a concern. If the source is modified, the watermark along with it is also modified. We call this kind of watermark a fragile watermark. The difference between the original and extracted watermarks is used to authenticate the source.

- **Broadcast monitoring:** In television or video broadcast, advertisers want to make sure that they receive all of the airtime for which they are paid. Owners of copyright programs need to know any illegal broadcast. Digital watermarking is one convenient technique for the purpose of broadcast monitoring. In this application, the program or the advertisement to be monitored is embedded with a watermark before broadcast. During broadcast period, a computer monitor broadcasts and detects the watermark in certain time intervals. This application requires high data payload and low computational cost in decoder. Imperceptibility of the watermark is also a major concern.

- **Copy control:** This application is used to prevent illegal copies of recordable DVDs, digital VCRs, or any other digital video recording technologies. A watermark is embedded in the content. It is used to tell the recording equipment whether this content could be recorded. If the recording device were fitted with a watermarking detector, the device could be made to prohibit recording whenever a never-copy watermark is detected in the content.

- **Fingerprinting:** In this application, the watermark is used to trace the originator or recipients of a particular copy of multimedia data. For example, the owner of the multimedia product could place a different watermark in each copy. If the product is subsequently redistributed illegally, the owner could find out who was responsible for it. Therefore, the watermark could identify people who obtain content legally but illegally redistribute it.

Attacks to Audio Watermarking Systems

In this section, we introduce a classification of attacks against digital audio watermarking algorithms. Attacks can be categorized into removal attacks, geometric attacks, cryptographic attacks, and protocol attacks. This classification is generic. However, the details of each category may differ for different types of host signals, especially in removal attacks and geometric attacks. In this section, we focus our attention only on audio watermarking systems. Figure 2 shows the classification of attacks an audio watermarking system may encounter.

Figure 2. Classification of attacks on digital audio watermarking systems

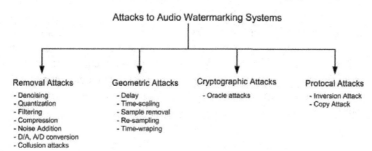

Removal Attacks

The goal of removal attacks is to remove the watermark from the watermarked signal completely without cracking the security of the watermarking system. Signal processing operations, such as noise addition, quantization, filtering, denoising, and compression, can be used to remove watermarks. Note that not all of these attacks could remove the watermark completely, but they may damage the watermark information significantly.

Collusion attack is another type of removal attack. If the attacker has more than one watermarked audio, he or she can either estimate the embedded watermark or estimate the original audio. In both cases, an estimated original audio can be produced. In other words, the watermark information is then "removed" from the protected audio.

Estimation of the watermark is possible if the attacker has a number of watermarked audios with the same watermark embedded. Furthermore, the watermark is not a function of original audios. In this case, assume the attacker has n watermarked audios $A'_1, A'_2, ... A'_n$, where $A'_i = A_i + W$, A_i is the original audio and W is the watermark. The attacker can estimate the watermark (denoted as W') by averaging these n watermarked audios:

$$W' = \frac{1}{n} \sum_{i=1}^{n} A'_i = W + \frac{1}{n} \sum_{i=1}^{n} A_i. \tag{3}$$

Estimation of the original audio is possible if the attacker has the same original audio watermarked with different watermarks. The estimated original audio $\tilde{A}$ is obtained by using the same averaging algorithm described previously:

$$\tilde{A} = \frac{1}{n} \sum_{i=1}^{n} A'_i = A + \frac{1}{n} \sum_{i=1}^{n} W_i, \tag{4}$$

where $A'_i = A + W_i$.

Geometric Attacks

In contrast to removal attacks, geometric attacks do not actually remove the watermark itself, but do destroy the synchronization between detector and the watermark. The detector could recover the embedded watermark information once perfect synchronization is achieved. However, the complexity of achieving synchronization is too high to be practical. For audio watermarking systems, geometric attacks include delay, time-scaling, sample removal, re-sampling, and time-warping.

Cryptographic Attacks

Cryptographic attacks aim at cracking the security of the watermarking schemes and thus finding a way to remove the embedded watermark or to embed misleading watermarks (Voloshynovskiy, Miller, & Bloom, 2001). One such technique is exhaustive search for the embedded information. Another type of attacks is called oracle attack. This attack is for the case that attackers have access to a watermark detector. The detector is treated as an "oracle." Attackers can apply this detector to a modified watermarked audio and find out whether the watermark can be detected. After iterations of slightly modifying the audio and using the detector to check the watermark from the modified audio, it is possible for attackers to estimate the original audio signal. A major disadvantage for cryptographic attacks is high computational complexity.

Protocol Attacks

In this category, there are two types of attacks. One is inversion attacks. The idea behind inversion attacks is that the attacker embeds his or her own watermark to the watermarked data and claims to be the owner of the data. This can create ambiguity with respect to the true ownership of the data. Another protocol attack is copy attack. This attack occurs when an adversary copies a watermark from one watermarked audio to another audio. During this process, removal attack may be applied to the watermarked audio to obtain the estimated watermark.

Stirmark Benchmark for Audio

Stirmark benchmark for audio (SBMA) is a benchmark for evaluating the performance of different audio watermarking algorithms, especially for robust watermarking algorithms. SBMA contains 39 different removal and geometric attacks. These attacks are categorized into add or remove attacks, filter attacks, and modification attacks (Lang, Dittmann, Spring, & Vielhauer, 2005). The goal of SBMA is to apply various attacks to watermarked audios. Extraction results indicate the performance of the algorithm.

Robust Audio Watermarking

There are several techniques for robust audio watermarking. The first technique is spread spectrum. This technique is derived from communication community and is originally proposed for image watermarking algorithms. Three unique techniques for robust audio watermarking are then introduced. They are echo hiding, masking, and phase coding. These techniques make use of special properties of audio signals and characteristics of HAS. Watermarking algorithms based on these techniques could achieve better robustness or imperceptibility. Note that the techniques introduced in this section are not the only ones for robust audio watermarking. There are many watermarking algorithms that employ different techniques to achieve robustness. The techniques that we will introduce are some typical ones.

In this section, we describe each technique in detail. A number of robust watermarking algorithms using these techniques are also provided.

Spread Spectrum Watermarking

The use of spread spectrum techniques to robustly encode data is borrowed from the communication community. In spread spectrum communications, one transmits a narrowband signal over a much larger bandwidth such that the signal energy present in any single frequency is undetectable. In other words, the narrowband data is spread across a large frequency band. It is often done through either the use of frequency hopping spread spectrum (FHSS)—taking a narrow-band signal and hopping it around the wide band—or direct-sequence spread spectrum (DSSS), where a signal is modulated at low intensity across the entire bandwidth. In the field of watermarking, we usually use the latter approach.

Cox, Kilian, Leighton, and Shanmoon (1997) first introduced spread spectrum into the watermarking system. Their approach is originally designed for image. However, the authors mentioned that this algorithm can be adapted to many other sources such as audio and video. In their approach, a watermark consists of a sequence of real numbers $W = w_1,...w_n$. Each value of w_i is chosen independently from a normal distribution with mean equal to 0 and its variance is 1. $X = x_1,...x_n$ is a sequence of coefficients selected from the host signal. The watermark W is then added into coefficients X by using one of the following formulas:

$$x_i' = x_i + \alpha w_i, \tag{5}$$

$$x_i' = x_i(1 + \alpha w_i), \tag{6}$$

$$x_i' = x_i(e^{\alpha w_i}). \tag{7}$$

α is a scalar parameter. It determines the extent to which the watermark W alters the sequence X. The resulting output sequence is attenuated and added back to original host signal.

Equation (5) may not be appropriate when the range of x_i varies widely. Insertion based on equation (6) or equation (7) is more robust against such differences in scale. Note that equation (6) and equation (7) give similar results when αw_i is smaller. Also, when x_i is positive, equation (7) is equivalent to $\ln x_i' = \ln x_i + \alpha w_i$. It then may be viewed as an application of equation (5) to the case where the logarithms of the original values are used. In the proposed approach by Cox et al. (1997), equation (6) is used to add watermarks to a signal. A single scaling parameter α may not be applicable for perturbing all the values x_i, since different spectral components may exhibit more or less tolerance to modification. Using multiple scaling parameters $\alpha_1 ... \alpha_n$ and using update rules such as $x_i' = x_i(1+\alpha_i w_i)$ might be more appropriate.

The extraction procedure is the inverse of the embedding algorithm. After we get the extracted watermark W', we measure the similarity between W' and the original watermark W using the following equation:

$$sim(W,W') = \frac{W \times W'}{\sqrt{W \times W'}}. \tag{8}$$

To decide whether W and W' match, one determines whether $sim(W,W') > t$, where t is a threshold. If $sim(W,W') > t$, we claim that W and W' matches. Setting the detection threshold is a decision estimation problem in which we wish to minimize both the false negative and false positive value, where false negative is the case that a watermark detector fails to detect a watermark that is present, and false positive occurs when a watermark detector detects a watermark in an unwatermarked audio.

Experimental results show that this approach is robust to many signal processing operations such as filtering, requantizaton, digital-analog, and analog-digital conversion. However, it also has some deficiencies. First, the marked signal and the watermark have to be perfectly synchronized at watermark detection. Next, to achieve a sufficiently small error probability, the length of the watermark should be sufficiently long.

Many improved approaches of spread spectrum watermarking for audio have been proposed. In these algorithms, spread spectrum has been used in various transform domain of the audio. Kirovski and Malvar (2003) developed a set of technologies to improve the effectiveness of embedding and detecting watermarks in audio. In their system, the signal is transformed to its frequency domain by using modulated complex lapped transform (MCLT). Watermark is added to the magnitudes of the signal. The watermarked signal is obtained by inverse MCLT with new magnitude values and original phase values. Block repetition coding is used to prevent against de-synchronization attacks and psycho-acoustic frequency masking. This algorithm is evaluated to be strongly robust to common audio editing procedures.

Cheng and Sorensen (2001) employed spread spectrum into the application of speech watermarking. Compared to the audio signal, the speech signal is a considerably narrower bandwidth signal. The long-time-averaged power spectral density of speech indicates that the signal is confined to a range of approximately 10 Hz to 8 kHz (Cheng & Sorensen, 2001). In order to make the watermark survive typical transformation of speech signals, including speech codecs, it is important to limit the watermark to the perceptually important portions of the spectra. A spread-spectrum signal with an uncharacteristically narrow bandwidth will be used in this algorithm as the watermark. In this way, the watermark will remain imperceptible. In this work, the message sequence and the psudo-random noise (PN) sequence are modulated using simple binary phase shift keying (BPSK). It then passes through a low-pass filter with frequency cutoff at 3400Hz. These make the PN sequence being fit within a typical telephone channel, which ranges from 250 Hz to 3800 kHz.

Audio Watermarking with Echo Hiding

The idea of using echo hiding is introduced by Gruhl, Bender, and Lu (1996). The basic idea is to add a repeated version of a component of the audio signal with a small offset to make the echo imperceptible. The watermark in this algorithm is a binary string. A watermark bit is embedded by echoing a segment of audio with certain delay time and echo amplitude. Figure 3 shows the relationship between the original signal and its echo. Binary one and zero are represented by different echo amplitudes and offsets. As the offset between the original and the echo decreases, the two signals blend. At a certain point the human ear hears not an original signal and an echo, but rather a single distorted signal.

The watermarking algorithm has a system function, which consists of configurations for two echo kernels: one kernel for binary 1 and the other one for binary 0. Figure 4 shows the process of embedding a watermark. In order to embed more than one bit, the host audio is divided into smaller segments. Each segment is considered as an individual signal and can then be echoed according to the watermark bit to be embedded. In Figure 4(a), the example signal is divided into six equal segments; each segment corresponds to one watermark bit. Then two echoed versions of the host audio are created using the system function. This is equivalent to embedding either all ones or all zeros to the signal. The resulting signals are shown in Figure 4(b).

In order to combine the two resulting signals, two mixer signals are created. The mixer signals are either one or zero, which depends on the watermark bit. The "one" mixture signal is multiplied by the "one" echo signal, while the "zero" mixer signal is multiplied by the "zero" echo signal. The two results are added. This mixer multiplication process

Figure 3. Echo kernels (Gruhl, 1996)

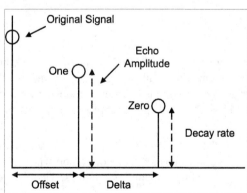

Figure 4. The echo watermarking technique (Gruhl, 1996)

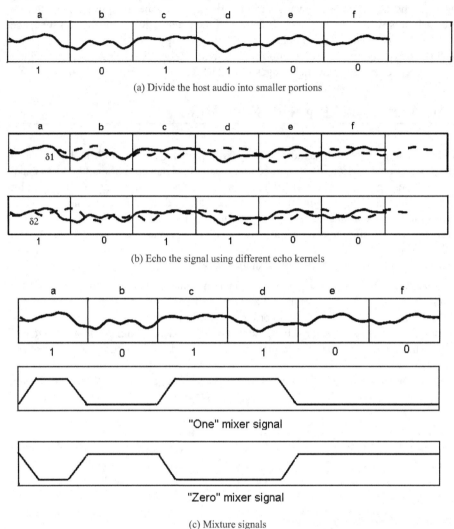

(a) Divide the host audio into smaller portions

(b) Echo the signal using different echo kernels

"One" mixer signal

"Zero" mixer signal

(c) Mixture signals

is demonstrated in Figure 4(c). Since the "zero" mixer signal is the binary inverse of the "one" mixer signal and the transitions within each signal are ramps, the resulting sum of the two mixer signals is always unity. This gives us a smooth transition between segments embedded with different bits. A block diagram representing the entire encoding process is illustrated in Figure 5.

In the extraction procedure, the autocorrelation of each signal segments' cepstrum value is calculated. This technique is called cepstrum autocorrelation. The cepstrum autocorrelation produces a signal with two pronounced amplitude humps. The distance between the two

Figure 5. Echo embedding (Gruhl, 1996)

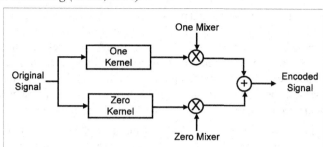

humps offsets between the original signal and the echo. We can use the value of this offset to determine whether a one or zero bit was encoded in the segment.

The echo hiding technique works for certain types of signals because very-shot-delay echoes are either imperceptible or heard only as resonance. It may be acceptable for certain classes of audio signals, but audio signals with large gaps of silence are not appropriate with this technique. A nice property of this technique is that it does not require the use of the original signal during extraction.

Several improved approaches have been proposed based on echo hiding. Oh, Seok, Hong, and Youn (2001) proposed multiple echo kernels in watermarking systems. The multiple echo kernels comprise both positive and negative pulses but with different offsets. A negative echo has negative initial amplitude and, thus, does not add the copied signal but subtract it from host signal. Subjective evaluation and robustness tests showed that this method is possible to embed echoes whose energies are two times larger than those in the conventional approach and, thus, to acquire robustness without degrading host signal quality.

Ko, Nishimura, and Suzuki (2002) combined echo hiding and the spread spectrum technique to embed the watermark. In their approach, an echo is temporally spread in the impulse response domain using a PN sequence, which also acts as a secret key to detect the embedded information from the watermarked signal. By spreading an echo, the amplitude of each component of the echo becomes small. However, it still maintains a high detection ratio. Another advantage is that it is possible to embed multi-information using uncorrelated PN sequences, which is useful for multi-authorities.

Audio Watermarking with Masking

Masking is the effect by which a faint but audible sound becomes inaudible in the presence of another louder audible sound. The masking effect depends on both spectral and temporal characteristics of both the masked signal and the masker. Frequency masking refers to masking that occurs in the frequency domain. If two signals occurred simultaneously and are close together in frequency, the stronger signal will make the weaker signal inaudible. The masking threshold of a masker depends on the frequency, sound pressure level, and tone-like or noise-like characteristics of both the masker and the masked signal. It is easier for a broadband noise to mask a tonal than for a tonal signal to mask out a broadband noise.

Moreover, higher frequency signals are more easily masked.

Temporal masking refers to both pre- and post-masking. Pre-masking effects make weaker signals inaudible before the stronger masker is turned on, and post-masking effects make weaker signals inaudible after the stronger masker is turned off. Pre-masking occurs from 5-20 msec. before the masker is turned on, while post-masking occurs from 50-200 msec. after the masker is turned off. Note that temporal and frequency masking effects have dual localization properties. Specifically, frequency- masking effects are localized in the frequency domain, while temporal masking effects are localized in the time domain.

Boney, Tewfik, and Hamdy (1996) first introduced masking phenomenon to watermarking algorithm for audios. The watermark is generated by filtering a PN sequence with a filter that approximates the frequency masking characteristics of HAS. It is then weighted in time domain to account for temporal masking.

In Boney et al.'s (1996) watermarking scheme, the basic watermarking step starts with generating a PN sequence. In order to make an inaudible watermark, the masking threshold of the signal is calculated using the moving picture expert group audio psychoacoustic model 1 (MPEG-1). The masking threshold is determined on consecutive audio segments of 512 samples. Each segment is weighted with a Hamming window. Consecutive blocks overlap by 25%. The masking threshold is then approximated with a 10th order all-pole filter $M(\omega)$ using a least squares criterion. The PN sequence W is filtered with the approximate masking filter $M(\omega)$ in order to ensure that the spectrum of the watermark is below the masking threshold. In each block, the perceptually shaped watermark is added directly to the audio signal. Since the embedded watermark lies below the frequency masking threshold, the imperceptibility of the watermark can be achieved well. This algorithm is also evaluated to be robust against additive noise, MP3 compression, multiple watermarks, re-sampling, and time-scaling.

Swanson, Zhu, Tewfik, and Boney (1998) improved Boney et al.'s (1996) approach by shaping the PN sequence not only with frequency masking effect, but also with temporal masking effect.

The audio signal with length N is first segmented into blocks of length 512 samples. The block with a size of 1024 samples has also been used. For each audio segment, the power spectrum is first computed. Then the frequency mask of the power spectrum is calculated using MPEG-1 psychoacoustic model. This frequency mask is used to weight the noise-like watermark for that audio block. The shaped watermark is then transformed back to temporal domain using the inverse Fourier transform. The next step is to compute the temporal mask using the envelope of the host audio. This temporal mask is used to further shape the frequency shaped noise, creating the watermark for that audio segment. The watermark is finally added to the block.

The overall watermark for a signal is simply the concatenation of the watermark segments for all of the audio blocks of length 512. The watermark detection uses linear correlation between the extracted signal and the original watermark (refer to equation (8)). The dual localization effects of the frequency and temporal masking control the watermark in both domains. This makes the watermarking algorithm have much better imperceptibility while it is robust to more attacks.

Muntean, Grivel, and Najim (2002) presented an algorithm to embed watermarks by substituting spectral components of the original signal that lie under the psycho-acoustical mask.

This algorithm is frame-based. The analyzed frames last from 20 to 30 ms. The embedding process is defined as:

$$S_w(f) = \begin{cases} S(f), & if \ \ P_s(f) \geq M(f) \\ \alpha W(f), & if \ \ P_s(f) < M(f) \end{cases}, \tag{9}$$

where $S_w(f)$ is the watermarked signal spectrum. $S(f)$ is the spectrum of analyzed frame of original signal. $W(f)$ is the spectrum of the spread watermark. $P_s(f)$ is the power spectrum density of the original signal. $M(f)$ is psycho-acoustical mask of the original signal. And α is a parameter to adjust the power of inserted spectral components.

In watermark retrieval, the input audio is first synchronized with the insertion process. Then we only consider the spectral components under the psycho-acoustical mask, estimated from the watermarked signal. At that stage, the extracted spectral components are linearly correlated with the watermark sequence to make the detection.

Foo, Yeo, and Huang (2001) proposed a scheme that combines the echo hiding and masking technique. Unlike conventional echo hiding techniques, the amplitude of echoes are set below a mask. In this way, it can make sure that the embedded watermark is under the masking threshold of HAS. In this approach, the echo kernel could be only one echo, or it can contain several echoes. This method is robust to common signal processing operations such as noise addition, re-sampling, cropping, filtering, and MP3 compression.

Audio Watermarking with Phase Distortion

Bender, Gruhl, Morimoto, and Lu (1996) introduce the phase coding method for audio watermarking. This method works by substituting the phase of an initial audio segment with a reference phase that represents the watermark. The phase of subsequent segment is adjusted in order to preserve the relative phase between segments.

Phase coding, when it can be used, is one of the most effective coding methods, in terms of signal-to-noise ratio. A phase altered audio signal may sound different from its original signal if each frequency component is dramatically changed. However, as long as the modification of the phase is sufficiently small, an inaudible coding can be achieved. It is due to the characteristic of HAS. Human auditory perception is insensitive to audio phase distortion in a certain range of audible frequencies.

The procedure of phase coding is illustrated in Figure 6. The original audio $S(i)$ is broken into a series of N short segments $S_n(i)$. In the second step, a K-points discrete Fourier transform (DFT) is applied to n^{th} segment $S_n(i)$. The matrix of the phase ϕ and magnitude M are created. In the next step, phase difference between each adjacent segment is stored as $\Delta\phi_n = \phi_n - \phi_{n-1}$. For segment S_0, an artificial absolute phase ϕ_0' is created according to the binary number to be embedded. $\phi_0' = \Pi/2$ if binary 0 is embedded. Otherwise $\phi_0' = -\Pi/2$. The phase matrix is re-created by using the phase difference $\phi_n' = \phi_{n-1}' + \Delta\phi_n$. The final step is to reconstruct the audio signal by applying the inverse DFT with the modified phase matrix ϕ' and the original magnitude matrix M.

Figure 6. Phase coding based watermarking algorithm (Bender, 1996)

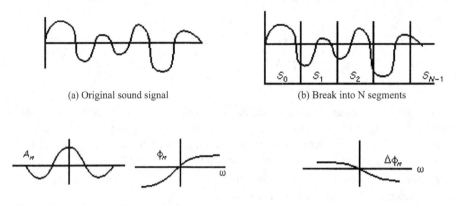

(a) Original sound signal   (b) Break into N segments

(c) Transform each segment into magnitude and phase   (d) Calculate the phase difference between consecutive segments

(e) For segment create an artificial absolute phase   (f) For all other segments, create new phase frames

For the decoding process, the synchronization of the sequence is done before decoding. The length of the segment, the DFT points, and the data interval must be known at the receiver. The value of the underlying phase of the first segment is detected as 0 or 1, which represents the coded binary string.

Since ϕ_0' is modified, the absolute phases of the following segments are modified respectively. However, the relative phase difference of each adjacent frame is preserved. It is this relative difference in phase to which the human ear is most sensitive.

Phase coding can achieve better imperceptibility. However, its robustness against various distortions is poor. The data payload typically varies from 8bps to 32bps.

Besides using DFT in phase coding, all-pass filters can also be employed in phase coding. The system in presented by Yardymcy, Cetin, and Ansari (1997) utilizes all-pass filters to embed watermark data into a speech or audio signal. All-pass filters having different poles or zeros operate on the consecutive blocks of the signal with the intention of modifying the phase without affecting the magnitude. Specifically, the system uses two all-pass filters, $H_0(z)$ and $H_1(z)$, with different poles or zeros:

$$H_i(z) = \frac{za_i + 1}{z + a_i}, \qquad i = 0,1. \tag{10}$$

Filtering a block by one of these filters corresponds to embedding a binary value i into the block. The encoding operation is started by dividing the audio signal into consecutive blocks of length N. Each block is filtered with the filter $H_i(z)$ corresponding to the value to be embedded. Finally, the blocks are merged together and output the watermarked audio.

Formally, let $s_k[n]$ be the kth block and $S_k(z)$ be its z-transform, then the watermarked block, $w_k[n]$, has the z-transform $W_k(z) = H_i(z)S_k(z)$. Hence the sequence $w_k[n]$ has a zero and a pole at $-a_i^{-1}$ and $-a_i$, respectively. The detection of the embedded data is accomplished by checking for the expected zeros of the sequence. The system evaluates the z-transform of the block at the two zero locations $w_k(-a_0^{-1})$ and $w_k(-a_1^{-1})$. Then the local minimum is estimated.

The data payload of this algorithm depends on the degree of the filter used, the number of possible zero locations, and the number of samples in each data block. The author indicated that it is possible to achieve a data payload of 100bps.

In the previous two algorithms, a process of synchronization is performed at the beginning of watermark detection. The algorithm presented by Ansari, Malik, and Khokhar (2004) is a novel phase coding algorithm with self-synchronization. The basic idea of this algorithm is to make use of silent points for synchronization.

The watermark embedding algorithm consists of the following steps. First, a list of salient points is extracted for a given audio signal. There are four to six salient points that are extracted per second on average in order to allow an adequate synchronization rate. Starting from the first salient point, the audio signal is segmented into frames of 10ms duration. Each frame is decomposed using a 5-level discrete wavelet packet analysis filter bank (DWPA-FB) and output 25 subbands. Twelve subbands in the middle frequency range, that is, from sb_4 to sb_{15}, are selected for data embedding. One bit data is embedded in each selected subband in a frame by processing it with the filter $H_0(z)$ for bit 0 or $H_1(z)$ for bit 1. The transfer function $H_i(z)$ is given by:

$$H_i(z) = \frac{(z^{-1} + p_i)(z^{-1} + p_i^*)}{(p_i z + 1)(p_i^* z^{-1} + 1)}. \tag{11}$$

All frames that contain salient points are embedded with a synchronization code consisting of a specific sequence. After data embedding, each frame is re-synthesized using a discrete wavelet packet synthesis filter bank. This scheme can reliably embed about 1200 bits in an audio segment of one-second duration, which is 10-30 times more compared with the previous two algorithms. Since the watermark is embedded in the middle frequency of the audio, perceptibility and robustness can be achieved at the same time. Experimental results show that it is robust to additive noise, lossy compression, random chopping, and re-sampling.

Fragile Audio Watermarking

Fragile audio watermarking algorithms are always designed for applications of authentication. In such applications, modifications on the signal should cause the watermark to be undetectable.

A number of fragile watermarking algorithms for image have been proposed in recent years. Most of these algorithms make use of quantization technology to embed watermarks. Audio watermarking adapted the same idea to embed fragile watermarks. Watermarks can be embedded in different domains. However, for audio authentication, watermarks are usually embedded in wavelet transform domain. Because this domain provides both temporal and frequency information at the same time, watermarks embedded in this domain are sensitive to various attacks, including attacks in frequency and temporal domain. Quan and Zhang (2004) presented such an audio fragile watermarking algorithm. The watermark is embedded by quantizing coefficients of wavelet transform.

Besides robust and fragile watermarking, there is a third type of watermarking algorithms called semi-fragile watermarking, which can be used for both copyright verification and content authentication. We will introduce two such schemes in the following.

Lu, Liao, and Chen (2000) proposed a multipurpose audio watermarking for both protection and authentication. In this scheme, two complementary watermarks are embedded in fast Fourier transform (FFT) coefficients of the host audio. Watermarks are embedded by quantizing FFT coefficients with corresponding masking threshold. No matter what kind of attack the audio encounters, this scheme guarantees that at least one watermark can survive well. At the same time, this approach can also locate the part of the audio that has been tampered with using the fragile watermark.

Tu and Zhao (2003) proposed a semi-fragile watermarking algorithm. Different from the previous approach, this algorithm embeds only one watermark to the audio. Watermarks are embedded into wavelet transform coefficients with quantization technology. This algorithm embeds watermarks into several levels of wavelet decomposition instead of using only one level. The experimental results show that this algorithm is robust against additive noise, filtering, and MP3 compression. Meanwhile, it has good performance for authentication.

Note that the algorithm introduced earlier is another example of semi-fragile watermarking. Different from the previous two algorithms, this watermarking approach is designed specially for applications of objective speech quality evaluation.

Audio and Speech Quality Evaluation

Audio and speech quality evaluation is of great interest in the research area of audio processing, mainly because of the fast increasing use of network as the media. Quality is a key determinant of customer satisfaction and key indication of computer network condition. Traditionally, the only way to measure the perception quality of a speech or an audio was through the use of subjective testing. Several different subjective testing methods have been proposed by ITU-T (1996a, 1996c). The simplest one is the absolute category rating (ACR) method. In this testing method, people are gathered to listen to a recorded conversation together with its reference, and they assign a rating to it. Mean opinion score (MOS) is calculated and is used to indicate the quality of the speech. This was the most reliable way to evaluate audio or speech quality. But subjective testing is expensive and time-consuming. Most importantly, with the rapid growth of networks, subjective testing becomes highly unsuitable for online monitoring applications. Due to these reasons, objective testing methods have been developed in the recent years.

An objective testing method takes both original and degraded audio or speech as its inputs. A perceptual model or a computational model is always involved for perceptual quality prediction. The goal of objective testing is to estimate subjective testing result. There are two types of approaches in objective testing: signal-based methods and parameter-based ones.

Signal-based algorithms take the reference and distorted signals as input. The two signals are compared based on some perceptual model, and the prediction of subjective test results is generated. In order to achieve an estimate of the perceived quality, a measurement should employ as much of an understanding of human auditory system and human judgment as possible. The common idea is to mimic a subjective test. Since 1993, there have been several perceptual measurement algorithms (ITU-R, 1999; ITU-T, 1996, 2001) recommended by the international telecommunication union (ITU).

Parameter-based algorithms predict the speech quality through a computational model instead of using real measurement. Approaches based on Gaussian mixture models (Falk & Chan, 2004), artificial neural networks (Samir Mohanmed & Afifi, 2001), and e-model (Ding & Goubran, 2003) are examples of recently published parameter-based algorithms for audio or speech quality assessment.

Compared to subjective approaches, objective testing methods are cheap and less time-consuming. Most of their applications are for networking monitoring, such as accessing voice quality in voice over internet protocol (VoIP). The predicted subjective test results are highly correlated with the real subjective results. At the same time, objective testing overcomes all the major shortcomings subjective testing has. However, algorithms for objective testing always involve design of complicated perceptual model or heavy computation. The reference audio or speech should always be provided for such algorithms as the input.

Cai and Zhao (2004) first presented an audio and speech quality evaluation algorithm based on digital watermarking technique. A watermark can be used to predict the perceptual quality because the carefully embedded watermark in a speech will suffer the same distortion as the speech does. This algorithm needs neither reference speech, nor any complicated perceptual model or computational model. It is simple and less computational. The experimental results show that this watermark-based approach can provide accurate quality evaluation, using perceptual evaluation of speech quality (PESQ), a speech quality evaluation model recommended by ITU, as the reference.

Mean Opinion Score

MOS is one of the most widely used subjective methods for speech quality evaluation. It provides a numerical measure of the quality of human speech. The algorithm generates a mean opinion score of voice quality after collecting scores from human listeners.

To determine MOS, a number of listeners are required to listen to a set of testing speeches. A listener gives a rating to each testing speech as follows: Excellent = 5; Good = 4; Fair = 3; Poor = 2; Bad = 1. The MOS is the arithmetic mean of the collection of these opinion scores. Subjective testing is very hard to repeat. In each test, the MOS value may differ, even with the same collection of listeners and the same condition.

Perceptual Evaluation of Speech Quality (PESQ)

In 2001, ITU standardized a new method—PESQ—for objective speech quality measurement (ITU-T, 2001). This method has good performance for a very wide range of applications, both in codec assessment and also in end-to-end testing of networks of all types (Rix, Beerends, Hollier, & Hekstra, 2000).

The basic idea behind the PESQ algorithm is to simulate the subjective listening test ACR and to predict MOS values of subjective testing. In PESQ, the reference and degraded signals are mapped onto an internal representation using a perceptual model. The difference between the internal representations is used to predict the perceived speech quality of the degraded signal, which is expressed in terms of MOS. We call the predicted MOS value as PESQ MOS. Defined by ITU recommendation P.862, the PESQ MOS ranges from -0.5 (worst) to 4.5 (best). This range is slightly different from the range of MOS values. This is due to the fact that the objective of PESQ is to optimize the average result of all listeners, but not the result of an individual listener. Statistics prove that the best average result one can expect from a listening test is 4.5.

Figure 7 illustrates the overall structure of PESQ (Rix et al., 2000). The method first aligns the reference and degraded signals in time space. An auditory transform is then used on the two signals. The difference between the transforms is aggregated in frequency and time and mapped to a prediction of subjective MOS value.

The PESQ is designed to accurately measure the distortions of waveform codecs and CELP/hybrid codecs, transmission error, packet losses, multiple transcoding, environmental noise, and variable delay. Benchmark tests of PESQ have yielded an average correlation of 0.935 with the corresponding MOS values under these conditions (Beerends, Hekstra, Rix, & Hollier, 2002). However, it has unknown accuracy for low rate vocoders (below 4kbit/s), multiple talkers, background noise, artificial speech, or music as input.

A Watermark-Based Algorithm for Objective Quality Evaluation

A carefully embedded watermark will undergo the same distortions as the host speech does. Based on this fact, Cai and Zhao (2004) proposed a watermark-based algorithm for objec-

Figure 7. Overall structure of PESQ

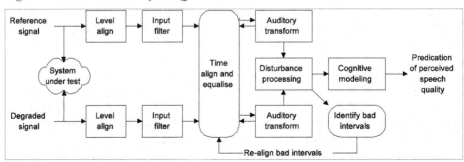

tive speech quality evaluation.

This watermark-based approach is based on the quantization technique. To evaluate the quality of speech that has undergone MP3 compression, additive noise, and low-pass filtering, the watermark is embedded in the discrete wavelet transform (DWT) domain (referred to as the DWT domain-based algorithm hereafter). To evaluate the quality of speech that has undergone packet loss, the watermark is embedded in the temporal domain (referred to as temporal domain-based algorithm hereafter). The PESQ MOS value of the distorted speech can be predicted from the value of percentage of correctly extracted watermark bit (PCEW). Figure 8 illustrates the overall watermarking scheme for audio and speech quality evaluation. The following describes the watermark embedding and extraction for both the DWT domain-based algorithm and the temporal domain-based algorithm.

- **Watermark embedding for DWT domain-based algorithm:** In this algorithm, the watermark W is a pseudo-random noise (PN) sequence. The seed of the PN code generator is treated as a secrete key. Before embedding the watermark, an adaptive control algorithm is used to obtain the optimal quantization scale (QS). With this optimal QS, it is possible to achieve both good fidelity of the watermarked signal and approximately 100% watermark detection before any distortion applied. The watermark is embedded in the DWT coefficients of the speech with quantization.

The block of watermark embedding consists of the following steps:

Step 1 (DWT decomposition): The DWT is applied to the original speech and Lth-level discrete wavelet decomposition is obtained.

Step 2 (Block division): On each DWT level, divide the decomposition coefficients into blocks. Each block will embed one watermark bit.

Step 3 (Coefficient selection): The larger the coefficient, the stronger watermark bit it can accommodate. Therefore, in each block, the 50 largest coefficients are chosen to embed the same watermark bit.

Step 4 (Coefficient quantization): Every selected coefficient in one block is quantized to binary 0 or 1 by using the following quantization rule:

$$Q(e) = \begin{cases} 0, & if \quad k \times \Delta \leq e < (k+1) \times \Delta \quad (k = 0, \pm 2, \pm 4) \\ 1, & if \quad k \times \Delta \leq e < (k+1) \times \Delta \quad (k = 1, \pm 3, \pm 5) \end{cases}, \tag{12}$$

where e is the value of the selected coefficient. The quantization step is denoted by Δ. It is a positive real number that is derived from optimal QS:

Figure 8. Watermarking scheme for objective quality evaluation

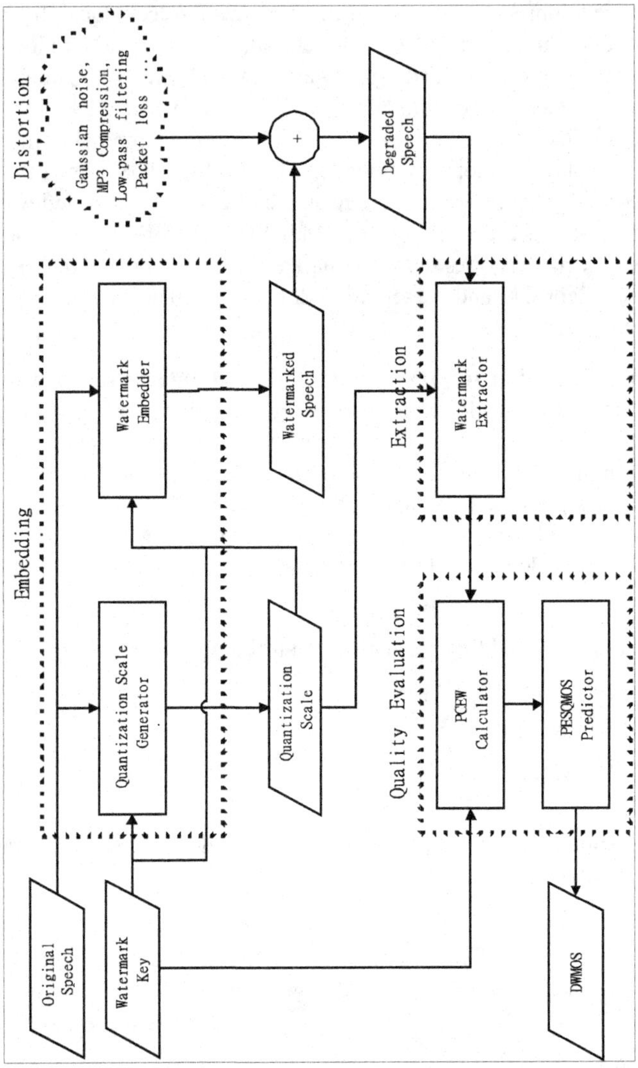

$$\Delta = \frac{\max_V - \min_V}{QS},$$ (13)

where $\min_V$ and $\max_V$ are the minimum and maximum values of the coefficients respectively in a specific decomposition level. Therefore, different decomposition level has different value of Δ.

Step 5 (Watermark embedding): A watermark bit W_i is embedded to a selected coefficient e by making $Q(e) = W_i$.

- If $Q(e) = W_i$, no change will be made to the coefficient e;
- If $Q(e) \neq W_i$, the coefficient e will be forcibly changed so that $Q(e) = W_i$, using $e = e + \Delta$.

Step 6 (Iteration): Iterate from step 3 to step 5 until the watermark bits are embedded to all the decomposition levels.

Step 7 (Inverse DWT reconstruction): The inverse DWT is applied to reconstruct the watermarked speech with the watermarked wavelet coefficients.

- **Watermark extraction for DWT domain-based algorithm:** The watermark extraction is carried out in a similar procedure of embedding. The distorted speech is first transformed into its discrete wavelet domain with the same mother wavelet and the same number of parameter L used in watermark embedding. Blocks are then divided on each decomposition level, and the 50 largest coefficients in each block are quantized to binary numbers by using equation (12). The estimated watermark bit $W_i{}'$ is obtained as follows:

$$W_i' = \begin{cases} 0, & if & N_0 > N_1 + 8 \\ 1, & if & N_1 > N_0 + 8, \\ 2, & o.w. \end{cases} \tag{14}$$

where N_0 is the number of binary zeros in 50 quantization values of the selected coefficients in one block, and N_1 is the number of binary ones. $W_i{}' = 2$ is the case that a decision cannot be made.

The extracted watermark sequence is denoted as W'.

- **Watermarking algorithm for temporal domain-based algorithm:** In the watermarking scheme for evaluating the effects of packet-loss, the authors still employ the technique of quantization that is used for the DWT domain-based watermarking algorithm. Because packet-loss affects the speech quality in temporal domain, over the speech file, the spectrum information has the equal opportunity to be lost. The advantage of using the frequency information to embed the watermark is not obvious here. Therefore, the watermark is directly embedded in temporal domain of the speech. The random and normal distributed watermark embedded in temporal domain gives more correct assessment of the effects on packet-loss attack.

In order to embed a watermark bit W_i to a selected sample, the sample value s is quantized and is assigned with a new value based on the quantized sample value $Q(s)$. The watermarked sample value s' is calculated as follows

$$s' = \begin{cases} s, & if \quad Q(s) = W_i \\ s + \Delta, & if \quad Q(s) \neq W_i \end{cases}.$$ (15)

For the only considering of packet-loss distortion, the watermark is very robust if there is no packet lost. So the same quantization step can be used for all speeches. Based on the experiment, the authors choose $\Delta = 1000$, on which the watermark disturbances on host speech signal are beyond the sensing of human ears and the watermark can still be extracted with 100% before the watermarked speech passes into the network.

Watermark extraction for the **temporal domain based algorithm** is simple. After the watermarked samples are located, the quantization results of these samples are the watermark

Figure 9. Predicted MOS vs. ITU-T P.862 PESQ MOS

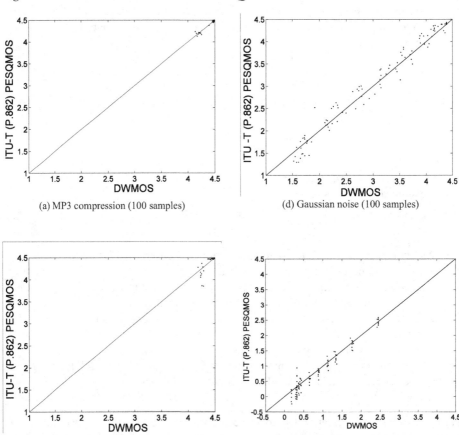

(a) MP3 compression (100 samples)

(d) Gaussian noise (100 samples)

(c) Low-pass filtering (80 samples)

(d) Packed-loss (80 samples)

to be extracted.

- **Speech quality evaluation:** The value of PECW is calculated by comparing the extracted watermark W' with the embedded watermark W as follows:

$$PCEW = \frac{1}{N}\sum_{i=1}^{N} W_i \oplus W_i',$$
(16)

where N is the length of the watermark, and $\oplus$ is the exclusive-OR operator for binary numbers. The PCEW is a real number that lies between 0 and 1.

In order to predict the PESQ MOS value of the distorted speech, a mapping from PESQ MOS and PCEW is built. In this mapping, the ranges of PESQ MOS and PCEW are both divided into 10 even segments. If $p \leq PCEW < p+0.1$, $p = 0,0.1,...0.9$, we set the starting point of the mapping segment $P_S = p$ and the end point $P_E = P_S + 0.1$. The predicted PESQ MOS is denoted as DW MOS, which is obtained as follows:

$$DWMOS = MOS_S + \frac{MOS_E - MOS_S}{P_E - P_S} \times PCEW,$$
(17)

where MOS_S and MOS_E are PESQ MOS values at the starting and end point of the mapping segment.

Figure 9 shows the correlation between the PESQ MOS and DW MOS for different kind of distortions. If DW MOS and PESQ MOS have an absolute match, all the sample points in the figures should be on the solid line from point $(1,1)$ to point $(4.5, 4.5)$. The closer the sample points to the solid line, the better the performance of DW MOS is.

Figure 9 indicates that no matter which distortion is applied, MP3 compression, Gaussian noise addition, low-pass filtering, or packet loss, the values of DW MOS and PESQ MOS are always matched perfectly.

Although this algorithm is only evaluated with speech signals, it can also be applied for audio quality measurements.

Summary

This chapter discussed several aspects of digital audio watermarking. We gave out the generic watermarking framework, properties, and applications of watermarking algorithms. Attacks to watermarking algorithms, especially to audio watermarking algorithms, were listed. With the classification of robust and fragile watermarking, several major techniques for each category and example watermarking algorithms were introduced. Finally we described the traditional ways for audio and speech quality evaluation, together with a watermark-based objective quality evaluation algorithm.

References

Ansari, R., Malik, H., & Khokhar, A. (2004). Data hiding in audio using frequency-selective phase alteration. In *Proceedings of IEEE International Conference on Acoustics, Speech, and Signal Processing* (vol. 5), (pp. 389-392). Montreal, Canada.

Beerends, J. G., Hekstra, A. P., Rix, A. W., & Hollier, M. P. (2002). Perceptual evaluation of speech quality (PESQ): The new ITU standard for end-to-end speech quality assessment part II—Psychoacoustic model. *Journal Audio Engineering Society, 50*(10), 765-778.

Bender, W., Gruhl, D., Morimoto, N., & Lu, A. (1996). Techniques for data hiding. *IBM System Journey, 35*(3), 313-336.

Boney, L., Tewfik, A., & Hamdy, K. N. (1996). Digital watermarks for audio signals. In *Proceedings of the Third IEEE International Conference on Multimedia Computing and Systems* (pp. 473-480). Hiroshima, Japan.

Brassil, J. T., Low, S., Maxemchuk, N. F., & O'Gorman, L. (1995). Electronic marking and identification techniques to discourage document copying. *IEEE Journal on Selected Areas in Communications, 13*(8), 1495-1504.

Cai, L., & Zhao, J. (2004). Evaluation of speech quality using digital watermarking. *IEICE Electronics Express (ELEX), 1*(13), 380-385.

Cox, I. J., Kilian, J., Leighton, F. T., & Shanmoon, T. (1997). Secure spread spectrum watermarking for multimedia. *IEEE Transactions on Image Processing, 6*(12), 1673-1687.

Cheng, Q., & Sorensen, J. (2001). Spread spectrum signaling for speech watermarking. In *Proceedings of International Conference on Acoustics, Speech, and Signal Processing* (vol. 3) (pp. 1337-1340). Phoenix, AZ.

Cox, I. J., Miller, M. L., & Bloom, J. A. (1999). *Digital watermarking*. San Francisco: Morgan Kaufmann Publishers.

Ding, L., & Goubran, R. (2003). Assessment of effects of packet loss on speech quality in voIP. *Proceedings of the Second IEEE International Workshop on Haptic, Audio and Visual Environments and Their Applications* (pp. 49-54). Ottawa, Canada.

Falk, T., & Chan, W.-Y. (2004). Objective speech quality assessment using Gaussian Mixture Models. In *Proceedings of the 22nd Biennial Symposium on Communications* (pp. 169-171). Kinston, Canada.

Foo, S. W., Yeo, T. H., & Huang D. Y. (2001). An adaptive audio watermarking system. In *Proceedings of IEEE Region 10th International Conference on Electrical and Electronic Technology* (vol. 2), (pp. 509-513). Singapore.

Gruhl, D., Bender, W., & Lu, A. (1996). Echo hiding. In *Proceedings of the First International Workshop on Information Hiding* (pp. 293-315). London.

ITU-R. (1999). Method for objective measurements of perceived audio quality. *ITU-R Recommendation BS.1387.*

ITU-T. (1996a). Methods for subjective determination of transmission quality. *ITU-T Recommendation P. 800.*

ITU-T. (1996b). Objective quality measurement of telephone-band (300-3400hz) speech codecs. *ITU-T Recommendation P.861.*

ITU-T. (1996c). Subjective performance assessment of telephone-band and wideband digital codecs. *ITU-T Recommendation P.830.*

ITU-T. (2001). Perceptual evaluation of speech quality (intrusive). *ITU-T Recommandation P.862.*

Kirovski, D., & Malvar, H. S. (2003). Spread-spectrum watermarking of audio signals. *IEEE Transactions on Signal Processing, 51*(4), 1020-1033.

Ko, B.-S., Nishimura, R., & Suzuki, Y. (2002). Time-spread echo method for digital audio watermarking using PN sequences. In *Proceedings on IEEE International Conference on Acoustics, Speech, and Signal Processing* (vol. 2), (pp. 2001-2004). Orlando, FL.

Lang, A., Dittmann, J., Spring, R., & Vielhauer, C. (2005). Audio watermark attacks: From single to profile attacks. In *Proceedings of the Seventh Workshop on Multimedia and Security* (pp. 39-50). New York.

Lu, C., Liao, H. M., & Chen, L. (2000). Multipurpose audio watermarking. In *Proceedings of IEEE International Conference on Pattern Recognition* (vol. 3), (pp. 282-285). Barcelona, Spain.

Muntean, T., Grivel, E., & Najim, M. (2002). Audio digital watermarking based on hybrid spread spectrum. In *Proceedings of the Second International Conference on WEB Delivering of Music* (pp. 150-155). Darmstadt, Germany.

Oh, H. O., Seok, J. W., Hong, J. W., & Youn, D. H. (2001). New echo embedding technique for robust and imperceptible audio watermarking. In *Proceedings of IEEE International Conference on Acoustics, Speech, and Signal Processing* (vol. 3), (pp. 1341-1344). Salt Lake City, UT.

Quan, X., & Zhang, H. (2004). Perceptual criterion based fragile audio watermarking using adaptive wavelet packets. In *Proceedings of the 17th International Conference on Pattern Recognition* (vol. 2), (pp. 867-870). Cambridge, UK.

Rix, A. W., Beerends, J. G., Hollier, M. P., & Hekstra, A. P. (2000). PESQ—The new ITU standard for end-to-end speech quality assessment. In *Preprints of the 109th Convention of the Audio Engineering Society* (p. 5260). Los Angeles, CA.

Rix, A. W., Hollier, M. P., Hekstra, A. P., & Beerends, J. G. (2002). Perceptual evaluation of speech quality (PESQ): The new ITU standard for end-to-end speech quality assessment part I—Time-delay compensation. *Journal Audio Engineering Society, 50*(10), 755-764.

Samir Mohanmed, F.C.-P., & Afifi, H. (2001). Audio quality assessment in packet networks: An inter-subjective neural network model. In *Proceedings of the 15th International*

Conference on Information Networking (pp. 579-586). Beppu City, Japan.

Swanson, M. D., Zhu, B., Tewfik, A. H., & Boney, L. (1998). Robust audio watermarking using perceptual masking. *Signal Processing Special Issue on Copyright Protection and Control, 66*(3), 337-344.

Tu, R., & Zhao, J. (2003). A novel semi-fragile audio watermarking scheme. In *IEEE International Workshop on Haptic, Audio and Visual Environments and their Applications* (pp.89-94). Ottawa, Canada.

Voloshynovskiy, S., Pereira, S., Pun, T., Eggers, J. J., & Su, J. K. (2001). Attacks on digital watermarks: Classification, estimation-based attacks, and benchmarks. *IEEE Communications Magazine, 39*(8), 118-127.

Wu, M. (2001). *Multimedia data hiding*. Unpublished doctoral dissertation, Princeton University.

Xu, C., Wu, J., & Sun, Q. (1999). Digital audio watermarking and its application in multimedia database. In *Proceedings of the Fifth International Symposium on Signal Processing and Its Applications* (vol. 1), (pp. 91-94). Brisbane, Australia.

Yardymcy, Y., Cetin, A. E., & Ansari, R. (1997). Data hiding in speech using phase coding. In *Proceedings of the Fifth European Conference on Speech Communication and Technology* (pp. 1679-1682). Rhodes, Greece.

Section III

Adaptive Filter Algorithms

Section III provides a review of some successful adaptive filter algorithms, together with two of the most successful applications of this technology such as the echo and active noise cancellers.

Chapter VII

Adaptive Filters:
Structures, Algorithms,
and Applications

Sergio L. Netto, Federal University of Rio de Janeiro, Brazil

Luiz W.P. Biscainho, Federal University of Rio de Janeiro, Brazil

Abstract

This chapter focuses on the main aspects of adaptive signal processing. The basic concepts are introduced in a simple framework, and its main applications (namely system identification, channel equalization, signal prediction, and noise cancellation) are briefly presented. Several adaptive algorithms are presented, and their convergence behaviors are analyzed. The algorithms considered in this chapter include the popular least-mean square (LMS), its normalized-LMS version, the affine-projection with the set-membership variation, the recursive least-squares (RLS), the transform-domain, the sub-band domain, and some IIR-filter algorithms such as the equation-error (EE) and the output-error (OE) algorithms. The main purpose of all this presentation is to give general guidelines for the reader to choose the most adequate technique for the audio application at hand.

Introduction to Adaptive Signal Processing

A Foreword

The unprecedented advances in Microelectronics along the last quarter of the 20th century, and after, made digital systems ubiquitous in signal processing. Increasing speed and miniaturization of devices gave rise to complex and modular processors that turned easier the design of large systems, providing robust and reliable solutions for demanding problems. Most of digital signal processing is carried out by the so-called digital filters—referring in general to FIR (finite-impulse-response) or IIR (infinite-impulse-response) linear time-invariant discrete systems (Diniz, da Silva, & Netto, 2002). The representation and operation of digital filters is inherently built on simple mathematical operations, thus allowing software- as well as hardware-based implementations. Once the digital processing chain is conceived algorithmically, a natural development is allowing the filters to be modified according to the system current needs, making them *adaptive* (Diniz, 2002; Haykin, 2001; Widrow & Stearns, 1985).

Adaptive systems are not a novelty, nor a result of digital signal processing techniques. They could be already found in radio receivers by the 1930s: the analog AGC (automatic gain control) is a simple adaptive system. But modern applications like the equalization of mobile communications channels require a level of flexibility and complexity that only digital processing systems can cope with, and digital adaptive filtering has become an autonomous research area: different structures and algorithms try to balance complexity and speed requirements.

This chapter aims at giving an overview of digital adaptive filtering, and is organized as follows. The remainder of this section establishes the general framework of adaptive filtering. The next two sections are dedicated to the most important adaptive algorithms applied to FIR direct-form filters: the LMS (least-mean-square) as well as some LMS-based algorithms are covered first, followed by the RLS (recursive least-squares) algorithm. Another section approaches alternative structures, including transform-domain implementations, sub-band systems, and IIR filters. The chapter concludes with practical issues: computer simulations on system identification illustrate the convergence of several algorithms, and some audio applications are discussed.

Basic Concepts

The distinctive quality of an adaptive system is its capacity to follow environmental changes. The general structure of a digital adaptive system can be seen in Figure 1 (Diniz, 2002; Haykin, 2001; Widrow & Stearns, 1985).

The adaptive system processes the input $x[k]$, generating an output $y[k]$. An error measurement $\varepsilon[k]$ between the output and a given reference $d[k]$ (somehow related to $x[k]$) is taken along the time. The system is properly modified to turn the error minimum. In a certain way, this makes the system trainable and self-designing, and obviously non-linear and time-variant.

Figure 1. Block diagram of an adaptive system

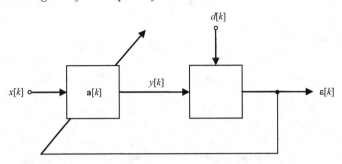

The adaptation itself can be treated as a general optimization problem. The design implies defining the following entities:

The *structure*, which dictates the dependence of $y[k]$ on $x[k]$ and the set of coefficients in vector $\mathbf{a}[k]$: $y[k] = g(x[k], \mathbf{a}[k])$. Constraining the system to be a structurally linear digital filter, for example, one could think of recursive and non-recursive implementations, as well as direct, cascade, parallel, and lattice-forms.

The *error* measurement, which can be any relationship between output and reference, the most common being the direct output error $e[k] = d[k] - y[k]$.

The function $F[\varepsilon[k]]$ to be minimized (*objective function*), for example, the MSE (mean square error) $E[E^2[k]]$, expected value of the random process $E[k]$, which generates the error $\varepsilon[k]$; and the WLS (weighted least-squares) function $\sum_{i=0}^{k} \lambda^{k-i} \varepsilon^2[i]$, sum of the squared errors subjected to a forgetting factor λ.

The *optimization method* employed in the minimization. In adaptive filtering, usually any practical method is an approximated or modified version of either the steepest-descent method, which updates the coefficient vector by the expression:

$$\mathbf{a}[k+1] = \mathbf{a}[k] - \mu \mathbf{g}_\mathbf{a}(F[\varepsilon[k]]), \tag{1}$$

or the Newton Method, which updates the coefficient vector by the expression:

$$\mathbf{a}[k+1] = \mathbf{a}[k] - \mu \mathbf{H}_\mathbf{a}^{-1}(F[\varepsilon[k]]) \mathbf{g}_\mathbf{a}(F[\varepsilon[k]]). \tag{2}$$

The convergence factor μ controls the adaptation step size; $\mathbf{g}_\mathbf{a}(F[\varepsilon[k]])$ is the gradient vector, and $\mathbf{H}_\mathbf{a}(F[\varepsilon[k]])$ is the Hessian matrix of $F[\varepsilon[k]]$ with respect to $\mathbf{a}[k]$.

All these issues will be addressed in this chapter.

Wiener Filter

The standard adaptive system consists of an Nth-order direct-form FIR filter with varying coefficients, as can be seen in Figure 2 (Diniz, 2002; Haykin, 2001; Widrow & Stearns, 1985).

At a given instant k, the input vector $\mathbf{x}[k] = [x[k] \quad x[k-1] \quad \cdots \quad x[k-N]]^T$ contains the $(N+1)$ most recent input samples, and the coefficient vector $\mathbf{w}[k] = [w_0[k] \quad w_1[k] \quad \cdots \quad w_N[k]]^T$ the current filter weights. The current output sample is given by:

$$y[k] = \sum_{i=0}^{N} w_i[k]x[k-i] = \mathbf{w}^T[k]\mathbf{x}[k].$$

(3)

In a more general case the input vector $\mathbf{x}[k] = [x_0[k] \quad x_1[k] \quad \cdots \quad x_N[k]]^T$ is formed by N current inputs, and the structure is just an *adaptive linear combiner*.

Having defined the output error $e[k] = d[k] - y[k]$ between the output and the desired signal $d[k]$, the MSE can be computed as:

$$\begin{aligned}
\xi[k] &= E[E^2[k]] \\
&= E[D^2[k]] - 2\,E[D[k]\mathbf{W}^T[k]\mathbf{X}[k]] \\
&\quad + E[\mathbf{W}^T[k]\mathbf{X}[k]\mathbf{X}^T[k]\mathbf{W}[k]],
\end{aligned}$$

(4)

Figure 2. Adaptive FIR filter

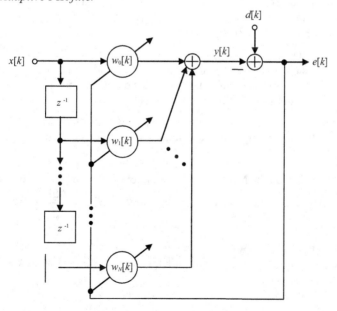

where capital letters indicate the random processes of which the defined signals and coefficients are samples.

The minimum MSE is the most usual criterium to obtain the optimum filter. Assuming fixed coefficients,

$$\xi = E[E^2[k]]$$
$$= E[D^2[k]] - 2\mathbf{w}^T E[D[k]\mathbf{X}[k]]$$
$$+ \mathbf{w}^T E[\mathbf{X}[k]\mathbf{X}^T[k]]\mathbf{w}. \tag{5}$$

Since the objective function ξ is a non-negative quadratic function of $\mathbf{w}$, it has a unique minimum point, which can be easily obtained by equating the gradient-vector $\mathbf{g_w}(\xi)$ to zero. Supposing the processes are jointly stationary, one can define the input autocorrelation matrix $\mathbf{R} = E[\mathbf{X}[k]\mathbf{X}^T[k]]$ and the cross-correlation vector $\mathbf{p} = E[D[k]\mathbf{X}[k]]$ between the desired signal and the input. Then, if $\mathbf{R}$ is non-singular, the optimum coefficient vector is:

$$\mathbf{w}_o = \mathbf{R}^{-1}\mathbf{p}, \tag{6}$$

leading to the minimum MSE:

$$\xi_{min} = E[D^2[k]] - \mathbf{p}^T\mathbf{R}^{-1}\mathbf{p}. \tag{7}$$

Practical models include an additive noise term in the actual reference signal $d[k] = d'[k] + n[k]$, where $d'[k]$ is the ideal desired signal.

An important property can be derived from the previous results. At the Wiener solution, the output error is *orthogonal* to the input signal, that is, $E[E[k]\mathbf{X}[k]] = \mathbf{0}$, and as a consequence, to the output signal, that is, $E[E[k]Y[k]] = 0$.

A simple interpretation of the operation principle of the described filtering can be drawn. The filter takes advantage of the correlation between $D[k]$ and $X[k]$ to equate $Y[k]$ to the correlated part of $D[k]$, thus minimizing $E[k]$. When the desired signal is orthogonal to the input, equations (6) and (7) show the filter has no effect.

This is the background against which adaptive filters perform their task. The practical algorithms available try to estimate $\mathbf{w}_o$ within a minimum of iterations and spending minimum computational effort.

Two measurements based on the MSE assess the solution deviation from its optimum: the *excess of MSE* $\Delta\xi[k] = \xi[k] - \xi_{min}$ and the *misadjustment* $M[k] = \dfrac{\Delta\xi[k]}{\xi_{min}}$. Alternatively, the quality of a given estimator $\mathbf{W}[k]$ for $\mathbf{w}_o$ can be measured by two properties: the *bias* $E[\mathbf{W}[k]] - \mathbf{w}_o$ (deviation of the estimator from the estimated parameter, in the mean) and the *mean-square consistency*, that is the fact of $E\left[(\mathbf{W}[k] - \mathbf{w}_o)^2\right] \to \mathbf{0}$ when $k \to 0$, along a sequential estimation procedure.

It can be insightful to write the excess of MSE as a function of the coefficient-error deviation. Assuming the *input vectors* $\mathbf{X}[k]$ are *mutually independent*, it can be shown that:

$$\Delta\xi[k] = \mathrm{E}[(\mathbf{W}[k] - \mathbf{w}_\mathrm{o})^\mathrm{T} \mathbf{R}(\mathbf{W}[k] - \mathbf{w}_\mathrm{o})]. \tag{8}$$

Although the independence assumption is not easily justifiable, it is behind important derivations in the context of adaptive filtering.

The time-variant case can be more easily examined if one attributes the time-variance exclusively to the Wiener solution, that is, the optimum coefficient vector is called $\mathbf{w}_\mathrm{o}[k]$. The overall coefficient-vector deviation can be decomposed as:

$$\mathbf{w}[k] - \mathbf{w}_\mathrm{o}[k] = (\mathbf{w}[k] - \mathrm{E}[\mathbf{W}[k]]) + (\mathrm{E}[\mathbf{W}[k]] - \mathbf{w}_\mathrm{o}[k]). \tag{9}$$

The first deviation term is due to additional noise, while the second one arises from lag. Considering $\mathbf{w}_\mathrm{o}[k]$ as a non-random vector, equation (8) can be rewritten as:

$$\begin{aligned}
\Delta\xi[k] = {}& \mathrm{E}[(\mathbf{W}[k] - \mathrm{E}[\mathbf{W}[k]])^\mathrm{T} \mathbf{R}(\mathbf{W}[k] - \mathrm{E}[\mathbf{W}[k]])] \\
& + \mathrm{E}[(\mathrm{E}[\mathbf{W}[k]] - \mathbf{w}_\mathrm{o}[k])^\mathrm{T} \mathbf{R}(\mathrm{E}[\mathbf{W}[k]] - \mathbf{w}_\mathrm{o}[k])],
\end{aligned} \tag{10}$$

where the overall excess of MSE is also decomposed in two terms: the former due to noise, the latter due to lag.

Two Standard Solutions

For the minimum-MSE problem just described, $\mathbf{g}_\mathbf{w}(\xi) = -2\mathbf{p} + 2\mathbf{R}\mathbf{w}$ and $\mathbf{H}_\mathbf{w}(\xi) = 2\mathbf{R}$. According to equation (2), the application of the *Newton algorithm* with $\mu=1$ leads to the updating formula:

$$\begin{aligned}
\mathbf{w}[k+1] &= \mathbf{w}[k] - \mathbf{H}_\mathbf{w}^{-1}(\xi)\mathbf{g}_\mathbf{w}(\xi) \\
&= \mathbf{w}[k] - \frac{1}{2}\mathbf{R}^{-1}(-2\mathbf{p} + 2\mathbf{R}\mathbf{w}[k]) \\
&= \mathbf{w}_\mathrm{o}.
\end{aligned} \tag{11}$$

This is an expected result. As a second-order method, the Newton approach yields the optimum solution in one step for any quadratic problem.

Alternatively, according to equation (1), the following updating formula applies to the steepest-descent algorithm:

$$\mathbf{w}[k+1] = \mathbf{w}[k] - \mu \mathbf{g}_w(\xi)$$
$$= \mathbf{w}[k] - \mu(-2\mathbf{p} + 2\mathbf{R}\mathbf{w}[k])$$
$$= (\mathbf{I} - 2\mu\mathbf{R})\mathbf{w}[k] + 2\mu\mathbf{p}. \tag{12}$$

After diagonalizing the autocorrelation matrix in the form:

$$\mathbf{Q}^T\mathbf{R}\mathbf{Q} = \Lambda = \begin{bmatrix} \lambda_0 & 0 & \cdots & 0 \\ 0 & \lambda_1 & \ddots & \vdots \\ \vdots & \ddots & \ddots & 0 \\ 0 & \cdots & 0 & \lambda_N \end{bmatrix},$$

with $\mathbf{Q}^T\mathbf{Q} = \mathbf{I}$, equation (9) can be rewritten as:

$$\mathbf{w}[k+1] - \mathbf{w}_0 = \mathbf{Q}(\mathbf{I} - 2\mu\Lambda)^{k+1}\mathbf{Q}^T(\mathbf{w}[0] - \mathbf{w}_0). \tag{13}$$

Then, given the eigenvalues λ_i of $\mathbf{R}$, $0 \le i \le N$, the convergence factor must be chosen in the interval $0 < \mu < \dfrac{1}{\max(\lambda_i)}$ to guarantee that $\mathbf{w}[k] \to \mathbf{w}_0$ when $k \to \infty$. On the other hand, the convergence speed is determined by the worst-case factor $(1 - 2\mu \min(\lambda_i))$. That means the convergence behavior of the steepest-descent algorithm depends strongly on the eigenvalue spread of the input autocorrelation matrix.

The behavior of the MSE can be traced by modifying equation (5):

$$\xi[k] = \mathrm{E}[D^2[k]] - 2\mathbf{w}[k]^T\mathbf{p} + \mathbf{w}^T[k]\mathbf{R}\mathbf{w}[k]. \tag{14}$$

Using again the decomposition of $\mathbf{R}$, one arrives at:

$$\xi[k] = \xi_{\min} + \sum_{i=0}^{N} \lambda_i(1 - 2\lambda_i)^{2k}v_i^2[0], \tag{15}$$

where $\xi_{\min}$ is given by equation (7) and $v_i[0]$ is the i-th element of $\mathbf{Q}^T(\mathbf{w}[0] - \mathbf{w}_0)$. The MSE convergence to $\xi_{\min}$ is dictated by the worst-case factor $(1 - 2\mu \min(\lambda_i))^2$. Therefore, the MSE evolves faster than the coefficient vector.

This analysis considered the $\mathbf{g}_w(\xi)$ and $\mathbf{H}_w(\xi)$ as precisely known quantities, and this is why $\mathbf{w}[k]$ could be treated as a non-random vector. In practice, even if the environment can be considered stationary, they can only be estimated. Different approaches lead to different adaptive algorithms.

Typical Applications

This section describes briefly four adaptive filter applications that encompass most practical cases (Diniz, 2002; Haykin, 2001; Widrow & Stearns, 1985).

System Identification

This application is illustrated by Figure 3. Both the system with unknown impulse response $h[k]$ and the adaptive filter are excited by the same input $x[k]$. After convergence, one expects the coefficients $w_i[k]$ approximate the system response samples $h[i]$. The input signal must be wide-band in order to excite every possible mode of the system's natural response.

Assuming $x[k]$ is white noise and the adaptive filter has order N, it can be shown that the optimum coefficient vector in the MSE sense is $\mathbf{w}_o = [h[0] \quad h[1] \quad \cdots \quad h[N]]^T$, regardless of the system order. For sufficient-order identification, given the input signal is a sufficiently persistent excitation, the optimum coefficients equate the impulse response. The signal $x[k]$ is a persistent excitation of order N if it cannot be set to zero by an order-N FIR filter.

In practical cases, an additional term of measurement noise $n[k]$ appears at the unknown system output, being responsible by the variance of the estimator $\mathbf{W}[k]$ after convergence. However, if the measurement noise is uncorrelated with the input and the filter has sufficient order, an unbiased estimate of $\mathbf{w}_o$ can still be obtained.

Almost every conventional application of adaptive filters can be transformed into a system identification scheme. Therefore, this is the most widely referred application in literature. It will be further explored in the later section on Computer Simulations, for didactic reasons.

Channel Equalization

This application is illustrated in Figure 4. In fact, the scheme can describe any system inversion application: given a system with transfer function $H(z)$, the adaptive filter target response $W(z)$ is such that $H(z)\,W(z)=1$.

In order to avoid a non-causal solution, requiring the adaptive filter also predicts the input signal, a delay of L samples is included in the system. Now, $H(z)W(z) = z^{-L}$. If $H(z)$ is an

Figure 3. System identification

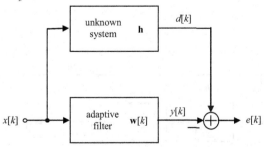

Figure 4. Channel equalization

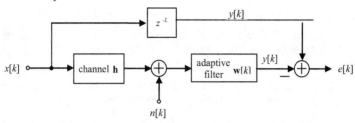

FIR system or modeled as such, then $W(z)$ results IIR. Typical FIR equalizers reach very high orders. The presence of channel noise $n[k]$ disturbs the equalizer convergence, since the filter tries to cancel the noise effects as well.

Modern channel equalizers employ increasingly complex structures, always based on this standard case.

Signal Prediction

This application is illustrated in Figure 5. The idea is to estimate $x[k+L]$ through a linear combination of $x[k]$ and N past samples, for an Nth order adaptive filter. This is the forward-prediction case. A similar scheme but with the delay moved to the upper branch performs a backward prediction.

A practical use of this structure is the LPC (linear-prediction coder) for speech signals. Also, an adaptive predictor can separate a narrowband signal from a wideband signal, given their sum: since the former is easily predictable, in contrast with the latter, they show up in $y[k]$ and $e[k]$, respectively.

Signal Enhancement

This application, also known as noise canceling, is illustrated in Figure 6. Here, the reference signal is composed by the effectively desired signal $x[k]$ corrupted by an additive interference $n[k]$. The input signal is formed by another noise signal $n'[k]$, sampled from a process $N'[k]$ statistically correlated with $N[k]$. The target is to turn $n'[k]$ into a replica of $n[k]$, so that $x[k]$ shows up in $e[k]$. In order to adequately synchronize both interferences, a delay of L samples can be included in either branch.

Figure 5. Signal prediction

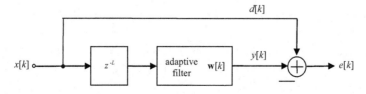

Figure 6. Signal enhancement

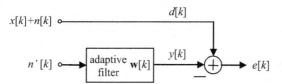

Acoustic echo cancellation in auditoriums and restoration of recordings from multiple copies are two possible occurrences of this scheme in audio.

The Least-Mean Square (LMS) and Some LMS-Based Algorithms

The LMS is by far the most popular and employed adaptive filtering algorithm, due to its inherent simplicity. Fast implementation is traded by convergence speed, which in the LMS depends strongly on the input signal statistical properties. As a desirable issue, the LMS exhibits guaranteed and unbiased convergence under stationary conditions. Several attempts to increase its convergence speed have originated an entire family of alternative LMS-based algorithms. In the following, the LMS is depicted, along with a set of selected variants, presented in an accumulative fashion (Diniz, 2002; Haykin, 2001; Widrow & Stearns, 1985).

The LMS Algorithm

The Least-Mean Square algorithm blends the instantaneous square output error $F[e[k]] = e^2[k]$ as an objective function with the steepest-descent search method, described by equation (1). Since:

$$\mathbf{g}_w(F[e[k]]) = 2e[k]\frac{\partial e[k]}{\partial \mathbf{w}[k]}$$

$$= 2e[k]\frac{\partial(d[k] - \mathbf{w}^T[k]\mathbf{x}[k])}{\partial \mathbf{w}[k]}$$

$$= -2e[x]\mathbf{x}[k], \tag{16}$$

the coefficient update can be performed iteratively by:

$$\mathbf{w}[k+1] = \mathbf{w}[k] + 2\mu e[k]\mathbf{x}[k], \tag{17}$$

where the convergence factor μ must be adequately chosen.

The coefficient-vector evolution along the LMS iterations can be studied along the same steps followed for the steepest-descent algorithm earlier in this chapter, except for using $E[\mathbf{W}[k]]$ instead of $\mathbf{w}[k]$, and assuming the input vectors $\mathbf{x}[k]$ are mutually independent. Adapting the results from equation (13), the coefficient vector converges *in the mean* to (i.e. it is an unbiased estimator for) the Wiener solution $\mathbf{w}_0$ when $k \to \infty$, as long as $0 < \mu < \dfrac{1}{\max(\lambda_i)}$; and the convergence speed is determined by the worst-case factor $(1 - 2\mu \min(\lambda_i))$. This makes clear that the convergence speed in the LMS is limited by the eigenvalue spread of $\mathbf{R}$.

Further insight can be gained by examining the coefficient-error-vector covariance, which coincides with its correlation $E[(\mathbf{W}[k] - \mathbf{w}_0)(\mathbf{W}[k] - \mathbf{w}_0)^T]$, since $E[\mathbf{W}[k] - \mathbf{w}_0] = \mathbf{0}$. After invoking again the independence assumption, it can be shown that the covariance converges to a non-zero matrix when $k \to \infty$ (i.e., is not a mean-square consistent estimator for $\mathbf{w}_0$) for an adequate choice of μ. This fact accounts for an excess of MSE after convergence, since equation (8) leads directly to the following result:

$$\Delta\xi[k] = \mathrm{tr}[\mathbf{R}\, E[(\mathbf{W}[k] - \mathbf{w}_0)(\mathbf{W}[k] - \mathbf{w}_0)^T]]. \tag{18}$$

Assuming the implied processes are jointly Gaussian, one obtains a sufficient condition for MSE stability:

$$0 < \mu < \frac{1}{2\max(\lambda_i) + \sum_{i=0}^{N}\lambda_i} \ ,$$

which is usually simplified to $0 < \mu < \dfrac{1}{\mathrm{tr}(\mathbf{R})}$. Additionally, considering $\mu\lambda_i \ll 1$ very small leads to a simple expression for the LMS misadjustment:

$$M = \mu\,\mathrm{tr}(\mathbf{R}), \text{ for } k \to \infty. \tag{19}$$

As seen in equation (10), under non-stationary conditions the excess of MSE is increased by an additional term $\Delta\xi_{\mathrm{lag}}[k] = E[(E[\mathbf{W}[k]] - \mathbf{w}_0[k])^T \mathbf{R}(E[\mathbf{W}[k]] - \mathbf{w}_0[k])]$. An interesting (although much simplified) analysis of this term can be done by taking $\mathbf{w}_0$ as sampled from a very slow first-order Markov process. Assuming again $\mu\lambda_i \ll 1$, one concludes that $\Delta\xi_{\mathrm{lag}}[k] \propto \mu^{-1}$. As a consequence, it is possible to compute an optimum μ that balances the two terms in equation (10), thus minimizing the overall excess of MSE.

The LMS algorithm is summarized in the following box. The error $e[k]$ can be called an *a priori* error, since it refers to the non-updated coefficient vector.

LMS Algorithm

Initialize

$\mathbf{x}[-1]=\mathbf{0}$

$\mathbf{w}[0]=\mathbf{0}$

Do for $k>0$

$e[k] = d[k] - \mathbf{w}^{\mathrm{T}}[k]\mathbf{x}[k]$

$\mathbf{w}[k+1] = \mathbf{w}[k] + 2\mu e[k]\mathbf{x}[k]$

The LMS algorithm requires around $2N$ additions and multiplications per iteration cycle.

The Normalized LMS Algorithm

The target of the so-called normalized LMS algorithm is to increase the LMS convergence speed by allowing a variable convergence factor $\mu[k]$ in the updating rule given by equation (17). After defining the a posteriori error:

$$e_+[k] = d[k] - \mathbf{w}^{\mathrm{T}}[k+1]\mathbf{x}[k], \tag{20}$$

the chosen criterion is the maximum reduction of the square error after updating the coefficient vector, that is the minimum difference $e_+^2[k] - e^2[k]$ between the a posteriori and a priori square errors. The solution consists of making $\mu[k] = \dfrac{1}{2\mathbf{x}^{\mathrm{T}}[k]\mathbf{x}[k]}$, yielding the new updating rule:

$$\mathbf{w}[k+1] = \mathbf{w}[k] + \frac{1}{\mathbf{x}^{\mathrm{T}}[k]\mathbf{x}[k]} e[k]\mathbf{x}[k]. \tag{21}$$

It can be easily verified that this solution leads to $e_+[k] = 0$. While at first glance it may seem an excellent situation, this is not the case. Zeroing the instantaneous a posteriori error means compensating sample-by-sample every error component, even those uncorrelated with the input signal, for example, the measurement noise $n[k]$ mentioned earlier in the subsection on System Identification. The effect of this tracking is an increase in misadjustment, thus disturbing the solution around its optimum state.

The balance between speed and misadjustment can be controlled by the reinsertion of a constant convergence factor in equation (21), as can be seen in the next box. The factor 2μ in equation (17) is changed to $\dfrac{\mu}{\mathbf{x}^{\mathrm{T}}[k]\mathbf{x}[k]}$ in the new algorithm. By coefficient matching and

---

Normalized LMS Algorithm

Initialize

$\mathbf{x}[-1]=\mathbf{0}$

$\mathbf{w}[0]=\mathbf{0}$

Do for $k \geq 0$

$e[k] = d[k] - \mathbf{w}^T[k]\mathbf{x}[k]$

$\mathbf{w}[k+1] = \mathbf{w}[k] + \dfrac{\mu}{\mathbf{x}^T[k]\mathbf{x}[k]} e[k]\mathbf{x}[k]$

---

making $\mathrm{tr}(\mathbf{R}) \approx \mathbf{x}^T[k]\mathbf{x}[k]$, the convergence range for the normalized LMS can be obtained as $0 < \mu < 2$.

Another practical consideration suggests the addition of a small constant $\delta > 0$ to the denominator in equation (21), which then becomes $\mathbf{x}^T[k]\mathbf{x}[k]+\delta$. This limits the updating steps if $\mathbf{x}^T[k]\mathbf{x}[k] \to 0$.

The normalized LMS as described previously requires around $3N$ additions and multiplications per iteration cycle. The term $p[k] = \mathbf{x}^T[k]\mathbf{x}[k]$ can be recursively computed as:

$$p[k] = p[k-1] + x^2[k] - x^2[k-(N+1)], \tag{22}$$

thus reducing the number of operations to just N per iteration.

As a last observation, the normalized LMS can be loosely viewed as an approximate Newton-type algorithm (see around equation [11]), if the input signal $\mathbf{x}[k]$ is white noise and at the same time one makes instantaneous approximations for $\mathbf{p}$ and $\mathbf{R}$.

The Affine-Projection Algorithm

Reusing past data is a procedure that can improve the convergence of adaptive algorithms. The affine-projection algorithm is an LMS-based reusing algorithm, in that it includes L older input vectors in the updating rule and results in a generalization of the normalized LMS algorithm.

It is useful to build the desired-signal vector $\mathbf{d}[k] = [d[k] \quad d[k-1] \quad \cdots \quad d[k-L]]^T$, the input matrix $\mathbf{X}[k] = [\mathbf{x}[k] \quad \mathbf{x}[k-1] \quad \cdots \quad \mathbf{x}[k-L]]$, the a priori error vector $\mathbf{e}[k] = \mathbf{d}[k] - \mathbf{X}^T[k]\mathbf{w}[k]$, and the a posteriori error vector $\mathbf{e}_+[k] = \mathbf{d}[k] - \mathbf{X}^T[k]\mathbf{w}[k+1]$, both formed by current and L past errors, computed with non-updated and updated coefficient vectors, respectively.

The affine-projection algorithm minimizes $\left\| \mathbf{w}[k+1] - \mathbf{w}[k] \right\|^2$ subject to $\mathbf{e}_+[k] = \mathbf{0}$. The idea is zeroing the a posteriori error vector through the minimum disturbing solution, thus avoiding unnecessary deviations of $\mathbf{w}[k]$. The optimum solution can be shown to be:

$$\mathbf{w}[k+1] = \mathbf{w}[k] + \mathbf{X}[k](\mathbf{X}^T[k]\mathbf{X}[k])^{-1}\mathbf{e}[k]. \tag{23}$$

It is exactly in the same form of the normalized LMS algorithm updating rule in equation (21), which corresponds to the case $L=0$, that is, without data reuse. Obviously, it suffers from the same increased misadjustment resulting from the null a posteriori error, which can be once more controlled by the inclusion of $0<\mu<2$.

In practical implementations, it is convenient to limit the updating step by adding $\delta\mathbf{I}$ (where $\delta > 0$ is a small constant) to the matrix to be inverted in equation (23), which then becomes $\mathbf{X}^T[k]\mathbf{X}[k] + \delta\mathbf{I}$.

The algorithm costs about $(L+1)(2N+L)$ additions and multiplications plus the inversion of an $(L+1)$-by-$(L+1)$ matrix per iteration cycle. Since $L \leq 4$ in practice and $\mathbf{X}^T[k]\mathbf{X}[k]$ is symmetrical, the cost of its inversion can be kept within low limits.

The affine-projection algorithm owes its name to the fact of searching the solution $\mathbf{w}[k+1]$ as the vector in the intersection of the hyperplanes defined by $\mathbf{d}[k] - \mathbf{w}^T[k+1]\mathbf{x}[k-L] = \mathbf{0}$ nearest to $\mathbf{w}[k]$, through successive orthogonal projections. Under the same considerations made in the subsection before regarding the normalized LMS, the affine-projection can be considered a Newton-like algorithm.

The Set-Membership Affine-Projection Algorithm

The last LMS-based algorithm detailed in this section gives one further step toward generalization. The set-membership concept relaxes the constraint on the a posteriori error, which is allowed to be within a given non-negative bound γ instead of being forced to zero. Besides mitigating the disturbance caused by the null a posteriori error, being data selective the set-

---

Affine-Projection Algorithm

Initialize
$\mathbf{x}[-1]=\mathbf{0}$
$\mathbf{w}[0]=\mathbf{0}$

Do for $k \geq 0$
$\mathbf{e}[k] = \mathbf{d}[k] - \mathbf{X}^T[k]\mathbf{w}[k]$
$\mathbf{w}[k+1] = \mathbf{w}[k] + \mu\mathbf{X}[k](\mathbf{X}^T[k]\mathbf{X}[k])^{-1}\mathbf{e}[k]$

---

membership algorithm reduces the average complexity per iteration cycle, since not every iteration requires updating the coefficient vector (Werner & Diniz, 2001).

The name of the algorithm refers to the set containing all solutions $\mathbf{w}$ such that $\left| d[k] - \mathbf{w}^T \mathbf{x}[k] \right| \leq \gamma$ at a given instant k. After defining the error bound vector $\mathbf{g}[k] = [g_0[k] \quad g_1[k] \quad \cdots \quad g_L[k]]^T$, $g_i[k] \leq \gamma$, the set-membership affine-projection minimization problem can be stated as: minimize $\left\| \mathbf{w}[k+1] - \mathbf{w}[k] \right\|^2$ subject to $\mathbf{e}_+[k] = \mathbf{g}[k]$. The general solution is given by:

$$\mathbf{w}[k+1] = \begin{cases} \mathbf{w}[k] + \mathbf{X}[k](\mathbf{X}^T[k]\mathbf{X}[k])^{-1}(\mathbf{e}[k] - \mathbf{g}[k]), & |e[k]| > \gamma \\ \mathbf{w}[k], & \text{otherwise} \end{cases} \qquad (24)$$

It can be easily verified that making $\gamma = 0$ the algorithm reduces to the previous affine-projection algorithm (see equation [23]).

A clever choice of $\mathbf{g}[k]$ will conclude the algorithm derivation. First, it is known that from the previous iteration $\left| e_{+_{i-1}}[k-1] \right| \leq \gamma$, $1 \leq i \leq L$. But $e_{+_{i-1}}[k-1] = e_i[k]$, $1 \leq i \leq L$; then, one can choose $g_i[k] = e_i[k]$, $1 \leq i \leq L$, thus keeping those a posteriori errors constant. This zeroes all except the first element in vector $\mathbf{e}[k] - \mathbf{g}[k]$, which of course saves a lot of operations. Now, the less restrictive choice for the remaining parameter can be made: $g_0[k] = \text{sign}[e_0[k]]\gamma = \text{sign}[e[k]]\gamma$, on the set boundary. The resulting algorithm is described in the following box, where $\mathbf{u}_1 = [1 \quad 0 \quad \cdots \quad 0]^T$.

Once more, in practical implementations, it is convenient to modify the matrix to be inverted in equation (24) into $\mathbf{X}^T[k]\mathbf{X}[k] + \delta\mathbf{I}$, where $\delta > 0$ is a small constant, to avoid overflow.

The algorithm costs about $2N(L+1)$ additions and multiplications plus the inversion of an $(L+1)$-by-$(L+1)$ matrix per update—which, as it was already pointed out, does not occur at every iteration.

The set-membership affine-projection can also be seen as a Newton-like algorithm.

Set-Membership Affine-Projection Algorithm

Initialize

$\mathbf{x}[-1]=\mathbf{0}$

$\mathbf{w}[0]=\mathbf{0}$

Do for $k \geq 0$

$\mathbf{e}[k] = \mathbf{d}[k] - \mathbf{X}^T[k]\mathbf{w}[k]$

$$\mathbf{w}[k+1] = \begin{cases} \mathbf{w}[k] + \mathbf{X}[k](\mathbf{X}^T[k]\mathbf{X}[k])^{-1}[e[k] - \text{sign}(e[k])\gamma]\mathbf{u}_1, & |e[k]| > \gamma \\ \mathbf{w}[k], & \text{otherwise} \end{cases}$$

Other Algorithms

Several other variants compose the LMS-type family of adaptive algorithms.

The quantized-data algorithms form an interesting group of modified LMS algorithms that employ quantized versions of $e[k]$ and/or $x[k]$ in equation (17), in order to save operations, however, incurring slow convergence, large misadjustment, or even instability, depending on the algorithm.

Another attempt to mitigate the dependence of the LMS convergence rate from the input signal correlation (which, of course, cannot be always made white noise) is the so-called LMS-Newton algorithm, which combines an instantaneous gradient estimate with a sequential estimate for the input autocorrelation matrix, based on time-correlation. It can be easily rewritten as an RLS algorithm (presented in the next section). Variable convergence factors were proposed for the LMS-Newton algorithm.

Closing this section, one should mention the transform-domain LMS family. The input vector $\mathbf{x}[k]$ is operated via a block unitary transform, and the LMS updating rule is applied on the power-normalized transformed sequence. The main idea behind this procedure is to decorrelate the input signal, thus accelerating the LMS convergence, as will be discussed in further subsections on transform-domain and sub-band adaptive algorithms.

The Recursive Least-Squares Algorithm

As seen previously, the LMS algorithm follows a steepest-descent path in search for the objective function minimum value. As a consequence, the LMS convergence speed is determined by the eigenvalue spread of the input-signal autocorrelation matrix $\mathbf{R}$. It was already mentioned that a faster convergence process can be obtained if one uses a Newton-type algorithm during the adaptation process, as indicated in equation (11). Such an iterative process, however, requires the computation of the inverse of $\mathbf{R}$, which is prohibitive in most online practical applications.

This section deals with the so-called recursive least-squares algorithm, which attempts to follow a Newton-like direction using an iterative procedure to estimate the inverse of $\mathbf{R}$ (Diniz, 2002; Haykin, 2001).

The RLS Algorithm

The main idea behind the RLS is to work with an alternative cost function defined as the WLS (weighted least-squares) function $\sum_{i=0}^{k} \lambda^{k-i} e_+^2[i]$, which is the sum of the squared a posteriori error subjected to a forgetting factor $0 << \lambda < 1$. For this cost function, the optimal weight vector at time $k+1$ is the solution of the deterministic normal equation:

$$\mathbf{\Phi}[k+1]\mathbf{w}[k+1] = \mathbf{\theta}[k+1], \tag{25}$$

where $\mathbf{\Phi}[k+1]$ is an $(N+1)\times(N-1)$ matrix and $\mathbf{\theta}[k+1]$ is an $(N+1)\times1$ vector defined as:

$$\mathbf{\Phi}[k+1] = \sum_{i=0}^{k+1} \lambda^{k+1-i} \mathbf{x}[i]\mathbf{x}^{\mathrm{T}}[i], \tag{26}$$

$$\mathbf{\theta}[k+1] = \sum_{i=0}^{k+1} \lambda^{k+1-i} \mathbf{x}[i]d[i], \tag{27}$$

respectively, such that:

$$\mathbf{\Phi}[k+1] = \lambda\mathbf{\Phi}[k] + \mathbf{x}[k+1]\mathbf{x}^{\mathrm{T}}[k+1], \tag{28}$$

$$\mathbf{\theta}[k+1] = \lambda\mathbf{\theta}[k] + \mathbf{x}[k+1]d[k+1]. \tag{29}$$

Assuming that $\mathbf{\Phi}[k+1]$ is nonsingular, its inverse $\mathbf{P}[k+1] = \mathbf{\Phi}^{-1}[k+1]$ can be determined, and by plugging recursion (29) into equation (25), one gets that:

$$\begin{aligned} \mathbf{w}[k+1] &= \mathbf{P}[k+1]\mathbf{\theta}[k+1] \\ &= \lambda\mathbf{P}[k+1]\mathbf{\theta}[k] + \mathbf{P}[k+1]\mathbf{x}[k+1]d[k+1]. \end{aligned} \tag{30}$$

Now, by applying the matrix recursion lemma, $\mathbf{P}[k+1]$ can be determined as:

$$\mathbf{P}[k+1] = \lambda^{-1}\mathbf{P}[k] - \frac{\lambda^{-2}\mathbf{P}[k]\mathbf{x}[k+1]\mathbf{x}^{\mathrm{T}}[k+1]\mathbf{P}[k]}{1+\lambda^{-1}\mathbf{x}^{\mathrm{T}}[k+1]\mathbf{P}[k]\mathbf{x}[k+1]}, \tag{31}$$

which, when used into the first term after the second equal sign in equation (30), yields the following updating procedure:

$$\mathbf{w}[k+1] = \mathbf{w}[k] + e[k+1]\mathbf{r}[k+1], \tag{32}$$

where the auxiliary vector $\mathbf{r}[k+1]$ is defined as:

$$\mathbf{r}[k+1] = \frac{\lambda^{-1}\mathbf{P}[k]\mathbf{x}[k+1]}{1+\lambda^{-1}\mathbf{x}^{\mathrm{T}}[k+1]\mathbf{P}[k]\mathbf{x}[k+1]}, \tag{33}$$

and the a priori error signal $e[k+1]$ is given by:

$$e[k+1] = d[k+1] - \mathbf{w}[k]^{\mathrm{T}}\mathbf{x}[k+1]. \tag{34}$$

RLS Algorithm

Initialize
$$\mathbf{P}[0] = \delta \mathbf{I}$$
$$\mathbf{w}[0] = \mathbf{0}$$

Do for $k \geq 0$:
$$\mathbf{r}[k+1] = \frac{\mathbf{P}[k]\mathbf{x}[k+1]}{\lambda^{-1} + \mathbf{x}^{\mathrm{T}}[k+1]\mathbf{P}[k]\mathbf{x}[k+1]}$$
$$e[k+1] = d[k+1] - \mathbf{w}^{\mathrm{T}}[k]\mathbf{x}[k+1]$$
$$\mathbf{w}[k+1] = \mathbf{w}[k] + e[k+1]\mathbf{r}[k+1]$$
$$\mathbf{P}[k+1] = \lambda^{-1}\mathbf{P}[k] - \lambda^{-1}\mathbf{r}[k+1]\mathbf{x}^{\mathrm{T}}[k+1]\mathbf{P}[k]$$

The previous procedure requires an initial estimate for $\mathbf{P}[k]$. Setting it to a null matrix would not correspond to an invertible $\mathbf{\Phi}[k]$. Therefore, the simplest initialization procedure is to make $\mathbf{P}[0]$ a multiple of the identity matrix. In addition, to avoid some numerical problems during the adaptation process, a convergence parameter μ can be included in equation (32).

The standard RLS algorithm is presented next.

One should notice that even though the RLS algorithm was devised to minimize the WLS of the a posteriori error $e_+[k]$, its updating equations can be put in terms of the a priori error $e[k]$.

RLS Convergence Characteristics

The convergence process associated to the RLS algorithm presents the following characteristics:

- The RLS produces an asymptotically unbiased estimate of the optimal coefficient vector. The weight-vector convergence to its optimal value is linear in time.

- The RLS convergence is about one order of magnitude faster than the one associated to the LMS algorithm. In practice, the RLS converges, in the mean-squared error sense, within $2(N+1)$ iterations, where N is the filter order.

- In a stationary environment, the RLS presents zero misadjustment when $\lambda = 1$. For $0 \ll \lambda < 1$, the RLS misadjustment is given by

$$M = \frac{1-\lambda}{1+\lambda}(N-1). \tag{35}$$

- As mentioned before, the parameter λ controls the memory length for the RLS algorithm. The longer the memory, the closer to 1 the parameter λ is, and, from equation (35), the smaller the misadjustment becomes. Hence, a longer memory is associated to a less noisy RLS convergence process, as would be expected.

- In non-stationary situations, it may seem at a first glance that the RLS outperforms the LMS algorithm, since the former has a faster convergence process. However, in practice, the algorithm performance is also determined by its steady-state behavior due to measurement and algorithm noise. When both the LMS and RLS algorithms are tuned to present the same steady-state performance, the LMS tends to present a superior tracking ability when compared to the RLS algorithm.

Other RLS-Type Algorithms

The RLS algorithm is mainly characterized by its fast convergence, which is achieved by an increase on the computational complexity of the corresponding implementation, especially when compared to the LMS algorithm. In fact, the standard RLS requires something in the order of N^2 multiplications, divisions, and additions. To reduce such computational burden, a few variations of the RLS algorithm were devised. Amongst such RLS-type algorithms, one can find, for instance, the fast RLS algorithms (also known collectively as fast transversal filter [FTF] algorithms) and the RLS lattice algorithms that can be implemented with or without error feedback (Diniz, 2002; Haykin, 2001).

In addition, a numerical analysis of the RLS algorithm shows that it can become unstable due to numerical errors in its implementation. To avoid such problem, systolic-array variations of the standard RLS and the lattice-based RLS were derived. These variations, due to their intrinsically modular structure, also allow efficient RLS implementations, ideal for online practical applications.

The main idea behind the RLS concept is to follow a Newton-like path during the optimization procedure. Alternative adaptation algorithms can be devised by following a similar approach. In particular, we can mention other quasi-Newton adaptive algorithms that are based on the Davidon-Fletcher-Power or Broyden-Fletcher-Goldfarb-Shannon forms of estimating the inverse of the Hessian matrix (Diniz, 2002; Haykin, 2001).

Other Adaptive Filter Structures

All adaptive algorithms seen so far in this chapter are associated to the standard direct-form FIR structure, also known as the tapped delay-line. This section covers some adaptation algorithms that, for one reason or another, relate to different digital filter structures.

Transform-Domain Adaptive Algorithms

The frequency domain was first employed in adaptive filtering in an attempt to increase the convergence speed of the LMS algorithm (Dentino, McCool, & Widrow, 1978). The original idea was to perform a fast Fourier transform (FFT) to the input signal, and add the frequency components, each one multiplied by a distinct filter weight $\mathbf{w}_i[k]$. The result is an output-signal estimate, which is compared to the reference signal to generate the error signal. This signal is then employed by an LMS-type adaptation algorithm to adjust the $\mathbf{w}_i[k]$ coefficients, as depicted in Figure 7.

The main idea is that the frequency domain whitens the input signal, thus decreasing the eigenvalue spread of its autocorrelation matrix. That, in consequence, leads to a faster convergence process for the associated adaptation algorithm. Possible transforms proposed in the literature include, for instance, the discrete cosine transform and the Hartley transform, both based solely on real operations (Marshall, Jenkins, & Murphy, 1989).

Ferrara (1980), presents an adaptive algorithm completely equivalent to the LMS but using the frequency domain, achieving reduced computational complexity for large values of N. The idea was to perform the input-signal convolution with the adaptive filter weights in the frequency domain with the aid of the FFT.

Sub-Band LMS Algorithm

Initialize
$\mathbf{w}[0] = \mathbf{0}$

Do for $k \geq 0$
$\mathbf{X}[k] = N\text{-point FFT}\{\mathbf{x}[k]\}$
$\mathbf{D}[k] = N\text{-point FFT}\{\mathbf{d}[k]\}$
$\mathbf{E}[k] = \mathbf{X}[k] - \mathbf{D}[k]$
$w_i[k+1] = w_i[k] + 2\mu_i E_i[k] X_i[k]$

Figure 7. Basic frequency-domain LMS algorithm

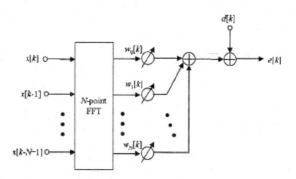

Sub-Band Adaptive Algorithms

The sub-band algorithms appear as a generalization of the transform-domain algorithms, seen in the previous subsection. In the sub-band scheme, the desired signal is also decomposed in several frequency bands, and individual convergence factors are employed to adjust each filter weight (Narayan, Peterson, & Narasimha, 1983). In this manner, this approach allows further increase in the overall convergence speed, at the expense of a more complicated algorithm specification. This scheme can also be modified to incorporate different input-signal transformations instead of the FFT.

The previous sub-band algorithm has an intrinsic delay, for accumulating the required N samples of the input and desired-output signals, before computing their respective FFTs. This can be avoided by implementing the orthogonal transformation with a filter bank, resulting in the scheme shown in Figure 8.

IIR Adaptive Algorithms

In general, adaptive algorithms associated to FIR structures are simple, well behaved, and present a fast convergence process. Unfortunately, FIR realizations tend to require a large number of coefficients to achieve good modeling of practical systems, increasing the algorithm computational cost in a prohibitive way. An alternative approach in such cases is to apply an adaptive IIR filter, which will tend to require much fewer coefficients to achieve a certain performance level (Johnson, 1984; Netto, Diniz, & Agathoklis, 1995; Regalia, 1994; Shynk, 1989).

The general input-output relationship of an Nth order adaptive IIR (infinite-duration impulse response) filter is given by:

$$y[k] = \frac{B[q^{-1},k]}{A[q^{-1},k]} x[k]$$
$$= \left[\frac{b_0[k] + b_1[k]q^{-1} + \cdots + b_N[k]q^{-N}}{1 + a_1[k]q^{-1} + \cdots + a_N[k]q^{-N}} \right] x[k], \qquad (36)$$

where q^{-1} represents the unit-delay operator defined by $q^{-1}x[k] = x[k-1]$. Equation (36) can be rewritten as:

$$y[k] = b_0[k]x[k] + b_1[k]x[k-1] + \cdots + b_N[k]x[k-N]$$
$$-a_1[k]y[k-1] - \cdots - a_N[k]y[k-N] \qquad , \qquad (37)$$

or equivalently:

$$y[k] = \boldsymbol{\theta}^T[k]\boldsymbol{\varphi}[k], \qquad (38)$$

Figure 8. Basic sub-band LMS algorithm

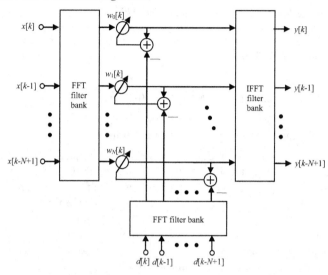

where $\boldsymbol{\theta}[k]$ and $\boldsymbol{\varphi}[k]$ are the so-called adaptive-filter coefficient and regression vectors, respectively defined as:

$$\boldsymbol{\theta}[k] = [b_0[k], b_1[k], \cdots, b_N[k]; a_1[k], \cdots, a_N[k]]^{\mathrm{T}}, \tag{39}$$

$$\boldsymbol{\varphi}[k] = [x[k], x[k-1], \cdots, x[k-N]; -y[k-1], \cdots, -y[k-N]]^{\mathrm{T}}. \tag{40}$$

In that context, some algorithms for adaptive IIR filters can be devised, as described in the following subsections.

The Equation-Error Algorithm

A simple adaptive IIR algorithm can be obtained by defining an auxiliary error signal, commonly referred to as the *equation error* (Johnson, 1984; Netto et al., 1995; Regalia, 1994; Shynk, 1989), by the relationship

$$d[k] = b_0[k]x[k] + \cdots + b_N[k]x[k-N]$$
$$-a_1[k]d[k-1] - \cdots - a_N[k]d[k-N] + e_{\mathrm{EE}}[k]. \tag{41}$$

In that framework, if one attempts to minimize the mean-squared equation error, following a steepest descent optimization scheme, one gets that

$$\boldsymbol{\theta}[k+1] = \boldsymbol{\theta}[k] - \mu' \nabla_{\boldsymbol{\theta}}[e_{EE}^2[k]]$$
$$= \boldsymbol{\theta}[k] - \mu e_{EE}[k] \nabla_{\boldsymbol{\theta}}[e_{EE}^2[k]] = \boldsymbol{\theta}[k] + \mu e_{EE}[k] \boldsymbol{\varphi}_{EE}[k], \qquad (42)$$

with $\mu = 2\mu'$ and $\boldsymbol{\varphi}_{EE}[k]$ given by:

$$\boldsymbol{\varphi}_{EE}[k] = [x[k], x[k-1], \cdots, x[k-N]; -d[k-1], \cdots, -d[k-N]]^{\mathrm{T}}. \qquad (43)$$

Equation (42) defines the so-called equation error algorithm.

From its definition, one can clearly notice that the mean-squared equation error is a quadratic function with respect to all adaptive filter coefficients, thus exhibiting a single optimal solution. This property yields a smooth convergence process for the equation-error algorithm. However, it does not necessarily minimize our standard objective function, which is the mean-squared value of the output-error signal. In fact, it can be shown that when the desired output signal contains any form of measurement or modeling noise, the optimal solution given by the equation-error algorithm is biased with respect to the optimal output-error solution. This prevents the spread use of this algorithm in case of practical applications where noise plays a major role.

The Output-Error Algorithm

The standard adaptive algorithm for direct-form IIR filters is the so-called *output-error* algorithm (Johnson, 1984; Netto et al., 1995; Regalia, 1994; Shynk, 1989), characterized by the updating equation:

Equation-Error IIR Algorithm

Initialize

$$\boldsymbol{\theta}[0] = \boldsymbol{0}$$

Do for $k \geq 0$

$$\boldsymbol{\varphi}_{EE}[k] = [x[k], x[k-1], \cdots, x[k-N]; -d[k-1], \cdots, -d[k-N]]^{\mathrm{T}}$$
$$\boldsymbol{\varphi}[k] = [x[k], x[k-1], \cdots, x[k-N]; -y[k-1], \cdots, -y[k-N]]^{\mathrm{T}}$$
$$y[k] = \boldsymbol{\theta}^{\mathrm{T}}[k] \boldsymbol{\varphi}[k]$$
$$e_{EE}[k] = y[k] - \boldsymbol{\theta}^{\mathrm{T}}[k] \boldsymbol{\varphi}_{EE}[k]$$
$$\boldsymbol{\theta}[k+1] = \boldsymbol{\theta}[k] + \mu e_{EE}[k] \boldsymbol{\varphi}_{EE}[k]$$

$$\mathbf{\theta}[k+1] = \mathbf{\theta}[k] + \mu e[k]\mathbf{\varphi}_{OE}[k], \tag{44}$$

where $e[k]$ is the standard a priori error and $\mathbf{\varphi}_{OE}[k]$ is the modified regressor vector defined as:

$$\mathbf{\varphi}_{OE}[k] = [x^f[k], x^f[k-1], \cdots, x^f[k-N]; y^f[k-1], \cdots, y^f[k-N]]^T, \tag{45}$$

where:

$$x^f[k-i] = \left[\frac{1}{A[q^{-1}, k-i]}\right] x[k-i], \text{ for } i = 0, 1, \ldots, N, \tag{46}$$

$$y^f[k-j] = \left[\frac{1}{A[q^{-1}, k-j]}\right] y[k-j], \text{ for } j = 1, \ldots, N, \tag{47}$$

are the small-step approximations for the derivatives of $e[k]$ with respect to the adaptive-filter coefficients b_i and a_j, respectively.

The output-error algorithm is a steepest-descent procedure for minimizing the mean squared error. In the case of IIR filters, this objective function is a non-quadratic function of the filter coefficients. Therefore, the minimization problem at hand is associated to a complicated performance surface, possibly presenting flat regions, which slow down the convergence

---

Output Error IIR Algorithm

Initialize

$\mathbf{\theta}[0] = \mathbf{0}$

Do for $k \geq 0$

$\mathbf{\varphi}[k] = [x[k], x[k-1], \cdots, x[k-N]; -y[k-1], \cdots, -y[k-N]]^T$

$y[k] = \mathbf{\theta}^T[k]\mathbf{\varphi}[k]$

$x^f[k] = \left[\dfrac{1}{A[q^{-1}, k]}\right] x[k]$

$y^f[k] = \left[\dfrac{1}{A[q^{-1}, k]}\right] y[k]$

$\mathbf{\varphi}_{OE}[k] = [x^f[k], x^f[k-1], \cdots, x^f[k-N]; y^f[k-1], \cdots, y^f[k-N]]^T$

$e[k] = d[k] - y[k]$

$\mathbf{\theta}[k+1] = \mathbf{\theta}[k] + \mu e[k]\mathbf{\varphi}_{OE}[k]$

---

process, and one or more local minima, which may guide the adaptive filter to sub-optimal solutions. The output-error algorithm is summarized in the following table.

Other Direct-Form Algorithms

There is a plethora of adaptive IIR algorithms that can be found in the literature (Johnson, 1984; Netto et al., 1995; Shynk, 1989). Such algorithms include, for instance, the Steiglitz-McBride algorithm, the modified output-error algorithm, the SHARF (simple hyperstable algorithm for recursive filters) algorithm, and the combination-error algorithms. In general, these routines present convergence properties that are a mixture of EE and OE characteristics: fast convergence, but not guaranteed to the optimal minimum, or global optimal solution, with possible local traps and slow convergence.

All algorithms named previously, including the presented EE and OE schemes, have a quasi-Newton variation, in addition to the steepest descent procedure seen previously. The extension to the quasi-Newton follows a similar scheme as for the FIR algorithms, where the respective regression vector plays the role of the FIR input vector. Naturally, quasi-Newton IIR algorithms tend to converge in a smaller number of iterations, at the cost of an increased number of operations in each iteration.

Alternative IIR Structures

In the previous subsections, we have described some algorithms for the direct-form adaptive IIR filter described in equation (36). Other realizations, however, can be used to describe the input-output relationship of the adaptive IIR filter. Some of these alternative structures include, for example, the parallel, the cascade, and the lattice, to name a few. Such variations introduce a new relationship of the error signal with respect to the adaptive filter coefficients, which will represent a new performance surface associated to the optimization problem at hand. Hence, alternative structures can be employed in an attempt to speed up the convergence process or to avoid local minima, by a proper morphing of the corresponding performance surface.

Another issue related to adaptive IIR filters is that the adaptive system may become unstable at a given iteration due to its stochastic behavior. This issue calls for a stability monitoring system that must be performed during the entire adaptation process. The direct form, however, is not suitable for this sort of procedure, as the determination of its poles is not straightforward. Hence, alternative structures may be used also to simplify the stability monitoring routine. The parallel and cascade IIR structures would seem the good choices, due to their organization in second-order subsystems; however, they tend to present slow convergence, due to the several equivalent minima obtained by a simple permutation of their poles. In this scenario, the IIR lattice structure represents a better alternative structure for allowing a simple stability monitoring without introducing multiple minima in the overall objective function.

Computer Simulations

In this section, we illustrate the convergence properties of some of the algorithms introduced in the previous sections, by using the system identification framework described in the subsection on Typical Applications.

Example 1: LMS Algorithm

Consider a system whose transfer function is given by $H(z)= 2-3z^{-1}$, and an input signal consisting of a zero-mean unit-variance white noise. This system can be identified by a first-order FIR adaptive filter, described by $\hat{H}(z,k) = a_0[k]+a_1[k]z^{-1}$, whose weights are adjusted by the LMS algorithm.

The resulting convergence process of the squared-error signal (in dB), when $\mu = 0.01$, is depicted in Figure 9, for several levels of measurement noise $v[k]$ in the reference (desired-output) signal. From this figure, one can notice that the additive noise variance defines the minimum value achieved by the squared-error signal.

Figure 10 illustrates the effect of the adaptation parameter μ on the LMS convergence process, when the measurement noise level was set to $\sigma_v^2 = -100\text{dB}$. From this figure, one easily concludes that a larger μ yields a faster convergence, at the cost of a higher misadjustment, as previously discussed in the section on LMS algorithms.

For a simpler visualization, the curves shown in Figures 9 and 10 represent the ensemble average of 30 and 200 experiments, respectively, using distinct input signals of similar statistics.

Example 2: LMS × RLS

As mentioned in the section on LMS algorithms, the LMS convergence behavior is highly dependent on the eigenvalue spread of the input autocorrelation matrix. To verify this assertion, consider the identification of the same system as in Example 1, but this time using a colored noise as input signal. For that purpose, assume that a zero-mean unitary-variance white noise is processed by an auxiliary filter $G(z)= 1+z^{-1}$ to form the input signal in the system identification setup. In this example, the measurement noise level was set to $\sigma_v^2 = -40\text{dB}$.

The resulting adaptive-filter coefficient trajectories are shown in Figures 11 and 12, for several initial conditions, using the LMS and RLS algorithms. For the LMS algorithm, we set $\mu = 0.01$, whereas for the RLS algorithm we used $\mu = 0.1$, $\gamma = 1$, and $\lambda = 0.95$. From Figure 11, one notices that the LMS coefficient trajectory is highly dependent on its initial position, which affects the algorithm's convergence speed. Meanwhile, Figure 12 clearly illustrates how the RLS algorithm follows a straight path to the optimum solution, regardless of the initial position of its coefficient vector, thus being able to achieve a steady-state solution in a smaller number of iterations than the LMS algorithm. Naturally, as stated in the section on the RLS algorithm, this faster convergence comes at a price of a larger number of arithmetic operations in each RLS iteration.

Figure 9. Example 1—LMS squared-error convergence. (1): $\sigma_v^2 = -50\text{dB}$; *(2)* $\sigma_v^2 = -100\text{dB}$; *(3)* $\sigma_v^2 = -200\text{dB}$; *(4)* $\sigma_v^2 = -\infty\text{dB}$: *In this case, the error level reaches machine precision.*

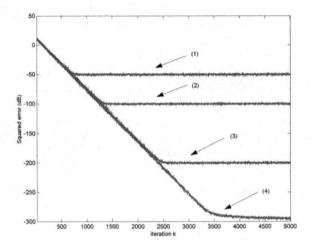

Figure 10. Example 1—LMS squared-error convergence when $\sigma_v^2 = -100\text{dB}$: *(1)* $\mu = 0.002$ *; (2)* $\mu = 0.3$. *Notice how a faster convergence corresponds to a higher level in the mean squared error after algorithm convergence.*

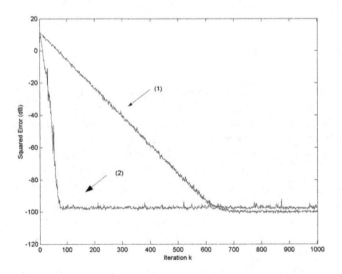

Example 3: Set-Membership

The set-membership technique is a powerful tool for reducing the overall computational complexity of any given adaptive algorithm. Its main idea is to avoid updating the coefficient vector if the error signal becomes too small, in its absolute value, at a given iteration. This simplification can decrease power consumption in mobile systems, greatly increasing the recharging period for its power-cell device.

In this example, the set-membership feature is incorporated to the LMS algorithm, in the same system identification setup employed in Example 1 with $\mu = 0.002$. The resulting squared-error signal, averaged over an ensemble of 30 experiments, for distinct values of the set-membership parameter γ is shown in Figure 13. From this figure, one may conclude that increasing the value of γ slightly increases the excess squared-error after convergence and greatly reduces the total number of filter adaptations, as indicated in Table 1.

Example 4: FIR x IIR

In this example, we attempt to compare the performances of FIR and IIR adaptive filters in the identification of the plant $H(z) = \dfrac{1}{1 - 0.6z^{-1}}$. Initially, an IIR adaptive filter $\hat{H}(z, k) = \dfrac{b_0[k]}{1 + a_1[k]z^{-1}}$ is used with the equation-error and the output-error algorithms presented in the subsection

Figure 11. Example 2—Coefficient trajectories for the adaptive filter for several initial conditions indicated by 'o.' LMS algorithm with $\mu = 0.01$.

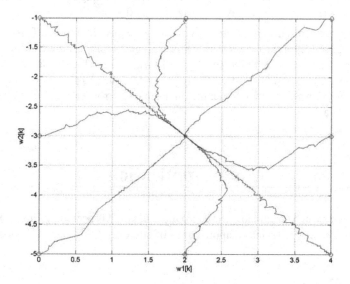

Figure 12. Example 2—Coefficient trajectories for the adaptive filter for several initial conditions indicated by 'o.' RLS algorithm with $\mu = 0.1$, $\gamma = 1$, *and* $\lambda = 0.95$.

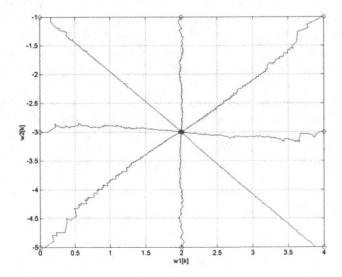

on IIR algorithms. Figures 14 and 15 show the coefficient evolution in time for these two algorithms with $\mu = 0.002$, and in the presence or not of additive measurement noise of level in the desired output signal. Figure 14 shows how the EE solution becomes biased, particularly the coefficient, in the presence of noise, whereas Figure 15 indicates that this noise does not affect the mean behavior of the OE coefficient solution.

The LMS performance in this example depends on the adaptive filter order. This relationship is shown in Figure 16, for the case where the measurement noise is absent, which indicates that the larger the filter order the lower the final mean value of the squared-error signal. Figure 16 also shows that a 60th order FIR would be necessary to perfectly match the first-order IIR plant. Above this order value, the final squared-error reached machine precision and becomes erratic.

Audio Applications

Adaptive systems can be found in several instances of audio processing. This section gives a brief discussion of some selected applications of interest.

Figure 13. Example 3—LMS squared-error convergence with $\sigma_v^2 = -40dB$, $\mu = 0.002$, *and set-membership feature: (1)* $\gamma = 0.3$; *(2)* $\gamma = 0.1$; *(3)* $\gamma = 0.001$.

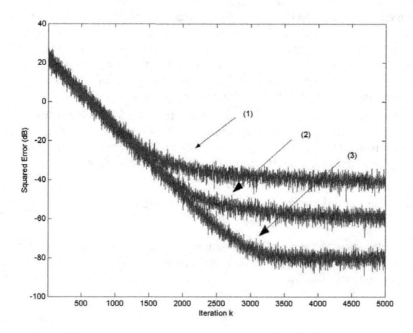

Table 1. Average number of adaptation iterations, out of a possible 5000, as a function of set-membership parameter γ *for the LMS algorithm in Example 3*

γ	Number of Iterations
$\gamma=0.3$	1033
$\gamma=0.1$	1563
$\gamma=0.05$	1944
$\gamma=0.02$	2516
$\gamma=0.01$	3315
$\gamma=0.001$	4801

HRTF Modeling

Head-Related Transfer Functions, or HRTFs, are key elements in binaural generation of three-dimensional sound. An HRTF describes a linear system that models the modifications suffered by a given sound along the path from the emitter source to each of the listener's ears, in an anechoic environment (see Figure 17). Typical measurements correspond to an FIR system with an impulse response (a Head-Related Impulse Response, or HRIR) of 128 samples at 44.1 kHz. (Gardner & Martin, 1994). Alternative IIR models of orders as low as 10 have been reported in the literature (Huopaniemi & Karjalainen, 1997).

An obvious identification scheme could be devised to obtain lower-order IIR models for measured FIR HRIRs. Special constraints can be added to the system to account for psychoacoustic issues. Of course this off-line procedure is simply an alternative to any other generic optimization tool, and it is mentioned here for this very reason.

Audio Restoration from Multiple Copies

A simple adaptation of the signal enhancement scheme presented in the subsection on Typical Applications can be useful in audio restoration whenever multiple noisy copies of a given recording are available.

Figure 14. Example 4—Coefficient trajectories for the adaptive IIR filter. EE algorithm: (1) without noise; (2) with noise; (3) without noise; (4) with noise.

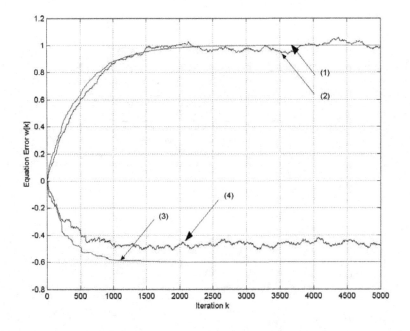

Figure 15. Example 4—Coefficient trajectories for the adaptive IIR filter. OE algorithm: (1) without noise; (2) with noise; (3) without noise; (4) with noise.

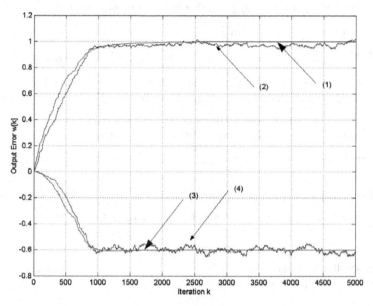

Figure 16. Example 4—Steady-state value of the squared error for the LMS algorithm with $\mu = 0.01$ as a function of the filter order.

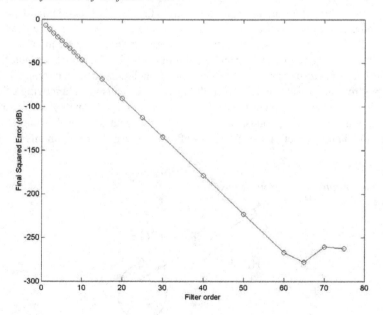

The model consists of two different copies of an ideal audio signal $s[n]$, respectively corrupted by additive noise signals $n_1[k]$ and $n_2[k]$. The processes $N_1[k]$ and $N_2[k]$ of which they are samples are assumed uncorrelated to each other and to $s[n]$, and zero-mean with variances $\sigma_{N_1}^2$ and $\sigma_{N_2}^2$, respectively. It is easy to show that when $\dfrac{1}{3} < \dfrac{\sigma_{N_1}^2}{\sigma_{N_2}^2} < 3$ the simple averaging $\dfrac{(s[k]+N_1[k])+(s[k]+N_2[k])}{2}$ yields a process with a higher signal-to-noise ratio than each preceding copy. This suggests that an adaptive structure (Vaseghi & Rayner, 1988), as shown in Figure 18, is capable of producing an enhanced version of $s[k]$.

One expects $y[k]$ is turned maximally correlated to $d[k]$. Ideally, $y[k] \rightarrow s[k-M]$. The delay of M samples compensates for the adaptive filter inherent delay.

Some practical considerations:

- The filter complexity can reach more than 1000 taps for this kind of application.

- The correlation between signal and noise degrades seriously the system performance.

- It has been assumed perfect synchronization between the two signal copies. In practice, if they are digitized signals independently acquired from analog sources, the adaptive system itself must provide synchronization in a time-variant basis.

Other Applications

Some of the most important applications of adaptive filtering to audio are *acoustic echo cancellation* systems (Breining, Dreiseitel, Hänsler, Mader, Nitsch, Puder, Schertler, Schmidt, & Tilp, 1999), which are usually associated to this simple situation: loudspeakers and microphones in a closed environment. Typical situations can be hands-free telephony or voice-over-IP. One can think, for example, of someone maintaining a conversation via cell phone while driving or in a teleconference through an office personal computer. The need for echo canceling results from the feedback path from loudspeaker to microphone: the signal coming from the remote side is transmitted back, thus causing an annoying echo or even instability. Modern voice systems extend to at least two audio channels. A stereo set-up, with two microphones and two loudspeakers, requires that four loudspeaker-microphone paths be cancelled out: left-left, left-right, right-left, and right-right. One can infer that the

Figure 17. Head-related transfer functions

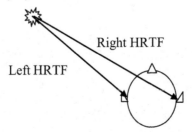

Right HRTF

Left HRTF

Figure 18. Adaptive noise suppressor

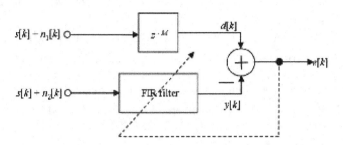

complexity grows accordingly. An interesting application derived from the stereophonic echo canceller is the generation of 3D sound through two loudspeakers (Garas, 2000): the desired binaural excitation can be driven to the ears from two common loudspeakers, provided the room response from the loudspeakers to the ears is compensated. The drawback of this system is to plug microphones into the users' ears.

Another important family of adaptive audio systems is intended to perform the so-called *active noise control* (Kuo & Morgan, 1999). In the usual situation, a given place is disturbed by some noise $n[k]$ generated by a source located elsewhere. The idea consists of placing a microphone near the noise source, picking up the primary noise $n_0[k]$; trying to model the path from the noise source to the place disturbed by its modified version; and generating its negative version $-n[k]$ acoustically in that place, through loudspeakers. The error signal must be captured by another microphone. This setup can be easily adapted to the case of headphones with room noise canceling.

Both acoustic echo cancellation and active noise control are detailed in other chapters of this book.

References

Breining, C., Dreiseitel, P., Hänsler, E., Mader, A., Nitsch, B., Puder, H., Schertler, T., Schmidt, G., & Tilp, J. (1999). Acoustic echo control: An application of very-high-order adaptive filters. *IEEE Signal Processing Magazine, 16*(4), 42-69.

Dentino, M., McCool, J. M., & Widrow, B. (1978). Adaptive filtering in the frequency domain. *Proceedings of IEEE, 66*(12), 1658-1659.

Diniz, P. S. R. (2002). *Adaptive filtering: Algorithms and practical implementations* (2nd ed.). Norwell, MA: Kluwer.

Diniz, P. S. R., da Silva, E. A. B., & Netto, S. L. (2002). *Digital signal processing—System analysis and design.* Cambridge, UK: Cambridge.

Ferrara, E. R. (1980). Fast implementation of LMS adaptive filters. *IEEE Transactions on Acoustics, Speech, and Signal Processing, 28*(4), 474-475.

Garas, J. (2000). *Adaptive sound systems.* Norwell, MA: Kluwer.

Gardner, W. G., & Martin, K. D. (1994). *HRTF measurements of a KEMAR dummy-head microphone* (Tech. Rep. No. 280). Cambridge, MA: MIT, Media Lab Perceptual Computing.

Haykin, S. (2001). *Adaptive filter theory* (4th ed.). Englewood Cliffs, NJ: Prentice-Hall.

Huopaniemi, J., & Karjalainen, M. (1997). Review of digital filter design and implementation methods for 3-D sound. In *Proceedings of the 102nd Convention of the Audio Engineering Society.* AES Preprint 4461. Munich, Germany.

Johnson, Jr., C. R. (1984). Adaptive IIR filtering: Current results and open issues. *IEEE Transactions on Information Theory, 30*(2), 237-250.

Kuo, S. M., & Morgan, D. R. (1999). Active noise control: A tutorial review. *Proceedings of the IEEE, 87*(6), 943-973.

Marshall, D. F., Jenkins, W. K., & Murphy, J. J. (1989). The use of orthogonal transforms for improving performance of adaptive filters. *IEEE Transactions on Circuits and Systems, 36*(4), 474-484.

Narayan, S. S., Peterson, A. M., & Narasimha, N. J. (1983). Transform-domain LMS algorithm. *IEEE Transactions on Acoustics, Speech, and Signal Processing, 31*(3), 609-615.

Netto, S. L., Diniz, P. S. R., & Agathoklis, P. (1995). Adaptive IIR filtering algorithms for system identification: A general framework. *IEEE Transactions on Education, 38*(1), 54-66.

Regalia, P. (1994). *Adaptive IIR filtering in signal processing and control.* New York: Marcel Dekker.

Shynk, J. J. (1989). Adaptive IIR filtering. *IEEE Acoustics, Speech, and Signal Processing Magazine, 6*(2), 4-21.

Vaseghi, S. V., & Rayner, P. J. W. (1988). A new application of adaptive filters for restoration of archived gramophone recordings. In *Proceedings of the International Conference on Acoustics, Speech and Signal Processing* (vol. 5) (pp. 2548-2551). New York: IEEE.

Werner, S., & Diniz, P. S. R. (2001). Set-membership affine projection algorithm. *IEEE Signal Processing Letters, 8*(8), 231-235.

Widrow, B., & Stearns, S. D. (1985). *Adaptive signal processing.* Englewood Cliffs, NJ: Prentice-Hall.

Chapter VIII

Adaptive Digital Filtering and Its Algorithms for Acoustic Echo Canceling

Mohammad Reza Asharif, University of the Ryukyus, Japan

Rui Chen, University of the Ryukyus, Japan

Abstract

In this chapter, we shall study adaptive digital filtering (ADF) and its application to acoustic echo canceling (AEC). At first, Wiener filtering and algorithms such as LMS in the time domain for ADF are explained. Then, to decrease the computational complexity, the frequency domain algorithms such as FDAF and FBAF will be studied. To challenge the double-talk problem in AEC, we will also introduce various algorithms by processing the correlation function of the signal. The proposed algorithms here are CLMS, ECLMS, and using frequency domain is FECLMS, and using wavelet transform is WECLMS. Each of these algorithms has its own merits, and they will be evaluated. At the end of this chapter a new system for room-acoustic partitioning is proposed. This new system is called smart acoustic room (SAR). The SAR will also be used in AEC with double-talk condition. The authors wish to gather all aspects in studying ADF and their use in AEC by going very deep into theoretical details as well as considering more practical and feasible applications considering real-time implementation.

Introduction to Adaptive Digital Filter and Its Various Structures

In analog devices usually we use analog filters, which are contained of resistances, capacitances, inductances, and so on. We use filter in signal analysis to extract a certain portion of the frequency spectrum, for instance LPF, HPF, or BPF. BSFs are very common in electronics & communications circuits. But, once we design these filters and make the hardware, it would be quite impossible to renew or change it unless we replace some parts by a new one. In *digital filters*, we do not need a specific electric device such as RLC; instead we just use the computations such as additions and multiplications on extracted samples of the digital signal. So, at first we need an A/D converter to go to the digital world. Then, there we just have numbers or stream of samples corresponding to the signal, which contains information. So, another thing that we need in digital filter is a delay line. In Figure 1 a simple structure of FIR (Finite Impulse Response) digital filter is shown. The input-output relation for this digital filter is as follows:

$$y(n) = \sum_{i=1}^{N-1} h(i)x(n-i), \tag{1}$$

where $y(n)$ and $x(n)$ are output and input of the filter and $h(i)$'s are called tap *coefficients*. Now imagine that we want to change the frequency response of this filter to another. Here, by just changing the values of the tap coefficient $h(i)$, we could achieve this goal. That is, we can change the characteristic of the *digital filter* just by values changing, not by device changing. And, of course, this could be done both in software or hardware easily (in hardware you can use a dip-switch to change the values in binary code for example). This capability of digital filters makes them quite promising for another job, which is not only

Figure 1. FIR digital filter structure

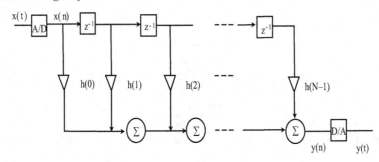

its versatility in digital form and to be flexible with our desire characteristics, but also it is promising for "adaptation." Adaptation means to make the system change its performance according to a desired environment. Therefore, here we define the *adaptive digital filter* as a *digital filter* with variable tap *coefficients*. This possibility to change the *coefficients* is not at random, but rather it should be according to some rule. We call the rule "algorithm." The desired *algorithm* is the one that could guide the filter to a specific and desired response. This changing rule for tap adaptation could be done in two ways: (1) by solution of some equation to find the best values (for instance by minimization of mean squared-error [MSE]), and (2) by gradually changing coefficients in a direction that the filter can approach to a desired performance. In latter case, we should have an algorithm to guarantee the convergence of the filter. Here, we call this gradual changing "iterations." Iteration could be done based on sample, that is, renewing the tap coefficients at each sample or at a bulk of samples or a frame (in speech processing a sample is 0.125 ms and a frame is 8 ms for 8kHz sampling frequency). Another structure for adaptive digital filter is Infinite Impulse Response (IIR). Basically the two structures FIR and IIR are used in vast applications, but also we have other structures such as lattice. This structure is usually used in Linear Prediction Coding (LPC) of *speech signal* (Rabiner & Schafer, 1978).

In later sections of this chapter we will discuss utilization of the adaptive digital filter in the *echo canceling*. First, we introduce the phenomenon that causes echo in telecommunication and audio system. Then we explain Wiener solution. The various algorithms such as LMS, FDAF, and FBAF are the subjects of the following sections. One important problem in echo cancellation is the Double-Talk problem, which will be addressed in the last part of this chapter. Various algorithms here also will be discussed such as CLMS, ECLMS, FECLMS, and WECLMS. The ending part of this chapter is introducing Smart Acoustic Room (SAR), which will be used in a new type of echo canceling.

Phenomenon in Producing Echo in Telecommunications and Audio Systems

An echo is the repetition of a sound caused by the reflection of sound waves. In a telecommunications network, echoes are problematic if the speaker hears a delayed version of his utterance. The telecommunications industry has sought means to control echo since the late 1950s. In a telephone network that involves both four-wire and two-wire links, echoes arise due to insufficient return signal suppression in the so-called hybrid that connects the four- to a two-wire link. It becomes more annoying as the signal path delay increases. When satellite links were introduced in the telephone network in the 1960s, communication delays increased, and the resulting echoes became so serious that the problem had to be re-examined. The human ear is extremely sensitive to echo, perceiving it even when round trip delay is as short as 10 milliseconds. However, not all echoes reduce voice quality. In order for phone conversations to sound natural, callers must be able to hear themselves speaking. For this reason, a short instantaneous echo called "side tone" is deliberately inserted, coupling the caller's speech from the telephone mouthpiece to the earpiece so that the line sounds connected. However, longer round trip delays (exceeding 30 ms) become annoying. Such an echo is typically heard as a hollow sound, "like talking into a well." Almost all callers find echoes annoying if round trip delay exceeds 50 ms. Echoes must also be loud enough to be heard. Those less than -40 decibels (dB) are unlikely to be noticed. However, above these levels (30 ms and -40 dB), echoes become steadily more disruptive with longer round trip delays and louder sounds.

Hybrid Echo

The four-wire trunk circuits were converted to two-wire local cabling, using a device called a "hybrid" (see Figure 2) (http://www.iec.org/online/tutorials/echo_cancel/topic02.html).

Unfortunately, the hybrid is by nature a leaky device. As voice signals pass from the four-wire to the two-wire portion of the network, the energy in the four-wire section is reflected back on itself, creating the echoed speech. Provided that the total round-trip delay occurs within just a few milliseconds (i.e., within 10 ms), it generates a sense that the call is live by adding side tone, which makes a positive contribution to the quality of the call.

In cases where the total network delay exceeds 25 ms, however, the positive benefits disappear, and intrusive echo results. The actual amount of signal that is reflected back depends on how well the balance circuit of the hybrid matches the two-wire line. In the vast majority of cases, the match is poor, resulting in a considerable level of signal reflecting back. This is measured as echo return loss (ERL). The higher the ERL, the lower the reflected signal back to the talker, and vice versa.

Acoustic Echo

Acoustic echo is generated with analog and digital handsets, with the degree of echo related to the type and quality of equipment used. This form of echo is produced by acoustic cou-

Figure 2. Hybrid echo in PSTN

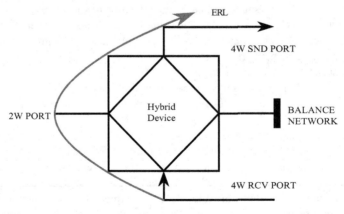

ERL is the echo return loss

Figure 3. Acoustic echo in the hand-free telephone system

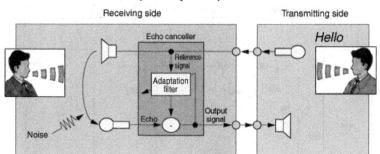

pling between the loudspeaker and microphone in hands-free devices. Acoustic echo was first encountered with the early video/audio conferencing studios and as Figure 3 shows now also occurs in typical mobile situations, such as when people are taking a call using the hands-free telephone. In this situation, sound from a loudspeaker is heard by a listener, as intended. However, this same sound also is picked up by the microphone, both directly and indirectly, after bouncing off the roof, windows, and seats of the room. The result of this reflection is the creation of multi path echo and multiple harmonics of echo, which, unless eliminated, are transmitted back to the distant end and are heard by the talker as echo.

The Wiener Solution and Its Convergence in Finding Echo Path

A signal, which is transmitted from the sender to the receiver, is often impaired by various forms of distortions. Wiener filtering is a method to recover the original signal as close as possible from the received signal. The Wiener filter is a filter proposed by Norbert Wiener during the 1940s and published in 1949 (Wiener, 1949). The theory for Wiener filter is formulated for the general case of time series with the filter specified in terms of its impulse response. Solutions to the Wiener-Hopf equations are then given for the case of filtering, smoothing, prediction, noise cancellation, and echo canceling.

In Figure 4 the block diagram of the Wiener solution in finding echo path is shown. The input of the filter is $x(0), x(1), x(2), ...,$ and the *acoustic impulse response* of near-end room is $r_0, r_1, r_2, ...,$ $\tilde{w}_0, \tilde{w}_1, \tilde{w}_2, ...$ denotes the M-by-1 optimum tap-weight vector of the transversal filter. At some discrete time n, the filter produces an output denoted by $y(n)$. The output is used to provide an estimate of a desired response denoted by $d(n)$. In particular, the estimation error, denote by $e(n)$, is defined as the difference between the desired response $d(n)$ and the filter output $y(n)$. The requirement is to make the estimated error $e(n)$"as small as possible" in some statistical sense.

Figure 4. Block diagram of the Wiener solution in finding echo path

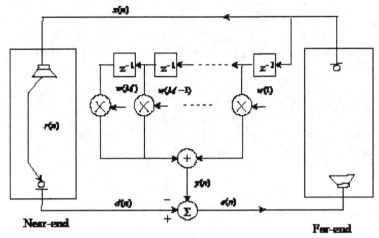

Principle of Orthogonality and Minimum Mean-Squared Error

Consider again the statistical filtering problem described in Figure 4. The filter output $y(n)$ at the discrete time n is defined by the linear convolution sum:

$$y(n) = \sum_{k=0}^{M} \tilde{w}_k x(n-k), \qquad n = 0, 1, 2, \ldots \tag{2}$$

The purpose of the filter in Figure 4 is to produce an estimate of the desired response $d(n)$. We assumed that the filter input and the desired response are both with zero mean. Accordingly, the estimation of $d(n)$ is accompanied by an error, defined by the difference:

$$e(n) = d(n) - y(n) \tag{3}$$

The estimation error $e(n)$ is the sample value of a random variable. To optimize the filter design, we choose to minimize the mean-square value of the estimation error $e(n)$. We may thus define the cost function as the mean-squared error:

$$J = E[|e(n)|^2], \tag{4}$$

where E denotes the statistical expectation operator. The problem is therefore to determine the operating condition for which J attains its minimum value. For the cost function J to attain its minimum value, all the elements of the gradient vector ∇J must be simultaneously equal to zero, as shown by:

$$\nabla_k J = 0 \qquad K = 0, 1, 2, ... \tag{5}$$

Under this set of conditions, the filter is said to be optimum in the mean-squared-error sense. According to equation (4), the cost function J is a scalar independent of time n. Hence, we get:

$$\nabla_k J = E\left[\frac{\partial e(n)}{\partial w_k} e(n)\right]. \tag{6}$$

We finally get the result:

$$\nabla_k J = -2E\{x(n-k)e(n)\}. \tag{7}$$

We are now ready to specify the operating conditions required for minimizing the cost function J. Let e_0 denote the special value of the estimation error that results when the filter operates in its optimum condition. We then find that the conditions specified in equation (5) are indeed equivalent to:

$$E\{x(n-k)e_o(n)\} = 0 \qquad k = 0, 1, 2, ... \tag{8}$$

In word, equation (8) stated the following:

The necessary and sufficient condition for the cost function J to attain its minimum value is that the corresponding value of the estimation error $e_0(n)$ is orthogonal to each input sample that enters into the estimation of the desired response at time n.

When the linear discrete-time filter in Figure 4 operates in its optimum condition, equation (3) takes on the following special form:

$$e_0(n) = d(n) - y_0(n)$$
$$= d(n) - \tilde{d}(n), \tag{9}$$

where $\tilde{d}(n)$ denotes the estimate of the desired response that is optimized in the mean-squared-error sense. Let the J_{min} denote the minimum mean-squared error, defined by

$$J_{min} = E[|e_0(n)|^2]. \tag{10}$$

Hence, we can get:

$$J_{min} = \sigma_d^2 - \sigma_{\tilde{d}}^2,$$ (11)

where σ_d^2 is the variance of the desired response, and $\sigma_{\tilde{d}}^2$ is the variance of the estimate $\tilde{d}(n)$; both of these random variables are assumed to be of zero mean.

This relation shows that for the optimum filter, the minimum mean-squared error equals the difference between the variance of the desired response and the variance of the estimate that the filter produces at its output.

It is convenient to normalize the expression in equation (11) in such a way that the minimum value of the mean-squared error always lies between zero and one. We may do this by dividing both sides of equation (11) by σ_d^2, obtaining:

$$\varepsilon = \frac{J_{min}}{\sigma_d^2} = 1 - \frac{\sigma_{\tilde{d}}^2}{\sigma_d^2},$$ (12)

where the quantity ε is called the normalized mean-squared error. We note that (1) the ratio ε can never be negative, and (2) the ratio $\sigma_{\tilde{d}}^2 / \sigma_d^2$ is always positive. We therefore have:

$$0 \le \varepsilon \le 1.$$ (13)

If ε is zero, the optimum filter operates perfectly in the sense that there is complete agreement between the estimate $\tilde{d}(n)$ at the filter output and the desired response $d(n)$. On the other hand, if ε is unity, there is no agreement whatsoever between these two quantities; this corresponds to the worst possible situation.

On the other hand, we can write the minimum mean-squared error J_{min} by using the Wiener-Hopf equation (Wiener & Hopf, 1931). The Wiener-Hopf equation can be defined as follows:

$$\sum_{i=0}^{\infty} w_{o\,i} r_{xx}(k-i) = r_{dx}(k) \qquad k = 0, 1, 2, \ldots$$ (14)

$$E[x(n-i)x^*(n-k)] = r_{xx}(k-i)$$

$$E[d(n)x^*(n-k)] = r_{dx}(k),$$

where $r_{xx}(k-i)$ is the autocorrelation function of the filter input $x(n-k)$ for a lag of $k-i$. $r_{dx}(k)$ is the cross-correlation function between the filter input $x(n-k)$ and the desired response $d(n)$ for a lag of k. $w_{o\,i}$ is the ith coefficient in the impulse response of the optimum filter. The system of equation (14) defines the optimum filter coefficients, in the most general setting, in terms of two correlation functions: the autocorrelation function of the filter input, and the cross-correlation function between the filter input and the desired response. In the Matrix form, using the fact that the autocorrelation sequence is conjugate symmetric, $r_{xx}(k) = r_{xx}^*(-k)$, equation (14) becomes:

$$
\begin{bmatrix}
r_{xx}(0) & r_{xx}(1) & \cdots & r_{xx}(M-1) \\
r_{xx}^*(1) & r_{xx}(0) & \cdots & r_{xx}(M-2) \\
\vdots & \vdots & \ddots & \vdots \\
r_{xx}^*(M-1) & r_{xx}^*(M-2) & \cdots & r_{xx}(0)
\end{bmatrix}
\begin{bmatrix}
w_{o\,0} \\
w_{o\,1} \\
\vdots \\
w_{o\,M-1}
\end{bmatrix}
=
\begin{bmatrix}
r_{dx}(0) \\
r_{dx}(1) \\
\vdots \\
r_{dx}(M-1)
\end{bmatrix},
\tag{15}
$$

which is the matrix form of the Wiener- Hopf equation. Equation (15) may be written more concisely as:

$$
\mathbf{R}_{xx}\mathbf{w}_o = \mathbf{R}_{dx} \Rightarrow \mathbf{w}_o = \mathbf{R}_{xx}^{-1}\mathbf{R}_{dx}
$$
$$
\mathbf{R}_{dx} = [r_{dx}(0), r_{dx}(1), \ldots r_{dx}(M-1)]^T,
\tag{16}
$$

where $\mathbf{R}_{xx}$ is a $M \times M$ Hermitian Toeplitz matrix of autocorrelation. $\mathbf{w}_o$ denotes the M-by-1 optimum tap-weight vector of the transversal filter. That is:

$$
\mathbf{w}_0 = [w_{o\,0}, w_{o\,1}, \ldots w_{o\,M-1}]^T.
$$

The minimum mean-square error in the estimate of $d(n)$ may be evaluated from equation (4) as follows:

$$
J = E[e(n)e^*(n)] = E\{[d(n) - \sum_{k=0}^{M-1} w_k^* x(n-k)]^2\}.
\tag{17}
$$

By using the definition for the correlation matrix $\mathbf{R}_{xx}$ and the cross-correlation vector $\mathbf{R}_{dx}$, we may rewrite equation (17) in matrix form, as follows:

$$
J(\mathbf{w}) = \sigma_d^2 - \mathbf{w}^H \mathbf{R}_{dx} - \mathbf{R}_{dx}^H \mathbf{w} + \mathbf{w}^H \mathbf{R}_{xx}\mathbf{w},
\tag{18}
$$

where the mean-squared error is written as $J(\mathbf{w})$ to emphasize its dependence on the tap-weight vector $\mathbf{w}$. Because of the correlation matrix, $\mathbf{R}_{xx}$ is almost always positive definite, so that the inverse matrix $\mathbf{R}_{xx}^{-1}$ exists. Accordingly, expressing $J(\mathbf{w})$ as a "perfect square" in $\mathbf{w}$, we may rewrite equation (18) in the form:

$$
J(\mathbf{w}) = \sigma_d^2 - \mathbf{R}_{dx}^H \mathbf{R}_{xx}^{-1}\mathbf{R}_{dx} + (\mathbf{w} - \mathbf{R}_{xx}^{-1}\mathbf{R}_{dx})^H \mathbf{R}_{xx}(\mathbf{w} - \mathbf{R}_{xx}^{-1}\mathbf{R}_{dx}).
\tag{19}
$$

From this equation, we now immediately see that if the $\mathbf{w}$ is the solution to the Wiener-Hopf equations, then the minimum mean-square error may be written as:

$$
J_{\min} = \sigma_d^2 - \mathbf{R}_{dx}^H \mathbf{R}_{xx}^{-1}\mathbf{R}_{dx}
\tag{20}
$$

since:

$$\mathbf{w}_o = \mathbf{R}_{xx}^{-1}\mathbf{R}_{dx}. \tag{21}$$

The main result here is that the Wiener-Hopf equations specified the coefficients of the optimum (minimum MSE) filter.

Various Algorithms for Adaptive Digital Filters

Least Mean Square (LMS) Algorithm

The *LMS* (least-mean square) *algorithm* is an approximation of the steepest descent algorithm, which uses an instantaneous estimate of the gradient vector of the cost function. The estimate of the gradient is based on sample values of the tap-input vector and the error signal. The algorithm iterates over each coefficient in the filter, moving it in the direction of the approximated gradient (Haykin, 1996).

For the LMS algorithm it is necessary to have a reference signal $d(n)$ representing the desired filter output. The difference between the reference signal and the actual output of the transversal filter is the error signal:

$$e(n) = d(n) - \mathbf{w}^T(n)\mathbf{x}(n)$$

where:

$$\mathbf{w}(n) = [w_0(n), w_1(n)\ldots w_{M-1}(n)]^T$$
$$\mathbf{x}(n) = [x(n), x(n-1),\ldots x(n-M+1)]^T. \tag{22}$$

$w(n)$ is the tap-coefficients of the filter, and $\mathbf{x}(n)$ is the tap-input vector of the filter. A schematic of the learning setup is depicted in Figure 5. The task of the LMS algorithm is to find a set of filter coefficients $w(n)$ that minimize the expected value of the quadratic error signal, that is, to achieve the least *mean squared error*. The squared error and its expected value are

$$e^2(n) = d^2(n) - 2d(n)\mathbf{w}^T(n)\mathbf{x}(n) + \mathbf{w}^T(n)\mathbf{x}(n)\mathbf{x}^T(n)\mathbf{w}(n), \tag{23}$$

$$E[e^2(n)] = E[d^2(n)] - 2\mathbf{w}^T(n)E[d(n)\mathbf{x}^T(n)] + \mathbf{w}^T E[\mathbf{x}(n)\mathbf{x}^T(n)]\mathbf{w}(n). \tag{24}$$

Note that the squared error e^2 is a quadratic function of the coefficient vector $\mathbf{w}(n)$, and thus has only one (global) minimum (and no other [local] minima), that theoretically could be found if the correct expected values in equation (24) were known. The gradient descent approach demands that the position on the error surface according to the current *coefficients* should be moved into the direction of the "steepest descent," that is, in the direction of the negative gradient of the cost function $J = E[e^2(n)]$ with respect to the coefficient vector.

$$-\nabla_w J = 2E[d(n)\mathbf{x}^T(n)] - 2E[\mathbf{x}(n)\mathbf{x}^T(n)]\mathbf{w}(n) \tag{25}$$

In the LMS algorithm, however, a very short-term estimate is used by only taking into account the current samples $E[d(n)\mathbf{x}^T(n)] \approx d(n)\mathbf{x}^T(n)$ and $E[\mathbf{x}(n)\mathbf{x}^T(n)] \approx \mathbf{x}(n)\mathbf{x}^T(n)$ leading to an updated equation for the filter coefficients:

$$\begin{aligned}\mathbf{w}(n+1) &= \mathbf{w}(n) + \mu[-\nabla_w J(e(n))]\\ &= \mathbf{w}(n) + \mu\mathbf{x}(n)e(n)\end{aligned} \tag{26}$$

Here, we introduced the "step-size" parameter μ, which controls the distance we move along the error surface. In the LMS algorithm the update of the coefficients, equation (26), is performed at every time instant n:

$$\mathbf{w}(n+1) = \mathbf{w}(n) + \mu\mathbf{x}(n)e(n). \tag{27}$$

The "step-size" parameter μ introduced in equations (26) and (27) controls how far we move along the error function surface at each update step. In the standard form of LMS algorithm, the correction $\mu\mathbf{x}(n)e(n)$ applied to the tap weight vector $\mathbf{w}(n)$ at the iteration $n+1$ is directly proportional to the tap-input vector $\mathbf{x}(n)$. Therefore, when $\mathbf{x}(n)$ is large, the LMS algorithm experiences a gradient noise amplification problem. To overcome this difficulty, we may use the normalized LMS algorithm, which is the companion to the ordinary LMS algorithm. In particular, the correction applied to the tap weight vector $\mathbf{w}(n)$ at iteration $n+1$ is "normalized" with respect to the squared Euclidean norm of the tap-input vector $\mathbf{x}(n)$ at iteration n, hence the term "normalized."

Figure 5. Adaptive transversal filter

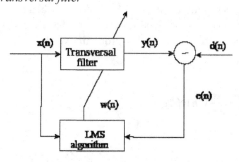

We may formulate the normalized LMS (NLMS) algorithm as a natural modification of the ordinary LMS algorithm. The formulation can be written as follows:

$$\mathbf{w}(n+1) = \mathbf{w}(n) + \frac{\widetilde{\mu}}{\|\mathbf{x}(n)\|^2}\mathbf{x}(n)e(n). \tag{28}$$

This is the desired recursion for computing the M-by-1 vector in the normalized LMS algorithm. The important point to note from the analysis presented previously is that given new input data (at time n) represented by the tap-input vector $\mathbf{x}(n)$ and desired response $d(n)$, the normalized LMS algorithm updates the tap-weight vector in such a way that the value $\mathbf{w}(n+1)$ computed at time $n+1$ exhibits the minimum change of input (in a Euclidean norm sense) with respect to the known value $\mathbf{w}(n)$ at time n; for example, no change may represent minimum change. Hence, the normalized LMS algorithm (and for that matter the conventional LMS algorithm) is a manifestation of the principle of minimal disturbance (Widrow & Lehr, 1990). The principle of minimal disturbance states that, in the light of new input data, the parameters of an adaptive system should only disturbed in a minimal fashion. Moreover, comparing of the recursion of equation (28) for the normalized LMS algorithm with that of equation (26) for the conventional LMS algorithm, we may make the following observations: the adaptation constant $\widetilde{\mu}$ for the normalized LMS algorithm is dimensionless, whereas the adaptation constant μ for the LMS algorithm has the dimensions of inverse power. Setting:

$$\mu(n) = \frac{\widetilde{\mu}}{\|\mathbf{x}(n)\|^2}, \tag{29}$$

we may view the normalized LMS algorithm as an LMS algorithm with a time-varying step-size parameter. The normalized LMS algorithm is convergent in the mean square if the adaptation constant $\widetilde{\mu}$ satisfies the following condition (Weiss & Mitra, 1979):

$$0 < \widetilde{\mu} < 2. \tag{30}$$

Most importantly, the normalized LMS algorithm exhibits a rate of convergence that is potentially faster than that of the standard LMS algorithm for both uncorrelated and correlated input data (Nagumo & Noda, 1967). Another point of interest is that in overcoming the gradient noise amplification problem associated with the LMS algorithm, the normalized LMS algorithm introduces a problem of its own. Specifically, when the tap-input vector $\mathbf{x}(n)$ is small, numerical difficulties may arise because then we have to divide by a small value for the squared norm $\|\mathbf{x}(n)\|^2$. To overcome this problem, we slightly modify the recursion of equation (28) as follows:

$$\mathbf{w}(n+1) = \mathbf{w}(n) + \frac{\widetilde{\mu}}{\alpha + \|\mathbf{x}(n)\|^2}\mathbf{x}(n)e(n), \tag{31}$$

where $\alpha > 0$, and as before $0 \leq \tilde{\mu} \leq 2$. For $\alpha = 0$, equation (31) reduces to the previous form given in equation (28).

Convergence of the LMS Algorithm and Gradient Noise Effect

In this section we present a stability analysis of the LMS algorithm that is largely based on the mean-squared value of the estimation error $e(n)$. For this analysis, we find it to be convenient to work with the weight-error vector rather than the tap-weight vector itself. The weight-error vector in the LMS algorithm may be denoted as

$$\varepsilon(n) = \mathbf{w}(n) - \mathbf{w}_o, \tag{32}$$

where, $\mathbf{w}_o$ denotes the optimum Wiener solution for the tap-weight vector, and $\mathbf{w}(n)$ is the estimate produced by the LMS algorithm at iteration n. Subtracting the optimum tap-weight vector $\mathbf{w}_o$ from both sides of equation (26), and using the definition of equation (32) to eliminate $\mathbf{w}(n)$ from the correction term on the right-hand side of equation (26), we may rewrite the LMS algorithm in the terms of the weight-error vector $\varepsilon(n)$ as follows:

$$\varepsilon(n+1) = [\mathbf{I} - \mu\mathbf{x}(n)\mathbf{x}^H(n)]\varepsilon(n) + \mu\mathbf{x}(n)e_o^*(n), \tag{33}$$

where $\mathbf{I}$ is the identity matrix, and $e_o(n)$ is the estimation error produced in the optimum Wiener solution:

$$e_o(n) = d(n) - \mathbf{w}_o^H \mathbf{x}(n). \tag{34}$$

Equation (33) is a stochastic equation in terms of the weight-error vector $\varepsilon(n)$ with the following characteristic feature: A system matrix equal to $[\mathbf{I} - \mu\mathbf{x}(n)\mathbf{x}^H(n)]$, which is approximately equal to the identity matrix $\mathbf{I}$ for all n, provided that the step-size parameter μ is sufficiently small. To study the convergence behavior of such a stochastic algorithm in an average sense, we may invoke the direct-averaging method described by Kushner (1984). According to this method, the solution of the stochastic difference equation (33), operating under the assumption of a small step-size parameter μ, is close to the solution of another stochastic difference equation whose system matrix is equal to the ensemble average:

$$E[\mathbf{I} - \mu\mathbf{x}(n)\mathbf{x}^H(n)] = \mathbf{I} - \mu\mathbf{R}, \tag{35}$$

where $\mathbf{R}$ is the correlation matrix of the tap-input vector $\mathbf{x}(n)$.

$$\mathbf{R} = E[\mathbf{x}^H(n)\mathbf{x}(n)]$$

More specifically, we may replace the stochastic difference equation (33) with another stochastic difference equation described by:

$$\boldsymbol{\varepsilon}(n+1) = (\mathbf{I} - \mu\mathbf{R})\boldsymbol{\varepsilon}(n) + \mu\mathbf{x}(n)e_o^*(n). \tag{36}$$

Taking the expected value of equation (36) gives:

$$E[\boldsymbol{\varepsilon}(n+1)] = (\mathbf{I} - \mu\mathbf{R})E[\boldsymbol{\varepsilon}(n)], \tag{37}$$

since $e_o(n)$ and $\mathbf{x}(n)$ are uncorrelated. By choosing μ to be sufficiently small, it is always possible to make the matrix $(\mathbf{I} - \mu\mathbf{R})$ stable, guaranteeing that the error will go asymptotically to zero. To see more clearly the convergence behavior of the error vector, we transform equation (37) into a set of N decoupled scalar equation. To do this we first note that the correlation matrix $\mathbf{R}$, being symmetric and positive definitive, can be decomposed as:

$$\mathbf{R} = \mathbf{U}\mathbf{D}\mathbf{U}^T, \tag{38}$$

where $\mathbf{U}$ is an orthonormal matrix $(\mathbf{U}^T\mathbf{U} = \mathbf{U}\mathbf{U}^T = \mathbf{I})$ and $\mathbf{D}$ is a diagonal matrix containing the eigenvalues of $\mathbf{R}$.

$$\mathbf{D} = diag\{\lambda_1 \cdots \lambda_M\}. \tag{39}$$

Inserting equations (38) and (37) and multiplying by $\mathbf{U}^T$, we get:

$$\mathbf{U}^T E[\boldsymbol{\varepsilon}(n+1)] = (\mathbf{I} - \mu\mathbf{D})\{\mathbf{U}^T E[\boldsymbol{\varepsilon}(n)]\}. \tag{40}$$

Denoting the transformed error vector by:

$$\mathbf{G}(n) = \begin{bmatrix} g_1(n) \\ \vdots \\ g_M(n) \end{bmatrix} = \mathbf{U}^T E[\boldsymbol{\varepsilon}(n)], \tag{41}$$

we get,

$$g_i(n+1) = (1 - \mu\lambda_i)g_i(n). \tag{42}$$

For convergence, it is necessary to have $|1 - \mu\lambda_i| < 1$, for all the eigenvalues λ_i. This condition will be certainly satisfied if

$$0 < \mu < \frac{2}{\lambda_{MAX}}, \tag{43}$$

where λ_{MAX} is the largest eigenvalue of $\mathbf{R}$. Note also that as long as $\mu < 1/\lambda_{MAX}$, the convergence rates of all the models will increase as μ increase. Once $\mu = 1/\lambda_{MAX}$, however, the mode corresponding to λ_{MAX} will begin to slow down again. Thus the choice of μ in the vicinity of λ_{MAX} will generally yield the best convergence rate for the difference equation (37). The condition for the LMS algorithm to be convergent in the mean square sense, described in equation (43), requires knowledge of the largest eigenvalue λ_{MAX} of the correlation matrix R. In a typical application of the LMS algorithm, knowledge of λ_{MAX} is not available. To overcome this practical difficulty, the trace of R may be taken as a conservative estimate for λ_{MAX}, in which case the condition of equation (43) may be reformulated as:

$$0 < \mu < \frac{2}{tr[\mathbf{R}]}, \tag{44}$$

where $tr[\mathbf{R}]$ denotes the trace of the matrix $\mathbf{R}$. We may go one step further by noting that the correlation matrix $\mathbf{R}$ is not only positive definite but also Toeplitz with all of the elements on the main diagonal equal to $r(0)$. Since $r(0)$ is itself equal to the mean-square value of the input at each of the M taps in the transversal filter, we have:

$$tr[R] = M\ r(0)$$
$$= \sum_{k=0}^{M-1} E[|x(n-k)|^2]. \tag{45}$$

Thus, using the term "tap-input power" to refer to the sum of the mean-square values of the tap inputs, we may restate the condition of equation (45) for convergence of the LMS algorithm in the mean square as:

$$0 < \mu < \frac{2}{tap-input\ power}. \tag{46}$$

In order to calculate the misadjustment, first, we may define the correlation matrix of the weight-error vector $\boldsymbol{\varepsilon}(n)$ as:

$$\mathbf{K}(n) = E[\boldsymbol{\varepsilon}(n)\boldsymbol{\varepsilon}^H(n)]. \tag{47}$$

Hence, applying this definition to the stochastic difference equation (36) and then invoking the independence assumption, we get:

$$\mathbf{K}(n+1) = (\mathbf{I} - \mu\mathbf{R})\mathbf{K}(n)(\mathbf{I} - \mu\mathbf{R}) + \mu^2 J_{min}\mathbf{R}, \tag{48}$$

where $J_{\min}$ is the minimum mean-squared error produced by the optimum Wiener filter. Let $J(n)$ denote the mean-squared error due to the LMS algorithm at iteration n. Invoking independence assumption, we get:

$$J(n) = E[e(n)^2] = E\{[d(n) - \mathbf{w}(n)\mathbf{x}(n)]^2\}$$
$$= J_{\min} + E[\boldsymbol{\varepsilon}^H(n)\mathbf{x}(n)\mathbf{x}^H(n)\boldsymbol{\varepsilon}(n)] \quad . \tag{49}$$

Our next task is to evaluate the expectation term in the final line of equation (49). Here we note that this term is the expected value of a scalar random variable represented by a triple vector product, and the trace of a scalar is the scalar itself. We may therefore rewrite it as:

$$E[\boldsymbol{\varepsilon}^H(n)\mathbf{x}(n)\mathbf{x}^H(n)\boldsymbol{\varepsilon}(n)] = E[tr\{\boldsymbol{\varepsilon}^H(n)\mathbf{x}(n)\mathbf{x}^H(n)\boldsymbol{\varepsilon}(n)\}]$$
$$= tr\{E[\mathbf{x}(n)\mathbf{x}^H(n)\boldsymbol{\varepsilon}(n)\boldsymbol{\varepsilon}^H(n)]\} \quad . \tag{50}$$

Invoking the independence assumption again, we reduce this expectation to:

$$E[\boldsymbol{\varepsilon}^H(n)\mathbf{x}(n)\mathbf{x}^H(n)\boldsymbol{\varepsilon}(n)] = tr\{E[\mathbf{x}(n)\mathbf{x}^H(n)]E[\boldsymbol{\varepsilon}(n)\boldsymbol{\varepsilon}^H(n)]\}$$
$$= tr[\mathbf{R}\mathbf{K}(n)] \quad , \tag{51}$$

where $\mathbf{R}$ is the correlation matrix of the tap inputs and $\mathbf{K}(n)$ is the weight-error correlation matrix. Accordingly, using equation (51) in (49), we may rewrite the expression for the mean-squared error in the LMS algorithm simply as:

$$J(n) = J_{\min} + tr[\mathbf{R}\mathbf{K}(n)]. \tag{52}$$

Equation (52) indicates that for all n, the mean-square value of the estimation error in the LMS algorithm consists of two components: the minimum mean-squared error $J_{\min}$, and a component depending on the transient behavior of the weight-error correlation matrix $\mathbf{K}(n)$.

We now formally define the excess mean-squared error as the difference between the mean-squared error, $J(n)$, produced by the adaptive algorithm at time n and the minimum value, $J_{\min}$, pertaining to the optimum Wiener solution. Denoting the excess mean-squared error by $J_{ex}(n)$, we have:

$$J_{ex}(n) = J(n) - J_{\min} = tr[\mathbf{R}\mathbf{K}(n)]. \tag{53}$$

For $\mathbf{K}(n)$ we use the recursive relation of equation (48). However, when the mean-squared error is of primary interest, another form of this equation obtained by a simple rotation of coordinates is more useful. We may write it as

$$\mathbf{Q}^H \mathbf{R} \mathbf{Q} = \Lambda \tag{54}$$

and,

$$\mathbf{Q}^H \mathbf{K}(n) \mathbf{Q} = \mathbf{U}(n), \tag{55}$$

where Λ is a diagonal matrix consisting of the eigenvalues of the correlation matrix $\mathbf{R}$, and $\mathbf{Q}$ is the unitary matrix consisting of the eigenvectors associated with these eigenvalues. Note that the matrix Λ is real valued.

In general, $\mathbf{U}(n)$ is not a diagonal matrix. Using equations (54) and (55), we get:

$$
\begin{aligned}
tr[\mathbf{R}\mathbf{K}(n)] &= tr[\mathbf{Q}\Lambda\mathbf{Q}^H \mathbf{Q}\mathbf{U}(n)\mathbf{Q}^H] \\
&= tr[\Lambda\mathbf{U}(n)]
\end{aligned}
\tag{56}
$$

Accordingly, we have:

$$J_{ex}(n) = tr[\Lambda\mathbf{U}(n)]. \tag{57}$$

Since Λ is a diagonal matrix, we may also write:

$$J_{ex}(n) = \sum_{i=1}^{M} \lambda_i u_i(n), \tag{58}$$

where $u_i(n)$, $i = 1,2,\ldots,M$ are the diagonal elements of the matrix $\mathbf{U}(n)$, and λ_i are the eigenvalues of the correlation matrix $\mathbf{R}$. Next, using the transformations described by equations (54) and (55), we may rewrite equation (48) in terms of $\mathbf{X}(n)$ and Λ as follows:

$$\mathbf{U}(n+1) = (\mathbf{I} - \mu\Lambda)\mathbf{U}(n)(\mathbf{I} - \mu\Lambda) + \mu^2 J_{min}\Lambda. \tag{59}$$

We observe from equation (58) that $J_{ex}(n)$ depends on the $u_i(n)$. This suggests that we need only look at the diagonal terms of the equation (59). Because of the form of this equation, the u_i decouple from the off-diagonal terms, and so we have

$$u_i(n+1) = (1 - \mu\lambda_i)^2 u_i(n) + \mu^2 J_{min}\lambda_i \qquad i = 1,2,\ldots,M. \tag{60}$$

The misadjustment may be defined as the ratio of the steady-state value $J_{ex}(\infty)$ of the excess mean-squared error to the minimum mean-squared error J_{min}. To find the final value of the excess mean-squared error, $J_{ex}(\infty)$, we may go back to equation (60). In particular, setting $n = \infty$ and then solving the resulting equation for $u_i(\infty)$, we get:

$$u_i(\infty) = \frac{\mu J_{min}}{2 - \mu\lambda_i} \qquad i = 1,2,\ldots,M. \tag{61}$$

Hence, evaluating equation (58) for $n = \infty$ and then substituting equation (61) in the resultant, we get:

$$
\begin{aligned}
J_{ex}(\infty) &= \sum_{i=1}^{M} \lambda_i u_i(\infty) \\
&= J_{min} \sum_{i=1}^{M} \frac{\mu\lambda_i}{2 - \mu\lambda_i}.
\end{aligned}
\tag{62}
$$

Finally, the misadjustment may be written as:

$$\mathsf{M} = \frac{J_{ex}(\infty)}{J_{min}} = \sum_{i=1}^{M} \frac{\mu\lambda_i}{2 - \mu\lambda_i}. \tag{63}$$

In this present form, this formula is impractical, for it requires knowledge of all the eigenvalues of the correlation matrix $\mathbf{R}$. However, assuming that the step-size parameter μ is small compared to the largest eigenvalue λ_{max}, we may approximate equation (63) as follows:

$$
\begin{aligned}
\mathsf{M} &= \frac{\mu}{2} \sum_{i=1}^{M} \lambda_i \\
&= \frac{\mu}{2} (tap - input\ power).
\end{aligned}
\tag{64}
$$

Define an average eigenvalue for the underlying correlation matrix $\mathbf{R}$ of the tap inputs as:

$$\lambda_{avg} = \frac{1}{M} \sum_{i=1}^{M} \lambda_i. \tag{65}$$

Then, we use the methods of the steepest descent, to define the following average time constant for the LMS algorithm:

$$(\tau)_{mse,avg} \approx \frac{1}{2\mu\lambda_{avg}}. \tag{66}$$

Hence, we may redefine the misadjustment approximately as follows (Widrow & Stearns, 1985):

$$M = \frac{\mu M \lambda_{avg}}{2}$$

$$= \frac{M}{4\tau_{mse,avg}}.$$ (67)

On the basis of this formula, we may now make the following observations:

The misadjustment M increases linearly with the filter length (number of taps) denoted by M, for a fixed $\tau_{mse,avg}$. The settling time of the LMS algorithm is proportional to the average time constant $\tau_{mse,avg}$. It follows, therefore, that the misadjustment M is inversely proportional to the settling time. The misadjustment M is directly proportional to the step-size parameter μ, whereas the average time constant $\tau_{mse,avg}$ is inversely proportional to μ. We therefore have conflicting requirements in that μ is reduced so as to reduce the misadjustment, and then settling time of the LMS algorithm is increased. Conversely, if μ is increased so as to reduce the settling time, then the misadjustment is increased.

Frequency Domain LMS Algorithm (FDAF)

There are two principle advantages to the frequency-domain implementations of the adaptive filters. In certain applications, such as acoustic echo cancellation in teleconferencing, for example, the adaptive filter is required to have a long impulse response (i.e., long memory) to cope with equally long echo duration (Murano, Unagami, & Amano, 1990). When the LMS algorithm is adapted in the time domain, we find that the requirement of a long memory results in a significant increase in the computational complexity of the algorithm. How then do we deal with this problem? There are two options available to use. We may choose an infinite-duration impulse response (IIR) filter and adapt it in the time domain (Regalia, 1994; Shynk, 1989); the difficulty with this approach is that we inherit a new problem, namely, that of filter instability. Alternatively, we may use a particular type of frequency-domain adaptive filtering that combines two complementary methods widely used in digital signal processing (Clark, Mitra, & Parker, 1981; Clark, Parker, & Mitra, 1983; Ferrara, 1980, 1985; Shynk, 1992): block implementation of FIR filter, which allows the efficient use of parallel processing and thereby results in a gain in computational speed, and fast Fourier transform (FFT) algorithms for performing fast convolution, which permits adaptation of filter parameters in the frequency domain in a computationally efficient manner. Frequency-domain adaptive filtering is used to improve the convergence performance of the standard LMS algorithm.

One of the simplest frequency-domain adaptive filters is that shown in Figure 6 (Bershad, & Feintuch, 1979; Dentino, McCool, & Widrow, 1978). The input signal $x(n)$ and desired response $d(n)$ are accumulated in buffer memories to form N-point data blocks. They are then transformed by N-point FFTs. Each of the FFT outputs comprised a set of N complex numbers. The desired response transform values are subtracted from the input transform values at corresponding frequencies to form N complex error signals. There are N complex weights, one corresponding to each spectral bin. Each weight is independently updated once for each data block. The weighted outputs are fed to an inverse FFT operator to produce the output signal $y(n)$. To analyze this algorithm, define the frequency-domain weight vector for the kth block by:

$$\mathbf{H}^T(k) = [H_1(k)H_2(k)...H_M(k)], \tag{68}$$

and the diagonal matrix of the input FFT coefficients by:

$$\mathbf{X}(k) = \begin{bmatrix} X_1(k) & & & 0 \\ & X_2(k) & & \\ & & \ddots & \\ 0 & & & X_M(k) \end{bmatrix}. \tag{69}$$

Similarly, let $\mathbf{Y}(k)$, $\mathbf{D}(k)$, *and* $\mathbf{E}(k)$ be vectors containing the frequency-domain of output, desired response, and error for k[th] block. Note that:

$$\mathbf{Y}(k) = \mathbf{X}(k)\mathbf{H}(k) \tag{70}$$

and,

$$\mathbf{E}(k) = \mathbf{D}(k) - \mathbf{Y}(k). \tag{71}$$

Figure 6. Frequency-domain adaptive filter

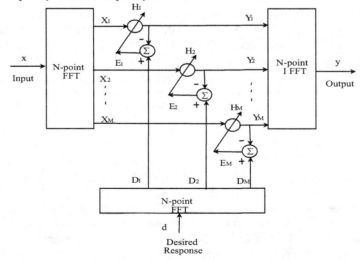

The frequency-domain weight update equation may be expressed as:

$$\mathbf{H}(k+1) = \mathbf{H}(k) + \mu \mathbf{X}^*(k)\mathbf{E}(k). \tag{72}$$

Frequency Bin Adaptive Filtering (FBAF) Algorithm

The intelligibility of speech in teleconferencing systems is of great importance. Acoustic feedback between speaker and microphone in the far-end room causes echo in the near-end and vice versa, which degrades the intelligibility. To eliminate this echo we need adaptive control to estimate path and to continue to estimate again as the echo path changes. However, due to the long reverberation time of the echo (several hundred milliseconds) it is necessary to use several thousand-tap coefficients. This results in a heavy computational load making it practically almost impossible to use FIR time domain adaptive filter (TDAF) in echo path replica estimation control section. Frequency domain adaptive filtering (FDAF) based on the block LMS (BLMS) algorithm can reduce the number of multiplications (Clark et al., 1981; Clark et al., 1983; Ferrara, 1980). However, the transmission delay between input and output is not a single sample like in the TDAF, but rather a block of several thousand samples since the FDAF is based on block processing. This transmission delay is also harmful for communication. To solve this problem, we have introduced a new algorithm called frequency bin adaptive filtering (FBAF) (Asharif, Amano, Unagami, & Murano, 1986, 1987). By using a short block of data, the FBAF algorithm achieves a very short transmission delay without losing computational efficiency. In the FBAF, each frequency bin is processed by an independent FIR filter rather than being weighted by a single tap as in the FDAF algorithm. To increase the convergence rate, we have used an algorithm for normalizing the convergence factor in the FBAF algorithm. This has proved to be effective when the input is a correlated signal. In this section we also present the design and implementation of the FBAF algorithm and evaluate it for echo canceling. The hardware was built using 12 VSP chips and one DSP chip (Asharif & Amano, 1990).

Dividing the Impulse Response

Suppose that the length of the *acoustic impulse response* of the room is N samples. Dividing this impulse response into M sub-blocks of N' samples ($N = MN'$, where M is an integer) is shown in Figure 7. Then, the output $y(\cdot)$ of the echo-canceller, which is the convolution between input $x(\cdot)$ and weight $w(\cdot)$, is derived as follows (Asharif et al., 1986, 1987):

$$y(kN'+r) = \sum_{m=0}^{M-1}\sum_{i=0}^{N'-1} w_m^i(k)x(kN'+r-mN'-i), \tag{73}$$

where k is the number of the sub-block, which contains N' samples, and r is the samples number in one sub-block ($r = 0,1,\cdots,N'-1$). The subscript m and the superscript i in the weight w_m^i correspond to the ith element in the mth sub-block. In order to implement equation (73) in the frequency domain, first take fast Fourier transform (FFT) of both sides of equation (73):

$$FFT[y(kN'+r)] = \sum_{m=0}^{M-1} FFT\left[\sum_{i=0}^{N'-1} w_m^i(k)x(kN'+r-mN'-i)\right] \tag{74}$$

The weight vector is padded by N' zeros and is transformed to the frequency domain by FFT. The half-overlapped input vector for each sub-block also is transformed to the frequency domain using FFT as follows (T means transpose):

$$\mathbf{W}_m^T(k) = FFT[w_m^0(k), w_m^1(k), \cdots, w_m^{N'-1}(k), \overbrace{0, 0, \cdots 0}^{N'}], \tag{75}$$

$$\mathbf{X}_m^T(k) = FFT[x(kN'-N'-mN'), x(kN'-(N'-1)-mN'), \cdots,$$
$$x(kN'-1-mN'), x(kN'-mN'), \cdots, x(kN'+N'-1-mN')]. \tag{76}$$

The output vector $y(kN'+r)$ in equation (73), which is the sum of the convolution between tap coefficients and input sub-blocks, is obtained by taking the inverse fast Fourier transform (IFFT) of the sum of the element by element multiplication ($\otimes$) of $\mathbf{W}_m(k)$ and $\mathbf{X}_m(k)$, as follows:

$$[y(kN'), y(kN'+1), \cdots, y(kN'+N'-1)]^T$$
$$= last\ N'\ elements\ of\ IFFT\left[\sum_{m=0}^{M-1} \mathbf{W}_m(k) \otimes \mathbf{X}_m(k)\right]. \tag{77}$$

In equation (77) we can see that the N' output samples are computed once after taking IFFT and that the delay is only N' samples. For tap coefficients updating, we use the BLMS algorithm (Clark et al., 1981) in each sub-block as follows:

$$w_m^i(k+1) = w_m^i(k) - 2\mu \sum_{r-0}^{N'-1} e(kN'+r) \cdot x(kN'+r-i-mN'). \tag{78}$$

For $r = 0, 1, \cdots, n'-1$ (the ith element in the mth sub-block). Where μ is convergence factor and $e(\cdot)$ is the error signal:

$$e(kN'+r) = y(kN'+r) - d(kN'+r), \tag{79}$$

and $d(\cdot)$ is the desired response. The cross correlation between error and input signal in equation (78), which is the gradient part $\nabla_m(k)$, can be realized using the Fourier transform as follows (superscript * means complex conjugate):

Figure 7. Dividing the impulse response

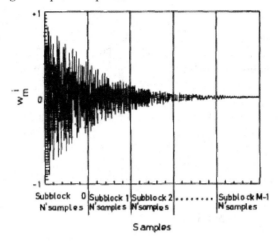

$$\nabla_m(k) = First \ N' \ elements \ of \ IFFT \ [\mathbf{E}(k) \otimes \mathbf{X}_m^*(k)], \tag{80}$$

where $\mathbf{E}(k)$ is the Fourier transform of the error vector preceded by N' zeroes as follows:

$$\mathbf{E}^T(k) = FFT[\overbrace{0,0,\cdots,0}^{N'}, \overbrace{e(kN'), e(kN'+1), \cdots, e(kN'+N'-1)}^{N'}]. \tag{81}$$

The weight vector of mth sub-block is updated by zero padding the gradient vector and transforming into the frequency domain as follows:

$$W_m^T(k+1) = W_m^T(k) - 2\mu FFT[\nabla_m(k), \overbrace{0,0,\cdots,0}^{N'}]. \tag{82}$$

From equations (77), (80), (81), and (82) the structure in Figure 8 can be obtained. In the input signal $x(kN'+r-i-mN')$ there are mN' samples delayed for the mth sub-block, and in each sub-block there are N' samples that are overlapped. Thus, in the frequency domain the successive sub-blocks are separated from each other by one delay element in each frequency bin. The structure in Figure 8 is very similar to an adaptive filtering in each frequency bin. Therefore, we call this structure frequency bin adaptive filtering (FBAF). According to the derivation of the FBAF algorithm, in each sub-block we have applied the BLMS algorithm with a short block length of N', that is, decomposing the original N sample's block length into M sub-blocks. It is known that the BLMS algorithm with block length of N samples converges to the Weiner solution when the convergence factor is limited to $1/N$ times the inverse of the maximum eigenvalue of the input signal autocorrelation matrix λ_{max} (Asharif et al., 1987):

$$0 < \mu < (1/N)(1/\lambda_{max}).$$
(83)

Since the FBAF algorithm is a sum of M BLMS algorithms in the frequency domain, it is also convergent under the previous condition and the fact that $N' < N$. In the special case, when $M=1$, the FBAF algorithm is reduced to the FDAF algorithm with a block length of N samples. The required number of multiplications for FBAF algorithm is:

$$Z_{FBAF} = (2M+3)[2(\log_2 N'+2)]+8M$$
$$= (4M+6)\log_2 N'+16M+12 .$$
(84)

For FDAF algorithm the required number of multiplications is:

$$Z_{FDAF} = (N/N')[5\times 2(\log_2 N+2)+8]$$
$$= (N/N')(10\log_2 N+28) .$$
(85)

In Figure 9, the plots for Z_{FBAF} and Z_{FDAF} versus sub-block length N' or sub-block number M are given. Also, the transmission delay for various sub-block length N', assuming a 16kHz sampling frequency, is plotted. Assuming a 128 sample-sub-block, and 32 sub-blocks for a 4096-sample echo-impulse response, the FBAF algorithm requires only 18% of the multiplications of an FIR time domain adaptive filter. In this case, using a 256-point FFT, the transmission delay for the FBAF is only 8 ms, which is less than the delay for the FDAF algorithm for the same number of computations.

Normalization of the FBAF Algorithm

To improve the convergence speed and tracking of the FBAF algorithm for a correlated input signal, such as a *speech signal*, we have adaptively normalized the convergence factor $\mu_i(k)$ to the power of the signal in each frequency bin, $\sigma_i^2(k)$. The motivation for the *normalization* to the power of each bin independently is the fact that the FBAF structure can be viewed as a subband structure that processes each subband (bin) independently. The power of each bin is calculated using the following recursive equation:

$$\sigma_i^2(k+1) = (1-\beta)\sigma_i^2(k) + \beta \sum_{m=0}^{M-1} X_m^{i\ 2}(k).$$
(86)

Therefore, the convergence factor is normalized according to the following equation:

$$\mu_i(k) = \frac{\alpha}{\sigma_i^2(k)},$$
(87)

where $0 \le \alpha \le 1$ is a constant factor and β is a forgetting factor between zero and one.

Computer Simulation Results

The FBAF algorithm is simulated on a computer by using a Gaussian random signal with zero mean and 0.5 standard deviations, and by using actual speech data as input. The echo-path impulse response with a length of *4001* samples was generated using the following equation:

$$Echo\ path = \sum_{i=0}^{4000} R_i \exp\left[-\frac{i+1}{880}\right]\delta(n-i),$$ (88)

where $\delta(n)$ is the Dirac function and Ri, is a random number within -1, +1. This echo path resembles the actual room *acoustic impulse response*. We defined the echo return loss enhancement (ERLE) as follows:

$$ERLE = 10\log_{10}\frac{E[d^2(n)]}{E[e^2(n)]}.$$ (89)

The input signal to the FBAF structure will be switched from noise to the actual speech data. In Figure 10, this input signal switching is done after sufficient convergence (ERLE

Figure 8. The FBAF algorithm

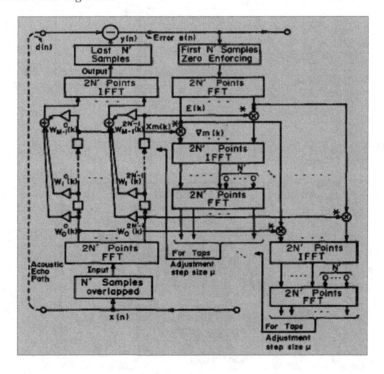

Figure 9. Multiplication per sample (MPS) and transmission delay for FBAF algorithm

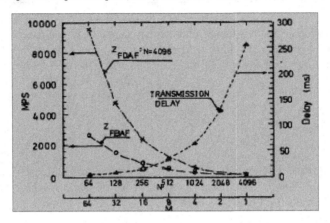

Figure 10. Convergence characteristics trained by noise for the FBAF algorithm

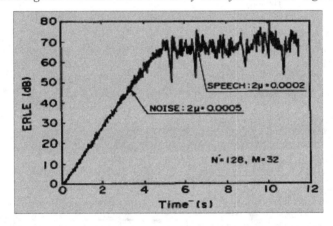

Figure 11. Normalized effect in the FBAF algorithm with speech input signal

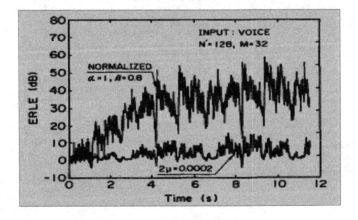

= 70 dB) is obtained. To investigate the effect of the normalization in the FBAF algorithm, we choose α=1 and β=0.8. The result of the simulation is shown in Figure 11. An ERLE of 35 dB is achieved within 4 s, with a speech input data. If we had used a fixed step size 2μ=0.0002, the convergence speed would be reduced, as shown in the same figure. Therefore, step size *normalization* with speech input data, by always changing the step size according to the power of corresponding bin, provides faster convergence.

Hardware Design of the FBAF Algorithm

To confirm the feasibility and the actual performance of the FBAF algorithm, we have designed and implemented the echo canceller hardware using zoran vector signal processor chips (VSP ZR34161) and a Fujitsu digital signal processor (FDSP-3 MB8764) (Asharif, & Amano, 1990). The *VSP* performs a 128-point *FFT* with one instruction in 237 μs. It has a complex internal RAM of 128 x 16 bit words. The internal memory can be split into two *64* word complex vectors (Bran, 1987). FDSP-3 is a general purpose DSP with two 128 word internal RAM'S (Fujitsu, 1984). The frame period for processing is 8 ms per block of data (one block contains 128 samples, that is, a 16 kHz sampling frequency). All FFTs have a 256-point size, using the half overlap-save method. The number of sub-blocks *M* is

Figure 12. FBAF hardware design block diagram

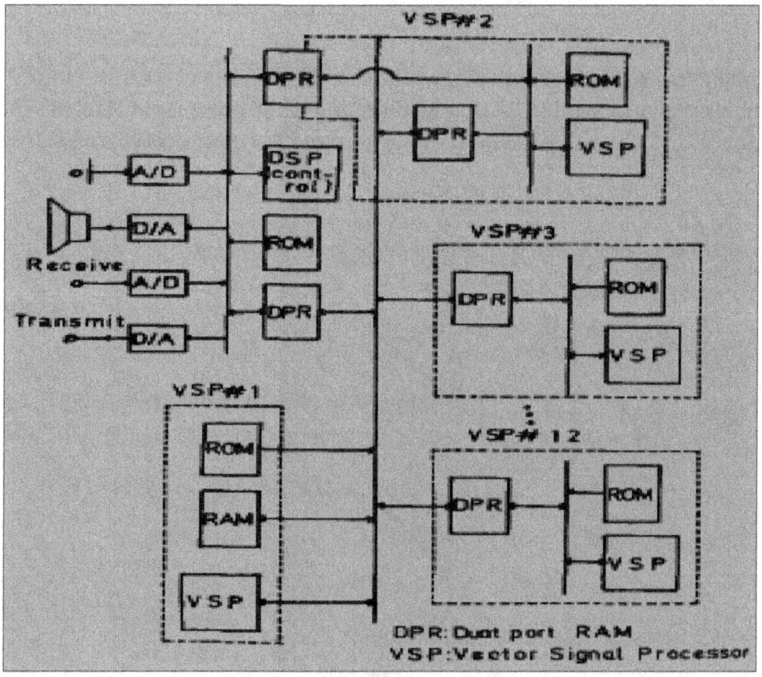

33 in this design. Due to the tightness of the 8 ms frame period, it is necessary to use more chips in parallel. A master-slave arrangement was used to perform the algorithm effectively with 12 VSP chips.

Figure 12 shows the conceptual block diagram of the hardware design. VSP#1 is the master processor. Each slave processor (VSP#3-#12) processes three tapped delay elements for all frequency bins. Due to symmetry property, the calculations are made for only a 129-point FFT. The slave processors use their own buses and Dual Port RAM (DPR) to calculate segmental convolution. They also update the three corresponding taps according to equations (80) and (82), and they shift data within the three delay elements. Aside from main processing, the master processor, VSP#1, processes another three tapped delay elements same as slave processors. Therefore, a total of 11 VSPS process all of the 33 tapped delay elements. To save more time another VSP (VSP#2) was used to perform the input 256-point FFT. Thus, the 12 chip VSP covers the complete job of processing the FBAF algorithm in parallel. To control data flow and for interfacing the VSPs with the rest of the world (input, output, microphone, and speaker) through the DPR, one of Fujitsu's FDSP-3 (MB8764) chips was used as a control processor. The prototype hardware for the FBAF algorithm requires 40 k-words of RAM, which is about 50% of the size of memory required for the FDAF algorithm. The prototype echo canceller is realized by four breadboards, to achieve an equivalent of a 4224-tap FIR time domain adaptive filter. A time domain echo canceller with the same number of taps would require 40-50 DSP chips. In other words, the FBAF-based echo canceller we designed requires only 25% of the hardware required for the time domain approach, considering the number of processors.

Hardware Measurement Results

Using the implemented hardware prototype echo canceller, the signal-to-noise ratio (S/N) and echo return loss enhancement (ERLE) with changing white noise input level are shown in Figure 13. The FBAF algorithm with a 256-point FFT and 33 tapped delay elements was used.

Figure 13. Measured ERLE and S/N versus noise input level

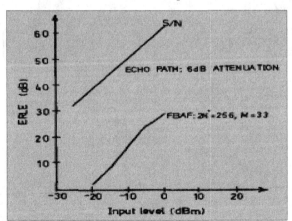

When the echo path is a simple 6 dB attenuation, the ERLE reaches 30 dB. We investigated that the ERLE remains at the same level when we increase the echo path reverberation up to 260 ms. The limitation of ERLE to 30 dB in hardware measurement (against the result of computer simulation of Figure 10, which achieved 70 dB) is due to the limitation of the 16-bit fixed-point arithmetics of the VSP and DSP, which accumulate the quantization error during the computation of the algorithm. The convergence characteristics of the hardware prototype are plotted in Figure 14. The echo path is a 6 dB attenuation, and the convergence factor is 0.001. The ERLE reaches 30 dB after 1000 iterations (8 s).

Using white noise as the training input signal to achieve a 30 dB ERLE, then switching to a speech signal (like the simulation in Figure 10), the 260 ms reverberated echo is almost undetectable. That is, listening to the actual echo canceller performance confirms its practical effectiveness.

Double-Talk Echo Canceling

Double-Talk Problem in Echo Canceling

In the *echo canceling* system shown in Figure 15, the *acoustic impulse response* of the teleconference room is estimated by an adaptive *algorithm* such as LMS algorithm. The output of the FIR filter, $\tilde{y}(n)$, is presented by:

$$\tilde{y}(n) = \sum_{i=0}^{N-1} h_i x(n-i), \tag{90}$$

where N is the number of tap, h is the tap coefficient of the adaptive FIR filter, and $x(n)$ is the far-end signal at sample n. The echo signal is obtained from echo impulse response, r, as follows (N is the acoustic impulse response length):

$$y(n) = \sum_{i=0}^{N-1} r_i x(n-i). \tag{91}$$

The output signal $\tilde{y}(n)$ is the estimation of the echo component signal $y(n)$, which is the result of passing $x(n)$ through the acoustic echo impulse response, r, of the loudspeaker enclosure microphone system (LEMS) (see Figure 15). $d(n)$ is the microphone signal, which is called the desired signal. Then the error signal between the desired signal $d(n)$ and the output signal $\tilde{y}(n)$ becomes the loudspeaker signal in the far-end side. This error signal, $e(n)$, is calculated as follows:

$$e(n) = d(n) - \tilde{y}(n), \tag{92}$$

Figure 14. Convergence characteristic using the hardware prototype

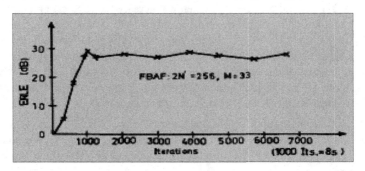

which is used to adapt the tap *coefficients* of the adaptive filter by the LMS algorithm, say, to minimize an estimation of the *mean squared error* as follows:

$$h_i(n+1) = h_i(n) + 2\mu.e(n)x(n-i), \tag{93}$$

where μ is the step size for tap coefficients adaptation.

The condition of double-talk in the echo canceling is occurred when both the near-end signal $s(n)$ and the noise signal $v(n)$ from the near-end come to exist simultaneously with the far-end signal $x(n)$ (generally the near-end and far-end room are under a noisy environment). In this condition the microphone signal consists of both the echo returned signal $y(n)$, the near-end signal $s(n)$, and the noise signal $v(n)$, that is:

$$d(n) = y(n) + s(n) + v(n). \tag{94}$$

Thus, the error signal $e(n)$ contains also the near-end signal $s(n)$, which is uncorrelated with the input signal $x(n)$, and therefore, the gradient search is misled to estimate the correct echo path impulse response. In this situation, we say the double-talk has occurred and the efficiency of the conventional algorithm such as the LMS algorithm will be destroyed.

Double-Talk Detection Based Algorithms

In general to solve the double-talk problem, a double-talk detector (DTD) has been implemented that stops the echo canceller from adapting its coefficients when double-talk occurs. The structure of the conventional echo canceling is shown in Figure 16.

The basic double-talk detection scheme starts with computing a detection statistic and comparing it with a preset threshold. Different methods have been proposed to form the detection statistic. The Geigel algorithm (Duttweiler, 1978) has proven successful in the line echo cancellers; however, it does not always provide reliable performance when used in AECs. Recently, cross-correlation based methods (Benesty, Morgan, & Cho, 2000; Cho,

Morgan, & Benesty, 1999; Gansler, Hansson, Invarsson, & Salomomsson, 1996; Ye & Wu, 1991) have been proposed, which appear to be more appropriate for AEC's applications. In this section, we will introduce three kinds of double-talk detection schemes briefly. Usually, double-talk is handled in the following way: A detection statistic ξ is formed using available signals, for example, x,y,e, and so forth, and the estimated filter coefficients h. The detection statistic ξ is compared to a preset threshold T, and double-talk is declared if $\xi > T$. Once double-talk is declared, the detection is held for a minimum period of time T_{hold}. While the detection is held, the filter adaptation is disabled. If $\xi \leq T$ consecutively over a time T_{hold}, the filter resumes adaptation, while the comparison of ξ to T continues until $\xi > T$ again. The hold time T_{hold} in steps 3 and 4 is necessary to suppress detection dropouts due to the noisy behavior of the detection statistic.

Geigel Algorithm

One simple algorithm due to A. A. Geigel is to declare the presence of near-end speech whenever:

$$\xi^{(g)} = \frac{|d(n)|}{\max\{|x(n-1)|,\cdots,|x(n-N)|\}} > T, \tag{95}$$

where N and T are suitably chosen constants (Duttweiler, 1978). This scheme is based on a waveform level comparison between the microphone signal $d(n)$ and the far-end speech $x(n)$, assuming the near-end speech $s(n)$ in the microphone signal will be typically stronger than the echo $y(n)$. The maximum of the N most recent samples of $x(n)$ is taken for the comparison because of the undetermined delay in the echo path. The threshold T is to compensate for the energy lever of the echo path response $\mathbf{r}$, and is often set to 1/2 for line echo cancellers because the hybrid loss is typically about 6 dB. For an AEC, however, it is not easy to set a universal threshold to work reliably in all the various situations because the loss through the acoustic echo path can vary greatly depending on many factors.

Figure 15. Double-talk condition in echo canceller system

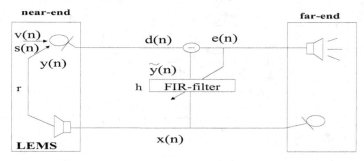

Cross-Correlation Methods

Ye and Wu (1991) proposed a double-talk detection algorithm based on the cross-correlation between $x(n)$ and $e(n)$. A similar idea using the cross-correlation between $x(n)$ and $d(n)$ has also been suggested by Wesel (Cho et al., 1999). The cross-correlation vector between $x(n)$ and $d(n)$ and between $x(n)$ and $e(n)$ are defined as:

$$\mathbf{c}_{xd}^{(1)} = [c_{xd,0}^{(1)} \ c_{xd,1}^{(1)} \cdots c_{xd,L-1}^{(1)}]^T, \tag{96}$$

where:

$$c_{xd,i}^{(1)} = \frac{E[x(n-i)d(n)]}{\sqrt{E[x^2(n-i)]E[d^2(n)]}} \tag{97}$$

and,

$$\mathbf{c}_{xe}^{(1)} = [c_{xe,0}^{(1)} \ c_{xe,1}^{(1)} \cdots c_{xe,L-1}^{(1)}]^T, \tag{98}$$

where:

$$c_{xe,i}^{(1)} = \frac{E[x(n-i)e(n)]}{\sqrt{E[x^2(n-i)]E[e^2(n)]}}. \tag{99}$$

The operator $E[\cdot]$ denotes statistical expectation. The detection statistic ξ is formed by taking the inverse norm of the cross-correlation vector. The detection statistic ξ may be defined as:

$$\xi_{xd}^{(1)} = [\max_i |\tilde{c}_{xd,i}^{(1)}|]^{-1}, \tag{100}$$

Figure 16. Structure of the conventional echo canceling

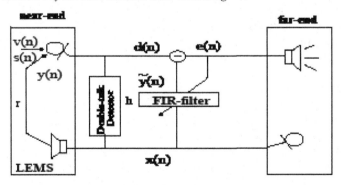

and,

$$\xi_{xe}^{(1)} = [\max_i \left| \tilde{c}_{xe,i}^{(1)} \right|]^{-1}, \tag{101}$$

where $\tilde{c}_{xd,i}^{(1)}$ and $\tilde{c}_{xe,i}^{(1)}$ are estimates of $c_{xd,i}^{(1)}$ and $c_{xe,i}^{(1)}$, respectively. A time average or exponentially windowed sum is used for the estimation of these statistic quantities, for example,

$$E[x(n-i)d(n)] \approx (1 - e^{-1/W}) \sum_{j=0}^{\infty} x(n-i-j)d(n-j)e^{-j/W} \tag{102}$$

and other statistic expectation are estimated analogously. The effective window length W needs be long enough for smooth estimation, but should not be too long because of the non-stationary nature of the *speech signal* and the desirability of rapid response.

Normalized Cross-Correlation Method

A new method based on the cross-correlation vector is proposed by Benesty et al. (2000). That method achieves proper *normalization* in the sense that the detection statistic is equal to one when the near end signal is zero. The normalized cross-correlation vector is defined as:

$$\mathbf{c}_{xd}^{(2)} = (\sigma_d^2 \mathbf{R}_x)^{-1/2} \mathbf{R}_{xd}, \tag{103}$$

where $\sigma_d^2 = E[d^2]$ is the variance of d, $\mathbf{R}_x = E[\mathbf{x}\mathbf{x}^T]$ is the autocorrelation matrix of x, and $\mathbf{R}_{xd} = E[\mathbf{x}d]$ is the cross-correlation vector between $\mathbf{x}$ and d. The corresponding detection statistic may be written as:

$$\xi_{xd}^{(2)} = \left\| \tilde{c}_{xd}^{(2)} \right\|^{-1}. \tag{104}$$

Now if $\tilde{c}_{xd}^{(2)} \approx c_{xd}^{(2)}$, we have:

$$\xi_{xd}^{(2)} \approx [\mathbf{R}_{xd}^T (\sigma_d^2 \mathbf{R}_x)^{-1} \mathbf{R}_{xd}]^{-1/2}. \tag{105}$$

For computational simplicity, it can be modified as follows. Assuming that the length of the adaptive filter L is long enough to accurately model the room response, that is, $L=M$ (M is the length of the room impulse response), we have $\mathbf{R}_x^{-1} \mathbf{R}_{xd} = r \approx h$ when the filter is converged. In this case, equation (105) can be rewritten as:

$$\xi_{xd}^{(2)} = \frac{\tilde{\sigma}_d}{\sqrt{\tilde{\mathbf{R}}_{xd}^T \mathbf{r}}} = \frac{\tilde{\sigma}_d}{\sqrt{\tilde{\mathbf{R}}_{xd}^T \mathbf{h}}}. \tag{106}$$

This form is significantly easier to compute than equation (105), but may incur some loss in accuracy substituting **h** for **r** when the filter is not yet converged. Again, we use exponentially windowed time averages to estimate R_{xd} and σ_d as in equation (102).

Several double-talk detection schemes are introduced in this section. Usually, conventional *echo canceling* uses the double-talk detector to detect the presence of the near end speech, and then halts filter adaptation. This is the important role of the double-talk detector. However, in many cases, the DTD fails to detect double-talk so the achieved echo suppression is not sufficient and speech is distorted and echo becomes apparent. And, also stopping the tap adaptation is just a passive action to handle the double-talk condition, and it causes lowering speed of adaptations and/or totally misleads when the echo path changed in the period of halting tap adaptation. Other works for challenging the double-talk problem in the echo canceling can be found by (Gansler, Gay, Sondhi, & Benesty, 2000; Hansler & Schmidt, 2004; Heitkamper, 1997) that cause much more complexity adding to a simple LMS *algorithm*.

Then, we proposed a new class of acoustic echo canceling based on the correlation functions to challenge the double-talk condition. These algorithms are different to the conventional DTD echo canceling, and it can continue the tap adaptation in double-talk condition.

Correlation LMS Algorithm

In this section, we introduce a new algorithm to continue the adaptation even in the presence of double-talk without freezing taps and/or misleading the performance. The proposed method is called correlation LMS (CLMS) algorithm (Asharif & Hayashi, 1999; Asharif, Hayashi, & Yamashita, 1999; Asharif, Rezapour, & Ochi, 1998), which utilizes the correlation functions of the input signal instead of the input signal itself, to process and find the echo path impulse response. The idea behind this is that we suppose the far-end signal is not correlated with the near-end signal, so the gradient for tap adaptation that is obtained from autocorrelation function does not carry the undesired near-end signal to misadjust the adaptive digital filter for echo path identification.

In Figure 17, new structure is shown. In this structure, we assume the double-talk exists.

Figure 17. Structure of correlation LMS algorithm

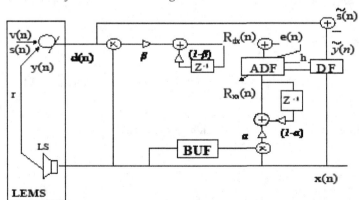

Since the new structure is based on the processing of autocorrelation function of the input signal (Loudspeaker in the near-end) and the cross-correlation of the input and microphone signal, we should, first, estimate them. The autocorrelation function for the input signal data, $x(n)$ with time-lag k, is defined as follows:

$$R_{xx}(n,k) = \sum_{j=0}^{n} x(j)x(j-k). \tag{107}$$

Also, the cross-correlation between the desired and the input signal is calculated as follows:

$$R_{dx}(n,k) = \sum_{j=0}^{n} d(j)x(j-k). \tag{108}$$

Substituting from equations (91), (94), and (107) into (108),

$$\begin{aligned} R_{dx}(n,k) &= E[d(n)x(j-k)] = E\{[y(n)+s(n)+v(n)]x(j-k)\} \\ &= E[y(n)x(j-k)] + E[s(n)x(j-k)] + E[v(k)x(j-k)]. \end{aligned} \tag{109}$$

Here, we assume that there is no correlation between the far-end $x(n)$ and the near-end signal $s(n)$.

$$R_{sx}(n,k) = E[s(n)x(j-k)] = E[x(n)s(j-k)] = 0$$
$$R_{vx}(n,k) = E[v(n)x(j-k)] = E[x(n)v(j-k)] = 0, \tag{110}$$

so the cross-correlation will be obtained as follows:

$$R_{dx}(n,k) \cong \sum_{i=0}^{N-1} r_i R_{xx}(n,k-i). \tag{111}$$

To estimate $R_{dx}(n,k)$ we need to process the autocorrelation values of the input by an adaptive filter. It can be defined as follows:

$$\widetilde{R}_{dx}(n,0) = \sum_{i=0}^{N-1} h_i(n)R_{xx}(n,i), \tag{112}$$

where $R_{dx}(n,0)$ is the output of the filter that is estimation of the cross-correlation for time-lag k=0. The MSE between the desired cross-correlation function $R_{dx}(n,0)$ and its estimated value $\widetilde{R}_{dx}(n,0)$ (assuming only for the lag component k=0) is defined as:

$$J=E[e^2(n)], \tag{113}$$

where:

$$e(n) = R_{dx}(n) - \tilde{R}_{dx}(n). \tag{114}$$

The gradient vector of MSE is:

$$\nabla J = \frac{\partial J}{\partial h} = -2E \begin{bmatrix} e(n)R_{xx}(n,0) \\ e(n)R_{xx}(n,1) \\ \vdots \\ e(n)R_{xx}(n,N-1) \end{bmatrix}$$

$$= -2E[e(n)\mathbf{P}_{xx}(n)] \qquad . \tag{115}$$

Then we obtained the steepest descent algorithm as follows:

$$\mathbf{h}(n+1) = \mathbf{h}(n) + 2\mu E[e(n)\mathbf{P}_{xx}(n)], \tag{116}$$

where,

$$\mathbf{h}(n) = [h_0(n), h_1(n), \cdots, h_{N-1}(n)]^T \tag{117}$$

$$\mathbf{P}_{xx}(n) = [R_{xx}(n,0), R_{xx}(n,1), \cdots, R_{xx}(n,N-1)]^T. \tag{118}$$

As with LMS algorithm, here we substitute the instantaneous MSE instead of its statistical expectation. The CLMS algorithm, which is normalized to the power of the input correlation function to ensure sufficient conditions for convergence, then becomes:

$$\mathbf{h}(n+1) = \mathbf{h}(n) + \frac{2\mu}{1 + \mathbf{P}_{xx}^T(n)\mathbf{P}_{xx}(n)} e(n)\mathbf{P}_{xx}(n), \tag{119}$$

where μ is the step size for tap *coefficients* adaptation. It will be shown in simulation that the CLMS algorithm has good performance compared to the LMS algorithm in double-talk situation. However, the CLMS algorithm does not give a sufficient convergence characteristic yet. Then, we extend the CLMS algorithm in order to obtain a sufficient convergence characteristic.

Extended CLMS Algorithm

In extended CLMS algorithm (Asharif, Shimabukuro, Hayashi, & Yamashita, 1999), we assume the double-talk condition exists. The autocorrelation function and the cross-correlation function are given by equation (107) and equation (108), respectively. Also we assume that there is no correlation between the far-end and the near-end signals. In the extended CLMS algorithm, we estimate all components of the cross-correlation. Therefore, based on equation (112), the output of the adaptive filter is defined here by:

$$\tilde{R}_{dx}(n,k) = \sum_{i=0}^{N-1} h_i(n).R_{xx}(n,k-i), \tag{120}$$

where $\tilde{R}_{dx}(n,k)$ is the estimation value of $R_{dx}(n,k)$. In contrast with equation (112) where only the main component of the cross-correlation was estimated, in equation (120), we try to estimate all lags up to N. In contrast with the cost function in the CLMS algorithm, the cost function in the ECLMS algorithm is defined by the sum of the lagged squared errors as follows:

$$J = E[\mathbf{e}^T(n)\mathbf{e}(n)], \tag{121}$$

where the error signal vector is shown by:

$$\mathbf{e}(n,k) = [e(n,0),e(n,1),\cdots e(n,N-1)]^T, \tag{122}$$

with,

$$\mathbf{e}(n,k) = R_{dx}(n,k) - \tilde{R}_{dx}(n,k). \tag{123}$$

The gradient vector of MSE is:

$$\begin{aligned} \nabla J &= \frac{\partial}{\partial h} E[\mathbf{e}^T(n)\mathbf{e}(n)] \\ &= -2E[\mathbf{Q}_{xx}(n)\mathbf{e}(n)], \end{aligned} \tag{124}$$

where,

$$\mathbf{Q}_{xx}(n,k) = \begin{bmatrix} R_{xx}(n,0) & R_{xx}(n,1) & \cdots & R_{xx}(n,N-1) \\ R_{xx}(n,1) & R_{xx}(n,0) & \cdots & R_{xx}(n,N-2) \\ \vdots & \vdots & & \vdots \\ R_{xx}(n,N-1) & R_{xx}(n,N-2) & \cdots & R_{xx}(n,0) \end{bmatrix}. \tag{125}$$

Here $\mathbf{Q}_{xx}(n,k)$ is a Toeplitz matrix. Therefore we obtain the steepest descent algorithm as follows:

$$\mathbf{h}(n+1) = \mathbf{h}(n) + 2\mu E[\mathbf{Q}_{xx}(n)\mathbf{e}(n)], \tag{126}$$

As in the LMS algorithm, here we substitute the instantaneous MSE instead of its statistical expectation. The adaptation for ECLMS algorithm, which is normalized to the power of the input correlation function to ensure sufficient conditions for convergence, then becomes:

$$\mathbf{h}(n+1) = \mathbf{h}(n) + \frac{2\mu_0 \mathbf{Q}_{xx}(n)\mathbf{e}(n)}{1 + tr[\mathbf{Q}_{xx}(n)\mathbf{Q}_{xx}(n)]}, \tag{127}$$

where μ_0 is the step size for tap coefficients adaptation and $tr[\cdot]$ means the trace operator. In order to adapt the tap coefficients according to the ECLMS algorithm, we need to compute $R_{xx}(n,k)$ and $R_{dx}(n,k)$. Then we have used the following recursion formulas for these computations:

$$R_{xx}(n,i) = (1-\alpha)R_{xx}(n-1,i) + \alpha x(n)x(n-i), \tag{128}$$

$$R_{dx}(n,i) = (1-\beta)R_{dx}(n-1,i) + \beta d(n)x(n-i), \tag{129}$$

where α and β are limited to $0 < \alpha, \beta < 1$. In the CLMS algorithm the gradient search algorithm is simply obtained by the *correlation function* of the input signal. In order to achieve the Wiener solution, in the ECLMS algorithm we estimate all components of the cross-correlation function by using the Toeplitz matrix of the auto-correlation function; therefore, the cost function in the ECLMS algorithm can be defined by the sum of the lagged squared errors. The computer simulation results have shown the improvement of the performance than the CLMS algorithm as it was expected. However, for a large number of tap coefficient, the ECLMS algorithm is very complex in the computation. In next section we try to implement this algorithm in the frequency and wavelet transform domain.

Frequency-Domain ECLMS Algorithm

As discussed in the previous section, the ECLMS algorithm shows a better convergence than the CLMS algorithm, but the computational complexity is also a problem. In order to reduce the computation complexity of the ECLMS algorithm, we try to implement the

ECLMS algorithm into the frequency domain, because in the frequency domain the *convolution* operation can be simplified to the multiplication operation. This algorithm is called frequency domain ECLMS (FECLMS) algorithm (Asharif, Shiroma, & Yamashita, 2000), (Asharif, Chen, & Yamashita, 2004). In Figure 18, the structure of the FECLMS algorithm is shown. First, we take N-point of the FFT correlation function based on the time-lag, k, in the fast Fourier transform kernel as follows:

$$F_{xx}(n,p) = \sum_{k=0}^{N-1}\left[\sum_{j=0}^{n} x(j)x(j-k)\right]W^{kp}, \tag{130}$$

$$F_{dx}(n,p) = \sum_{k=0}^{N-1}\left[\sum_{j=0}^{n} d(j)x(j-k)\right]W^{kp}, \tag{131}$$

where W shows complex exponential $e^{-j(2\pi/N)}$, $F_{xx}(n,p)$ shows the FFT of $R_{xx}(n,k)$ at the sample-time n, and p is the frequency variable of the FFT. $F_{dx}(n,p)$ shows the FFT of $R_{dx}(n,k)$. As described in the previous section, the FFT of the cross-correlation function, $F_{dx}(n,p)$, between $d(n)$ and $x(n)$ signal will be obtained as follows:

$$F_{dx}(n,p) \cong H_p F_{xx}(n,p), \tag{132}$$

where H_p is p^{th} element of the FFT of the echo impulse response vector $r = [r_0 r_1 \cdots r_{N-1}]$. Then on the basis of equation (132), the adaptive filter in which the input signal is the FFT of the autocorrelation function of the far-end signal is defined by:

$$\tilde{F}_{dx}(n,p) = \tilde{H}_p(n)F_{xx}(n,p), \tag{133}$$

where $\tilde{H}_p(n)$ is the adaptive filter tap coefficient in the frequency domain and $\tilde{F}_{dx}(n,p)$ is the estimation value of $F_{dx}(n,p)$. Next, we define the cost function for adapting tap coefficients as follows:

$$J(n,p) = E[\varepsilon^*(n,p)\varepsilon(n,p)], \tag{134}$$

where:

$$\varepsilon(n,p) = F_{dx}(n,p) - \tilde{F}_{dx}(n,p). \tag{135}$$

The superscript * shows the Hermitian transposition. To obtain the gradient value of equation (134) we differentiate equation (134) with respect to tap coefficient $\tilde{H}_p(n)$:

$$\nabla J = \frac{\partial}{\partial \tilde{H}_p(n)} E[\varepsilon^*(n,p)\varepsilon(n,p)]$$

$$= -2E[\varepsilon(n,p)F_{xx}^*(n,p)] \qquad . \qquad (136)$$

From equation (136) we derive the steepest descent FECLMS algorithm as follows:

$$\tilde{H}_p(n+1) = \tilde{H}_p(n) + \frac{2u_f \varepsilon(n,p)F_{xx}^*(n,p)}{1 + tr[F_{xx}(n,p)F_{xx}(n,p)]} \qquad (137)$$

where μ_f is the convergence parameter and $tr[\cdot]$ means the trace operator. As we can see, the structure of the FECLMS algorithm is similar to the ECLMS algorithm, but we process the algorithm in the frequency domain. In FECLMS algorithm, the FFT of the correlation function is obtained corresponding to the lag-time, not sampling time in the FFT kernel as usually used in conventional methods. And also, we do not need a Toeplitz matrix to estimate all the components of the cross-correlation function, such as in ECLMS algorithm, so the computation complex is reduced.

Wavelet-Domain ECLMS Algorithm

In Figure 19, the structure of the WECLMS algorithm is shown (Asharif, Chen, & Yamashita, 2003; Chen, Asharif, Ardekani, & Yamashita, 2004). As shown in Figure 19, first, we take the N-point discrete wavelet transform (DWT) of the cross-correlation function and the autocorrelation function, respectively. The coefficients vector (N/2-point) can be written as:

$$DWT(R_{dx}(n,k)) = [\mathbf{W}_{Ldx}(n), \mathbf{W}_{Hdx}(n)], \qquad (138)$$

$$DWT(R_{xx}(n,k)) = [\mathbf{W}_{Lxx}(n), \mathbf{W}_{Hxx}(n)], \qquad (139)$$

where,

$$\mathbf{W}_{Ldx}(n) = [W_{Ldx}(n,0), W_{Ldx}(n,1) \cdots W_{Ldx}(n,N/2-1)] \qquad (140)$$

$$\mathbf{W}_{Hdx}(n) = [W_{Hdx}(n,0), W_{Hdx}(n,1) \cdots W_{Hdx}(n,N/2-1)] \qquad (141)$$

$$\mathbf{W}_{Lxx}(n) = [W_{Lxx}(n,0), W_{Lxx}(n,1) \cdots W_{Lxx}(n,N/2-1)] \qquad (142)$$

$$\mathbf{W}_{Hxx}(n) = [W_{Hxx}(n,0), W_{Hxx}(n,1) \cdots W_{Hxx}(n,N/2-1)]. \qquad (143)$$

$\mathbf{W}_{Ldx}(n)$ is an approximation of the cross-correlation function. $\mathbf{W}_{Hdx}(n)$ is a detail part of cross correlation function. $\mathbf{w}_{Ldx}(n)$ is an approximation of the autocorrelation function. $\mathbf{W}_{Hdx}(n)$ is a detail part of autocorrelation function.

As in the ECLMS algorithm, the error signal is shown by:

$$\mathbf{e}_L(n) = \mathbf{W}_{Ldx}^T(n) - \mathbf{G}_{Lxx}(n) * \mathbf{H}_L(n), \tag{144}$$

$$\mathbf{e}_H(n) = \mathbf{W}_{Hdx}^T(n) - \mathbf{G}_{Hxx}(n) * \mathbf{H}_H(n), \tag{145}$$

where * means the *convolution* operator. $\mathbf{e}_L(n)$, $\mathbf{e}_H(n)$ are vertical vector errors for estimation of the approximation and detail of the cross-correlation function, respectively. $\mathbf{H}_L(n)$, $\mathbf{H}_H(n)$ are the estimation of the room impulse response in wavelet domain for the low-pass band and high-pass band, respectively. And

$$\mathbf{G}_{Lxx}(n) = \begin{bmatrix} W_{Lxx}(n,0) & W_{Lxx}(n,1) & \cdots & W_{Lxx}(n,N/2-1) \\ W_{Lxx}(n,1) & W_{Lxx}(n,0) & \cdots & W_{Lxx}(n,N/2-2) \\ \vdots & \vdots & \vdots & \vdots \\ W_{Lxx}(n,N/2-1) & W_{Lxx}(n,N/2-2) & \cdots & W_{Lxx}(n,0) \end{bmatrix}, \tag{146}$$

Figure 18. Echo canceller using FECLMS algorithm

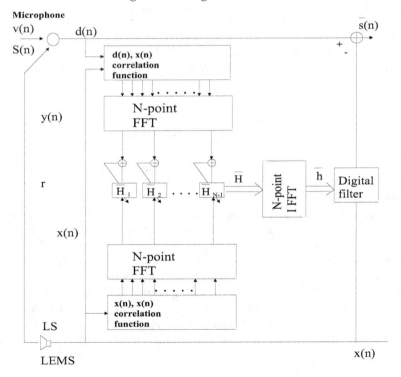

$$\mathbf{G}_{Hxx}(n) = \begin{bmatrix} W_{Hxx}(n,0) & W_{Hxx}(n,1) & \cdots & W_{Hxx}(n,N/2-1) \\ W_{Hxx}(n,1) & W_{Hxx}(n,0) & \cdots & W_{Hxx}(n,N/2-2) \\ \vdots & \vdots & \vdots & \vdots \\ W_{Hxx}(n,N/2-1) & W_{Hxx}(n,N/2-2) & \cdots & W_{Hxx}(n,0) \end{bmatrix}. \tag{147}$$

$\mathbf{G}_{Lxx}(n)$ and $\mathbf{G}_{Hxx}(n)$ are both Toeplitz matrix.

We can update the tap coefficients as:

$$\mathbf{H}_L(n+1) = \mathbf{H}_L(n) + \frac{2\mu_L \mathbf{G}_{Lxx}(n)\mathbf{e}_L(n)}{1 + tr[\mathbf{G}_{Lxx}(n)\mathbf{G}_{Lxx}(n)]}, \tag{148}$$

$$\mathbf{H}_H(n+1) = \mathbf{H}_H(n) + \frac{2\mu_H \mathbf{G}_{Hxx}(n)\mathbf{e}_H(n)}{1 + tr[\mathbf{G}_{Hxx}(n)\mathbf{G}_{Hxx}(n)]}, \tag{149}$$

where μ_L and μ_H are the convergence parameters, $tr[\cdot]$ means the trace operator. Then we use the H_L and H_H to do the inverse discrete wavelet transform (IDWT).

$$IDWT(H_L, H_H) = \tilde{h} \tag{150}$$

Finally, we copied $\tilde{h}$ from correlation filter into the tap *coefficients* of the *digital filter* (DF in Figure 19), to cancel the echo signal. In the WECLMS algorithm, the correlation functions are decomposed by the high-pass and low-pass filters and down sample by two. Therefore, we can adapt the estimation impulse response by using the different step-sizes in two bands, simultaneously, so that the convergence speed is improved. Also the computation complexity is reduced, because of the down-sampling process.

Computational Complexity

In this section, we briefly discuss the computational complexity of the correlation-based algorithms. Consider first the standard LMS algorithm with N tap weight operating on real data. In this case, N multiplications are performed to compute the output, and further N multiplications are performed to update the tap weights, making for a total of $2N$ multiplications per iteration. For all kind of correlation-based algorithms, first we need extra $2N$ multiplications to compute the correlation functions $\mathrm{R}_{xx}(n,k)$ and $\mathrm{R}_{dx}(n,k)$, respectively. Then, we also need extra N multiplications to compute the output of digital filter $\tilde{y}(n)$. So for all kind of correlation-based algorithms, totally we need extra $3N$ multiplications, compared with the LMS algorithm. In CLMS algorithm we need N multiplications to estimate the cross-correlation function $\tilde{R}_{dx}(n,k)$ and N multiplications to update the tap coefficients; totally we need $5N$ multiplications. In the ECLMS algorithm considering tap coefficients adaptation computations as well as calculation for the estimation of the cross-correlation $\tilde{R}_{dx}(n,k)$ between $d(n)$

and $x(n)$, we need $2N^2$ multiplications; totally we need $2N^2+3N$ multiplications. On the other hand, in the FECLMS algorithm we need three N-point FFTs and only $2N$ multiplications to estimate the cross-correlation function and the tap coefficients adaptation, so that in total the number of multiplication for the FECLMS algorithm is as follows:

$$3 \times \frac{N}{2} \log_2 N + 2N + 3N. \qquad (151)$$

In the WECLMS algorithm we need three N-point DWT process. As we know the computation of the wavelet decomposition can be written as $2(L+1)N$, where L is the number of non-zero values of the scaling function (for Haar, $L=2$, and for the Daubechies2, $L=4$). We only need N^2 multiplications to estimate the cross-correlation function and the tap coefficients adaptation, because of the downsampling process, so that in total the number of multiplication for the WECLMS algorithm is as follows:

$$3 \times 2 \times (L+1) \times N + N^2 + 3N. \qquad (152)$$

As we can see, the CLMS algorithm is just 2.5 times more complex than the LMS algorithm. The ECLMS algorithm is very complex compared with the LMS algorithm; however, the FECLMS algorithm is proposed to reduce the computational complexity. In Table 1, the ratios of the computational loads for the CLMS, FECLMS, and WECLMS to the ECLMS

Figure 19. Echo canceller using WECLMS algorithm

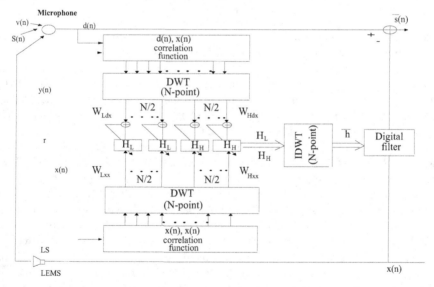

algorithms are given with respect to various numbers of tap coefficients N. For this comparison we need only to compare the computational loads in the different parts of the proposed algorithms. For instance, in N=512 the WECLMS algorithm requires 51.7% of computational loads for the ECLMS algorithm. The computational complexity is reduced. The FECLMS algorithm requires only 1.5% of computational loads for the ECLMS algorithm. This makes the hardware implementation of the FECLMS algorithm a realistic matter using a fewer chips of DSP, or in considering of the mass production, it requires less LSI area.

Simulation Results

To demonstrate the validity and the robustness of the proposed algorithm, some simulations were done. Because we do like to make a comparison with all proposed algorithms, in these simulations we implemented the proposed algorithms under the same environments. The acoustic echo impulse response, r_i, of the room is assumed to have exponential decaying shape that decreases to -60 dB after N samples as follows:

$$r_i = Rand[\exp(-8i/N)]. \tag{153}$$

To measure the performance of the convergence of the algorithm, we use the ratio of distance of weight and impulse response, $DW(n)$, which is defined as follows:

$$DW(n) = 10\log_{10}[\sum_{i=0}^{N-1} \| r_i - \tilde{h}_i(n) \|^2 / \sum_{i=0}^{N-1} \| r_i \|^2]. \tag{154}$$

In order to show the capability and robustness of the proposed algorithms, we have performed several computer simulations by using the real speech data. Here, we use two independent speech signals: one is in English, and another is in Japanese. The far-end signal $x(n)$ is the voice of a woman in her 20s and pronounced as "Good morning and welcome to IF I ONLY KNEW…" in English. The double-talk signal $s(n)$ is the voice of a woman in her 30s and pronounced as "KA RE GA IZEN KA RA, KAGA KU GIJYUTSU…" in Japanese. The sampling frequency is 8kHz for both. The waveforms of the speech signals are shown in Figure 20 and Figure 21. The noise $v(n)$ is a Gaussian noise signal with zero mean. In LMS, CLMS, ECLMS, and FECLMS algorithms we set the step size equal to 0.01. In WECLMS algorithm, we use two different step sizes (μ_L=0.001, μ_H=0.01) to estimate the room impulse response in the two bands. In Figure 22, the convergence characteristics for LMS and proposed algorithms in noisy single-talk condition have been shown. The CLMS algorithm converges to -8dB, the ECLMS algorithm reaches -16dB, the FECLMS algorithm converges to -18dB, and the LMS algorithm reaches -31dB. The WECLMS algorithm is better than the CLMS, ECLMS, and FECLMS algorithms, and it converges to -22dB. In Figure 23, the proposed algorithms are compared with LMS algorithm in the noisy double-talk condition. As shown in Figure 23, the LMS algorithm hardly converges and is totally blown up in the double-talk situation. The CLMS gives a better convergence than the LMS algorithm, and it converges to about -6dB. The ECLMS algorithm reaches -16dB, and the FECLMS algorithm converges to -18dB. The WECLMS algorithm, which is the best among all algorithms, shows a steady convergence under noisy double-talk condition, and it converges to -22dB. Here, the convergence speed was also improved. Then, we note that the new class of algorithms is robust in the double-talk condition. In the next simulation in Figure 24, we started with the noisy single-talk condition; then, at 10000-th iteration, we changed to double-talk condition, but the acoustic echo impulse response has not been changed here. We can see the robustness of proposed algorithm. These algorithms can continue the adaptation even after we changed the single-talk to the double-talk condition. In Figure 25, we started with the single-talk condition. Then, at 10000th iteration, we changed the echo path impulse response and imposed the double-talk condition at the same time. As shown in Figure 25, the WECLMS algorithm has superior convergence characteristics compared to the LMS, CLMS, ECLMS, and FECLMS algorithm.

Smart Acoustic Room System for Partitioning Room Acoustically

Study of the room acoustics is an important topic in all kinds of speech processing and audio systems. In hands free telephony or in teleconferencing systems, acoustic echo canceller (Haykin, 1996) is used to remove the echo signal from speech. Here, echo is generated due to acoustic couplage between loudspeaker and microphone in a room. The echo degrades the intelligibility of the communication. Therefore, AEC tries to estimate the room acoustic response and make a replica of the echo signal and remove it. The acoustic noise control (ANC) (Kuo & Morgan, 1996) system is another example to reduce acoustic noise in a location of the room. Here, the acoustic noise is propagated through room acoustics, and ANC tries to estimate this acoustic path to generate an opposite signal similar to noise and reduce it appropriately. In all kinds of previously mentioned examples, we need to estimate and control the room acoustic response between two locations. Nevertheless, this control could be imposed electrically (AEC) or acoustically (ANC); the adaptive digital filter is used to perform this job with an appropriate algorithm. In this section, we want to introduce a room with smart acoustic. That is, the acoustic response between two (or more) points could be controlled smartly. By control, we mean to have a good estimation of the acoustic path between two points and then to make the appropriate signal to cancel an unwanted signal or to emphasis to a desired signal (speech or music). And also, we apply the smart

Table 1.

N	CLMS / ECLMS	FECLMS / ECLMS	WECLMS / ECLMS
32	0.031	0.148	0.781
128	0.008	0.049	0.572
256	0.004	0.027	0.535
512	0.002	0.015	0.517

acoustic room (SAR) system into the double-talk echo canceling. That is, by smartly controlling the impulse response in the room, the signals from the loudspeakers will be cancelled at the microphone position. This is a new type of echo canceling; it is different from the conventional echo cancellation, which cancels the echo signal in the telephone system electronically. Suppose that we want to listen to jazz music in one portion of a room, and at the same time another person wants to listen to classical music on the other side of the room. Also, we do not want to use headphones, as it totally isolates the person from the surroundings. Another example is in a conference room or big hall, where we have two kinds of audiences. In one section, audiences want to listen in Japanese, while in another section international audiences are seated and want to listen to the speech in English. Again, we do not want to use headphones, as here is very costly to manage the system for each person,

Figure 20. The input speech signal from far-end

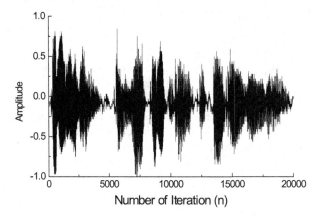

Figure 21. The double-talk speech signal from near-end

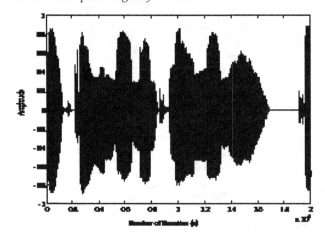

and the hall should be designed for that or we need transceiver, which is also costly. But if we design the acoustic response such that Japanese loudspeakers cover the desired location while English loudspeakers cover the other part, just by sitting in the right place one can hear the desired language. There are many more applications of SAR systems. ANC is a special case of SAR, because in a room we want to reduce the noise source propagation to a location. In more general case, we can define acoustic channels similar to radio or TV channels. Imagine you want to change the channel of TV by using a remote control. The same is possible to be performed for acoustic channel. But, the difference here is location dependency of the remote control. That is, depending on place of the remote control, one can push a button to listen to a specific program that will be propagated to that place only.

Figure 22. Comparison between LMS, CLMS, ECLMS, FECLMS, and WECLMS in noisy single-talk condition

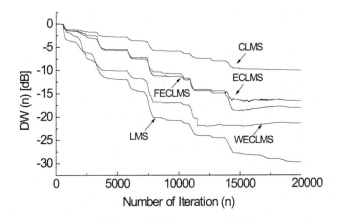

Figure 23. Comparison between LMS, CLMS, ECLMS, FECLMS, and WECLMS in noisy double-talk condition

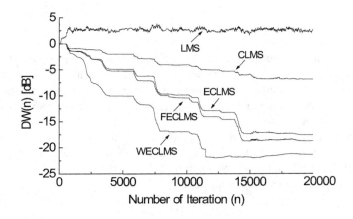

Figure 24. Switching from single- to double-talk with the same echo path

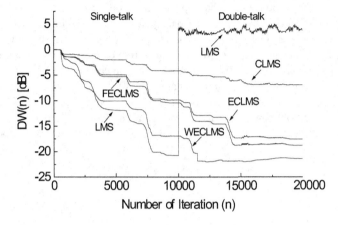

Figure 25. Switching from single- to double-talk with the echo path changed

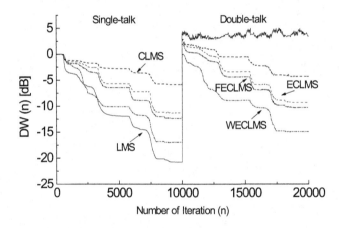

If we move the remote control to another location in the room, we can select another program and set the acoustic path to listen only to a specified program. Therefore, in SAR we require changing and controlling of the acoustic impulse response of the room, as we desire. Of course, sound propagation through acoustic channel from one loudspeaker could cause perturbation for the other one. This is because in contrast to electromagnetic propagation and frequency division multiplexing (by using proper modulation technique), it is not possible in acoustic wave propagation. Therefore, by using a powerful algorithm in adaptive digital filter, one can make the null point (zero point) of an acoustic source to be set in a specific location and/or move it to any other location.

SAR by Using Virtual Microphone Method

In this section, we are challenge to control the acoustic response between two points as shown in Figure 26, that is, by using two speakers and one microphone to make an acoustic null point at the microphone position. In Figure 27, a SAR model by using the virtual microphone (Asharif, Chen, & Higa, 2005; Asharif, Higa, & Chen, 2004; Ohana & Kohna, 2002) is shown. The source signal $x(n)$ is for instance a record player output or any audio electric signal. This signal is usually converted to acoustic signal through an amplifier and a loudspeaker in order to propagate in a room for listening. The acoustic paths from speaker S1 to the microphone M is $w_1(n)$, and the one from speaker S2 is $w_2(n)$. We want to make a null point at the place of microphone M. For this purpose, we put one adaptive filter estimator $h(n)$ in order to predict the acoustic paths and to zero-enforce the signal of M. The signal of microphone is called the error signal, $e(n)$, and it is obtained as follows:

$$e(n) = x(n) * w_1(n) + x(n) * h(n) * w_2(n). \tag{155}$$

Aside from speakers S1 and S2, we imagine that we have two virtual speakers S̃1 and S̃2 in parallel with S1 and S2, respectively. Also, we define two virtual acoustic paths for S̃1 and S̃2 as $\tilde{w}_1(n)$ and $\tilde{w}_2(n)$ from each virtual speaker to a virtual microphone M̃ (see Figure 27). The signal of the virtual microphone is $\tilde{e}(n)$. According to Figure 27, we can write the following relation for the virtual paths:

$$\tilde{e}(n) = x(n) * \tilde{w}_1(n) + x(n) * h(n) * \tilde{w}_2(n). \tag{156}$$

If $h(n)$ is adapted perfectly, then the virtual error signal will be diminished to zero. Therefore, in Z transform we have:

$$X(z) * \tilde{W}_1(z) + X(z) * H(z) * \tilde{W}_2(z) = 0, \tag{157}$$

that is,

$$H(z) = -\frac{\tilde{W}_1(z)}{\tilde{W}_2(z)}. \tag{158}$$

From equation (155) and equation (157), we conclude that

$$\frac{W_1(z)}{W_2(z)} = \frac{\tilde{W}_1(z)}{\tilde{W}_2(z)} \Rightarrow \frac{W_1(z)}{\tilde{W}_1(z)} = \frac{W_2(z)}{\tilde{W}_2(z)} = a(z). \tag{159}$$

Function $a(z)$ describes the relation between the real and virtual part of the system. Then we can use two simple LMS adaptive filters to estimate the impulse responses w_1 and w_2. For estimation of the w_1, the error signal can be written

$$E_{w1}(z) = [W_1(z) - a(z)\tilde{W}_1(z)]X(z)$$
$$= W_1(z)X(z) - \frac{W_2(z)}{\tilde{W}_2(z)}\tilde{W}_1(z)X(z) = E(z). \qquad (160)$$

As the same for estimation the w_2, the error signal can be written:

$$E_{w2}(z) = -E(z). \qquad (161)$$

That is, the acoustic paths $w_1(n)$ and $w_2(n)$ can be estimated by using the real error $e(n)$. In order to reduce the computational complexity at this time all the computation will be done in the frequency domain (Asharif & Amano, 1994). First, the FFT of the input signals $x(n)$, $y(n)$ are calculated:

Figure 26. Two speakers SAR system

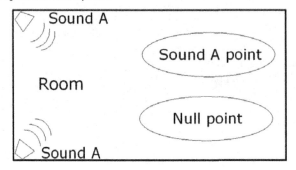

Figure 27. SAR model by using the virtual microphone

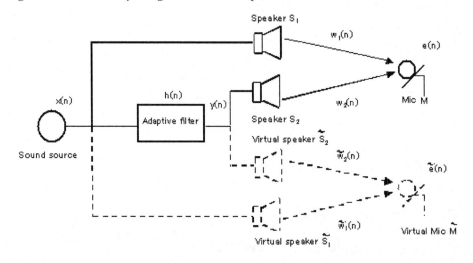

$$F_x(n,p) = \sum_{k=0}^{N-1} x(n-k)W^{kp}, \tag{162}$$

$$F_y(n,p) = \sum_{k=0}^{N-1} y(n-k)W^{kp}, \tag{163}$$

where W shows complex exponential $e^{-j(2\pi/N)}$, and N is the impulse response length. Then, the FFT transform of the error signal is calculated:

$$F_e(n,p) = \sum_{k=0}^{N-1} e(n-k)W^{kp}. \tag{164}$$

So, the acoustic impulse response can be estimated by:

$$\tilde{W}_1(n+1,p) = \tilde{W}_1(n,p) + \frac{2\mu F_e(n,p)F_x^*(n,p)}{1 + tr[F_x(n,p)F_x(n,p)]}, \tag{165}$$

$$\tilde{W}_2(n+1,p) = \tilde{W}_2(n,p) - \frac{2\mu F_e(n,p)F_y^*(n,p)}{1 + tr[F_y(n,p)F_y(n,p)]}. \tag{166}$$

The superscript * in equation (166) shows the Hermitian transposition, and $tr[\cdot]$ means the trace operator. Finally H(z) is calculated by equation (158), and $h(n)$ can be calculated by using the inverse FFT transform.

Figure 28. Four speakers SAR system

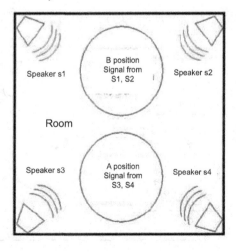

SAR Algorithm Based on Correlation Function

In this section, the SAR *algorithm* based on the *correlation function* is presented (Chen, Asharif, & Yamashita, 2005). The SAR system is shown in Figure 28. The aim of this system is that by control the *acoustic impulse responses* the signals in the room can be separated. The person can choose the desired signal just by sitting at the different positions. As shown in Figure 28, the person who sitting at the position A just can hear the desired signals from speakers S3 and S4, because the signals from speakers S1 and S2 were cancelled. The same process will be done for the position B. The person who seating at the position B just can hear the desired signal from the speakers S1 and S2.

Because the processes for positions A and B are the same, here just the process for the position A will be introduced. In Figure 29 the structure of the proposed SAR algorithm is shown. The desired signal from speakers S3 and S4 are assumed as the double-talk signals. Also the proposed algorithm will be implemented in the frequency domain. For the double-talk condition the signal from the microphone will be defined as follows:

$$d(n) = e(n) + s(n)$$
$$= x(n) * w_1(n) + x(n) * h(n) * w_2(n) + s(n). \tag{167}$$

First, the auto-correlation of the input signal is calculated:

$$R_{xx}(n,k) = \sum_{j=0}^{n} x(j)x(j-k), \tag{168}$$

$$R_{yy}(n,k) = \sum_{j=0}^{n} y(j)y(j-k). \tag{169}$$

Then, the cross-correlation function is calculated:

Figure 29. Structure of the SAR system based on correlation function

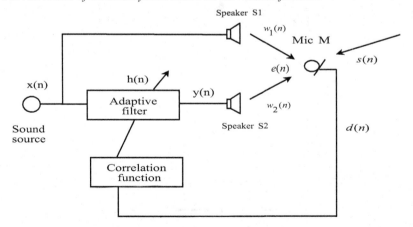

$$R_{dx}(n,k) = \sum_{j=0}^{n} d(j)x(j-k),$$ (170)

$$R_{dy}(n,k) = \sum_{j=0}^{n} d(j)y(j-k).$$ (171)

The fast Fourier transform is shown as follows:

$$F_{xx}(n,p) = \sum_{k=0}^{N-1}\left[\sum_{j=0}^{n} x(j)x(j-k)\right]W^{kp},$$ (172)

$$F_{yy}(n,p) = \sum_{k=0}^{N-1}\left[\sum_{j=0}^{n} y(j)y(j-k)\right]W^{kp},$$ (173)

$$F_{dx}(n,p) = \sum_{k=0}^{N-1}\left[\sum_{j=0}^{n} d(j)x(j-k)\right]W^{kp},$$ (174)

$$F_{dy}(n,p) = \sum_{k=0}^{N-1}\left[\sum_{j=0}^{n} d(j)y(j-k)\right]W^{kp}.$$ (175)

So the acoustic paths can be updated by:

Figure 30. Echo canceling base on SAR system and correlation function

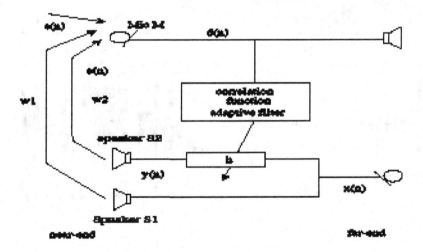

$$\tilde{W}_1(n+1, p) = \tilde{W}_1(n) + \frac{2\mu F_{dx}(n, p)F_{xx}^*(n, p)}{1 + tr[F_{xx}(n, p)F_{xx}(n, p)]},$$ (176)

$$\tilde{W}_2(n+1, p) = \tilde{W}_2(n, p) - \frac{2\mu F_{dy}(n, p)F_{yy}^*(n, p)}{1 + tr[F_{yy}(n, p)F_{yy}(n, p)]}.$$ (177)

The superscript * shows the Hermitian transposition, and $tr[\cdot]$ means the trace operator. Finally the $h(n)$ can be calculated by using the inverse FFT transform from the $H(z)$.

A New Method of Acoustic Echo Canceling Based on Room Partitioning System

In this section, we combine ANC with AEC to improve echo canceller performance. In ANC, as we know the acoustic noise is supposed to be cancelled by generating an opposite phase signal that is generated by adaptive filtering of reference (main) noise signal. Now, if we use this ANC structure at near end room in the AEC system, then echo signal will be diminished at the microphone position. That is, a very week feedback exists between loud-speaker and microphone. In a sense, we cancel echo signal before it enters the microphone, acoustically by using ANC system. In Figure 30, the proposed echo canceling system by using the smart acoustic room and correlation function is shown (Chen, Asharif, & Yamashita, 2005). This algorithm uses two speakers and one microphone; by smartly controlling the

Figure 31. Waveform of signals

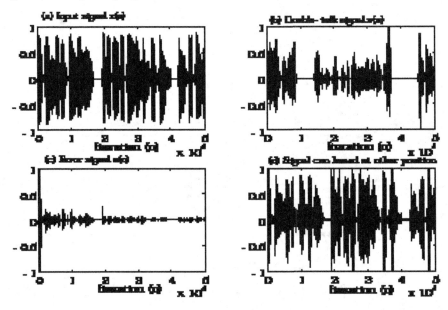

acoustic impulse responses, the speaker signals will be cancelled at the microphone position locally. That is, the microphone cannot receive any echo signal. For the double-talk, the correlation function in the frequency domain also is used. As shown in Figure 30, $x(n)$ is the input signal from the far-end room. $y(n)$ is the output signal of the adaptive filter. $e(n)$ is the signal from the speakers, which is called as error signal. $d(n)$ is the signal picked up by the microphone, including the error signal and double-talk signal. $s(n)$ is the double-talk signal from the near-end room. For the double-talk condition, the signal from the microphone will be defined as follows:

$$d(n) = e(n) + s(n)$$
$$= x(n) * w_1(n) + x(n) * h(n) * w_2(n) + s(n). \qquad (178)$$

As in the SAR system, which is presented in the previous section, if $h(n)$ is adapted perfectly, then the error signal $e(n)$ will be diminished to zero. That is, the signal from speakers will be cancelled at the microphone position. The microphone cannot receive any echo signal. First, the auto-correlation of the input signal is calculated:

$$R_{xx}(n,k) = \sum_{j=0}^{n} x(j)x(j-k), \qquad (179)$$

$$R_{yy}(n,k) = \sum_{j=0}^{n} y(j)y(j-k). \qquad (180)$$

Then, the cross-correlation function is calculated:

Figure 32. Waveform of signals

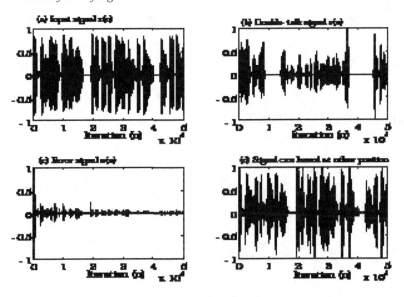

Figure 33. The MSE of the proposed algorithm in double-talk condition

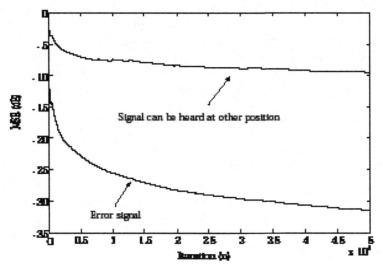

$$R_{dx}(n,k) = \sum_{j=0}^{n} d(j)x(j-k), \tag{181}$$

$$R_{dy}(n,k) = \sum_{j=0}^{n} d(j)y(j-k). \tag{182}$$

The fast Fourier transform of the correlation functions are shown as follows:

$$F_{xx}(n,p) = \sum_{k=0}^{N-1} \left[\sum_{j=0}^{n} x(j)x(j-k) \right] W^{kp}, \tag{183}$$

$$F_{yy}(n,p) = \sum_{k=0}^{N-1} \left[\sum_{j=0}^{n} y(j)y(j-k) \right] W^{kp}, \tag{184}$$

$$F_{dx}(n,p) = \sum_{k=0}^{N-1} \left[\sum_{j=0}^{n} d(j)x(j-k) \right] W^{kp}, \tag{185}$$

$$F_{dy}(n,p) = \sum_{k=0}^{N-1} \left[\sum_{j=0}^{n} d(j)y(j-k) \right] W^{kp}. \tag{186}$$

So, the acoustic paths can be updated by:

$$\tilde{W}_1(n+1,p) = \tilde{W}_1(n) + \frac{2\mu F_{dx}(n,p)F_{xx}^*(n,p)}{1+tr[F_{xx}(n,p)F_{xx}(n,p)]},$$ (187)

$$\tilde{W}_2(n+1,p) = \tilde{W}_2(n,p) - \frac{2\mu F_{dy}(n,p)F_{yy}^*(n,p)}{1+tr[F_{yy}(n,p)F_{yy}(n,p)]}.$$ (188)

Simulation Results

In this section, we first explain the simulation results of the SAR system for partitioning room acoustically; we then apply the SAR system into the double-talk echo canceling, and of course the simulation results will be explained. In simulation for the SAR system, we assume that the person is sitting at the position A. We want to cancel the signals from speakers S1 and S2. And the signal from the speakers S3 and S4 will be heard as a desired signal. As shown in Figure 29, the signals $x(n)$ and $y(n)$ are the input signals of speakers S1 and S2, respectively. The signal $s(n)$ is the output signal from speakers S3 and S4. Here, the signal $s(n)$ is assumed as the double-talk signal. The microphone M is set at the position A to pick up the error signal. The input signal $x(n)$ is a speech signal of a woman in English, and the double-talk signal $s(n)$ is a speech of a woman in Japanese as shown in Figure 31a and 31b, respectively. The adaptive filter has 32 taps. The step size is 0.01. The acoustic paths $w_1(n)$ and $w_2(n)$ of the room are assumed to have an exponential decaying shape that decreases to -60dB after M sample, which is defined as follows:

$$w_{1,2}(i) = Rand[\exp(-8i/M)],$$ (189)

where Rand is a normal distributed random number between +1 and −1 with zero mean and unit variance. $w_{1,2}$ is the impulse response from the speakers S1 and S2 to the microphone, respectively. In Figure 31c, the waveform of the error signal at the microphone position is shown. The signals are canceled at the microphone position locally. In Figure 31d, the waveform of the signal, that is, what can be heard by the person at position A, is shown. Compared with the waveforms of the double-talk signal and the signal that can be heard in position A, which is shown in Figure 31b and 31d, we can see that there are not many differences between the two waveforms. That is, the person who is sitting at the position A can just hear the signals from the speakers S3 and S4, clearly.

The simulation results of the double-talk echo canceling based on the SAR system and correlation function are shown in Figure 32. As in previous simulations, the input signal $x(n)$ is a speech signal of a woman in English, and the double-talk signal $s(n)$ is a speech of a woman in Japanese as shown in Figures 31a and 31b, respectively. The adaptive filter has 32 taps. The step size is 0.01. In Figure 31c, the waveform of the error signal at the microphone position is shown. The signals are canceled at the microphone position locally. That means there is not signal feedback from the speakers to the microphone, and there is no echo signal generated in the telephone system. In Figure 31d, the waveform of the signal, that is, what can be heard by the person in the near-end room, is shown. Compared with the waveforms of the input signal and the signal that can be heard by the person, which is shown in Figures 31a and 31d, we can see that there are not many differences between the two waveforms. That is, the person who talking in the near-end room can hear the signals from the speakers clearly.

To measure the performance of the algorithm, also the MSE is used. The MSE of the algorithms is shown. The MSE can be defined as:

$$MSE = \frac{1}{M} \sum_{k=1}^{M} e(k)^2. \tag{190}$$

In the double-talk condition, the proposed algorithm converges to -32 dB of at the microphone position, and a -8db signal can be heard at another position, which is shown in Figure 33. That is, the echo can be cancelled in the microphone position by using the smart acoustic control and correlation function. Also, the person who is talking in the near-end room can hear the signal from the speakers clearly.

Conclusion

In this chapter, we explained the merits of adaptive digital filter. ADFs are very useful in modeling an unknown system just by knowing input-output information. On the other hand, the problem of acoustic echo canceling was addressed. The optimum solution for finding best coefficients is derived by using Wiener-Hopf equation. Then we applied ADF to AEC using various algorithms such as LMS, NLMS, FDAF, and FBAF. A very important problem in AEC is double-talk echo canceling. This challenging problem was treated by using a new approach in digital signal processing. That is, instead of processing a sampled signal, we introduced the processing of the correlation of the signal (this is in a sense second-ordered statistical signal processing). Various algorithms such as CLMS, ECLMS, FECLMS, and WECLMS are introduced and evaluated for challenging DTEC. At the end of this chapter, a new system called smart acoustic room to control room acoustic impulse response was introduced. Using the SAR system, we could reach to a very robust algorithm for DTEC.

References

Asharif, M. R., & Amano, F. (1990). Hardware implementation of acoustic echo canceller based on FBAF algorithm. In *Proceedings of the IEEE Workshop on VLSI Signal Processing* (pp. 191-200). San Diego, CA.

Asharif, M. R., & Amano, F. (1994). Acoustic echo-canceller using the FBAF algorithm. *IEEE Trans. Communications, 42*(12), 3090-3094.

Asharif, M. R., Amano, F., Unagami, S., & Murano, K. (1986). A new structure of echo canceller based on frequency bin adaptive filtering (FBAF). *DSP Symp. (in Japan), A3.1.* (pp. 165-169).

Asharif, M. R., Amano, F., Unagami, S., & Murano, K. (1987). Acoustic echo canceller based on frequency bin adaptive filtering (FBAF). In *Proceedings of the IEEE Int. Con5 Global Telecommun* (pp. 1940-1944).

Asharif, M. R., Chen, R., & Yamashita, K. (2003). Acoustic echo canceling in the double-talk condition. In *Proceedings of the IEEE, EURASIP, Eighth International Workshop on Acoustic Echo and Noise Control* (pp. 39-42). Kyoto, Japan.

Asharif, M. R., Chen, R., & Higa, R. (2005). Smart acoustic room (SAR) system by using virtual microphone. *International Symposium on Telecommunications (IST)*. Shiraz, Iran.

Asharif, M. R., Chen, R., & Yamashita, K. (2004). A new class of adaptive algorithm based on correlation functions for double-talk acoustic echo canceling. *Journal of Mathematics and Computer in Simulation, Elsevier Publisher, 65*(6), 599-605.

Asharif, M. R., & Hayashi, T. (1999). Correlation LMS for double-talk echo canceling. In *Proceedings of the IASTED International Conference, Modeling and Simulation* (pp. 249-253). Philadelphia, PA (Cherry Hill, NJ).

Asharif, M. R., Hayashi, T., & Yamashita, K. (1999). Correlation LMS algorithm and its application to double-talk echo canceling. *ELECTRONICS LETTERS, 35*(3), 194-195.

Asharif, M. R., Higa, R., & Chen, R. (2004). Smart acoustic room. *The 2004 autumn meeting of the acoustical society of Japan* (pp. 601-602).

Asharif, M. R., Rezapour, A., & Ochi, H. (1998). Correlation LMS algorithm for double-talk echo canceller. In *Proceedings of the IEICE National Conference, A-4-13.* (p. 122). Japan.

Asharif, M. R., Shimabukuro, A., Hayashi, T., & Yamashita, K. (1999). Expanded CLMS algorithm for double-talk echo canceling. In *Proceedings of the IEEE, SMC'99, Japan* (vol. 1) (pp. 998-1002).

Asharif, M. R., Shiroma, M., & Yamashita, K. (2000). Design of echo canceller with frequency domain ECLMS algorithm. In *Proceedings of the IEEE Global Telecommunications Conference* (vol. 1), (pp. 1649-1653).

Benesty, J., Morgan, D. R., & Cho, J. H. (2000). A new class of double-talk detectors based on cross-correlation. *IEEE Transactions on Speech and Audio Processing, 8*(2), 168-172.

Bershad, N. J., & Feintuch, P. L. (1979). Analysis of the frequency domain adaptive filter. *Processing IEEE, 67*(12), 1658-1659.

Bran VSP ZR34161 data book, Zoran Corporation, Santa Clara, CA, 1987.

Chen, R., Asharif, M. R., Ardekani, I. T., & Yamashita, K. (2004). A new class of acoustic echo canceling by using correlation LMS algorithm for double-talk condition. *IEICE Transactions on Fundamentals, Special Section Issue on Digital Signal Processing, E87-A*(8), 1933-1940.

Chen, R., Asharif, M. R., & Yamashita, K. (2005a). A new type echo canceling by using the smart acoustic room (SAR) system & correlation function for the double-talk condition. In *IEEE, EURASIP, Ninth International Workshop on Acoustic Echo and Noise Control* (pp. 29-32). Eindhoven, The Netherlands.

Chen, R., Asharif, M. R., & Yamashita, K. (2005b). Smart acoustic room (SAR) system. In *Symposium on Information Theory and its Applications (SITA) conference* (pp. 913-916). Okinawa, Japan.

Cho, J. H., Morgan, D. R., & Benesty, J. (1999). An objective technique for evaluating double-talk detectors in acoustic echo cancellers. *IEEE Transactions on Speech and Audio Processing, 7*(6), 718-724.

Clark, G. A., Mitra, S. K., & Parker, S. R. (1981). Block implementation of adaptive digital filters. *IEEE Transaction on Circuits and Systems, CAS-28*, 584-592.

Clark, G. A., Parker, S. R., & Mitra, S. K. (1983). A unified approach to time and frequency-domain realization of FIR adaptive digital filters. *IEEE Transaction on Acoustic Speech Signal Processing, ASSP-31,* 1073-1083.

Dentino, M., McCool, J., & Widrow, B. (1978). Adaptive filtering in the frequency domain. *Proceeding IEEE, 66*(12), 1658-1659.

Duttweiler, D. L. (1978). A twelve-channel digital echo canceller. *IEEE Transaction on Communications, COMM-26*, 647-653.

Ferrara, E. R. (1980). Fast implementation of LMS adaptive filters. *IEEE Transaction on Acoustic Speech Signal Processing, ASSP-28*(4), 474-475.

Ferrara, E. R. (1985). Frequency-domain adaptive filtering. In C. F. N. Cowan & P. M. Grant (Eds.), *Adaptive filters* (pp. 145-179). Englewood Cliffs, NJ: Prentice-Hall.

Fujitsu FDSP-3 MB8764 data manual, Fujitsu Ltd, Tokyo, Japan, 1984.

Gansler, T., Gay, S. L., Sondhi, M. M., & Benesty, J. (2000). Double-talk robust fast converging algorithm for network echo cancellation. *IEEE Transaction on Speech and Audio Processing, 8*(6), 656-663.

Gansler, T., Hansson, M., Invarsson, C. J., & Salomomsson, G., (1996). A double-talk detector based on coherence. *IEEE Transaction on Communications, 44,* 1421-1427.

Hansler, E., & Schmidt, G. (2004). *Acoustic echo and noise control: A practical approach.* John Wiley & Sons.

Haykin, S. (1996). *Adaptive filter theory* (3rd ed.). Prentice Hall.

Heitkamper, P. (1997). An adaptation control for acoustic echo cancellers. *IEEE Signal Processing Letters, 4*(6), 170-172.

Kuo, S. M., & Morgan, D. R. (1996). *Active noise control systems.* John Wiley & Sons.

Kushner, H. J. (1984). *Approximation and weak convergence methods for random processes with applications to stochastic system theory.* Cambridge, MA: MIT Press.

Murano, K., Unagami, S., & Amano, F. (1990). Echo cancellation and application. *IEEE Communications Magazine, 28,* 49-55.

Nagumo, J. I., &. Noda, A. (1967). A leaning method for system identification. *IEEE Transaction on Automatic Control, 12,* 282-287.

Ohana, Y., & Kohna, T. (2002). Direct fully adaptive active noise control algorithms without identification of secondary path dynamics. In *IEEE International Conference on Control Application*. Scotland.

Rabiner, L. R., & Schafer, R. W. (1978). *Digital processing of speech signal*. Prentice Hall.

Regalia, P. A. (1994). *Adaptive IIR filtering in signal processing and control*. New York: Dekker.

Shynk, J. J. (1989). Adaptive IIR filtering. *IEEE Signal Processing Magazine, 6,* 4-21.

Shynk, J. J. (1992). Frequency-domain and multirate adaptive filtering. *IEEE Signal Processing Magazine, 9*(1), 14-37.

Weiss, & Mitra, D. (1979). Digital adaptive filter: Condition for convergence, rate of convergence, effects of noise and errors arising from the implementation. *IEEE Transactions on Information Theory, IT-25,* 637-652.

Widrow, B., & Lehr, M. (1990). 30 years of adaptive neural networks: Perceptron, madaline and backpropagation. *Proc. IEEE, Special Issue on Neural networks I, 78*(9), 1415-1442.

Widrow, B., & Stearns, S. D. (1985). *Adaptive signal processing*. Englewood Cliffs, NJ: Prentice-Hall.

Wiener, N. (1949). *Extrapolation, interpolation, and smoothing of stationary time series*. New York: Wiley.

Wiener, N., & Hopf, E. (1931). On a class of singular integral equations. In *Proceedings of the Prussian Acad. Math-Phys. Ser* (p. 696).

Ye, H., & Wu, B. X. (1991). A new double-talk detection algorithm based on the orthogonality theorem. *IEEE Transaction on Communications, 39,* 1542-1545.

Chapter IX

Active Noise Canceling:
Structures and Adaption Algorithms

Hector Perez-Meana, National Polytechnic Institute, Mexico

Mariko Nakano-Miyatake, National Polytechnic Institute, Mexico

Abstract

Some of the main problems present in active noise cancellations are the feedback distortion due to the acoustic feedback between the cancellation speaker and the input microphone; the high computational complexity when recursive least square algorithms are used; and the secondary path estimation. This chapter presents a review of some successful solutions to these problems, such as a hybrid structure to reduce the feedback distortion; active noise cancellation (ANC) FxRLS algorithms in which the filter input signal is decomposed into a finite number; and mutually near orthogonal signal components, as well as successful secondary path estimation algorithms. Computer simulation results confirm the desirable properties of presented ANC structures.

Introduction

Acoustic noise problem becomes more and more important as the use of large industrial equipment such as engines, blowers, fans, transformers, air conditioners, motors, and so forth increases. Due to its importance, several methods have been proposed to solve this problem (Kuo & Morgan, 1996, 1999), such as enclosures, barriers, silencers, and other passive techniques that attenuate the undesirable noise (Beranek & Ver, 1992; Harris, 1991; Kuo & Morgan, 1999). There are mainly two types of passive techniques: the first type uses the concept of impedance change caused by a combination of baffles and tubes to silence the undesirable sound. These types of passive techniques, usually called reactive silencers, are commonly used as mufflers in internal combustion engines.

The second type, called resistive silencers, uses energy loss caused by sound propagation in a duct lined with sound-absorbing material (Aoki & Morishita, 2001; Erickson, Allie, & Bremigon, 1988; Kuo & Morgan, 1999; Nelson & Elliot, 1992; Usagawa & Shimada, 2001). These silencers are usually used in ducts for fan noise (Kuo & Morgan, 1999). Both types of passive silencers have been successfully used during many years in several applications; however, the attenuation of passive silencers is low when the acoustic wavelength is large compared with the silencer's dimension (Erickson et al., 1988). In an effort to overcome these problems, single- and multi-channel active noise cancellation (ANC), which uses a secondary noise source that destructively interferes with the unwanted noise, has received considerable attention during the last several years (Erickson et al., 1988; Kuo & Morgan, 1999). In addition, because the characteristics of the environment and acoustic noise source, as well as the amplitude, phase, and sound velocity of the undesirable noise are non-stationary, the ANC system must be adaptive in order to cope with these variations (Kuo & Morgan, 1999; Nelson & Elliot, 1992).

Widely used ANC systems are the single channel ANC systems that typically use two microphones. The first microphone is used to measure the noise signal, and the second microphone is used to measure the attenuated noise or error signal. Both signals are then used to update the ANC parameters such that error power becomes a minimum (Figure 1) (Kuo & Morgan, 1999; Nelson & Elliot, 1992). In this kind of ANC systems, the adaptive filter, $W(z)$, estimates the time varying unknown acoustic path from the reference microphone to the point where the noise attenuation must be achieved, $P(z)$.

Figure 1. Single-channel broadband feed forward ANC in a duct

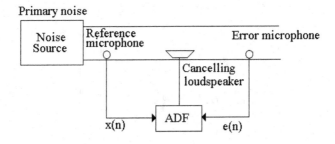

The active noise canceller system is quite similar to the traditional noise canceller system (Widrow & Stearns, 1981) because in both cases the purpose of the adaptive filter is to minimize the power of the residual error, such that the filter output becomes the best estimate of the disturbance signal in the mean square sense. However, in the active noise canceller system an acoustic summing point is used instead of the electrical subtraction of signals. Then after the primary noise is picked up by the reference microphone, the adaptive filter will require some time to estimate the right output of the canceling loudspeaker. Thus, if the electrical delay becomes longer than the acoustic delay from the reference microphone to the canceling loudspeaker, the system performance will be substantially degraded, because in this situation, the ANC impulse response becomes non-causal. However, when the causality

Figure 2. Block diagram of an active noise canceling structure with a system identification configuration and a secondary path estimation (SPE) stage

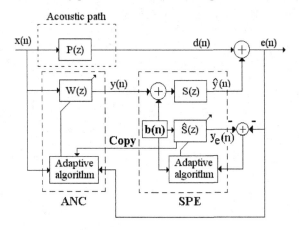

Figure 3. Active noise canceller with acoustic feedback

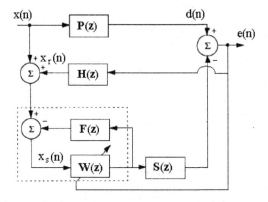

condition is met, the ANC system is able to cancel the broadband random noise (Nelson & Elliot, 1992). Note that if it is not possible to meet the causality condition, the system can effectively cancel only narrowband or periodic noise. To avoid this problem, it is necessary to compensate for the secondary-path transfer function, $S(z)$, from $y(n)$ to $\hat{y}(n)$(Figure 2), which includes the digital-to-analog (D/A) converter, the reconstruction filter, the power amplifier, the loudspeaker, and the acoustic path from loudspeaker to the error microphone, as well as the error microphone, the preamplifier, the anti-aliasing filter, and the analog-to-digital (A/D) converter. A key advantage of this approach is that with a proper model of the plant, $P(z)$, and the secondary-path, $S(z)$, the ANC system can respond instantaneously to change in the statistics of noise signal (Kuo & Morgan, 1999; Nelson & Elliot, 1992). Besides the secondary path explained previously and denoted by $S(z)$, the loudspeaker on a duct wall, shown in Figure 1, will generate plane waves that propagate to both the error and reference microphones. Therefore the anti-noise not only cancels the primary noise source, but also radiates upstream to the reference microphone resulting on a corrupted reference signal $x(n)$ as shown in Figure 3. This effect is called acoustic feedback.

The ANC structure with a system identification configuration presents a good cancellation performance in most applications because it is able to cancel both narrow and wide band noise. However, in some situations the signal produced by the canceling speaker is also captured by the reference microphone, leading to a performance degradation of the ANC system (Kuo & Morgan, 1996, 1999). A possible choice to avoid this distortion is to use another adaptive filter structure, F(Z), as shown in Figure 3. However, to develop this filter it is necessary to take into account potential instability problems. Another widely used adaptive structure for active noise cancellation generates internally its own input signal using the adaptive filter output and the error signals, as shown in Figures 4 and 5. This approach, if the disturbing noise samples are strongly correlated among them and the secondary-path, $S(z)$, is properly estimated, provides a fairly good cancellation of the disturbing noise (Bustamante & Perez-Meana, 2001; Kuo & Morgan, 1996; Nelson & Elliot, 1992; Tapia, Bustamante, Pérez-Meana, & Nakano-Miyatake, 2005), and because it only uses the error microphone, it does not present the feedback problem, making it suitable for applications in which the position of error and reference microphone is close from each other and the noise to be cancelled is narrow band. However, the system performance will degrade if the correlation among consecutive samples of noise signal weakens because in this situation the prediction of the disturbing signal becomes less accurate (Kuo & Morgan, 1996; Tapia et al., 2005).

Figure 4. A single channel ANC system in a duct using a predictive structure

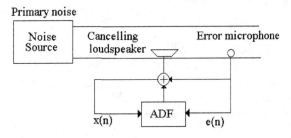

To reduce the ANC distortion produced by the acoustic feedback, a single sensor ANC system in which it is required to cancel wideband noise, and an identification configuration, together with a predictive structure, can be used to reduce the feedback interference (Muneyasu, Wakasugi, Hisayasu, Fujii, & Hinamoto, 2001). In addition, because the characteristics of the acoustic noise and the environment may be time varying, and the frequency content, amplitude, phase, and sound velocity of the undesired noise are non-stationary, the ANC must be adaptive in order to cope with these variations.

Most active noise canceller systems use the FxLMS adaptive algorithm, or some variation of it, mainly due to its low computational complexity. However, the convergence of FxLMS is slow when the input signal autocorrelation matrix presents a large eigenvalue spread. In addition, the FxLMS algorithm is sensitive to additive noise. These facts may limit the use of FxLMS adaptive algorithm when fast convergence rates and low sensitivity to additive noise are required (Petraglia & Mitra, 1993; Tapia et al., 2005). On the other hand, the FxRLS adaptive algorithms have the potential to provide a much faster convergence rate with a much lower sensitivity to additive noise than the FxLMS algorithm, while its computational complexity is very high. Thus, due to the desirable properties of FxRLS algorithm, several efforts have been carried out to reduce the computational complexity of RLS-based algorithms while keeping its desirables properties.

On the other hand, in real time signal processing, a significant amount of computational effort can be saved if the input signals are represented in terms of a set of orthogonal signal components (Nakano-Miyatake & Perez-Meana, 1999; Perez-Meana, Nakano-Miyatake, Martinez, & Sanchez, 1996; Perez-Meana & Tsujii, 1991). That is because the system admits processing schemes in which each signal component can be independently processed. Taking this fact into account, parallel form active noise cancellation algorithms using a single sensor with system identification and predictive configurations were proposed (Tapia et al.,

Figure 5. Block diagram of an ANC algorithm with a predictive structure and an SPE stage

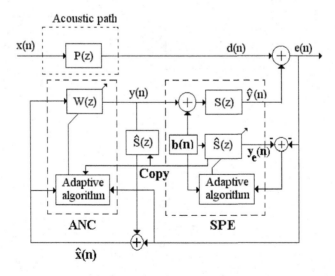

2005), in which the input signal is split into a set of approximately orthogonal signal components by using the discrete cosine transform. Subsequently these signal components are fed into a bank of adaptive transversal filters (FIR-ADF) whose parameters are independently updated to minimize a common error (Perez-Meana et al., 1996; Perez-Meana, Nakano-Miyatake, & Niño de Rivera, 2002; Tapia et al., 2005). The DCT-based schemes, provided in a later section, are attractive alternatives to the conventional filtered-x recursive least squares transversal algorithms, FxRLS, because they reduce the computational complexity of conventional algorithms and keep similar convergence performance.

Hybrid Structure

The feedforward and feedback control structures are called a hybrid ANC system, whereby the canceling signal is generated based on the outputs of both the reference sensor and the error sensor. Significant performance improvements occurred when the secondary-to-reference feedback was present. Figure 6 shows the classical block diagram of a hybrid ANC system. In the hybrid ANC system, the reference microphone is situated near the primary source in order to provide a coherent reference signal, where the error microphone is placed downstream and senses the residual noise. It is then used to synthesize the reference signal for the adaptive feedback ANC filter, as well as to adapt the coefficients of both the feedforward and the feedback ANC filters. The feedforward ANC attenuates the primary noise that is correlated with the reference signal, while the feedback ANC cancels the narrowband components and the secondary-to-reference feedback effect. Figure 7 shows the ANC hybrid structure, which increases the level of cancellation and reduces the feedback effects. As shown in Figure 7, the ANC hybrid structure can be split into two main parts, the identifier part and the predictive part. Here the identifier part, $A(z)$, intends to cancel the primary noise based on an ANC feedforward scheme, using the filtered input signal $x'(n)$ to adapt the coefficients system, together with the residual error picked up by the reference sensor. Using these signals, the feedforward filter is updated using FxRLS algorithm. The second part of the ANC system is the predictive structure, in which the filter output and the output error are used to synthesize the feedback filter input signal, whose output signal will be used to predict and cancel in such way the secondary-to-reference error and the remaining narrow band noise. In this part the algorithm used to update the filter coefficients is the FxLMS. Here the FxLMS is used instead of the FxRLS to reduce the computational complexity of the prediction stage.

Filtered X Least Mean-Square Algorithm (FxLMS)

The main problem present in the adaptation of $W(z)$, which does not appear in the conventional noise canceling schemes, is the introduction of the secondary path that may cause instability if it is not properly compensated because the error signal is not correctly "aligned" in time with the reference signal due to the presence of $S(z)$. To compensate the secondary path effect, a filter of the same characteristics of $S(z)$ is placed on the path of the reference signal of the adaptive algorithm (Kuo & Morgan, 1996). Consider the residual error, which from Figure 2 is given by:

Figure 6. Hybrid ANC system with a combination of feedforward and feedback ANC

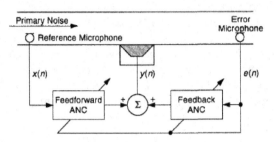

Figure 7. Hybrid ANC structure

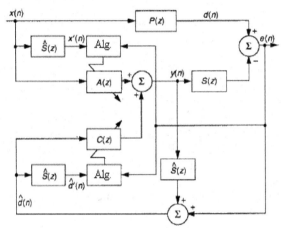

$$e(n) = d(n) - s(n) * [\mathbf{W}^T(n)\mathbf{X}(n)], \qquad (1)$$

where n is the time index, $s(n)$ is the impulse response of secondary path $S(z)$, * denotes linear convolution, $W(n)$ is the filter coefficients vector, at the time n is given by

$$\mathbf{W}(n) = [w_0(n), w_1(n),..., w_{N-1}(n)]^T, \qquad (2)$$

$$\mathbf{X}(n) = [x(n), x(n-1),..., x(n-N+1)]^T, \qquad (3)$$

and N is the filter order that must be large enough to accurate the model of the response of physical system. When a gradient-search-based algorithm is used to update the filter coefficients, the coefficients vector $W(n)$ at time instant $n+1$ is given by (Kuo & Morgan, 1999; Nelson & Elliot, 1992):

$$\mathbf{W}(n+1) = \mathbf{W}(n) + \mu e(n)\mathbf{X}'(n), \tag{4}$$

where $X'(n)$ is the filtered input vector whose k^{th} component is given by:

$$x'(n-k) = \hat{s}(n) * x(n-k). \tag{5}$$

We cannot forget that the secondary path, $\hat{S}(z)$, is inherent to the characteristics of the physical system; thus this factor is unknown beforehand, and then $\hat{S}(z)$ should be estimated from the input data using either an "online" or an "off-line" technique.

Filtered X Recursive Least-Square Algorithm (FxRLS)

To update the coefficients of the adaptive filter $W(z)$, the FxRLS algorithm uses an approach similar to the FxLMS to derive the adaptation equation because the secondary path is presented also in the system, but it uses a gain matrix including the filtered reference signal instead of directly using the filtered reference signal. The FxRLS algorithm combines a correlation of the filtered reference signal and a minimization of a weighted sum of the passed squared errors. Thus the FxRLS algorithm is given by:

$$\mathbf{W}(n) = \mathbf{W}(n-1) + \mathbf{K}(n)e(n), \tag{6}$$

where $e(n)$ is the output error given by (1),

$$\mathbf{K}(n) = \frac{\mathbf{Q}(n-1)\mathbf{X}'(n)}{\lambda + \mathbf{X}'^{T}(n)\mathbf{Q}(n-1)\mathbf{X}'(n)} \tag{7}$$

is the "Kalman Gain", $X'(n)$ is the filtered input vector whose k^{th} component is given by (5), λ is the "forgetting factor" that permits RLS type algorithms track slowly time varying statistics of the input signal, and $Q(n)$ is the inverse autocorrelation matrix given by:

$$\mathbf{Q}(n) = \frac{1}{\lambda}[\mathbf{Q}(n-1) - \mathbf{K}(n)\mathbf{X}^{T}(n)\mathbf{Q}(n-1)]. \tag{8}$$

The FxRLS algorithm, given by equations (6) through (8), has a computational complexity proportional to N^2, $O(N^2)$, where N is the order of the filter, as compare with the computational complexity of the FxLMS algorithm that is proportional to N, $O(N)$.

ANC Structures Based on Subband Decomposition

Some of the most widely used active noise canceling structures use the system identification configuration, predictive configurations, or a combination of both, as shown in Figures 2,

5, and 7, which differ among them only in the way used to derive the input signal. Thus the orthogonalized active noise (SBD-ANC) structure will be developed without assuming any particular configuration. To this end, consider the output signal, $y(n)$, of an Nth order transversal filter which is given by:

$$y(n) = \mathbf{X}_F^T(n)\mathbf{H}_F, \tag{9}$$

where,

$$\mathbf{X}_F(n) = [\mathbf{X}^T(n), \mathbf{X}^T(n-M), \mathbf{X}^T(n-2M),...,$$
$$....., \mathbf{X}^T(n-(L-2)M), \mathbf{X}^T(n-(L-1)M)]^T, \tag{10}$$

$$\mathbf{X}(n-kM) = [x(n-kM), x(n-kM-1),...,$$
$$x(n-(k+1)M+2), x(n-(k+1)M+1)]^T, \tag{11}$$

is the input vector, and:

$$\mathbf{H}_F = [\mathbf{H}_0^T, \mathbf{H}_1^T, \mathbf{H}_2^T,..., \mathbf{H}_{L-1}^T]^T, \tag{12}$$

$$\mathbf{H}_k = [h_{kM}, h_{kM+1}, h_{kM+2},..., h_{(k+1)M-1}]^T, \tag{13}$$

is the adaptive filter coefficients vector. Substituting equations (10) and (12) into (9), defining (Tapia et al., 2005):

$$\mathbf{H}_k = \mathbf{C}^T \mathbf{A}, \tag{14}$$

where $\mathbf{C}$ denotes the discrete cosine transform, and interchanging the summation order it follows. Substituting equation (14) into (9) it follows that (Tapia et., al.):

$$y(n) = \sum_{r=0}^{M-1} \mathbf{W}_r^T \mathbf{V}_r(n), \tag{15}$$

$$\mathbf{V}_r(n) = [u_r(n), u_r(n-M), u_r(n-2M),...,$$
$$u_r(n-(L-2)M), u_r(n-(L-1)M)]^T, \tag{16}$$

$$\mathbf{W}_r = [a_{0,r}, a_{1,r}, a_{2,r},..., a_{(L-1),r}]^T. \tag{17}$$

Equation (15), whose realization form is show in Figure 8, denotes the output signal of the subband decomposition-based filter structure proposed by Tapia et al. (2005), which has perfect reconstruction properties without regarding the statistics of the input signal or the adaptive filter order.

Adaptation Algorithm

Consider the output error, which, from equations (1) and (15) is given by (Tapia et. al.):

$$e(n) = d(n) - \left(\sum_{r=0}^{M-1} \mathbf{W}_r^T \mathbf{V}_r(n) \right) * s(n), \qquad (18)$$

$$e(n) = d(n) - \left(\sum_{r=0}^{M-1} \mathbf{W}_r^T \hat{\mathbf{V}}_r(n) \right), \qquad (19)$$

where $\mathbf{W}_r$ is given by (17), and

$$\hat{\mathbf{V}}_r(n) = [\hat{v}_r(n), \hat{v}_r(n-M), ..., \hat{v}_r(n-(L-1)M)]^T, \qquad (20)$$

$$\hat{v}_r(n) = s_r(n) * u_r(n), \qquad (21)$$

Figure 8. Proposed active noise canceller structure using subband the decomposition method

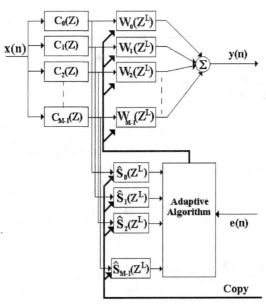

Figure 9. r^{th} stage of proposed ANC structure

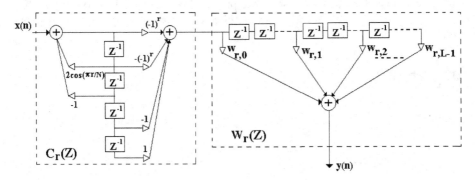

$u_r(n)$ is the orthogonal transformation of input signal, and * denotes the convolution operation.

The performance of the subband decomposition-based ANC structure strongly depends on the selection of the orthogonal transformation, because in the development of adaptive algorithm it is assumed that the transformation components are fully decorrelated. Among the several orthogonal transformations that approximately satisfy this requirement, the DCT appears to be an attractive alternative because it is a real transformation and has better orthogonalizing properties than other orthogonal transformations. Besides, it can be estimated in a recursive form by using a filter bank whose rth output signal is given by (Narayan, Peterson, & Narasimha, 1983; Perez-Meana et al.; Tapia, Perez-Meana, & Nakano Miyatake, 2003):

$$u_r(n) = 2\cos\left(\frac{\pi r}{M}\right) u_r(n-1) - u_r(n-2) \cdot \cos\left(\frac{\pi r}{2M}\right)$$

$$\{x(n-M-1) - (-1)^r x(n-1) - x(n-M) + (-1)^r x(n)\}. \tag{22}$$

To achieve fast convergence rates, the coefficients vector, $\mathbf{W}_r$, $r = 0, 1, 2,.., M-1$ will be updated such that $\varepsilon(n)$, given as:

$$\varepsilon(n) = \sum_{k=1}^{n} \left(d(k) - \mathbf{W}^T \hat{\mathbf{V}}(k)\right)^2, \tag{23}$$

becomes a minimum, where:

$$\mathbf{W} = [\mathbf{W}_1^T, \mathbf{W}_2^T, \mathbf{W}_3^T, ..., \mathbf{W}_{L-1}^T]^T, \tag{24}$$

$$\hat{\mathbf{V}}(n) = [\mathbf{V}_0^T(n), \hat{\mathbf{V}}_1^T(n), \hat{\mathbf{V}}_2^T(n), ..., \hat{\mathbf{V}}_{M-1}^T(n)]^T, \tag{25}$$

V_r and $W_r(n)$ are given by equations (16) and (17), respectively. Next, taking the derivative of equation (23) with respect to W it follows that:

$$\left[\sum_{k=1}^{n}\hat{V}(k)\hat{V}^{T}(k)\right]W(n) = \sum_{k=1}^{n}d(k)\hat{V}(k). \tag{26}$$

Finally, assuming that the DCT coefficients of input signals are fully decorrelated among them (Perez-Meana et al.; Tapia et al., 2003; Tapia et al., 2005), equation (25) becomes:

$$\left[\sum_{k=1}^{n}\hat{V}_r(k)\hat{V}_r^{T}(k)\right]W_r(n) = \sum_{k=1}^{n}d(k)\hat{V}_r(k), \tag{27}$$

$$W_r(n) = \left[\sum_{k=1}^{n}\hat{V}_r(k)\hat{V}_r^{T}(k)\right]^{-1}\sum_{k=1}^{n}d(k)\hat{V}_r(k), \tag{28}$$

where $r = 0,1,2,3,\ldots, M-1$. Equation (28) is the solution of the Wiener-Hopf equation, which can be solved in a recursive way by using the matrix inversion lemma as follows (Stearns, 1988):

$$W_r(n+1) = W_r(n) + \mu\, K_r(n)e(n), \tag{29}$$

where $e(n)$ is the output error given by equation (1), μ is the convergence factor that controls the stability, and convergence rate (Stearns, 1988),

$$K_r(n) = \frac{P_r(n)\hat{V}_r(n)}{\lambda + \hat{V}_r^{T}(n)P_r(n)\hat{V}_r(n)}, \tag{30}$$

$$P_r(n+1) = \frac{1}{\lambda}[P_r(n) - K_r(n)\hat{V}_r^{T}(n)P_r(n)], \tag{31}$$

and $\hat{V}_r(n)$ is given by equation (20).

The orthogonalized structure describe in this section can be used in active noise canceller structures using either system identification, predictive, or hybrid configurations. In the first case, the input signal is picked up by the reference microphone, while when a predictive configuration is used, the input signal is estimated from the output error and the adaptive filter output signal.

Computational Complexity

The proposed structure requires 2LM multiplication and 5LM additions for DCT estimation, and LM multiplication and LM+M additions to compute the filter output. Next, for adaptation each stage requires L_s multiplies and L_s additions to estimate the secondary-path

Figure 10. Computational complexity of full band and subband decomposition ANC

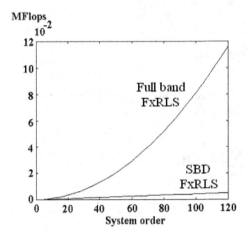

Figure 11. Secondary path estimation method proposed by Eriksson

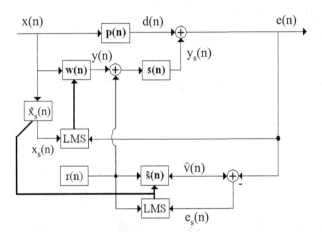

output signals, where L_s is the rth secondary-path stage order. L^2+L multiplication and L^2+L+1 addition are required for Kalman to gain estimation. The estimation of the inverse autocorrelation matrix requires $3L^2$ multiplication and $2L^2$ additions. Finally, for coefficients vectors update are required L multiplication and L additions. Thus, because the proposed structure consists of M stages, for filtering and update it requires $7L^2M+12LM+(L_s+2)M$ flouting point operations. This computational complexity is far fewer than the $8(LM)^2+8(LM)+1$ floating point operations required by the conventional FIR structure. Figure 10 shows a comparison of the number of floating point operations required, respectively, by the proposed and conventional FxRLS algorithms. From this figure it is clear that the proposed algorithms require far fewer operations per sample period than conventional algorithms, especially for large filter order. In all cases L was fixed to 4.

Secondary Path Estimation Method

To obtain a good cancellation level, accurate secondary path estimation is required, which can be achieved using an internally generated white noise sequence together with an adaptive filter operating with a system identification configuration (Kuo & Morgan, 1996, 1999; Zhang, Lan, & Ser, 2003), as shown in Figure 11.

To analyze the performance, the secondary path estimation proposed by Eriksson (Zhang et al., 2003) considers the output error $e(n)$, which is given by:

$$e(n) = (p(n) + w(n) * s(n)) * x(n) + s(n) * r(n). \tag{32}$$

Assuming that the secondary path has been correctly estimated, that is $w(n) * s(n) \rightarrow p(n)$, the first term of the right hand of equation (32) denotes the residual noise, while the second term denotes the additive noise due to the random signal used to estimate the secondary path. Next, consider the error signal $e_s(n)$, which is given by:

$$e_s(n) = (\hat{s}(n) - s(n)) * r(n) - v(n), \tag{33}$$

Figure 12. Secondary path estimation method proposed by Bao

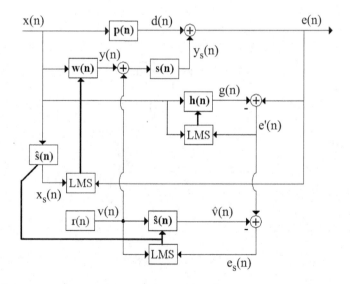

where:

$$v(n) = d(n) + w(n) * s(n) * x(n), \tag{34}$$

denotes the additive noise during the secondary path estimation. Thus, to obtain a reasonable good estimation of $s(n)$, the power of $r(n)$ should be larger than the power of $v(n)$, or the convergence factor much smaller than one.

To reduce this problem, Bao proposed the system shown in Figure 12 (Zhang et al., 2003), where the output error used to estimate $\hat{s}(n)$ is given by:

$$e_s(n) = e'(n) - \hat{s}(n) * x(n), \tag{35}$$

where,

$$e'(n) = (p(n) + s(n) * w(n) - h(n)) * x(n) + s(n) * x(n). \tag{36}$$

Substituting equation (36) into (35), it follows that:

$$e_s(n) = (p(n) + s(n) * w(n) - h(n)) * x(n) + (s(n) - \hat{s}(n)) * x(n). \tag{37}$$

Figure 13. Secondary path estimation method proposed by Zhang

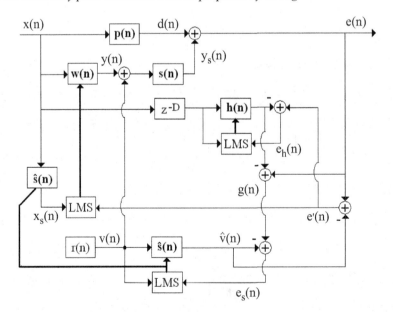

Figure 14. Signal power for the hybrid and the identifier ANC with the sound of a bike: (a) original signal power, (b) cancellation performance with a system identification structure, (c) cancellation performance with a hybrid structure

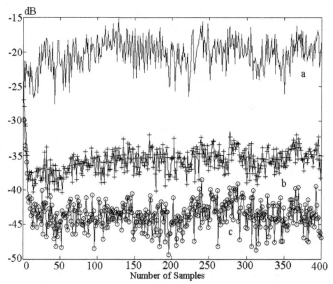

Figure 15. Power spectral density for the hybrid and the identifier structures for the airplane sound: (a) original signal power spectrum, (b) error signal power spectrum with a system identification configuration, (c) error signal power spectrum with a hybrid configuration

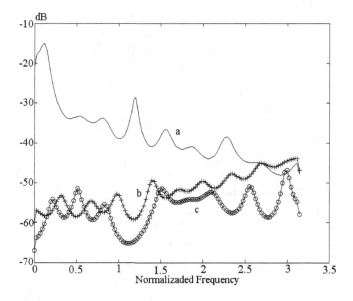

Figure 16. Power spectral density for the hybrid and the identifier structures for the bike sound: (a) original signal power spectrum, (b) error signal power spectrum with a system identification configuration, (c) error signal power spectrum with a hybrid configuration

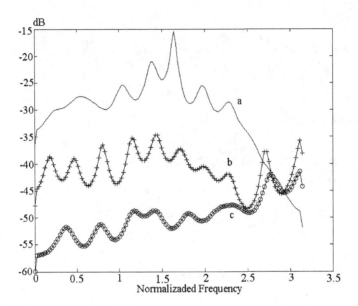

Figure 17. Convergence performance of proposed and conventional algorithm when required to cancel an actual bell noise signal

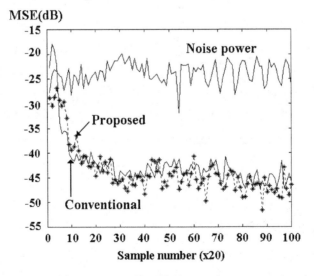

Figure 18. Convergence performance of proposed and conventional algorithm when required to cancel an actual motor noise signal

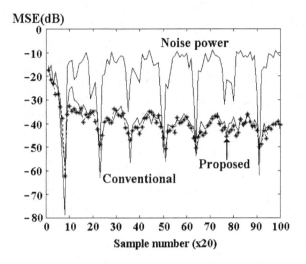

Figure 19. Convergence performance of proposed, _____, and conventional --*-- algorithms with a predictive configuration: the noise signal was the airplane noise signal, airplane_2. The time variations of noise power, --•--, is shown for comparison.

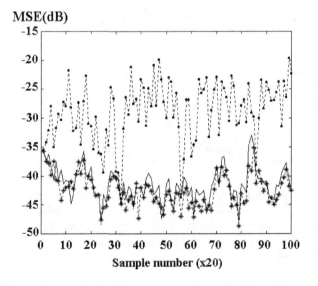

Figure 20. Convergence performance of SBD-ANC, _____ , and conventional --*-- algorithms with a predictive configuration: the noise signal was a motor noise signal. The time variations of noise power, --•--, is shown for comparison.

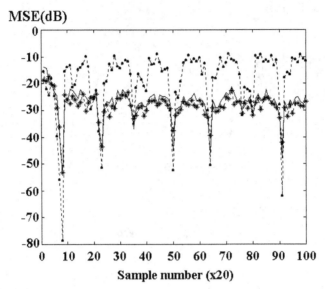

Under suitable conditions we can assume that $h(n) \rightarrow p(n) + s(n) * w(n)$, and then from (37) it follows that $e_s(n) \rightarrow (s(n) - \hat{s}(n)) * x(n)$ which allows a better estimation of secondary path, with a lower power of the additive noise, as compared with the method proposed by Eriksson whose performance is more sensitive to the additive noise. In a similar form, from Figure 13 it follows that the method proposed by Zhang provides similar performance to the Bao algorithms when $h(n - D) \rightarrow p(n) + s(n) * w(n)$.

Simulation Results

The cancellation performance of ANC algorithms was evaluated by computer simulations using system identification, predictive, and hybrid configurations that are required to cancel actual airplane, bell, motors, and bike noise signals. In all cases, the noise path, $P(z)$, the feedback path, and the secondary, $S(z)$, paths are all simulated using FIR filters of order 20 with impulse responses given by:

$$p(n) = \exp(-kn)r(n), \quad n = 0, 1, 2, ..., N, \tag{38}$$

where N is the filter order, n is the time index, k is a constant chosen such that $\exp(-kN)=0.01$, and $r(n)$ is a uniformly distributed random sequence with zero mean and unit variance.

ANC Structure with a Hybrid Configuration

Figure 14 shows the performance of hybrid structure when it is required to cancel a bike noise signal. The performance of conventional ANC without feedback cancellation is shown for comparison. Figures 14 and 15 show the power spectral density obtained when the hybrid structure and conventional structures are required to cancel airplane and bike signals.

ANC Based on Subband Decomposition with System Identification Configuration

Figures 17 and 18 show the cancellation performance of the orthogonalized ANC (SBD-ANC) and conventional ANC algorithms, operating with a system identification configuration, when required to cancel actual noises bell and a motor noise signals, respectively. In both cases the sparse filters order was equal to 4 and the overall filter order equal to 20. Figures 17 and 18 show that the SBD-ANC scheme provides quite similar performance to conventional ANC algorithm with much less computational complexity. In all cases the forgetting factor λ is equal to 0.99 and the convergence factor μ is equal to 0.1.

ANC Based on Subband Decomposition with Predictive Configuration

Figures 19 and 20 show the cancellation performance of the SBD-ANC with predictive configuration when it is required to cancel actual airplane and motor noise signals whose samples are highly correlated among them. These figures show that a fairly good cancellation performance is achieved when the noise signals present a strong correlation among their samples.

Conclusion

In this chapter we have presented alternative structures for active noise cancellation, ANC, to reduce the feedback distortion present in the ANC structures using system identification configuration, as well as to reduce the computational complexity of ANC algorithms using the FxRLS. In the first case, the hybrid ANC systems is based on the combination of both a system identification configuration updated using the FxRLS algorithm and a predictive configuration updated using the FXLMS algorithm. Simulation results show that the hybrid structure improves the performance of conventional ANC structures operating with a broadband noise because in this situation a system identification configuration must be used.

This chapter also presented active noise cancellation algorithms, based on a subband decomposition approach, with system identification and predictive configurations in which the input signals are split into M near orthogonal signal components using the discrete cosine transform. Subsequently a sparse FIR adaptive filter is inserted in each subband whose coefficients are independently updated using the FxRLS algorithm. SBD-ANC algorithms with system identification and predictive configurations were evaluated using different kinds of actual noise signals. In all cases, simulation results show that the proposed approaches allow a significant reduction of the computation of the adaptive FxRLS algorithms, while keeping quite similar convergence performance than the conventional ones. Simulation results also show that the ANC with system identification configuration can properly handle signals with strong correlation as well as with a weak correlation among their samples. On the other hand, using an ANC with predictive configuration of a fairly good cancellation level is achieved if the samples of noise signals are strongly correlated among them, as happens with the airplanes, bells, and motor signals. However, when the samples of input signal are weakly correlated among them, the cancellation level is smaller. This is because as the correlation among consecutive samples of noise signal becomes stronger, the ANC system may estimate the noise signal with more accuracy achieving in such a way for a better cancellation performance.

Acknowledgments

The authors thank the National Council of Science and Technology (CONACYT) for the financial support provided during the realization of this research.

References

Aoki, T., & Morishita, T. (2001). Active noise control system in a duct with partial feedback canceller. *IEICE Trans. on Fundamentals of Electronics, Communications and Computer Science, 84*(2), 400-405.

Beranek, L., & Ver, I. L. (1992). *Noise and vibration control engineering: Principles and applications.* New York: Wiley & Sons.

Bustamante, R., & Perez-Meana, H. (2001). Development, simulation and comparison of orthogonalized LMS algorithms for active noise control. *Journal of Electromagnetics Waves and Electronic Systems, 8*(7), 44-49.

Erickson, L. J., Allie, M. C., Bremigon, C. D., & Gilbert, J. A. (1988). Active noise control and specifications for noise problems. *Proceedings of Noise Control*, 273-278.

Farhang-Boroujeny, B. (2000). *Adaptive filters: Theory and applications.* New York: John Wiley & Sons.

Harris, C. M. (1991). *Handbook of acoustical measurements and noise control.* New York: McGraw Hill.

Kuo, S. M., & Morgan, D. (1996). *Active noise control systems.* New York: John Wiley & Sons.

Kuo, S. M., & Morgan, D. (1999). Active noise control: A tutorial review. *Proceedings of the IEEE, 87*(6), 943-973.

Muneyasu, M., Wakasugi, Y., Hisayasu, O., Fujii, K., & Hinamoto, T. (2001). Hybrid active noise control system based on simultaneous equation method. *IEICE Trans. on Fundamentals of Electronics, Communications and Computer Science, 84*(2), 479-481.

Nakano-Miyatake, M., & Perez-Meana, H. (1999). Fast orthogonalized FIR adaptive filter structure using a recurrent Hopfield-Like network. In *Lectures in computer science 1606: Foundations and tools for neural modeling* (pp. 478-487). Berlin: Springer Verlag.

Narayan, S., Peterson, A., & Narasimha, J. (1983). Transform domain LMS algorithm. *IEEE Trans. Acoustic, Speech, Signal Processing, 31*(6), 609-615.

Nelson, P. A., & Elliot, S. J. (1992). *Active control of sound.* San Francisco: Academic Press.

Omoto, A. (2002). Active noise control: Adaptive signal processing and algorithms. *IEICE Trans. Fundamentals, 85*(3), 548-557.

Perez-Meana, H., Nakano-Miyatake, M., Martinez, A., & Sanchez, J. (1996). A fast block type adaptive filter algorithm with short processing delay. *IEICE Trans. on Fundamentals of Electronics, Communications and Computer Science, 79*(5), 721-726.

Perez-Meana, H., Nakano-Miyatake, M., & Niño de Rivera, L. (2002). Speech and audio signal application. In G. Jovanovic (Ed.), *Multirate systems: Design and application* (pp. 200-224). Idea Publishing Group.

Perez-Meana, H., & Tsujii, S. (1991). A fast parallel form IIR adaptive filter. *IEEE Trans. on Signal Processing, 39*(9), 2118-2122.

Petraglia, M., & Mitra, S. (1993). Adaptive FIR filter structure based on the generalized subband decomposition of FIR filters. *IEEE Trans. on Circuits and Systems-II, 40*(6), 354-362.

Stearns, S. (1988). Fundamentals of adaptive signal processing. In J. Lim & A. V. Oppenheim (Eds.), *Advanced topics on signal processing.* Englewood Cliffs, NJ: Prentice Hall.

Tapia, D., Bustamante, R., Pérez-Meana, H., & Nakano-Miyatake, M. (2005). Single channel active noise canceller algorithm using discrete cosine transform. *Journal of Signal Processing, 9*(2), 141-151.

Tapia, D., Perez-Meana, H., & Nakano-Miyatake, M. (2003). Orthogonal methods for filtered X algorithms applied to active noise control using the discrete cosine transform. *Zarubezhnaya Radioelektronika, 2003*(6), 59-67.

Tobias, O., & Bermudez, J. (2000). Mean weight behavior of the filtered-X LMS algorithm. *IEEE Transactions on Signal Processing, 48*(4), 1061-1075.

Usagawa, T., & Shimada, Y. (2001). An active noise control headset for crew members of ambulance. *IEICE Trans. on Fundamentals of Electronics, Communications and Computer Science, 84*(2) 475-478.

Widrow, B., & Stearns, S. (1981). *Adaptive signal processing.* Englewood Cliffs, NJ: Prentice Hall.

Zelinski, R., & Noll, P. (1977). Adaptive transform coding of speech. *IEEE Trans. on Acoustic, Speech and Signal Processing, 25*(2), 299-309.

Zhang, M., Lan, H., & Ser, W. (2003). A robust on line secondary path modeling method with auxiliary noise power scheduling strategy and norm constrain manipulation. *IEEE Trans. on Speech and Audio Processing, 11*(1), 45-53.

Chapter X

Differentially Fed Artificial Neural Networks for Speech Signal Prediction

Manjunath Ramachandra Iyer, Banglore University, India

Abstract

Speaker authentication has become increasingly important. It goes with the other forms of security checks such as user login and personal identification number and has a say in the final decision about the authenticity. One of the issues with the authentication algorithms is that the automated devices that take the call have to work with a limited data set. In this chapter, a new class of intelligent element called differentially fed artificial neural network has been introduced to predict the data and use it effectively. It keeps the model simple and helps in taking online and crisp decisions with the available limited data.

Introduction

Online authentication of speakers has turned into a challenging task, especially with the kind of decisions to be taken based on the speaker authentication. This calls for an intelligent element that can make use of minimum data set and arrive at the meaningful conclusion.

Artificial neural networks can be conveniently used for pattern matching with a known set of data. The conventional neural networks, however, suffer with the drawback of a lengthy training period and reduced signal to noise ratio at the output. To address these issues, a differential feedback from the output of the network to the input is suggested and discussed. Intuitively, appropriate feedback from the output to the input of a system results in change in the system behavior, including the improved stability and noise immunity. A differential feedback ends up in more interesting properties. They require a reduced training set and provide better noise immunity. Some of the features are unique to these networks that are not found in a conventional neural network.

With the differentially fed neural network in place, a portion of the challenge data is taken for training data. The other part is synthesized based on this. It is then matched with the actual data and the difference is computed. By setting threshold on difference, the speaker identity may be endorsed.

The knowledge base queries would consist of audio or speech samples. Sophisticated pattern matching algorithms would be required to generate the match online. Based on the outcome of the match, decisions would be taken. Such knowledge bases would be used in banks, industries, airport surveillance systems, crime detection and prevention, and so forth. It can prevent unauthorized entries. Online evaluation of the patterns is the biggest challenge. It calls for the usage of sophisticated algorithms. An intelligent algorithm based on differential feedback is discussed in this chapter.

Background

There are various techniques for speaker identification and verification. The model-based algorithms with built-in auto regression can work with limited available data. Hence the stress in this chapter is for the data prediction models. In this section, different models are introduced for speaker verification. Basically two processes are involved with speech signal processing: speaker identification and verification.

Speaker identification is basically the task of determining who is speaking from a set of known voices or speakers. It is a pattern-matching problem. To perform identification, the system must perform a 1:N classification. Generally it is assumed the unknown voice comes from a known set of speakers. Often artificial neural network classifiers are used to accomplish this task. The matching of signal can happen with respect to a scale or shape of the waveform and not necessarily with respect to the numerical values.

Speaker verification or speaker authentication or detection is the task of determining whether a certain speech sample really comes or originates from a certain individual.

In another method of classification, there will be a closed set of users. It would be required to pick up one speaker out of a set. On the other hand, in an open set the speaker need not match with any of the known speakers.

Speaker identification involves the process of recognizing the speaker based on the information extracted from a part of the speech signal. The remaining part may be used to verify the authenticity. There are two classes of identification techniques: text dependent and text independent recognition. In a text dependent technique, the speaker is urged to pronounce a predetermined set of sentences. The text in both training and testing is the same or it is known in advance. In a text independent technique, the speaker identification happens without restricting the pronunciations of the speaker. The latter technique is more complex, as the target matching data will not be readily available. There will not be a known pattern of the spoken string. It has to be synthesized based on some other set of speech spoken by the speaker earlier. This chapter concentrates on the text dependent technique.

Speaker recognition system consists of two steps including feature extraction and feature matching. Feature extraction refers to parameterize the speech sample that is required later for feature matching. Feature matching involves the comparison of the features associated with a certain speech signal with the stored features and thereby identifies the speaker.

A speaker recognition system works on phases—the training phase and the deployment phase. During the training phase, the speakers, who are supposed to be recognized in future, are required to render voice samples. Based on these samples, individual speech models are built. It involves the extraction of the voice features and their storage. The deployment phase involves the classification of features of a certain speech signal into one of the sample sets. One of the major problems with the deployment phase is that the training data and the challenge data do not match most of the time. It is because the characteristics of the speaker as well as the speech signal vary over time and space. The other issues are noise associated with the acquisition and transfer of the speech signal that result in distorted features. They call for the usage of sophisticated signal processing techniques and models.

A speech signal is characterized with short time spectrum. Over a short period of the order of one fifth of a second, the speech waveform envelope relatively remains constant and corresponds to a particular phonetic sound. If the bandwidth of the signal is large, a filter bank may be used to get the various flat envelop components.

For the text independent identification, various techniques based on the neural networks are available. They include auto associative neural networks, radial basis function, and so forth, as explained by Oglesby and Mason (1991) and Yegnanarayana and Kishore (2002). The other common techniques include vector codebooks and Gaussian mixture models.

The Gaussian mixture model (Reynold & Rose, 1995) is reasonably successful and accurate in identification. However, it is computationally complex. This model is generally used in complicated systems such as in-vehicle speaker verification (Abut, Hansen, & Tekeda, 2004).

Speech signal consists of frames. Each frame is of a fixed duration. Mel frequency cepstral coefficients are computed for each frame. The magnitude spectrum of each frame is passed through a Mel scale filter bank. The technique makes use of the characteristics of the human ear. The human ear critical bandwidth varies over frequencies. The filters are spread linearly at the low frequencies and logarithmically at the high frequencies. The scale is called the Mel frequency scale. The scale is linear below 1 Kilohertz and logarithmic above that. The topic is discussed in detail by Furui (1994). The log energy filter bank outputs are cosine transformed to get the cepstral coefficients. The cepstral coefficients are taken as feature vectors. Cepstral coefficients (Oppenheim & Schafer, 1989) are generally used in speaker recognition problems because it is easy to compute them using recursive formulae.

The Gaussian mixture model (GMM) is the weighted sum of feature vectors given by:

$$p(\vec{X} \mid \lambda) = \sum_{i=1}^{M} p_i b_i(\vec{x}). \tag{1}$$

Here $\vec{x}$ is a D dimensional feature vector, b is the component density, and p_i are the mixture weights. The component density is a D dimensional Gaussian probability density function (pdf) given by:

$$b_i(\vec{x}) = \frac{1}{(2\pi)^{D/2} |\Sigma_i|^{1/2}} \exp\{-(\frac{1}{2}(\vec{x} - \vec{\mu}_i)' \Sigma_i^{-1} (\vec{x} - \vec{\mu}_i)\}. \tag{2}$$

Here $\vec{\mu}$ is mean vector and Σ is the covariance matrix. The mixture weights add up to 1.ie $\sum_{i=1}^{M} p_i = 1$. The speakers are represented by the GMM λ_i such that:

$$\lambda_i = \{p_i, \vec{\mu}, \Sigma_i\}. \tag{3}$$

The corresponding parameters of the speech sample under question are then compared with the stored values.

In another technique, a wide band speech signal is subjected to sub band processing by passing it through a set of band pass filters, and the output of each filter is processed separately. As the envelop of the sub band signals very slowly compared to the relatively wideband input, it would be easy to process the same. Detailed discussion on the same is provided by Besacier and Bonastre (1997, 2000). The technique may be blended with hidden Markov model (HMM) for better performance. Such a multi-classifier provides accurate results, especially in the presence of noise. Finally, the outputs of the various classifiers are combined with a rule such as lLog likelihood model (LLM) or multi-layer perceptron (MLP).

Artificial neural networks are used as the general classifiers (Morgan & Bourlard, 1995; Wouhaybi, 1996). They are trained with the known features of the different individuals. They can adapt and throw out the decisions in the presence of the noisy inputs that they have not encountered. The power of decision-making and the accuracy may be improved substantially by adding one or more hidden layers to the neural network. With this they can learn any type of non-linearities accurately. A hard limiter may be used in the output stage to throw out the decision of types of yes or no, that is, matching or not matching.

The differentially fed artificial neural networks introduced in this chapter can learn the non-linearities with reduced training set. In addition, they merge a set of rules removing the redundancies. In fact, a set of classifiers such as sub band filters may be replaced by a single differentially fed neural network. It reduces the power requirement and the hardware apart from saving time and computation power.

A Markov model basically emits a sequence or chain of symbols on the output for each state. The state-to-state transition is governed by the transition probability. This makes the Markov model probabilistic and statistical. For example, the probability of spelling "o" after "b" is different for different words with such sequences. This factor plays a crucial role when one of the words from the speaker is known and the other word has to be authenticated. With the observable sequence of outputs from the model, one can infer the most likely dynamical system. The result is a model for the underlying process. Conversely, from a sequence of outputs, it is possible to infer the most likely sequence of states. The model also predicts the most appropriate next state. The speaker recognition problem with Markov model is formulated as follows:

$$w^* = \arg \left(\max \left(\{w \text{ in } W\}^* \Pr \left(\sigma \mid \lambda_w \right) \right) \right), \tag{4}$$

given a set W of words and a separate training set for each of these words. It is required to build a Markov model for each word using the associated training set. Let λ_w represent the Markov model parameters associated with the word w. Along with a sequence of words σ observed or provided, it is required to choose the word with the most likely model.

Speaker authentication finally involves the authorization and proving the identity of the supposed speaker.

Differentially Fed Artificial Neural Network

When a feedback is applied from the output to the input of a system appropriately, it results in increased stability. The system turns auto regressive with enhanced predictability.

In a typical autoregressive moving average model, the output and the input are related by:

$$y(n) = a_0 * x(n) + a_1 * x(n-1) + \ldots\ldots + b_1 * y(n-1) + \ldots\ldots \tag{5}$$

The differentials of the output (and input) can be written in similar linear combinations of present and previous outputs (inputs):

$$\frac{dy}{dt} = y(n+1) - y(n). \tag{6}$$

By equations (5) and (6) it is clear that:

$$y(n) = f(x(n), x(n-1)......, \frac{dy}{dt}_{t=n}, \frac{d^2y}{dt^2}_{t=n} .....) \tag{7}$$

The function f accounts for the non-linearities of the system. The system that generates output (7) is also called as a differentially fed artificial neural network. It is referred to as DANN throughout the chapter. Like a neural network, it does the summation and passes the output into a non-linear network. However, there is a minor difference. The differentials of the output are also considered as additional inputs.

This small change to the artificial neural network or any system that does similar operations brings out major changes to the output. Even if the system were not intelligent, a certain degree of intelligence would get added with differential feedback. The following important properties have been observed with this network.

Properties of Differentially Fed System

Equation (5) geometrically represents a hyper plane. With the increase in the order of the differential, a set or manifold of hyper planes would be formed. These planes would be parallel to one another. As the order of the differential feedback increases, the planes get closer, that is, the distance or difference between them gets reduced. When the order of the feedback is increased to infinity, it appears as though they merge. The corresponding plane is called an eigen plane.

The differentially fed neural networks are extremely useful in estimation and learning probabilistic data. When a set of estimators is used to learn a certain data set, each of them would start throwing out its own output and associated probability distribution. The ideal estimator happens to be the weighted sum of the outputs of the individual estimators. Each of these estimators may be realized by a differentially fed neural network with different degrees of feedback. The near-ideal estimator may be generated with higher order feedback.

The estimators may be used for classification. Classifier is an integral part of an authentication system. The input applied to the system is matched to one of the set of available, pre-stored classes. Estimators can also throw out the decision based on a rule. An ideal estimator out happens to be the outcome of a merger of all the rules.

The output of the differentially fed neural network consists of two parts—the data independent part and the data dependent part. The data independent part is generated totally based on the inputs and is free from feedback. The data dependent part, on the other hand, takes its form with the previous outputs. Any errors or variations in the data independent part of the output contribute toward the bias in the measured output. The variance in the output may be attributed to the data dependent terms. Any of the data dependent terms may be obtained from the other by convolving the same with a Gaussian pulse of appropriate scale factor. For the same reason, any of the hyper planes may be written as a weighted sum of other planes. Gaussian estimators are known for avoiding over fitting of the data, that is, only a small data set is good enough for these estimators to make decisions.

The information content of the different hyper planes varies monotonically. The higher the order of the hyper plane, the lower the information content would be. This is because the total information in it would get smoothened out or averaged. It would be more of a history. The characteristics of the input, output, and the data would have changed by then. In any case, the hyper planes represent a hierarchy of abstractions in the data. The hyper planes are orthogonal to each other. Hence it provides a complete view of the signal when resolved into hyper planes.

The spectrum of prediction error shows interesting behavior. It becomes more and more flat with increase in the order of the feedback. This is because with increase in abstraction, the data turns whiter, occupying more bandwidth.

The multi resolution property of the hyper planes has been established by Manjunath (2006). The simulation results actually prove that the increase in abstraction in the hyper planes is the same as that of the wavelets.

When a differentially fed neural network controller is inserted in a system, it will have a profound effect on the system. Consider a system with feed forward path consisting of the data flow from an information system to the client, a feedback path carrying the feedback signals of the client, and a neural network sitting in the loop as a controller.

The differentially fed neural network sits as a controller, as a part of the loop comprising of the source, the forward path, the destination, and the feedback path.

The differentially fed neural networks make use of a large number of previous samples for decision-making. Decisions thrown out by such a system contribute to long-range dependency in the output. The abstract levels of the output contribute to self-similarity of data when observed over different time scales. The presence of long-range dependency in the differential feedback output may be attributed to the usage of a long history of the output as the additional inputs for decision making. The presence of long-range dependency or self-similarity improves predictability of the system. The systems and data that are inherently self-similar such as earthquake data or metrological data can be modeled by a differentially fed neural network. To model these systems, the first step is to extract the underlying and hidden patterns from the past data. These patterns are later transformed into useful information such as rules. The rules need to be carefully merged. These rules are useful for predicting decisions in similar events.

Increase in the order of feedback results in increased entropy in the output. The entropy reaches its maximum when infinite order feedback is provided. The entropy maximization technique is often used in pattern recognition. The principle of maximum entropy originates from the statistical thermodynamics. The same concept enriches the information theory and has been applied to pattern recognition tasks including speaker authentication, language modeling, and text classification. In the context of classification, the basic idea is to choose the distribution such that it fulfils all the constraints given by that information and has the highest possible entropy. This constraint avoids over fitting of the data. The additional advantage of the maximum entropy approach is that it is scalable and extensible. It is quite easy to include new feature functions into the classifiers.

The data from time varying systems such as speech signal lead to time varying clusters. The data need to be pruned for the true negatives before being processed.

Unlike the speaker identification, some applications target at eliminating duplicates in the data. Here, the pattern whose duplicate has to be found out in a data set is applied to a classifier. The class with the lowest conditional probability is selected as the disjoint data. Together they share the least information in common. In a differentially fed neural network classifier, it corresponds to the lowest entropy state. The data corresponding to the class of a certain conditional probability may be taken as the duplicate if the value of the probability is more than a threshold value.

The clustering process is basically an unsupervised learning process, as there is no previously known reference for this. Clusters are often done hierarchically where smaller clusters are merged into larger ones. The hierarchies in the cluster may be generated with a differentially fed neural network

It is desired to keep the variance of the prediction error in the signal as low as possible. As explained earlier, the variance can be brought down with the increase of the differential feedback order.

Architecture of Differentially Fed Neural Network

The architecture of a differentially fed neural network is shown in Figure 1. Here the set of previous outputs are being used as additional inputs.

The output of a differentially fed artificial neural network is generated as:

$$Y' = f(y) = 0 \text{ if } |y| < Th$$
$$\text{Else } 1 \tag{8}$$

Figure 1. Differentially fed artificial neural network

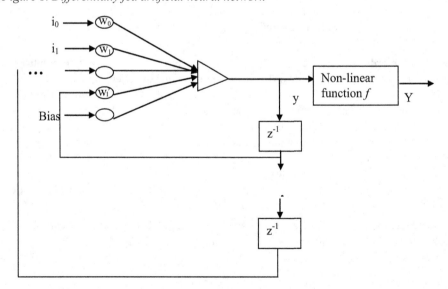

with Th being the threshold. Different non-linear functions such as sigmoid and hard limiter are used in practice. The linear intermediate output is generated as:

$$y(n) = w_0 * i_0 + w_1 * i_1 + \dots\dots + w'_0 * y(n-1) + \dots\dots \qquad (9)$$

The network learns the training data before deployment. The weights are adjusted during the training. A detailed description is provided by Manjunath and Gurumurthy (2003). Error back propagation technique is used for the incremental changes in the weight.

$$\Delta w = \xi.(error).i \qquad (10)$$

Here i is the input driving the node, and ξ is the learning rate. The error represents the difference between the desired and the obtained outputs.

Table 1. Square error in training for different orders

No.	Differential order	Square error
1	0	0.1943
2	1	0.1860
3	2	0.1291

Figure 2. Actual signal and predicted signal with no feedback

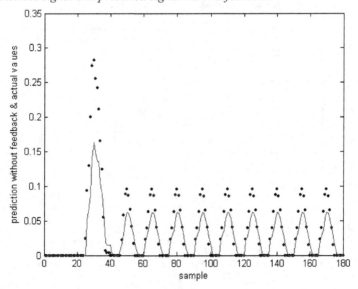

Performance of Differentially Fed Neural Network

The differentially fed neural network is trained to learn Ex-OR function.

The prediction error for different orders of feedback is shown in Table 1. As the order of differential feedback increases, the error reduces. Simulation time is set to 60 seconds, and 180 samples are taken. Matlab version 6 and Simulink have been used to carryout the simulation.

Figure 3. Actual signal and predicted signal with first order feedback

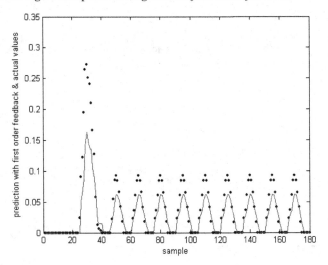

Figure 4. Actual signal and predicted signal with second order feedback

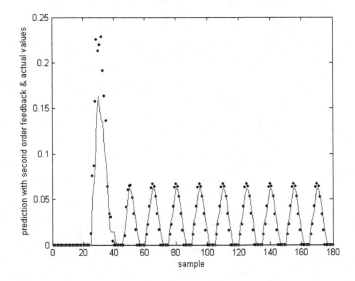

Figure 5. Instantaneous values of actual signal and predicted signal with a first order feedback

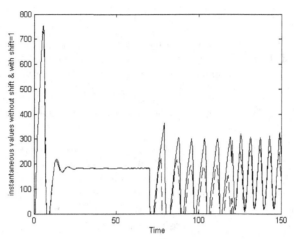

The plots of actual auto correlation of the speech signal and its predicted versions with different orders of feedback are shown in Figures 1, 2, and 3. The prediction power of second order differential feedback is evident from the graph.

It may be noted here that the first few samples will be used for training the neural network.

In another experiment, a differentially fed neural network of first order time shift was used for white noise excited speech signal prediction. The results are shown in Figure 5. Here DC bias has been removed for simplicity. The predicted output matched for a scale. The initial exact matching happens for the training period data.

Issues and Solutions

Human voice is subjected to changes under the environmental conditions such as open-air, closed auditorium, and biological conditions such as cold, cough, emotions, and so forth. In these extreme circumstances, speaker identification or authentication does not result in success. If such failures are common, then it makes sense to store the features corresponding to these commonly encountered situations.

The other limitation is the variation in the speech characteristics with age. So, regular updating of the parameters is required. Even variations in the microphone characteristics would lead to mismatching results. Hence, the systems rather than relying on voice systems alone for verification need to use supplementing techniques such as personal identification number (PIN), and so forth. The voice system is generally used for authentication.

The other factor that seriously hampers the result is the change in accent at the time of recording and usage. The speed of pronunciation during verification and generation of the training data has to match.

The verification and authentication algorithms are to be rigid and sensitive to changes in the speech characteristics. Otherwise a pre-recorded or imitated voice would pass the identification test. However, it is difficult to record the voice with very high fidelity with the commercially available general-purpose microphones, and the HiFi devices are very costly.

Another issue with the speech signal processing is power. The complexity of computations required during the speech signal authentication makes it unsuitable for mobile applications.

For most of these issues, as a solution, a portion of the challenge data is taken for training, and the other part is synthesized with a differentially fed neural network. It is then matched with the actual data, and the difference is computed. By setting threshold on the difference, the speaker identity may be endorsed. Alternatively, the challenge data may be sieved through a neural network. The same would be compared with the data stored in the knowledge base for every level of abstraction. The usage of a differentially fed neural network in the place of a conventional neural network would be helpful, as it provides an increased signal to noise ratio.

If the challenge data is the distorted version of the data in the knowledge base, the lower order hyper planes match better, as they carry more information. The degree of matching falls with the increased abstractions or with the higher order differential planes. By setting threshold for each level, it would be possible to endorse the identity of the challenge data. The degree of distortion can be given.

The spectrum of the distorted signal obtained by subtracting each of the corresponding hyper planes and then taking the Fourier transform would fall under different regions. Based on the amount of the noise energy in each of these regions, it would be possible to identify the source of the corrupting noise.

As the speech signal happens to be the superposition of bursts with different time scales, it results in self-similarity in the spectrum of the speech signal. The feature of this self-similarity is the localization of the energy contents. The long bursts tend to have large amplitude, while the short ones, though frequent, would have small amplitudes. The localization of energy in long pulses makes the Fourier transforms inaccurate. The hierarchical organization or generation of the data provides a powerful alternative.

Future Trends

The usage of neural networks for speaker recognition and verification would surpass the conventional software techniques. Unlike the other algorithms, a neural network can tolerate a certain degree of noise and handles the unforeseen or untrained test patterns.

The neural networks blended with Bayesian decisions can work as the best classifier in the presence of probabilistic input patterns. Decisions in the presence of conditional inputs may be taken by the Bayes' network, while the associated neural network provides the necessary prediction of the data. A differential feedback in such a network would provide the requisite historical data for the appropriate inference. With an increase in the previous history in the feedback, the outcome or decision would be more accurate.

The output data from a differentially fed neural network exhibits multiple resolutions or a hierarchy of different levels of abstraction. To speed up the pattern matching, parallel algorithms may be implemented with each of these levels, and the final result may be collated so that the real time performance is achieved. With this, it would be possible to have lengthy words or sentences for authentication.

The proliferating usage of speaker authentication technology requires appropriate automation techniques. Clustering of speech or voice samples is an important area that requires a certain degree of automation. The words uttered by the individual may be collected from a large set of documents and grouped together. It takes practically impossible time for manual clustering. An intelligent element is required for computing the distance between the clusters and generates the most optimal one. The data that can be automatically generated from a speech signal has many characteristics that make it suitable for processing with a neural network.

The methods given here are not confined for the applications such as speaker verification. In the future, multimedia browsers will become common. The documents and album containing the sample speech or voice pattern may be recovered from databases. MPEG-7 has provided the requisite framework for multimedia query.

The speech sample signal to be organized as a database of speakers consists of two components—the structured and the unstructured. The structured part corresponds to the abstraction without feedback. It carries the major chunk of the speech signal. The unstructured part consists of a hierarchy of abstract data. Each of them may be obtained from the other by convolving with a Gaussian pulse of arbitrary scale factor. It throws up new models of vocal tract and consequently opens market for a family of voice coders and speech synthesizers.

Speaker identification algorithms may be built into mobile phones. It may be coupled with remote login and enable access to the workplace while traveling. Alternatively, the songs stored in a streaming server at home may be fed into the mobile phone through a voice command.

Based on the speaker, it would be possible to fire the auto responses as appropriate. Different responses may be stored for friends, colleagues, relatives, strangers, and so forth, and provision must be there to customize the same.

The differential feedback provided among the different speakers would be extremely useful for building up a crisp database. Such a feedback is resistant for over training. A small set of data from a small set of sources or the data provided over a small duration would be good enough for global learning. The differential feedback architecture that operates on multiple scales is useful for modeling this problem. The forecasting strategy is interpreted as the subdivision of the prediction task into elementary tasks. Like wavelets, it is possible to express the signal as a weighted sum of the different resolution levels.

The decision taken during the comparison of attributes of the waveforms is quite interesting. It calls for the usage of a large set of IF-ELSE statements. Each of these statements excites a rule. In effect, all these rules together would give out a single output. A differentially fed neural network can merge the rules by removing the redundancies associated with the rules.

Alternatively, the decision rule may be split into a set of rules, each operating over the different abstractions of the dataset. With this, it is possible to perform the operations in parallel. Like data, the rules are similar but for a scale.

Semantic speech or voice searching would be an interesting application in the future. In the query of speech or utterance, rather than a single output corresponding to an individual, there could be multiple outputs for a given sample or query input waveform. For example, the query input could be a part of the national anthem. The output would be the national anthem sung by different singers.

Conclusion

Real time speaker identification and verification are challenging. They call for the usage of intelligent elements. In this chapter, a differentially fed neural network is employed to accomplish the same. A certain degree of feedback from the output to the input of the system brings in interesting properties to the system. The system can make out the otherwise undetected patterns in the speech signal. These patterns would be unique to the speakers and are associated with the identity of the speaker.

The speaker identification is finding increased applications in banks, security, forensic, biometric login, telephone banking, and so forth. They call for model-based approaches to work with a limited available data and take online decisions. The model needs to have built-in predictive power to extrapolate the data.

The structure of the speech in any language is such a way that the individual words or syllable do not vary abruptly. There is some gradation that binds the different words of a sentence or different phonetics within a sentence. Nobody speaks a sentence as a collection of words. Languages generally provide punctuations up to which there will be a free flow of words. This smooth transition is associated with the information redundancy. In a speech coder, this redundancy is exploited for compression. In a speech recognition system, the same may be used for prediction or extrapolation.

References

Abut, H., Hansen, J.H., & Tekeda, K. (2004). *DSP for in-vehicle and mobile system*. Kluwer/Springer-Verlag Publishing.

Besacier, L., & Bonastre, J.-F. (1997). Sub band approach for automatic speaker recognition: Optimal division of the frequency domain. In Bigün et al. (Eds)*Proceedings of the First International Conference on Audio- and Visual-Based Biometric Person Authentication* (AVBPA), Crans-Montana, Switzerland (pp. 195-202). New York: Springer LNCS.

Besacier, L., and Bonastre, J.-F. (2000). Sub band architecture for automatic speaker recognition. *Signal Processing, 80*(7), 1245-1259.

Doddington, G. R. (1986). Speaker recognition-identifying people by their voices. In *Proceedings of IEEE, 73*(11), 1651-1644.

Furui, S. (1994). An overview of speaker recognition technology (tutorial). ESCA Workshop on Automatic *Speaker Recognition, Identification and Verification,* Martigny, Switzerland, (pp. 1-9).

Haykin, S. (1994). *Neural networks, a comprehensive foundation.* New York: Macmillan College Publishing.

Manjunath, R. (2006). *Compact architecture for the analysis and processing of subnet signals using differentiators as building block*s. Unpublished doctoral dissertation, University of Bangalore, India.

Manjunath, R., & Gurumurthy, K. S. (2003). System design using differentially fed artificial neural network. In R. Akerkar (Eds.) *Proceedings of ICAAI'03.* Kolhapur, India.

Morgan, N., & Bourlard, H. (1995). Neural networks for statistical recognition of continuous speech. In *Proceedings of the IEEE, 83*(5), 741-770.

Oglesby, J., & Mason, J. (1991). Radial basis function networks for speaker recognition. *IEEE ICASSP* Toronto, Canada, (pp. 393-396).

Oppenheim, A. V., & Schafer, R. W. (1989). Discrete-time signal processing. Englewood Cliffs, NJ: Prentice-Hall.

Reynold, D., & Rose, R. C. (1995). Robust text independent speaker identification using Gaussian Mixture Speaker Models. In *Proceedings of IEEE Tran. Speech and Audio Processing, 3*(1), 72-83.

Wouhaybi, R. H. (1996). *Speaker recognition using neural networks.* Unpublished master's thesis, Department of Electrical and Computer Engineering, American University of Beirut, Lebanon.

Yegnanarayana, B., & Kishore, S. (2002). AANN: An alternative to GMM for pattern recognition. *Neural Networks, 15*(3), 459-469.

Section IV

Feature Extraction Algorithms and Speech Speaker Prediction

This section provides a review of some of the most widely used feature extraction algorithms together with some of the successful paradigms used in speech and speaker recognition. Finally, the use of speech recognition technology to develop a language therapy system is provided.

Chapter XI

Introduction to Speech Recognition

Sergio Suárez-Guerra, National Polytechnic Institute, Mexico

Jose Luis Oropeza-Rodriguez, National Polytechnic Institute, Mexico

Abstract

This chapter presents the state-of-the-art automatic speech recognition (ASR) technology, which is a very successful technology in the computer science field, related to multiple disciplines such as the signal processing and analysis, mathematical statistics, applied artificial intelligence and linguistics, and so forth. The unit of essential information used to characterize the speech signal in the most widely used ASR systems is the phoneme. However, recently several researchers have questioned this representation and demonstrated the limitations of the phonemes, suggesting that ASR with better performance can be developed replacing the phoneme by triphones and syllables as the unit of essential information used to characterize the speech signal. This chapter presents an overview of the most successful techniques used in ASR systems together with some recently proposed ASR systems that intend to improve the characteristics of conventional ASR systems.

Introduction

Automatic speech recognition (ASR) has been one of the most successful technologies allowing the man-machine communications to request some information from it or to request to carry out some given task using the natural oral communication. The artificial intelligence field has contributed in a remarkable way to the development of ASR algorithms.

The more widely used paradigm in ASR systems has been the phonetic content of the speech signal, which varies from language to language, but there are no more than 30 different phonemes without some variations, such as accentuation, duration, and the concatenation. The last one includes the co-articulation such as demisyllables and triphones. Considering all variations, the number of phonetic units will be increased considerably. Recently some researchers have considered the use of syllables instead of phonemes as an alternative for development of the ASR systems, because in general, the natural way to understand the language by the human brain is to store and recognize syllables not phonemes.

The automatic speech recognition is a very complex task due to the large amount of variations involved in it, such as intonation, voice level, health condition and fatigue, and so forth (Suárez, 2005). Therefore, in the automatic speech recognition system, for specific or general tasks, there is an immense amount of aspects to be taken into account. This fact has contributed to increase the interest in this field, and as a consequence, several ASR algorithms have been proposed during the last 60 years.

A brief review of ASR systems can be summarized as follows. At the beginning of 1950s, the Bell Laboratories developed an ASR system that was able to recognize isolated digits. The RCA Laboratories developed a single-speaker ASR for recognition of 10 syllables. The University College in England developed a phonetic recognizer, and in the MIT Lincoln Laboratory a speaker independent vowel recognizer was developed. During the 1960s, some basic tools for ASR systems were developed. The dynamic time warping is developed by the NEC Laboratories and Vintsyuk of the Soviet Union. In the Carnegie Mellon University, the automatic continuous speech recognition system with small vocabularies HAL 9000 was developed. During the 1970s, several isolated word recognition systems were developed, such as a large vocabulary ASR system by IBM. During this time also there was an important increase on the investment to develop ASR systems, such as the DARPA and HARPY project in the U.S. During the decade of the 1980s, the first algorithms for continuous speech recognition system with large vocabularies appeared. Also during this time the hidden Markov model (HMM) and neural networks were introduced in (development of) the ASR systems; one of these types of systems is a SPHINX system. The ASR systems have appeared as commercial systems during the decade of the 1990s thanks to the development of fast and cheap personal computers that allow the implementation of dictation systems and the integration between speech recognition and natural language processing. Finally, during recent years, it was possible to use the voice recognition systems in the operating systems, telephone communication system, and Internet sites where Internet management using voice recognition, Voice Web Browsers, as well as Voice XML standards are developed.

State-of-the-Art

During the last few decades, the study of the syllables as a base of language model has produced several beneficial results (Hu, Schalkwyk, Barnard, & Cole, 1996). Hu et al. (1996) realized an experiment where syllables belonging to the name of months in English were recognized. They created a corpus with a total of 29 syllabic units, and 84.4% efficiency was achieved in their system. Boulard (1996) realized similar works using the syllables in German. Hauenstein (1996) developed a hybrid ASR system: HMM-NN (hidden Markov models-neural networks) using syllables and phonemes as basic units for the model. He realized a performance comparison between the system using only syllables and another one using only phonemes, and he concluded that the system that combined both units (syllables and phonemes) presents higher performance than the system using syllables or phonemes separately. Wu, Shire, Greenberg, and Morgan (1997) proposed an integration of information at syllables level within the automatic speech recognizer to improve their performance and robustness (Wu, 1998; Wu et al., 1997), taking 10% of the recognition error for digits voices of OGI (Oregon Graduate Institute) corpus. In a work by Wu (1998), 6.8% of recognition error rate for digits data using corpus of digits from telephone conversation was reported; here, the RSA system was a phoneme-syllable hybrid system. Jones, Downey, and Mason (1999) experimented with HMM to obtain the representations of the units at the syllable level. From these experiments they concluded that it is possible to substantially improve the performance of the ASR using a medium size database comparing with the monophonic models (Jones et al., 1999). In this case, the recognition rate was 60% compared with 35% obtained when a monophonic model was used, concluding that the practical applications must be satisfied by a hybrid system (Fosler-Lussier, Greenberg, & Morgan, 1999). They found that a great amount of phonetic phenomena that appeared in the spontaneous speech have syllabic features, and it is necessary to use more phonetic contextual windows for phonetic-based ASR systems (Fosler et al., 1999).

Weber (2000), in his experiments using segmentation of speech signal with different duration, found the recognition error rate of word (WER: Word Error Rate) is increased when the speech signal is distorted by noise. WER can be reduced increasing segmentation size using syllabic-based ASR. Meneido and Neto (2000) used the information at the syllable level to apply an automatic word segmentation system to improve ASR systems, which was applied to the Portuguese, and the WER was reduced. Some works began to consider a language model to improve the ASR system. The work of Meneido in Portuguese showed a method of incorporation of the speech information at the syllable level with Spanish language, because both languages share common features in the syllable level (Meneido & Neto, 2000; Meneido, Neto, & Almeida, 1999). Also the work of Menido et al. (1999) reports a successful detection of starting point of the syllable with about 93%, and they considered that wide range windows of context entrance (260m) are most appropriate.

In 1996, a summer meeting about continuous speech recognition was held in the Language and Speech Processing Center of Johns Hopkins University, where it was demonstrated that the use of the syllable level and the use of the individual internal pressure can reduce the WER of the triphones-based ASR systems (Wu, 1998). In the same year, Hauenstein (1996) introduced the syllabic units into the continuous speech recognition systems and realized a performance comparison with a phonetic units-based system. His experiments showed that a phonetic-based system presents better performance for the continuous speech recognition system, while a syllabic-based system is better for the discontinuous speech recognition system, reaching more than 17.7% of a recognition error.

Five years later, Ganapathiraju, Hamaker, Picone, and Doddington (2001) showed that the syllabic-based system reaches a similar performance to the phonetic-based system for continuous speech recognition task. Firstly, they observed that there are a considerable number of triphones with little information to construct an appropriate speech model. In addition, they noticed that in the triphones, there is minimum integration of the spectral and temporal dependencies due to the short duration of masks, and one by one mapping of the words to its corresponded phonemes caused a great amount of different categories for the same sound. To solve this problem, they proposed an integrated system with syllables model and an acoustic model. The proposed system reduced 1% of WER with respect to a triphones-based system; here a switchboard database was used. They reported an 11.1% error rate when the syllable of the context was used independently. In 1997, the project generated by Edinburgh, "Improvement of the speech recognition using syllabic structure" (Project ESPRESSO), which is motivated by the fact that the conventional HMM-based ASR system no longer provided the expected performance, and it is necessary to find more efficient models than the conventional one that used phonemes of the context. The project intended to find a suitable model to capture the context dependency without requiring an excessive number of parameters for its representation. Its first stage, in which the use of the phonetic syllables characterized for speech recognition was researched by King, Taylor, Frankel, and Richmond (2000), was finished in 1999, while in the second phase, new models for the speech recognition were developed, taking into account the continuous nature of the schemes found in the previous phase. This phase still is in the accomplishment process.

For the Spanish, speech recognizers for specific applications have been developed. Córdoba, Menéndez-Pidal, and Macías Guasara (1995) worked in an ASR system for digits for telephony applications. Also the problem of variation by the emotional state of the speaker was analyzed (Montero, Gutiérrez Arreola, & Colás, 1999). In Mexico the authors have worked on the development of an ASR version for the Spanish spoken in Mexico, which is based on a platform developed originally by the English language (Fanty, 1996; Munive, Vargas, Serridge, Cervantes, & Kirschnning, 1998). Regarding the study about the syllables, Feal (2000) mentioned the idea to use them as a unit for the synthesis of the Spanish spoken speech, and presents a list of the syllables that are used in this language, using a database created from books of Spanish Literature (Feal, 2000). Also, he proposed an algorithm for syllables segmentation in continuous text from the phonetic transcription of the words.

For languages like the Cantonés, spoken in China, which are also based on syllabic units, several experiments have been carried out to analyze the performance of a speech recognition system based on syllables (Lee & Ching, 1997; Peskin, Gillick, & Liberman, 1991). Lee and Ching (1997) used a speaker dependent speech recognition system, with a vocabulary of between 40 and 200 syllables. In the case of the 200 syllables, a recognition rate of 81.8% was obtained. Some languages, such as Cantonese, are mainly based on tones with mono-syllabic features; thus the ASR systems suitable for this kind of language were developed. The system proposed by Peskin et al. (1991) consists of two essential parts: a detector of tones and a basic syllables recognizer using a multilayer perceptron neuronal network. The vocabulary used to evaluate the ASR system was of 40 to 200 syllables, which represent the 6.8% and 34.4% of the total of the syllables of such language. The number of speakers was equal of 10: five men and five women. Another language that has been the object of study is Mandarin language (Chang, Zhou, Di, Huang, & Lee, 2000), which is similar to the previous one; it is based on tones and syllables, but unlike Cantonese, the tone at the end of the syllable is emphasized. Within the main features of this language is that it inserts the fundamental tone ("pitch") as a recognition parameter. The database used in this case included a total of 500 speakers and 1000 phrases; the algorithm obtains the "pitch" in real time, adding also the delta and double delta components. They obtained an error rate of 7.32% when no pitch processing was made. When they added the pitch for the analysis of tones, the error rate was reduced to 6.43%. When the information of the pitch and the set of syllables were combined, the error rate was 6.03%, which represents a reduction of an accumulated error of 17.6%.

These results denote that factors such as the signal energy and the duration can contribute to reduce the ambiguity problem of different tones. As mentioned in some references of this chapter, it can be applied to the Spanish language such as the works of Meneido, Neto and Almeida (1999) and Meneido and Neto (2000), which were done for the Portuguese. Meneido et al. (1999) show that recent developments have allowed the observance that the syllable can be used like a unit of recognition for the Portuguese language, which is a highly syllabic language, because the borders of the syllables are better defined than the phonemes borders. Among their main works, the segmentation of speech signal to syllabic units is proposed; it is realized by means of the feature extraction oriented to perception. These features were post-processed by means of a simple threshold-based system or neural networks based on the syllables borders estimation. The experimental results showed 93% of correct detection of beginning of syllables with 15% of insertion rate, using a window of approximately 260 ms. The obtained results showed that, with a window of approximately 260 ms, 93% of correct detection of the beginnings was reached, with an insertion rate of 15%. The inclusion of the triphones on part of the study of the syllables is another excellent aspect mentioned by Meneido and Neto (2000). As an introduction to their research, they considered that an exact knowledge of the beginnings of the syllable can be useful to increase the recognition rate obtained until now. The database used for testing the ASR system was the BD-PUBLIC, from which they obtained a segmentation adapted of the same one of the order of 72%. In this work they propose four methods to segment the signal in syllabic units. Using the database under analysis they extracted a corpus with a total of 750 phrases, containing a total of 3408 words, from which 1314 were different with a total of 616 different syllables. It is possible to emphasize that the work of Meneido and Neto (2000) looks strongly influenced by the work of Villing, Timoney, Ward, and Costello (2004), in which the utility that has the syllabic unit is mentioned. These results were obtained from a set of experiments using digits of the database SWITCHBOARD. In such experiments they demonstrated that the syllables have better execution than the triphones in approximately 1.1%. Also, the analysis of an algorithm used for the segmentation of syllabic units appears, which are compared with the results of the algorithms of Mermelstein and Howitt used to make the same activity. A recognition rate of 93.1% reported is greater than the 76.1% obtained by the algorithm of Mermelstein and the 78.9% obtained by the Howitt algorithm. Another contribution of Meneido (Meneido & Neto, 2000) consists in the performance analysis that used the neuronal network and the Hidden Markov Models, and in the recognition of phrases of the Portuguese by means of a new method of segmentation in syllabic units. Hartmut et al. (1996) proposed an algorithm for the segmentation of the word in syllabic units, providing a segmentation error of the 12.87% for isolated words and of the 21.03% for the spontaneous speech. This algorithm used a great amount of digital filters to perform the corresponding segmentation.

Fundamentals of Voice Recognition

The automatic speech recognition is a complex pattern recognition task in which the speech signal is analyzed to extract the most significant features, once the speech signal has been digitalized with a sampling rate between 8 and 16 kHz. This section describes some of the most used feature extraction methods reported in the literature (Jackson, 1996; Kirschning-Albers, 1998; Kosko, 1992; Sydral, Bennet, & Greenspan, 1995). The first method is the Fourier analysis, which can be observed from Figure 1, which consists of applying the fast Fourier transform (FFT) to the set of samples under analysis. Regularly, this representation in the frequency domain is distributed by using the well-known MEL scale, where the frequencies smaller than 1KHz are analyzed using a linear scale, and the frequencies larger than 1kHz use a logarithmic scale (Bernal, Bobadilla, & Gomez, 2000), with the purpose of creating an analogy with the internal cochlea of the ear that in its natural way works like a frequencies splitter. This can be observed in the expression of equation 1.

Linear predictive coding (LPC) is a method whose purpose is to find a set of representative vectors denominated vectors code, from which it forms a matrix of representative vectors that as well conforms what book is denominated code. Based on its hypothesis in the fact that sample XT of a signal can be predetermined from the k previous samples, if we know

Figure 1. Filters banks implementation for cepstral-based system proposed by Suk and Flanagan

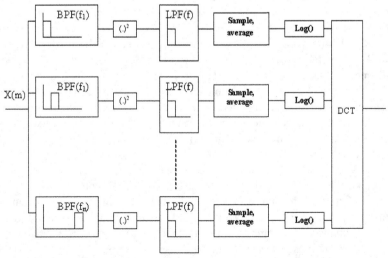

the weight by which each one of them is affected by all the XT-K, previous XT-K-1, XT-K-2, and so forth, samples.

Cepstrales coefficients analysis is another method used for feature extraction of speech signals that represent the inverse Fourier transform of the logarithm of power spectral density of the speech signal (Rabiner & Biing-Hwang, 1993). Finally, the perceptual linear prediction analysis (PLP) is another widely used method, resulting of the physiological characteristics, but that cannot be represented graphically (Kirschning-Albers, 1998).

$$Mel(f) = b \log_{10} (1 + \frac{f}{c}), \tag{1}$$

The essential characteristic of the speech signal is its excessive time varying characteristics. At the present time, the speech signal is analyzed from two different points of view: the acoustic level and the temporary level (Tebelskis, 1995). From the acoustic point of view, the aspects to be analyzed are the accent, the pronunciation, the frequency resonance of vocal tract ("pitch"), and the volume, among others, while in the case of the temporary variation, the different durations presented in a set of speech samples are analyzed. Although in general, both previously mentioned aspects are not independent, they are assumed to independent among them. Between both aspects mentioned before, the time variation is easier to handle. In principle, a linear deformation type of an unknown speech signal was used to compare with a given reference signal. In this case the obtained result was not optimal. Next, a non-linear type deformation was used, which gave as a consequence the appearance of DTW (Dynamic Time Warping) algorithm (Rabiner & Levinson, 1990). At the present time, such algorithm has yet to be used to a great extent. The acoustic variation is more difficult to model, due to its heterogeneous nature. Therefore, the study of the speech recognition has extended its field in this aspect. The different perspectives to analyze the speech recognition are reduced to the following ones: models of reference or groups, knowledge, stochastic or statistical models, artificial neuronal networks, and hybrid methods. Among them the most widely used method is the statistical method that makes use of the hidden Markov model (Kita, Morimoto, & Sagayama, 1993). Several developed systems using such methods appear in specific domains, although these present some limitations that suggest the necessity to develop new methods.

The speech is a continuous time signal and then in order to be processed by a digital processor is indispensable in its digitalization, with an appropriate sampling rate. This factor is very important, however, although a high quality digitalized speech signal could be available since there are still many factors that must be taken in account to be able to develop reliable ASR systems (Kirschning-Albers, 1998) such as the vocabulary size, if the system is speaker dependent or speaker independent, if the ASR is required to recognize isolate words or continuous speech, if the ASR is intended for a particular task, or for general applications, and so forth.

The number of words that the ASR system is required to recognize is a very important factor because the system performance decreases when the vocabulary size increases. Reports of an acceptable recognition average show that most ASR performs fairly well when the word numbers is smaller than 1000 and that the performance worsens when the word number is beyond 1000.

The ASR, depending on the particular application, can be speaker dependent and the speaker independent. The speaker dependent ARS is commonly used when a high recognition rate is required, although its use is restricted to one particular speaker, while the speaker independent ASR can be used in applications that require handling a relatively large number of users, although its recognition performance degrades when the number of speakers increases. Also, both ASR systems can be classified into isolated and continuous speech ASR, depending on the particular application. In the first case, the ASR is required to recognize isolated words or short sentences without relation with other previous speech. In continuous speech recognitions, the system is required to recognize long sentences and even a conversation. In this case, the relations among the different components of a given sentence become very important. Because both situations are quite different, the ASR systems required in both applications are substantially different. Besides the characteristics mentioned previously, the ASR systems can be divided also into ASR systems for particular applications such as to recognize some specific commands, or for general applications.

Another aspect that must be taken in account to develop reliable ARS systems is the distortion introduced by the additive noise as well as variation introduced in the speaker voice due to sickness, possible stress, and so forth.

General Framework for Speech Recognition

All researches related with speech recognition require carrying out a set of tasks to be performed independently of the goal to be reached; some of them are summarized as follows: (a) to prepare the speech corpus to use in the research; (b) analysis of the required conditions to obtain a corpus of good quality; (c) to define the preprocessing to be applied to the corpus file; (d) determine the algorithms and methods that will be used for features extraction to be use in speech recognition; (e) estimate the cepstrals or melspec and so forth; (f) to train the recognition system; and g) to verify the system performance using the correct recognition average.

Prepare the Speech Corpus to Use in the Research

The speech corpus is a set of files with digitized speech that are used for feature extraction during training and evaluation of the developed ASR system. Independently of the application, isolated word recognition, that is, words or short phrases, speaker dependent or independent approach, as well as speaker recognition application, which will be analyzed in an accompanying chapter, the method to construct a reliable speech corpus is basically the same one. The continuous speech problem is not analyzed in this chapter.

To construct a reliable speech corpus, the followings aspects must be considered: (a) a codebook must be designed containing the words or phrase to be recognized by the ASR system. Here the codebook size depends on the application; (b) for each speaker working in the developing of the system (K speakers), N files of each command will be recorded;

Figure 2. Three-dimensional representation speech corpus

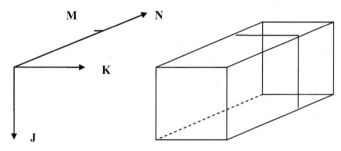

(c) the recorded files are divided into sets, M commands, will be used to train the system, and N-M for testing the behavior of the system using the recognition rate.

Requirements to Obtain a Good Quality Corpus

It is very important, during the sound recording stage, to consider the recording conditions, such as distance to the microphone and adjustment of the gain and sensitivity of the microphone. All recorded commands must be monitored graphically to be sure that they fulfill the minimum requirements such as the signal level. It is important that all recorded signals have similar average amplitude and that these must not be saturated nor have very little amplitude. An example of these two cases is shown by Figure 3(a) and 3(b), respectively, while Figure 3(c) shows the same signal with a good amplitude level. It is very important to avoid the situations shown in Figure 3(a) and 3(b), which can be a cause of performance degradation. The amplitude normalization, in the preprocessing stage, can be used to reduce this problem; however, it is important to avoid the recording and storage of files in the corpus with very low or very large amplitude. In Figure 3, three examples of recorded signals are shown. The first one (Figure 3[a]) is saturated; the second one (Figure 3[b]) has very low amplitude; and the third (Figure 3[c]) is an amplitude normalized signal.

Preprocessing Applied to the Corpus Files

The preprocessing stage is commonly used to improve the system during the training and normal operation stages. It is usually carried out in a series of steps that standardize the characteristics of the speech signals recorded in the time domain. This stage can be summarized as follows: (a) normalization of the recorded signal amplitude, (b) pre-emphasizing the standardized signal, and (c) detection of the starting and final speech signal point, with the purpose of eliminating the silent intervals at the beginning and ending of the words.

The file amplitude normalization is done with the purpose of obtaining a greater similarity between files that contain the same command, avoiding variations of the amplitude during the recording process due to speaker position with respect to the microphone, fatigue, or distraction.

Figure 3. Examples of recording with amplitude: (a) saturate, (b) low, and (c) medium

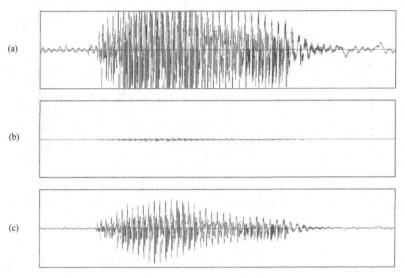

The pre-emphasis is used to compensate the lost that suffer the high speech signal frequencies by effect of the propagation and radiation from the vocal cavity to the microphone. The pre-emphasis is performed by filtering the speech signal with a first order filter whose output signal is given by passing the speech signal through a first order filter as shown in Figure 4. This filter improves the efficiency of the stages used to calculate the speech spectrum, increasing, from the hearing point of view, the sensibility of the frequencies components larger than 1 KHz. Note that the pre-emphasis is not applied if the task consists of the analysis and extraction of the fundamental tone.

The detection of beginning and final point of a word is done by taking into account the activity, the energy activity, and zero crossing of the speech signal, $S(n)$, with respect to the values that are in silence conditions. The duration of the segment under analyze is of 5 ms approximately. The behavior of the energy increase or the zero crossing indicates that a speech signal is present. Clearly, this activity can be due to additive noise; however, in most cases the ASR system can control the presence of it during the recordings. The zero

Figure 4. Pre-emphasis filter response

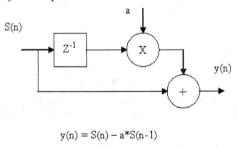

$$y(n) = S(n) - a*S(n-1)$$

Figure 5. Start and end point detection in (a) Spanish word "ahora," (b) Spanish word "silos"

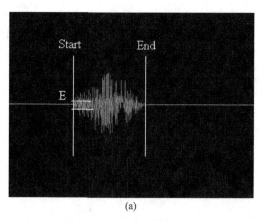

(a)

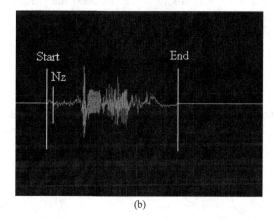

(b)

crossing variation is mainly due to the emission of an explosive signal (`p', `t', `k', `b') or random noise (`s', `f', `ch', `j', `z'), while the energy variation happens in the presence of loudness vowels (`á', `é', `í', `ó', `ú'), semivowels, or consonants (`m', 'n', `ñ', `w', `d', `l', `g', `y'). In order to detect the presence of isolated words, the same procedure is done, but in this occasion the detection starts at the end of the data set and proceeds toward the principle. If the task of determining beginning and end involves a phrase where several words exist, the process is done by determining where there are segments larger than, usually between 30 and 50 milliseconds, according to the characteristics of the speaker who produces the voice.

In Figure 5 we can observe the necessity of working with the energy threshold and zero crossing, according to the type of sound to be analyzed at the initial word: (a) sonorous sound "ahora," (b) noise sound "silos." How it is possible to be appreciated. For the case of the word "silos," the energy threshold does not detect the beginning of the word, and the same happens for the end.

Energy analysis: Consider the energy contained in a silence segment of 1s duration, which for $N = f_s$, where f_s is the sampling frequency has an energy given by:

$$E_{sil} = \sum_{i=0}^{N-1} (S_i)^2, \tag{2}$$

while tl200nergy average is given by:

$$Ep_{sil} = \frac{E_{sil}}{20}. \tag{3}$$

It is the average energy in a 5 ms segment, that is, the size of segment that is used to estimate the time interval i lvhich tl5, ice activity is present. Next the energy threshold use to determine the starting and ending point of the speech segment is given by:

$$Eu = Ep_{sil}(1+\%), 0.1 < \% < 0.2, \tag{4}$$

where the parameter $\%$ is chosen by the user. This is the value that must be considered during the analysis. The first sample of the segment that fulfills that condition is considered as the starting point of the speech segment under analysis, while the last sample of the last segment that satisfies this condition is considered as the ending point.

Analysis of zero crossing: Consider the number of zero crossings of a silence segment of 1s length, assuming that $N = f_s$ samples:

$$NZ_{sil} = \sum_{0}^{N-1} Signo(Si+1) - Signo(Si) > 0. \tag{5}$$
$$NZ_{sil}$$

In a similar way the average value for a segment of 5 ms is given by:

$$NZP_{sil} = \frac{NZsil}{20}. \tag{6}$$

This value represents the average of zero crossing in a 5 ms segment, which is the size of the segment used to analyze and to determine the starting point of speech segment when it begins with a noise consonant. Next, NZu, which is the zero crossing threshold, is given by:

$$NZu = MZp_{sil}(1+\%), \tag{7}$$

where the value of % is chosen by the ASR user. This value must be considered by the analysis. Here, as in the energy average method, the first sample of the first segment that fulfills this condition is considered as the first sample of the speech signal segment. Once the starting point is detected, a segment of 20 or 25 ms is used for feature extraction.

Feature Extraction Algorithms

Some authors consider the feature extraction as part of the preprocessing stage; however, because of the importance that the feature extraction has in the performance of ASR systems, the feature extraction is presented separately. Several methods have been proposed to feature extraction; among them, the autoregressive parameters obtained using the linear prediction method, a_p, provides the better results to characterize the human speech. Using these parameters we can assume that the speech signal can be represented as the output signal of an all pole digital filter whose excitation is an impulse sequence with a frequency equal to the pitch of speech signal under analysis, when the segment is voiced, or with noise when the segment is unvoiced. A variant is to use the cepstrales coefficients of the speech signal, which can be obtained from the LPC coefficients; both of them have been shown to perform fairly well in feature extraction in speech recognition system. The speech production model is shown in Figure 6.

The speech production model shown in Figure 6 is strongly dependent on the estimation of the autoregressive parameters, a_p, which can be obtained using the linear prediction method, which can be summarized as follows: (a) firstly the input signal is segmented to obtain the useful signal, without silence, in segments from 25 to 20 ms overlapping the segments; (b) apply the Hamming window to the segmented signal (Childers, 2000; Williams, 1996); (c) estimate the prediction order, that is, the amount of p values for each segment; (d) calculate the autoregressive coefficients or linear prediction coefficients, LPC, for each segment; (e)

Figure 6. Speech signal production model

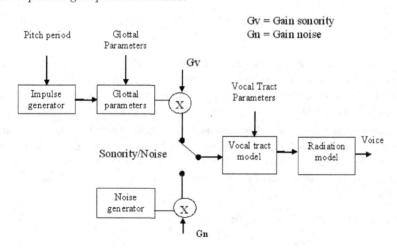

using the estimated LPC parameters estimate the cepstrales coefficients, (f) finally obtain the coefficients average.

To obtain the features vector, firstly the speech signal is divided in segments of 20 to 25 ms, which is an established standard to characterize the dynamics of the operation of the phonate system. From multiple observations one concludes that the change from a phoneme to another one in the speech happens approximately in that time interval, although there are phonemes like the explosives that are a little shorter. The overlapping of segments is necessary to obtain the dynamics of change of the most representative segment characteristics. Usually the overlapping is applied with a 50% overlap. If the objective using the autocorrelation is to determine the existence of the pitch, FO, in the segment under analysis, the segment duration is taken with a length of 40 ms.

To avoid distortion of the segmented speech due to the discontinuities introduced during the segmentation process, a window function, typically the Hamming window, given by following equation, is used:

$$W(n) = 0.54 - 0.46\cos(2\pi n / N), \text{ for } 0 \leq n \leq N - 1,$$

where N is the number of samples of the used segment.

After the speech signal is segmented, the p autocorrelation coefficients are estimated, where p is the linear predictor order. The autocorrelation function can be estimated using the unbiased autocorrelation or the biased autocorrelation algorithms (Childers, 2000), where for the biased case we have:

$$Rss(k) = \frac{1}{N - |k|} \sum_{i=0}^{N-1-|k|} S(i + |k|)S(i), \quad \text{where } |k| < \mathbf{p} + 1, \tag{8}$$

and for the unbiased case;

$$Rss(k) = \frac{1}{N} \sum_{i=0}^{N-1-|k|} S(i + |k|(S(i), \quad \text{where } |k| < \mathbf{p} + 1, \tag{9}$$

where N is the number of speech data and $\mathbf{p}$ the linear prediction order. The more widely used autocorrelation estimation method is the unbiased one, although solutions exist using the biased algorithm. However, in such a case the calculation of LPC coefficients is done using the covariance matrix.

Once p autocorrelation coefficients are estimated for each segments I, the linear prediction coefficients, a_p, coefficients for each segment, are estimated minimizing the mean square value of prediction error as follows (Childers, 2000): consider that the signal at time n is estimated as a linear combination of the pass samples of input signal, such that:

$$\hat{s}(n) = -(a_1 s(n-1) + a_2 s(n-2) + ... + a_p (n-p)), \tag{10}$$

$$\hat{s}(n) = -\sum_{k=1}^{p} a_k s(n-k),\tag{11}$$

where a_k, $k=1,2,\dots,p$ are the linear prediction coefficients. Notice that with this model a real value sampled data at time n is predicted, using a linear combination from the previous sampled data. Therefore, it is valid to affirm that a filter can be designed that be able to estimate the data at time n only using the previous data at times $n-1$, because:

$$\hat{s}(n) = -a_e s(n-1),\tag{12}$$

where a_e is the linear prediction coefficient and $s(n)$ and $\hat{s}(n)$ are discrete samples. The error sequence between both sequences is given by:

$$e(n) = s(n) - \hat{s}(n) = s(n) + a_e\, s(n-1),\tag{13}$$

where the linear predictor coefficients are estimated such that mean square value of prediction error becomes a minimum. Consider:

$$E_T^2 = \sum_{n=0}^{N-1} e^2(n) = \sum_{n=0}^{N-1} (s(n) - \hat{s}(n))^2$$

$$= \sum_{n=0}^{N-1} (s(n) + a_e s(n-k))^2.\tag{14}$$

In order to obtain the linear predictor coefficient, a_e, we take the partial derivative of E_T^2 with respect to a_k and set it to zero, that is,

$$\frac{\partial E_T^2}{\partial a_e} = 0 = 2\sum_{n=0}^{N-1} (s(n) + a_e s(n-1))s(n-1),\tag{15}$$

to obtain,

$$a_e = \frac{-\dfrac{1}{N}\displaystyle\sum_{n=0}^{N-1} s(n)s(n-1)}{\dfrac{1}{N}\displaystyle\sum_{n=0}^{N-1} s(n-1)s(n-1)} = -\frac{Rss(1)}{Rss(0)}.\tag{16}$$

In order to generalize the previous result for p coefficients, it is necessary firstly to consider that (13) and (15) show that the prediction error is orthogonal to the input data (Figure 7).

Consider a general case in which the speech sample at time n is estimated as a linear combination of p previous samples as follows:

Figure 7. Orthogonally between the data and error

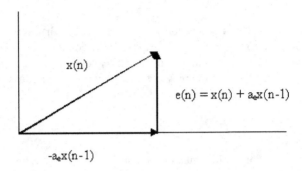

$$\hat{s}(n) = -\sum_{k=1}^{p} a_k s(n-k) \tag{17}$$

$$s(n) = -\sum_{k=1}^{p} a_k s(n-k) + e(n) = \hat{s}(n) + e(n). \tag{18}$$

Next consider the Z transform of equation (18), which is given as:

$$S(z) = -\left[\sum_{k=1}^{p} a_k z^{-k}\right] S(z) + E(z) = \hat{S}(z) + E(z). \tag{19}$$

Then,

$$S(z) = \frac{E(z)}{1 + \left[\sum_{k=1}^{p} a_k z^{-k}\right]} = \frac{E(z)}{A(z)}, \tag{20}$$

where,

$$A(z) = 1 + \sum_{k=1}^{p} a_k z^{-k}. \tag{21}$$

Equation (20) denotes the transfer function of an all pole filter shown in Figure 8. The total quadratic error for this interval is:

$$E_T^2 = \sum_{n=0}^{N-1} e^2(n) = \sum_{n=0}^{N-1} (s(n) - \hat{s}(n))^2 = \sum_{n=0}^{N-1} \left(s(n) + \sum_{k=1}^{p} a_k s(n-k) \right)^2, \tag{22}$$

where $s(n)$ are the windowed data. Next consider the minimization of equation (22) that is

Figure 8. AR filter

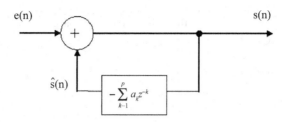

obtained taking the derivate of E_T with respect to the filter coefficients and setting it equal to zero, that is,

$$\frac{\partial E_T^2}{\partial a_k} = 0, \quad k = 1, 2, ...p.$$
(23)

Thus, from equations (22) and (23) it follows that:

$$\sum_{k=1}^{p} a_k \sum_{n=0}^{N-1} s(n-k)s(n-i) = -\sum_{n=0}^{N-1} s(n)s(n-i), \quad k = 1, 2, ...p,$$
(24)

which can be expressed in terms of the autocorrelation function of input signal as follows:

$$\sum_{k=1}^{p} a_k Rss(i-k) = -Rss(i), \quad k = 1, 2, ...p,$$
(25)

where,

$$Rss(k) = \frac{1}{N} \sum_{n=0}^{N-1-|k|} s(n)s(n+|k|).$$
(26)

The term $1/N$, not mentioned previously, is the scale factor of the partial autocorrelation, which is a guarantee for the stability of the estimated LPC coefficients. Writing equation (25) in a matrix form it follows that:

$$\begin{bmatrix} Rss(0) & Rss(-1) & \cdots & Rss(-(p-1)) \\ Rss(1) & Rss(0) & \cdots & Rss(-(p-2)) \\ \vdots & \vdots & \cdots & \vdots \\ Rss(p-1) & Rss(p-1) & \cdots & Rss(0) \end{bmatrix} \begin{bmatrix} a_1 \\ a_2 \\ \vdots \\ a_p \end{bmatrix} = - \begin{bmatrix} Rss(1) \\ Rss(2) \\ \vdots \\ Rss(p) \end{bmatrix}.$$
(27)

Taking into account that autocorrelation coefficients are real and even, that is, $Rss(k-m)=Rss(m-k)$, for $k=1,2,3,..p$ and $m=1,2,3,...,p$, the matrix on the left part becomes a Toeplitz type matrix (left part), and then the terms a_k can be obtain by using the Levinson-Durbin algorithm. An additional equation for the estimation of a_k is based on total quadratic prediction error, which is given by:

$$E_T^2 = Rss(0)a_0 + \sum_{k=1}^{p} a_k Rss(-k), \tag{28}$$

where $a_0=1$. Again assuming that the autocorrelation coefficients are even, as in equation (27), from equation (28), it follows that:

$$\begin{bmatrix} Rss(0) & Rss(-1) & \cdots & Rss(-p) \\ Rss(1) & Rss(0) & \cdots & Rss(-(p-1)) \\ \vdots & \vdots & \cdots & \vdots \\ Rss(p) & Rss(p-1) & \cdots & Rss(0) \end{bmatrix} \begin{bmatrix} a_0 \\ a_1 \\ \vdots \\ a_p \end{bmatrix} = -\begin{bmatrix} E_T^2 \\ 0 \\ \vdots \\ 0 \end{bmatrix}. \tag{29}$$

Finally, the linear predictor coefficients can be obtained solving the normal equations given by equations (27) or (29), using the Leveinson-Durbin algorithm.

Levinson-Durbin Algorithm

Given: $p, Rss[0,p]$

Calculate: $\{\alpha_m, a_{k,m}, c_m: 1 \le m \le p, 1 \le k \le p\}$

Begin: $\alpha_0 = Rss[0,0]$

                    $a_{0,0} = 1$

Body of the program: for $m=0$ to $p-1$, do

$$\gamma_m = \sum_{k=0}^{m} Rss[m+1-k] \, a_{k,m}$$

$$c_{m+1} = -gamma_m / \alpha_m$$
$$\alpha_{m+1} = \alpha_m (1 - c_{m+1}^2)$$
$$a_{m+1,m} = 0$$

        for $k=0$ to $m+1$, do

$$a_{k,m+1} = a_{k,m} + c_{m+1} \, a_{m+1-k,m}$$

        end loop k

    end loop m

Within the second loop, the one of k, is formed the a_p LPC coefficients.

The advantage of estimating the coefficients of the all pole filter using the partial correlation coefficients α is that the resulting filter is always stable. Thus from the previous process it follows that the LPC coefficients are estimated in a recursive form as shown in Table 1 for a predictor order equal to $p=10$.

From the table it follows that the terms $a_{0,m} = 1$, because the estimation task due to in each iteration, the terms $a_{\#,m}$ and $a_{m,\#}$, are different, $a_{1,2} \neq a_{1,2}$; the columns value are the result of the vector a_p of LPC coefficients $a_p = a_0, a_1, \cdots, a_p$, in each iteration.

Depending on the ARS application, it may be useful to take the LPC averages of each word or word sections of each word. This a_p coefficients average may be used as the behavior model of each word or section (Buzo & Gray, 1980). Thus in the case of all word, the mth LPC becomes:

$$\hat{a}_m = \hat{a}_m = \frac{1}{I}\sum_{i=1}^{I} a_{i,m}, \quad 1 \leq m \leq p. \tag{30}$$

The cepstral coefficients, which are widely used in both speech as well as speaker recognition problems, can be directly obtained from the LPC coefficients, or by means of the inverse Fourier transform of input signal power spectral density. These coefficients have shown to be very good parameters for the development of speech recognition, sometimes better than the LPC.

The ceptrals coefficients can be estimated from the LPC coefficients applying the following expression:

$$c_n = -a_n - \frac{1}{n}\sum_{i=1}^{n-1}(n-i)a_i c_{n-i}, \text{ for } n > 0, \tag{31}$$

Table 1. Vector a_p in iteration p selected

Iteration Coefficients	0	1	2	3	...	9	10
a_0	1	1	1	1	...	1	1
a_1	-	$a_{1,1}$	$a_{1,2}$	$a_{1,3}$	...	$a_{1,p-1}$	$a_{1,p}$
a_2	-	-	$a_{2,2}$	$a_{2,3}$	...	$a_{2,p-1}$	$a_{2,p}$
a_3	-	-	-	$a_{3,3}$	...	$a_{3,p-1}$	$a_{3,p}$
a_4	-	-	-	-	...	$a_{4,p-1}$	$a_{4,p}$
a_5	-	-	-	-	...	$a_{5,p-1}$	$a_{5,p}$
a_6	-	-	-	-	...	$a_{6,p-1}$	$a_{6,p}$
a_7	-	-	-	-	...	$a_{7,p-1}$	$a_{7,p}$
a_8	-	-	-	-	...	$a_{8,p-1}$	$a_{8,p}$
a_9	-	-	-	-	-	$a_{9,p-1}$	$a_{9,p}$
a_{10}	-	-	-	-	-	-	$a_{p,p}$

where c_n is the nth LPC-cepstral coefficients (CLPC), a_i are the LPC coefficients, and n is the cepstral index.

Another form to carry out the cepstrals estimation is use of the power spectral density of the input signal. To this end we can use the homomorphic techniques of signal processing, which have had great importance within the speech recognition field. The homomorphic systems are a class of non-linear systems that obey to a superposition principle. The motivation to do a homomorphic processing of the speech signal is shown in Figure 9.

The cepstrum estimation involves firstly the calculation of the power spectral density of input signal. Once the power spectral density of the input signal in the selected interval is obtained, next the logarithm of the previous power spectral density is calculated, and the inverse Fourier transform is applied to the resulting signal, which is all defined positive. This procedure is illustrated in Figure 10.

The cepstrum of a speech signal can be divided in two parts: the lower portion of time that corresponds to the transfer function of the vocal track and the high portion that corresponds to the excitation. To smooth the cepstral estimation of the vocal track, the high portion of it can do zero and the Fourier transform applied to the low portion part of the ceptrum, resulting in a smoothed cepstral spectrum. This represents the magnitude of vocal tract response when the excitation effect has been removed, including the fundamental tone. Whereas the LPC analysis represents only the poles of the system, the use of the cepstrales is better like the solution to represent the nasalized voice (Chen, 1988).

Usually the number of cepstrales coefficients that are used is similar to the number of LPC coefficients, by convenience and to avoid noise.

Consider the inverse Fourier transform of the logarithm of input signal power spectral density given by:

$$c(n) = \frac{1}{N} \sum_{k=0}^{N-1} \log_{10} \left| S_{med}(k) \right| e^{j\frac{2\pi}{N}kn}, \quad 0 \le n \le N-1. \tag{32}$$

In equation (32), the $c(n)$ is known as the nth cepstral coefficient derived from the Fourier transform and N is the number of points used to calculate the discrete Fourier transform (DFT). This equation is also known as the inverse DFT of the logarithmic spectrum. It can be properly simplified considering that the spectrum of the logarithm is a symmetrical real function, thus equation (32) becomes:

Figure 9. The homomorphic technique can be use to separate the vocal tract action of the excitation signal (lineal filter on the time variable)

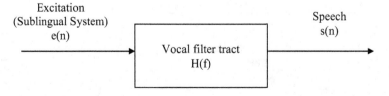

Figure 10. Algorithm for cepstrum estimation

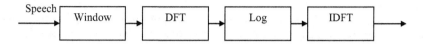

$$c(n) = \frac{2}{N} \sum_{k=1}^{N} S_{med}(I(k)) \cos\left(\frac{2\pi}{N} kn\right),$$ (33)

where *n* is the coefficient index, which is usually keep lower than 20, that is, $(n \le 20)$. $I(k)$ denotes a function that translates the position of a value in frequency at the interval where it is contained. It is in fact the measurement of the period of the frequencies that contains the signal. The cepstrum is also useful for the detection of the pitch in voiced segments. In such a case, as shown by Veeneman (1998), the distance from the origin of the graph to its maximum value is the period of the fundamental tone (T0). Usually, to this end, a segment signal of 64 ms, sampled to 8000 Hertz, is used. The election of the maximum point to determine the position of the fundamental tone is based on the fact that for standard voices the pitch takes place between 80 and 250 Hertz, corresponding to the maximum level with the frequency for women and the minimum for the men. That in time is equivalent to an interval between 4 and 12.5 ms.

For isolated words recognition, it is possible to take the average from the LPC or cepstrales coefficients (CLPC) of the total of segments contained in the word to generate an averaged feature vector to be used during the ASR training or during normal operation parameters to determine their similarity with the training models.

System Training

The system training has the purpose to provide the ASR system the capacity to recognize isolated words depending on the speaker or independently of the speaker. In the first case the system will be trained with a corpus consisting of all words that the system must recognize spoken by all possible users of the system; in the second case, the system is trained with a corpus containing all words spoken by a specific speaker. In both cases it is desirable that each word be repeated several times by each speaker, if possible, during different days. Usually some part of the recorded speech signal is used for training and another part is used for testing.

The technique used for the training is chosen by the system designers and can be vector quantization (Barrón, Suárez-Guerra, & Moctezuma, 1999), neuronal networks, self-organized maps, Gaussian mixtures model, hidden Markov models, or combinations of the previous ones, with applications of vocalized segments, continuous speech, and so forth.

ASR Testing

Following the ASR training, system verification will be done using the N-M words not used for ASR training; the recognition success will be verified using these commands.

During the case of training, a question that must be considered is when we must stop the training process to avoid the overtraining phenomenon. It is understood like overtraining, the moment from which the system instead of reducing the error with respect to the testing set when the training time increase, the recognition error increases when the training time increases. From the methodology point of view, to detect this moment of increase of the error of recognition in the system due to overtraining, it is recommendable to perform a system test at the end of each training session. Also it is recommend that, for the case of neuronal networks to initiate the training of the system with different weights from probability in the vectors that interconnect the cells of the system and to remain in the end with the network that provides the smaller error of trained recognition after.

Conclusion

This chapter presents an overview of the speech recognition technology, analyzing the main components of a speech recognition system. Topics such as signal capture, consideration that must be taken to construct a reliable corpus for system training, as well as different methods used for features extraction are analyzed in detail. This chapter complements Chapter XII provided in this book, related to advanced topics of speech and speaker recognition algorithms.

References

Barrón, R., Suárez-Guerra, S., & Moctezuma, C. (1999). *Reconocimiento de comandos verbales utilizando cuantización vectorial y redes neuronales* (Tech. Rep. Serie Roja, No. 40). Computing Research Center, The National Polyechnic Institute of Mexico.

Bernal, J., Bobadilla, J., & Gomez, P. (2000). *Reconocimiento de voz y fonética acústica.* Madrid, España: Alfa-Omega.

Boulard, D. S. (1996). A new ASR approach based on independent processing and recombination of frequency bands. In *Proceedings of the International Conference on Spoken Language Processing* (ICSLP 1996) (Vol 1. pp. 426-429) ACM Digital Library.

Buzo, A., & Gray, R. (1980). Speech coding based upon quantization. *IEEE Transaction on Communications, COM-28*(1).

Chang, E., Zhou, J., Di, S., Huang, C., & Lee, K. (2000). Large vocabulary Mandarin speech recognition with different approaches in modeling tones. In *Proceedings of the International Conference on Spoken Language Processing,* Beijing, China (pp. 983-986). ACM Digital Library.

Childers, D. G. (2000). *Speech processing and synthesis toolboxes.* New York: John Wiley & Sons.

Córdoba, R., Menéndez-Pidal, X., & Macías Guasara, J. (1995). Development and improvement of a real-time ASR system for isolated digits in Spanish over the telephone line. In *Proceedings of Eurospeech '95* (pp. 1537-1540). Madrid.

Fanty, M. (1996). *Overview of the CSLU toolkit,* (Tech. Rep. No. CSLU-011-1995). Center for Spoken Language Understanding, Oregon Graduate Institute of Science & Technology.

Feal, L. (2000). *Sobre el uso de la sílaba como unidad de síntesis en el español* (Tech. Rep. No. IT-DI-2000-0004). Informatics Department, Universidad de Valladolid.

Fosler-Lussier, E., Greenberg, S., & Morgan, N. (1999). Incorporating contextual phonetics into automatic speech recognition. In *Proceedings of the ESCA Workshop on Modeling Pronunciation Variation for Automatic Speech Recognition* (pp. 611-614). San Francisco.

Ganapathiraju, A., Hamaker, J., Picone, J., & Doddington, G. (2001). Syllable-based large vocabulary continuous speech recognition. *IEEE Transactions on Speech and Audio Processing, 9*(4), 358-366.

Harmut, R., Pfitzinger, S. B., & Heid, S. (1996) Syllable detection in read and spontaneous speech. In *Proceedings of 4th International Conference on Spoken Language Processing*, Philadelphia (pp. 1261-1264). Washington, DC: IEEE Computer Society.

Hauenstein, A. (1996). *The syllable re-revisited* (Tech. Rep. No. tr-96-035). Munich, Germany: Siemens AG, Corporate Research and Development.

Hu, Z., Schalkwyk, J., Barnard, E., & Cole, R. (1996). Speech recognition using syllable-like units. In *Proceedings of the International Conference on Spoken Language Processing,* Philadelphia, PA, (vol. 2, pp. 1117-1120). Washington DC: IEEE Computer Society.

Jackson, L. B. (1996). *Digital filters and signal processing.* New York: Kluwer Academic Publishers.

Jones, R., Downey, S., & Mason, J. (1999). Continuous speech recognition using syllables. In *Proceedings of Eurospeech '96* (vol. 3, pp. 1171-1174). Rhodes, Greece.

King, S., Taylor, P., Frankel, J., & Richmond, K. (2000). Speech recognition via phonetically featured syllables. *PHONUS, 5,* 15-34.

Kirschning-Albers, I. (1998). *Automatic speech recognition with the parallel cascade Neural Network.* Unpublished doctoral dissertation, University of Tokushima, Japan.

Kita, K., Morimoto, T., & Sagayama, S. (1993). LR parsing with a category reachability test applied to speech recognition. *IEICE Trans. Information and Systems, E76-D*(1), 23-28.

Kosko, B. (1992). *Neural networks for signal processing.* Englewood Cliffs, NJ: Prentice Hall.

Lee, T., & Ching, P. (1998). A neural network based speech recognition system for isolated Cantonese syllables. In *Proceedings of the 1997 IEEE International Conference on Acoustics, Speech, and Signal Processing (ICASSP'97) Hong Kong* (vol. 4, p. 3269). Washington DC: IEEE Computer Society.

Meneido, H., & Neto, J. (2000). Combination of acoustic models in continuous speech recognition hybrid systems. In *Proceedings of the International Conference on Spoken Language Processing,* Beijing, China (vol. 9, pp. 1000-1029). ACM Digital Library.

Meneido, H., Neto, P., & Almeida, L. (1999). Syllable onset detection applied to the Portuguese language. In *Proceedings of Eurospeech'99* (p. 81). Budapest, Hungry.

Montero, H., & Neto, J. (2000). Combination of acoustic models in continuous speech recognition hybrid systems. In *Proceedings of Eurospeech'99* (pp. 2099-2102). Budapest.

Munive, N., Vargas, A., Serridge, B., Cervantes, O., & Kirschnning, I. (1998). Entrenamiento de un reconocedor fonético de digitos para el español mexicano usando el CSLU toolkit. *Revista de Computación y Sistemas, 3*(2), 98-104.

Peskin, B., Gillick, L., & Liberman, N. (1991). Progress in recognizing conversational telephone speech. In *Proceedings of the IEEE International Conference on Acoustics, Speech, and Signal Processing* (ICASSP'97) Toronto, Canada (vol. 3, pp. 1811-1814). Washington, DC: IEEE Computer Society.

Rabiner, L., & Biing-Hwang, J. (1993). *Fundamentals of speech recognition.* Englewood Cliffs, NJ: Prentice Hall.

Rabiner, L. R., & Levinson, S. E. (1990). Isolated and connected word recognition-theory and selected applications. In A. Waibel & K. Lee (Eds.), *Readings in speech recognition* (pp. 115-153). New York: Morgan Kaufman Publishers.

Suárez-Guerra, S. (2005). ¿100% de reconocimiento de voz? Unpublished.

Sydral, A., Bennet, R., & Greenspan, S. (1995). *Applied speech technology.* New York: CRC.

Tebelskis, J. (1995). *Speech recognition using neural networks.* Unpublished doctoral dissertation, School of Computer Science, Carnegie Mellon University, Pittsburgh, PA.

Veeneman, D. E. (1988). Speech signal analysis. In C. H. Chen (Ed) *Signal processing handbook.* New York: Marcel Dekker, Inc.

Villing, R., Timoney, J., Ward, T., & Costello, J. (2004). Automatic blind syllable segmentation for continuous speech. In *Proceedings of the Irish Signals and Systems Conference 2004.* Belfast, UK (pp. 41-46). IET Digital Library.

Weber, K. (2000). Multiple timescale feature combination towards robust speech recognition. In *Konferenz zur Verarbeitung natürlicher Sprache KOVENS2000.* Ilmenau, Germany.

Williams, C. S. (1986). *Designing digital filters.* Englewood Cliffs, NJ: Prentice Hall.

Wu, S. (1998). *Incorporating information from syllable-length time scales into automatic speech recognition.* Unpublished doctoral dissertation, Berkeley University.

Wu, S., Shire, M., Greenberg, S., & Morgan, N. (1997). Integrating syllable boundary information into automatic speech recognition. In *Proceedings of the IEEE International Conference on Acoustics, Speech and Signal Processing (ICASSP),* Munich, Germany (vol. 1, pp. 987-990). Washington, DC: IEEE Computer Society.

Chapter XII

Advanced Techniques in Speech Recognition

Jose Luis Oropeza-Rodriguez, National Polytechnic Institute, Mexico

Sergio Suárez-Gerra, National Polytechnic Institute, Mexico

Abstract

During the last 30 years, people have tried to communicate in an oral form with the computers, developing for this end an important amount of automatic speech recognition algorithms. Because of this, software such as the Dragon Dictate and the IBM Via Voice are already available to interact easily with the computer in oral form. However, during the last several years ASR has not reported important advances, not only due to the advances obtained until now, but also because the scientific community working in this area does not have founded another tool so powerful as HMM, despite a great number of alternatives that have been proposed since HMM appeared. This chapter presents the main elements required to create a practical ASR using HMM. The basic principles of the continuous density hidden Markov models (CDHMM) are also given.

Introduction

From readings in speech recognition such as those provided in the previous chapter or those provided by Waibel and Lee (1990), it follows that automatic speech recognition (ASR) is based mainly by the following approaches: template-based, knowledge-based, stochastic, and connectionist, principally. During a long time, 20 years ago, the interest was based on the data time warping (DTW) algorithm; it was used for a long time because it represented a good alignment between the speech signal and the time.

The template-based approach was mentioned in the previous chapter, and its most representative algorithm is the linear coding predictive (LPC). The LPC was widely used to solve problems of the verbal commands with a set of limited instructions. After that, in the 1980s, the stochastic approach using hidden Markov models was used to efficiently solve the alignment mentioned previously and the relationship with the significance of the word or message that corpus of voices needed. Actually, research centers are interested in realizing studies about the interaction of neural networks (connectionist approach) with ASR.

This chapter is focused on hidden Markov models because their applications actually are vast; HTK is the most important result of that. The discussion presented in this chapter pretends to give to the reader an idea of automatic speech recognition using HMMs, in both continuous and discontinuous speech recognition.

Finally, we present a new approach used in the training stage; the inclusion of the knowledge-based system has the goal of adding a priori knowledge to this stage, so that not only the segmentation of the corpus is important, but also the knowledge of the grammatical structure. For that, we use the 10 rules identified into the Spanish language that permit splitting a word into the syllables that it constitutes.

The Units and Models into
Automatic Speech Recognition

Automatic speech recognition systems (ASRs) are implemented using the phoneme-like fundamental speech unit, being the more applications based on the hidden Markov models

Figure 1. Concatenation in hidden Markov models

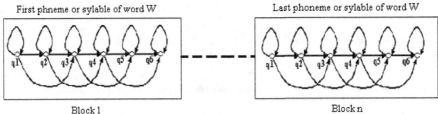

(HMMs) that concatenate themselves as show Figure 1 (Savage, 1995) to obtain words or phrases.

The present requirements within the field of speech recognition converge in increasing the reliability of the type of system that is used; these have found in the phoneme the base of their modeling, coverall in systems of recognition with an extensive vocabulary and therefore applied to the necessities of the continuous speech system.

hidden Markov models must find an optimal model for each word belonging to a defined vocabulary. Next the typical example of the urn and ball model is explained to understand its operation.

The Urn and Ball Model

Rabiner and Biing-Hwang (1993) mention this example. Considering that there are N glass urns in a room, as in Figure 2, within each one exist balls of M distinct colors; the physical process to obtain the observations is as follows.

A person is in a room, according to a random procedure, and chooses an initial urn; of this urn, a ball is selected randomly, and its color is registered like an observation. Then, the ball is replaced in the urn from which it was selected. A new urn according to a random process is chosen, and the process of ball selection is repeated; of this form is generated a sequence of finite observations of colors, which we could model as the observable output of a HMM.

It should be obvious that the simplest HMM in the process of the urn and the ball is in which each state belongs to a specific urn and for which the probability of a color ball is defined by each state. The election of urns is dictated by the transition state matrix of the HMM. We must to take into account that the balls into each urn must be the same and the distinction on several urns is in the way of the collection of balls of colors that compose it. Therefore, an isolated observation of a ball of color individually does not indicate immediately which urn comes.

Figure 2. The urn and ball model

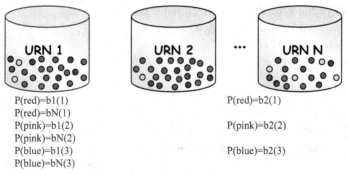

The Elements of a Hidden Markov Model

Rabiner and Biing-Hwang (1993) and Resch (2001b) mention that a hidden Markov model for observations of discreet symbols, such as an urn and a ball model, is characterized by the following aspects:

Number of States in the Model (N)

Because the states are hidden, for many practical applications some meaning related to the states or sets of states of the model exists. In the urn and ball model, each state corresponds to the urns. Generally, the states are interconnected in such a form that any state can be reached from any other state; as we see, a great amount of interconnections between interest states exists, and this can be transferred to applications of speech recognition. We denote the individual states like $\{S_1, S_2, S_3, \ldots, S_N\}$, and the state to time t like q_t.

Number of Distinct Observation Symbols per State (M)

The observation symbols correspond to the physical output of the system being modeled. For the urn and ball model they were the colors of the selected balls from the urns. The individual symbols are denoted by $V = \{v_1, v_2, \ldots, v_M\}$.

The State Transition Probability Distribution (A)

The probability distribution of stage transition is $A = \{a_{ij}\}$, where a_{ij} is defined as in equation (1).

$$a_{ij} = P\left[q_{t+1} = j \mid q_t = i\right], \quad 1 \leq i, j \leq N \tag{1}$$

For the special case where any state can reach any another state in a single step, we have $a_{ij} > 0$ for all i, j. For other types of HMM, we would have a_{ij} for one or more (i, j) pairs.

Observation Symbol Probability Distribution $B = \{b_j(k)\}$

The observation symbol probability distribution is $B = \{b_j(k)\}$, in which $b_j(k)$ is defined by equation (2), where $j=1, 2\ldots N$.

$$b_j(k) = P[o_t = v_k \mid q_t = j], \quad 1 \leq k \leq M, \tag{2}$$

Initial State Distribution (π)

Initial state distribution $\pi = \{\pi_i\}$, is defined by equation (3)

$$\pi_i = P[q_1 = i], \quad 1 \leq i \leq N \tag{3}$$

It is possible that HMM requires the specification of two parameters for a number of states (N) and a number of different observations from each symbol by state (M), the specification of the observation symbols, and the specification of the three measured probability states A, B and π. By convenience, we use the compact notation:

$$\lambda = (A, B, \pi), \tag{4}$$

to indicate the complete parameter set of the model. This set of parameters, of course, defines a measurement of probability for O, for example $P(O \mid \lambda)$.

The Three Basic Problems for Hidden Markov Models

Given the form of HMM from the previous section, there are three basic problems that must be solved for the model. These problems are the following:

Problem 1

Given the observation sequence $O_T = (O_1, O_2,..., O_T)$, and a model $\lambda = (A, B, \pi)$, how do we efficiently compute $P(O \mid \lambda)$?, where $P(O \mid \lambda)$ is the probability of the observation sequence, given the model?

Problem 2

Given a observation sequence $O_T = (O_1, O_2,..., O_T)$, and a model λ, how do we choose a corresponding state sequence $Q = (q_1, q_2,..., q_T)$, that is optimal in some sense?

In this problem we tried to conceal the hidden part of the model, that is to say, to find the correct state sequence.

Problem 3

How do we adjust the model parameters $\lambda = (A, B, \pi)$ to maximize $P(O \mid \lambda)$?

In this problem we attempt to optimize the model parameters to properly describe how a given observation sequence comes about. The observation sequence is called a training sequence since it is used to train the HMM. The training problem is crucial for most HMM applications, since it allows us to optimally adapt the model parameters to an observing training data.

Solution to Problem 1

We wish to calculate the probability of the observation sequence, $O=(O_1, O_2,..., O_T)$, given the model, for example, $P(O \mid \lambda)$. The most straightforward way of doing this is through enumerating of length T (the number of observations). Consider one such fixed state sequence:

$$Q=(q_1 q_2, \ldots, q_T),$$ (5)

where q_1 is the initial state. The probability of the observation sequence for the state sequence of the last equation is:

$$P(O|Q,\lambda) = \prod_{t=1}^{T} P(O_t | q_t, \lambda),$$ (6)

where we have assumed statistical independence of the observations. Thus we get

$$P(O|q,\lambda)=bq_1(O_1) \cdot bq_2(O_2) \ldots bq_T(O_T).$$ (7)

The probability of such a state sequence Q can be written as equation (8):

$$P(Q|\lambda)=\pi_{q1} a_{q1q2} a_{q2q3} \ldots a_{qT-1qT}$$ (8)

The probability that O and Q occur simultaneously is showed in equation (9), which is simply the product of the two previous equations:

$$P(O,Q|\lambda)=P(O|Q, \lambda)P(Q|\lambda).$$ (9)

The probability of O (given the model) is obtained by summing this joint probability over all possible state sequences q giving by equation (10):

$$P(O,Q|\lambda)=\sum_{allQ} P(O|Q, \lambda)P(Q|\lambda)$$

$$= \sum_{q1,q2,\cdots,qT} \pi_{q1} b_{q1}(O_1) a_{q1q2} b_{q2}(O_2) \ldots a_{qT-1qT} b_{qT}(O_T).$$ (10)

The interpretation of the computation in the previous equation is the following. Initially (at time $t=1$) we are in state q_1 with probability π_{q1}, and generate the symbol O_1 (in this state) with probability $b_{q1}(O_1)$. The clock changes from time t to $t+1$ ($t=2$) and we make a transition to state q_2 from state q_1 with probability a_{q1q2}, and generate symbol O_2 with probability $b_{q2}(O_2)$. This process continues in this manner, whereas it becomes, is carried out the transferring previous (to time T) of the state q_{T-1} to state q_T with probability a_{qT-1qT} and generate symbol O_T with probability $b_{qT}(O_T)$.

A small analysis allows us o verify that if we calculate $P(O|\lambda)$ according to this definition, in equation (10) it involves $2T*N^T$ calculations, since in each $t=1,2\ldots,T$, there are N possible states that can be reached, and for each such state sequence about $2T$ calculations are required for each term in the sum of the equation. To be precise, we need $(2T-1)N^T$ multiplications, and N^T-1 additions. This calculation is unrealizable from the computational point of view, since for small values of N and T, for example $N=5$ (*states*), $T=100$ (observations), then we have around 10^{72} calculations. A more efficient procedure is required clearly to solve problem 1. Fortunately such a procedure exists and is called the forward-backward procedure.

The Forward-Backward Procedure

Consider the forward variable defined as in equation (11):

$$\alpha_t(i) = P(O_1 O_2 ... O_t, q_t = S_i | \lambda).$$ (11)

This is the probability of the partial observation sequence, $O_1 O_2 ... O_t$, (until time t) and state S_i to the time t, given the λ model. Zhang (1999) mentioned that we can solve for $\alpha_t(i)$ inductively, using the following equations:

1. **Initialization:**

    $$\alpha_1(i) = \pi_i b_i(O_1) \qquad\qquad 1 \leq i \leq N$$ (12)

2. **Induction:**

    $$\alpha_{t+1}(j) = b_j(O_{t+1}) \sum_{i=1}^{N} \alpha_t(i) a_{ij} \qquad 1 \leq j \leq N, \ 1 \leq t \leq T-1$$ (13)

3. **Termination:**

    $$P(O|\lambda) = \sum_{i=1}^{N} \alpha_T(i)$$ (14)

Solution to Problem 2

The Viterbi algorithm finds the single best state sequence $Q=\{q_1, q_2..., q_T\}$, for the given observation sequence $O=\{O_1, O_2..., O_T\}$. The following equations show that.

1. **Initialization:**

    $$\delta_1(i) = \pi_i b_i)(O_1) \qquad\qquad 1 \leq i \leq N$$ (15)

2. **Recursion:**

    $$\delta_{t+1}(j) = b_j(O_{t+1}) \left[\max_{1 \leq i \leq N} \delta_t(i) a_{ij} \right] \quad 1 \leq j \leq N, \ 1 \leq t \leq T-1$$ (16)

3.   **Termination:**

$$p^* = \max[\delta_T(i)] \qquad\qquad 1 \le i \le N \qquad\qquad (17)$$

$$q^* = \arg\max[\delta_T(i)] \qquad\qquad 1 \le i \le N$$

Solution to Problem 3

In order to be able to give solution to problem 3, we use the Baum-Welch algorithm, which, like others, does by induction the determination of values that optimize the transition probabilities in the mesh of possible transitions of the states of the Markov Model. The sequence of events leading to the conditions required is illustrated in Figure 3.

An efficient way to optimize the values of the transition matrices in the Baum-Welch algorithm is given by Oropeza (2000) and Rabiner and Biing-Hwang (1993):

$$a_{ij}Z = \frac{expected\ number \quad of\ transitions\ from\ state\ s_i\ to\ state\ s_j}{expected\ number\ of\ times\ from\ state\ s_i}$$

$$b_i(k) = \frac{expected\ number \quad of\ times\ in\ state\ j\ and\ observing\ symbol\ v_k}{expected\ number\ of\ times\ in\ state\ j}$$

Gaussian Mixtures

Gaussian mixtures are combinations of normal distributions or functions of Gaussian. A Gaussian mixture can be written as a weighted sum of Gaussian densities (Kamakshi, Prasad, Nagarajan, & Murthy, 2002; Mermelstein, 1975; Resch, 2001a, 2001b), where the

Figure 3. Illustration of the sequence of operations required for the computation of the joint event that the system is in state S_i at time t and state S_j at time t+1

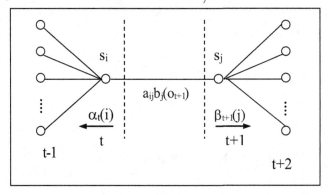

probability density function of the Gaussian mixture is written as:

$$g(\mu, \Sigma)(x) = \frac{1}{\sqrt{2\pi}^d \sqrt{\det(\Sigma)}} e^{-\frac{1}{2}(x-\mu)^T \Sigma^{-1}(x-\mu)}.$$ (18)

A weighted mixture of k Gaussians can be written as:

$$gm(x) = \sum_{k=1}^{K} w_k * g(\mu_k, \Sigma_k)(x),$$ (19)

where the weights are all positives and sum to one:

$$\sum_{i=1}^{K} w_i = 1 \quad \forall \quad i \in \{1, \ldots\ldots, K\} \quad : w_i \geq 0.$$ (20)

In Figure 4, a Gaussian mixture is plotted, consisting of three single Gaussians.

By varying the number of k Gaussians, the weights w_k and the parameters of each of the density functions, the mixtures of Gaussians can be used to describe some *probability density function* (*pdf*). The parameters of the *pdf* are the number of Gaussian, its factors of weight,

Figure 4. Gaussian mixture of three single Gaussians

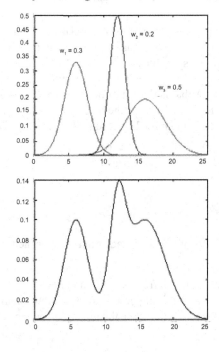

and the parameters of each Gaussian function of such as the average and the covariance matrix. In order to find these parameters to describe a given probability density function of a data set an iterative algorithm, expectation-maximization (EM) is used.

Applying the Gaussian mixture models together with a hidden Markov model leads to the so-called continuous density hidden Markov models (CDHMMs) (Peskin, Gillick, & Liberman, 1991).

Statistical Speech Recognition

The speech signal is represented by sequences of words that are described of the form $W=(w_1, w_2, ..., w_t)$, where w_t is the pronounced generic word in discreet time "t." The word sequences are connected through the speech that is a sequence of acoustic sounds, according to Becchetti and Prina (1999).

In mathematical terms, the recognition is an operation "f" that maps an X data set, that belongs to the complete set of acoustic χ sequences, to a joint W included in the set ϖ, according to Becchetti and Prina (1999):

$$f : X \to W, \quad X \in \chi \quad y \quad W \in \varpi. \tag{21}$$

The Deterministic Approach

The ASR problem, like many others, can be solved by relating a model Θ to the phenomenon. The strategy consists of building a model that returns all the possible "emissions" X to all the admissible events W. In the speech case, it returns all the possible acoustic sequences X that can be associated to a given W. Recognition is performed by finding the sequence of words that return a sequence X that is related of better form. In essence, the recognition is performed by relying on prior knowledge of the mapping of acoustic and word sequences. This knowledge is embedded in the model, according to Becchetti and Prina (1999).

In mathematical form, defining $d(X', X'')$ as the distance between two sequences X' & X'', the recognized sequence of words associated to X is given by:

$$W^* = ArgMin_{W \in \varpi} d(h(W, \Theta), X). \tag{22}$$

The general procedure consists of two steps, according to Becchetti and Prina (1999):

- **Training:** The model is build from a large number of different correspondences (X', W'). This it is the same training procedure of a human being in his early age: the greater the number of couples (X', W'), the greater is the recognition accuracy.

- **Recognition:** All the possible sequences of words are tested to find the best sequence whose acoustic sequence $X = h(W^*, \Theta)$ best matches the one given.

The Stochastic Framework

First note that in statistical recognition the recognized sequence of words can be obtained like the maximization of the probability given by the present acoustic sequence. Well known with the name of "observation," the acoustic sequence and introducing the (a posteriori) probability $P(W/X)$ to have W conditioned to the fact that if X is observed, the recognized sequence of words is defined as follows:

$$W^* = ArgMax_{W \in \varpi} P(W \mid X). \tag{23}$$

We consider that the conditional probability has a stochastic variable x conditioned to a particular value of a second variable w related to the joint probability, but using the Bayes formula, according to Becchetti and Prina (1999), becomes:

$$P(W \mid X) = \frac{P(X,W)}{P(X)} = \frac{P(X,W)P(W)}{P(X)}. \tag{24}$$

Equation (24) becomes:

$$W^* = ArgMax_{W \in \varpi} P(X,W) = ArgMax_{W \in \varpi} P(X \mid W)P(W), \tag{25}$$

where the term $P(X)$ is dropped since it does not change the result of the maximization, according to Becchetti and Prina (1999). Equation (25) allows a model to be introduced, using concepts that are similar to those outlined in the previous section. From equation (25) we have according to Becchetti and Prina (1999):

$$W^* = ArgMax_{W \in \varpi} P(X \mid W, \Theta)P(W \mid \Theta). \tag{26}$$

Although similar, equations (25) and (26) have very different meanings; equation (25) tell us that, following a maximum a posteriori (MAP) criterion, the recognized sequence can be found by maximizing the a posteriori probability. The probabilities must be found somehow, according to Becchetti and Prina (1999).

Equation (26) suggests that a model can be selected and two sets of probabilities must be considered:

- The probabilities $P(X \mid W, \Theta)$ that the model Θ produces the acoustic sequence X when communicating the sequence of words W.
- The probability $P(W, \Theta)$ that the model communicates the words W.

Stochastic Model Simplifications

The recognition procedure can be simplified by considering that an uttered word is basically composed of a sequence of acoustic states S belonging to a set. The X associated to existing words can be modeled as a sequences of such states, which, for instance, may correspond to the set of the similar acoustic data of each phoneme, according to Becchetti and Prina (1999).

For example, vowels can be modeled by three acoustic similar states: the beginning, the central, and the ending (the present work makes use of this same scheme by employing syllables as unit recognition). A certain word can be contained to different sequences of units. The main simplification is that the number of possible units is limited. A total of 138 units (46 phonemes x 3 states) are generally sufficient to obtain high performance for most languages (Becchetti & Prina, 1999). In mathematical form, the recognized sequence is given by:

$$
\begin{aligned}
W^* &= ArgMax_{W \in \varpi, S \in \delta} P(X, W, S \mid \Theta) = \\
&= ArgMax_{W \in \varpi, S \in \delta} P(W, S \mid \Theta) P(X \mid W, S, \Theta) = \\
&= ArgMax_{W \in \varpi, S \in \delta} P(W \mid \Theta) P(S \mid W, \Theta) P(X \mid W, S, \Theta).
\end{aligned} \tag{27}
$$

The last term of equation (27) is a product of three probabilities. These probabilities can be simplified to make recognition feasible as outlined next.

Simplifications of $P(W \mid \Theta)$

The probability of word sequences can be simplified considering that a word at time "t," w_t statistically depends only on a limited number L of past uttered words $w_{t-1}, w_{t-2}, ..., w_{t-L}$, the reason why the process does not depend on the time. Assuming $L=2$ we have, according to Becchetti and Prina (1999):

$$
P(W = w_1, w_2, ..., w_T \mid \Theta) \equiv P(w = w_1 \mid \Theta) \prod_{t=2,.....,T} P(w_t \mid w_{t-1}, \Theta). \tag{28}
$$

Equation (28) states that the probability of a sequence of words $P(W = w_1, w_2, ..., w_T)$ can be computed by the probability that a particular word is emitted and the probability that a word w_t is emitted after uttering of the word w_{t-1}.

Simplifications of $P(S \mid W, \Theta)$

Simplifications similar to this expression can be made. We must to consider that the probability of emitting a unit s_t depends only on the present word, and it is independent of the time in which it is uttered. In addition, the probability of a unit can be assumed independent of the future uttered units, depending only on the previously uttered unit. Therefore, $P(S | W, \Theta)$ takes the form, according to Becchetti and Prina (1999):

$$P(S = s_1, s_2, \ldots, s_T | W = w_1, w_2, \ldots, w_T, \Theta)$$

$$= P(s_1 | w_1, \Theta) \prod_{t=2,\ldots,T} P(s_t | s_{t-1}, w_t, \Theta). \tag{29}$$

Simplifications of $P(X | W, S, \Theta)$

The last term of equation (29) undergoes major simplifications. The first simplification is derived from the fact that the sequence of acoustic samples X is not the best observations to estimate W. Therefore, a sufficient statistic $g(X)$ must be found. Heuristically, a data set: $Y = y_1, y_2, \ldots, y_T = g(X)$ that contains all the information of X that is relevant for the estimation of W. Hopefully Y should contain less data than X in the sense that $g(X)$ should discard all the useless information to estimate W. For example, the pitch and the volume are not particularly significant for recognition and can be discarded in the information carried Y. Introducing $g(X)$, the probability in $P(X | W, S, \Theta)$ of equation (29) is replaced by $P(g(X)/W, S, \Theta) = P(Y | W, S, \Theta)$, according to Becchetti and Prina (1999).

Other assumptions can be defined on the process Y to simplify the computation of $P(Y | W, S, \Theta)$. In particular, it is assumed that:

- Y is statistically independent of W.
- y_t only depends of the current state S_t.
- The conditional process y_t/s_t is independent and identically distributed.

These considerations imply that the probability that y_t is emitted when the model is in the acoustic unit s_t must be computed only:

$$P(Y | W, S, \Theta) = \prod_{t=1,\ldots,T} P(y_t | s_t, \Theta). \tag{30}$$

The Syllables like Basic Units

For the study of the syllables we must have a set of important concepts and to consider the following aspects:

The auditory human system can perceive approximately 200 ms of speech signal without significant loss of information, which has a suitable correlation with the duration of the syllables. This characteristic of the human perception can be modeled if we use syllables instead of the phonemes.

- The relative duration of the syllables depends to a lesser extent on the variations of the pronunciation in the duration of the phonemes.

- It is considered that analysis time of 250 ms is adequate for the cepstrales vectors extraction methods. Using this consideration, the stationary noise signal can be discriminated. Shorter times of capture (of 100 ms, for example) can capture the stationary part of a vowel. It shows the potential advantage for use of syllable, when using windows between 200 and 250 ms for each classification unit.

- The arguments mentioned previously allow supposing that the automatic speech recognition systems based in syllables can be more robust than the ones based in phonemes.

Definition of the Syllable

The syllable is a joint sound or articulated sounds that constitute a single sonic nucleus between two successive depressions of the speech emission.

For a long time, researchers had been mentioning that the syllable is constructed around a nucleus that generally is the component of greater intensity within the structure and generally the only one.

Within the linguistic study, the syllable has a vowel in the middle, and its ends are consonants, although this does not always happen because sometimes the syllables can have a nucleus consonant and the sides a consonant and a vowel. Also, related to the fact that the syllables represent the loudness tips, which are analogous to the regions of greater energy of sound and are thought to correspond to the nucleus of the syllable.

Figure 5 demonstrates the behavior of the energy for a sample of speech uttered; you must to observe the behavior of the energy when the high loudness of the speech signal is pronounced.

From an abstracted point of view, a syllable unavoidably is constituted by a set of phonemes and has acoustic manifestations. A syllable can be analyzed in terms of its properties and

Figure 5. Graph of the behavior of the speech signal and its energy

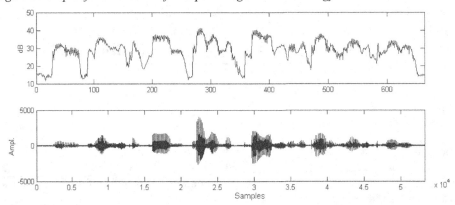

sounds that constitute it or in terms of its manifestation when it emerges from the speaker. In the Spanish language there is a classification defined for the syllables; such classification unlike other languages is framed by students of the language.

The Rules of the Syllable in the Spanish Language

Monosyllabic words: They are those that are formed by a syllable: "luz," "mar."

Two-syllabic words: They are those that are formed by two syllables: "silla," "mesa."

Three-syllabic words: They are those that are formed by three syllables: "ventana," "cabeza."

Disyllables words: They are those that are formed by four or more syllables: "Argentina," "Polideportivo."

Feal (2000) mentioned that 27 letters exist in the Spanish language, which are classified according to his pronunciation in two groups: vowels and consonants. Figure 6 shows a scheme of the classification of the letters for a better understanding. The group of the vowels is formed by five; its pronunciation does not make the exit of the air difficult. The mouth acts like a box of resonance opened in minor or greater degree, and according to this the vowels classify themselves in open, semi open, and closed (Oropeza, 2000; Rabiner & Biing-Hwang, 1993).

The other group of letters, the consonants, is formed by 22, with which three form consonants are composed, called thus, being simple letters in their pronunciation and doubles in their writing. The remaining letters are called consonant simple, being simple in their pronunciation and its writing.

Figure 6. Used notations to express the rules of syllabic division

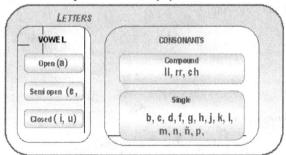

Table 1. Symbol description

+	Used to concatenate syllables
()	Used for grouping
|	Will be applied to the rule at issue; used to establish alternative possibilities

Rules of the Spanish Language for the Formation of Syllables

In the Spanish language, 10 rules exist, which determine the segmentation of a word in syllables. These rules are listed showing immediately exceptions at the same one:

- **Rule 1:** In the syllables, it must always at least have a vowel. Without vowel there is no syllable. Exception: This rule is not fulfilled when "y" appears.

- **Rule 2:** Each element of the group of inseparable consonants shown in Figure 7 cannot be separated when dividing a word in syllables.

- **Rule 3:** When a consonant is between two vowels, it is associated with the second vowel.

- **Rule 4:** When there are two consonants between two vowels, each vowel is associated with a consonant.

    Exception: This does not happen in the group of inseparable consonants (rule 2).

- **Rule 5:** If there are three consonants placed between two vowels, the two first consonants will be associated with the first vowel and the third consonant with the second vowel.

    Exception: This rule is not fulfilled when the second and third consonant is member of the group of inseparable consonants.

- **Rule 6.** The words that contain "h" preceded or followed by another consonant are divided separating both letters.

- **Rule 7:** Diphthong is the inseparable union of two vowels. Three types of possible diphthongs are the following:

Figure 7. Group of inseparable consonants

br, bl, cr, cl, dr, fr, fl,
gr, gl, kr, ll, pr, pl, tr,
rr, ch

- An open vowel + a closed vowel.
- A closed vowel + an open vowel.
- A closed vowel + a closed vowel.

The following pairs of vowels are diphthongs: ai, au, ei, eu, io, ou, ia, ua, ie, ue, oi, uo, ui, iu, ay, ey, oy.

The union of two open or semi opened vowels does not form a diphthong. They can be single or united to a consonant.

- **Rule 8:** The "h" between two vowels does not destroy a diphthong.
- **Rule 9:** The accentuation on the vowel closed of diphthong causes its destruction.
- **Rule 10:** The union of three vocals conform a tripthong. The only possible disposition for the formation of a tripthong is the following: closed vowel + (vocal opened | vocal semi-opened) + closed vowel. Only the following combinations of vowels form tripthongs: iai, iei, uai, uei, uau, iau, uay, uey.

A Based Knowledge System Implementation

The case of study that we presented is referent to the syllables for the Spanish Language; therefore, we treat in this topic concerning how to introduce a based knowledge system, also named expert system, which contemplates the previous enunciated rules. In our case, the knowledge base is constituted by all the rules of classification of syllables of the Spanish Language that were previously analyzed. Here the task is to understand and to put in the appropriate programming language such rules to reach the system requirements. The input of the expert system is the set of phrases or words, which constituted a determined vocabulary to recognize (speech corpus).

After the application of the rules mentioned before, the application of the energy in short time of the signal and the energy in short time of parameter RO is necessary to make the syllable splitting of each one of the utterance, with which the beginnings and ends of the syllables are managed (Giarratano & Riley, 2001; Russell & Norvig, 1996).

The energy function of the high frequency (ERO parameter) is the energy level of the speech signal at high frequencies. The fricative letter, s, is the most significant example. When we use a high-pass filter, we obtain the speech signal above a given cut-off frequency f_c, the RO signal. In our approach, a cut-off frequency f_c = 3500 Hz is used as the threshold frequency for obtaining the RO signal. The speech signal at a lower frequency is attenuated. Afterward, the energy is calculated from equation (30) for the ERO parameter in each segment of the resultant RO signal. Figure 8 shows graphically the results of this procedure for short-term total energy function (STTEF) and ERO parameter in the case of any word pertains to some corpus.

Figure 8. Block diagram of the system of proposed recognition, making use of an expert system

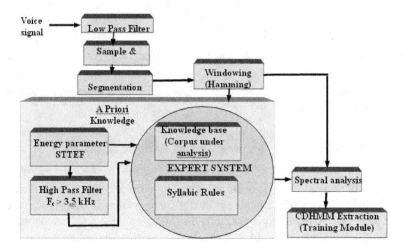

$$ERO = \sum_{i=0}^{N-1} ROi^2 \tag{31}$$

We can summarize the incorporation of an expert to the training task in the following block diagram, which demonstrates the purpose and function of the same one.

The previous analysis extracts the syllables that conform a corpus to study; also, it provides the amount of blocks that will be used in the labeled stage of speech signals. With a previous analysis we can indicate a few parameters of reference as the following:

- It come to agree the number of syllables obtained by the work of the expert, with the number of segments obtained after the determination of the energy in short time of the speech signal and the energy extracted to the same signal. This after have applied a digital filter finite impulse filter (FIR) and have obtained the energy of RO parameter.

- In the case of not agreeing, the analyzed sample is rejected and a new one is taken. For the case of the continuous speech, the expert has the same relevance in the training task, because it allows extracting the syllabic units according to the dictionary at issue. Once the representative units are obtained, the expert makes the training using concatenation of the word models obtained and the model language from corpus employed.

The purpose is to create the expert system that reconciled to the necessities of the problem that we are trying to solve. To demonstrate the last concepts, a program using C language was implemented. The main characteristics of such program are described as follows:

- It has to take a qualitative and quantitative decision about syllables that is being granted, storing the results in the database of the expert system (SQL Server was used for that).
- In the case of being phrases, the system can make its separation in words for later to separate them into syllables.
- The knowledge base is used to be able to make the segmentation task, it had as reference, the rules of the Spanish for the splitting of syllables. The use of if-then sentences is the standard used in this layer of the system.
  - ° The programming base was made using dynamic data structures (linked lists, for this work). Therefore, allow us to be acceding to each one of the elements of the word, later to make the splitting of syllables according to the Spanish Language rules mentioned before.

Here we show two segments of the code of the expert system at issue:

```
void CDivide_elemento::inicializa (void)
{
          posiciones_corte[0]=elemento;
           elemento++;
           for (i=0;i<20;i++)   reglas[i]=false;
           cons_insepa="brblcrcldrfrflgrglkrllprpltrrrchtl";
  vocal_diptongo="aiaueieuioouiauaieueoiuouiiuayeyoy";
  vocal_abierta="íaíoíeíuúaúeúoúiooaeaoeaeooaoeee";
vocales = "aeiouíúáéó";
}
/* rule 2 analyzed*/
 r=inicio;
do
{
 ptr1=*r->fonema;
  if (ptr1==*"C")
  {
          p2=r->next;
           ptr2=*p2->fonema;
            if(ptr1==ptr2)
     {
       for (i=0;i<int(strlen(cons_insepa));i+=2)
              {
if(cons_insepa[i]==palabra[contador]&& cons_insepa[i+1]==palabra[contador+1])
      {
       conta_conso_insepa[cuenta_insepa]=contador;
       cuenta_insepa++;
```

```
reglas[1]=true;
        if (verifica_existencia(posiciones_corte,elemento,contador))
        {
                        posiciones_corte[elemento]=contador;
                        elemento++;
                }
        }
        }
        }
}
                r=r->next;
  contador+=1;
} while (r->next!=NULL);
```

The previous sentences allow observing the form in which the program works on a determined set of utterance. The flags (that represent the rules that activate) conform to the results of the application of the inference mechanisms and are the base of the expert decision making. When these rules are satisfied, it is come to analyze them in another later stage of the same system, at the end to give the suitable results. The process follows the logic of four inference trees showed in Figure 9.

Figure 9. Inference trees of the expert system

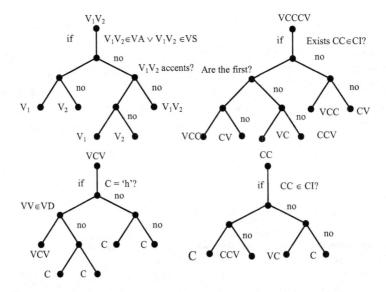

Conclusion

This chapter provided a guide for those professionals who have the intention of making the design or to use a speech recognition system for a specific application. The variants in the model structure are due to the special applications where the speech training and recognition depend strongly on the objectives to reach.

All the techniques used are strongly related within thematic of pattern recognition and statistical mathematics. In successive works many efforts must be made to approach, at the same time the results that contribute to the recognition and their reaches. The use of different models has been the work of various researchers. Their contributions have reported so much information and statistics data around the speech recognition. Finally, the people that work with applications have taken the concepts developed by the researchers to develop efficient commercial systems.

This chapter showed a summary of the techniques and methods that are used for the signal speech processing and for the extraction of parameters to be used in speech recognition. The same techniques are used in the context independent commands recognition systems. They can also be used for speaker recognition using the proposed methodology. The phonetic segmentation, or in syllables, is a subject attached to the speech recognition that we did not discuss here. In that case it is necessary to work with patterns of sonorous energy and spectral density. This topic will be a subject of further research.

References

Becchetti, C., & Prina, L. (1999). *Speech recognition theory and C++ implementation.* Fundazione Ugo Bordón, Rome, Italy: John Wiley & Sons.

Feal, L. (2000). Sobre el uso de la sílaba como unidad de síntesis en el español (Tech. Rep.). Informatics Department, Universidad de Valladolid.

Giarratano, J., & Riley, G. (2001). *Expert systems, principles and programming.* New York: International Thompson Editors.

Kamakshi, V., Prasad, Nagarajan, T., & Murthy, A. (2002). *Continuous speech recognition automatically segmented data at syllabic units.* In Proceedings IEEE 6th International Conference on Signal Processing (Vol. 1, pp. 235-238). Washington, DC: IEEE Computer Society.

Mermelstein, P. (1975). Automatic segmentation of speech into syllabic snits. *The Journal of the Acoustical Soceity of America, 58*(4), 880-883.

Oropeza, J. (2000). *Reconocimiento de comandos verbales usando HMM.* Unpublished master's theses, Computing Research Center. The National Polytechnic Institute, Mexico.

Peskin, B., Gillick, L., & Liberman, N. (1991). Progress in recognizing conversational telephone speech. In *Proceedings IEEE International Conference on Acoustic, Speech, and*

Signal Processing (ICASSP), Toronto, Canada (Vol. 3, pp. 1811-1814). Washington, DC: IEEE Computer Society.

Rabiner, L. (1989). *Fundamentals of speech recognition.* Englewood Cliffs, NJ: Prentice Hall.

Rabiner, L., & Biing-Hwang, J. (1993). *Fundamentals of speech recognition.* Englewood Cliffs, NJ: Prentice Hall.

Resch, B. (2001a). *Gaussian statistics and unsupervised learning: A tutorial for the course.* Computational Intelligence Signal Processing and Speech Communication Laboratory. Retrieved from www.igi.turgaz.at/lehre/CI/tutorials/Gaussian/, last updated, October 13, 2006

Resch, B. (2001b). *Hidden Markov Models: A tutorial for the course.* Computational Laboratory Signal Processing and Speech Communication Laboratory. Retrieved from www.igi.turgaz.at/lehre/CI/tutorials/HMM/index/html, last updated, October 13, 2006

Russell, S., & Norvig, P. (1996). *Artificial intelligence a modern scope.* Englewood Cliffs, NJ: Prentice Hall.

Savage, J. (1995). *A hybrid system with symbolic AI and statistical methods for speech recognition.* Unpublished doctoral dissertation, University of Washington, Seattle.

Waibel, A., & Lee, K. (1990). *Readings in speech recognition.* San Mateo, CA: Morgan Kaufman Publishers, Inc.

Zhang, J. (1999). *On the syllable structures of Chinese relating to speech recognition.* In *Proceedings of 4th International Conference on Spoken Language, 1996 (ICSLP '96)* (Vol. 4, pp. 2450-2453). Philadelphia: IEEE.

Chapter XIII

Speaker Recognition

Shung-Yung Lung, National University of Taiwan, Taiwan

Abstract

This chapter presents some of the main contributions in several topics of speaker recognition since 1978. Representative books and surveys on speaker recognition published during this period are listed. Theoretical models for automatic speaker recognition are contrasted with practical design methodology. Research contributions to measure process, feature extraction, and classification are selectively discussed, including contributions to measure analysis, feature selection, and the experimental design of speaker classifiers. The chapter concludes with a representative set of applications of speaker recognition technology.

Introduction

Before addressing the various speaker recognition technologies and systems, it is appropriate to review the acoustical bases for speaker recognition. Research on speaker recognition, including identification and verification, has been an active area for several decades. The distinction between identification and verification is simple: the speaker identification task is to classify an unlabeled voice token as belonging to (having been spoken by) one of a set of N reference speakers (N possible outcomes), whereas the speaker verification task is to decide whether or not an unlabeled voice token belongs to a specific reference speaker (two possible outcomes: the token is either accepted as belonging to the reference speaker or is rejected as belonging to an impostor). Note that the information in bits, denoted I, to be gained from the identification task is in general greater than that to be gained from the verification task.

Speaker identification as just defined is also sometimes called "closed-set" identification, which contrasts it from "open-set" identification. In open-set identification the possibility exists that the unknown voice token does not belong to any of the reference speakers. The number of possible decisions is then $N + 1$, which includes the option to declare that the unknown token belongs to none of the reference speakers. Thus open-set identification is a combination of the identification and verification tasks that combines the worst of both—performance is degraded by the complexity of the identification task, and the rejection option requires good characterization of speech feature statistics.

During the past few years, text-independent (or "free-text") speaker recognition has become an increasingly popular area of research, with a broad spectrum of potential applications. The free-text speaker recognition task definition is highly variable, from an acoustically clean and prescribed task description to environments where not only is the speech linguistically unconstrained, but also the acoustic environment is extremely adverse. Possible applications include forensic use, automatic sorting and classification of intelligence data, and passive security applications through monitoring of voice circuits. In general, applications for free-text speaker recognition have limited control of the conditions that influence system performance. Indeed, the definition of the task as "free-text" connotes a lack of complete control. (It may be assumed that a fixed text would be used if feasible, because better performance is possible if the text is known and calibrated beforehand.) This lack of control leads to corruption of the speech signal and consequently to degraded recognition performance. Corruption of the speech signal occurs in a number of ways, including distortions in the communication channel, additive acoustical noise, and probably most importantly through increased variability in the speech signal itself. (The speech signal may be expected to vary greatly under operational conditions in which the speaker may be absorbed in a task or involved in an emotionally charged situation.) Thus the free-text recognition task typically confers upon the researcher multiple problems—namely, that the input speech is unconstrained, that the speaker is uncooperative, and that the environmental parameters are uncontrolled.

What is it about the speech signal that conveys information about the speaker's identity? There are, of course, many different sources of speaker identifying information, including high-level information such as dialect, subject matter or context, and style of speech (including lexical and syntactical patterns of usage). This high-level information is certainly valuable as an aid to recognition of speakers by human listeners, but it has not been used in automatic recognition systems because of practical difficulties in acquiring and using such information. Rather, automatic techniques focus on "low-level" acoustical features. These low-level features include such characteristics of the speech signal as spectral amplitudes, voice pitch frequency, formant frequencies and bandwidths, and characteristic voicing aperiodicities. These variables may be measured as a function of time, or the statistics of long-term averages may be used as recognition variables. But the real question, the essence of the problem, is this: How stable are these speaker discriminating features? Given a speech signal, is the identity of the speaker uniquely decodable?

The fact is, however, that different individuals typically exhibit speech signal characteristics that are quite strikingly individualistic. We know that people sound different from each other, but the differences become visually apparent when comparing spectrograms from different individuals. The spectrogram is by far the most popular and generally informative tool available for phonetic analysis of speech signals. The spectrogram is a running display of the spectral amplitude of a short-time spectrum as a function of frequency and time. The amplitude is only rather crudely plotted as the level of darkness, but the resonant frequencies of the vocal tract are usually clearly represented in the spectrogram. Note the differences between the individual renditions of this linguistic message. Segment durations, formant frequencies, and formant frequency transitions, pitch and pitch dynamics, formant amplitudes, all exhibit gross differences from speaker to speaker. Thus these speakers would be very easy to discriminate by visual inspection of their spectrograms. This is especially impressive in view of the fact that two sound quite similar to each other. Yet their spectrograms look very different.

In this chapter, we focus on the problem of text independent speaker recognition systems. All of the methods discussed have an underlying basis in probabilistic modeling of the features of the speakers. Prior to the development of probabilistic algorithms, methods based on template matching were employed and can still be useful under constrained circumstances. By template matching, we mean decomparison of all averages computed on lest data to a collection of stored averages developed for each of the speakers in training. Also termed statistical feature averaging, the template matching approach employs the mean of some feature over a relatively long utterance to distinguish among speakers. For text-independent recognition, ideally one has utterances of several seconds or minutes in order to ensure that a voice is modeled by mean features of a broad range of sounds, rather than by a particular sound or phone. Test utterances are compared to training templates by the distance between feature means. All variations to the leclmicme arise from the choices of features vectors and distance metrics.

Background

Much of the theory and techniques of speaker identification is common to speaker verification. These are adequately covered in the paper by Lung in this issue. However, we will review them again here with emphasis on techniques and issues peculiar to speaker identification.

Figure 1. The structure of a speaker recognition system

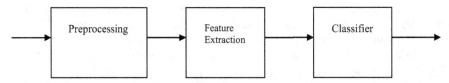

The period 1978-2002 witnessed extensive activity on decision theoretic multivariate statistical procedures for the design of classifiers. However, the statistical decision theory approach was justly criticized for focusing entirely on statistical relationships among scalar features and ignoring other structural properties that seemed to characterize patterns. The general feature extraction classification model, shown in Figure 1, was also criticized for performing too severe data compression, since it provided only the class designation of a pattern rather than a description that would allow one to generate patterns belonging to a class.

These criticisms led to proposals for a linguistic model for pattern description whereby patterns are viewed as sentences in a language defined by a formal grammar. By 1978 these proposals together with the success of syntax-directed compilers had attracted many to research in pattern grammars. The linguistic or syntactic model for pattern recognition uses a "primitive extractor," which transforms the input data into a string of symbols or some general relational structure. The primitive extractor may itself be a feature extractor classifier. Then a structural pattern analyzer uses a formal grammar to parse the string and thus constructs a description of the pattern.

The system consists of three major blocks. The preprocessing block that analyzes the incoming speech signal and produces a sequence of spectral vectors is common in virtually every recognition system.

Speech Signal Preprocessing

The most frequently used preprocessor for speaker recognition systems is the filter bank. The filter bank, widely used in other areas of speech analysis, is a series of contiguous bandpass filters spanning the useful frequency range of speech. The output of each filter is rectified, smoothed, and sampled say every 10 ms to obtain the energy of the signal over the specified passband. The summed output of the filter bank can be considered as the short time power spectrum of the input speech signal. Filter banks can provide a highly efficient and comprehensive analysis of speech signals. Although digital representations of filter banks are potentially computationally superior and provide reproducible measurements, analog configurations provide an online analysis of speech, which can be input to a digital computer for further processing.

Feature Extraction

Feature extraction follows the basic processing. The goal of extraction is considered to be the process in which the raw measurements, from a filter bank for example, are combined or restricted to certain speech segments in such a way as to reduce the dimensionality of the original measurement space, while at the same time preserving or enhancing speaker discriminability according to a prescribed system design. It is a central process in a system, the process that makes the most of the designer's intuitive ideas or theoretical knowledge.

Classifier Techniques

Decision techniques are all based on the computation of a distance that quantifies the degree of dissimilarity between the feature vectors associated with pairs of utterances. There are many distance metrics that have been investigated. The simplest decision rule is that of the nearest neighbor. For speaker recognition this means that distances are calculated from the unknown vector to each reference vector, and the speaker corresponding to the minimum distance is designated the identified speaker.

In feature space, the data are compressed and represented in such an effective way that objects from the same class behave similarly, and a clear distinction among objects from different classes exists. The classifier takes the features computed by the feature exactor and performs either template matching or probabilistic likelihood computation on the features, depending on the type of algorithm employed. Before it can be used for classification, the classifier has to be trained so that a mapping from the feature to the label of a particular class is established.

In the past, much has been made of the apparent difference between the two models. The stress on the distinction between the two models hides many similarities: in practice, in the syntactic model, the extraction of "primitives" can involve statistical classification procedures, and the association of patterns with generative grammars is equivalent to the classification of patterns into categories.

A major evolution that has occurred during the last few years is to view design of a speaker recognition system as a highly iterative process. Figure 2 illustrates the complex nature of this design process. The theoretical models, in which the flow of data and decisions is only one direction, from the input pattern environment to the categorizer/structural analyzer, are indicative of the operational speaker recognition system one seeks as an end result.

Figure 2. The development of speaker recognition systems

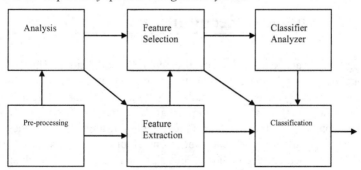

There are many different combination models in Figure 2. Each model has selected four, five, or six blocks. In recent research, speaker recognition systems are focused on analysis, feature selection, and classifier analyzer. For example, the feature selection and analyzer functions are treated independently, which prevents the structural information available to the analyzer from influencing the primitive extraction. Without this feed back the representation provided by the extractor may not be well suited to the patterns being examined. Noting this limitation, models that incorporate feedback between the classifier analyzer and the selection have recently been proposed.

The analysis block is a vector quantization-based speaker recognition, with a decision logic that provides a list of tentative candidates for further processing. The goal of the analysis part is to reduced storage and computation for spectral analysis information.

Statistical feature selection is an important element of any speaker recognition scheme. The most common statistical feature selection technique is that of the F-ratio or variance. For this purpose several statistics are computed over the set of training of reference utterances provided by each speaker. These methods are called N best (Kuo, Chen, & Lung, 1999; Morgera & Datta, 1984).

A different approach to statistical feature selection is to select those features which from processing a set of training or reference utterances through the designated speaker recognition system provide the lowest error rate. One such approach is that of the knock out tournament (Lung, 2001; Sambur, 1975).

The classifier analyzer, the main stages of this approach, is the following:

a.   Knowledge based segmentation.

b.   A priori knowledge is represented by means of decision trees, graph models, and decision graphs.

c.   Several levels of structural information are utilized.

d.   Parsing is bottom-up and top-down and non-left-to-right.

In this chapter, the aim of the selective discussion of topics and contributions that I present here is to provide a perspective on how speaker recognition theories, techniques, and applications have evolved during the last few years.

Speaker Recognition Systems

Speaker recognition is an example of biometric personal identification. This term is used to differentiate techniques that base identification on certain intrinsic characteristics of the person (such as voice, fingerprints, retinal patterns, or genetic structure) from those that use artifacts for identification (such as keys, badges, magnetic cards, or memorized passwords). This distinction confers upon biometric techniques the implication of greater identification reliability, perhaps even infallibility because the intrinsic biometrics are presumed to be more reliable than artifacts, perhaps even unique. Thus a prime motivation for studying speaker recognition is to achieve more reliable personal identification. This is particularly true for security applications, such as physical access control (a voice-actuated door lock for your home or ignition switch for your automobile), computer data access control, or automatic telephone control (airline reservations or bank-by-phone). Convenience is another benefit that accrues to a biometric system, since biometric attributes cannot be lost or forgotten and thus need not be remembered.

The problem of speaker recognition, like most problems in pattern recognition, may be considered to be divided into three parts: measurement, feature extraction, and classification (in Figure 3).

In the pre-processing of the measurement part, all speech signal processing applications, it is necessary to work with sampling, frames, windows, endpoint detection, and so on. The input signals are changed to suit the speaker recognition system by these works.

In the analysis works, it is a data compression processing, we are selection the useful information from speech data. There are many technologies in this part. Generally, vector quantization and codebook design are used in speaker recognition system.

The process of feature extraction consists of obtaining characteristic parameters of a signal to be used to classify the signal. The extraction of salient features is a key step in solving any pattern recognition problem. For speaker recognition, the features extracted from a speech signal should be invariant with regard to the desired speaker while exhibiting a large deviation from the features of an imposter. The selection of speaker unique features from a speech signal is an ongoing issue. It has been found that certain features yield better performance for some applications than do other features. Thus far, no feature set has been found to allow perfect discrimination for all conditions.

A large number of feature extraction techniques involving linear transformations are based in one way or another on the eigenvectors of the correlation or covariance matrices, for example, Karhunen-Loeve transform and wavelet feature extraction. Some of the more general results will be derived here, for example, cepstrum, cepstral derivatives, and cepstral weighting.

Figure 3. Speaker recognition system

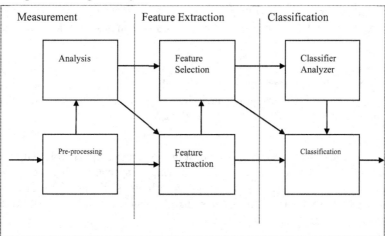

Decision trees are well known analyzers in the field of classification. A decision tree represents a collection of rules, which are organized in a hierarchical fashion, that implement a decision structure. In general, decision trees only consider one element at a time when making a decision. This constrains the partitioning of feature space to using discriminants that are perpendicular to the feature axes. This can be a severe limitation for problems that require more flexibility in the discriminant positioning.

There are two basic classes of methods upon which almost all contemporary speaker recognition algorithms using sequential computation are based. The first class is based on a form of template matching. These methods draw heavily upon conventional feature-based approaches developed for general statistical pattern recognition problems. In this chapter, three probability models of classifications—hidden wavelet Markov model (HWMM), Gaussian mixture model (GMM), and wavelet neural network (WNN)—are described.

One of the key issues in developing a text independent speaker recognition system is to identify appropriate measures and features that will support good recognition performance.

The aim of the selective discussion of topics and contributions presented here is to provide a perspective on how speaker recognition theories, techniques, and applications have evolved during the last few years. This chapter is organized as follows. Firstly, the measurement analysis of speaker recognition is described; next the feature extraction of speaker recognition is provided. Next the selection of feature extraction methods is described, together with several classifiers. Here the classifiers for the individual speaker models can use either supervised or unsupervised training. For supervised training methods, the classifier for each speaker model is present with the data for all speakers. For unsupervised training, each speaker model is presented with only the data for that speaker. In this section, we introduce three unsupervised speaker recognition models: the classifier included hidden wavelet Markov model (WMM), Gaussian mixture model (GMM), and wavelet neural network (WNN).

Measurement Analysis

A speaker recognition system basically consists of a front-end measurement, feature exaction, and a classifier, as shown in Figure 3. The measurement and feature extraction normalize the collected data and transform them to the feature space. During the past few years, pre-processing of text independent speaker recognition system has become normalization formula.

Filter Banks: Since the purpose of the filter bank analyzer is to give a measurement of the energy of the speech signal in a given frequency band, each of the bandpass signals is passed through a non-linearity, such as a full wave or half wave rectifier.

Frame: In all practical signal processing applications, it is necessary to work with frames of the signal, unless the signal is of short duration. This is especially true if we are to use conventional analysis techniques on speech signals with non-stationary dynamics. In this case it is necessary to select a portion of the signal that can reasonably be assumed to be stationary.

Window: Window is a finite length sequence used to select a desired frame of the original signal by a simple multiplication process. Some of the commonly used window sequences are rectangular, Hamming, Hanning and Blackman, and so on.

Endpoint Detection: The goal of speech detection is to separate acoustic events of interest in a continuously recorded signal from other parts of the signal. Many methods have been proposed for endpoint detection for use in speech recognition systems. These methods can be broadly classified into three approaches according to their interaction with the pattern-matching paradigm: explicit, implicit, and hybrid.

Fourier Transform: At the heart of much engineering analysis are various frequency domain transforms. Three transforms—discrete time Fourier transform (DTFT), discrete Fourier series (DFS), and fast Fourier transform (FFT)—on discrete time data will be used throughout this chapter, and it will be assumed that the reader is familiar with their properties and usage.

The results of either preprocessing stage are a series of vectors characteristic of the time varying spectral characteristics of the speech signal. The goal of the analysis part is to reduced storage and computation for spectral analysis information. If we compare the information rate of the vector representation to that of the raw speech waveform, we see that the spectral analysis has significantly reduced the required information rate. Generally speaking, vector quantization and codebook design are used in the analysis part of speaker recognition system.

Vector Quantization

In this section, we address the problem of closed-set speaker identification based on the vector quantization (VQ) speaker model. VQ-based speaker recognition is a conventional and successful method (Buck, Burton, & Shore, 1985; Haydar, Demirekler, Nakipoglu, & Thzun, 1995; Linde, Buzo, & Gray, 1980). Due to its simplicity, the VQ speaker model is often used as a reference when studying other methods (Haydar et al., 1995). In VQ-based speaker recognition, each speaker is characterized with several prototypes known as code vectors, and the set of code vectors for each speaker is referred to as that speaker's codebook. Normally, a speaker's codebook is trained to minimize the quantization error for the training data from that speaker. The most commonly used training algorithm is the Linde-Buzo-Grey (LBG) Algorithm (Linde et al., 1980). The codebook trained based on the criterion of minimizing the quantization error tends to approximate the density function of the training data. A straightforward extension to the VQ speaker model is the matrix quantization (MQ) in which a block of frames is considered each time during the quantization procedure (Furui, 1991). The same algorithm that is used for training a VQ model can also be used for generating MQ codebooks; the only difference is that instead of a single vector, a block of vectors is used as a single training sample.

Kohonen (1990) proposed a discriminative training procedure called learning vector quantization (LVQ). The goal of LVQ training is to reduce the number of misclassified vectors. The

LVQ trained codebook is used to define directly the classification borders between classes. It was shown that after applying LVQ training, the correct classification rate for feature vectors increases significantly (Rosenberg & Soong, 1987). However, we found that even though the LVQ codebook can give a better frame level performance than the corresponding LBG codebook, the sentence level performance may not be improved. Sometimes it may even be degraded. This is because the speech feature vectors are highly correlated, and this correlation has not been taken into account if a model is optimized for individual vectors.

To overcome this weakness, we propose a modified version of the LVQ, group vector quantization (GVQ). The GVQ training procedure is similar to that of LVQ, but in each iteration a number of vectors rather than a single vector are considered. The average quantization error of this vector group is used to determine whether the speaker models should be modified or not. The goal of GVQ training is to reduce the number of misclassified vector groups. The GVQ training procedure can be viewed as a combination of the LVQ training method and the idea of matrix quantization.

In principle, the training vectors contain all available information and can be used directly to represent a speaker. However, such a direct representation is not practical when there is a large amount of training vectors. VQ provides an effective means for compressing the short-term spectral representation of speech signals. In vector quantization, mapping vector $\mathbf{x}$ into its nearest code vector y_{NN} leads to a quantization error $e(x) = |x - y_{NN}|$. Suppose there are N vectors, $\{x_t\}_1^N$, to be quantized; the average quantization error is given by:

$$E = \frac{1}{N} \sum_{t=1}^{N} e(x_t). \tag{1}$$

The task of designing a codebook is to find a set of code vectors so that E is minimized. However, since a direct solution is not available, one has to rely on an iterative procedure to minimize E. The commonly used method is the LBG algorithm (Linde et al., 1980).

In the identification phase, a vector sequence can be obtained from a given test sentence by using short-time analysis techniques. The classification for the vector sequence is determined using a decision rule. Usually, the test sentence is classified as from the speaker whose model gives the smallest average quantization error. This sentence level decision rule is known as the average distance decision rule. Alternatively, the identity of the unknown speaker can be determined by taking a majority voting from all test vectors. With this decision rule, each test vector is assigned to a speaker whose model contains the global nearest code vector to this vector. Since the majority voting decision rule can be regarded as a special case of the average distance decision rule, we will rely on the latter in the following discussions.

The LBG trained codebook is optimal in the sense that the quantization error is minimized. If the codebook is used for applications such as speech coding, this criterion is a proper one. However, in speaker identification, the codebook is used for classification. Minimizing the quantization error does not necessarily lead to the best classification performance. A more suitable criterion for training a VQ-based classifier is to minimize the classification error rate. The LVQ algorithm is a well-known discriminative training procedure in which the codebooks of all classes are trained together and the code vectors are modified depending on the local difference of density functions (Furui, 1991; Kohonen, 1990; Rosenberg & Soong, 1987). There are three variants of the basic algorithm; we will use the LVQ because it usually gives better performance.

As mentioned before, the identity of a speaker is determined from a vector sequence rather than from a single vector. In our previous studies, we encountered the problem that LVQ trained codebooks perform better at the frame level, but at the sentence level, they often give a lower speaker identification rate than the corresponding LBG codebooks. It is known from the sequential hypothesis testing theory that the classification performance improves with the length of sequences; however, the rate of this improvement depends on the degree of correlation between individual scores (Pellom & Hansen, 1998; Rosenberg, DeLong, Juang, & Soong, 1992). It might be that the frame scores from an LVQ trained codebook are highly correlated. To reduce this correlation, we develop the following training procedure, the GVQ, to optimize the codebooks for speaker identification.

Like LVQ, the GVQ algorithm also needs a good initialization to the codebooks. This can be done with LBG method. Suppose all codebooks are initialized and the code vectors are labeled with their corresponding class membership; the following procedure is used to fine-tune the positions of code vectors to create GVQ codebooks.

1.   Randomly choose a speaker; designate its ID as p.

2.   From the training date belonging to p, the N vectors $X = \{x_t\}_1^N$ as a group.

3.   Calculate average quantization errors E_i using (1) for all speaker models (i indicates the model's ID). If speaker q's codebook ($q \neq p$) gives the smallest quantization error, go to step 4; otherwise go to step 5.

4.   If $(E_p - E_q)/E_p < w$, where w is a pre-selected threshold, for each vector x_t in the group, find its nearest code vector from speaker p's codebook (denoted as y_{NN}^p), and the nearest code vector from speaker q's codebook (denoted as y_{NN}^q); adjust the two code vectors simultaneously by:

$$y_{NN}^p \Leftarrow y_{NN}^p + \alpha(x_t - y_{NN}^p),\tag{2}$$

$$y_{NN}^q \Leftarrow y_{NN}^q + \alpha(x_t - y_{NN}^q),\tag{3}$$

where α is a small constant known as the learning rate. If the ratio $(E_p - E_q)/E_p < w$ is larger than the threshold w, this vector group is simply ignored. After finishing this step, go to step 6.

5.   In this case, the current vector group is correctly classified. To keep the codebook still approximating the density function, the code vectors are moved closer to their training date. For each vector in the group, adjust its nearest code vector in speaker p's codebook by:

$$y_{NN}^p \Leftarrow y_{NN}^p + 0.1\alpha(x_t - y_{NN}^p).\tag{4}$$

After processing all vectors, go to step 6.

6.   If the number of iterations is less than the desired number, go to step 1; otherwise the training procedure stops.

Codebook Design

VQ-based speaker recognition is a conventional and successful method. The well-known technique of VQ is called the Linde-Buzo-Grey (LBG) algorithm. Combined genetic algorithm with LBG algorithm, a new model of codebook design for speaker recognition is proposed. The basic idea behind the codebook is to replace split-and-merge algorithm with vector quantization (VQ) using genetic algorithm(GA) at the same space.

A genetic algorithm (Chen, Lung, Yang, & Lee, 2002; Kuo et al., 1999; Lung, 2006) as a modern search/optimization technique is introduced to data compression design in codebook. Generally, codebook design (Kohonen, 1990) is carried out in two steps: (1) initialization, that is, looking for the desired number of initial code vectors in a training space and (2) optimization, that is, improve these code vectors in an iterative learning process to find an optimal set that minimizes the average quantization error.

Several processing steps occur in the front-end speech analysis. First, the speech is segmented into frames by a 20 ms window progressing at a 10 ms frame rate. A codebook combining LBG and GA is then used to select code vector on the fast Fourier transform (FFT) (Mammon & Eichmann, 1982; Therrien, 1992) coefficients. Next, KLT (Lung & Chih-Chien, 1998) feature vectors are extracted from the speaker covariance matrix on the code vectors.

In the identification phase, a vector sequence can be obtained from a given test sentences by using short-time analysis technique. The classification for the vector sequence is determined using a decision rule (Gish & Schmidt, 1994; Stern, Liu, Moreno, & Acero, 1994).

There are two major aims of this study. The first aim is to establish how well text independent speaker identification can perform under long distance telephone line conditions for 100 populations. The second aim is to use GA to codebook design for optimal search. In this present study, a system is based on maximal likelihood decision models (Gish & Schmidt, 1994; Stern et al., 1994) that are used for speaker identification, and experiments are conducted for telephone speech databases.

Genetic algorithms (Chen et al., 2002; Kuo et al., 1999) are heuristic search/optimization techniques based on Darwin's theory of natural selection. In our problem domain we describe the chromosomes as strings of indices that number the representing code vectors, that is, the chromosome length is defined by the number of training vectors. The chromosomes must be evaluated by a fitness value depending on the average distortion in our case.

Algorithm

Step 1 (Initial): Create an initial N-level codebook y for the given vector space using the binary splitting method, where the number of iterations in each initial step is set to 2. Build S chromosomes of the first population in the same way as in Step 3; copy one chromosome as the best solution g_{best} and continue with step 4.

Step 2 (Calculation of code vectors):

$$y_i = \frac{\sum_{k=1}^{n} \mu_{ik} x_k}{\sum_{k=1}^{n} \mu_{ik}} \qquad 1 \leq i \leq c, \tag{5}$$

where n is the chromosome length. c is a code vector index.

Step 3 (Coding): Build S chromosomes $g_s = \{g_{s,k}, k = 1, 2, ..., n\}$ of the current population as follows:

$$d(x_k, y_i) = \sum_{p=1}^{P} (x_{kp} - y_{ip})^2 for\ d(x_k, y_i) \leq d(x_k, y_j)$$

$$\forall 1 \leq i, j \leq c, 1 \leq k \leq n. \tag{6}$$

If $g_{s,k} = i$ then $\mu_{ik} = 1$, *otherwise* $\mu_{ik} = 0$.

Step 4 (Evaluation): Evaluate the current population by calculating the fitness values F_s of the chromosomes. If the desired distortion or number of generations is not reached, continue:

$$D_s = \frac{1}{nP} \sum_{k=1}^{n} d(x_k, y(g_{s,k})) = \frac{1}{nP} \sum_{k=1}^{n} \sum_{i=1}^{c} \mu_{i,k} d(x_k, y_i) \tag{7}$$

$$F_s = \frac{1}{1 + D_s}. \tag{8}$$

Step 5 (Survival of fittest chromosome): If $F_s > F_{best}$ $(s = 1, 2, ..., S)$, then copy fittest g_s into g_{best}. Include the best solution g_{best} as an additional chromosome in the gene pool.

Step 6 (Selection): Select S from $(S+1)$ chromosomes of the gene pool for reproduction with probabilities in direct proportion to their fitness values by roulette wheel selection.

Step 7 (Crossover): Build pairs of neighboring chromosomes. Address a certain number of gene positions for each mate, and exchange L gene values from the sites addressed before. The crossover points are addressed randomly in the range $[1, n{-}L]$.

Step 8 (Mutation): Choose one gene in each chromosome randomly and change its value in the range $[1, N]$ at random.

Step 9 (Replacement): Replace a certain number of chromosomes by the members of the previous population obtained after Step 5. Use a random number generator in the range $[1,S]$ to determine how many and which chromosomes are replaced. Continue with Step 2.

A distributed genetic algorithm (Lung, 2003) has been introduced to vector quantization for text-independent speaker recognition. Strictly speaking we have combined DGA and the Markov random field to avoid typical local minima and decrease the search time. The proposed method is easy to implement, can readily be integrated into existing GMM-based systems, and requires no additional overhead.

Feature Extraction

In the feature extraction, a number of parameters are abstracted from the pattern under test. These parameters characterize the pattern. The resulting set of numbers in turn acts as the input to a classification scheme, which compares them with stored information on known reference patterns and makes a decision as to the class membership of the tested pattern.

As the performance of speaker recognition systems generally correlates strongly with the classification accuracy of the acoustic model, one possibility is to design the feature vector in such a way that the classes can be unambiguously predicted by observing the feature vector. In other words, the feature vector should have the power to discriminate between different classes, and our hope is that this will be lead to better speaker recognition accuracy.

The techniques to be described are very closely related to the topic in statistics known as principle component analysis and to the Karhunen-Loeve expansion in stochastic process theory. In fact, because of the latter relations, these feature extraction techniques are often called Karhunen-Loeve methods.

Karhunen-Loeve Transform

A well-known method for feature extraction is based on the Karhunen-Loeve transform (KLT). These models have been applied to text-independent speaker recognition cases (Morgera & Datta, 1984; Reynolds, 1995) with excellent results. Karhunen-Loeve Transform is the optimal transform in the minimum mean square error and maximal energy packing sense. The transformed data are totally uncorrelated, and it contains most of the classification information in the first few coordinates.

Suppose that it is desired to approximate a random vector x of dimension by a linear combination of $m < n$ vectors from some orthonormal basis $\{u_j \mid j = 1, 2,, \cdots n\}$. The approximation is:

$$\bar{x} = y_1 u_1 + y_2 u_2 + y_3 u_3 + \cdots + y_m u_m, \tag{9}$$

where,

$$y_j = u_j^T x.$$ (10)

Equations (9) and (10) can be written more concisely as $\bar{x} = U_m y$ and $y = U_m^T x$, where y is the m-dimensional vector whose components are y_j and U_m is the matrix of basis vectors:

$$U_m = \begin{bmatrix} \vdots & \vdots & & \vdots \\ u_1 & u_2 & \cdots & u_m \\ \vdots & \vdots & & \vdots \end{bmatrix}.$$ (11)

Since it is an orthonormal basis, the residual error in representing x by $\bar{x}$ is given by:

$$\varepsilon = x - \bar{x} = \sum_{j=m+1}^{n} y_j u_j,$$ (12)

where the y_j for $j > m$ are still defined according to equation (12). The problem now is to choose the basis $\{u_j\}$ such that the mean-square error:

$$\eta = E[|\varepsilon|^2] = E[|x - \bar{x}|^2],$$ (13)

is as small as possible. The y_j can then be regarded as features derived from the random vector x, and equation (13) represents the feature transformation.

It follows from equations (12) and (13) and the condition that the basis is orthonormal, that is,

$$\eta = E[\varepsilon^T \varepsilon] = E[(\sum_{i=m+1}^{n} y_i u_i^T)(\sum_{j=m+1}^{n} y_j u_j)].$$ (14)

If one writes:

$$y_j^2 = (y_j)(y_j) = (u_j^T x)(x^T u_j),$$ (15)

it then follows that:

$$E[y_j^2] = u_j^T E[xx^T] u_j = u_j^T R u_j,$$ (16)

where R is the correlation matrix for x. By substituting equation (16) into equation (14), one finds that the quantity to be minimized is:

$$\eta = \sum_{j=m+1}^{n} u_j^T R u_j,$$ (17)

subject, of course, to the constraint,

$$u_j^T u_j = 1 \quad j=m+1, ..., n. \tag{18}$$

The constraints of equation (18) can be incorporated directly into the minimization problem by using a set of Lagrange multipliers and seeking to minimize the quantity:

$$\eta' = \sum_{j=m+1}^{n} u_j^T R u_j + \sum_{j=m+1}^{n} \lambda_j (1 - u_j^T u_j). \tag{19}$$

A necessary condition for the minimum is that:

$$\frac{\partial \eta'}{\partial u_j} = 2(R u_j - \lambda u_j) = 0, \quad j=m+1, ..., n. \tag{20}$$

Equation (18) states that the u_j must be eigenvectors of R. Under the condition that the u_j are eigenvectors,

$$\eta = \sum_{j=m+1}^{n} \lambda_j, \tag{21}$$

and the solution to the minimization problem is now obvious. To minimize E, the eigen-vectors $u_{m+1}, u_{m+2}, \cdots, u_n$ must be those corresponding to the smallest eigenvalues. Thus the vectors used for equation (20) should be the eigenvectors of R corresponding to the m largest eigenvalues. In the KLT process, the transformed data are calculated from the inner products of the original spectral samples and the selected eigenvectors whose basis vectors correspond to the maximum variance directions in the original space.

The KLT method uses the statistical distribution of input samples to seek a projection that best represents the data in a least squares sense. In relevant research (Lung & Chen, 2000), a reduced form of KLT is proposed. The reduced form of KLT is based on split-and-merge algorithm. The multi-resolution singular value decomposition (MSVD) (Lung, 2002) is applied to the speaker data compression and feature extraction. The basic idea behind the MSVD is to replace split-and-merge algorithm and KLT with MSVD at not square matrix.

However, these schemes may lead to an eigenvalue decomposition of a very large covariance matrix, which is computationally expensive. Moreover, if too many samples are taken, the covariance matrix may be numerically ill conditioned. As a suitable means for analyzing the ill conditioned of covariance matrix, wavelet transforms can be used.

Wavelet Feature Extraction

A wavelet transform (WT) can simultaneously have orthogonality, regularity, symmetry, approximation order, and compact support, and these properties are very useful in signal processing. For example, recent studies show wavelet eigenvector applied to speech signal processing (Goldberg, 1989; Hsieh, Lai, & Wang, 2003; & Lung, 2004) with excellent results. In a recent paper (Lung, 2004), we presented some initial results on fuzzy C-means algorithm (FCM), and wavelet eigenvectors are based on feature extraction. The FCM approaches have been attempted for designing feature extraction in the spatial domain. The similarity between two patterns is measured by a weight distance between them. The weight coefficients are used to denote the degree of importance of the individual features. The detail can be seen in work by Lung (2004).

On the basis of the time-frequency multiresolution analysis, the effective and robust MSVD is used as the front end of the speaker identification system. First, the MSVD is extracted from the full band input signal. Then the wavelet transform technique is applied to decompose the input signal into two frequency subbands: a lower frequency approximated subband and a higher frequency detailed subband. For capturing the characteristics of a speaker, the MSVD of the lower frequency subband is calculated.

The main reason for using the MSVD parameters is their good representation of the envelope of the speech spectrum of vowels and their simplicity. On the basis of this mechanism, one can easily extract the multiresolution features from all approximated subbands simply by iteratively applying the wavelet transform to decompose the approximated subband signals.

A set of scaling functions $\{\phi_i(x)\}$ is interpolating if there exists a set of interpolating points $\{x_k\}$ such that $\phi_k(x_{k'})=1$ if $k=k'$ and $\phi_k(x_{k'})=0$ otherwise.

Suppose we have a set of pth-order polynomial approximating interpolating scaling functions $\{\phi_i(x)\}$, and let V be defined as the following subspace $V=span\{\phi_i(x)\}$. Let $\{\tilde{\phi}_i(x)\}$ be the corresponding dual scaling functions such that the following biorthogonal $\tilde{V}=span\{\tilde{\phi}_i(x)\}$.

As a first step, assume $u^i(x)\in V$ and $\varphi(x)\in\tilde{V}$. Thus, it is desirable that the basis that spans $\tilde{V}$ has piecewise polynomial approximation capabilities equal to V. Assuming $u^i(x)\in V$, we thus have $u(x)=D\phi(x)$, where:

$$
D=\begin{bmatrix}
u_1^1 & u_2^1 & \cdots & u_L^1 \\
u_1^2 & u_2^2 & \cdots & u_L^2 \\
\vdots & \vdots & \cdots & \vdots \\
u_1^M & u_2^M & \cdots & u_L^M
\end{bmatrix},
\tag{22}
$$

$u_l^i=u^i(l\Delta x)$, and $\Delta x = x_k - x_{k-1}$. Since the primary scaling functions are interpolating, the coefficients u_l^i are just samples of $u(x)$. Now, expand $\varphi(x)$ in terms of the dual basis functions, and denote this expansion as:

$$
\varphi(x)=[\tilde{\phi}(x)]^T\tilde{v},
\tag{23}
$$

where $\tilde{v}=[\tilde{v}_1\tilde{v}_2...\tilde{v}_L]^T$ and $\tilde{\phi}(x)=[\tilde{\phi}_1(x)\tilde{\phi}_2(x)...\tilde{\phi}_L(x)]^T$.

We obtained a $L\times L$ covariance matrix such that:

$$\tilde{C}\tilde{v} = \lambda\tilde{v}, \tag{24}$$

where,

$$\tilde{C} = \frac{1}{M}D^T D. \tag{25}$$

The M is then truncated to samples of the autocorrelation matrix. Notice that the coefficients $\tilde{v}_i$ are independent of the choice of $\phi(x)$ and $\tilde{\phi}(x)$, where $\phi(x)$ is an interpolation scaling function.

Cepstrum (Atal, 1974; Furui, 1981; Schroeder & Yarlagadda, 1989)

Consider a signal $x(n)$ whose z-transform $X(z)$ exists and has a region of convergence that includes the unit circle. Suppose $C(z) = \log X(z)$ has a convergent power series expansion in which, again, the region of convergence includes the unit circle. The cepstrum is defined as the inverse z-transform of $C(z)$, that is, $C(z) = \sum_n c(n)z^{-n}$. Note that $c(n)$ is also not necessarily causal. Let us continue by assuming that $X(z)$ is a rational function of z that is completely described by its poles, zeros, and gain. Then, the cepstrum $C(z)$ will have the following properties:

1. The sample $c(0)$ is the natural algorithm of the gain.
2. The poles and zeros of $X(z)$ inside the unit circle contribute only to the casual part of $c(n)$ starting at $n=1$.
3. The poles and zeros of $X(z)$ outside the unit circle contribute only to the anticausal part of $c(n)$.
4. The cepstrum is causal if and only if $X(z)$ is minimum phase.
5. The cepstrum is anticausal if and only if $X(z)$ is maximum phase.
6. The cepstrum $c(n)$ decays as fast as $1/|n|$ as n approaches ∞ and $-\infty$.
7. The cepstrum has infinite duration whether $x(n)$ is of finite or infinite duration.
8. If $x(n)$ is real, $c(n)$ is real.

As a special case of the more general $X(z)$, consider the minimum phase all-pole LP filter $H(z)$ obtained by the autocorrelation method. Given that all the poles $z=z_i$ are inside the unit circle and the gain is 1, the causal LP cepstrum $c_{lp}(n)$ of $H(z)$ is given by (Furui, 1981; Schroeder & Yarlagadda, 1989):

$$c_{lp}(n) = \begin{cases} \dfrac{1}{n}\sum_{i=1}^{p} z_i^n & n > 0 \\ 0 & n < 0. \end{cases} \tag{26}$$

A recursive relation between the LP cepstrum and the predictor coefficients is given as (Schroeder & Yarlagadda, 1989):

$$c_{lp}(n) = a_n + \sum_{i=1}^{n-1} \frac{i}{n} c_{lp}(i) a_{n-i}. \tag{27}$$

The use of this recursion allows for an efficient computation of $c_{lp}(n)$ and avoids polynomial factorization. Since $c_{lp}(n)$ is of infinite duration, the feature vector of dimension p consists of the components $c_{lp}(1)$ to $c_{lp}(p)$, which are the most significant due to the decay of the sequence with increasing n. Even with this truncation, the mean square difference between two LP cepstral vectors is approximately equal to the mean square difference between the log spectra of the corresponding all pole LP filters (Schroeder & Yarlagadda, 1989).

Cepstral Derivatives (Furui, 1981; Rosenberg, Lee, & Soong, 1994; Vergin, O'Shaughnessy, & Farhat, 1999)

The LP cepstrum represents the local spectral properties of a given frame of speech. However, it does not characterize the temporal or transitional information in a sequence of speech frames. For text related applications such as speech recognition and text dependent speaker recognition, improved performance has been found by introducing cepstral derivatives into the feature space because the cepstral derivatives capture the transitional information in the speech. The first derivative of the cepstrum is defined as (Furui, 1991):

$$\frac{\partial c_{lp}(n,t)}{\partial t} = \Delta c_{lp}(n,t) \approx u \sum_{k=-K}^{K} k c_{lp}(n,t), \tag{28}$$

where $c_{lp}(n,t)$ denotes the nth LP cepstral coefficients at time t, u is an appropriate normalization constant, and $(2K+1)$ is the number of frames over which the computation is performed. The LP cepstrum and the delta cepstrum together have been used to improve speaker recognition performance (Vergin et al., 1999).

Cepstral Weighting (Lockwood & Boudy, 1992; Vergin et al., 1999)

The basic idea behind cepstral weighting is to account for the sensitivity of the low order cepstral coefficients to overall spectral slope and the sensitivity of the high order cepstral coefficients to noise (Vergin et al., 1999). Weighting is accomplished by multiplying $c_{lp}(n)$ by a window $w(n)$ and using the weighted cepstrum as the feature vector. This weighting operation is also known as liftering. The first consequence of liftering is in extracting a finite dimensional feature vector from an infinite duration $c_{lp}(n)$. Also, careful choices of $w(n)$ enhance robustness. There are several schemes of weighting that differ in the type of cepstral window $w(n)$ that is used. The simplest one is the rectangular window as given by:

$$w(n) = \begin{cases} 1, & n = 1, 2, \cdots, L \\ 0, & otherwise , \end{cases}$$ (29)

where L is the size of the window. The first L samples, which are the most significant due to the decaying property, are kept. Other forms of $w(n)$ include quefrency liftering (Lockwood & Boudy, 1992; Vergin et al., 1999), where:

$$w(n) = \begin{cases} n, & n = 1, 2, \cdots, L \\ 0, & otherwise , \end{cases}$$ (30)

and bandpass liftering (Lockwood & Boudy, 1992; Vergin et al., 1999), where:

$$w(n) = \begin{cases} 1 + \frac{1}{2}\sin(\frac{\pi n}{L}), & n = 1, 2, \cdots, L \\ 0, & otherwise \end{cases}$$ (31)

Note that the weighting schemes described are fixed in the sense that the weights are only a function of the cepstral index and have no explicit bearing on the instantaneous variations in the cepstrum that are introduced by different environmental conditions.

Feature Selection

Feature selection is a process of selection of a map of the form $x' = f(x)$ by which a sample $x(x_1, x_2, \cdots, x_n)$ in a n-dimensional measurement space is transformed into a point $x'(x_1', x_2', \cdots, x_m')$ in an m-dimensional ($m<n$) feature space. The problem of feature selection deals with choosing some of the x_is from the measurement space to constitute the feature space.

Optimal feature selection is an important problem and has been studied by several researchers (Cohen & Froind, 1989; Ma, Kamp, & Willems, 1993). The knockout procedure by Ma et al. (1993) is symmetrical to the ascendant selection procedure. These algorithms begin with evaluating the N given features one at a time and knock out the most effective one. This step-by-step procedure also requires $\frac{N(N+1)}{2}$ evaluations (Ma et al., 1993). Selection of dynamic programming (Ma et al., 1993) is a multistage optimization technique. This procedure is bounded by $\frac{1}{k!} \frac{N^{k-2}}{k-1}$ evaluations (Ma et al., 1993). In selection by genetic algorithm (Chen, Chang, & Lung, 1999), not only may the parameters selected be different, but also the number of parameters selected could vary. The feature without which "universally good features" are obtained is discarded. In the training phase, the optimal feature selection using genetic algorithm procedure is prohibitive when N is large.

Dynamic Feature Selection Method

Recently, dynamic programming has been applied to feature selection in speaker recognition. Cheung and Eisenstein (1978) employed a multistage decision process to choose features that had acquisition costs associated with them. However, in most feature selection applications, the computation time is very prohibitive.

In this section, the authors introduce the use of a split-and-merge algorithm in the constraint multistage of a dynamic programming (DP) searched. This technique can be reducing the computational complex of identifying a speaker within a multistage decision process. The experimental data used in the evaluation were collected over a two-year period and afforded the opportunity to investigate the variation over time of the features. Before considering the merits of the features selected, we shall discuss the method used in this section to investigate the measurements.

An important step in the speaker recognition process is to extract sufficient information for good discrimination, and, at the same time, to have captured the information in a form and size that is amenable to effective modeling. In Figure 4, a set of 64 acoustic attributes was determined from the input speech, namely, 16 PARCOR coefficients, 16 cepstral coefficients, 16 normalized absolute prediction error energy, and 16 normalized autocorrelation coefficients.

The split-and-merge algorithm is a top-down method that begins with the entire parameter set. Some parameter is selected as a criterion to decide whether everything is uniform. This criterion is often based on the statistics from the region. If the region is high standard deviation, then the region is assume to be non-uniform and is divided into four quadrants. Each quadrant is examined in the same way and subdivided again if necessary. The procedure continues until the individual data level is reached.

In our problem domain, each parameter set of speakers is an 8×8 matrix. This matrix can be represented as a region. The criteria may also depend on relative, rather than absolute, uniform. We merge with if $V(R_1 \cup R_2)/V(R)$ is small compared with $V(R_1)/V(R)$ and $V(R_2)$

Figure 4. Extraction of features from speech in text-independent speaker identification

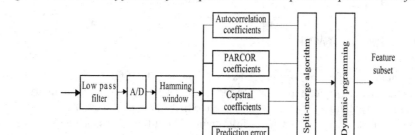

/$V(R)$, where is a measure of standard deviation and R is a total region. For a detailed treatment as well as split-and-merge algorithm, readers are referred to Lung (2001).

This criterion of split-and-merge is similar the F ratio (Cheung & Eisenstein, 1978). We called this criterion a region ratio (R ratio). This means that R ratio has an important variation between speakers and a little intra-speaker variations; hence, a good feature has a high R ratio, because the value of different parameter sets have obvious differences. Therefore, split-and-merge algorithms can be easy segmentation original region in four strip sub-groups. In Figure 4, every potential parameter matrix is regarded as a regional calculation on the basis of split-and-merge algorithm. Rearrange the features according to the size of the sub-regions. In this way, a constraint multistage is formed to show the potential parameter.

Through split-and-merge algorithm, M features are obtained, where M is the number of sub-regions. It is found that decreasing the number of potential parameters over 48 does not significantly decrease the recognition rate due to the parameter property of split-and-merge algorithm, as mentioned earlier.

The time complexity of the cost of split-and merge algorithm is determined by the size of the potential parameter. Let K be the number of regions created by the split algorithm, and let m be the number of regions that are merged. Then, the time complexity of the cost of split-and merge algorithm is O(K+mlogK).

Genetic Feature Selection Method (Goldberg, 1989; Haydar, Demirekler, & Yurtseven, 1998)

In this section, each speaker is modeled by two Gaussian distributions. The first mean vector μ_i and the covariance matrix Σ_i are obtained using the data for the ith speaker; the second mean vector $\bar{\mu}_i$ and the covariance matrix $\bar{\Sigma}_i$ are obtained using the collection of data from the rest of the speakers in the identification system. Therefore the model of the ith speaker is:

$$M^i = \{\mu_i, \bar{\mu}_i, \Sigma_i, \bar{\Sigma}_i\}. \tag{32}$$

For a population of N speakers, and $N \times N$ matrix, $B = [\bar{b}_{ij}]$ is obtained where $\bar{b}_{ij}$ can be defined as follows:

$$\bar{b}_{ij} = \sum_{K=1}^{T_j} u \left(\begin{array}{c} \left(x_j(k) - \bar{\mu}_i \right)^T \bar{\Sigma}_i^{-1} \left(x_j(k) - \bar{\mu}_i \right) - \\ (x_j(k) - \mu_i)^T \Sigma_i^{-1} (x_j(k) - \mu_i) \end{array} \right) / T_j \tag{33}$$

Here, T_j is the number of feature vectors used as the training data of the jth speaker, u is the unit step function, and $x_j(k)$ corresponds to the kth vector of the jth speaker. This matrix is further normalized by dividing its ith row to obtain the matrix $B = [b_{ij}]$. B can be viewed as a 'fitness matrix' since its $(i, j)^{th}$ entry gives information about the fitness of the jth speaker data to the ith model.

To form a similar fitness matrix, say $\hat{B}$, for the reduced set of features, the criterion that must be maximized is modified as:

$$\max_{t_i \subset t_{all}} (\hat{b}_{ii}(t_i)) - \max_{j,k} \frac{\hat{b}_{ij}(t_i) + \hat{b}_{ik}(t_i)}{2}). \tag{34}$$

Here, t_i is the reduced set of features with cardinality z_i, and t_{all} is the set of all (ordered) features with cardinality z_{all}. The aim is to select the number of features from a set $S = \{5, 6, 7, 8, 10\}$ in such a way that a person is discriminated from his or her two closest neighbors, rather than discriminating him or her from all the other speakers in the set.

The argument of the previous optimization problem gives us the best reduced order model represented as follows:

$$\hat{M}^i = \{\hat{\mu}_i, \hat{\mu}_i, \hat{\Sigma}_i, \hat{\bar{\Sigma}}_i\}. \tag{35}$$

To give a better explanation of the genetic algorithm developed to solve the optimization problem, the problem is simplified to a constant 'z' case ($z_i = z$ for all i). The algorithm basically uses mutation and can be defined as follows:

Step 1 (initialization): Form a binary vector of size z_{all}, which exactly contains a number, z, of ls. The positions of these ls denote that the corresponding feature is selected for the reduced set; call this vector, $V_{initial}$. Set $V_{initial} = V_{final}$; calculate the value of the objective function given equation (3) using $V_{initial}$, say *MaxVal*.

Step 2 (mutation): Obtain a new binary vector, V, from $V_{initial}$ by interchanging randomly selected '1' and '0' entries of $V_{initial}$. By this process, number M ($M = 25$ *in our application*) of new candidate sets for the reduced set are generated using $V_{initial}$.

Step 3 (selection of new $V_{initial}$): Calculate the objective function given in equation (3) for these new M vectors and choose that which has the maximum value, say *MaxNew*. Replace $V_{initial}$ with the vector that corresponds to the value *MaxNew*. *MaxNew* > *MaxVal*, replace V_{final} with the vector that corresponds to value *MaxNew* and equate *MaxVal* to *MaxNew*. Go to step 2 (elitist approach).

Iterate step 2 and step 3 for 24 times. V_{final} gives the selected subset t. Note that in this algorithm, to generate the new population, only mutation is used.

Testing is performed after a different number of features are selected for each person. From now on, the same symbol B will be used instead of the normalized $\hat{B}$ and B as described in the preceding sections. In the testing phase, using each model, N fitness values are obtained for the test data and normalized using the normalizing constants of each model used in the normalization of B. This new vector is denoted by c_{test}, which is very similar to a column of the matrix B. The N values, $\bar{c}_{test}(i)$, $1 \le i \le N$, are used to eliminate the candidate speakers one at a time until only one candidate is left. Elimination is based on the normalized matrix B, and the vector c_{test}. This elimination process is described next.

At the first step of the elimination process, speaker 1 is compared with speaker 2, and the winner of this step is compared with speaker 3. In general, the winner of the nth step is compared with speaker $n+1$. For the comparison of the ith speaker with the kth speaker, we are using the following distance measure in order to decide which one is going to be eliminated:

$$\left(\left(b_{ii}-\bar{c}_{test}(i)\right)^2 + \left(b_{ki}-\bar{c}_{test}(k)\right)^2\right) -$$
$$\left(\left(b_{ik}-\bar{c}_{test}(i)\right)^2 + \left(b_{kk}-\bar{c}_{test}(k)\right)^2\right) \begin{cases} > 0 & \text{If Speaker } k \\ < 0 & \text{If Speaker } i. \end{cases} \tag{36}$$

The unknown speaker is identified as the final candidate.

Fuzzy Feature Selection Method

One of the commonly used features set is a wavelet feature (Fowler, 2005; Lung, 2004). Wavelet spaces are a series of function spaces that are highly decorrelated from each other and are particularly suitable for the representation of signals and operators at different resolution scales that exhibit speech and speaker feature behaviors. The discrete wavelet transform (DWT) (Lung, 2004) has been used with limited success because of its left recursive nature. However, as the number of DWT bases grows, the time required to correctly classify the database will become non-linear. Therefore, dimensionality reduction becomes a significant issue.

Our aim here is to select the features from a 32 DWT parameter set so that the separability of one speaker from all others is maximized. To achieve this, a novel approach for speaker identification is applied for text-independent speaker identification systems. The new approach is a fuzzy feature evaluation index for a set of features and is defined in terms of membership values denoting the degree of similarity between two patterns. The similarity between two patterns is measured by a weighed distance between them.

The DWT performs the recursive decomposition of the lower frequency band obtained by the previous decomposition in dyadic fashion, thus giving a left recursive binary tree. The two wavelet orthogonal bases generated from a parent node are defined as:

$$\psi_{j+1}^{2p}(k) = \sum_{n=-\infty}^{\infty} h[n]\psi_j^p(k-2^j n), \tag{37}$$

$$\psi_{j+1}^{2p+1}(k) = \sum_{n=-\infty}^{\infty} g[n]\psi_j^p(k-2^j n), \tag{38}$$

where $h[n]$ is the lowpass filter, $g[n]$ is the highpass filter, and $\psi[n]$ is the wavelet function (Vergin et al., 1999). $\psi_j^p(k - 2^j n)$, where j is the depth of decomposition, p is the number of nodes to the left of the parent node, and k is an integer.

For a full j level wavelet decomposition there will be over $2^{2^{j-1}}$ orthogonal bases in which all of them are not useful as features for recognition. Therefore, from the previous library of bases, a selection criterion for best basis needs to be derived.

To overcome the previous problems, DW feature selection derived by using fuzzy evaluation index for speaker identification is described. The new approach is a fuzzy feature evaluation index for a set of features and is defined in terms of membership values denoting the degree of similarity between two patterns.

Let, μ_{pq}^o be the degree that both the pth and q^{th} patterns belong to the same cluster in the n-dimensional DW space, and μ_{pq}^T be that in the m-dimensional transformed space ($m < n$). μ values determine how similar a pair of patterns are in the respective DW features spaces. Let s be the number of samples on which the feature evaluation index is computed. The feature evaluation index is defined as:

$$E = \frac{1}{s(s-1)} \sum_p \sum_{q \neq p} \mu_{pq}^T (1 - \mu_{pq}^o) + \mu_{pq}^o (1 - \mu_{pq}^T), \tag{39}$$

where O is the original space (DW features space) and T is the transform space.

Therefore, the feature evaluation index decreases as the membership value representing the degree of belong of the pth and qth patterns to the same cluster in the transformed feature space tends to either 0 ($\mu^o < 0.5$) or 1 ($\mu^o > 0.5$). Our objective is to select those features for which the evaluation index becomes minimum, thereby optimizing the decision on the similarity of a pair of patterns with respect to their belonging to a cluster.

The membership function (μ) in a feature space may be defined as:

$$\mu_{pq} = \begin{cases} 1 - d_{pq}/D, & if \ d_{pq} \leq D. \\ 0, & othwewise \end{cases} \tag{40}$$

d_{pq} is a distance measure that provides similarity between the pth and qth patterns in the feature space. D is the parameter that reflects the minimum separation between a pair of patterns belonging to two different clusters. The distance d_{pq} in equation (28) is the Eucldian distance between the two patterns. Then,

$$d_{pq} = [\sum_i (x_{pi} - x_{qi})^2]^{1/2}. \tag{41}$$

The task of feature subset selection requires selecting the subset from a given set of n features for which E is a minimum. This is done by computing the E values for all possible ($2n-1$) subsets of features using equations (39) through (41) and ranking them accordingly. In our problem domain, the algorithm has been modified by reducing the set of 32 DWT features ($n=32$) to 16 features ($m=16$).

Classification

The basic assumption underlying statistical classification is that there exists a multivariate probability distribution for each class. Members of a pattern class are then treated as samples from a population, which are distributed in an n-dimensional feature space according to the distribution associated with that population. This theoretical framework leads to subcategories ranging from complete statistical knowledge of the distributions to no knowledge except that which can be inferred from samples. The subcategories are:

a.   Known distributions;

b.   Parametric families of distributions for which the functional forms are known, but some finite set of parameters are estimated;

c.   The non-parametric case in which the distributions are not known.

This section surveyed work on statistical classification algorithms presented in the engineering literature on pattern recognition through early 1978. Some topics under categories (a) and (b) that were considered in some detail are sequential and non-sequential statistical decision theoretic algorithms, hidden Markov model procedures for "learning with a teacher" when labeled samples are available, and the Gaussian mixture model formulation of "learning without a teacher" when unlabeled samples are available. Under category (c) this section described algorithms for learning the coefficients of linear decision functions based on iterative deterministic optimization procedures for solving neural network under some criterion function; extensions of these procedures to deal with neural network; algorithms based on stochastic approximation methods to find the coefficients of orthonormal series representations for the difference between the unknown a posteriori probability distributions for each class; and some clustering algorithms for unlabeled samples.

In this section, a new classifier is introduced and evaluated for speaker recognition. The new classifier is the modified hidden wavelet Markov model (WMM). The WMM incorporates modifications to the learning rule of the original stochastic process and uses an initial state criterion. In addition, wavelet coefficients are an initial state input of HMM.

Wavelet Markov Model

Hidden Markov models (HMMs) (Gauvain & Lee, 1994; Tishby, 1991) are widely used in many fields where temporal dependencies are present in the data. HMMs are doubly stochastic processes, in which a sequence of observed random variables is drawn conditionally on the sequence of states of an M state hidden Markov chain.

There are two main approaches to form hidden wavelet Markov models (Tishby, 1991; Vidakovic, 1999). In the first approach, the wavelet component is decoupled from the learning component of the perception architecture. In essence, a signal is decomposed on some wavelet, and wavelet coefficients are fed to the Markov model. In the second approach, the multi-wavelet theory and Markov model are combined into a single method. We first review the wavelet-based density estimation in the i.i.d. case. In the multi-wavelet case, we applied the ensemble functions $\{u^i(x)\}$ onto V_j and form the matrix $A = BM^{-\frac{1}{2}}$ (Lung, 2004), where B can be a matrix of dimensional $M \times L$ derive from ensemble functions $\{u^i(x)\}$ and M is the threshold to samples of autocorrelation matrix. Therefore, the covariance matrix $\tilde{C}$ is equal to A^TA. The decompose V_j is written as:

$$V_j = W_{j-1} \oplus W_{j-2} \oplus \cdots \oplus W_{j-n} \oplus V_{j-n}, \tag{42}$$

to obtain an n-level multi-scale representation of A. The n level wavelet transform is denoted by $A^{j,n}$, which is written as:

$$
\begin{aligned}
A^{j,n} &= [\overline{s}_{(j-n),1} \cdots \overline{s}_{(j-n),2^{q}-n} \mid \overline{d}_{(j-n),2^{q}-n+1} \cdots \overline{d}_{(j-n),2^{q}-n+1} \overline{d}_{(j-n+1),2^{q}-n+1} \cdots \\
&\quad \overline{d}_{(j-n+1),2^{q}-n+2} \mid \overline{d}_{(j-n+1),2^{q}-n+1}{}_{+1} \cdots \overline{d}_{(j-n+1),2^{q}-n+2} \overline{d}_{(j-n+2),2^{q}-n+2} \cdots \\
&\quad \overline{d}_{(j-n+2),2^{q}-n+3} \mid \overline{d}_{(j-n+2),2^{q}-n+2}{}_{+1} \cdots \overline{d}_{(j-n+2),2^{q}-n+3} \overline{d}_{(j-n+3),2^{q}-n+3} \cdots \\
&\quad \overline{d}_{(j-n+3),2^{q}-n+4} \mid \cdots \mid \overline{d}_{(j-1),2^{q}-1}{}_{+1} \cdots \overline{d}_{(j-1),2^{q}}] \\
&= [\overline{S}_{j-n} \mid \overline{D}_{j-n} \mid \overline{D}_{j-n+1} \mid \overline{D}_{j-n+2} \mid \cdots \mid \overline{D}_{j-1}] = AW^{T}
\end{aligned}
\tag{43}
$$

where the ith row of the vectors $\overline{s}$ and $\overline{d}$ contains the average and detail wavelet coefficients of the multi-scale representation of $u^i(x)$. The matrix W and $\tilde{W}$ represents the dual wavelet transform of each other. Suppose $\tilde{C}_{j,n} = (A^{j,n})^T A^{j,n}$ is a covariance matrix, and we have the equation:

$$\tilde{C}_{j,n} = WA^T AW^T. \tag{44}$$

The vector $\tilde{v}$ may now be expressed in its multi-scale form as $\tilde{v}_{j,n} = W\tilde{v}$. The final orthonormal eigenvalue problem then has the form:

$$\tilde{W}A^T A\tilde{W}^T \tilde{W}\tilde{v} = \tilde{W}\tilde{v}. \tag{45}$$

The wavelet component is decoupled from the learning component of the perception architecture. In essence, a signal is decomposed on some wavelet, and wavelet coefficients are fed to the Hidden Markov Model.

in the Wavelet Markov Model-based estimator, let $S = \{(i,j) \mid 1 \le i \le M_1, 1 \le j \le M_2\}$ denote the $M_1 \times M_2$ lattice such that an element in S might index a wavelet component data. We can define a neighborhood on S as $\Gamma = \{\eta_{ij}\}$, where η_{ij} is a set of sites neighboring (I,j). Let $\Lambda = \{\lambda_1, ..., \lambda_R\}$ denote the label set and $X = \{X_{ij}\}$ be a family of random variables defined on S. Furthermore, let Ω denote the set of all possible realizations of X, and let ω be a realization of Ω. X is an MRF on S with respect to the neighborhood system if the two following conditions hold (Tishby, 1991): $P(X = \omega) > 0$ for all $\omega \in \Omega$, and

$P(X_{ij} = \omega_{ij} \mid X_{kl} = \omega_{kl}, (i,j) \neq (k,l)) = P(X_{ij} = \omega_{ij} \mid X_{kl} = \omega_{kl}, and(k,l) \in \eta_{ij})$. Our goal is to find ω that maximizes the posterior distribution for a fixed input data g. That is, we want to determine:

$$\arg\ \max_{\omega}\ P(X = \omega \mid G = g) = \arg\ \max_{\omega} \frac{P(g \mid \omega)P(\omega)}{P(g)}. \tag{46}$$

Equation (46) is divided into two components of the following:

$$P(g \mid \omega) = \prod_{(i,j)\in S} P(n_{ij} = g_{ij} - f_{ij} \mid \omega_{ij}) = \prod_{(i,j)\in S} \frac{1}{\sqrt{2\pi\sigma^2}} \exp[-\frac{(g_{ij} - f_{ij})^2}{2\sigma^2}], \tag{47}$$

$$P(\omega) = \exp(-U(\omega)) = \exp\{-\sum_{(i,j)\in S}\sum_{c\in\rho_{ij}} [V_c(f \mid l) + E_c(l)]\}. \tag{48}$$

In equation (48), C is a possible set of two pair cliques in a second order neighborhood (Tishby, 1991), and ρ_{ij} is a set of cliques containing data (i,j). Then, the potential function $E_c(l) = -\alpha$ if all labels in c are equal and $E_c(l) = \alpha$ otherwise. V_c is described in detail by Lung (2004). Equation (1) can be defined as the energy function:

$$\arg\ \min_{(f,l)}\ \sum_{(i,j)\in S} \{\sum_{C\in\rho_{ij}} [V_c(f \mid l) + E_c(l)] + \frac{(g_{ij} - f_{ij})^2}{2\sigma^2} + \log 2\pi\sigma^2\}, \tag{49}$$

where the energy function is the sum of the local energy U_{ij} at data (i,j).

Such an HMM is completely characterized by A and $\tilde{W}$. The initial probabilities vector ρ is simply the eigenvector associated with the unit eigenvalue of the stochastic matrix A. If the state sequence were available, $\hat{A}$ could be directly calculated, and $\tilde{W}$ could be obtained by applying the wavelet-based estimator equation (41) through (48) to the set of conditional i.i.d. for each state. The EM iterative algorithm can be used for posteriori state probabilities.

Some variants are possible in order to limit the computational burden. For instance, the Viterbi approximation may be postulated, taking into account only the most likely state path instead of considering all the possible state sequences. We illustrate the proposed algorithm with a simple example. All the computer simulations have been performed in MATLAB with the *wavelab* toolbox (Donoho, 1999).

Gaussian Mixture Model

Gaussian mixture models (GMMs) (Digalakis, Rtischev, & Neumeyer, 1995; Miyajima, Hattori, Tokuda, Masuko, Kobayashi, & Kitamura, 2001; Reynolds & Rose, 1995) recently have become the dominant approach in text independent speaker recognition. One of the powerful attributes of GMMs is their capability to form smooth approximations to arbitrarily shaped densities (Reynolds & Rose, 1995). Although for text dependent applications, HMMs can have some advantages when incorporating temporal knowledge, GMMs still show the best performance to date for text independence speaker recognition with high accuracy.

As a typical model-based approach, GMM has been used to characterize speaker's voice in the form of probabilistic model. It has been reported that the GMM approach outperforms other classical methods for text-independent speaker identification. In this section, we briefly review the GMM-based speaker identification scheme that will be used in our simulations.

Given $Y = \{Y_1 Y_2 \cdots Y_k\}$, where $Y = \{y_{t_1 = T_1}, y_{t_2 = T_2}, \cdots y_{t_j = T_j}\}$ is a sequence of T_j feature vectors in j^{th} cluster R^j, the complete GMM for speaker model λ is parameterized by the mean vectors, covariance matrices and mixture weights from all component densities. The parameters of the speaker model are denoted as:

$$\lambda = \{p_{j,i} u_{j,i} \Sigma_{j,i}\}, \qquad i = 1, 2, \cdots, M_j \text{ and } j = 1, 2, \cdots, K. \tag{50}$$

Then, the GMM likelihood can be written as:

$$p(Y \mid \lambda) = \prod_{t_1}^{T_1} p(y_{t_1} \mid \lambda) \cdots p(y_{t_K} \mid \lambda). \tag{51}$$

In equation (51), $p(y_{t_j} \mid \lambda)$ is the Gaussian mixture density for j^{th} cluster and defined by a weighted sum of M_j component densities as:

$$p(y_{t_j} \mid \lambda) = \sum_{i=1}^{M_j} p_{j,i} b(y_{t_j}), \tag{52}$$

where,

$$b_i(y_{tj}) = \frac{1}{(2\pi)^{\frac{1}{2}} \mid \Sigma_{j,i} \mid^{\frac{1}{2}}} \exp\{-\frac{1}{2}(y_{tj} - u_{j,i})^T \Sigma_{j,i}^{-1} (y_{tj} - u_{j,i})\}, \tag{53}$$

with mean $u_{j,i}$ and variance matrix $\Sigma_{j,i}$.

The mixture weights satisfy the constraint that $\sum_{j=1}^{K} \sum_{i=1}^{M_j} p_{j,i} = 1$. In here, we assume that the mixture number in each cluster is constant and the same: $M_1 = \cdots = M_K = M$.

The parameter set λ is obtained by maximizing the likelihood of equation (52). The λ could not be solved directly. However, it can be obtained iteratively using EM algorithm (Miyajima et al., 2001; Digalakis et al., 1995). Each iteration consists of expectation step (E-step) and maximization step (M-step).

E-Step: Compute the expected value of the complete log-likelihood, conditioned on the data and the current parameter estimate,

$$Q(\lambda; \overline{\lambda}) = \sum_{j=1}^{K} \sum_{i=1}^{Mj} \sum_{tj=1}^{Tj} p(j, i \mid y_{t_j}, \overline{\lambda}) p(j, i, y_{t_j} \mid \lambda)$$

$$= \sum_{j=1}^{K} \sum_{i=1}^{Mj} \sum_{tj=1}^{Tj} p(j, i \mid y_{t_j}, \overline{\lambda}) \{\log p_{j,i} + \log p_i(y_{t_j})\} \tag{54}$$

where $\overline{\lambda}$ is an initial model and λ is a new model to estimate.

M-Step: The new model parameters are estimated by maximizing the expectation of log-likelihood as $\lambda = \arg\max Q(\overline{\lambda}; \lambda)$.

In EM algorithm, the new model becomes the initial model for the next iteration, and the process is repeated until some convergence threshold is reached.

Wavelet Neural Network

Being non-linear classifiers, neural networks possess the ability to discriminate the characteristics of different speakers. But when the dimensionality of the input feature space is high and the network structure becomes sophisticated, the convergence during training is slow. For the purpose of achieving both computational efficiency and identification performance, we propose an integrated system with structural wavelet and a multilayer feed forward neural network. In this way the acoustic space is partitioned into multiple regions in different levels of resolution.

The network consists of an input, a hidden and output layer (Figure 5). The input layer consists of a pair of nodes corresponding to each feature, for an n dimensional feature space. The hidden layer consists of n nodes, which compute the part in equation (47) for each pair of patterns. The output layer consists of two nodes. One of them computes μ^O, and the other μ^T. The feature evaluation index $E(W)$ in equation (44) is computed from these μvalues off the network. For convenience we use the following notation to describe the functions of the nodes in each of the three layers.

Layer 1: The nodes of this layer directly transmit input signals to the next layer. When the pth and q^{th} patterns are presented to the input layer, the activation produced by ith input node is $u_i^{(0)}$, where $u_i^{(0)} = x_{pi}$ and $u_{i+n}^{(0)} = x_{qi}$ for $1 \leq i \leq n$, the total activations received by the ith and $(i+n)^{th}$ input node, respectively.

Layer 2: The total activations received by the jth hidden node is given by:

$$u_j^1 = 1 \times u_i^{(0)} + (-1) \times u_{i+n}^{(0)} \text{ for } 1 \leq i \leq n. \tag{55}$$

Layer 3: The node in this layer computes the output signal of the NF model. The total activations received by the output node, which computes the u^T values, is:

Figure 5. Neural network model

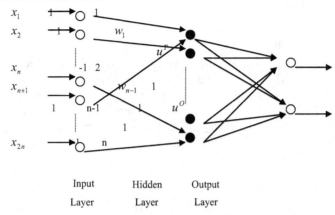

| | Input | Hidden | Output |
| | Layer | Layer | Layer |

$$u_T^{(2)} = \sum_j w_j u_j^{(1)}, \tag{56}$$

and that received by the other node which computes the u^O values, is:

$$u_o^{(2)} = \sum_j u_j^{(1)}. \tag{57}$$

Therefore,

$$v_T^{(2)} = \begin{cases} 1 - (u_T^{(2)})^{1/2} / D & \text{if } (u_T^{(2)})^{1/2} \le D \\ 0 & \text{otherwise} \end{cases}, \tag{58}$$

and,

$$v_O^{(2)} = \begin{cases} 1 - (u_O^{(2)})^{1/2} / D & \text{if } (u_O^{(2)})^{1/2} \le D \\ 0 & \text{otherwise} \end{cases}. \tag{59}$$

D is the parameter that reflects the minimum separation between a pair of patterns belonging to two different clusters. Let s be the number of samples on which the feature evaluation index is computed. The fuzzy evaluation index, in terms of these actions, is written as:

$$E(W) = \frac{1}{s(s-1)} \sum_p \sum_{q \neq p} v_T^{(2)}(1 - v_O^{(2)}) + v_O^{(2)}(1 - v_T^{(2)}). \tag{60}$$

The task of minimization of $E(W)$ is used a gradient descent technique (Farrell, Mammone, & Assaleh, 1994; Oppenheim & Schafer, 1989) in a connectionist framework in unsupervised mode. The gradient-descent technique, where the change in W_j is computed as:

$$\Delta W_j = -\eta \frac{\partial E}{\partial W_j}, \qquad \forall j, \tag{61}$$

where η is the learning rate.

Gradient-based algorithms, especially the backpropagation algorithm (Farrell et al., 1994) and its revised versions (Gori & Petrosino, 2004), are well known as a type of learning for multilayered neural networks. Initial and transition probabilities are estimated via Baum-Welch (Oppenheim & Schafer, 1989), while gradient descent techniques aimed at the termination of the minimization criteria were developed. The detailed can be seen in work by Farrell et al. (1994) and Oppenheim and Schafer (1989).

Conclusion

The task of automatic speaker identification is to determine the identity of a speaker by machine. In order for humans to recognize voices, the voices must be familiar; similarly for machines. The process of "getting to know" speakers is referred to as training and consists of collecting data from utterances of people to be identified. The second component of speaker identification is testing; namely the task of comparing unidentified utterances to the training data and making the identification. The speaker of test utterances is referred to as the target speaker. The terms speaker identification and speaker recognition are used interchangeably.

This chapter has presented a review of some of the techniques used in robust speaker recognition with an emphasis on measure analysis, feature extraction, feature selection, and classifier. Most of the measurement analyses are described based on vector quantization or codebook design model. The well-known technique of VQ is called the LBG algorithm, which is based on three necessary conditions: code word splitting, the centroid, and the nearest neighbor rule.

For feature extraction, in this chapter, Karhunen-Loeve transform, cepstrum, cepstral derivatives, and wavelet transform are described. The wavelet transform is a very recent and promising technique for mapping the feature space from one region to another to correct for deviations caused by the corruption of the speech signal by channel and noise. But, more effort is needed in finding features for achieving very high recognition performance.

Since this chapter technique provides a weighting of the components of the feature vector, it is, in effect, providing statistical feature selection. In fact, the weighting is decided by the dynamic, genetic, or fuzzy method, and so on. The aim of selection is to determine the feature space in which the seperability of speakers from each other is maximized.

For classifier assessment, estimates of the Bayes error probability are of interest, as are estimates of the probability of misclassification of any "suboptimal" classifier that is used. Very often, little is known about the underlying probability distributions, and performance must be estimated using whatever samples are available. In this context various questions arise concerning the relationships between the number of features, the estimation of its performance. Here we summarize some recent results concerning:

1. Quantitative estimation of the bias in the error estimate based on the design sample set;
2. Whether statistical independence of measurements allows performance to be improved by using additional measurements;
3. How to best use a fixed size sample in designing and testing a classifier;
4. Comparison of error estimation procedures based on counting misclassified samples with non-parametric estimation of the Bayes error probability using density estimation techniques;
5. Use of unclassified test samples in error estimation.

"Testing on the training set" and "re-substitution" are names for the approach in which the entire set of available samples is first used to design the classifier, and future performance is predicted to be that obtained on the design set. The well-known optimistic bias of this approach was confirmed by various theoretical and experimental demonstrations. A classical alternative is the sample-partitioning or "hold-out" method, whereby some samples are used to design the classifier and the remaining to test it. Usually half the samples are held out. An attempt at analytically determining the optimal partitioning in order to minimize the variance of the estimated error rate has been shown to rest on shaky assumptions. Based on experimental comparisons reported by Lachenbruch and Mickey (1968) and elsewhere, the conclusion at the end of 1968 seemed to be that one should use the "leave-one-out" method. In this method, given N samples, a classifier is designed on $N - 1$ samples, tested on the remaining sample, and then the results of all such partitions of size $N - 1$ for the design set and one for the test set are averaged. Except in some special cases, this method takes N times computation of the hold-out method.

In Glick (1972) it is shown that the re-substitution method is consistent for general non-parametric density estimation schemes, and Wagner (1973) proved that the leave-one-out method is consistent in the non-parametric case under certain mild conditions. As pointed out by Foley (1972), even if a sample partitioning scheme is used during the experimental phase of designing a classifier, the entire set of samples is likely to be used for the final design. Thus one would like to know the conditions under which the estimate using re-substitution is a good predictor of future performance, and the relationship between that and the optimal probability of error achievable by a Bayes classifier.

For learning with various types of teachers and for many other problems in statistical pattern classification, for example, automatic threshold adjustment, taking context into account, inter-symbol interference, and distribution-free learning, at least conceptually, compound decision theory provides an integrated theoretical framework.

In past studies for recognition models, dynamic time warping (DTW), the hidden Markov model, GMM, and neural network (NN) are used in speaker recognition. The DTW technique is effective in text dependent speaker recognition, but it is not suitable for text independent speaker recognition. The HMM is widely used in speech recognition, and it is also commonly used in text dependent speaker verification. The HMM models are not only the underlying speech sounds, but also the temporal sequence among these sounds. The GMM provides a probabilistic model of the underlying sounds of a person's voice, but unlike HMM it does not impose any Markov constraints among the sound classes. It is computationally more efficient than HMM and has been widely used in text independent speaker recognition.

For speaker recognition, typically, a sequence of test vectors is available. For the neural network method, the labels are found for all test vectors. The score for each class is recorded. For speaker identification, the speaker corresponding to the largest score is selected. NN classifiers require the storage of all training data and an exhaustive search to find the closest neighbor among all the data. Hence, they are very costly with respect to memory and computation requirements.

A new classifier is introduced and evaluated for speaker recognition. The new classifier is the modified hidden wavelet Markov model. The WMM is decomposed on some wavelet and wavelet coefficients are fed to the Markov model.

That the future will bring new and improved systems is certain. There is a ready market for practical systems in many areas where it is desired to extend and automate valuable informational and transactional services to larger and larger groups of customers, while at the same time ensuring that these services are provided only to those who are authorized to receive them.

References

Atal, B. S. (1974). Effectiveness of linear prediction characteristics of the speech wave for automatic speaker identification and verification. *J. Acoust. Soc. Amer., 55*, 1304-1312.

Buck, J., Burton, D., & Shore, J. (1985). Text-dependent speaker recognition using vector quantization. *Proc. IEEE ICASSP-85, 1*, 391-394.

Chen, C.-T., Fu-Rui, F.-R., & Lung, S.-Y. (1999). Genetic algorithm for text independent speaker recognition. *The Second International Conference on Multimodal Interface (ICMI'99)* (pp. 57-61). Hong Kong.

Chen, C., Lung, S.-Y., Yang, C., & Lee, M. (2002). Speaker recognition based on 80/20 genetic algorithm. In *IASTED International Conference on Signal Processing, Pattern Recognition, and Application* (pp. 547-549). Greece.

Cheung, R., & Eisenstein, B. (1978). Feature selection via dynamic programming for text-independent speaker identification. *IEEE Trans. on Acoustics, Speech, and Signal Processing, ASSP-26*, 397-403.

Cohen, A., & Froind, I. (1989). On text-independent speaker identification using a quadratic classifier with optimal features. *Speech Commun.*, 35-44.

Digalakis, V., Rtischev, D., & Neumeyer, L. (1995). Speaker adaptation using constrained re-estimation of Gaussian mixtures. *IEEE Trans. Speech Audio Processing, 3*, 357-366.

Donoho, D. (1999). WaveLab 7.01 Toolbox for MATLAB. Retrieved from http://www.stat.stanford.edu

Farrell, K. R., Mammone, J., & Assaleh, K. (1994). Speaker recognition using neural networks versus conventional classifiers. *IEEE Trans. Speech Audio Processing, 2*, 194-205.

Fowler, J. E. (2005). The redundant discrete wavelet transform and additive noise. *IEEE Signal Processing Letters, 12*, 629-632.

Furui, S. (1981a). Comparison of speaker recognition methods using statistical features and dynamic features. *IEEE Trans. Acoust. Speech Signal Process, ASSP-29*(3), 342-350.

Furui, S. (1981b). Cepstral analysis technique for automatic speaker verification. *IEEE Trans. Acoust. Speech Signal Process, ASSP-29*(2), 254-272.

Furui, S. (1991). Vector-quantization-based speech recognition and speaker recognition techniques. *Proc. IEEE ICASSP-91*, 954-958.

Gauvain, J. L., & Lee, C. H. (1994). Maximum a posteriori estimation for multivariate Gaussian mixture observations of Markov chains. *IEEE Trans. Speech Audio Processing, 2*, 291-298.

Gish, H., & Schmidt, M. (1994). Text-independent speaker identification. *IEEE Signal Processing Magazine*, 18-32.

Goldberg, D. (1989). *Genetic algorithms in search, optimization, and machine learning.* Addison-Wesley

Gori, M., & Petrosino, A. (2004). Encoding nondeterministic fuzzy tree automata into recursive neural networks. *IEEE Trans. Neural Networks, 15*, 1435-1449.

Haydar, A., Demirekler, M., Nakipoglu, B., & Thzun, B. (1995). Text independent speaker identification using Bayes decision rule and vector quantizer. *5th Int. Conf. on Advances in Communication and Control* (pp. 56-60).

Haydar, A., Demirekler, M., & Yurtseven, M. K. (1998). Feature selection using genetic algorithm and its application to speaker verification. *Electronics Letters, 34*(15), 1457-1459.

Hsieh, C., Lai, E., & Wang, Y. (2003). Robust speaker identification system based on wavelet transform and Gaussian Mixture Model. *J. Information Science and Engineering, 19*, 267-282.

Juang, B. H., & Chen, T. (1998). The past, present, and future of speech processing. *IEEE Signal Processing Magazine, 15*, 24-48.

Kohonen, T. (1990). The self-organizing map. *Proc. IEEE, 78*, 1464-1480.

Kuo, D.-Y., Chen, C.-T., & Lung, S.-Y. (1999). Speaker identification through use of features selected using genetic algorithm. *IASTED International Conference on Applied Modeling and Simulation,* Australia (pp. 563-566).

Linde, Y., Buzo, A., & Gray, R. (1980). An algorithm for vector quantizer design. *IEEE Trans. Communications, 28*(1), 84-95.

Lockwood, P., & Boudy, J. (1992). Experiments with a nonlinear spectral subtractor (NNS), Hidden Markov Models and the projection for robust speech recognition in cars. *Speech Commun., 11*(2), 215-228.

Lung, S.-Y. (2001). Feature selected using R ratio to text independent speaker recognition. *IASTED International Conference on Artificial Intelligence and Soft Computing.* Mexico. Accepted.

Lung, S.-Y. (2002a). An eigenspace estimation of KLT for text independent speaker identification. In *IASTED International Conference on Signal Processing, Pattern Recognition, and Application* (pp. 516-518). Greece.

Lung, S.-Y. (2002b). Multi-resolution form of SVD for text independent speaker recognition. *Pattern Recognition, 35,* 1637-1639.

Lung, S.-Y. (2003). Distributed genetic algorithm for Gaussian Mixture Model based speaker identification. *Pattern Recognition, 36,* 2479-2481.

Lung, S.-Y. (2004a). Adaptive fuzzy wavelet algorithm for text independent speaker recognition. *Pattern Recognition, 37,* 2095-2096.

Lung, S.-Y. (2004b). Further reduced form of wavelet feature for text independent speaker recognition. *Pattern Recognition, 37,* 1569-1570.

Lung, S.-Y. (2004c). Applied multi-wavelet feature to text independent speaker identification. *IEICE Trans. on Fundamentals of Electronics, Communications, and Computer Sciences, E87-A*(4), 944-945.

Lung, S.-Y. (2006). Wavelet codebook design using genetic algorithm for text independent speaker recognition. In *IASTED International Conference on Signal Processing, Pattern Recognition, and Application* (pp. 1257-1259). Innsbruck, Austria.

Lung, S.-Y., & Chen, C.-C. T. (1998). Further reduced form of Karhunen-Loeve transform for text independent speaker recognition. *Electronics Letters, 34,* 1380-1382.

Lung, S.-Y., & Chen, C.-C. T. (2000). A new approach for text independent speaker recognition. *Pattern Recognition, 33,* 1401-1403.

Ma, C., Kamp, Y., & Willems, L. (1993). Robust signal selection for linear prediction analysis of voiced speech. *Speech Commun., 12*(2), 69-82.

Mammon, R., & Eichmann, G. (1982). Restoration of discrete Fourier spectra using linear programming. *J. Opt. Soc. Amer., 72,* 987-992.

Miyajima, C., Hattori, Y., Tokuda, K., Masuko, T., Kobayashi, T., & Kitamura, T. (2001). Text-independent speaker identification using Gaussian Mixture Models based on multi-space probability distribution. *IEICE Trans. Inf. & Syst., E84-D*(7), 847-855.

Morgera, S. M., & Datta, L. (1984). Toward a fundamental theory of optimal feature selection: Part I. *IEEE Trans. Acoust., Speech, Signal Process, PAMI-6,* 601-616.

Oppenheim, A. V., & Schafer, R. W. (1989). *Discrete-time signal processing.* Englewood Cliffs, NJ: Prentice-Hall.

Pellom, B. L., & Hansen, J. H. (1998). An effective scoring algorithm for Gaussian Mixture Model based speaker identification. *IEEE Signal Process. Lett., 5*(11), 281-284.

Reynolds, D. (1995). Large population speaker identification using clean and telephone speaker. *IEEE Signal Processing Lett., 2,* 46-48.

Reynolds, D., & Rose, R. (1995). Robust text-independent speaker identification using Gaussian mixture speaker models. *IEEE Trans. Speech Audio Processing, 3*(1), 72-83.

Rosenberg, A., DeLong, J., Juang, B. H., & Soong, F. (1992). The use of cohort normal-ized scores for speaker verification. In *Proc. ICSLP'92* (pp. 599-602). Banff, Alta., Canada.

Rosenberg, A., Lee, C. H., & Soong, F. (1994). Cepstral channel normalization techniques for HMM-based speaker verification. *Proc. Int. Conf. on Spoken Language Process-ing* (pp. 1835-1838).

Rosenberg, A., & Soong, F. (1987). Evaluation of a vector quantization talker recognition system in text independent and text dependent modes. *Comp. Speech Language, 22*, 143-157.

Sambur, M. R. (1975). Selection of acoustic features for speaker identification. *IEEE Trans. Acoust., Speech, Signal Processing, ASSP-23*, 176-182.

Schroeder, J., & Yarlagadda, R. (1989). Linear predictive spectral estimation via the L_1 norm. *Signal Processing, 17*, 19-29.

Stern, R., Liu, F., Moreno, P., & Acero, A. (1994). Signal processing for robust speech recognition. In *Proc. ICSLP'94* (vol. 3) (pp. 1027-1030). Yokohama, Japan.

Therrien, C. (1992). *Discrete random signals and statistical signal processing*. Englewood Cliffs, NJ: Prentice-Hall.

Tishby, N. Z. (1991). On the application of mixture AR Hidden Markov Models to text independent speaker recognition. *IEEE Trans. Signal Process, 39*(3), 563-570.

Vergin, R., O'Shaughnessy, D., & Farhat, A. (1999). Generalized mel frequency cepstral coefficients for large-vocabulary speaker-independent continuous-speech recognition. *IEEE Trans. Speech Audio Process, 7*(5), 525-532.

Vidakovic, B. (1999). *Statistical modeling by wavelets*. New York: Wiley.

Chapter XIV

Speech Technologies for Language Therapy

Ingrid Kirschning, University de las Americas, Mexico

Ronald Cole, University of Colorado, USA

Abstract

This chapter presents the development and use of speech technologies in language therapy for children with hearing disabilities. It describes the challenges that must be addressed to design and construct a system to support effective interactions. The chapter begins with an introduction to speech and language therapy and discusses how speech-based systems can provide useful tools for speech and language therapy and to overcome the lack of sufficient human resources to help all children who require it. Then it describes the construction of adequate speech recognition systems for children, using artificial neural networks and hidden Markov models. Next, a case study is presented with the system we have been developing for speech and language therapy for children in a special education school. The chapter concludes with an analysis of the obtained results and the lessons learned from our experiences that will hopefully inform and encourage other researchers, developers, and educators to develop learning tools for individuals with disabilities.

Introduction: Language Acquisition and Hearing Disability

Hearing is the means by which humans acquire their spoken language (Flores & Berruecos, 1991; McAleer, 1995). It is mainly through spoken language that a child learns about hi or her world, and this is where the development of the intellect begins.

Hearing impairment can range from partial to complete loss of hearing. Hearing impairment or deafness in infants poses a big problem for language acquisition and requires special attention. Although sign language exists, about 90% of all children with profound hearing loss are born to hearing parents, and many parents want their children to be able to communicate with them and others using speech. Therefore, it is very important to find the means for these children to learn to express themselves orally (Delgado, 1999).

Each year thousands of deaf children receive cochlear implants. In many countries, screening newborns for hearing loss before they leave the hospital has become mandatory, and this process is identifying important numbers of infants with significant bilateral hearing loss. Early detection and intervention for these children, including cochlear implants, has dramatically improved the chances for these individuals to lead a normal and productive life in a hearing world. Once these devices are implanted, the children need help learning to perceive and produce speech and language, so speech and language therapy is critically important. Because they are hearing language for the first time, these children often have difficulty making sense of sounds and enunciating clearly.

Speech and language therapy at special education schools typically focuses on three general topics (Valadéz & Espinosa, 2002):

- **Articulation of vowels and consonants:** This refers to the positions of lips, tongue, and teeth to pronounce each vowel or consonant. This is taught by the teacher pointing to her or his mouth and showing the movements, although many of them remain invisible inside the mouth.

- **Intonation, modulation, and rhythm:** These are taught through repetitions, trial, and error, where the teacher corrects each student when speaking. Intonation is marked on a blackboard or on words painted on papers, pinned to the walls using circles that show the syllable that has to be spoken with more emphasis than the others. Rhythm is practiced by clapping while pronouncing certain words.

- **Individualized, one-on-one instruction:** Because each child will have special needs, children in special education programs typically receive individual training sessions with a speech and language pathologist who will focus on the particular problems he or she has, to complement their training along with other children in the classroom.

Baldi: A Virtual Teacher for Students at Tucker Maxon School

Scientists at the OGI School of Science & Engineering (formerly the Oregon Graduate Institute of Science & Technology) have developed a special computer program called the CSLU Toolkit, which provides both an authoring and runtime environment for speech and language training applications in which students interact with a lifelike talking head (Cole, Sutton, Yan, Vermeulen, & Fanty, 1998; Sutton & Cole, 1998; Sutton, Novick, Cole, & Fanty, 1996). These scientists have worked with students who attend Tucker Maxon School in Portland, Oregon, most of whom were born with severe hearing loss and have received cochlear implants. To help them learn how to listen to and recognize sounds and speak clearly, OGI students and faculty used a "talking" head named Baldi (Massaro, 1997) that produces accurate lip movements synchronized with synthetic speech. Baldi has been incorporated into many applications at the Tucker Maxon School to teach student vocabulary, speech perception, and speech production skills, as well as classroom subjects (Connors, Davis, Fortier, Gilley, Rundle, Soland, & Tarachow, 1999).

Most of the children warm up to Baldi's giant smiling face, which was created at the Perceptual Science Laboratory at the University of California, Santa Cruz (Massaro, 1997).

Instructors at Tucker Maxon have embraced Baldi and the vocabulary tutoring program, which has been part of Tucker Maxon's curriculum for several years now. The students are highly motivated to use the technology, and so they spend a significant amount of time independently engaged in speech and language practice. Most of the students who work with Baldi are severely to profoundly deaf and received a cochlear implant at an early age. Interaction with Baldi has made a dramatic difference in the speech and language skills of these children. They acquire and use new vocabulary, perceive speech more accurately, and produce speech more accurately and intelligibly. They are enrolled in a program focusing on the development of auditory skills and are now demonstrating excellent listening skills and a high level of spoken communication. Baldi is a great example of what speech technology and computer graphics can do to enhance education (Barker, 2003; Cole, 1999; Tucker Maxon, 2001). This work was featured on national television in the United States, and a video showing this program can be downloaded (UCSC-PSL, 2006; Payson, 2001).

Bringing Spanish-Speaking Baldi to Mexico

For the past several years, the CSLU Toolkit and Baldi have been integrated into the curriculum at the Jean Piaget Special Education School in Puebla, Mexico. "The children are always eager to work with Baldi because he's the most patient teacher," said Rosario Espinosa, director of the school. "The students, even the very young ones, are highly motivated to use the technology during their language therapy sessions. They compete with each other to practice their speech production and trying to make Baldi smile," she added. In this school children with cochlear implants are very rare, because of the high cost involved. The school received 10 personal computers two years ago thanks to a donation from the Mexican Teletón, which provided these children a chance to interact with Baldi in multimedia learning exercises two or three times a week.

In the remainder of this chapter, we present the development and use of speech technologies for language therapy for children with hearing disabilities. We describe the issues involved in order to construct the adequate elements for an effective interaction. We present the current state of the art concerning computer assisted learning, followed by a case study describing the system that has been developed and which is presently being used for language therapy for small children in a special education school. We also describe some issues on the construction of robust speech recognition systems for children voices, using artificial neural networks (with the CSLU Toolkit) and hidden Markov models (SONIC). The chapter concludes with an analysis of the obtained results and the experiences that will hopefully encourage more developers to work on applications for individuals with disabilities.

Computer Aided Language Therapy

Over the last few years, there has been a surge in interest in the intelligent tutoring systems that incorporate computer speech recognition. This interest is fueled by at least three factors:

1. An increase in the performance and accuracy of speech recognition systems.
2. A greater incorporation of students and learners with some disability into the educational sector.
3. An increase of the legal obligations to provide accessible information technology.

As a result one can find that several university Web sites now offer access to speech recognition software for access to information, especially to support blind or visually impaired students (e.g., //cslr.colorado.edu/beginweb/speech_recognition/sonic.html; //cslu.cse.ogi.edu; Kirriemuir, 2003).

There are several programs and applications in the market for language therapy, especially for English, and one or two for Spanish (Castilian). These programs usually focus on one type of therapy: articulation, repetition, intonation, or rhythm.

These programs range in their use from simple tutoring systems to ones that support language therapists and doctors to establish the appropriate therapies. Some of the exercises in most of these applications can be used independently of a language, as are those that practice the control of the voice volume, pitch, and modulation. However, for other cases where correct pronunciation and vocabulary are important, the system has to be developed for a specific language. Additionally, most of these systems do not work for Mexican Spanish, and they can also be very expensive.

Some impressive advances have been made in the development of learning environments and tutoring systems to support the acquisition of vocabulary and reading skills. Examples of commercially or publicly available systems include:

- **Electronic Books:** The center for special education "El buen pastor" in Spain has developed an electronic book that supports the learning process with a content that intends to intensify the stimulus in students (Gómez, 1999).

- **Aphasia Tutor Sights 'n Sounds:** This is a system for language therapy to train articulation and word identification through auditory discrimination and repetitions (Bungalow Software, 2000).

- **Speech Sounds on Cue:** This system focuses on independent language practice: individual phonemes (sounds) and complete words. This is appropriate for children that need to hear and see the production of sounds (with difficulty to articulate) (Bungalow Software, 2000).

- **Language Therapy with IBM's Dr. Speech 4:** This system has a series of interactive game-like sessions designed to train pitch and tone changes, volume, and so forth, allowing the storage of statistical data on performance of each child to be used by doctors and speech therapists in diagnostics and treatments (Zaoming, 1990).

- **Kurzweil Educational Systems Group of L&H**: They offer a series of products that read aloud (Kurzweil 3000) and take dictates (L&H Voice Xpress Professional) to support people with physical disabilities or learning disabilities (Bradburn, 2000).

- **Soliloquy Reading Assistant:** See //www.soliloquylearning.com/

- **Animated Speech Corporation:** This is the company that uses Baldi technology for kids with autism and other disabilities (http://www.animatedspeech.com/).

- **CSLU Vocabulary Tutor:** The Tucker Maxon Oral School in Portland, Oregon, uses this system, which is based on the CSLU Toolkit (Cole, 1999; Tucker Maxon, 2001) developed by the Center for Spoken Language Understanding (CSLU). The vocabulary Tutor contains tools for instructors to build their own sessions (Stone, 1999). These sessions are aimed to practice vocabulary, using speech synthesis and an animated three-dimensional face, called Baldi, who pronounces each word with accurate lip and tongue movements. The CSLU Toolkit allows programmers to create new lessons and add language specific features, such as speech recognizers and synthesizers.

Animated Pedagogical Agents that Teach and Conduct Therapy

Intelligent learning systems built around animated pedagogical agents have been the subject of much recent attention (e.g., Barker, 2003; Baylor & Ryu, 2003; Cole, Van Vuuren, Pellom, Hacioglu, Ma, Movellan, Schwartz, Wade-Stein, Ward, & Yan, 2003; Graesser, Wiemer-Hastings, Wiemer-Hastings, Kreuz, & the Tutoring Research Group, 1999; Gratch, Rickel, André, Badler, Cassell, & Petajan, 2002). We have developed computer-based learning systems at the Center for Spoken Language Research (CSLR) that use pedagogical agents to teach reading and to conduct speech therapy. These systems (a) faithfully implement an instructional program or treatment, and (b) use an animated pedagogical agent to emulate, to the extent possible, the behaviors of an expert teacher or therapist conducting the treatment. In each case, we worked with experts who developed the original program or treatment to design an initial prototype, and then refined the system through a series of "design-and-test"

Figure 1. Screen images of virtual therapists for (a) Parkinson disease and (b-d) aphasia interventions: (a) a pitch exercise in the LSVT-VT; (b) cue selection during script practice in the C-Costa-VT, (c) treatment for underlying forms exercise in the Sentactics-VT; (d) sentence reading exercise in the ORLA-VT

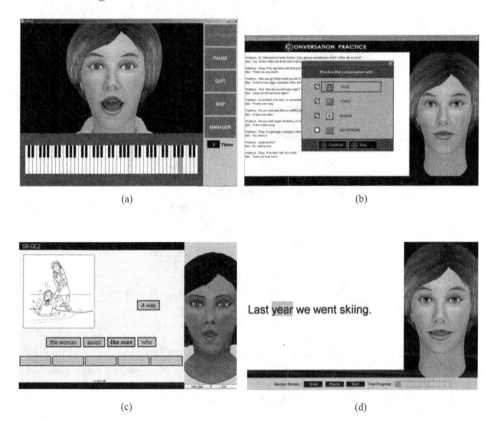

(a) (b)

(c) (d)

cycles with users partaking in this effort. This process, called *participatory design*, ensures treatment fidelity and good user experiences. Independent users of our systems have given them high ratings, saying the agent is believable and helps them learn (Cole, Wise, & Van Vuuren, 2007).

We are developing virtual speech therapy systems for four independent treatments (Figure 1), including a system for individuals with Parkinson's disease (*LSVT*™-VT [Cole, Halpern, Lorraine, Van Vuuren, Ngampatipatpong, Yan, 2007; Halpern, Cole, Ramig, Yan, Petska, Vuuren, & Spielman, 2006]), and separate treatments for individuals with aphasia (*Sentactics*™-VT [Thompson, 2003], *ORLA*™-VT [Cherney, Halper, Babbit, Holland, Cole, Van Vuuren, & Ngampatipatpong, 2005], and *C-Costa*™-VT [Cherney et al., 2005]).

We are also developing virtual tutors for reading instruction (*Foundations to Literacy*™ [Wise, Cole, & Van Vuuren., 2005; Cole, Wise, & Van Vuuren, 2007]) and reading assessment (*ICARE*™ [Wise et al., 2005]). *Foundations to Literacy* is a comprehensive, scientifically-based program that teaches reading and comprehension skills to students in Kindergarten

Figure 2. Screen images of the Foundations to Literacy program showing reading skills activity, interactive book, and multiple choice question activity

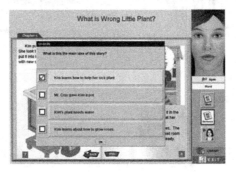

through second grade. A virtual tutor, *Marni*, guides students through reading skill exercises and books (Figure 2). During the last three years, this program has been fielded in over 50 classrooms in Colorado schools with summative evaluation of the program using standardized tests showing significant gains in letter and word recognition in Kindergarten and first grade.

Why and How to use Pedagogical Agents

When human computer interfaces are based on the social conventions and expectations that govern our daily interactions with each other, they provide engaging, satisfying, and effective user experiences (Johnson, Rickel, & Lester, 2000; Nass & Brave, 2005; Reeves & Nass, 1996). Such programs foster *social agency,* enabling users to interact with the program like they interact with people. Programs that incorporate pedagogical agents, represented by talking heads or human voices, especially inspire social agency in interactive media (Atkinson, 2002; Baylor & Kim, 2005; Baylor & Ryu, 2003; Mayer, 2001; Moreno, Mayer, Spires, & Lester, 2001; Nass & Brave, 2005; Reeves & Nass, 1996). In comparisons of programs with and without talking heads or human voices, children learned more and reported more satisfaction using programs that incorporated virtual humans (e.g., Atkinson, 2002; Baylor & Kim, 2005; Baylor & Ryu, 2003; Moreno et al., 2001). Students tend to work hard to please a virtual teacher much as they would respond to a real teacher (Lester, Converse, Kahler,

Barlow, Stone, & Boghal, 1997). The demonstrated power of individualized instruction with expert human tutors (Bloom, 1984; Cohen, Kulik, & Kulik, 1982) further motivates the use of realistic animated pedagogical agents in tutoring systems to produce effective learning experiences in homes and schools.

Our work builds on theory and research in three areas to inform the design of computer-based learning tools that optimize learning. These areas include (1) research demonstrating benefits of individualized instruction, (2) theory and research on the design of multimedia learning environments, and (3) theory and research on benefits of fostering social agency in computer-based learning tasks.

1. **Individualized Instruction:** There is clear evidence that individualized instruction benefits learning for both human tutoring and intelligent tutoring systems. In his classic work, Benjamin Bloom (1984) and his students demonstrated two sigma learning gains for one-on-one or small group instruction, and replicated these results in different content areas for students in different age groups. These results are supported by meta-analyses of a large number of experiments that compare different methods of human tutoring (including peer tutoring) to "standard" classroom instruction (Cohen et al., 1982). Intelligent tutoring systems that provide individualized and adaptive instruction have been shown to produce a one-sigma gain in teaching students algebra (Koedinger, Anderson, Hadley, & Mark, 1997).

2. **Multimedia Design:** Mayer (2001) and his colleagues have conducted an extensive series of experiments designed to identify principles for optimizing learning in multimedia environments. These experiments, which led to the cognitive theory of multimedia learning, compared learning gains of different tasks (e.g., how lighting forms, how pumps work, how brakes work, etc.) in terms of both retention of information and transfer of knowledge to new problems. For example, a series of experiments compared learning when text was presented with illustrations or when narration (identical to the text) was presented with the same illustrations; these experiments demonstrated that learning gains are greatest, with large effect sizes, when spoken explanations are accompanied by informative visual displays. Mayer's cognitive theory of multimedia learning holds that learning is optimal when complementary information is presented in independent (and limited capacity) auditory and visual channels. Students can construct and combine auditory and visual channels to construct rich mental models, whereas presenting both verbal (text) and pictorial information in the visual channel splits limited visual attention between two sources, resulting in impoverished representations relative to the two-modality situation.

3. **Social Agents:** A significant body of research, stimulated by the seminal work of Reeves and Nass (1996), has demonstrated that individuals apply the same fundamental rules and social conventions during their interactions with computers and people. Reeves and Nass termed this phenomenon, supported by dozens of experiments, *the media equation*: people interact with computers like they interact with people. In recent years, converging evidence from several studies has demonstrated that learning gains can be achieved by designing computer programs that use pedagogical agents (either voices or talking heads) that foster social agency (e.g., Atkinson, 2002; Lester et al., 1997; Moreno et al., 2001). Learning programs with well-designed animated pedagogical

agents appear to engage and motivate students, produce greater learning gains, and students report that they find the program more likable, trustworthy, and credible. Our own work with animated agents strongly supports this idea. In a survey given to 129 Kindergarten, first grade, and second grade students who used the *Foundations to Literacy* program this past school year, over 90% gave the highest possible rating scores to questions like "Do you think Marni is a good teacher?" "Does Marni act like a real human teacher?" and "How well does Marni help you learn to read?" Similar results were obtained using a 3-D talking head to teach speech and vocabulary skills to students with hearing challenges (Barker, 2003; Cole et al., 1999). This work was also featured on ABC TV's Prime Time Thursday (Payson, 2001) and the NSF Home page in 2001.

ICATIANI: A Computer-Based Speech Therapy Program

Rationale for ICATIANI

In Mexico we have few special education schools with specialized personnel (speech therapists, physical therapists, etc.). We began working together with one particular school, the Jean Piaget Special Education School in Puebla, Mexico. The Jean Piaget school is known as a "Multiple Attention Center" (CAM), which is an institute for children with hearing and language disorders due to different problems, including Down syndrome. This school has around 250 students and a staff of 30 teachers, which includes special education teachers, psychologists, and therapists. The curriculum is given by the Mexican Ministry of Education "SEP" (Secretaría de Educación Pública), which also establishes that the teaching methods shall be oral, avoiding sign language. Language therapy is given individually, but there are only three therapists (social service workers) for all the students of the school, and very few families can afford private sessions (Valadéz & Espinosa, 2002).

By instructions of SEP the learning method is focused on verbal communication and lip reading. There is not one established method that has proven best, but this focus helps to integrate the hearing impaired into the social group, and he or she is not isolated. According to Perelló and Tortosa (1978), the aim of this method is to develop the cognitive processes of individuals with hearing impairments to become identical to individuals with normal hearing, so they can communicate normally and express their feelings and thoughts to others despite imperfect speech production. Additionally the children use a workbook that contains phonemes and pictures to practice. They use mirrors, posters that illustrate situations, concepts, phrases with intonation marks, colored cards that are used to define gender, and temporal frames of reference. Most of the material is created by the teachers themselves to support a specific task the class has to do.

The Jean Piaget School received a donation of 11 fully equipped Pentium III PCs. Although 11 machines are far from enough, they enable teachers to use software tools for their classes and therapies. They are using software for reading practice, math, and some games to apply logic. Recently the school acquired IBM's SpeechView. It is an excellent tool, but there are some difficulties: the type of microphone it requires is expensive, so they only have one, and the system is so sensitive that it cannot be used when a whole group is in the room working on the other computers, it has to be used in quiet classroom environments and during individual therapy hours.

The TLATOA[1] Speech Processing Group at the Universidad de las Americas, Puebla (UDLA-P) has developed several applications using the CSLU Toolkit (de Villiers, 2002; Cole et al., 1998; Stone, 1999) to support language acquisition for hearing impaired children at the Jean Piaget School. These applications guide the practice of the pronunciation of vowels and diphthongs and a set of simple short words. The system uses an animated 3D face together with a Mexican Spanish text-to-speech system developed at UDLA-P (Barbosa, 1997; Kirschning, 2001b; Meza, Cervantes, & Kirschning, 2001) and Mexican Spanish speech recognizer (Clemente, Vargas, Olivier, Kirschning, & Cervantes, 2001; Kirschning, 2001).

One of the main goals of the instructors at the Jean Piaget School is to be able to personalize and optimize instruction for each child. Unfortunately, this goal cannot be achieved because of the lack of personnel required to provide the level of individualized attention that each child requires. We thus worked with the Jean Piaget staff to develop an automated tool that students could learn to use independently to support individual language practice. This tool is called ICATIANI and uses speech technology and computer graphics to support pronunciation practice of Mexican Spanish (Kirschning, 2004; Kirschning & Toledo, 2004; Toledo, 2002).

Due to the lack of enough speech therapists and the increasing demand of early special education for these children to incorporate them as soon as possible into classrooms in regular schools, the teachers require tools to elicit speech production from the children. The system, which has been developed during the last three years through participatory design between teachers, therapists, and speech technology researchers and students from the TLATOA Group, focuses on the practice of speech production in a semi-personalized way.

Designing the Lessons: After a large number of interviews and discussions with teachers and the school's therapist, it was decided to work first on vowel pairs, indicating points and manner of articulation. In a second series of exercises, the students work with diphthongs

Figure 3. The system lets the student choose a pair of vowels to practice

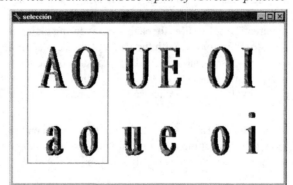

Figure 4. The system lets the student choose a vowel to practice the diphthongs that begin with that vowel

using the same schema. The five vowels in Spanish are grouped in pairs: /a/ with /o/, /u/ with /e/, and /o/ with /i/, based on similar tongue positions, using their representation in capitals and small caps letters. The diphthongs are grouped by their beginning vowel (see Figures 1a and 1b).

The system targets children between ages 3 to 8 years, and keeps a personalized registry of each student, their practice sessions, success rate, and errors when pronouncing vowels.

The system is not intended to replace a teacher or therapist; rather, it provides the teacher with an important tool to support their work and give them a little more time to focus on specific problems of each student while the others can practice with the system on their own.

As mentioned before, the method to be used is the oral method, focusing on the explanations of the points of articulation and using lip-reading, with no sign language used.

Program Structure

The system identifies two types of users: the instructor and the student. The instructor can register new students, review the results of each student in their personal log-files, and also modify lessons.

The logic sequence of the lessons runs in three phases:

1. **Student login:** The student logs into the system with his or her full name, and then selects a lesson. After logging in, Baldi greets the student with his or her name. This step initiates the creation of log-files for each student during their whole work session. The log files are stored in folders with the name of the corresponding student. Each session creates a new log-file that is named with the date of the session and contains a list of the practiced vowels and the systems recognition result, as well as the number of trials for each vowel. Each utterance can also be recorded for later review by an instructor.

    After greeting the student, Baldi says the instructions for each step of the learning exercises. The fact that the student is greeted with his or her name gives the whole session a more personal touch and is highly accepted by the students.

Figure 5. Baldi pronouncing /u/, frontal, solid view, and lateral, semi-transparent view

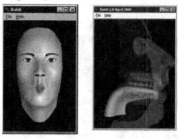

Figure 6. Baldi pronouncing the diphthong "ao" by first speaking each phoneme separately and then together.

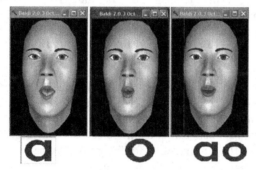

2.   **Presentation:** The student first selects whether to work on vowels or diphthongs and then selects the specific pair of vowels or a set of diphthongs to practice by clicking on the selected stimuli on the computer screen, (Figures 3 and 4). Baldi then displays the pronunciation of each vowel or diphthong to be practiced (Figures 5 and 6).

3.   **Practice:** After repeating the item three times, Baldi asks the child to say the vowel or diphthong and then asks the student to speak. The utterance is then processed by the speech recognizer. If the recognizer is able to match the utterance correctly, Baldi will congratulate the student and smile; otherwise he will say that it was not the correct sound and ask the student to try again (see Figure 7). The recognizers and the male voice for Mexican Spanish were developed by TLATOA (Kirschning, 2001a; Kirschning, 2001b)

A loudness meter (that measures sound pressure level) displayed on the screen is used to provide feedback to help the students learn if they are producing a sound and how loudly they are saying it (de Villiers, 2002).

To elicit pronunciation of each vowel or diphthong, the printed version of the vowel is shown on the screen as Baldi says it in both natural and semi-transparent mode. Then Baldi tells the child to say the sound. The speech recognizer evaluates the child's utterance and tries to match the results to the vowel or diphthong that were supposed to be said.

Figure 7. Baldi smiling for correct answers and with a sad face when the utterance was not recognized

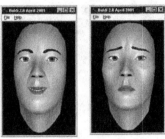

Another part of the exercises with diphthongs asks the child to fill in the blank in a word by clicking on a diphthong and dragging and dropping it into its correct place within the word. When the exercise is done correctly a small animation of two hands clapping appears, and Baldi says "¡Bravo!"

Feedback: The same face provides the feedback on the correct and incorrect answers of the child, smiling if the answer was correct and otherwise making a sad face and explaining that the pronunciation was wrong (Figure 7). We found that it was better to avoid the children being distracted by other images appearing on the screen, such as medals, smiling or sad face icons, and so forth, so Baldi provides all feedback using verbal and non-verbal cues, such as the sad and happy facial expressions shown in Figure 7.

Baldi has been designed to produce accurate lip movements during speech production, and to produce accurate movements of the tongue for English (Cole, 1999; Cole et al., 1999; Massaro, 1997; Massaro & Light, 2005). In very few cases, we have observed that the tongue movement is not completely accurate for Spanish, one example being the pronunciation of an "a." Baldi lifts the tip of the tongue at the end of the sound. (These details have already been reported to Massaro for their correction).

Speech synthesis is used even if most of the students cannot hear it. But they sometimes place their hand on the speakers to feel the vibration of the sound when Baldi speaks.

To support the understanding of what Baldi says, we added a captioning window. The students that can read can confirm what they understood by re-reading what was said in this window.

Robust Speech Recognition

It is a major challenge to use speech recognition effectively with hearing impaired children. In initial research with Baldi at the Tucker Maxon School in the U.S., speech recognition capabilities were disabled after parents complained that the program often rejected excellent pronunciations of utterances by children. While computer speech recognition has been used recently to track speech of normally hearing children while reading out loud (Hagen, Pellom,

& Cole, 2003; Hagen, Pellom, van Vuuren, & Cole, 2004), to our knowledge, computer speech recognition has not been used effectively in speech and language training with children with severe and profound hearing loss. The reason for this is that the speech production of children with hearing problems typically varies enormously within a child and from child to child. Their utterances can sometimes be interpreted correctly by a human listener, even if the pronunciation is not correct, but an automated system will determine the result by using a fixed threshold. Negative recognition results can discourage the learners.

But still, the teachers at the Jean Piaget School decided to use the recognizer. They spent the first sessions with each student, explaining why the results were often not good, and this surprisingly motivated the kids to try harder.

Two types of speech recognizers were trained to be used for speech-based educational software, one using artificial neural networks, developed using the CSLU Toolkit and the other using SONIC, a hidden Markov model (HMM) recognizer developed by Pellom (2001) at the University of Colorado.

Children Speech Corpus for Mexican Spanish

The data used to train the recognizers for child speech in Mexican Spanish is a corpus consisting of the recordings of 1016 speakers. These children were all native speakers, ages between 8 and 12 years, in grades between 2nd and 5th from six different schools of the area around Puebla (Mexico). Each child recorded 32 phrases: short sentences, digits, numbers, isolated words, names, and one segment of spontaneous speech. The duration of the recordings vary between one second and three minutes (for the spontaneous speech segment).

For all experiments we use speech data and associated transcriptions from 700 children (grades 2nd to 6th) who were asked to answer a set of questions. The 16 kHz audio data contains 2700 different words.

Neural Network Speech Recognizer Trained with the CSLU Tookit

The neural network-based recognizer was created using the CSLU Toolkit. It uses a three-layer feed-forward neural network trained with standard back propagation.

Using 450 recordings, a child speech recognizer was trained, obtaining the best results in the 16th iteration (see Table 1).

HMM Speech Recognizer Trained with SONIC

Baseline Training:

The recognizer trained with SONIC (Pellom, 2001) implements an efficient time-synchronous, beam-pruned Viterbi token-passing search through a static re-entrant lexical prefix

Table 1. Results of the training process of the artifical neural network. These results correspond to the 16th iteration, which obtained the best word accuracy and correct sentence rate.

Number of Sentences	Number of Words	Sub. %	Ins. %	Del. %	Word Accuracy %	Correct Sentences %
1883	11283	0.82%	2.63%	0.08%	96.47%	85.71%

tree while utilizing continuous density mixture Gaussian HMMs. For children's speech, the recognizer has been trained on 500 users (above 10 hours of data) from Mexican children in grades 2nd to 6th, but excluding the spontaneous speech segments. In this experiment 80% of the child speech corpus was used for training and 20% for evaluation, that is, 400 speakers were selected for training and 100 for testing.

The obtained models were evaluated with NIST, obtaining a **41.4% WER** (word error rate).

Adaptation experiments:

In order to obtain a high accuracy in child speech recognition it is necessary to apply some normalization techniques. The vocal tract of a child (0 to 14 years) is different from the one of an adult, affecting the characteristics of the voice, requiring thus a recognizer trained specially for child speech.

By applying different adaptation techniques such as VTLN (Vocal Tract Length Normalization), MLLR (Maximum Likelihood Linear Regression), and MAPLR (Maximum A-Posteriori Linear Regression), error rates decreased down to a **31% WER.** The following table (Table 2) summarizes the obtained results.

As mentioned before, it should seem obvious that for an application for children a child-speech recognizer is required. However, we tested several settings for the different recognizers at our disposal for children voices and for adults.

When the level of speech production of the hearing impaired child is advanced (i.e. it has a better control over the pitch, volume, and intonation), a child-speech recognizer yields good results. But, when this is not the case, when the child has difficulty producing speech, we found that an adult-speech recognizer works better. The latter is the more common case for the students at the Jean Piaget School, since those that do have a better control of their speech usually join other non special education schools.

Table 2. Summary of the result obtained with the training of the HMM'S with different techniques

Number of Words	Baseline WER(%)	VTLN WER(%)	MLLR WER(%)	MAPLR WER(%)
14076	41.4%	42.6%	41.2%	31.9%

The teachers have thus the choice of two recognizers that they can select according to their perception of the child's level of speech production, or if during the initial sessions the recognition is bad.

Another option is to collect a very small corpus from hearing impaired children and train and test a recognizer with these samples. However, some attempts were made and then discarded, because the collected speech samples were so highly heterogeneous that the training never reached a point where it could reasonably generalize and produce acceptable recognition rates.

Evaluation

During the initial stages of development at the TLATOA laboratory at UDLA-P, functionality and usability tests were performed with three children of different ages and abilities to read

Figure 8a. Pictures of students of the Jean Piaget School testing ICATIANI the first time, together with their parents

Figure 8b. Pictures of students of the Jean Piaget School testing ICATIANI the first time, together with their parents

lips. Here, issues like the speed of Baldi's speech and the maximum number of repetitions for each vowel were adjusted.

Then another test was made at the Jean Piaget School, after parents tried it with their children, approving the system's use for sessions after school hours (see Figures 8a and 8b).

Initial Assessment

Assessment Questions: "What is the change, if any, in students' vowel production after using the Toolkit for speech practice for six months of the regular school year? Does vowel production come closer to canonical form?"

In order to investigate changes in performance caused by the treatment, we collected baseline data. The baseline test was performed with 55 students of four different groups. The chart in Figure 9a shows the intelligibility rate for each vowel per group. Vowels /e/ and /o/ are those with best results, and /u/ and /i/ have the lowest rates overall with the recognizer. When evaluated by a human listener (Figure 9b) these rates increased drastically because,

Figure 9a. Intelligibility rates evaluating each utterance with the speech recognizer

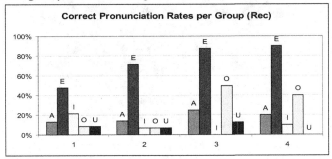

Figure 9b. Intelligibility rates of the same utterances of Figure 9a, but evaluated by a human listener

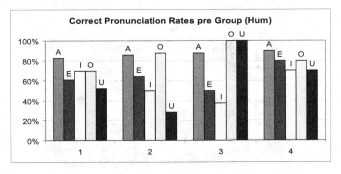

we believe, often pronunciation was close, barely audible, but still enough for the evaluators to guess the correct vowel.

The following section presents the second assessment and compares the results.

Second Assessment

A second test was performed one year after the first tests to assess if the speech production of the children had improved. Figures 10a and 10b show the comparison of the results obtained from five children in the two tests in May 2003 and June 2004. The reason why only five children are shown here is that after a year our test group, as well as the control group consisting of 19 children, had changed its composition dramatically. Some children had been transferred to other schools to be integrated into groups of non special education schools. Others had stopped language therapy after school. The result of attrition from

Figure 10a. Comparing speech production—vowels—of five children (recognizer). Percentages from the tests in May 2003 are shown in blue versus the pronunciation in June 2004 shown in the red bars.

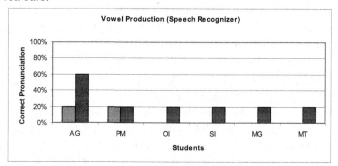

Figure 10b. Comparing speech production—vowels—of five children (human listener). Percentages from the tests in May 2003 are shown in blue versus the pronunciation in June 2004 shown in the red bars.

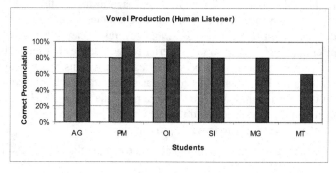

these and other causes resulted in only five children who had taken the first test and could be tested again.

The charts in Figures 10a and 10b show an increase of the intelligibility of the vowel pronunciation. It should be noted that all five children suffered total loss of hearing and do **not** have cochlear implants.

It is difficult to determine if the improvement in their speech production is due to ICATIANI. But what the teachers have noticed as a direct result of the children interacting with ICATIANI is that they have increasingly gained more courage to elicit speech. Most of the children arrive at the school and are either completely rebellious children or extremely shy. "Baldi has successfully shown them that it is OK to speak, even if others have trouble understanding" (Valadéz & Espinosa, 2002).

Conclusion

We have developed a set of applications using the CSLU Toolkit (Cole et al., 1998; de Villiers, 2002; Stone, 1999) to support language acquisition for hearing impaired children of the Jean Piaget Special Education School. These applications practice the pronunciation of pairs of vowels, diphthongs, and a set of simple short words.

The system is not intended to provide a substitute for a teacher or therapist, but to supplement and support their work by providing several children with useful instruction while the teacher can devote more individualized attention to specific children.

The reason for using the CSLU Toolkit is because it is publicly available for research use and because it is a well-designed authoring and runtime environment for developing learning applications that incorporate state-of-the-art speech recognition and character animation technologies. The tools developed with the CSLU Toolkit for English language acquisition have been evaluated and the results published recently, encouraging us to continue in this pursuit. Barker (2003) states in her paper, which reviewed outcomes of using the CSLU Toolkit and Baldi at the Tucker Maxon School in the U.S., that the results indicate that the CSLU vocabulary tutors may be an efficient way to increase vocabulary and literacy in oral-deaf education. Pat Stone, the schools director, considers the use of Baldi to be a revolution in oral deaf education, similar in its potential future benefits to infant screening and cochlear implants (Stone, 1999).

ICATIANI has been developed with a similar approach to that of the CSLU Vocabulary Tutors, with the addition that ICATIANI includes computer speech recognition. Speech recognition creates a high rate of rejections, and several researchers consider it too disturbing for the children. However, so far, experiences with these children at this particular school have been positive from the perspective of teachers, parents, and students, and initial results are encouraging. The initial assessment has shown that the level of oral production of the children is extremely low and they require more than ICATIANI, but Baldi seems to motivate them to produce speech, and teachers have said that even if production is not improving fast, they are less shy to try and speak in class.

Thanks to ICATIANI, groups of 11 children at a time can practice their vowel production, and every time Baldi smiles it evokes a big smile in the children, motivating us to continue this work. We note that relative to children at Tucker Maxon School, who receive state-of-the-art amplification and often receive cochlear implants, many of the children at the Jean Piaget school, many of whom are profoundly deaf, have not received these benefits, and the challenges of educating them to perceive and produce speech are significantly greater. It is thus remarkable that speech recognition has produced initial positive results.

After the system was released and the students began to use it, a group of children was tested last year to assess their speech production. The tests showed a small improvement in the first group's speech production.

We attribute success in this project, as indicated by the widespread acceptance of the program and its continued use by teachers and students in the Jean Piaget School, to the use of participatory design methodology, which engages language therapists, software developers, educators, parents, and the students in all stages of the design and development process: from conception and planning of the learning tools, through iterative design and test cycles, and through monitoring and refinement of problems identified following deployment of the program in classrooms. It is a very important process and crucial for success.

The success of this program is due to the enthusiastic and voluntary participation of members of both TLATOA and the Jean Piaget School. It has been through participatory design that each detail has been reviewed, tested, and re-designed as often as necessary until it could fit completely into the requirements.

In summary, teachers and therapists who have seen and worked with ICATIANI agree that the system poses an interesting and different option for language therapy. The animated character captures the students' attention and they become engaged and often immersed in the activities the system presents.

Testing ICATIANI with Children with Significant Cognitive Disabilities

In a recent test, children with intellectual disability were included in the groups using ICATIANI to see how they respond to it. They have problems with speech production due to other factors: Down syndrome causes about 70% of children to have a larger than normal tongue, which makes it harder for them to speak clearly. Other children have neural lesions in the language area.

The students' first contact with the program was not very successful, as the system did not appear to be a game, like other software they had seen and played with. However, it caught their attention, and the further they advanced through the lessons, the children became curious to see what happened when they pronounced correctly.

The interest and motivation toward this system (and any other) vary on a day-by-day basis with the emotional state of the children, and it is impossible to predict it. Nevertheless, ICATIANI has managed to hold their interest over time and motivates them to work on their speech production. It is often difficult to make the children stop when their time is up.

The fact that the animated character rewards them for a correct pronunciation makes the children smile, and sometimes they clap, especially those with intellectual disability. It motivates them, and they put all their effort into getting a positive result.

ICATIANI successfully helps in the conceptualization of words through objects displayed on the screen. The children broaden their vocabulary, and it helps them to work on the co-ordination of their motor skills. The children put all of their attention into this system and try their best to correct their pronunciation of the combination of vowels, just so Baldi says "Bravo" and smiles at them.

Problems to be Solved and Future Work

After language therapists verified the system, they found that in some cases the visemes of the animated character do not correspond to the movements of a Spanish-speaking person. This is the case of the viseme for the phoneme /a/ in Spanish. Baldi lifts the tongue at the end, which distorts the image significantly.

Another aspect that is considered incorrect is that Baldi does not close the mouth completely after an utterance, not marking the end or signaling silence. This confuses the children that try to interpret the lip movements for better understanding of the movements they are supposed to make themselves. They are not sure if Baldi finished speaking. We also observed that the TTS rules for the pronunciation of certain combinations of vowels have to be revised, as in some cases the emphasis of the intonation is not situated correctly.

The teachers have suggested that for any work in this area it is important to select a vo-cabulary that has a real meaning to the children, that is, words they need in daily life. Also, for the next step, we will include other phonemes of groups of consonants, using the semi-transparent Baldi to show the point and manner of articulation.

In summary, there are compelling reasons to explore the potential of computer-based speech and language treatments for individuals with neurological disorders. While effective clinical treatments exist, there are significant barriers to scaling up treatments to provide widespread treatment. Effective treatments are typically both intensive and extensive, whereas reim-bursed face-to-face treatment is usually insufficient in terms of both its intensity and length. Barriers to introducing behavioral treatments for neurological disorders include informing and convincing physicians about the value of the treatment, and developing reimbursement models that assure access to treatment by patients. Even if all of these problems could be solved, the problem remains of training a sufficient number of therapists to treat those in need of treatment. Computer-based *virtual therapist systems* have the potential to provide accessible, affordable, engaging, and effective treatment to individuals.

Acknowledgments

This work was supported in part by grants from the Coleman Foundation, National Science Foundation, Department of Education, and National Institutes of Health: NSF/ITR IIS-

0086107, NSF/IERI EIA-012\1201, NICHD/IERI 1R01HD-44276.01, IES R305G040097, NIH 1R21DC007377-01, NIH 5R21DC006078-02, NIDRR H133B031127, NIDRR H133G040269, NIDRR H133E040019. We would like to thank Barbara Wise and our other colleagues, cited herein, for their invaluable contributions and feedback.

We would also like to thank the teachers and therapists of the Jean Piaget Special Education School for their constant interest and support in this project.

References

Atkinson, R. K. (2002). Optimizing learning from examples using animated pedagogical agents. *Journal of Educational Psychology, 94*(2), 416-427.

Barbosa, A. (1997). *Desarrollo de una nueva voz en Español de México para el Sistema de Texto a Voz Festival.* Unpublished master's thesis, Universidad de las Américas, Department of Computer Systems Engineering, Puebla.

Barker, L. (2003). Computer-assisted vocabulary acquisition: The CSLU vocabulary tutor in oral-deaf education. *Journal of Deaf Studies and Deaf Education, 8*(2), 187-198.

Baylor, A. L., & Kim, Y. (2005). Simulating instructional roles through pedagogical agents. *International Journal of Artificial Intelligence in Education, 15*(1), 95-115.

Baylor, A. L., & Ryu, J. (2003). Does the presence of image and animation enhance pedagogical agent persona? *Journal of Educational Computing Research, 28*(4), 373-395.

Bloom, B. S. (1984). The 2 sigma problem: The search for methods of group instruction as effective as one-on-one tutoring. *Educational Researcher, 13*, 4-16.

Bradburn, D. (2000). *Speech technology in education.* Retrieved January 15, 2006, from www.csun.edu/cod/conf/2000/proceedings/csun00.htm

Bungalow Software. (2000). *Speech sounds on cue and AphasiaTutor: Sights 'n sounds.* Retrieved August 21st, 2000, from http://www.bungalowsoftware.com/sights.htm

Cherney, L., Halper, A., Babbit, E., Holland, A., Cole, R., Van Vuuren, S., & Ngampatipatpong, N. (2005). *Learning to converse: Script training, virtual tutors, and aphasia treatment.* American Speech-Language Hearing Association (ASHA), San Diego.

Clemente, E., Vargas, A., Olivier, A., Kirschning, I., & Cervantes, O. (2001). Entrenamiento y evaluación de reconocedores de voz de propósito general basados en redes neuronales feed-forward y modelos ocultos de harkov. In *Proceedings of ENC* (Encuentro Nacional de Computación) (pp. 177-186). Aguscalientes: Sociedad Mexicana de Ciencias de la Computación.

Cohen, P. A., Kulik, J. A., & Kulik, C. L. C. (1982). Educational outcomes of tutoring: A meta-analysis of findings. *American Educational Research Journal, 19*(2), 237-248.

Cole, R. (1999). *Tools for research and education in speech science.* 14th International Congress of Phonetic Sciences. San Francisco. Retrieved January 20th, 2006, from http://www.tmos.org/tech/papers/ron_icphs1.html

Cole, R., Halpern, A., Lorraine, R., Van Vuuren, S., Ngampatipatpong, N., & Yan, J. (2007). A virtual speech therapist for individuals with Parkinson's disease. *Educational Technology 47*(1), 51-55.

Cole, R., Massaro, D., de Villiers, J., Rundle, B., Shobaki, K., Wouters, J., Cohen, M., Beskow, J., Stone, P., Connors, P., Tarachow, A., & Solcher, D. (1999). New tools for interactive speech and language training: Using animated conversational agents in the classrooms of profoundly deaf children. In *Proceedings of the ESCA/SOCRATES Workshop on Method and Tool Innovations for Speech Science Education* (pp. 45-52). London.

Cole, R., Sutton, S., Yan, Y., Vermeulen, P., & Fanty, M. (1998). Accessible technology for interactive systems: A new approach to spoken language research. In *Proceedings of the International Conference on Acoustics, Speech and Signal Processing*, 2 (pp. 1037-1040). IEEE Seattle, WA.

Cole, R., Van Vuuren, S., Pellom, B., Hacioglu, K., Ma, J., Movellan, J., Schwartz, S., Wade-Stein, D., Ward, W., & Yan, J. (2003). Perceptive animated interfaces: First steps toward a new paradigm for human-computer interaction. *Proceedings of the IEEE: Special Issue on Human-Computer Multimodal Interface, 91*(9), 1391-1405.

Cole, R., Wise, B., & Van Vuuren, S. (2007). How Marni teaches children to read. *Educational Technology, 47*(1), 14-18.

Connors, P., Davis, A., Fortier, G., Gilley, K., Rundle, B., Soland, C., & Tarachow, A. (1999). Participatory design: Classroom applications and experiences. *Invited talk at the International Conference of Phonetic Sciences*. San Francisco.

Delgado, J. J. (1999). *Hipoacuia infantil*. PrevInfad: Spain.

de Villiers, J. (2002). CSLU vocabulary tutor. Retrieved June 2, 2002, from http://www.cslu.ogi.edu/toolkit/docs/2.0/apps/vocabulary/

Espinosa, M. R. (2001). *Personal communication*. General Director of Jean Piaget Special Education School. Mexico.

Flores, L., & Berruecos, P. (1991). *El niño sordo de edad preescolar*. México: Ed. Trillas.

Gómez, M. (1999). *Las nuevas tecnologías de la información y la comunicación y su aplicación a las necesidades educativas especiales. Cómo generar recursos didácticos para el aula*. Almeces. No. 5 June 1999, at CPR de Cieza y en Magisterio Español (n° 41; 9, June 1999). Retrieved May 7, 2000, from http://paidos.rediris.es/needirectorio/tema21.htm#inicio

Graesser, A., Wiemer-Hastings, K., Wiemer-Hastings, P., Kreuz, R., & the Tutoring Research Group. (1999). AutoTutor: A simulation of a human tutor. *Journal of Cognitive Systems Research, 1*, 35-51.

Gratch, J., Rickel, J., André, E., Badler, N., Cassell, J., & Petajan, E. (2002). Creating interactive virtual humans: Some assembly required. *IEEE Intelligent Systems, 17*(4), 54-63.

Hagen, A., Pellom, B., & Cole, R. (2003). Children's speech recognition with application to interactive books and tutors. In *Proceedings of ASRU* (International Conference on Automactic Speech Recognition and Understanding) 2003. St. Thomas, Virgin Islands. (pp. 186-191).

Hagen, A., Pellom, B., van Vuuren, S., & Cole, R. (2004). Advances in children's speech recognition within an interactive literacy tutor. In *Proceedings of HLT NAACL 2004* (Human Language Technology Conference-North American chapter of the Assocation for Computational Linguistics), (pp. 25-28).

Halpern, A. E., Cole, R., Ramig, L. O., Yan, J., Petska, J., Vuuren, S., & Spielman, J. (2006). Virtual speech therapists—Expanding the horizons of speech treatment for Parkinson's disease. *Invited talk at the Conference on Motor Speech*. Austin, TX.

Wise, B. (PI), Cole, R., Pellom, B., & Van Vuuren, S. (2004-2008). *ICARE: Independent Comprehensive Adaptive Reading Evaluation*. IES ED, grant no. R305G040097.

Johnson, W., Rickel, J., & Lester, J. (2000). Animated pedagogical agents: Face to face interaction in interactive learning environments. *International Journal of Artificial intelligence in Education, 11*, 47-78.

Kirriemuir, J. (2003). *Speech recognition technologies*. TSW 03-03. Retrieved March 5, 2006, from http://www.ceangal.com/

Kirschning, I. (2001a). Research and development of speech technology & applications for Mexican Spanish at the Tlatoa group. In *Development Consortium at CHI 2001* (pp. 49-50). Seattle, WA: ACM Press.

Kirschning, I. (2001b). Tlatoa: Developing speech technology & applications for Mexican Spanish. In *Proceedings of the SLPLT-2 (2nd Intl.Workshop on Spanish Language Processing and Language Technologies)*. Spain (pp. 115-119).

Kirschning, I. (2004). CSLU Toolkit-based vocabulary tutors for the Jean Piaget Special Education School. In *International Conference InSTIL/ICALL2004-NLP and Speech Processing Technologies in Advanced Language Learning Systems* (pp. 165-168). Venice, Italy: UNIPRESS.

Kirschning, I., & Toledo, T. (2004). Language training for hearing impaired children with CSLU vocabulary tutor. *WSEAS Transactions on Information Science and Applications, 1*(1), 20-25.

Koedinger, K. R., Anderson, J. R., Hadley, W. H., & Mark, M. A. (1997). Intelligent tutoring goes to school in the big city. *International Journal of Artificial Intelligence in Education, 8*, 30-43.

Lester, J., Converse, S., Kahler, S., Barlow, S., Stone, B., & Boghal, R. (1997). The persona effect: Affective impact of animated pedagogical agents. In *Proceedings of CHI(Computer-Human Interaction)'97 Human Factors in Computer Systems* (pp. 359-366). New York: Association for Computing Machinery.

Mayer, R. (2001). *Multimedia learning*. Cambridge, UK: Cambridge University Press.

Massaro, D. (1997). *Perceiving talking faces: From speech perception to a behavioral principle*. MIT Press.

Massaro, D. W., & Light, J. (2005). Improving the vocabulary of children with hearing loss. *The Volta Review, 104*(3), 141-174.

McAleer, P. (1995). *Childhood speech, language & listening problems*. John Wiley & Sons.

Meza, H., Cervantes, O., & Kirschning, I. (2001). Estimation of duration models for phonemes in Mexican Speech synthesis. In *Proceedings of ICSLP (International Conference on Spoken Language Processing), 1*, 685-688. Beijing China.

Moreno, R., Mayer, R. E., Spires, H. A., & Lester, J. C. (2001). The case for social agency in computer-based teaching: Do students learn more deeply when they interact with animated pedagogical agents? *Cognition and Instruction, 19*(2), 177-213.

Nass, C., & Brave, S. (2005). *Wired for speech.* Cambridge, MA: MIT Press.

OHSU. (2002). *Deaf children learn to talk using speech technology.* OGI School of Science & Engineering, Ohsu News. Retrieved March 5, 2006, from www.ohsu.edu

Payson, J. (Producer). (2001). Look who's talking. *Prime Time Thursday, ABC Television Network.* Aired March 15, 2001. [Online]. Retrieved January 5th, 2006, from http://oak.colorado.edu/~spradhan/download/ron-videos/ABC-Primetime/

Perelló, J., & Tortosa, F. (1978). *Sordomudez* (3rd ed). Spain: Científico-Médica, Audiofoniatría y Logopedia, Barcelona.

Pellom, B. (2001). *SONIC: The University of Colorado continuous speech recognizer* (Tech. Rep. No. TR-CSLR-2001-01). CSLR, University of Colorado.

Reeves, B., & Nass, C. (1996). *The media equation: How people treat computers, television, and new media like real people and places.* New York: Cambridge University Press.

Stone, P. (1999). *Revolutionizing language use in oral deaf education.* 14th International Congress of Phonetic Sciences. San Francisco. Retrieved March 5th, 2006, from http://www.tmos.org/tech/papers/S0837.html

Sutton, S., & Cole, R. (1998). Universal speech tools: The CSLU toolkit. In *Proceedings of the International Conference on Spoken Language Processing* (pp. 3221-3224). Sydney, Australia.

Sutton, S., Novick, D., Cole, R., & Fanty, M. (1996). Building 10,000 spoken-dialogue systems. In *Proceedings of the International Conference on Spoken Language Processing.* Philadelphia. (pp. 709-712).

Thompson, C., Shapiro, L., Kiran, S., & Sobeks, J. (2003). The role of syntactic complexity in treatment of sentence deficits in agrammatic aphasia: The complexity account of treatment efficacy (CATE). *Journal of Speech, Language, and Hearing Research, 46*, 591-605.

Toledo, M. T. (2002). *Cómo enseñar a niños hipoacúsicos aprender a hablar utilizando reconocimiento de voz.* Unpublished master's thesis in Computer Systems, Universidad de las Américas, Puebla, Mexico.

Tucker Maxon. (2001). *Vocabulary tutor* (1998-2001). Retrieved March 5th, 2006, from http://www.tmos.org/tech/vocabulary_tutor/vt1.html

UCSC-PSL (2006). *PSL on ABC Primetime. University of California Santa Cruz, Perceptual Science Lab.* Retrieved on March 5, 2006, from http://mambo.ucsc.edu/psl/primetime

Valadéz, L., & Espinosa, M. R. (2002). *Personal communication.* Director and Teacher of the Jean Piaget Special Education School. Mexico.

Van Vuuren, S. (2007). Technologies that power animated agents that teach and conduct therapy. *Educational Technology, 47*(1), 4-10.

Wise, B., Cole, R. A., & Van Vuuren, S. (2005). Foundations to literacy: Teaching children to read through conversational interaction with a virtual teacher. In *Invited talk at 56th Annual Meeting of the International Dyslexia Association, Technology strand.* Denver, CO.

Zaoming, H. D. (1990). Speech skill builder for children. Tiger DRS Inc. Retrieved March 5th, 2006, from http://drspeech.com/Paper.html

Endnote

[1] TLATOA comes from Nahuatl, one of the main native languages of Mexico, and means "speech."

About the Authors

Hector Perez-Meana received his PhD degree in electrical engineering from Tokyo Institute of Technology, Tokyo, Japan, in 1989. From March 1989 to September 1991, he was a visiting researcher at Fujitsu Laboratories Ltd, Kawasaki, Japan. In February 1997, he joined the Graduate Department of The Mechanical and Electrical Engineering, School of the National Polytechnic Institute of Mexico, where he is now a professor. In 1991 he received the IEICE excellent Paper Award, and in 2000 the IPN Research Award. In 1998 was co-chair of the ISITA'98. He is a member of the IEEE, IEICE, The Mexican Researcher System and The Mexican Academy of Science. His principal research interests are adaptive filter systems, image processing, pattern recognition and related fields.

***

Mohammad Reza Asharif was born in Tehran, Iran, on December 15, 1951. He received the BSc and MSc degree in electrical engineering from the University of Tehran, Tehran, 1973, 1974, respectively and the PhD degree in electrical engineering from the University of Tokyo, Tokyo in 1981. He was Head of Technical Department of T.V. broadcasting college

(IRIB), Tehran, Iran from 1981 to 1985. Then, he was a senior researcher at Fujitsu Labs. Co. Kawasaki, Japan from 1985 to 1992. Then, he was an assistant professor in Department of Electrical and Computer Engineering, University of Tehran, Tehran, Iran from 1992 to 1997. Dr. Asharif is now a full professor at Department of Information Engineering, University of the Ryukyus, Okinawa, Japan since 1997. He has developed an algorithm and implemented its hardware for real time TV. Ghost canceling. He introduced a new algorithm for acoustic echo canceller and he released it on VSP chips. He also introduced a new algorithm for double-talk echo canceling based on correlation processing. Professor Asharif has contributed many publications to journals and conference proceedings. His research interests are in the field of digital signal processing, acoustic echo canceling, active noise control, adaptive digital filtering, image and speech processing. Professor Asharif is a senior member of IEEE since 1998.

Luiz W. P. Biscainho was born in Rio de Janeiro, Brazil, in 1962. He received the Elec Eng degree (*magna cum laude*) from the EE (now Poli) at Universidade Federal do Rio de Janeiro (UFRJ), Brazil, in 1985, and the MSc and DSc degrees in electrical engineering from the COPPE at UFRJ in 1990 and 2000, respectively. Dr. Biscainho is associate professor at DEL/Poli and PEE/COPPE, at UFRJ. His research area is digital signal processing, particularly audio processing and adaptive systems. He is currently a member of the IEEE, the Audio Engineering Society (AES), and the Brazilian Telecommunications Society (SBrT).

Rui Chen was born in Hunan, China, on March 10, 1974. He received the BE in information engineering from the South-Central University for Nationalities, China, in 1998, and the ME degree in electrical engineering and the DE degree in Interdisciplinary Intelligent systems engineering from the university of Ryukyu, Japan, in 2003, 2006, respectively. Now He works as an associate professor in the Central South University of Forestry and Technology. His research interests are in the field of digital signal processing, acoustic echo canceling, active noise control, blind signal separation, independent components analysis, digital image processing.

Ronald Allan Cole (PhD, psychology '71) is the director of the Center for Spoken Language Research (CSLR), which he co-founded in 1998, at the University of Colorado. Ron has published over 150 articles in scientific journals and published conference proceedings. In 1990, Ron founded the Center for Spoken Language Understanding (CSLU) at the Oregon Graduate Institute. The CSLU Toolkit, a platform for research and development of spoken dialogue systems using animated characters, has been distributed to 15,000 sites in over 100 countries, and research using this toolkit to teach language skills to children with profound hearing loss was featured on ABC TV's Prime Time Thursday and the NSF Home Page.

John R. (Jack) Deller Jr. is a fellow of the IEEE and a professor of electrical and computer engineering at Michigan State University where he directs the Speech Processing Laboratory. Deller holds the PhD (biomedical engineering, 1979), MS (electrical and computer engineering, 1976), and MS (biomedical engineering, 1975) degrees from the University of Michigan and the BS (electrical engineering, *Summa Cum Laude*, 1974) from the Ohio

State University. His research interests include statistical signal processing with application to speech processing, communications technologies, digital libraries, and biomedicine. He has co-authored two textbooks, is co-authoring a third, and has contributed chapters to numerous research volumes. Deller is a recipient of IEEE Millennium Medal for contributions in signal processing research and education, IEEE *Signal Processing* Best Paper Award in 1998, and the IEEE Signal Processing Society's 1997 Meritorious Service Award for his six-year service as editor-in-chief of *Signal Processing Magazine*.

Paulo A. A. Esquef was born in Campos dos Goytacazes, Rio de Janeiro, Brazil, in 1973. He received the engineering degree from Universidade Federal do Rio de Janeiro (UFRJ) in 1997, the MSc degree from COPPE/UFRJ in 1999, and the DSc (Tech) degree from Helsinki University of Technology, Finland, in 2004, all in electrical engineering. Dr. Esquef is currently working as a researcher for Nokia Institute of Technology in Manaus, Brasil. His main research interests are in digital audio signal processing, including topics such as audio restoration, sound source modeling, and model-based analysis/synthesis of audio signals. Dr. Esquef is an associate member of the IEEE and member of the Audio Engineering Society.

Alfonso Fernandez Vazquez received a BS degree from Technological Institute Puebla, an MSc degree and a PhD degree from Institute INAOE, Puebla, Mexico. Currently he has a postdoctoral position at University of Las Americas, UDLA, Puebla. His research interest includes digital signal processing and digital communications. He is author of more than 20 papers. He is a member of IEEE.

Aparna Gurijala received her MS degree in electrical engineering from Michigan State University, East Lansing, in 2001. She will be receiving her PhD degree in electrical engineering from Michigan State University in 2006. She served as a research assistant on the National Gallery of Spoken Word project from 2000 to 2004 and has been involved in the development of speech watermarking algorithms. Her research interests lie in the areas of multimedia security and signal processing, with a focus on speech watermarking and adaptive signal processing. Ms. Gurijala is a member of IEEE and has served as a reviewer for the IEEE Transactions on Image Processing, IEEE Transactions on Information Forensics and Security, and the IEEE Transactions on Audio, Speech, and Language Processing.

Gordana Jovanovic-Dolecek received a BS degree from the Department of Electrical Engineering, University of Sarajevo, an MSc degree from University of Belgrade, and a PhD degree from the Faculty of Electrical Engineering, University of Sarajevo. She was a professor at the Faculty of Electrical Engineering, University of Sarajevo until 1993, and from 1993-1995 she was with the Institute Mihailo Pupin, Belgrade. In 1995 she joined Institute INAOE, Department for Electronics, Puebla, Mexico, where she works as a professor and researcher. During 2001-2002 and 2006 she was at the Department of Electrical & Computer Engineering, University of California, Santa Barbara, as visiting researcher. She is the author of three books, editor of one book, and author of more than 200 papers.

Her research interests include digital signal processing and digital communications. She is a senior member of IEEE and the member of National Researcher System (SNI) Mexico and the regular member of Mexican Academy of Science.

Ingrid Kirschning (PhD, computer science '98) is the director of the TLATOA Laboratory for Speech Technology at the Universidad de las Américas, Puebla (UDLA-P). Ingrid is a faculty member of the Department of Computing, Electronics, Physics and Innovation at UDLA-P and currently the graduate advisor for the master's program in computer science. Ingrid is a member of the Research Group for Interactive and Collaborative Technologies and her research focuses on speech technologies for language learning and language acquisition. She has published in scientific journals and conference proceedings and promotes the research and development of speech based applications in Mexican Spanish.

Shung-Yung Lung was born in Taipei, Taiwan, in 1963. He received the BS degree in Department of Mathematics from Soochow University, Taiwan, in 1990, and the MS degree in Department of Applied Mathematics from National Chung-Kung University, Taiwan, in 1993. He received his PhD degree in Department of Electrical Engineering from National Sun Yat-Sen University, Kaohsiung, Taiwan, in 2000. His is presently a professor with the China University of Technology Department of Management Information Systems. His current research interests include image processing, speech processing, and pattern recognition.

Mariko Nakano-Miyatake received a ME degree in electrical engineering from the University of Electro-Communications, Tokyo, Japan in 1985, and her PhD in electrical engineering from The Universidad Autónoma Metropolitana (UAM), Mexico City, in 1998. From July 1992 to February 1997 she was with the Department of Electrical Engineering of the UAM Mexico. In February 1997, she joined the Graduate Department of The Mechanical and Electrical Engineering, School of The National Polytechnic Institute of Mexico, where she is now a professor. Her research interests are in adaptive systems, neural networks, pattern recognition and related field.

Manjunath Ramachandra Iyer is a research scholar from the university Visveswaraiah College of engineering, Bangalore University, India. He was born in 1971 in Kolar, India. His doctoral thesis spans signal processing, Neural networks, data transfer over the network and data integration. He has published about 55 papers in international conferences and journals in diverse areas involving the applications of signal processing. He has chaired many international conferences. His research interests include networking, Signal processing, supply chain, database architecture, and so forth. He has industrial and academic experience over eleven years in various fields including signal processing, data transfers, data organization and neural networks.

Sergio L. Netto was born in Rio de Janeiro, Brazil. He received the BSc (cum laude) and the MSc degrees from the Federal University of Rio de Janeiro (UFRJ), in 1991 and 1992, respectively, and the PhD degree from the University of Victoria, Canada, in 1996, all in electrical engineering. Dr. Netto is an associate professor at DEL/Poli and PEE/COPPE, at UFRJ. His research interests include digital signal processing, adaptive signal processing, and speech processing. Dr. Netto is the co-author (with Paulo S. R. Diniz and Eduardo A. B. da Silva) of *Digital Signal Processing: System Analysis and Design*, published by Cambridge University Press in 2002.

José Luis Oropeza-Rodríguez received the BS in telecommunication engineering from the Mechanical and Electrical Engineering School from the National Polytechnic Institute of Mexico. He received the MS and PhD in computer engineering from the Research Center in Computing, (CIC), of the National Polytechnic Institute, Mexico City, in 2000 and 2006 respectively where he is now an professor. His research interests are in speech processing, speech recognition and related fields.

Sergio Suarez-Guerra received the BS in electrical engineering from the Polytechnic Institute José Antonio Echeverria, La Havana Cuba in 1972 and the PhD degree in electrical engineering the Academic of Science in Soviet Union, Moscow 1979. Since 1998, he joined the Research Center in Computing of the National Polytechnic Institute, Mexico City, where he is now a professor. His research interests are in digital signal processing, speech processing and related fields.

Ronghui Tu received her BSc from Northern Jiaotong University, China, in 2001 and her MSc in computer science from University of Ottawa, Canada, in 2003. She is a PhD student of the School of Information Technology and Engineering (SITE) at University of Ottawa. Her current research interests are on audio processing, information theory and codes on graphs.

Jiying Zhao received his B Eng and M Eng in Computer Engineering, and PhD degree in electrical engineering from North China Electric Power University (NCEPU), China, respectively in 1983, 1988, and 1992, and his second PhD degree in computer engineering from Keio University, Japan, in 1998. He is an associate professor of the School of Information Technology and Engineering (SITE) at University of Ottawa. His current research interests are on image/video processing and multimedia communications. He is a member of Professional Engineers Ontario and a member of IEEE.

Index